An Introduction to

LITERATURE

FICTION   POETRY   DRAMA

Ruminants

—

He travels after the wintry sun,
Driving the cattle along the straight red road;
Calling to them in a voice they know,
He drives the cattle above Cabra

His voice tells them home is not far.
They low and make soft music with their hoofs
He drives them without labour before him,
Steam pluming their foreheads.

Herdsman, careful of the herd,
Tonight sleep well by the fire
When the herd too is asleep
And the door made fast.

Dublin : 1904

Holograph of James Joyce's "Ruminants"

An Introduction to

LITERATURE

FICTION   POETRY   DRAMA

THIRD EDITION

SYLVAN BARNET, *Tufts University*
MORTON BERMAN, *Boston University*
WILLIAM BURTO, *Lowell State College*

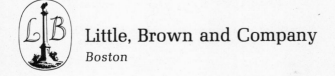

Little, Brown and Company
Boston

SEVENTH PRINTING

Published simultaneously in Canada
by Little, Brown & Company (Canada) Limited

PRINTED IN THE UNITED STATES OF AMERICA

ACKNOWLEDGMENTS

ANONYMOUS. The version of "De Titanic" used in this book is from the collection of Bessie Z. Jones.

W. H. AUDEN. "Musée des Beaux Arts" and "The Unknown Citizen," copyright, 1940, by W. H. Auden. "O What Is That Sound," copyright, 1937, and renewed 1964, by W. H. Auden. Reprinted from *Collected Poetry of W. H. Auden*, by permission of Random House, Inc., and from *Collected Shorter Poems* by W. H. Auden, by permission of Faber and Faber Ltd. (London).

JOHN MALCOLM BRINNIN. "Nuns at Eve" from *The Sorrows of Cold Stone* by John Malcolm Brinnin, copyright, 1951, by John Malcolm Brinnin. Reprinted by permission of Dodd, Mead & Company.

ALBERT CAMUS. "The Guest," copyright, 1957 1958, by Alfred A. Knopf, Inc. Reprinted from *Exile and the Kingdom*, by Albert Camus (Justin O'Brien, trans.) by permission of Alfred A. Knopf, Inc.

E. E. CUMMINGS. "next to of course god" by E. E. Cummings, copyright, 1926, by Horace Liveright; copyright, 1954, by E. E. Cummings. Reprinted from *Poems 1923-1954* by E. E. Cummings, by permission of Harcourt, Brace & World, Inc.

EMILY DICKINSON. "The Soul Selects" (No. 303) and "Because I Could Not Stop for Death" (No. 712) are reprinted by permission of the publishers from Thomas H. Johnson, Editor, *The Poems of Emily Dickinson* (Cambridge, Mass.: The Belknap Press of Harvard University Press). Copyright, 1951, 1955, by The President and Fellows of Harvard College.

T. S. ELIOT. "Journey of the Magi" and "The Love Song of J. Alfred Prufrock" from *Collected Poems 1909-1962* by T. S. Eliot, copyright, 1936, by Harcourt, Brace & World, Inc.; copyright, © 1963, 1964, by T. S. Eliot. Reprinted by permission of Harcourt, Brace & World, Inc., and by permission of Faber and Faber Ltd. (London).

WILLIAM FAULKNER. "The Bear," copyright, 1942, by The Curtis Publishing Co. Reprinted by permission of Random House, Inc. An expanded version of this story appears in *Go Down, Moses* by William Faulkner.

ARTHUR FREEMAN. "Cut Laurels" by Arthur Freeman, copyright © 1966, by Arthur Freeman, is reprinted from his volume *Estrangements* by permission of Harcourt, Brace & World, Inc.

ROBERT FROST. "Come In," "The Most of It," "The Silken Tent," "Design," "The Pasture," "Stopping By Woods on a Snowy Evening" from *Complete Poems of Robert Frost*. Copyright, 1923, 1930, 1939, by Holt, Rinehart and Winston, Inc. Copyright, 1936, 1942, 1951, © 1958, by Robert

Edwards and the Spider" from *Lord Weary's Castle* by Robert Lowell, copyright, 1944, 1946, by Robert Lowell. Reprinted by permission of Harcourt, Brace & World, Inc.

GEORGE MACBETH. "What Metre Is" is reprinted by permission of Mr. George MacBeth.

ARCHIBALD MACLEISH. "Ars Poetica" from *Collected Poems* by Archibald MacLeish is reprinted by permission of Houghton Mifflin Company.

WALTER DE LA MARE. "Epitaph" is reprinted by permission of The Literary Trustees of Walter de la Mare and The Society of Authors (London) as their representative.

W. SOMERSET MAUGHAM. "Mr. Know-All," copyright, 1924, by W. Somerset Maugham, from the book *Cosmopolitans* by W. Somerset Maugham. Reprinted by permission of Doubleday & Company, Inc. and A. P. Watt & Son (London), for the Literary Executor and William Heinemann Ltd.

MARIANNE MOORE. "Silence" and "Poetry" are reprinted with permission of The Macmillan Company from *Collected Poems* by Marianne Moore. Copyright, Marianne Moore, 1935, renewed 1963, by Marianne Moore and T. S. Eliot.

EDWIN MUIR. "The Enchanted Knight" from *Collected Poems* by Edwin Muir. Copyright © 1960, by Willa Muir. Reprinted by permission of the Oxford University Press, Inc. and Faber and Faber Ltd. (London).

FLANNERY O'CONNOR. "A Good Man is Hard to Find," copyright, 1953, by Flannery O'Connor. Reprinted from her volume *A Good Man is Hard to Find and Other Stories* by permission of Harcourt, Brace & World, Inc.

FRANK O'CONNOR. "Guests of the Nation" from *More Stories* by Frank O'Connor. Published, 1954, by Alfred A. Knopf, Inc. Reprinted by permission of Alfred A. Knopf, Inc., and A. D. Peters & Co., Literary Agents (London).

WILFRED OWEN. "Anthem for Doomed Youth" from *The Collected Poems* of Wilfred Owen. Copyright © Chatto & Windus, Ltd., 1963. Reprinted by permission of New Directions Publishing Corporation and Chatto & Windus, Ltd. (London).

PETRONIUS. The excerpt from *The Satyricon of Petronius*, translated by William Arrowsmith, is used by permission of the University of Michigan Press.

SYLVIA PLATH. "Daddy" from *Ariel* by Sylvia Plath, copyright © 1963, by Ted Hughes. Reprinted by permission of Harper & Row, Publishers, and Miss Olwyn Hughes on behalf of Ted Hughes.

KATHERINE ANNE PORTER. "The Jilting of Granny Weatherall," copyright, 1930, 1958, by Katherine Anne Porter. Reprinted from her volume *Flowering Judas and Other Stories* by permission of Harcourt, Brace & World, Inc.

EZRA POUND. "Immorality" from *Lustra* by Ezra Pound, copyright, 1917, by Ezra Pound. All rights reserved. Reprinted by permission of the author's agent, New Directions Publishing Corporation. "The Age Demanded" from "Hugh Selwyn Mauberley" from *Personae* by Ezra Pound, copyright, 1926, 1954, by Ezra Pound. Reprinted by permission of the publisher, New Directions Publishing Corporation.

JOHN CROWE RANSOM. "Bells for John Whiteside's Daughter," copyright, 1924, by Alfred A. Knopf, Inc. and renewed 1952, by John Crowe Ransom. "Piazza Piece," copyright, 1927, by Alfred A. Knopf, Inc. and renewed 1955, by John Crowe Ransom. Reprinted from *Selected Poems* by John Crowe Ransom, by permission of Alfred A. Knopf, Inc.

THEODORE ROETHKE. "Elegy for Jane," copyright, 1950, by Theodore Roethke, from the book, *Words for the Wind* by Theodore Roethke. Reprinted by permission of Doubleday & Company, Inc. "My Papa's Waltz" from *The Lost Son and Other Poems* is used by permission of the author.

WILLIAM SHAKESPEARE. Text and footnotes from *The Tragedy of Othello* by William Shakespeare, edited by Alvin Kernan. Copyright © 1963, by Alvin Kernan. Copyright © 1963, by Sylvan Barnet. All Rights Reserved. Published by arrangement with The New American Library, Inc., New York.

BERNARD SHAW. *Major Barbara* by Bernard Shaw is reprinted with the permission of the Public Trustee and The Society of Authors (London).

SOPHOCLES. *Antigone of Sophocles:* An English Version by Dudley Fitts and Robert Fitzgerald, copyright, 1939, by Harcourt, Brace & World, Inc., and reprinted with their permission.

WALLACE STEVENS. "Peter Quince at the Clavier" and "Anecdote of the Jar," copyright, 1923, and renewed 1951, by Wallace Stevens. "Of Modern Poetry," copyright, 1942, by Wallace Stevens. Reprinted from *The Collected Poems of Wallace Stevens*, by permission of Alfred A. Knopf, Inc.

JON SWAN. "The Opening" by Jon Swan is used with the permission of The New Yorker Magazine, Inc. Copyright, 1960, by The New Yorker Magazine, Inc.

JOHN M. SYNGE. *Riders to the Sea* is reprinted from *The Complete Works of John M. Synge*, courtesy of Random House, Inc., and George Allen & Unwin Ltd. (London). "Is It a Month" (both versions) from *Synge Poems*, Volume I of *Collected Poems*, edited by Robin Skelton, are reprinted by permission of the Oxford University Press (London). "The Curse" by John M. Synge is reprinted by permission of George Allen & Unwin Ltd. (London).

DYLAN THOMAS. "After the Funeral" and "Fern Hill" from *Collected Poems* by Dylan Thomas, copyright, 1953, by Dylan Thomas, © 1957, by New Directions. Reprinted by permission of the publisher, New Directions Publishing Corporation, and J. M. Dent & Sons Ltd. (London).

JAMES THURBER. "The Secret Life of Walter Mitty" by James Thurber, copyright © 1942, James Thurber. From *My World—And Welcome to It*, published by Harcourt, Brace & World, Inc. Originally printed in *The New Yorker*. Reprinted by permission of Mrs. Helen Thurber.

JOHN UPDIKE. "A & P," © copyright, 1962, by John Updike. Reprinted from *Pigeon Feathers and Other Stories*, by John Updike, by permission of Alfred A. Knopf, Inc. "Youth's Progress" from *The Carpentered Hen and Other Tame Creatures* by John Updike, copyright ©, 1955, by John Updike. Originally published in *The New Yorker*, and reprinted by permission of Harper & Row, Publishers.

EUDORA WELTY. "A Worn Path," copyright, 1941, by Eudora Welty, is reprinted from her volume *A Curtain of Green and Other Stories* by permission of Harcourt, Brace & World, Inc. "Livvie," copyright, 1942, by Eudora Welty, is reprinted from her volume *The Wide Net and Other Stories* by permission of Harcourt, Brace & World, Inc.

RICHARD WILBUR. "Mind," from *Things of This World*, copyright © 1956, by Richard Wilbur, and "Praise in Summer," from *The Beautiful Changes*, copyright, 1947, by Richard Wilbur. Reprinted by permission of Harcourt, Brace & World, Inc.

PREFACE

"A big book," said Callimachus, "is a big misfortune." He might have added that a big book is heavy. Aware that many instructors have found needlessly bulky most of the textbooks designed for introductory courses in literature, the editors and publisher of *An Introduction to Literature* have produced a book that is smaller than most books intended for such courses. They have kept in mind Dr. Johnson's maxim: "Books that you may. . . hold readily in your hand are the most useful after all."

The relative brevity of this volume has been achieved partly by omitting the essay, partly by assuming (hopefully) that much of what is here included will please the instructor and therefore need not be reinforced by numerous alternative selections, and partly by refusing to allow the editorial apparatus to usurp the province of the classroom. Each of these points deserves further comment.

We have omitted essays of all sorts, confining the selections to the central literary genres of the story, the poem, and the play. The affinities of the essay are commonly with history (*e.g.*, a biographical essay) or philosophy (*e.g.*, an analysis of the nature of poetry). To say that essays are not as central to literature as stories, poems, and plays is not to denigrate them; it is no affront to a cat to bar it from a dog show. Furthermore, whether the introductory course in literature is given in the second half of the freshman year, or in the sophomore year, it usually has behind it a course in which essays have been studied; if it is given as part of a freshman composition course, a rhetoric text with illustrative essays is customarily used as well. Finally, there are now available numerous inexpensive editions of essays (*e.g.*, *Great Essays in Science*, *A Collection of Essays by George Orwell*, or *Classic Essays in English*) that can easily supplement this book if essays are desired.

We have concentrated, for the most part, on material that can be called "classical," partly to keep the bulk down and partly because we strongly feel that students ought for the most part to read first-rate material. There is something wrong, we believe, with a book that includes half a dozen stories of the last year or two and nothing by Hawthorne. We include some very recent work, and almost half of the selections are from the twentieth century, but for the most part we rely on such classic writers as Hawthorne, Faulkner, Shakespeare, and Yeats. A classic, of course, is not the same thing as a chestnut. The former, Maurice Beebe explains in *College English*, January, 1957, "are in a sense the freshest of stories simply because they obviously may be seen in many different lights and even yet have not given up all their secrets. The chestnuts are those stories which—like 'Haircut,' 'The Necklace,' and 'The Furnished Room'—give up all their secrets on an initial reading and hence require as little classroom discussion as they have evoked published criticism. I see no objection to a text made up primarily of classics." We should add, too, that we have included in addition to a large number of classics and a smaller number of good contemporary pieces a few unusual pieces: the manuscript of Robert Frost's "The Silken Tent," Frost's "In White" (omitted from his collected poems), an early poem by James Joyce, and so forth.

The editorial material is brief and yet rather complete. The paradox is easily explained: this book does not try to do what only the teacher can really do. The proper place for a detailed discussion of the multiple meanings in a word or line is, we believe, the classroom. Textbook analyses that for pages drag the student through a short poem or story are often dull and irritating. The object of an anthology of literature is to allow the student to read and to think, and perhaps to write down his thoughts, but it is doubtful if a long exegesis does much to stimulate a student to think. We have tried in our editorial apparatus to give succinct definitions of the terms commonly used in talking about literature, and to *begin* (but by no means to finish) a critical reading of literature. About half of the selections in the book are briefly discussed or have questions appended; the other half are unsullied. We have kept in mind Frost's remark: "You don't chew a poem—macerate a poem—for an evening's pleasure, for a Roman holiday. You touch it. You are aware that a good deal of it is missed."

USING THE BOOK. Probably most instructors teach fiction, then poetry, and then drama—the order followed here. But the three sections can be taught in any sequence, because each is relatively independent; there is, for example, a discussion of symbolism in each of the three sections, and while the three discussions have a cumulative effect, any of the three can be used first. This flexibility runs throughout the book; we hope that instructors will not feel that the first chapter must be taught first. Indeed, the first chapter—a survey of some theories of literature—can be used effectively midway or even at the end. There is a similar flexibility within the three chief sections of the book: one can teach everything straight through a section, or skip one's way through a section, or bring in wherever one wishes the stories and poems that conclude the sections. One might, for example, jump from Maugham's and Maupassant's stories to Hemingway's story near the end of the section. Similarly, one might jump from Johnson's poem on the death of Levet (in the chapter on lyrics) to Roethke's "Elegy for Jane" (in the anthology of poems). If the instructor wishes to skip a good many poems, he can run through the first eight chapters in the poetry section in a few meetings; if, on the other hand, he wishes to examine closely most or all of the poems in these chapters, he could spend as much as half a semester with them.

Although comparatively brief, *An Introduction to Literature* contains ample material for a one-semester course; supplemented by a few paperback books, it can provide a core volume for a full-year course. Most instructors in a one-semester course will, however, wish to add a paperback novel, and possibly still another paperback. For example, one might wish to read a novel by Faulkner, and additional plays by Sophocles, Shakespeare, or Shaw. Or one might wish to go beyond Eliot's "The Love Song of J. Alfred Prufrock" and "Journey of the Magi," using the Harvest selection of Eliot's poems. But the present volume supplies the student with a basic selection of literature, and a basic introduction to the critical study of literature. Since we have not tried to predict what paperbacks might be added, we have not included questions on any novels. We have, however, included "Some Observations on the Novel," a few pages that attempt to distinguish the novel from other prose fiction. We have tried to make our apparatus sufficiently broad so that it can serve as an aid to whatever additional books are read. For example, the introduction to tragedy is not an introduction to *Antigone* or to *Othello* but is an introduction to *tragedy*; because it examines definitions of tragedy by a Jacobean dramatist, a Soviet critic, and an American dramatist, and discusses such terms as *hamartia*, *hybris*, and *catharsis*, it will be helpful in thinking about all tragedies, from Greek to contemporary American.

THE TEXTS. On the whole we have regularized and Americanized the spelling. There seems little point in confronting the student with:

> That time of yeeare thou maift in me behold,
> When yellow leaues, or none, or few doe hange
> Vpon thofe boughes which fhake againft the could,
> Bare rn'wd quiers, where late the fweet birds fang.

However, we have in a few cases retained un-American spellings: Eliot's poems are printed exactly as they appear in his *Collected Poems*; Shaw's *Major Barbara* is printed not only with its English spellings but with its odd Shavian spellings (orthography meant a lot to Shaw); Blake's "The Tyger" retains its other-worldly "y." We might also mention that despite alterations in spelling, many of the works are here presented in more accurate texts than usual. For example, Emily Dickinson's "Because I Could Not Stop for Death" is reprinted from the new edition by Thomas Johnson; "Western Wind" is deprived of the "O" that often precedes—without any authority—the first word; Milton's "When I Consider How My Light Is Spent" is called just that, instead of the unauthorized "On His Blindness." (A few unauthentic titles, sanctioned by tradition, are used, *e.g.*, "Western Wind," "Edward.")

The material on versification is reprinted with a few abridgments, from our handbook, *The Study of Literature*. Some of the ideas in the section on drama were earlier contributed, in slightly different form, to Newman P. Birk and Genevieve B. Birk, *Understanding and Using English*. We thank them for allowing us to make use of this material.

In preparing the third edition of this book, we have been mindful of the encouraging and gratifying comments from users of the first and second editions. If this new edition has been strengthened and enhanced, it is primarily because of their helpful suggestions. Among the new selections that will be found throughout the book are stories by Melville, Hemingway, and Updike, and poems by Wallace Stevens, Theodore Roethke, and Sylvia Plath. The drama section in particular has been much changed and enlarged.

Finally, after this elaborate explanation of what has been done, we wish to thank people who helped us do it: Peter Brown, Arthur Freeman, Martin Friedman, David Bonnell Green, Donald R. Hammonds, Doris Kirk Holmes, X. J. Kennedy, Ronald Q. Lewton, Bernard McCabe, Warren R. Stone, Marcia Stubbs, and Ruth Sullivan.

S. B.
M. B.
W.B.

CONTENTS

Eleven
FIGURATIVE LANGUAGE: IMAGERY AND SYMBOLISM

359

Twelve
IRONY AND PARADOX

368

Thirteen
RHYTHM

376

A COLLECTION OF POEMS   412

DRAMA

An Introduction to

LITERATURE

FICTION   POETRY   DRAMA

One

SOME THEORIES OF LITERATURE

WHAT IS LITERATURE? Although literature is sometimes defined as anything written, this definition is both too broad and too narrow. While it is true that a housewife can ask the Department of Agriculture for "literature" about canning artichokes, surely we can distinguish between literature in the sense of any writing, and literature in the sense of verbal works of art. And, on the other hand, to say that literature must be written or printed is too narrow, because it excludes oral literature, *e.g.*, ballads that are sung and stories that are recited.

We can begin by saying that literature is (to quote Robert Frost) a "performance in words." It has in it an element of entertaining display, and surely we expect literature to be in some sense entertaining, or, to put it in slightly different terms, to afford pleasure. That literature is an adult game, a sort of make-believe, is suggested in some of the words we apply to pieces of literature—"fiction," "story," "tale," "play."

Now, what is it that makes literature pleasant? Without attempting a complete answer, perhaps we can say that a literary work seizes our interest and more or less—at least for a moment—makes the rest of the world fade or vanish. If the writer has done his job well, our attention is focused on the work, and we are in some measure detached from our usual surroundings. Consider, as an analogy, our reaction when we suddenly get a whiff of new-mown hay. We are walking along a road, either fretting about a dozen things or engaged in a pleasant vague reverie, when suddenly we smell the hay. At once we are caught up, keenly interested in this experience, intensely aware of this one thing, a thing that seems complete and satisfying in itself. For the moment we forget about the time of day, the dust of the road, the heat of the sun, and we find in this thing which is complete, whole, independent, something that catches us up and delights us. A work of art has this power to catch us up momentarily, and to delight us.

But it may well be objected that *Hamlet* is surely more than a load of hay. Art, it is commonly said, offers truth as well as pleasure. Such a view is at least superficially plausible, but when we begin to think about it, we encounter problems. What "truth" is there in *Hamlet?* The characters in the play are fictional, so we cannot say that Shakespeare is giving us a true picture of Danish history. There is a ghost in the play, but many people today have serious doubts about the existence of ghosts. Perhaps we will seize on certain lines, such as "Neither a borrower nor a lender be," but even this much-quoted line can hardly be defended as an unquestioned truth: there are surely times when it is good to borrow or to lend. Let us leave *Hamlet* (though not with the implication that the concept of truth is irrelevant to it), and glance at a short poem, "Heart's-Ease," by Walter Savage Landor (1775-1864):

> There is a flower I wish to wear,
>   But not until first worn by you—
> Heart's-ease— of all earth's flowers most rare;
>   Bring it; and bring enough for two.

Is it true that the flower called Heart's-ease is the earth's rarest flower? If we want to know about flowers, hadn't we better listen to botanists than to poets? Poets may occasionally stumble on scientific truths, but aren't scientists the more likely ones to give us scientific truths? Isn't it apparent that whatever value Landor's poem has is not in its botany?

These are big problems, and they have not yet been solved to general satisfaction. Not only literary critics but creative artists themselves have held numerous theories about the nature of literature. A glance at an anthology of criticism reveals a confusing diversity. In *Writers at Work*, for example, a paperback collection (edited by Malcolm Cowley) of interviews with contemporary novelists, one finds a writer who holds that the artist presents experience and is not a teacher, a writer who holds that the artist presents experience and is a teacher incidentally, and a writer who holds that the artist is essentially (to use Frank O'Connor's own words) "a reformer." We may as well face the fact that there is a diversity of theories; nothing is gained by pretending that everyone knows or agrees what literature is or does. But most theories of literature can, without much distortion, be put into one of three pigeon-holes, and it is these three classifications—which can be called "imitative," "expressive," and "affective" —that we want to talk about at the outset. A glance at the chief ways in which professional students talk about literature may help sharpen a reader's perceptions. Good literature deserves to be talked about as well as read and enjoyed.

THE IMITATIVE THEORY. The imitative theory holds that art is an imitation of something. In his *Poetics*, Aristotle (384-322 B.C.) says, for example, that a tragedy is an imitation of an action that is serious and complete. Because imitation now has pejorative associations, it is well to think of Aristotle's *mimesis* as not only "imitation" but also "re-creation" or "re-presentation." In an artistic imitation, Aristotle holds, a form is presented in a substance not natural to it. Thus, Michelangelo (it can be said) imitated Moses in stone; Cézanne imitated Mont Sainte Victoire in pigment on canvas; Shakespeare imitated Caesar in an actor's words and gestures. Music, too, Aristotle holds, is imitative; Tchaikovsky, for example, imitates Napoleon's defeat in Russia in the "1812 Overture." Aristotle would have approved of Thomas De Quincey's remark that although no one whistled at Waterloo, one might whistle Waterloo. The imitative instinct, of course, is not the artist's private possession. A small boy says to another, "You be the cop and I'll be the robber and you say 'Halt' and I'll run away." This natural tendency to imitate is combined, Aristotle says, with a tendency toward rhythm or pattern, and the result can be a work of art. In its simplest form the imitative theory appeals to the naive: "How life-like that wax apple is!" "How like a Frenchman that actor looks!" But more sophisticated people may ask: "What is so pleasing about a wax apple or a fake Frenchman? There are plenty of real apples and real Frenchmen for us to look at." Aristotle's theory includes such a close copy of nature as a wax apple, but it goes farther. He says that art is superior to history because where history must stick to the facts, art refines nature, showing, one might say, not what happened but what should have happened in a world free from accident. The artist is a sort of greenhouse man, producing not the rose that grows wild, cankered, and stunted, but the rose that has fulfilled all its potential, the rose that is more a rose than any wild rose. The artist, in short, does not imitate servilely; he recreates reality and presents it to us in a fashion in which we see its essence more clearly.

It is only half-true, then, to say that Aristotle's imitator is a maker of an imitation. (This idea of the artist as a maker, by the way, survives dimly in the word "playwright"—"wright" being a maker, as in "shipwright," and having nothing to do with "write.") Because the artist's imitation is more than a copy of what is apparent to every eye, his imitation is in some measure a creation. It is imaginative and interpretive; it reflects a special view of reality. Thomas Mann, attributing such an inspired sort of imitating to Anton Chekhov, comments on the boy Chekhov's propensity for mimicking the dentist, the policeman, and other acquaintances: "What makes its appearance here is the primitive origin of all art, the inclination to ape, the jester's desire and talent to entertain; . . . it was to ally itself [in Chekhov's maturity] with spiritual principles, to undergo moral ennoblement, and to rise from merely amusing trifles to soul-searching achievements." Presumably, then, the reader of a work written by a Chekhov will learn something.

The imitative theory often includes the notion that art gives us not only pleasure but also knowledge, insight into the nature of reality. If you say that we enjoy wax apples simply because we enjoy seeing exhibitions of man's skill at imitation, you are not introducing the criterion of knowledge. If, however, you say that by looking at the imitation we come to know something about reality, you are saying that art furnishes knowledge, and that its value depends partly on its truth. This problem of truth does not arise in all the arts: no one asks the Taj Mahal to be true. But many people want their literature to be true—to be an illuminating reflection of reality. Milton, it might be said, in *Paradise Lost* imitated the fall of Adam and Eve, and he did so in an effort (he says) to "justify the ways of God to men." He was not merely trying to divert, he was trying to help his readers to understand certain facts. The danger, of course, is that the reader may turn literature into a message: he hunts for detachable tags ("Frailty, thy name is woman," "To thine own self be true"), or he reduces the whole work to a neat moral. He begins to neglect artistry and to give A's to those works whose messages (as he conceives them) seem right to him. But what does anyone really learn from a work of literature? Do we learn from *Julius Caesar* not to be a tyrant? Or not to assassinate a tyrant? Or the difficulty of assassinating a tyrant and getting away with it? Surely we knew all this before. Perhaps the answer to the question, "Does literature give knowledge?" is that we do not learn from literature how to act in a particular situation (we'll probably never get the chance to be Roman tyrants or assassins), but we do learn something about life in general. After seeing a play, we feel that we have achieved at least a momentary understanding of some of the facts of life. The happenings in the book or on the stage not only seem in some degree to resemble things in real life, but they also clarify real life, making us say: "Yes, people are like that, but I hadn't noticed it before." Or we may have known intellectually that this or that is so, but now what earlier had been a lifeless platitude is a vital part of our being. We may not translate this vivified knowledge into any specific action, but we may nevertheless feel that we have acquired new insight and that our lives will be in some degree changed. James Joyce expressed such a view when he complained to a publisher who refused to issue his book of stories, *Dubliners:*

It is not my fault that the odor of ashpits and old weeds and offal hangs round my stories. I seriously believe that you will retard the course of civilization in Ireland by preventing the Irish people from having one good look at themselves in my nicely polished looking-glass.

THE EXPRESSIVE THEORY. The second theory, usually called the expressive theory, can be treated more briefly. It holds that the artist is not essentially an imitator but a man who expresses his feelings. Two quotations from William Wordsworth will make this theory clear. "Poetry," he said, "is the spontaneous overflow of powerful feelings"; the poet's job is "to treat of things not as they *are* . . . but as they *seem* to exist to the *senses*, and the *passions*." (This is by no means a complete summary of Wordsworth's theories, but it is enough to illustrate the gist of expressive theories.) The artist's vision, the theory holds, is more inward than outward; the work of art is not an imitation of the external world but an expression of the internal world, the embodiment of an emotion. This theory sometimes holds that "truth" has nothing to do with literature; Landor's "Heart's-Ease," it might be said, expresses his feelings, and his feelings cannot be true or false. They simply exist. But sometimes an expressive theory insists that a work is true if it is sincere. We do not ordinarily say that laughter or tears are true or false, but if we discover that the laughter or tears are hypocritical rather than sincere, we call them false. Since, however, the reader of a piece of literature cannot know if the author was sincere when he wrote it, the criterion of sincerity is valueless. We cannot say that *Julius Caesar* is sincere; perhaps Shakespeare wrote it to a theater-owner's prescription. We cannot even say that his sonnets reflect his true feelings; though Wordsworth said that in them Shakespeare "unlocked his heart," how can we be sure? Furthermore, writing that is indubitably sincere is not necessarily good writing. Aldous Huxley is surely correct in his observation that "a bad book is as much labor to write as a good one; it comes as sincerely from the author's soul." Moreover, what value does expressive writing have? One can reply it is valuable for the writer: "If I don't write to empty my mind," Byron said, "I go mad." But if this relief from pressure is its only value, the written piece might just as well be left lying on the writer's desk. Most expressions of emotions, after all, are valueless to everyone but the person expressing them. Our laughter, mumblings, and cries of despair are all very expressive, and afford us a relief, but who would call them works of art that are of value to other people? Not all expressions of emotion, clearly, are works of art, and conversely, if a work of art is an expression of emotion, it must be a very special kind of expression.

Advocates of the expressive theory, however, have yet another argument, this one stronger: by showing us how he sees and feels something, the writer may pluck the blinders from our eyes and melt the ice around our heart. He may jolt us out of our usual rut, and widen the area of our sensibilities. Wordsworth's view of daffodils may force upon us the awareness that our own views are narrow. An awareness of how other people feel is, after all, a way of expanding and enriching one's own personality.

THE AFFECTIVE THEORY. Finally, there is the affective theory of art, which holds that a work of art ought to arouse a particular emotion, or affect (to use the psychologist's term), in the perceiver. This theory is often closely related to the expressive theory: the artist allegedly expresses his emotion, embodying it in a work of art, and this work evokes in the perceiver a similar or identical emotion. Presumably by describing certain things in a certain way the writer can evoke the proper response. The most famous presentation of this theory is Tolstoi's *What Is Art?*, a sentence of which is here quoted:

> Art is a human activity consisting in this, that one man consciously by means of certain external signs, hands on to others feelings he has lived through, and that others are infected by these feelings, and also experience them.

Here is another statement of the theory, this one by Alexander Pope:

> Let me for once presume to instruct the times,
> To know the poet from the man of rhymes:
> 'Tis he, who gives my breast a thousand pains,
> Can make me feel each passion that he feigns;
> Enrage, compose, with more than magic art,
> With pity and with terror tear my heart;
> And snatch me o'er the earth or through the air,
> To Thebes, to Athens, when he will, and where.

(It is worth mentioning, incidentally, that although Pope's lines say that poetry arouses passions in the reader or hearer, they themselves, like most of Pope's writing, do not arouse fierce passions, but rather arouse interest and attention.) Affective theories hold that the stimulation of certain emotions is, for some reason, good: we need an occasional release (a good cry), or we need to have our emotions organized into a pleasant pattern (as the fretful child needs his mother's smile, to induce in him good spirits). That some readers seek emotional stimulus from books is beyond doubt. Often the lady who asks the rental librarian to recommend a good novel is asking for a book that will allow her fully to identify herself with the heroine, experiencing bursts of love, sorrow, and so forth. But a good work of art neither invites this identification nor triggers stereotyped emotions. How many people have felt totally at one with Hamlet, Macbeth, Brutus?

Usually the affective theory insists that the aim is not to induce a temporary emotional state, but to induce an emotional state that will lead to action. Such a theory might hold, for example, that the artist should stimulate in people an awareness of the horror of war so that they will go out and do something about stopping wars. Tolstoi, who held such a view, regarded the evocation of emotion not as an end but as a means:

> The task of art is enormous. Through the influence of real art, aided by science, guided by religion, that peaceful co-operation of man which is now maintained by external means—by our law-courts, police, charitable institutions, factory inspection, and so forth—should be obtained by man's free and joyous activity. Art should cause violence to be set aside.

Pope, too, holds that the aim of art is to reform those whom it touches:

> To wake the soul by tender strokes of art,
> To raise the genius, and to mend the heart;
> To make mankind, in conscious virtue bold,
> Live o'er each scene, and be what they behold:
> For this the Tragic Muse first trod the stage,
> Commanding tears to stream through ev'ry age;
> Tyrants no more their savage nature kept,
> And foes to virtue wondered how they wept.

SOME TENTATIVE CONCLUSIONS. This chapter opened with the query, "What is literature?" and it has not yet given a satisfactory answer. Nor will it. No one has come up with a satisfactory answer so far. Textbooks and theoretical treatises are filled with neat definitions, but no definition has yet withstood all criticism. It would be nice to say that literature evokes emotion, but so does a good deal of non-literature (*e.g.*, a documentary account of the bombing of Hiroshima), and, as we suggest above, perhaps much literature evokes "attention" rather than "emotion." It would be nice to say that literature is essentially fictional, but is a poem on, say, the power of God, fictional? Is such a poem fictional to the believer who composes it or to the believer who reads it? It would be nice to say that in literature there is complexity and unity, but these are characteristics of a telephone book as well as of *Hamlet*. And so it goes, definition after definition failing when applied to specific works that we know are works of art.

The brief sketch of critical theories in the preceding pages, however, may help a reader toward a tentative definition. Surely we can agree that a piece of literature is a performance in words; it strongly holds our attention, seeming complete in itself; it is not primarily regarded as a source of factual information; it offers a unique delight or satisfaction. To these, most people would add that literature offers some sort of truth, though not the sort of truth found in factual propositions of the $E = mc^2$ variety. Finally, most people would say that it has a beneficial effect on the perceiver. Tolstoi and Pope may be claiming too much for the arts, but is it absurd to believe that they can play a role in civilizing man? Music has beneficial effects on animals: cows are said to give more milk when music is played in barns, race horses are soothed at the starting-gate at Aqueduct, and wolves reduce their howling when they hear classical music. Is there nothing in these lines from *The Merchant of Venice*:

Jessica. I am never merry when I hear sweet music.
Lorenzo. The reason is your spirits are attentive;
    For do but note a wild and wanton herd,
    Or race of youthful and unhandled colts,
    Fetching mad bounds, bellowing and neighing loud,
    Which is the hot condition of their blood—
    If they but hear perchance a trumpet sound,
    Or any air of music touch their ears,
    You shall perceive them make a mutual stand,
    Their savage eyes turned to a modest gaze
    By the sweet power of music. Therefore the poet
    Did feign that Orpheus drew trees, stones, and floods,
    Since nought so stockish, hard, and full of rage,
    But music for the time doth change his nature.
    The man that hath no music in himself,
    Nor is not moved with concord of sweet sounds,
    Is fit for treasons, stratagems, and spoils.

Is it not possible that works of art give us an insight into reality (as the imitative theory usually holds), that they broaden our awareness of the possibilities of experience (as the expressive theory usually holds), and that they valuably affect our nervous system (as the affective theory usually holds)? This is not to say that every work of art does all these things, but only that all of these theories may have something to contribute to a deeper and more conscious awareness of what is valuable in the works we read. If we look back into our experiences, can we not find moments that seem to verify aspects of each theory? This book will offer further experiences; as the reader encounters them, he is invited to test these theories.

FICTION

Some Elements of Fiction   •   Plausibility in Fiction   •
Narrative Point of View • Allegory and Symbolism • Style

Two

SOME ELEMENTS OF FICTION

With one exception, all the stories in this book were written during the last two centuries. Here is the exception, a brief tale from *The Satyricon*, a witty, cynical book attributed to Petronius, director-in-chief of Nero's entertainments.

PETRONIUS (*1st Century* A.D.)

The Widow of Ephesus

Translated by William Arrowsmith

"Once upon a time there was a certain married woman in the city of Ephesus whose fidelity to her husband was so famous that the women from all the neighboring towns and villages used to troop into Ephesus merely to stare at this prodigy. It happened, however, that her husband one day died. Finding the normal custom of following the cortege with hair unbound and beating her breast in public quite inadequate to express her grief, the lady insisted on following the corpse right into the tomb, an underground vault of the Greek type, and there set herself to guard the body, weeping and wailing night and day. Although in her extremes of grief she was clearly courting death from starvation, her parents were utterly unable to persuade her to leave, and even the magistrates, after one last supreme attempt, were rebuffed and driven away. In short, all Ephesus had gone into mourning for this extraordinary woman, all the more since the lady was now passing her fifth consecutive day without once tasting food. Beside the failing woman sat her devoted maid, sharing her mistress' grief and relighting the lamp whenever it flickered out. The whole city could speak, in fact, of nothing else: here at last, all classes alike agreed, was the one true example of conjugal fidelity and love.

"In the meantime, however, the governor of the province gave orders that several thieves should be crucified in a spot close by the vault where the lady was mourning her dead husband's corpse. So, on the following night, the soldier who had been assigned to keep watch on the crosses so that nobody could remove the thieves' bodies for burial suddenly noticed a light blazing among the tombs and heard the sounds of groaning. And prompted by a natural human curiosity to know who or what was making those sounds, he descended into the vault.

"But at the sight of a strikingly beautiful woman, he stopped short in terror, thinking he must be seeing some ghostly apparition out of hell. Then, observing the corpse and seeing the tears on the lady's face and the scratches her fingernails had gashed in her cheeks, he realized what it was: a widow, in inconsolable grief. Promptly fetching his little supper back down to the tomb, he implored the lady not to persist in her sorrow or break her heart with useless mourning. All men alike, he reminded her, have the same end; the same resting place awaits us all. He used, in short, all those platitudes we use to comfort the suffering and bring them back to life. His consolations, being unwelcome, only exasperated the widow more; more violently than ever she beat her breast, and tearing out her hair by the roots, scattered it over the dead man's body. Undismayed, the soldier repeated his arguments and pressed her to take some food, until the little maid, quite overcome by the smell of the wine, succumbed and stretched out her hand to her tempter. Then, restored by the food and wine, she began herself to assail her mistress' obstinate refusal.

" 'How will it help you,' she asked the lady, 'if you faint from hunger? Why should you bury yourself alive, and go down to death before the Fates have called you? What does Vergil say?—

Do you suppose the shades and ashes of the dead are by such sorrow touched?

No, begin your life afresh. Shake off these woman's scruples; enjoy the light while you can. Look at that corpse of your poor husband: doesn't it tell you more eloquently than any words that you should live?'

"None of us, of course, really dislikes being told that we must eat, that life is to be lived. And the lady was no exception. Weakened by her long days of fasting, her resistance crumbled at last, and she ate the food the soldier offered her as hungrily as the little maid had eaten earlier.

"Well, you know what temptations are normally aroused in a man on a full stomach. So the soldier, mustering all those blandishments by means of which he had persuaded the lady to live, now laid determined siege to her virtue. And chaste though she was, the lady found him singularly attractive and his arguments persuasive. As for the maid, she did all she could to help the soldier's cause, repeating like a refrain the appropriate line of Vergil:

> If love is pleasing, lady, yield yourself to love.

To make the matter short, the lady's body soon gave up the struggle; she yielded and our happy warrior enjoyed a total triumph on both counts. That very night their marriage was consummated, and they slept together the second and the third night too, carefully shutting the door of the tomb so that any passing friends or stranger would have thought the lady of famous chastity had at last expired over her dead husband's body.

"As you can perhaps imagine, our soldier was a very happy man, utterly delighted with his lady's ample beauty and that special charm that a secret love confers. Every night, as soon as the sun had set, he bought what few provisions his slender pay permitted and smuggled them down to the tomb. One night, however, the parents of one of the crucified thieves, noticing that the watch was being badly kept, took advantage of our hero's absence to remove their son's body and bury it. The next morning, of course, the soldier was horror-struck to discover one of the bodies missing from its cross, and ran to tell his mistress of the horrible punishment which awaited him for neglecting his duty. In the circumstances, he told her, he would not wait to be tried and sentenced, but would punish himself then and there with his own sword. All he asked of her was that she make room for another corpse and allow the same gloomy tomb to enclose husband and lover together.

"Our lady's heart, however, was no less tender than pure. 'God forbid,' she cried, 'that I should have to see at one and the same time the dead bodies of the only two men I have ever loved. No, better far, I say, to hang the dead than kill the living.' With these words, she gave orders that her husband's body should be taken from its bier and strung up on the empty cross. The soldier followed this good advice, and the next morning the whole city wondered by what miracle the dead man had climbed up on the cross."

Petronius tells us that the sailors who heard this tale greeted it "with great guffaws," surely the appropriate response. It is an amusing story, largely because it is well told. Let us look at it as a piece of craftsmanship. The happenings, as they are selected and arranged by the author, are the **plot**; the participants are the **characters**; the meaning or point is the **theme**.

The traditional plot has this structure:

(1) **exposition** (setting forth of the beginning)
(2) **conflict** (a complication that moves to a climax)

(3) **dénouement** (literally, "unknotting," the outcome of the conflict; the resolution)

Petronius' exposition is in the opening paragraph, which sets forth a situation that seems to be stable (the lady is resolved to die). We do not ask why she was so virtuous or of what her husband died; we simply accept the exposition, and wait for something to disturb the situation it describes. The second paragraph begins the conflict by introducing a complication (a soldier goes to the tomb). This complication (literally, folding or weaving together) is momentarily resolved when the lady exchanges widowhood for a new marriage, but the resolution gives rise to a greater complication, the disappearance of the thief's body. At this point the conflict is at its height, for the soldier's life is at stake. (Although at the start the widow's life was in danger, the tension was slight because she was doing what she wished; now that the lovers wish to live, the tension is greatest.) This moment of greatest tension is called the **climax**; it is here dissipated by an action of the lady, whose love for the soldier is as great as was her grief for her husband. Her suggestion to substitute her husband's corpse for the missing one unties the knot or the weaving begun with the complication. The soldier's acceptance of her suggestion, and the townsmen's bewilderment, constitute the dénouement. We have moved then, from a situation that seemed static (the widow's grief) through a complication that became acute, into a new situation that is stable. The lady may later leave the soldier for another man, but such happenings do not concern us; we feel that we have seen a unified action —something with a beginning, a middle, and an end.*

The things that happen are in large measure caused by the characters, who act believably. Although in Petronius' tale it is a coincidence that a thief has been crucified near the tomb containing the grieving wife, all the subsequent happenings arise from **character** (*i.e.*, the personality of each of the characters) : the soldier visits the tomb "prompted by a natural human curiosity," and, after he has consoled the widow and has eaten, he undergoes the

> temptations [that] are normally aroused in a man on a full stomach. So the soldier, mustering all those blandishments by means of which he had persuaded the lady to live, now laid determined siege to her virtue. And chaste though she was, the lady found him singularly attractive and his arguments persuasive.

* Though we have defined "plot" as the author's selection and arrangement of happenings, some critics define "plot" as the happenings in their chronological order. The term is further discussed on pages 463-65.

Similarly, there is **motivation** (a basis in character) for the disappearance of the thief's corpse; the fact that the soldier had been stationed to guard it gives us clear indication that the thief's family will bury it if given the chance. The soldier's fear and despair are similarly plausible, and, finally, so too is the lady's ingenious suggestion that saves the soldier, for her love for him is now as deep as it had been for her husband. The crucifixion of her husband's corpse, then, like the soldier's visit and the lady's change of heart, is motivated; we feel it is plausible in the light of the characters involved. And our interest in the tale is not only an interest in occurrences, but is also an interest in the people who engender the occurrences.

In some stories, of course, we are chiefly interested in plot (the arrangement of happenings or doings), in others we are chiefly interested in character (the personalities of the doers), but on the whole the two are so intertwined that interest in one involves interest in the other. Happenings occur (people cross paths), and personalities respond to them, engendering further happenings. As Henry James rhetorically asked, "What is character but the determination of incident? What is incident but the illustration of character?" Commonly, as a good story proceeds and we become increasingly familiar with the characters, we get intimations of what they may do in the future. We may not know precisely how they will act, but we have a fairly good idea, and when in fact we see their subsequent actions, we usually recognize the appropriateness. Sometimes there are hints of what is to come, and because of this **foreshadowing** we are not shocked by what happens, but rather we experience suspense as we wait for the expected to come about. Coleridge had Shakespeare's use of foreshadowing in mind when he praised him for giving us not surprise but expectation and then the satisfaction of perfect knowledge. E. M. Forster, in *Aspects of the Novel*, has a shrewd comment on the importance of both fulfilling expectation and offering a slight surprise: "Shock, followed by the feeling, 'Oh, that's all right,' is a sign that all is well with the plot: characters, to be real, ought to run smoothly, but a plot ought to cause surprise."

Finally, a few words about **theme**. Usually, a story is about something, it has a meaning, a point—a theme. The narrator of "The Widow of Ephesus" prefaced the tale by declaring that "no woman was so chaste or faithful that she couldn't be seduced," and his story was told in order to make this statement meaningful. A vulgar fellow, he interprets his story rather cheaply, even indecently. But the reader can more accurately restate the theme, giving it greater significance and making it more acceptable: life and love are too strong to be buried alive. A word of caution, however, is needed here: a story is not simply an illustration of a theme. A story has a variety of details that modify any abstract statement; in Petronius' story the lady was "weakened by her long days of fasting," and the soldier was "singularly attractive." Such details, not present in the narrator's own statement of his "theme," are important modifications of the theme. To state the theme either as the narrator stated it or as we have restated it is to falsify the story, for Petronius' story is about a particular widow's encounter with a particular soldier, under particular circumstances. And what lives in our memory is not an abstract statement, but an image that by every word in the story has convinced us that it is a representation if not of "reality" of at least an aspect of reality. Still, the artist was guided by a theme in his choice of details; of many possible details he chose to present only a few. What is it, Robert Frost asks, that prevents the writer from kicking himself "from one chance suggestion to another in all directions as of a hot afternoon in the life of a grasshopper?" Frost's answer: "Theme alone can steady us down."

We can, then, talk about the theme—what the story adds up to —as long as we do not think a statement of the theme is equivalent to or a substitution for the whole story.

QUESTIONS: *The Widow of Ephesus*

1. Most of the story is narrated, rather than dramatized through dialogue. Is the use of dialogue haphazard or is it in the right place?

2. What does the presence of the maid contribute to the story?

3. We are told that the lady decides to surrender the corpse because she is "no less tender than pure." Does the narrator mean exactly what he says? Explain.

4. The lady's virtue is set forth at some length; the desecration of the corpse is set forth very briefly. Why is this disparity effective?

5. The last sentence of the story is characteristic of the prevailing tone in which the story is told. How would you describe that tone, and how does it affect the theme?

Three

PLAUSIBILITY IN FICTION

Although the writer of fiction creates his own world, peopling it with such invented characters as David Copperfield, Silas Marner, Eustacia Vye, and Holden Caulfield, he is not altogether free. We have to feel that his fictional world hangs together, that one thing more or less leads to another. This is not to say that there can be nothing fantastic in a story: only that what is fantastic must be presented in a context that makes the fantastic seem plausible.

The following two stories may seem equally plausible or implausible upon a casual reading, but a closer reading will reveal a significant difference.

w. somerset maugham (1874-1965)

Mr. Know-All

I was prepared to dislike Max Kelada even before I knew him. The war had just finished and the passenger traffic in the ocean-going liners was heavy. Accommodation was very hard to get and you had to put up with whatever the agents chose to offer you. You could not hope for a cabin to yourself and I was thankful to be given one in which there were only two berths. But when I was told the name of my companion my heart sank. It suggested closed portholes and the night air rigidly excluded. It was bad enough to share a cabin for fourteen days with anyone (I was going from San Francisco to Yokohama), but I should have looked upon it with less dismay if my fellow passenger's name had been Smith or Brown.

When I went on board I found Mr. Kelada's luggage already below. I did not like the look of it; there were too many labels on the suitcases, and the wardrobe trunk was too big. He had unpacked his toilet things, and I observed that he was a patron of the excellent Monsieur Coty; for I saw on the washing-stand his scent, his hairwash, and his brilliantine. Mr. Kelada's brushes, ebony with his monogram in gold, would have been all the better for a scrub. I did not at all like Mr. Kelada. I made my way into the smoking room. I called for a pack of cards and began to play patience. I had scarcely started before a man came up to me and asked me if he was right in thinking my name was so and so.

"I am Mr. Kelada," he added, with a smile that showed a row of flashing teeth, and sat down.

"Oh, yes, we're sharing a cabin, I think."

"Bit of luck, I call it. You never know who you're going to be put in with. I was jolly glad when I heard you were English. I'm all for us English sticking together when we're abroad, if you understand what I mean."

I blinked.

"Are you English?" I asked, perhaps tactlessly.

"Rather. You don't think I look like an American, do you? British to the backbone, that's what I am."

To prove it, Mr. Kelada took out of his pocket a passport and airily waved it under my nose.

King George has many strange subjects. Mr. Kelada was short and of a sturdy build, clean-shaven and dark skinned, with a fleshy, hooked nose and very large, lustrous and liquid eyes. His long black hair was sleek and curly. He spoke with a fluency in which there was nothing English and his gestures were exuberant. I felt pretty sure that a closer inspection of that British passport would have betrayed the fact that Mr. Kelada was born under a bluer sky than is generally seen in England.

"What will you have?" he asked me.

I looked at him doubtfully. Prohibition was in force and to all appearance the ship was bone dry. When I am not thirsty I do not know which I dislike more, ginger ale or lemon squash. But Mr. Kelada flashed an oriental smile at me.

"Whisky and soda or a dry martini, you have only to say the word."

From each of his hip pockets he fished a flask and laid it on the table before me. I chose the martini, and calling the steward he ordered a tumbler of ice and a couple of glasses.

"A very good cocktail," I said.

"Well, there are plenty more where that came from, and if you've got any friends on board, you tell them you've got a pal who's got all the liquor in the world."

Mr. Kelada was chatty. He talked of New York and of San Francisco. He discussed plays, pictures, and politics. He was patriotic. The

Union Jack is an impressive piece of drapery, but when it is flourished by a gentleman from Alexandria or Beirut, I cannot but feel that it loses somewhat in dignity. Mr. Kelada was familiar. I do not wish to put on airs, but I cannot help feeling that it is seemly in a total stranger to put mister before my name when he addresses me. Mr. Kelada, doubtless to set me at my ease, used no such formality. I did not like Mr. Kelada. I had put aside the cards when he sat down, but now, thinking that for this first occasion our conversation had lasted long enough, I went on with my game.

"The three on the four," said Mr. Kelada.

There is nothing more exasperating when you are playing patience than to be told where to put the card you have turned up before you have had a chance to look for yourself.

"It's coming out, it's coming out," he cried. "The ten on the knave."

With rage and hatred in my heart I finished. Then he seized the pack.

"Do you like card tricks?"

"No, I hate card tricks," I answered.

"Well, I'll just show you this one."

He showed me three. Then I said I would go down to the dining room and get my seat at table.

"Oh, that's all right," he said. "I've already taken a seat for you. I thought that as we were in the same stateroom we might just as well sit at the same table."

I did not like Mr. Kelada.

I not only shared a cabin with him and ate three meals a day at the same table, but I could not walk round the deck without his joining me. It was impossible to snub him. It never occurred to him that he was not wanted. He was certain that you were as glad to see him as he was to see you. In your own house you might have kicked him downstairs and slammed the door in his face without the suspicion dawning on him that he was not a welcome visitor. He was a good mixer, and in three days knew everyone on board. He ran everything. He managed the sweeps, conducted the auctions, collected money for prizes at the sports, got up quoit and golf matches, organized the concert and arranged the fancy-dress ball. He was everywhere and always. He was certainly the best hated man in the ship. We called him Mr. Know-All, even to his face. He took it as a compliment. But it was at mealtimes that he was most intolerable. For the better part of an hour then he had us at his mercy. He was hearty, jovial, loquacious and argumentative. He knew everything better than anybody else, and it was an affront to his overweening vanity that you should disagree with him. He would not drop a subject, however unimportant, till he had brought you round to his way of thinking. The possibility that he could be mistaken never occurred to him. He was the chap who knew. We sat at the doctor's table. Mr. Kelada would certainly have had it all his own way, for the doctor was lazy and I was frigidly indifferent, except for a man called Ramsay who sat there also. He was as dogmatic as Mr. Kelada and resented bitterly the Levantine's cocksureness. The discussions they had were acrimonious and interminable.

Ramsay was in the American Consular Service and was stationed at Kobe. He was a great heavy fellow from the Middle West, with loose fat under a tight skin, and he bulged out of his ready-made clothes. He was on his way to resume his post, having been on a flying visit to New York to fetch his wife who had been spending a year at home. Mrs. Ramsay was a very pretty little thing, with pleasant manners and a sense of humor. The Consular Service is ill paid, and she was dressed always very simply; but she knew how to wear her clothes. She achieved an effect of quiet distinction. I should not have paid any particular attention to her but that she possessed a quality that may be common enough in women, but nowadays is not obvious in their demeanor. You could not look at her without being struck by her modesty. It shone in her like a flower on a coat.

One evening at dinner the conversation by chance drifted to the subject of pearls. There had been in the papers a good deal of talk about the culture pearls which the cunning Japanese were making, and the doctor remarked that they must inevitably diminish the value of real ones. They were very good already; they would soon be perfect. Mr. Kelada, as was his habit, rushed the new topic. He told us all that was to be known about pearls. I do not believe Ramsay knew anything about them at all, but he could not resist the opportunity to have a fling at the Levantine, and in five minutes we were in the middle of a heated argument. I had seen Mr. Kelada vehement and voluble before, but never so voluble and vehement as now. At last something that Ramsay said stung him, for he thumped the table and shouted:

"Well, I ought to know what I am talking about. I'm going to Japan just to look into this Japanese pearl business. I'm in the trade and there's not a man in it who won't tell you that what I say about pearls goes. I know all the best pearls in the world, and what I don't know about pearls isn't worth knowing."

Here was news for us, for Mr. Kelada, with all his loquacity, had never told anyone what his business was. We only knew vaguely that he was going to Japan on some commercial errand. He looked round the table triumphantly.

"They'll never be able to get a culture pearl that an expert like me can't tell with half an eye." He pointed to a chain that Mrs. Ramsay wore. "You take my word for it, Mrs. Ramsay, that chain you're wearing will never be worth a cent less than it is now."

Mrs. Ramsay in her modest way flushed a little and slipped the chain inside her dress. Ramsay leaned forward. He gave us all a look and a smile flickered in his eyes.

"That's a pretty chain of Mrs. Ramsay's, isn't it?"

"I noticed it at once," answered Mr. Kelada. "Gee, I said to myself, those are pearls all right."

"I didn't buy it myself, of course. I'd be interested to know how much you think it cost."

"Oh, in the trade somewhere round fifteen thousand dollars. But if it was bought on Fifth Avenue I shouldn't be surprised to hear that anything up to thirty thousand was paid for it."

Ramsay smiled grimly.

"You'll be surprised to hear that Mrs. Ramsay bought that string at a department store the day before we left New York, for eighteen dollars."

Mr. Kelada flushed.

"Rot. It's not only real, but it's as fine a string for its size as I've ever seen."

"Will you bet on it? I'll bet you a hundred dollars it's imitation."

"Done."

"Oh, Elmer, you can't bet on a certainty," said Mrs. Ramsay.

She had a little smile on her lips and her tone was gently deprecating.

"Can't I? If I get a chance of easy money like that I should be all sorts of a fool not to take it."

"But how can it be proved?" she continued. "It's only my word against Mr. Kelada's."

"Let me look at the chain, and if it's imitation I'll tell you quickly enough. I can afford to lose a hundred dollars," said Mr. Kelada.

"Take it off, dear. Let the gentleman look at it as much as he wants."

Mrs. Ramsay hesitated a moment. She put her hands to the clasp.

"I can't undo it," she said. "Mr. Kelada will just have to take my word for it."

I had a sudden suspicion that something unfortunate was about to occur, but I could think of nothing to say.

Ramsay jumped up.

"I'll undo it."

He handed the chain to Mr. Kelada. The Levantine took a magnifying glass from his pocket and closely examined it. A smile of triumph spread over his smooth and swarthy face. He handed back the chain. He was about to speak. Suddenly he caught sight of Mrs. Ramsay's face. It was so white that she looked as though she were about to faint. She was staring at him with wide and terrified eyes. They held a desperate appeal; it was so clear that I wondered why her husband did not see it.

Mr. Kelada stopped with his mouth open. He flushed deeply. You could almost *see* the effort he was making over himself.

"I was mistaken," he said. "It's a very good imitation, but of course as soon as I looked through my glass I saw that it wasn't real. I think eighteen dollars is just about as much as the damned thing's worth."

He took out his pocketbook and from it a hundred-dollar bill. He handed it to Ramsay without a word.

"Perhaps that'll teach you not to be so cocksure another time, my young friend," said Ramsay as he took the note.

I noticed that Mr. Kelada's hands were trembling.

The story spread over the ship as stories do, and he had to put up with a good deal of chaff that evening. It was a fine joke that Mr. Know-All had been caught out. But Mrs. Ramsay retired to her stateroom with a headache.

Next morning I got up and began to shave. Mr Kelada lay on his bed smoking a cigarette. Suddenly there was a small scraping sound and I saw a letter pushed under the door. I opened the door and looked out. There was nobody there. I picked up the letter and saw that it was addressed to Max Kelada. The name was written in block letters. I handed it to him.

"Who's this from?" He opened it. "Oh!"

He took out of the envelope, not a letter, but a hundred-dollar bill. He looked at me and again he reddened. He tore the envelope into little bits and gave them to me.

"Do you mind just throwing them out of the porthole?"

I did as he asked, and then I looked at him with a smile.

"No one likes being made to look a perfect damned fool," he said.

"Were the pearls real?"

"If I had a pretty little wife I shouldn't let her spend a year in New York while I stayed at Kobe," said he.

At that moment I did not entirely dislike Mr. Kelada. He reached out for his pocketbook and carefully put in it the hundred-dollar note.

GUY DE MAUPASSANT (1850-1893)

Hautot and His Son

Translated by the Editors

I

In front of the door of the house—part-farmhouse, part-manorhouse, one of those combined rural dwellings that were once almost manorial and that are now owned by big farmers—the dogs, tied to the apple trees in the courtyard, barked and howled at the game-bags carried by the gamekeeper and the boys. In the large dining room-kitchen, Hautot senior, Hautot junior, M. Bermont the tax-collector, and M. Mondrau the notary, were having a snack and a drink before starting out on the hunt, for it was the opening day of the season.

Hautot senior, proud of everything he owned, was boasting of the game his guests would find on his land. He was a tall Norman, one of those powerful, full-blooded, large-boned men, who can lift a cartload of apples onto their shoulders. Half-peasant, half-gentleman, rich, respected, influential, authoritative, he had sent his son, César, to school so that he would be educated, and then pulled him out of secondary school, afraid he might become a fine gentleman, indifferent to the farm.

César Hautot, almost as tall as his father, but thinner, was a good son, docile, content with everything, full of adoration, respect, and deference for the wishes and opinions of Hautot senior.

M. Bermont, the tax-collector, a fat little man whose red cheeks showed thin networks of purple veins like the tributaries and winding courses of rivers on a map, asked: "And hare—are there any hare?"

Hautot senior replied, "As many as you want, especially in the Puysatier bottoms."

"Where do we start?" asked the notary, a good-natured fellow, fat and pale, his paunch bulging out of his brand-new, tightly-laced hunting outfit, bought in Rouen last week.

"Why, that way, through the bottoms. We'll drive the partridges into the plain, and then we'll close in on them." Then Hautot senior got up. They all followed suit, took their guns from the corner, checked the locks, stamped their feet to get used to their stiff boots not yet softened by the warmth of their feet. Then they went out; and the dogs, straining at their leashes, let out shrill howls as they pawed the air.

They set out toward the bottoms, a small vale, or rather a large undulating stretch of poor land, which remained uncultivated, furrowed with ravines, overgrown with bracken—an excellent game preserve.

The hunters spread out, Hautot senior keeping to the right, Hautot junior to the left, the two guests in the middle. The game-keeper and the game-bag carriers followed. Now was that solemn moment when one awaits the first shot, when hearts beat a little faster, while nervous fingers keep feeling for the trigger.

Suddenly, the shot went off. Hautot senior had fired. They all stopped and saw a partridge drop from a covey in swift flight and fall into a ravine, disappearing in the thick brushwood. The excited hunter began running, stepping over and yanking at the brambles in his way, and he, in turn, disappeared into the thick brush, in search of his game.

Almost immediately, a second shot was heard.

"Ha! ha! the rascal," cried M. Bermont, "he must have routed out a hare in there."

They all waited, their eyes fixed on the heap of branches which their gaze could not penetrate.

The notary, cupping his hands, shouted out: "Did you get them?" Hautot senior didn't answer; then César, turning toward the game-keeper, said "Go, give him a hand, Joseph. We have to keep in line. We'll wait here."

And old Joseph, a dry, gnarled, old stump of a man, whose every joint was a lump, ambled off down to the ravine, searching for passable openings with the caution of a fox. Then, suddenly, he cried out: "Oh! c'm'ere, c'm'ere, there's been an accident."

They all rushed down and plunged through the brambles. Hautot senior lay on his side unconscious, both hands pressed to his belly. Through his canvas jacket, ripped by the bullet, long streams of blood flowed onto the grass. He had dropped his gun in setting it down to seize the dead partridge, which was just within his reach; it had gone off at the shock, the second discharge ripping open his entrails. They pulled him out of the ditch, undressed him, and saw a ghastly wound through which his intestines protruded. After binding him up as well as they could, they carried him back home and waited for the doctor, who had been sent for, along with a priest.

When the doctor arrived, he shook his head gravely, turned to Hautot junior, who was sitting in a chair, sobbing, and said: "My poor boy, it doesn't look too good."

But when the dressing was finished, the wounded man moved his fingers, opened his mouth, and cast a troubled, haggard look about him; then he seemed to search in his memory, recalling, grasping what had happened, and he murmured: "Good God, I'm finished."

The doctor was holding his hand. "Not at all, not at all. Just a few days' rest and you'll be all right."

Hautot continued: "I'm finished! My belly's ripped open! I know it." Then suddenly: "I want to speak to my son, if there's time."

Hautot junior was sobbing despite himself and repeating like a little boy: "Pappa, pappa, poor pappa!"

But his father, in a steadier voice, said: "Come on, stop crying, now's not the time for it. I've something to tell you. Come closer, it won't take long and then I'll feel easier. The rest of you, please give us a minute."

They all went out, leaving the son face to face with the father. As soon as they were alone, he said: "Listen, son, you're twenty-four. I can talk plain to you. And besides, there's not as much mystery about this sort of thing as we make of it. You know, of course, that your mother's been dead for seven years, right? And that I'm no more than forty-five myself, seeing I got married at nineteen. Right?"

The son stammered: "Yes, that's right."

"So, your mother's been dead for seven years, and I've stayed a widower. Well, I'm not a man to stay a widower at thirty-seven, right?"

The son answered: "Yes, that's right."

The father, gasping for breath, his face white and drawn with pain, continued: "God, how it hurts. Well, you understand. Man isn't made to live alone, but I wouldn't let anyone take your mother's place, seeing I gave her my word. So . . . you see?"

"Yes, father."

"So, I've kept a girl in Rouen, 18 rue de l'Éperlan, third floor, second door—I'm telling you all this, so don't forget it—and this girl's been as nice as she could be to me, affectionate, devoted, all in all, a real wife, you see? You follow me, my boy?"

"Yes, father."

"So, if I move on, I owe her something, but something substantial that'll take care of her. You understand?"

"Yes, father."

"I tell you she's a fine girl, really fine, and if it weren't for you and the memory of your poor mother, and the house where all three of us have lived together, I'd have brought her here. And I'd have married her, too . . . listen . . . listen . . . my boy . . . I could've made a will . . . but I didn't do it. . . I didn't want to . . . some things you don't put down in writing . . . they harm the family too much . . . and then everything gets all tangled up . . . it ruins everyone. Steer clear of legal documents, never use them. If I'm rich it's because I've never used them at all in my whole life. You understand, son?"

"Yes, father."

"Now listen . . . listen carefully . . . so I didn't make a will . . . I didn't want to . . . and anyway, I know you, you've got a good heart, you're not stingy, not tight-fisted, I mean. I said to myself that when I was near the end I'd tell you all about it and I'd ask you not to forget the girl:—Caroline Donet, 18 rue de l'Eperlan, third floor, second door, don't forget. And then . . . are you listening? Go there right after I'm gone—and fix it so she won't have any reason to complain about me.—You can afford it.—You can do it,—I'm leaving you enough . . . Listen . . . You won't find her at home every day. She works at Mme. Moreau's, rue Beauvoisine. Go see her on a Thursday. That's the day she expects me. That's been my day for six years. Poor little thing, how she'll cry! . . . I'm telling you all this because I know you so well, my son. Such things aren't let out, not even to the notary or the priest. They're done; everyone knows that, but they're not mentioned, unless they have to be. So there's no outsider in on the secret, only the family, because the family's all one. You understand?"

"Yes, father."

"You promise?"

"Yes, father."

"You swear?"

"Yes, father."

"I ask you, son, I beg you not to forget. It's important to me."

"No, father."

"You'll go there yourself. I want you to make sure of everything."

"Yes, father."

"And then, you'll see . . . you'll see what she'll explain to you. I can't tell you any more myself. You swear?"

"Yes, father."

"That's good, son. Kiss me. Good-bye. I'm burning out, I'm sure of it. Tell them to come in."

Hautot junior kissed his father, moaning as he did so. Then, always obedient, he opened the door, and the priest appeared in a white surplice, carrying the holy oils.

But the dying man had closed his eyes, and he refused to open them again, he refused to answer, he refused to show, even by a sign, that he understood.

Hautot had talked enough; he could not go on. Besides, his heart now felt at ease; he wanted to die in peace. What need was there to confess to God's deputy when he had just confessed to his own son, one of the family.

He was given the last rites, purified, absolved, surrounded by his kneeling friends and servants, without any expression on his face revealing that he was still alive.

He died toward midnight, after four hours of shuddering that revealed terrible suffering.

The hunting season having opened on Sunday, he was buried on Tuesday. Back home after having accompanied his father to the cemetery, César Hautot spent the rest of the day weeping. He hardly slept at all that night and felt so sad when he awoke that he wondered how he could go on living.

But all through the day he kept thinking that to obey his father's last wish he would have to go to Rouen the next day and see that girl, Caroline Donet, who lived at 18 rue de l'Éperlan, third floor, second door. Countless times he had repeated the name and address under his breath, as one mutters a prayer, so as not to forget it, and he ended up by muttering it incessantly, unable to stop or to think about anything else, so much were his tongue and mind obsessed by the words.

Accordingly, about eight the next morning, he ordered Graindorge to be harnessed to the gig, and set out behind the heavy Norman horse that trotted along the main road from Ainville to Rouen. He wore his black frock coat, his tall silk hat, and his trousers that strapped under his shoes. Under the circumstances, he didn't slip over his fine clothes the blue smock which swells out in the wind and protects clothes from dust and stains, and which can be quickly removed on arrival as soon as one has jumped from the carriage.

He got into Rouen just as it struck ten, stopped, as always, at the Hôtel des Bons Enfants, rue des Trois-Mares, endured the embraces of the landlord, his wife, and five sons, who had heard the sad news; then he had to give them the details of the accident, which made him weep; to refuse the helpful offers of all of them, zealous because they knew he was rich; and even to refuse luncheon, which offended them.

Then, having dusted off his hat, brushed his frock coat, and wiped his boots, he set out to find the rue de l'Éperlan, not daring to ask directions of anyone for fear of being recognized and arousing suspicion.

At last, unable to find the place, he caught sight of a priest, and trusting to the professional discretion of the clergy, he asked him. It was only a hundred yards off, just the second street to the right.

Then he hesitated. Up to this moment he had obeyed the dead man's wish like an unthinking animal. Suddenly he felt very disturbed, confused, humiliated at the idea of finding himself—him, the son—face to face with this woman who had been his father's mistress. All the morality that lies buried within us, crammed at the bottom of our feelings by centuries of inherited teaching, all he had learned about loose women from his catechism on, the instinctive contempt that every man feels for them, even if he marries one of them, all his narrow peasant propriety—all this worked within him, holding him back, making him blush with shame.

But he thought:—"I gave my word to father, I mustn't break it." So he pushed back the half-open door of the house marked number 18, found the dark stairway, went up three flights, saw one door, then a second, found the bell-cord and pulled it.

The tinkle in the neighboring room sent a shiver through his body. The door opened and he found himself face to face with a very well-dressed young woman, with dark hair and a ruddy complexion. She stared at him in astonishment.

He did not know what to say to her, and she, surmising nothing and expecting Hautot senior, did not invite him in. They stared at each other for nearly half a minute. Finally she asked: "Can I help you, sir?"

He mumbled: "I am young Hautot."

She started, turned pale, and stammered out as if she had known him for a long time: "Monsieur César?"

"Yes."

"Well?"

"I have something to say to you on my father's behalf."

She exclaimed, "Oh! my God!" and stepped back to let him in. He followed her in and closed the door.

Then he noticed a small boy of four or five, who was playing with a cat. He was sitting on the floor in front of a stove from which rose the steam of food being kept hot.

"Sit down," she said. He sat down. She asked: "Well?"

He no longer dared to speak, his eyes fixed on the table in the middle of the room, with three settings, one for a child. He stared at the chair with its back to the fire, at the plate, the napkin, the glasses, the open bottle of red wine and the untouched bottle of white wine. This was his father's chair, with its back to the fire. He was expected. It was his bread he saw—recognized—next to the fork, for the crust had been cut off because of Hautot's bad teeth. Then, looking up, he caught sight, on the wall, of his father's picture, the large photograph taken in Paris the year of the Exhibition, the same one that hung over the bed in his room at Ainville.

The young woman asked again: "Well, Monsieur César?"

He looked at her. Her face had darkened with anxiety, and she waited there, her hands trembling with fear.

Now he dared to speak: "Well, mam'zelle, papa died Sunday in opening the hunting season."

She was so overwhelmed that she did not move. After several moments of silence, she murmured, almost inaudibly: "Oh! It can't be!"

And suddenly her eyes welled with tears and, raising her hands, she covered her face and began to sob. The little boy turned and, seeing his mother in tears, began to wail. Then, understanding that the stranger was the source of this sudden grief, he rushed at César, seized his trousers with one hand and with the other kept hitting him on the thigh with all his might. César stood there, bewildered, full of pity, between this woman mourning for his father and this child defending its mother. He, too, felt the effect of the emotion, his eyes welling with grief; and, to regain his self-control, he started to talk.

"Yes," he was saying, "the accident happened Sunday morning about eight o'clock. . . ." And he went on to tell the story as if she were listening to him, forgetting no detail, recounting the most trivial points with the peasant's thoroughness. And the little boy kept on hitting him, now kicking his ankles.

When César reached the part where Hautot senior had spoken of her, she heard her name mentioned, uncovered her face, and said: "I'm sorry, I wasn't following you. But I really would like to know. . . . If you don't mind starting all over again."

He started over again in the same words: "The accident happened Sunday morning about eight o'clock. . . ."

He told everything, at great length, with short pauses, with full stops, with reflections of his own from time to time. She listened to him intently, perceiving with a woman's sharp sensitivity all the mishaps he was relating, shuddering with horror and exclaiming from time to time: "Oh, my God!" The little boy, believing she had calmed down, had stopped hitting César in order to take his mother's hand, and he, too, was listening as if he understood.

When Hautot junior ended his account, he said: "And now we must settle things according to his wishes. You see, I'm well-off; he's left me a good deal of property. I don't want you to have any reason to complain. . . ."

But she broke in abruptly: "Oh! Monsieur César, Monsieur César, not today. I'm too upset. . . . Some other time, some other day. . . . No, not today. . . . If I accept . . . you see . . . it's not for myself . . . no, no, no, I swear. It's for the little boy. The settlement will be for him."

Startled, César guessed, and stammered out: "Then . . . he's his . . . this little boy?"

And Hautot junior stared at his brother with confused emotion, both intense and pained.

"Of course," she said.

After a long silence, for she was weeping again, César, quite ill at ease, said: "Well, Mam'zelle Donet, I must be going. When would you like to talk this over?"

She cried out: "Oh! no, don't go, don't go, don't leave me and Émile all alone. I'll die of sorrow. I've no one anymore, no one but my little boy. Oh! how awful, how awful, Monsieur César. Look, sit down. Talk to me some more. Tell me what he used to do out there all week long."

And César sat down, accustomed to obeying. She drew up another chair for herself, next to his, before the stove where the food was still simmering, put Émile on her lap and asked César a thousand questions about his father, intimate questions about his everyday life, so that César felt without thinking that she had loved his father with all her poor heart.

And, the chain of his thoughts, rather limited in number, brought him back again to the accident and he began to relate it all over again with all the same details.

When he said, "He had a hole in his belly you could have put your two fists into," she uttered a sort of cry, and tears welled up in her eyes again. Caught up by her sorrow, César, too, began to weep, and as tears always soften the fibers of the heart, he leaned toward Émile, and kissed him on the forehead.

The mother, recovering her breath, murmured: "Poor little fellow, he's an orphan now."

"So am I," said César.

And they spoke no more.

But suddenly, the practical instinct of a housewife, accustomed to think of everything, revived in the young woman. "Perhaps you've had nothing to eat all morning, Monsieur César?"

"No, mam'zelle."

"Oh, you must be hungry. Do have something to eat."

"No, thank you," he said, "I'm not hungry. I've been too upset."

She replied: "In spite of sorrow, we have to go on living. Surely you won't refuse me. And besides, it'll keep you here a bit longer. When you go, I don't know what will become of me."

He yielded, after some further resistance, and sitting with his back to the fire, facing her, he ate a plateful of the tripe which had been crackling in the oven, and drank a glass of red wine. But he would not let her open the bottle of white wine.

Several times he wiped the mouth of the little boy, who had smeared gravy all over his chin. As he was getting up to leave, he asked: "When would you like me to come back to talk the matter over, Mam'zelle Donet?"

"If it's all the same to you, next Thursday, Monsieur César. That way I won't lose any time. My Thursdays are always free."

"That's fine for me. Next Thursday."

"You will come for lunch, won't you?"

"Oh! I can't make any promises about that."

"It's only that we can chat better while eating. And there's more time, too."

"Well, all right. Noon, then."

And he went off, after kissing little Emile again, and shaking hands with Mlle. Donet.

III

The week seemed long to César Hautot. Never before had he been alone, and the isolation seemed unbearable. Until now, he had lived at his father's side, like his shadow, following him to the fields, seeing to it that his father's orders were carried out, and when he would leave him for a short while, he would find him again at dinner. They would spend their evenings smoking their pipes, sitting opposite each other, discussing horses, cows, or sheep; and their morning handshakes seemed to signify their deep family affection.

Now César was alone. He wandered about in the autumn-ploughed lands, still expecting to see the tall, gesticulating figure of his father rise up at the far end of a field. To kill time, he stopped by his neighbors', told the story of the accident to all those who had not heard it, and sometimes told it again to those who had. Then, exhausted by work and by thinking, he would sit down by the roadside and wonder if such a life could go on for very long.

He often thought of Mlle. Donet. He had liked her. He had found her lady-like, gentle, and fine, just as his father had said. Yes, she certainly was a fine person. He was resolved to do the thing handsomely and give her two thousand francs income, settling the capital on the child. He even felt a certain pleasure at the thought of seeing her again the following Thursday and of arranging the whole matter with her. And then the thought of this brother, this little fellow of five, who was his father's son, would bother him, would worry him a little and, at the same time, would give him a warm feeling. He had a kind of family there in that little illegitimate urchin who would never bear the Hautot name, a family he could take or leave as he pleased, but which reminded him of his father.

So, when he found himself Thursday morning on the road to Rouen, carried along by the echoing trot of Graindorge, he felt his heart lighter, more at peace than he had felt at any moment since his misfortune.

Entering Mlle. Donet's apartment, he saw the table set as on the previous Thursday, with a single difference that the crust had not been removed from the bread.

He shook hands with the young woman, kissed Emile on both cheeks, and sat down, feeling somewhat at home, but with a heavy heart all the same. Mlle. Donet seemed a little thinner to him, a little paler. She must have wept a lot. She seemed ill at ease in his presence, as if she understood now what she had not realized the week before, under the initial impact of her misfortune, and she now treated him with excessive respect, with stricken humility, and with touching solicitude as if to repay him with attention and devotion for the kindness he had shown her. They spent a long time over lunch, talking about the matter which had brought him there. She didn't want so much money. It was too much, much too much. She earned enough to take care of herself; she only wanted Emile to have a little money he could look forward to when he grew up. But César stood fast, and even added a gift of one thousand francs for her mourning expenses.

When he had finished his coffee, she asked: "Do you smoke?"

"Yes . . . I have my pipe."

He felt his pocket. Damn it, he had forgotten it! He was getting upset about it when she offered him one of his father's pipes, which was kept in the cupboard. He accepted, took it, recognized it, sniffed it, praised its excellence with emotion in his voice, filled it with tobacco, and lit it. Then he set Émile astride his knee and played horse with him while she cleared away the table and set the dirty dishes off on the sideboard to be washed after he had left.

Toward three, he got up regretfully, distressed at the thought of leaving. "Well, Mam'zelle Donet," he said, "I wish you good afternoon. It was a pleasure to see you again."

She stood before him, flushed, very moved, and looked at him while she thought of his father. "Won't we ever see each other again?" she asked.

He replied, simply: "Why, yes, mam'zelle, if you wish."

"Certainly, Monsieur César. Would next Thursday suit you?"

"Yes, Mam'zelle Donet."

"You'll come for lunch, of course?"

"Well . . . if you really want me to, I won't say no."

"Then it's settled, Monsieur César, next Thursday, at noon, the same as today."

"Thursday noon, Mam'zelle Donet."

W. SOMERSET MAUGHAM said that his stories and those of his master, Guy de Maupassant, are basically anecdotes, each relating "an incident which is curious, striking and original." One can read such a story at least twice, Maugham says, first for "what happens" and second for "the cleverness of the telling." Let us see what happens in he two preceding stories, and let us see whether they are cleverly told. And then let us see whether they are meaningful.

Maugham's story is indeed very close to an anecdote. We have the feeling that we are listening to Maugham across a dinner table, recounting a curious happening that he witnessed. We learn of a happening that is curious because it concludes surprisingly: Mr. Kelada, who seemed to be imperceptive and boorish, is at the end revealed to us as a man who is shrewd and gallant. And there is a curious irony; whereas usually a decent act adds to one's reputation, Mr. Kelada's decent act lessens his reputation. But is Mr. Kelada's act plausible? Suppose we look at the story again, to admire "the cleverness of the telling." On re-reading it, are we convinced that the Mr. Kelada whom we meet at the outset would do what Mr. Kelada later does? Would a man who showed to an unwilling acquaintance three card tricks, a man who "would not drop a subject, however unimportant, till he had brought you round to his way of thinking," a man who might have been kicked downstairs without "the suspicion dawning on him that he was not a welcome visitor"—would this Mr. Kelada care enough, especially in a moment of "triumph," not only to notice Mrs. Ramsay's terrified expression but to put together in an instant the whole story of Mrs. Ramsay's infidelity? And would he care enough to be gallant, if it meant humiliating himself in order to protect the reputation of a casual acquaintance? (In fact, to conjecture—as apparently Mr. Kelada does—that Mrs. Ramsay's reputation will be ruined if he tells the truth about the pearls, is somewhat melodramatic, for his insistence that the pearls are genuine would probably not at all shake Mr. Ramsay's certainty; Mr. Ramsay "was as dogmatic as Mr. Kelada," and their discussions "were acrimonious and interminable.") Maugham tells us that certain things happened, but is the story compelling? Contrast it with "The Widow of Ephesus," which, at first thought, is also a story about the impossibility of judging a book by its cover. The widow's virtue is thoroughly established at the outset, yet within a few hundred words so convincing a picture has been drawn of the forces working on her that her surrender to the soldier is thoroughly plausible. The ironic contrast between her deep grief at the outset and her deep love at the conclusion is gained not by saying she wasn't at all what she seemed, but by vividly outlining a believable series of happenings that would lead her from grieving over her husband's body to desecrating it.

Of course, on re-reading "Mr. Know-All," we realize that the narrator is a snob (he is not Maugham, but a fictitious character, no less an imagined person than Mr. Kelada), and that his description of Mr. Kelada has not been entirely fair. But even if we allow for the narrator's bias, we have seen in the early part of the story that Mr. Kelada *is* a boor. Maugham's final effect is achieved, one feels, through the sudden introduction of an aspect of Mr. Kelada's personality for which we are entirely unprepared.

Related to this point (indeed, inseparable from it) is the problem of whether Maugham's story is meaningful. When we read "The Widow of Ephesus," we feel that it is not only plausible but meaningful: tears are shed, but life goes on. Virtuous young widows mourn, but they often remarry. Egomaniacs, however, do not usually humiliate themselves to save a lady's reputation. The effect that Maugham's story leaves, whether after one or several readings, is of cleverness; the effect that "The Widow of Ephesus" leaves is of truth.

Earlier it was suggested that irony is present when Mr. Kelada's gallant act loses for him whatever respect the passengers might have had. He is thoroughly shown up, yet he is in the right. Similarly, there is irony in Petronius' story; it is ironic that a widow devoted to the memory of her husband should use her husband's body as a means of preserving her lover. In this sense, **irony** denotes a contrast between original intentions and outcome.* Maupassant's story, too, is ironic; like Petronius' story, but unlike Maugham's, the irony does not seem tricky. The "incident which is curious" (to use Maugham's phrase) in Maupassant's story is the son's innocent inheritance of his father's mistress. The story does not suffer by re-reading; it is thoroughly plausible, as Maupassant presents it. Though neither the father nor the son would ever have conceived of the outcome, as Maupassant arranges his story the outcome seems inevitable. Maupassant skillfully identifies the son with the father: Hautot junior is "almost as tall as his father," and he is filled with "respect and deference for the wishes and opinions of Hautot senior." On the first visit to Caroline Donet he tells the story of his father's death while the meal intended for his father is kept warm on the stove, and then, when pressed, he eats the meal. Before the second visit, he draws some comfort from the fact that in Caroline and her son (his half-brother) he has "a kind of family." On the second visit the table is set as it was for his father, but now, quite reasonably, the crust has not been removed from the bread. After the meal he smokes his father's pipe and bounces Emile on his knee. A third visit is inevitable; we have moved, yet with no violence to character or probability, from filial reverence to something akin to filial usurpation. Because of this apparent inevitability, the story adds up to a believable representation of an aspect of life: sons grow up and replace their fathers. Hautot junior, on his father's death, acquires his father's name and all his property.

* Such irony is not to be confused with verbal irony. See pages 368-69.

1. How does Maugham prepare us to be cautious about totally accepting the narrator's attitude toward Mr. Kelada?

2. Does the description of Mr. Kelada's possessions and appearance help to substantiate the narrator's prejudice toward him?

3. Although Mr. Kelada says that he is "British to the backbone," wouldn't the phrase ordinarily apply more appropriately to the narrator? Why? Or is the conclusion of the story an ironic verification of Mr. Kelada's self-characterization?

4. Until the argument over the pearls, Mr. Kelada "had never told anyone what his business was." Is this a surprising fact?

5. What is the function of the last sentence?

6. Maugham says (in *The Summing Up*):

> The value of art, like the value of the Mystic Way, lies in its effects. If it can only give pleasure, however spiritual that pleasure may be, it is of no great consequence or at least of no more consequence than a dozen oysters and a pint of Montrachet. If it is a solace, that is well enough; the world is full of inevitable evils and it is good that man should have some heritage to which from time to time he may withdraw himself; but not to escape them, rather to gather fresh strength to face them. For art, if it is to be reckoned as one of the great values of life, must teach men humility, tolerance, wisdom and magnanimity. The value of art is not beauty, but right action.

Does this theory seem true? By this standard, is "Mr. Know-All" a work of art?

QUESTIONS: *Hautot and His Son*

1. About two pages are given to the preparation for the hunt and to the hunt itself. What would be lost by beginning, "Hautot senior was dying as a result of a hunting accident"?

2. Why does the woman not follow the account of the accident the first time it is related? Why are we told that the son often repeats the story, even to persons who know it?

3. Maupassant is frequently criticized for his cynical view of human nature. Is this story cynical? Is it immoral? Explain.

Four

NARRATIVE POINT OF VIEW

Every story is told by someone. "The Widow of Ephesus" was written by Petronius, but it is told by one Eumolpus, who makes no claim to having witnessed the happening; "Mr. Know-All" was written by Maugham, but it is told by an unnamed narrator who has witnessed the happening; "Hautot and His Son" was written by Maupassant, but it is told by a narrator who, although he does not participate in the story, not only knows all about Hautot's past and is able to record conversations, but also looks into men's minds and relates their thoughts. The narrator of "Hautot and His Son" tells us, for example, that Hautot "was a tall Norman, one of those powerful, full-blooded, large-boned men," and that Hautot's "heart now felt at ease; he wanted to die in peace."

An author must choose a point of view (or several points of view) from which he will narrate his story. His choice is perhaps analogous to the poet's choice of free verse, blank verse, or rhyme, and the choice will contribute to the total effect that the story will have. Take, for example, "The Widow of Ephesus." The teller, Eumolpus, recounts the tale with very little intrusion of himself, but just before the end he analyzes the lady's feelings: "Our lady's heart, however, was no less tender than pure." Now, this wry, inexact, seemingly ingenuous appraisal of her character is largely what gives the story its effect; if the story had been told by an outraged moralist or by the lady herself or by the soldier, it would have been a different story.

Narrative points of view can be divided into two sorts: **participant** (or **first person**) and **non-participant** (or **third person**). Each of these two divisions can be subdivided:

I. Participant (first person)
    (a) Narrator as a major character
    (b) Narrator as a minor character

II. Non-participant (third person)

    (a) Omniscient

    (b) Selective omniscient

    (c) Objective

PARTICIPANT POINTS OF VIEW. In the story by Frank O'Connor, at the end of this chapter, the narrator is a major character. He, and not O'Connor, tells the story, and the story is chiefly about him; hence one can say that O'Connor *uses* a first person (or participant) point of view. O'Connor has invented an Irishman who has fought against the English, and this narrator tells of the impact a happening had on him: "And anything happened me afterwards, I never felt the same about again." But sometimes a first-person narrator is telling a story that focuses on someone other than himself; he is a minor character, a peripheral witness, for example, to a story about Jones, and we get the story of Jones filtered through, say, the eyes of Jones's friend or brother or cat. Maugham's "Mr. Know-All" is narrated by "I," but it is about Mr. Kelada. One special kind of first-person narrator (whether major or minor) is the **innocent eye**: the narrator is naive (usually a child, an idiot, or a not-too-bright adult), telling what he sees and feels; the contrast between what he perceives and what the reader understands produces an ironic effect. Such a story, in which the reader understands more than the teller himself does, is Ring Lardner's "Haircut," a story told by a garrulous barber who does not perceive that the "accident" he is describing is in fact a murder.

NON-PARTICIPANT POINTS OF VIEW. In a non-participant (third-person) point of view, the teller of the tale does not introduce himself as a character. He has receded from the story. If the point of view is **omniscient**, the narrator relates what he wishes about the thoughts as well as the deeds of his characters (as in "Hautot and His Son"). When he chooses, the omniscient teller enters the mind of any or all of his characters; where the first-person narrator can only say, "I was angry," or "Jones seemed angry to me," the omniscient narrator can say, "Jones was inwardly angry but gave no sign; Smith continued chatting, but he sensed Jones's anger." Furthermore, a distinction can be made between **neutral omniscience** (the narrator recounts deeds and thoughts, but does not judge), and **editorial omniscience** (the narrator not only recounts but judges). The narrator in Hawthorne's "Young Goodman Brown," for example, knows what goes on in the mind of Brown, and he comments approvingly or disapprovingly: "With this excellent resolve for the future, Goodman Brown felt himself justified in making more haste on his present evil purpose."

Because a short story can scarcely hope to develop effectively a picture of several minds, an author may prefer to limit his omniscience to the minds of only a few of his characters, or even to one of his characters; that is, he may use **selective omniscience** as his point of view. Selective omniscience provides a focus, especially if it is limited to a single character. When thus limited, the author hovers over the shoulder of one of his characters, seeing him from outside and from inside, and seeing other characters from the outside and from the impact they make upon the mind of this selected receptor. In "Young Goodman Brown," for example, the reader sees things mostly as they make their impact upon the protagonist's mind:

> He could have well-nigh sworn that the shape of his own dead father beckoned him to advance, looking downward from a smoke wreath, while a woman with dim features of despair, threw out her hand to warn him back. Was it his mother? But he had no power to retreat one step, nor to resist, even in thought, when the minister and good old Deacon Gookin seized his arms and led him to the blazing rock.

When selective omniscience attempts to record mental activity ranging from consciousness to unconsciousness, it is sometimes labeled the **stream-of-consciousness** point of view. Example, from Katherine Anne Porter's "The Jilting of Granny Weatherall":

> Her eyelids wavered and let in streamers of blue-gray light like tissue paper over her eyes. She must get up and pull the shades down or she'd never sleep. She was in bed again and the shades were not down. How could that happen? Better turn over, hide from the light, sleeping in the light gave you nightmares. "Mother, how do you feel now?" and a stinging wetness on her forehead. But I don't like having my face washed in cold water!

In an effort to reproduce the unending activity of the mind, some authors who use the stream-of-consciousness point of view dispense with conventional syntax, punctuation, and logical transitions. In James Joyce's *Ulysses*, for example, the last forty-six pages are an unpunctuated flow of one character's thoughts.

Finally, sometimes a third-person narrator does not enter even a single mind, but records only what crosses a dispassionate eye and ear. Such a point of view is **objective** (sometimes called **the camera** or **fly-on-the-wall**). The absence of editorializing and of dissection of the mind often produces the effect of a play; we see and hear the characters in action. Much of Hemingway's "The Short Happy Life of Francis Macomber" is objective, consisting of bits of dialogue that make the story look like a play:

> "Good morning," she said. "Are we going after that lion?"
> "As soon as you deal with your breakfast," Wilson said. "How are you feeling?"
> "Marvellous," she said. "I'm very excited."
> "I'll just go and see that everything is ready," Wilson went off. As he left the lion roared again.

But the word "objective" is almost a misnomer, for to describe happenings is—by one's choice of words—to comment on them too, however unobtrusively. How objective is the point of view if a man is described as "fat" instead of "stout" or "stout" instead of "heavy" or "heavy" instead of "two hundred and fifty pounds in weight"? The objective point of view, even though it expressly enters no mind, often is a camouflaged version of the selective omniscient point of view. When Joyce writes, "Maria was a very, very small person indeed but she had a very long nose and a very long chin," he is not giving us her thought but he is (by his sentence structure and his repetition of "very") giving us the quality of her mind; the description is given in Maria's language though the line gives the impression of being objectively set down.

Generalizations about the effect of a point of view are risky, but two have already been made: that the innocent eye can achieve an ironic effect otherwise unattainable, and that an objective point of view is dramatic. Three other generalizations are often made: that a first-person point of view lends a sense of immediacy or reality, that an omniscient point of view suggests human littleness, and that the point of view must be consistent. To take the first of these: it is true that when a story begins "I was prepared to dislike Max Kelada even before I knew him," we feel that the author has gripped us by the lapels; but, on the other hand, we know we are only reading a piece of fiction, and we do not really believe in the existence either of the "I" or of Max Kelada; and, furthermore, when we pick up a story that begins with *any* point of view we agree (by picking up the book) to pretend to believe the fictions we are being told. That is, all fiction—whether in the first person or not—is known to be literally false but is read with the pretense that it is true. The writer must hold our attention, and make us feel that his fiction is meaningful, but the use of the first-person pronoun does not of itself confer reality. The second generalization, that an omniscient point of view can make puppets of its characters, is equally misleading; this point of view can also reveal in them a depth and complexity quite foreign to the idea of human littleness. The third generalization, that the narrator's point of view must be consistent lest the illusion of reality be shattered, has been much preached by the followers of Henry James. But E. M. Forster has suggested, in *Aspects of the Novel*, that what is important is not consistency but "the power of the writer to bounce the reader into accepting what he says." Forster notes that in *Bleak House* Dickens uses in Chapter I an omniscient point of view, in Chapter II a selective omniscient point of view, and in Chapter III a first-person point of view. "Logically," Forster says, "*Bleak House* is all to pieces, but Dickens bounces us, so that we do not mind the shiftings of the view-point."

Perhaps the only sound generalizations possible are that (1) because point of view is one of the things that give form to a story, a good author chooses the point (or points) of view that he feels best for his particular story, and (2) the use of any other point of view would turn the story into a different story.

FRANK O'CONNOR (1903-1966)

Guests of the Nation

I

At dusk the big Englishman, Belcher, would shift his long legs out of the ashes and say "Well, chums, what about it?" and Noble or me would say "All right, chum" (for we had picked up some of their curious expressions), and the little Englishman, Hawkins, would light the lamp and bring out the cards. Sometimes Jeremiah Donovan would come up and supervise the game and get excited over Hawkins's cards, which he always played badly, and shout at him as if he was one of our own "Ah, you divil, you, why didn't you play the tray?"

But ordinarily Jeremiah was a sober and contented poor devil like the big Englishman, Belcher, and was looked up to only because he was a fair hand at documents, though he was slow enough even with them. He wore a small cloth hat and big gaiters over his long pants, and you seldom saw him with his hands out of his pockets. He reddened when you talked to him, tilting from toe to heel and back, and looking down all the time at his big farmer's feet. Noble and me used to make fun of his broad accent, because we were from the town.

I couldn't at the time see the point of me and Noble guarding Belcher and Hawkins at all, for it was my belief that you could have planted that pair down anywhere from this to Claregalway and they'd have taken root there like a native weed. I never in my short experience seen two men to take to the country as they did.

They were handed on to us by the Second Battalion when the search for them became too hot, and Noble and myself, being young, took over with a natural feeling of responsibility, but Hawkins made us look like fools when he showed that he knew the country better than we did.

"You're the bloke they calls Bonaparte," he says to me. "Mary Brigid O'Connell told me to ask you what you done with the pair of her brother's socks you borrowed."

For it seemed, as they explained it, that the Second used to have little evenings, and some of the girls of the neighborhood turned in, and, seeing they were such decent chaps, our fellows couldn't leave the two Englishmen out of them. Hawkins learned to dance "The Walls of Limerick," "The Siege of Ennis," and "The Waves of Tory" as well as any of them, though, naturally, we couldn't return the compliment, because our lads at that time did not dance foreign dances on principle.

So whatever privileges Belcher and Hawkins had with the Second they just naturally took with us, and after the first day or two we gave up all pretense of keeping a close eye on them. Not that they could have got far, for they had accents you could cut with a knife and wore khaki tunics and overcoats with civilian pants and boots. But it's my belief that they never had any idea of escaping and were quite content to be where they were.

It was a treat to see how Belcher got off with the old woman of the house where we were staying. She was a great warrant to scold, and cranky even with us, but before ever she had a chance of giving our guests, as I may call them, a lick of her tongue, Belcher had made her his friend for life. She was breaking sticks, and Belcher, who hadn't been more than ten minutes in the house, jumped up from his seat and went over to her.

"Allow me, madam," he says, smiling his queer little smile, "please allow me"; and he takes the bloody hatchet. She was struck too paralytic to speak, and after that, Belcher would be at her heels, carrying a bucket, a basket, or a load of turf, as the case might be. As Noble said, he got into looking before she leapt, and hot water, or any little thing she wanted, Belcher would have it ready for her. For such a huge man (and though I am five foot ten myself I had to look up at him) he had an uncommon shortness—or should I say lack?—of speech. It took us some time to get used to him, walking in and out, like a ghost, without a word. Especially because Hawkins talked enough for a platoon, it was strange to hear big Belcher with his toes in the ashes come out with a solitary "Excuse me, chum," or "That's right, chum." His one and only passion was cards, and I will say for him that he was a good card-player. He could have fleeced myself and Noble, but whatever we lost to him Hawkins lost to us, and Hawkins played with the money Belcher gave him.

Hawkins lost to us because he had too much old gab, and we probably lost to Belcher for the same reason. Hawkins and Noble would spit at one another about religion into the early hours of the morning, and Hawkins worried the soul out of Noble, whose brother was a priest, with a string of questions that would puzzle a cardinal. To make it worse, even in treating of holy subjects, Hawkins had a deplorable tongue. I never in all my career met a man who could mix such a variety of cursing and bad language into an argument. He was a terrible man, and a fright to argue. He never did a stroke of work, and when he had no one else to talk to, he got stuck in the old woman.

He met his match in her, for one day when he tried to get her to complain profanely of the drought, she gave him a great come-down by blaming it entirely on Jupiter Pluvius (a deity neither Hawkins nor I had ever heard of, though Noble said that among the pagans it was believed that he had something to do with the rain). Another day he was swearing at the capitalists for starting the German war when the old lady laid down her iron, puckered up her little crab's mouth, and said: "Mr. Hawkins, you can say what you like about the war, and think you'll deceive me because I'm only a simple poor countrywoman, but I know what started the war. It was the Italian Count that stole the heathen divinity out of the temple in Japan. Believe me, Mr. Hawkins, nothing but sorrow and want can follow the people that disturb the hidden powers."

A queer old girl, all right.

II

We had our tea one evening, and Hawkins lit the lamp and we all sat into cards. Jeremiah Donovan came in too, and sat down and watched us for a while, and it suddenly struck me that he had no great love for the two Englishmen. It came as a great surprise to me, because I hadn't noticed anything about him before.

Late in the evening a really terrible argument blew up between Hawkins and Noble, about capitalists and priests and love of your country.

"The capitalists," says Hawkins with an angry gulp, "pays th priests to tell you about the next world so as you won't notice what th bastards are up to in this."

"Nonsense, man!" says Noble, losing his temper. "Before ever capitalist was thought of, people believed in the next world."

Hawkins stood up as though he was preaching a sermon.

"Oh, they did, did they?" he says with a sneer. "They believed all the things you believe, isn't that what you mean? And you believe that God created Adam, and Adam created Shem, and Shem created Jehoshophat. You believe all that silly old fairytale about Eve and Eden and the apple. Well, listen to me, chum. If you're entitled to hold a silly belief like that, I'm entitled to hold my silly belief—which is that the first thing your God created was a bleeding capitalist, with morality and Rolls-Royce complete. Am I right, chum?" he says to Belcher.

"You're right, chum," says Belcher with his amused smile, and got up from the table to stretch his long legs into the fire and stroke his moustache. So, seeing that Jeremiah Donovan was going, and that there was no knowing when the argument about religion would be over, I went out with him. We strolled down to the village together, and then he stopped and started blushing and mumbling and saying I ought to be behind, keeping guard on the prisoners. I didn't like the tone he took with me, and anyway I was bored with life in the cottage, so I replied by asking him what the hell we wanted guarding them at all for. I told him I'd talked it over with Noble, and that we'd both rather be out with a fighting column.

"What use are those fellows to us?" says I.

He looked at me in surprise and said: "I thought you knew we were keeping them as hostages."

"Hostages?" I said.

"The enemy have prisoners belonging to us," he says, "and now they're talking of shooting them. If they shoot our prisoners, we'll shoot theirs."

"Shoot them?" I said.

"What else did you think we were keeping them for?" he says.

"Wasn't it very unforeseen of you not to warn Noble and myself of that in the beginning?" I said.

"How was it?" says he. "You might have known it."

"We couldn't know it, Jeremiah Donovan," says I. "How could we when they were on our hands so long?"

"The enemy have our prisoners as long and longer," says he.

"That's not the same thing at all," says I.

"What difference is there?" says he.

I couldn't tell him, because I knew he wouldn't understand. If it was only an old dog that was going to the vet's, you'd try and not get too fond of him, but Jeremiah Donovan wasn't a man that would ever be in danger of that.

"And when is this thing going to be decided?" says I.

"We might hear tonight," he says. "Or tomorrow or the next day at latest. So if it's only hanging round here that's a trouble to you, you'll be free soon enough."

It wasn't the hanging round that was a trouble to me at all by this time. I had worse things to worry about. When I got back to the cottage the argument was still on. Hawkins was holding forth in his best style, maintaining that there was no next world, and Noble was maintaining that there was; but I could see that Hawkins had had the best of it.

"Do you know what, chum?" he was saying with a saucy smile. "I think you're just as big a bleeding unbeliever as I am. You say you believe in the next world, and you know just as much about the next world as I do, which is sweet damn-all. What's heaven? You don't know. Where's heaven? You don't know. You know sweet damn-all! I ask you again, do they wear wings?"

"Very well, then," says Noble, "they do. Is that enough for you? They do wear wings."

"Where do they get them, then? Who makes them? Have they a factory for wings? Have they a sort of store where you hands in your chit and takes your bleeding wings?"

"You're an impossible man to argue with," says Noble. "Now, listen to me—" And they were off again.

It was long after midnight when we locked up and went to bed. As I blew out the candle I told Noble what Jeremiah Donovan was after telling me. Noble took it very quietly. When we'd been in bed about an hour he asked me did I think we ought to tell the Englishmen. I didn't think we should, because it was more than likely that the English wouldn't shoot our men, and even if they did, the brigade officers, who were always up and down with the Second Battalion and knew the Englishmen well, wouldn't be likely to want them plugged. "I think so too," says Noble. "It would be great cruelty to put the wind up them now."

"It was very unforeseen of Jeremiah Donovan anyhow," says I.

It was next morning that we found it so hard to face Belcher and Hawkins. We went about the house all day scarcely saying a word. Belcher didn't seem to notice; he was stretched into the ashes as usual, with his usual look of waiting in quietness for something unforeseen to happen, but Hawkins noticed and put it down to Noble's being beaten in the argument of the night before.

"Why can't you take a discussion in the proper spirit?" he says severely. "You and your Adam and Eve! I'm a Communist, that's what I am. Communist or anarchist, it all comes to much the same thing." And for hours he went round the house, muttering when the fit took him. "Adam and Eve! Adam and Eve! Nothing better to do with their time than picking bleeding apples!"

III

I don't know how we got through that day, but I was very glad when it was over, the tea things were cleared away, and Belcher said in his peaceable way: "Well, chums, what about it?" We sat round the table and Hawkins took out the cards, and just then I heard Jeremiah Donovan's footstep on the path and a dark presentiment crossed my mind. I rose from the table and caught him before he reached the door.

"What do you want?" I asked.

"I want those two soldier friends of yours," he says, getting red.

"Is that the way, Jeremiah Donovan?" I asked.

"That's the way. There were four of our lads shot this morning, one of them a boy of sixteen."

"That's bad," I said.

At that moment Noble followed me out, and the three of us walked down the path together, talking in whispers. Feeney, the local intelligence officer, was standing by the gate.

"What are you going to do about it?" I asked Jeremiah Donovan.

"I want you and Noble to get them out; tell them they're being shifted again; that'll be the quietest way."

"Leave me out of that," says Noble under his breath.

Jeremiah Donovan looks at him hard.

"All right," he says. "You and Feeney get a few tools from the shed and dig a hole by the far end of the bog. Bonaparte and myself will be after you. Don't let anyone see you with the tools. I wouldn't like it to go beyond ourselves."

We saw Feeney and Noble go round to the shed and went in ourselves. I left Jeremiah Donovan to do the explanations. He told them that he had orders to send them back to the Second Battalion. Hawkins let out a mouthful of curses, and you could see that though Belcher didn't say anything, he was a bit upset too. The old woman was for having them stay in spite of us, and she didn't stop advising them until Jeremiah Donovan lost his temper and turned on her. He had a nasty temper, I noticed. It was pitch-dark in the cottage by this time, but no one thought of lighting the lamp, and in the darkness the two Englishmen fetched their topcoats and said good-bye to the old woman.

"Just as a man makes a home of a bleeding place, some bastard at headquarters thinks you're too cushy and shunts you off," says Hawkins, shaking her hand.

"A thousand thanks, madam," says Belcher. "A thousand thanks for everything"—as though he'd made it up.

We went round to the back of the house and down towards the bog. It was only then that Jeremiah Donovan told them. He was shaking with excitement.

"There were four of our fellows shot in Cork this morning and now you're to be shot as a reprisal."

"What are you talking about?" snaps Hawkins. "It's bad enough being mucked about as we are without having to put up with your funny jokes."

"It isn't a joke," says Donovan. "I'm sorry, Hawkins, but it's true," and begins on the usual rigmarole about duty and how unpleasant it is.

I never noticed that people who talk a lot about duty find it much of a trouble to them.

"Oh, cut it out!" says Hawkins.

"Ask Bonaparte," says Donovan, seeing that Hawkins isn't taking him seriously. "Isn't it true, Bonaparte?"

"It is," I say, and Hawkins stops.

"Ah, for Christ's sake, chum!"

"I mean it, chum," I say.

"You don't sound as if you meant it."

"If he doesn't mean it, I do," says Donovan, working himself up.

"What have you against me, Jeremiah Donovan?"

"I never said I had anything against you. But why did your people take out four of our prisoners and shoot them in cold blood?"

He took Hawkins by the arm and dragged him on, but it was impossible to make him understand that we were in earnest. I had the Smith and Wesson in my pocket and I kept fingering it and wondering what I'd do if they put up a fight for it or ran, and wishing to God they'd do one or the other. I knew if they did run for it, that I'd never fire on them. Hawkins wanted to know was Noble in it, and when we said yes, he asked us why Noble wanted to plug him. Why did any of us want to plug him? What had he done to us? Weren't we all chums? Didn't we understand him and didn't he understand us? Did we imagine for an instant that he'd shoot us for all the so-and-so officers in the so-and-so British Army?

By this time we'd reached the bog, and I was so sick I couldn't even answer him. We walked along the edge of it in the darkness, and every now and then Hawkins would call a halt and begin all over again, as if he was wound up, about our being chums, and I knew that nothing but the sight of the grave would convince him that we had to do it. And all the time I was hoping that something would happen;

that they'd run for it or that Noble would take over the responsibility from me. I had the feeling that it was worse on Noble than on me.

IV

At last we saw the lantern in the distance and made towards it. Noble was carrying it, and Feeney was standing somewhere in the darkness behind him, and the picture of them so still and silent in the bogland brought it home to me that we were in earnest, and banished the last bit of hope I had.

Belcher, on recognizing Noble, said: "Hallo, chum," in his quiet way, but Hawkins flew at him at once, and the argument began all over again, only this time Noble had nothing to say for himself and stood with his head down, holding the lantern between his legs.

It was Jeremiah Donovan who did the answering. For the twentieth time, as though it was haunting his mind, Hawkins asked if anybody thought he'd shoot Noble.

"Yes, you would," says Jeremiah Donovan.

"No, I wouldn't, damn you!"

"You would, because you'd know you'd be shot for not doing it."

"I wouldn't, not if I was to be shot twenty times over. I wouldn't shoot a pal. And Belcher wouldn't—isn't that right, Belcher?"

"That's right, chum," Belcher said, but more by way of answering the question than of joining in the argument. Belcher sounded as though whatever unforeseen thing he'd always been waiting for had come at last.

"Anyway, who says Noble would be shot if I wasn't? What do you think I'd do if I was in his place, out in the middle of a blasted bog?"

"What would you do?" asks Donovan.

"I'd go with him wherever he was going, of course. Share my last bob with him and stick by him through thick and thin. No one can ever say of me that I let down a pal."

"We had enough of this," says Jeremiah Donovan, cocking his revolver. "Is there any message you want to send?"

"No, there isn't."

"Do you want to say your prayers?"

Hawkins came out with a cold-blooded remark that even shocked me and turned on Noble again.

"Listen to me, Noble," he says. "You and me are chums. You can't come over to my side, so I'll come over to your side. That show you I mean what I say? Give me a rifle and I'll go along with you and the other lads."

Nobody answered him. We knew that was no way out.

"Hear what I'm saying?" he says. "I'm through with it. I'm a deserter or anything else you like. I don't believe in your stuff, but it's no worse than mine. That satisfy you?"

Noble raised his head, but Donovan began to speak and he lowered it again without replying.

"For the last time, have you any messages to send?" says Donovan in a cold, excited sort of voice.

"Shut up, Donovan! You don't understand me, but these lads do. They're not the sort to make a pal and kill a pal. They're not the tools of any capitalist."

I alone of the crowd saw Donovan raise his Webley to the back of Hawkins's neck, and as he did so I shut my eyes and tried to pray. Hawkins had begun to say something else when Donovan fired, and as I opened my eyes at the bang, I saw Hawkins stagger at the knees and lie out flat at Noble's feet, slowly and as quiet as a kid falling asleep, with the lantern-light on his lean legs and bright farmer's boots. We all stood very still, watching him settle out in the last agony.

Then Belcher took out a handkerchief and began to tie it about his own eyes (in our excitement we'd forgotten to do the same for Hawkins), and, seeing it wasn't big enough, turned and asked for the loan of mine. I gave it to him and he knotted the two together and pointed with his foot at Hawkins.

"He's not quite dead," he says. "Better give him another."

Sure enough, Hawkins's left knee is beginning to rise. I bend down and put my gun to his head; then, recollecting myself, I get up again. Belcher understands what's in my mind.

"Give him his first," he says. "I don't mind. Poor bastard, we don't know what's happening to him now."

I knelt and fired. By this time I didn't seem to know what I was doing. Belcher, who was fumbling a bit awkwardly with the handkerchiefs, came out with a laugh as he heard the shot. It was the first time I heard him laugh and it sent a shudder down my back; it sounded so unnatural.

"Poor bugger!" he said quietly. "And last night he was so curious about it all. It's very queer, chums, I always think. Now he knows as much about it as they'll ever let him know, and last night he was all in the dark."

Donovan helped him to tie the handkerchiefs about his eyes. "Thanks, chum," he said. Donovan asked if there were any messages he wanted sent.

"No, chum," he says. "Not for me. If any of you would like to write to Hawkins's mother, you'll find a letter from her in his pocket. He and his mother were great chums. But my missus left me eight years ago. Went away with another fellow and took the kid with her. I like the feeling of a home, as you may have noticed, but I couldn't start again after that."

It was an extraordinary thing, but in those few minutes Belcher said more than in all the weeks before. It was just as if the sound of the shot had started a flood of talk in him and he could go on the whole night like that, quite happily, talking about himself. We stood round like fools now that he couldn't see us any longer. Donovan looked at Noble, and Noble shook his head. Then Donovan raised his Webley, and at that moment Belcher gives his queer laugh again. He may have thought we were talking about him, or perhaps he noticed the same thing I'd noticed and couldn't understand it.

"Excuse me, chums," he says. "I feel I'm talking the hell of a lot, and so silly, about my being so handy about a house and things like that. But this thing came on me suddenly. You'll forgive me, I'm sure."

"You don't want to say a prayer?" asked Donovan.

"No, chum," he says. "I don't think it would help. I'm ready, and you boys want to get it over."

"You understand that we're only doing our duty?" says Donovan.

Belcher's head was raised like a blind man's, so that you could only see his chin and the tip of his nose in the lantern-light.

"I never could make out what duty was myself," he said. "I think you're all good lads, if that's what you mean. I'm not complaining."

Noble, just as if he couldn't bear any more of it, raised his fist at Donovan, and in a flash Donovan raised his gun and fired. The big man went over like a sack of meal, and this time there was no need of a second shot.

I don't remember much about the burying, but that it was worse than all the rest because we had to carry them to the grave. It was all mad lonely with nothing but a patch of lantern-light between ourselves and the dark, and birds hooting and screeching all round, disturbed by the guns. Noble went through Hawkins's belongings to find the letter from his mother, and then joined his hands together. He did the same with Belcher. Then, when we'd filled in the grave, we separated from Jeremiah Donovan and Feeney and took our tools back to the shed. All the way we didn't speak a word. The kitchen was dark and cold as we'd left it, and the old woman was sitting over the hearth, saying her beads. We walked past her into the room, and Noble struck a match to light the lamp. She rose quietly and came to the doorway with all her cantankerousness gone.

"What did ye do with them?" she asked in a whisper, and Noble started so that the match went out in his hand.

"What's that?" he asked without turning round.

"I heard ye," she said.

"What did you hear?" asked Noble.

"I heard ye. Do ye think I didn't hear ye, putting the spade back in the houseen?"

Noble struck another match and this time the lamp lit for him.

"Was that what ye did to them?" she asked.

Then, by God, in the very doorway, she fell on her knees and began praying, and after looking at her for a minute or two Noble did the same by the fireplace. I pushed my way out past her and left them at it. I stood at the door, watching the stars and listening to the shrieking of the birds dying out over the bogs. It is so strange what you feel at times like that you can't describe it. Noble says he saw everything ten times the size, as though there were nothing in the whole world but that little patch of bog with the two Englishmen stiffening into it, but with me it was as if the patch of bog where the Englishmen were was a million miles away, and even Noble and the old woman, mumbling behind me, and the birds and the bloody stars were all far away, and I was somehow very small and very lost and lonely like a child astray in the snow. And anything that happened me afterwards, I never felt the same about again.

QUESTIONS: *Guests of the Nation*

1. Although the narrator, Noble, and Donovan are all patriotic Irishmen, Donovan's attitude toward the English prisoners is quite different from that of the other two. How does that difference in attitude help point up the story's theme?

2. How does the constant bickering between Noble and Hawkins help to prepare us for the conclusion of the story? How does it contribute to the theme?

3. When he hears he is about to be shot, Hawkins, to save his life, volunteers to join the Irish cause. Is his turnabout simply evidence of his cowardice and hypocrisy? Explain.

4. Throughout most of the story Belcher is shy and speaks little; just before his execution, however, he suddenly becomes loquacious. Is he trying to stall for time? Would it have been more in character for Belcher to have remained stoically taciturn to the end, or do the narrator's remarks about Belcher's change make it plausible?

5. Does the old woman's presence in the story merely furnish local color or picturesqueness? If so, is it necessary or desirable? Or does her presence further contribute to the story's meaning? If so, how?

6. The following is the last paragraph of an earlier version:

So then, by God, she fell on her two knees by the door, and began telling her beads, and after a minute or two Noble went on his knees by the fireplace, so I pushed my way out past her, and stood at the door, watching the stars and listening to the damned shrieking of the birds. It is so strange what you feel at such moments, and not to be written afterwards. Noble says he felt he seen everything ten times as big, perceiving nothing around him but the little patch of black bog with the two Englishmen stiffening into it; but with me it was the other way, as though the patch of bog where the two Englishmen were was a thousand miles away from me, and even Noble mumbling just behind me and the old woman and the birds and the bloody stars were all far away, and I was somehow very small and very lonely. And anything that ever happened me after I never felt the same about again.

Which is the more effective conclusion? Why?

7. How does the point of view help to emphasize the narrator's development from innocence to disillusion? If the story had been told in the third person, how would it have affected the story's impact?

Five

ALLEGORY AND SYMBOLISM

That a story has a theme—a significance, a meaning—was suggested on pages 15-16. Here is a narrative whose theme has profoundly affected millions of people.

LUKE 10:30-37

Parable of the Good Samaritan

And Jesus answering said, "A certain man went down from Jerusalem to Jericho, and fell among thieves, which stripped him of his raiment, and wounded him, and departed, leaving him half dead. And by chance there came down a certain priest that way: and when he saw him, he passed by on the other side. And likewise a Levite, when he was at the place, came and looked on him, and passed by on the other side. But a certain Samaritan, as he journeyed, came where he was: and when he saw him, he had compassion on him, and went to him, and bound up his wounds, pouring in oil and wine, and set him on his own beast, and brought him to an inn, and took care of him. And on the morrow when he departed, he took out two pence, and gave them to the host, and said unto him, 'Take care of him; and whatsoever thou spendest more, when I come again, I will repay thee.' Which now of these three, thinkest thou, was neighbour unto him that fell among the thieves?"

And he said, "He that shewed mercy on him."

Then said Jesus unto him, "Go, and do thou likewise."

The narrative proper ends with the first paragraph; the theme, implicit there, is made explicit in the two lines that follow. Jesus' story has been "about" something; it has had a theme or meaning. It is a **parable,** a short narrative that enforces a moral.

Closely related to the parable is the allegory. An **allegory** presents items that are understood to have equivalents: Bunyan's allegory, *The Pilgrim's Progress*, tells of a man named Christian, who, on the road to the Celestial City, encounters, among others, Giant Despair, Mr. Worldly Wiseman, and Faithful. What these are equivalent to is clear from their names, and it is clear that Christian's journey stands for the trials of a soul in this world.

Modern short stories rarely have either the parable's explicit moral or the allegory's clear system of equivalents, but they nevertheless can be said to be about something. Take such detailed, realistic stories as "Hautot and His Son" and "Guests of the Nation." They may be very good pictures of French rural life and Irish military life, but they also imply or suggest things not limited to these subjects. This is not to say that after reading either story we discard the richly detailed narrative in favor of some abstraction that it implies—we do not throw away the narrative and cling to the theme. We feel that the narrative is meaningful. "Hautot and His Son" and "Guests of the Nation" present abundant precise details, and these details somehow add up to give the stories a generality or universality. The numerous details are so interrelated that they are a revelation of what is otherwise inexpressible.

In "Guests of the Nation," for example, the narrative forces into the edges of our minds thoughts of the inhumanity of officialdom, the power of hatred, the average man's impotence, the power of friendship, and the enormous aftereffect a deed can have. These thoughts are sharply controlled by the details of the story, and they do not separate themselves from the details. But the thoughts are there, though we scarcely think of them; in the story they are just under the surface. Quite properly we take small notice of the substratum and concentrate on the surface details. But in other stories—such as parables and allegories—the details are so presented that we are forced to look from them to their implied equivalents. Between these two extremes, of writing that is almost all surface and writing that is almost all implication, are stories in which we strongly feel both the surface happenings and their implication. In *Place in Fiction*, Eudora Welty uses an image of a china lamp to explain literature that presents an interesting surface texture filled with rich significance. Though she is talking about the novel, her words apply equally to the short story, as a reading of her story, "Livvie" (page 75), will show. Like a painted porcelain lamp which, when illuminated, reveals an inner picture shining through the outer (Miss Welty describes a lamp that unlit showed London and lit showed the Great Fire of London), the physical details in a work are illuminated from within by the author's imaginative vision. The outer painting, the literal details, presents "a continuous, shapely, pleasing, and finished surface to the eye," but this surface is not the whole: "The lamp alight is the combination of internal and external, glowing at the imagination as one; and so is the good novel. . . . The good novel should be steadily alight, revealing."

The unified picture, the details and what they suggest by virtue of the inner illumination with which the artist endows them, constitutes the symbolic level of a piece of literature. Here is Ishmael, in *Moby-Dick*, perceiving the symbolic meaning of Father Mapple's ascent into the pulpit:

> I was not prepared to see Father Mapple after gaining the height, slowly turn round, and stooping over the pulpit, deliberately drag up the ladder step by step, till the whole was deposited within, leaving him impregnable in his little Quebec.
> I pondered some time without fully comprehending the reason for this. Father Mapple enjoyed such a wide reputation for sincerity and sanctity, that I could not suspect him of courting notoriety by any mere tricks of the stage. No, thought I, there must be some sober reason for this thing; furthermore, it must symbolize something unseen. Can it be, then, that by that act of physical isolation, he signifies his spiritual withdrawal from the time, from all outward worldly ties and connections? Yes, for replenished with the meat and wine of the world, to the faithful man of God, this pulpit, I see, is a self-containing stronghold—a lofty Ehrenbreitstein, with a perennial well of water within the walls.

Ishmael's interpretation strikes the reader as well-stated and convincing, but many symbolic interpretations of literature (especially of *Moby-Dick*) are neither. An ingenious reader may overcomplicate or overemphasize the symbolism of a work, or he may distort it by omitting some of the details and by unduly focusing on others. In many works the details glow, but the glow is so gentle and subtle that even to talk about them is to overstate them and to understate other equally important aspects of the work.

Yet if it is false to overstate the significance of a detail, it is also false to understate a significant detail. For example, the let's-have-no-nonsense literal reader who holds that Faulkner's "The Bear" (which appears later in this chapter) is only an adventure story about a bear hunt impoverishes the story by neglecting the rich symbolic meaning just as much as the symbol-hunter impoverishes O'Connor's "Guests of the Nation" by slighting the literal meaning. Faulkner's insistence on the bear's magnificence (the beast is compared to King Priam, to a locomotive, to an immortal creature) compels the reader to attend to its symbolic meaning, as does his insistence that not until "the three lifeless mechanicals" (the watch, the compass, and the stick) are surrendered can the bear be fully seen. Near the end of the story Faulkner underlines the symbolic quality by having the boy's father explain that Keats's "Ode on a Grecian Urn" is not (as the son says) only "about a girl"; the talk about a girl, the father goes on, is a vehicle by which Keats communicates an insight about truth. "He had to talk about something. . . . He was talking about truth." Faulkner, too, had to talk about something in order to communicate his insight, so he chose as a meaningful vehicle a bear-hunt.

There has been a tendency, for about a century and a half now, to call **allegoric** those works whose images have precise equivalents that can be paraphrased with some accuracy, and to call **symbolic** those works whose images cast long shadows, give off multiple suggestions that do not allow for easy substitutions. This view might turn Father Mapple's gesture into an allegory and *Moby-Dick* (which Melville called an allegory) into a symbolic work. D. H. Lawrence's pronouncement can serve as an example of modern usage:

> You can't give a great symbol a "meaning," any more than you can give a cat a "meaning." Symbols are organic units of consciousness with a life of their own, and you can never explain them away, because their value is dynamic, emotional, belonging to the sense-consciousness of the body and soul, and not simply mental. An allegorical image has a *meaning*. Mr. Facing-both-ways has a meaning. But I defy you to lay your finger on the full meaning of Janus, who is a symbol.

Whether or not we like the modern distinction between allegory and symbol (much that today is called symbolic was in the Middle Ages called allegorical) the distinction seems here to stay. But we should recall that every piece of art—including allegory as well as writing that might be called "realistic"—is, in Robert Frost's words, "a symbol small or great of the way the will has to pitch into commitments deeper and deeper to a rounded conclusion."

A NOTE ON SETTING. The **setting** of a story—not only the physical locale but also the time of day or year or century—may or may not be symbolic. Sometimes the setting is lightly sketched, presented only because the story had to take place somewhere and at some time. "Mr. Know-All" takes place on a ship, shortly after the First World War, but it might equally well have taken place in a crowded hotel during the Cannes Film Festival. Sometimes, however, the setting is more important, giving us the feel of the people who move through it. "Hautot and His Son" has a good deal more landscape painting than "Mr. Know-All," not as added decoration but as a revelation of the sort of life a prosperous French farmer lives. If, however, scenery is drawn in detail, yet adds up to nothing, we share the impatience Robert Louis Stevenson expressed in a letter: " 'Roland approached the house; it had green doors and window blinds; and there was a scraper on the upper step.' To hell with Roland and the scraper." Yes, of course; but if the green doors and the scraper were to tell us something about the tenant, they could be important. And it might even be that the green doors and the scraper were so important that the story would be more or less about them. A rocky New England farm may be an analogue to the farmer who cultivates it, and the story may be as much about the farm as about the farmer. An obvious example is the setting in *The Return of the Native*. Oppressive Egdon Heath is so much a part of the novel that it almost takes on the role of a major character and, in large part, it is made responsible for the tragic fate of the novel's characters.

Though the wilderness in "The Bear" is described in little detail, it is not mere background but an important part of what the story is about. Take, for example, the following passage:

> On the second day he even found the gutted log where he had first seen the crooked print. It was almost completely crumbled now, healing with unbelievable speed, a passionate and almost visible relinquishment, back into the earth from which the tree had grown.

This is not just local color: it is also one of the ways by which Faulkner talks about the importance of contact with nature; it helps us understand what is involved when (a page or two later) the boy

> . . . stood for a moment, alien and small in the green and topless solitude. . . . He hung the watch and compass carefully on a bush and leaned the stick beside them and relinquished completely to it.

It is no accident that "relinquish" appears in both passages; like the gutted log, the boy derives his vitality by merging himself with the wilderness. What the wilderness stands for is something that can be grasped only by reading the story.

WILLIAM FAULKNER (1897-1962)

The Bear

He was ten. But it had already begun, long before that day when at last he wrote his age in two figures and he saw for the first time the camp where his father and Major de Spain and old General Compson and the others spent two weeks each November and two weeks again each June. He had already inherited then, without ever having seen it, the tremendous bear with one trap-ruined foot which, in an area almost a hundred miles deep, had earned itself a name, a definite designation like a living man.

He had listened to it for years: the long legend of corncribs rifled, of shotes and grown pigs and even calves carried bodily into the woods and devoured, of traps and deadfalls overthrown and dogs mangled and slain, and shotgun and even rifle charges delivered at point-blank range and with no more effect than so many peas blown through a tube by a boy—a corridor of wreckage and destruction beginning back before he was born, through which sped, not fast but rather with the ruthless and irresistible deliberation of a locomotive, the shaggy tremendous shape.

It ran in his knowledge before he ever saw it. It looked and towered in his dreams before he even saw the unaxed woods where it left its crooked print, shaggy, huge, red-eyed, not malevolent but just big—too big for the dogs which tried to bay it, for the horses which tried to ride it down, for the men and the bullets they fired into it, too big for the very country which was its constricting scope. He seemed to see it entire with a child's complete divination before he ever laid eyes on either—the doomed wilderness whose edges were being constantly and punily gnawed at by men with axes and plows who feared it because it was wilderness, men myriad and nameless even to one another in the land where the old bear had earned a name, through which ran not even a mortal animal but an anachronism, indomitable and invincible, out of an old dead time, a phantom, epitome and apotheosis of the old wild life at which the puny humans swarmed and hacked in a fury of abhorrence and fear, like pygmies about the ankles of a drowsing elephant: the old bear solitary, indomitable and alone, widowered, childless, and absolved of mortality—old Priam reft of his old wife and having outlived all his sons.

Until he was ten, each November he would watch the wagon containing the dogs and the bedding and food and guns and his father and Tennie's Jim, the Negro, and Sam Fathers, the Indian, son of a slave woman and a Chickasaw chief, depart on the road to town, to

Jefferson, where Major de Spain and the others would join them. To the boy, at seven, eight, and nine, they were not going into the Big Bottom to hunt bear and deer, but to keep yearly rendezvous with the bear which they did not even intend to kill. Two weeks later they would return, with no trophy, no head and skin. He had not expected it. He had not even been afraid it would be in the wagon. He believed that even after he was ten and his father would let him go too, for those two weeks in November, he would merely make another one, along with his father and Major de Spain and General Compson and the others, the dogs which feared to bay at it and the rifles and shotguns which failed even to bleed it, in the yearly pageant of the old bear's furious immortality.

Then he heard the dogs. It was in the second week of his first time in the camp. He stood with Sam Fathers against a big oak beside the faint crossing where they had stood each dawn for nine days now, hearing the dogs. He had heard them once before, one morning last week—a murmur, sourceless, echoing through the wet woods, swelling presently into separate voices which he could recognize and call by name. He had raised and cocked the gun as Sam told him and stood motionless again while the uproar, the invisible course, swept up and past and faded; it seemed to him that he could actually see the deer, the buck, blond, smoke-colored, elongated with speed, fleeing, vanishing, the woods, the gray solitude, still ringing even when the cries of the dogs had died away.

"Now let the hammers down," Sam said.

"You knew they were not coming here too," he said.

"Yes," Sam said. "I want you to learn how to do when you didn't shoot. It's after the chance for the bear or the deer has done already come and gone that men and dogs get killed."

"Anyway," he said, "it was just a deer."

Then on the tenth morning he heard the dogs again. And he readied the too-long, too-heavy gun as Sam had taught him, before Sam even spoke. But this time it was no deer, no ringing chorus of dogs running strong on a free scent, but a moiling yapping an octave too high, with something more than indecision and even abjectness in it, not even moving very fast, taking a long time to pass completely out of hearing, leaving then somewhere in the air that echo, thin, slightly hysterical, abject, almost grieving, with no sense of a fleeting, unseen, smoke-colored, grass-eating shape ahead of it, and Sam, who had taught him first of all to cock the gun and take position where he could see everywhere and then never move again, had himself moved up beside him; he could hear Sam breathing at his shoulder, and he could see the arched curve of the old man's inhaling nostrils.

"Hah," Sam said. "Not even running. Walking."

"Old Ben!" the boy said. "But up here!" he cried. "Way up here!"

"He do it every year," Sam said. "Once. Maybe to see who in camp this time, if he can shoot or not. Whether we got the dog yet that can bay and hold him. He'll take them to the river, then he'll send them back home. We may as well go back too; see how they look when they come back to camp."

When they reached the camp the hounds were already there, ten of them crouching back under the kitchen, the boy and Sam squatting to peer back into the obscurity where they had huddled, quiet, the eyes luminous, glowing at them and vanishing, and no sound, only that effluvium of something more than dog, stronger than dog and not just animal, just beast, because still there had been nothing in front of that abject and almost painful yapping save the solitude, the wilderness, so that when the eleventh hound came in at noon and with all the others watching—even old Uncle Ash, who called himself first a cook—Sam daubed the tattered ear and the raked shoulder with turpentine and axle grease, to the boy it was still no living creature, but the wilderness which, leaning for the moment down, had patted lightly once the hound's temerity.

"Just like a man," Sam said. "Just like folks. Put off as long as she could having to be brave, knowing all the time that sooner or later she would have to be brave to keep on living with herself, and knowing all the time beforehand what was going to happen to her when she done it."

That afternoon, himself on the one-eyed wagon mule which did not mind the smell of blood nor, as they told him, of bear, and with Sam on the other one, they rode for more than three hours through the rapid, shortening winter day. They followed no path, no trail even that he could see; almost at once they were in a country which he had never seen before. Then he knew why Sam had made him ride the mule which would not spook. The sound one stopped short and tried to whirl and bolt even as Sam got down, blowing its breath, jerking and wrenching at the rein, while Sam held it, coaxing it forward with his voice, since he could not risk tying it, drawing it forward while the boy got down from the marred one.

Then, standing beside Sam in the gloom of the dying afternoon, he looked down at the rotted over-turned log, gutted and scored with claw marks and, in the wet earth beside it, the print of the enormous warped two-toed foot. He knew now what he had smelled when he peered under the kitchen where the dogs huddled. He realized for the first time that the bear which had run in his listening and loomed in his dreams since before he could remember to the contrary, and which, therefore, must have existed in the listening and dreams of his father and Major de Spain and even old General Compson, too, before they began to remember in their turn, was a mortal animal, and that if they had departed for the camp each November without any actual hope of bringing its trophy back, it was not because it could not be slain, but because so far they had had no actual hope to.

"Tomorrow," he said.

"We'll try tomorrow," Sam said. "We ain't got the dog yet."

"We've got eleven. They ran him this morning."

"It won't need but one," Sam said. "He ain't here. Maybe he ain't nowhere. The only other way will be for him to run by accident over somebody that has a gun."

"That wouldn't be me," the boy said. "It will be Walter or Major or—"

"It might," Sam said. "You watch close in the morning. Because he's smart. That's how come he has lived this long. If he gets hemmed up and has to pick out somebody to run over, he will pick out you."

"How?" the boy said. "How will he know—" He ceased. "You mean he already knows me, that I ain't never been here before, ain't had time to find out yet whether I—" He ceased again, looking at Sam, the old man whose face revealed nothing until it smiled. He said humbly, not even amazed, "It was me he was watching. I don't reckon he did need to come but once."

The next morning they left the camp three hours before daylight. They rode this time because it was too far to walk, even the dogs in the wagon; again the first gray light found him in a place which he had never seen before, where Sam had placed him and told him to stay and then departed. With the gun which was too big for him, which did not even belong to him, but to Major de Spain, and which he had fired only once—at a stump on the first day, to learn the recoil and how to reload it—he stood against a gum tree beside a little bayou whose black still water crept without movement out of a canebrake and crossed a small clearing and into cane again, where, invisible, a bird—the big woodpecker called Lord-to-God by Negroes —clattered at a dead limb.

It was a stand like any other, dissimilar only in incidentals to the one where he had stood each morning for ten days; a territory new to him, yet no less familiar than that other one which, after almost two weeks, he had come to believe he knew a little—the same solitude, the same loneliness through which human beings had merely passed without altering it, leaving no mark, no scar, which looked exactly as it must have looked when the first ancestor of Sam Fathers' Chickasaw predecessors crept into it and looked about, club or stone ax or bone arrow drawn and poised; different only because, squatting at the edge of the kitchen, he smelled the hounds huddled and cringing beneath it and saw the raked ear and shoulder of the one who, Sam said, had had to be brave once in order to live with herself, and saw yesterday in the earth beside the gutted log the print of the living foot.

He heard no dogs at all. He never did hear them. He only heard the drumming of the woodpecker stop short off and knew that the bear was looking at him. He never saw it. He did not know whether it was in front of him or behind him. He did not move, holding the useless gun, which he had not even had warning to cock and which even now he did not cock, tasting in his saliva that taint as of brass which he knew now because he had smelled it when he peered under the kitchen at the huddled dogs.

Then it was gone. As abruptly as it had ceased, the woodpecker's dry, monotonous clatter set up again, and after a while he even believed he could hear the dogs—a murmur, scarce a sound even, which he had probably been hearing for some time before he even remarked it, drifting into hearing and then out again, dying away. They came nowhere near him. If it was a bear they ran, it was another bear. It was Sam himself who came out of the cane and crossed the bayou, followed by the injured bitch of yesterday. She was almost at heel, like a bird dog, making no sound. She came and crouched against his leg, trembling, staring off into the cane.

"I didn't see him," he said. "I didn't, Sam!"

"I know it," Sam said. "He done the looking. You didn't hear him neither, did you?"

"No," the boy said. "I—"

"He's smart," Sam said. "Too smart." He looked down at the hound, trembling faintly and steadily against the boy's knee. From the raked shoulder a few drops of fresh blood oozed and clung. "Too big. We ain't got the dog yet. But maybe someday. Maybe not next time. But someday."

So I must see him, he thought. *I must look at him.* Otherwise, it seemed to him that it would go on like this forever, as it had gone on with his father and Major de Spain, who was older than his father, and even with old General Compson, who had been old enough to be a brigade commander in 1865. Otherwise, it would go on so forever, next time and next time, after and after and after. It seemed to him that he could never see the two of them, himself and the bear, shadowy in the limbo from which time emerged, becoming time; the old bear absolved of mortality and himself partaking, sharing a little of it, enough of it. And he knew now what he had smelled in the huddled dogs and tasted in his saliva. He recognized fear. *So I will have to see him*, he thought, without dread or even hope. *I will have to look at him.*

It was in June of the next year. He was eleven. They were in camp again, celebrating Major de Spain's and General Compson's birthdays. Although the one had been born in September and the other in the depth of winter and in another decade, they had met for two weeks to fish and shoot squirrels and turkey and run coons and wildcats with the dogs at night. That is, he and Boon Hoggenbeck and the Negroes fished and shot squirrels and ran the coons and cats, because the proved hunters, not only Major de Spain and old General Compson, who spent those two weeks sitting in a rocking chair before a tremendous iron pot of Brunswick stew, stirring and tasting, with old Ash to quarrel with about how he was making it and Tennie's Jim to pour whiskey from the demijohn into the tin dipper from which he drank it, but even the boy's father and Walter Ewell, who were still young enough, scorned such, other than shooting the wild gobblers with pistols for wagers on their marksmanship.

Or, that is, his father and the others believed he was hunting squirrels. Until the third day, he thought that Sam Fathers believed that too. Each morning he would leave the camp right after breakfast. He had his own gun now, a Christmas present. He went back to the tree beside the bayou where he had stood that morning. Using the compass which old General Compson had given him, he ranged from that point; he was teaching himself to be a better-than-fair woodsman without knowing he was doing it. On the second day he even found the gutted log where he had first seen the crooked print. It was almost completely crumbled now, healing with unbelievable speed, a passionate and almost visible relinquishment, back into the earth from which the tree had grown.

He ranged the summer woods now, green with gloom; if anything, actually dimmer than in November's gray dissolution, where, even at noon, the sun fell only in intermittent dappling upon the earth, which never completely dried out and which crawled with snakes —moccasins and water snakes and rattlers, themselves the color of the dappling gloom, so that he would not always see them until they moved, returning later and later, first day, second day, passing in the twilight of the third evening the little log pen enclosing the log stable where Sam was putting up the horses for the night.

"You ain't looked right yet," Sam said.

He stopped. For a moment he didn't answer. Then he said peacefully, in a peaceful rushing burst as when a boy's miniature dam in a little brook gives way, "All right. But how? I went to the bayou. I even found that log again. I—"

"I reckon that was all right. Likely he's been watching you. You never saw his foot?"

"I," the boy said—"I didn't—I never thought—"

"It's the gun," Sam said. He stood beside the fence motionless—the old man, the Indian, in the battered faded overalls and the five-cent straw hat which in the Negro's race had been the badge of his enslavement and was now the regalia of his freedom. The camp—the clearing, the house, the barn and its tiny lot with which Major de Spain in his turn had scratched punily and evanescently at the wilderness—faded in the dusk, back into the immemorial darkness of the woods. *The gun,* the boy thought. *The gun.*

"Be scared," Sam said. "You can't help that. But don't be afraid. Ain't nothing in the woods going to hurt you unless you corner it, or it smells that you are afraid. A bear or a deer, too, has got to be scared of a coward the same as a brave man has got to be."

The gun, the boy thought.

"You will have to choose," Sam said.

He left the camp before daylight, long before Uncle Ash would wake in his quilts on the kitchen floor and start the fire for breakfast. He had only the compass and a stick for snakes. He could go almost a mile before he would begin to need the compass. He sat on a log, the invisible compass in his invisible hand, while the secret night sounds, fallen still at his movements, scurried again and then ceased for good, and the owls ceased and gave over to the waking of day birds, and he could see the compass. Then he went fast yet still quietly; he was becoming better and better as a woodsman, still without having yet realized it.

He jumped a doe and a fawn at sunrise, walked them out of the bed, close enough to see them—the crash of undergrowth, the white scut, the fawn scudding behind her faster than he had believed it could run. He was hunting right, upwind, as Sam had taught him; not that it mattered now. He had left the gun; of his own will and relinquishment he had accepted not a gambit, not a choice, but a condition in which not only the bear's heretofore inviolable anonymity but all the old rules and balances of hunter and hunted had been abrogated. He would not even be afraid, not even in the moment when the fear would take him completely—blood, skin, bowels, bones, memory from the long time before it became his memory—all save that thin, clear, immortal lucidity which alone differed him from this bear and from all the other bear and deer he would ever kill in the humility and pride of his skill and endurance, to which Sam had spoken when he leaned in the twilight on the lot fence yesterday.

By noon he was far beyond the little bayou, farther into the new and alien country than he had ever been. He was traveling now not only by the compass but by the old, heavy, biscuit-thick silver watch which had belonged to his grandfather. When he stopped at last, it was for the first time since he had risen from the log at dawn when he could see the compass. It was far enough. He had left the camp nine hours ago; nine hours from now, dark would have already been an hour old. But he didn't think that. He thought, *All right. Yes. But what?* and stood for a moment, alien and small in the green and topless solitude, answering his own question before it had formed and ceased. It was the watch, the compass, the stick— the three lifeless mechanicals with which for nine hours he had fended the wilderness off; he hung the watch and compass carefully on a bush and leaned the stick beside them and relinquished completely to it.

He had not been going very fast for the last two or three hours. He went no faster now, since distance would not matter even if he could have gone fast. And he was trying to keep a bearing on the tree where he had left the compass, trying to complete a circle which would bring him back to it or at least intersect itself, since direction would not matter now either. But the tree was not here, and he did as Sam had schooled him—made the next circle in the opposite direction, so that the two patterns would bisect somewhere, but crossing no print of his own feet, finding the tree at last, but in the wrong place—no bush, no compass, no watch—and the tree not even the tree, because there was a down log beside it and he did what Sam Fathers had told him was the next thing and the last.

As he sat down on the log he saw the crooked print—the warped, tremendous, two-toed indentation which, even as he watched it, filled with water. As he looked up, the wilderness coalesced, solidified—the glade, the tree he sought, the bush, the watch and the compass glinting where the ray of sunshine touched them. Then he saw the bear. It did not emerge, appear; it was just there, immobile, solid, fixed in the hot dappling of the green and windless noon, not as big as he had dreamed it, but as big as he had expected it, bigger, dimensionless, against the dappled obscurity, looking at him where he sat quietly on the log and looked back at it.

Then it moved. It made no sound. It did not hurry. It crossed the glade, walking for an instant into the full glare of the sun; when it reached the other side it stopped again and looked back at him across one shoulder while his quiet breathing inhaled and exhaled three times.

Then it was gone. It didn't walk into the woods, the undergrowth. It faded, sank back into the wilderness as he had watched a fish, a huge old bass, sink and vanish into the dark depths of its pool without even any movement of its fins.

He thought, *It will be next fall.* But it was not next fall, nor the next nor the next. He was fourteen then. He had killed his buck, and Sam Fathers had marked his face with the hot blood, and in the next year he killed a bear. But even before that accolade he had become as competent in the woods as many grown men with the same experience; by his fourteenth year he was a better woodsman than most grown men with more. There was no territory within thirty miles of the camp that he did not know—bayou, ridge, brake, landmark, tree and path. He could have led anyone to any point in it without deviation, and brought them out again. He knew the game trails that even Sam Fathers did not know; in his thirteenth year he found a buck's bedding place, and unbeknown to his father he borrowed Walter Ewell's rifle and lay in wait at dawn and killed the buck when it walked back to the bed, as Sam had told him how the old Chickasaw fathers did.

But not the old bear, although by now he knew its footprints better than he did his own, and not only the crooked one. He could see any one of three sound ones and distinguish it from any other, and not only by its size. There were other bears within these thirty miles which left tracks almost as large, but this was more than that. If Sam Fathers had been his mentor and the back-yard rabbits and squirrels at home his kindergarten, then the wilderness the old bear ran was his college, the old male bear itself, so long unwifed and child- less as to have become its own ungendered progenitor, was his alma mater. But he never saw it.

He could find the crooked print now almost whenever he liked, fifteen or ten or five miles, or sometimes nearer the camp than that. Twice while on stand during the three years he heard the dogs strike its trail by accident; on the second time they jumped it seemingly, the voices high, abject, almost human in hysteria, as on that first morn- ing two years ago. But not the bear itself. He would remember that noon three years ago, the glade, himself and the bear fixed during that moment in the windless and dappled blaze, and it would seem to him that it had never happened, that he had dreamed that too. But it had happened. They had looked at each other, they had emerged from the wilderness old as earth, synchronized to the instant by some- thing more than the blood that moved the flesh and bones which bore them, and touched, pledged something, affirmed, something more lasting than the frail web of bones and flesh which any accident could obliterate.

Then he saw it again. Because of the very fact that he thought of nothing else, he had forgotten to look for it. He was still hunting with Walter Ewell's rifle. He saw it cross the end of a long blow-down, a corridor where a tornado had swept, rushing through rather than over the tangle of trunks and branches as a locomotive would have, faster than he had ever believed it could move, almost as fast as a deer even, because a deer would have spent most of that time in the air, faster than he could bring the rifle sights up with it. And now he knew what had been wrong during all the three years. He sat on a log, shaking and trembling as if he had never seen the woods before nor anything that ran them, wondering with incredulous amazement how he could have forgotten the very thing which Sam Fathers had told him and which the bear itself had proved the next day and had now returned after three years to reaffirm.

And now he knew what Sam Fathers had meant about the right dog, a dog in which size would mean less than nothing. So when he returned alone in April—school was out then, so that the sons of farmers could help with the land's planting, and at last his father had granted him permission, on his promise to be back in four days—he had the dog. It was his own, a mongrel of the sort called by Negroes a fyce, a ratter, itself not much bigger than a rat and possessing that bravery which had long since stopped being courage and had become foolhardiness.

It did not take four days. Alone again, he found the trail on the first morning. It was not a stalk; it was an ambush. He timed the meeting almost as if it were an appointment with a human being. Himself holding the fyce muffled in a feed sack and Sam Fathers with two of the hounds on a piece of a plowline rope, they lay down wind of the trail at dawn of the second morning. They were so close that the bear turned without even running, as if in surprised amazement at the shrill and frantic uproar of the released fyce, turning at bay against the trunk of a tree, on its hind feet; it seemed to the boy that it would never stop rising, taller and taller, and even the two hounds seemed to take a desperate and despairing courage from the fyce, following it as it went in.

Then he realized that the fyce was actually not going to stop. He flung, threw the gun away, and ran; when he overtook and grasped the frantically pin-wheeling little dog, it seemed to him that he was directly under the bear.

He could smell it, strong and hot and rank. Sprawling, he looked up to where it loomed and towered over him like a cloudburst and colored like a thunderclap, quite familiar, peacefully and even lucidly familiar, until he remembered: This was the way he had used to dream about it. Then it was gone. He didn't see it go. He knelt, holding the frantic fyce with both hands, hearing the abashed wailing of the hounds drawing farther and farther away, until Sam came up. He carried the gun. He laid it down quietly beside the boy and stood looking down at him.

"You've done seed him twice now with a gun in your hands," he said. "This time you couldn't have missed him."

The boy rose. He still held the fyce. Even in his arms and clear of the ground, it yapped frantically, straining and surging after the fading uproar of the two hounds like a tangle of wire springs. He was panting a little but he was neither shaking nor trembling now.

"Neither could you!" he said. "You had the gun! Neither did you!"

"And you didn't shoot," his father said. "How close were you?"

"I don't know, sir," he said. "There was a big wood tick inside his right hind leg. I saw that. But I didn't have the gun then."

"But you didn't shoot when you had the gun," his father said. "Why?"

But he didn't answer, and his father didn't wait for him to, rising and crossing the room, across the pelt of the bear which the boy had killed two years ago and the larger one which his father had killed before he was born, to the bookcase beneath the mounted head of the boy's first buck. It was the room which his father called the office, from which all the plantation business was transacted; in it for the fourteen years of his life he had heard the best of all talking. Major de Spain would be there and sometimes old General Compson, and Walter Ewell and Boon Hoggenbeck and Sam Fathers and Tennie's Jim, too, were hunters, knew the woods and what ran them.

He would hear it, not talking himself but listening—the wilderness, the big woods, bigger and older than any recorded document of white man fatuous enough to believe he had bought any fragment of it or Indian ruthless enough to pretend that any fragment of it had been his to convey. It was of the men, not white nor black nor red, but men, hunters with the will and hardihood to endure and the humility and skill to survive, and the dogs and the bear and deer juxtaposed and reliefed against it, ordered and compelled by and within the wilderness in the ancient and unremitting contest by the ancient and immitigable rules which voided all regrets and brooked no quarter, the voices quiet and weighty and deliberate for retrospection and recollection and exact remembering, while he squatted in the blazing firelight as Tennie's Jim squatted, who stirred only to put more wood on the fire and to pass the bottle from one glass to another. Because the bottle was always present, so that after a while it seemed to him that those fierce instants of heart and brain and courage and wiliness and speed were concentrated and distilled into that brown liquor which not women, not boys and children, but only hunters drank, drinking not of the blood they had spilled but some condensation of the wild immortal spirit, drinking it moderately, humbly even, not with the pagan's base hope of acquiring the virtues of cunning and strength and speed, but in salute to them.

His father returned with the book and sat down again and opened it. "Listen," he said. He read the five stanzas aloud, his voice quiet and deliberate in the room where there was no fire now because it was already spring. Then he looked up. The boy watched him. "All right," his father said. "Listen." He read again, but only the second stanza this time, to the end of it, the last two lines, and closed the book and put it on the table beside him. "She cannot fade, though thou hast not thy bliss, forever wilt thou love, and she be fair," he said.

"He's talking about a girl," the boy said.

"He had to talk about something," his father said. Then he said, "He was talking about truth. Truth doesn't change. Truth is one thing. It covers all things which touch the heart—honor and pride and pity and justice and courage and love. Do you see now?"

He didn't know. Somehow it was simpler than that. There was an old bear, fierce and ruthless, not merely just to stay alive, but with the fierce pride of liberty and freedom, proud enough of the liberty and freedom to see it threatened without fear or even alarm; nay, who at times even seemed deliberately to put that freedom and liberty in jeopardy in order to savor them, to remind his old strong bones and flesh to keep supple and quick to defend and preserve them. There was an old man, son of a Negro slave and an Indian king, inheritor on the one side of the long chronicle of a people who had learned humility through suffering, and pride through the endurance which survived the suffering and injustice, and on the other side, the chronicle of a people even longer in the land than the first, yet who no longer existed in the land at all save in the solitary brotherhood of an old Negro's alien blood and the wild and invincible spirit of an old bear. There was a boy who wished to learn humility and pride in order to become skillful and worthy in the woods, who suddenly found himself becoming so skillful so rapidly that he feared he would never become worthy because he had not learned humility and pride, although he had tried to, until one day and as suddenly he discovered that an old man who could not have defined either had led him, as though by the hand, to that point where an old bear and a little mongrel of a dog showed him that, by possessing one thing other, he would possess them both.

And a little dog, nameless and mongrel and many-fathered, grown, yet weighing less than six pounds, saying as if to itself, "I can't be dangerous, because there's nothing much smaller than I am; I can't be fierce, because they would call it just a noise; I can't be humble, because I'm already too close to the ground to genuflect; I can't be proud, because I wouldn't be near enough to it for anyone to know who was casting the shadow, and I don't even know that I'm not going to heaven, because they have already decided that I don't possess an immortal soul. So all I can be is brave. But it's all right. I can be that, even if they still call it just noise."

That was all. It was simple, much simpler than somebody talking in a book about youth and a girl he would never need to grieve over, because he could never approach any nearer her and would never have to get any farther away. He had heard about a bear, and finally got big enough to trail it, and he trailed it four years and at last met it with a gun in his hands and he didn't shoot. Because a little dog— But he could have shot long before the little dog covered the twenty yards to where the bear waited, and Sam Fathers could have shot at any time during that interminable minute while Old Ben stood on his hind feet over them. He stopped. His father was watching him gravely across the spring-rife twilight of the room; when he spoke, his words were as quiet as the twilight, too, not loud, because they did not need to be because they would last. "Courage, and honor, and pride," his father said, "and pity, and love of justice and of liberty. They all touch the heart, and what the heart holds to becomes truth, as far as we know the truth. Do you see now?"

Sam, and Old Ben, and Nip, he thought. And himself too. He had been all right too. His father had said so. "Yes, sir," he said.

SEVERAL OF FAULKNER'S COMMENTS on "The Bear," made during interviews at the University of Virginia (printed in *Faulkner in the University*, ed. F. L. Gwynn and J. W. Blotner, 1959), though not necessarily definitive, are suggestive:

One symbol was the bear represented the vanishing wilderness. The little dog that wasn't scared of the bear represented the indomitable spirit of man. I'll have to dig back and get up some more of those symbols, because I have learned around an even dozen that I put into that story without knowing it. But there are two pretty good ones that you can hold to.

Asked the significance of the fyce, Faulkner said that it is

> . . . the antithesis of the bear. The bear represented the obsolete primitive. The fyce represents the creature who has coped with environment and is still on top of it, you might say. That he has—instead of sticking to his breeding and becoming a decadent degenerate creature, he has mixed himself up with the good stock where he picked and chose. And he's quite smart, he's quite brave. All's against him is his size. But I never knew a fyce yet that realized that he wasn't big as anything else he ever saw, even a bear.

Asked to explain what the "one thing" was that would enable the boy to learn "humility and pride," Faulkner replied: "Courage, it was. A little dog that never saw a bear bigger than he was."

QUESTIONS: *The Bear*

1. In the opening three paragraphs of the story, the pronoun "it" usually refers to Old Ben. But does "it" always have the same referent in this opening section of the story? How might the "it" be said to function ambiguously and thus prepare the reader for the symbolism in the story? How does the fact that the boy is nameless throughout the story add to the symbolic meaning?

2. Compare the characterizations of the bear in the second and third paragraphs. How do they affect our attitude toward the bear? Does the fact that it is given a name and does the name itself affect our attitude toward Old Ben?

3. What is the distinction Sam Fathers makes between being "scared" and being "afraid"? Aren't the words synonymous, or is there, in the context, some crucial difference? If so, what might it be?

4. The boy relinquishes the three lifeless mechanicals before he is permitted to see the bear. Why? Is Faulkner making some social comment about modern man that goes beyond the limits of a bear hunt? How is the following letter, written by Faulkner to *The New York Times* (26 December 1954), relevant to "The Bear"?

> This is about the Italian airliner which undershot the runway and crashed at Idlewild after failing three times to hold the instrument glide-path which would have brought it down to the runway.
>   It is written on the idea (postulate, if you like) that the instrument or instruments—altimeter-cum-drift-indicator—failed or

had failed, was already out of order or incorrect before the moment when the pilot committed irrevocably the aircraft to it.

It is written in grief. Not just for the sorrow of the bereaved ones of those who died in the crash, and for the airline, the public carrier which, in selling the tickets, promised or anyway implied security for the trip, but for the crew, the pilot himself, who will be blamed for the crash and whose record and memory will be tarnished by it; who, along with his unaware passengers, was victim not even of the failed instruments but victim of that mystical, unquestioning, almost religious awe and veneration in which our culture has trained us to hold gadgets—any gadget, if it is only complex enough and cryptic enough and costs enough.

I imagine that even after the first failure to hold the glide-path, certainly after the second one, his instinct—the seat of his pants, call it what you will—after that many hours in the air, told him that something was wrong. And his seniority as a four-engine over-water captain probably told him where the trouble was. But he dared not accept that knowledge and (this presumes that even after the second failure he still had enough fuel left to reach a field which he could see) act on it.

Possibly at some time during the four attempts to land, very likely at some one of the final rapid seconds before he had irrevocably committed the aircraft—that compounding of mass and weight by velocity—to the ground, his co-pilot (or flight engineer or whoever else might have been in the cockpit at the time) probably said to him: "Look. We're wrong. Get the flaps and gear up and let's get to hell out of here." But he dared not. He dared not so flout and affront, even with his own life too at stake, our cultural postulate of the infallibility of machines, instruments, gadgets—a Power more ruthless even than the old Hebrew concept of its God, since ours is not even jealous and vengeful, caring nothing about individuals.

He dared not commit that sacrilege. If he had, nothing would have remained to him save to open the cockpit hatch and (a Roman) cast himself onto the turning blades of one of the inboard air-screws. I grieve for him, for that moment's victims. We all had better grieve for all people beneath a culture which holds any mechanical superior to any man simply because the one, being mechanical, is infallible, while the other, being nothing but man, is not just subject to failure but doomed to it.

5. On page 68 the hunters pass around a bottle. What is symbolized by this action?

6. Why doesn't the boy kill the bear?

7. A careful reading of Keats's "Ode on a Grecian Urn" (pages 328-29) may illuminate the father's comments to his son. What is the particular relevance of the second stanza?

Six

STYLE

In the preface to *The Nigger of the "Narcissus"* Joseph Conrad wrote:

> My task which I am trying to achieve is, by the power of the written word, to make you hear, to make you feel—it is, before all, to make you see. That—and no more, and it is everything.

Most writers set themselves Conrad's task, attempting to make us "see" by their choice and arrangement of words into sentences. These sentences constitute the writer's style, and they are an important part of his meaning, just as a speaker's style—in addition to choice of sentences, his pace, tone of voice, gestures—helps communicate his meaning. What is good **style**? Jonathan Swift defined it as "proper words in proper places." But what are the proper words and the proper places? Shall the writer heap up details, or shall he be highly selective? Shall he call a spade a spade, or shall he understate, and allow the reader to leap to the meaning himself? Shall he use abundant dialogue, or shall he use abundant summaries? Shall he use short sentences or long ones? If long, shall they be constructed to suggest forethought and self-assurance, or improvisation and uncertainty? Contrast, for example, these two long sentences, chosen, for the sake of clarity, from expository prose rather than from fiction. The first is by Samuel Johnson:

> To search his plays for vigorous sallies and sententious elegances, or to fix the dates of any little pieces which he wrote by chance or by solicitation, were labor too tedious and minute.

The second is by John Donne:

> We study health, and we deliberate upon our meats and drink and air and exercises, and we hew and we polish every stone that goes to the building; and so our health is a long and regular work.

Johnson, by placing his finite verb near the end, indicates that his sentence has been formed before it is uttered; in contrast, Donne, by placing his finite verb near the beginning, and by adding modifications and parenthetical thoughts in clauses linked by semicolons and such a simple co-ordinate as "and," suggests a writer in the process of thinking.

What style shall a writer use?

Put this way, it is clear that there is no simple answer; anything can be right or wrong, depending on what effect is sought. James Joyce, in *A Portrait of the Artist as a Young Man*, uses a variety of styles, and each of them is right, beginning with a child-like style in describing the protagonist's infancy, moving to a luxuriant style in describing his adolescence, and concluding with a sparer style in describing his preparations for self-exile. Here are three passages from the novel— the opening sentence, a sentence from the middle, and the closing sentence:

(1) Once upon a time and a very good time it was there was a moocow coming down along the road and this moocow that was down along the road met a nicens little boy named baby tuckoo. . . .

(2) Only at times, in the pauses of his desire, when the luxury that was wasting him gave room to a softer languor, the image of Mercedes traversed the background of his memory.

(3) April 27. Old father, old artificer, stand me now and ever in good stead.

Consider the first two sentences in the opening paragraph of Eudora Welty's "Livvie":

Solomon carried Livvie twenty-one miles away from her home when he married her. He carried her away up on the Old Natchez Trace into the deep country to live in his house.

These sentences can easily be transposed and combined into:

When Solomon married Livvie, he carried her away up on the Old Natchez Trace into the deep country to live in his house, twenty-one miles away.

The words are the same, but everything is changed. By failing to repeat the structure of subject-verb ("Solomon carried," "He carried"), the suggestion of Livvie's own voice is lost. Though the lines, as Miss Welty wrote them, were not spoken by Livvie, they carry within them a suggestion of her simplicity. Take the first two sentences of the second paragraph:

It was a nice house, inside and outside both. In the first place, it had three rooms.

These can be combined into:

The three-room house was nice, inside and out.

Again, the innocence of Livvie's voice is missing. In these lines, Miss Welty is not communicating information only about Livvie's house; she is also giving us an image of Livvie's mind, and the paraphrases do not.

A more subtle example may be useful. When Miss Welty first published "Livvie," the third sentence of the opening paragraph was simply:

She was sixteen then.

But in the revision, printed in this book, the sentence runs:

She was sixteen—an only girl, then.

Of course the revision has an additional piece of information, but what is important for our present purpose is the difference in style. "She was sixteen then" is a quite ordinary sentence, such as any of us might write. But "She was sixteen—an only girl, then" presents us with a special mind. It almost seems to suggest that Livvie is no longer an only girl, yet this point is never made. What the revision adds is a hint of Livvie's slightly wistful, disjointed view of the past. Ordinarily the sentence might run, "She was sixteen then, an only girl"; by being placed at the end of the sentence, after some material that it does not logically follow, "then" is somewhat unexpected, rather like the last step down to the cellar. The slight jolt we feel in "then" both reveals Livvie's naive mind and gives the past an emphasis lacking in the original "She was sixteen then" and lacking in "She was sixteen then, an only girl."

These comments on some of Miss Welty's sentences do not come near to revealing their special power, but perhaps they have made clear that in good writing words cannot be rearranged without change in meaning. "I began to speak of style," Isaac Babel writes in one of his stories, "of the army of words, of the army in which all kinds of weapons may come into play. No iron can stab the heart with such force as a period put just at the right place."

A NOTE ON TONE. A speaker's tone of voice conveys part of his meaning: "Good Lord" can be a pious invocation; it can also be a blasphemous expletive, and the tone, quite as well as the context, can tell us which it is. **Tone** in a story is commonly defined as the author's voice (in distinction from the voices of his characters); it is, let us say, the author's attitude as the reader infers it. His characters may speak angrily, but the reader may rightly detect that the author's tone is gentle and compassionate. His characters may speak gaily and wittily, but the reader may rightly detect that the author's tone is scornful. When we talk about the author's sympathies and antipathies, his cynicism or his solemnity or his flippancy, we are talking about his tone. And it is through his pervasive style that his tone is heard.*

EUDORA WELTY (1909-   )

Livvie

Solomon carried Livvie twenty-one miles away from her home when he married her. He carried her away up on the Old Natchez Trace into the deep country to live in his house. She was sixteen—an only girl, then. Once people said he thought nobody would ever come along there. He told her himself that it had been a long time, and a day she did not know about, since that road was a traveled road with *people* coming and going. He was good to her, but he kept her in the house. She had not thought that she could not get back. Where she came from, people said an old man did not want anybody in the world to ever find his wife, for fear they would steal her back from him. Solomon asked her before he took her, "Would she be happy?"— very dignified, for he was a colored man that owned his land and had it written down in the courthouse; and she said, "Yes, sir," since he was an old man and she was young and just listened and answered. He asked her, if she was choosing winter, would she pine for spring, and she said, "No indeed." Whatever she said, always, was because he was an old man . . . while nine years went by. All the time, he got old, and he got so old he gave out. At least he slept the whole day in bed, and she was young still.

It was a nice house, inside and outside both. In the first place, it had three rooms. The front room was papered in holly paper, with green palmettos from the swamp spaced at careful intervals over the walls. There was fresh newspaper cut with fancy borders on the mantle-shelf, on which were propped photographs of old or very young men printed in faint yellow—Solomon's people. Solomon had a houseful of furniture. There was a double settee, a tall scrolled rocker and an organ in the front room, all around a three-legged table with a pink marble top, on which was set a lamp with three gold feet, besides a jelly glass with pretty hen feathers in it. Behind the front room, the other room had the bright iron bed with the polished knobs like a

*Although Chapter 9, "The Speaking Tone of Voice," draws its illustrative material from poems, the points it makes are relevant here. The reader may find it useful to consult the first half-dozen pages of that chapter now.

throne, in which Solomon slept all day. There were snow-white curtains of wiry lace at the window, and a lace bedspread belonged on the bed. But what old Solomon slept sound under was a big feather-stitched piece-quilt in the pattern "Trip Around the World," which had twenty-one different colors, four hundred and forty pieces, and a thousand yards of thread, and that was what Solomon's mother made in her life and old age. There was a table holding the Bible, and a trunk with a key. On the wall were two calendars, and a diploma from somewhere in Solomon's family, and under that Livvie's one possession was nailed, a picture of the little white baby of the family she worked for, back in Natchez before she was married. Going through that room and on to the kitchen, there was a big wood stove and a big round table always with a wet top and with the knives and forks in one jelly glass and the spoons in another, and a cut-glass vinegar bottle between, and going out from those, many shallow dishes of pickled peaches, fig preserves, water-melon pickles and blackberry jam always sitting there. The churn sat in the sun, the doors of the safe were always both shut, and there were four baited mouse-traps in the kitchen, one in every corner.

The outside of Solomon's house looked nice. It was not painted, but across the porch was an even balance. On each side there was one easy chair with high springs, looking out, and a fern basket hanging over it from the ceiling, and a dishpan of zinnia seedlings growing at its foot on the floor. By the door was a plow-wheel, just a pretty iron circle, nailed up on one wall and a square mirror on the other, a turquoise-blue comb stuck up in the frame, with the wash stand beneath it. On the door was a wooden knob with a pearl in the end, and Solomon's black hat hung on that, if he was in the house.

Out front was a clean dirt yard with every vestige of grass patiently uprooted and the ground scarred in deep whorls from the strike of Livvie's broom. Rose bushes with tiny blood-red roses blooming every month grew in threes on either side of the steps. On one side was a peach tree, on the other a pomegranate. Then coming around up the path from the deep cut of the Natchez Trace below was a line of bare crape-myrtle trees with every branch of them ending in a colored bottle, green or blue. There was no word that fell from Solomon's lips to say what they were for, but Livvie knew that there could be a spell put in trees, and she was familiar from the time she was born with the way bottle trees kept evil spirits from coming into the house—by luring them inside the colored bottles, where they cannot get out again. Solomon had made the bottle trees with his own hands over the nine years, in labor amounting to about a tree a year, and without a sign that he had any uneasiness in his heart, for he took as much pride in his precautions against spirits coming in the house as he took in the house, and sometimes in the sun the bottle trees looked prettier than the house did.

It was a nice house. It was in a place where the days would go by and surprise anyone that they were over. The lamplight and the fire-light would shine out the door after dark, over the still and breathing country, lighting the roses and the bottle trees, and all was quiet there.

But there was nobody, nobody at all, not even a white person. And if there had been anybody, Solomon would not have let Livvie look at them, just as he would not let her look at a field hand, or a field hand look at her. There was no house near, except for the cabins of the tenants that were forbidden to her, and there was no house as far as she had been, stealing away down the still, deep Trace. She felt as if she waded a river when she went, for the dead leaves on the ground reached as high as her knees, and when she was all scratched and bleeding she said it was not like a road that went anywhere. One day, climbing up the high bank, she had found a graveyard without a church; with ribbon-grass growing about the foot of an angel (she had climbed up because she thought she saw angel wings), and in the sun, trees shining like burning flames through the great caterpillar nets which enclosed them. Scarey thistles stood looking like the proph-ets in the Bible in Solomon's house. Indian paint brushes grew over her head, and the mourning dove made the only sound in the world. Oh for a stirring of the leaves, and a breaking of the nets! But not by a ghost, prayed Livvie, jumping down the bank. After Solomon took to his bed, she never went out, except one more time.

Livvie knew she made a nice girl to wait on anybody. She fixed things to eat on a tray like a surprise. She could keep from singing when she ironed, and to sit by a bed and fan away the flies, she could be so still she could not hear herself breathe. She could clean up the house and never drop a thing, and wash the dishes without a sound, and she would step outside to churn, for churning sounded too sad to her, like sobbing, and if it made her home-sick and not Solomon, she did not think of that.

But Solomon scarcely opened his eyes to see her, and scarcely tasted his food. He was not sick or paralyzed or in any pain that he mentioned, but he was surely wearing out in the body, and no matter what nice hot thing Livvie would bring him to taste, he would only look at it now, as if he were past seeing how he could add anything more to himself. Before she could beg him, he would go fast asleep. She could not surprise him any more, if he would not taste, and she was afraid that he was never in the world going to taste another thing she brought him—and so how could he last?

But one morning it was breakfast time and she cooked his eggs and grits, carried them in on a tray, and called his name. He was sound asleep. He lay in a dignified way with his watch beside him, on his back in the middle of the bed. One hand drew the quilt up high, though it was the first day of spring. Through the white lace curtains a little puffy wind was blowing as if it came from round cheeks. All night the frogs had sung out in the swamp, like a commotion in the room, and he had not stirred, though she lay wide awake and saying "Shh, frogs!" for fear he would mind them.

He looked as if he would like to sleep a little longer, and so she put back the tray and waited a little. When she tiptoed and stayed so quiet, she surrounded herself with a little reverie, and sometimes it seemed to her when she was so stealthy that the quiet she kept was for a sleeping baby, and that she had a baby and was its mother. When she stood at Solomon's bed and looked down at him, she would be thinking, "He sleeps so well," and she would hate to wake him up. And in some other way, too, she was afraid to wake him up because even in his sleep he seemed to be such a strict man.

Of course, nailed to the wall over the bed—only she would forget who it was—there was a picture of him when he was young. Then he had a fan of hair over his forehead like a king's crown. Now his hair lay down on his head, the spring had gone out of it. Solomon had a lightish face, with eyebrows scattered but rugged, the way privet grows, strong eyes, with second sight, a strict mouth, and a little gold smile. This was the way he looked in his clothes, but in bed in the daytime he looked like a different and smaller man, even when he was wide awake, and holding the Bible. He looked like somebody kin to himself. And then sometimes when he lay in sleep and she stood fanning the flies away, and the light came in, his face was like new, so smooth and clear that it was like a glass of jelly held to the window, and she could almost look through his forehead and see what he thought.

She fanned him and at length he opened his eyes and spoke her name, but he would not taste the nice eggs she had kept warm under a pan.

Back in the kitchen she ate heartily, his breakfast and hers, and looked out the open door at what went on. The whole day, and the whole night before, she had felt the stir of spring close to her. It was as present in the house as a young man would be. The moon was in the last quarter and outside they were turning the sod and planting peas and beans. Up and down the red fields, over which smoke from the brush-burning hung showing like a little skirt of sky, a white horse and a white mule pulled the plow. At intervals hoarse shouts came through the air and roused her as if she dozed neglectfully in the shade, and they were telling her, "Jump up!" She could see how over each ribbon of field were moving men and girls, on foot and mounted on mules, with hats set on their heads and bright with tall hoes and forks as if they carried streamers on them and were going to some place on a journey—and how as if at a signal now and then they would all start at once shouting, hollering, cajoling, calling and an-swering back, running, being leaped on and breaking away, flinging to earth with a shout and lying motionless in the trance of twelve o'clock. The old women came out of the cabins and brought them food they had ready for them, and then all worked together, spread evenly out. The little children came too, like a bouncing stream overflowing the fields, and set upon the men, the women, the dogs, the rushing birds, and the wave-like rows of earth, their little voices almost too high to be heard. In the middle distance like some white-and-gold towers were the haystacks, with black cows coming around to eat their edges. High above everything, the wheel of fields, house, and cabins, and the deep road surrounding like a moat to keep them in, was the turning sky, blue with long, far-flung white mare's-tail clouds, serene and still as high flames. And sound asleep while all this went around him that was his, Solomon was like a little still spot in the middle.

Even in the house the earth was sweet to breathe. Solomon had never let Livvie go any farther than the chicken house and the well. But what if she would walk now into the heart of the fields and take a hoe and work until she fell stretched out and drenched with her efforts, like other girls, and laid her cheek against the laid-open earth, and shamed the old man with her humbleness and delight? To shame him! A cruel wish could come in uninvited and so fast while she looked out the back door. She washed the dishes and scrubbed the table. She could hear the cries of the little lambs. Her mother, that she had not seen since her wedding day, had said one time, "I rather a man be anything, than a woman be mean."

So all morning she kept tasting the chicken broth on the stove, and when it was right she poured off a nice cupful. She carried it in to Solomon, and there he lay having a dream. Now what did he dream about? For she saw him sigh gently as if not to disturb some whole thing he held round in his mind, like a fresh egg. So even an old man dreamed about something pretty. Did he dream of her, while his eyes were shut and sunken, and his small hand with the wedding ring curled close in sleep around the quilt? He might be dreaming of what time it was, for even through his sleep he kept track of it like a clock, and knew how much of it went by, and waked up knowing where the hands were even before he consulted the silver watch that he never let go. He would sleep with the watch in his palm, and even holding it to his cheek like a child that loves a plaything. Or he might dream of journeys and travels on a steamboat to Natchez. Yet she thought he dreamed of her; but even while she scrutinized him, the rods of the foot of the bed seemed to rise up like a rail fence between them, and she could see that people never could be sure of anything as long as one of them was asleep and the other awake. To look at him dreaming of her when he might be going to die frightened her a little, as if he might carry her with him that way, and she wanted to run out of the room. She took hold of the bed and held on, and Solomon opened his eyes and called her name, but he did not want anything. He would not taste the good broth.

Just a little after that, as she was taking up the ashes in the front room for the last time in the year, she heard a sound. It was somebody coming. She pulled the curtains together and looked through the slit.

Coming up the path under the bottle trees was a white lady. At first she looked young, but then she looked old. Marvelous to see, a little car stood steaming like a kettle out in the field-track—it had come without a road.

Livvie stood listening to the long, repeated knockings at the door, and after a while she opened it just a little. The lady came in through the crack, though she was more than middle-sized and wore a big hat.

"My name is Miss Baby Marie," she said.

Livvie gazed respectfully at the lady and at the little suitcase she was holding close to her by the handle until the proper moment. The lady's eyes were running over the room, from palmetto to palmetto, but she was saying, "I live at home . . . out from Natchez . . . and get out and show these pretty cosmetic things to the white people and the colored people both . . . all around . . . years and years . . . Both shades of powder and rouge. . . . It's the kind of work a girl can do and not go clear 'way from home . . ." And the harder she looked, the more she talked. Suddenly she turned up her nose and said, "It is not Christian or sanitary to put feathers in a vase," and then she took a gold key out of the front of her dress and began unlocking the locks on her suitcase. Her face drew the light, the way it was covered with intense white and red, with a little patty-cake of white between the wrinkles by her upper lip. Little red tassels of hair bobbed under the rusty wires of her picture-hat, as with an air of triumph and secrecy she now drew open her little suitcase and brought out bottle after bottle and jar after jar, which she put down on the table, the mantelpiece, the settee, and the organ.

"Did you ever see so many cosmetics in your life?" cried Miss Baby Marie.

"No'm," Livvie tried to say, but the cat had her tongue.

"Have you ever applied cosmetics?" asked Miss Baby Marie next.

"No'm," Livvie tried to say.

"Then look!" she said, and pulling out the last thing of all, "Try this!" she said. And in her hand was unclenched a golden lipstick which popped open like magic. A fragrance came out of it like incense, and Livvie cried out suddenly. "Chinaberry flowers!"

Her hand took the lipstick, and in an instant she was carried away in the air through the spring, and looking down with a half-drowsy smile from a purple cloud she saw from above a chinaberry tree, dark and smooth and neatly leaved, neat as a guinea hen in the dooryard, and there was her home that she had left. On one side of the tree was her mama holding up her heavy apron, and she could see it was loaded with ripe figs, and on the other side was her papa holding a fish-pole over the pond, and she could see it transparently, the little clear fishes swimming up to the brim.

"Oh, no, not chinaberry flowers—secret ingredients," said Miss Baby Marie. "My cosmetics have secret ingredients—not chinaberry flowers."

"It's purple," Livvie breathed, and Miss Baby Marie said, "Use it freely. Rub it on."

Livvie tiptoed out to the wash stand on the front porch and before the mirror put the paint on her mouth. In the wavery surface her face danced before her like a flame. Miss Baby Marie followed her out, took a look at what she had done, and said, "That's it."

Livvie tried to say "Thank you" without moving her parted lips where the paint lay so new.

By now Miss Baby Marie stood behind Livvie and looked in the mirror over her shoulder, twisting up the tassels of her hair. "The lipstick I can let you have for only two dollars," she said, close to her neck.

"Lady, but I don't have no money, never did have," said Livvie.

"Oh, but you don't pay the first time. I make another trip, that's the way I do. I come back again—later."

"Oh," said Livvie, pretending she understood everything so as to please the lady.

"But if you don't take it now, this may be the last time I'll call at your house," said Miss Baby Marie sharply. "It's far away from anywhere, I'll tell you that. You don't live close to anywhere."

"Yes'm. My husband, he keep the *money*," said Livvie, trembling.

"He is strict as he can be. He don't know *you* walk in here—Miss Baby Marie!"

"Where is he?"

"Right now, he in yonder sound asleep, an old man. I wouldn't ever ask him for anything."

Miss Baby Marie took back the lipstick and packed it up. She gathered up the jars for both black and white and got them all inside the suitcase, with the same little fuss of triumph with which she had brought them out. She started away.

"Goodbye," she said, making herself look grand from the back, but at the last minute she turned around in the door. Her old hat wobbled as she whispered, "Let me see your husband."

Livvie obediently went on tiptoe and opened the door to the other room. Miss Baby Marie came behind her and rose on her toes and looked in.

"My, what a little tiny old, old man!" she whispered, clasping her hands and shaking her head over them. "What a beautiful quilt! What a tiny old, old man!"

"He can sleep like that all day," whispered Livvie proudly.

They looked at him awhile so fast asleep, and then all at once they looked at each other. Somehow that was as if they had a secret, for he had never stirred. Livvie then politely, but all at once, closed the door.

"Well! I'd certainly like to leave you with a lipstick!" said Miss Baby Marie vivaciously. She smiled in the door.

"Lady, but I told you I don't have no money, and never did have."

"And never will?" In the air and all around, like a bright halo around the white lady's nodding head, it was a true spring day.

"Would you take eggs, lady?" asked Livvie softly.

"No, I have plenty of eggs—plenty," said Miss Baby Marie.

"I still don't have no money," said Livvie, and Miss Baby Marie took her suitcase and went on somewhere else.

Livvie stood watching her go, and all the time she felt her heart beating in her left side. She touched the place with her hand. It seemed as if her heart beat and her whole face flamed from the pulsing color of her lips. She went to sit by Solomon and when he opened his eyes he could not see a change in her. "He's fixin' to die," she said inside. That was the secret. That was when she went out of the house for a little breath of air.

She went down the path and down the Natchez Trace a way, and she did not know how far she had gone, but it was not far, when she saw a sight. It was a man, looking like a vision—she standing on one side of the Old Natchez Trace and he standing on the other.

As soon as this man caught sight of her, he began to look himself over. Starting at the bottom with his pointed shoes, he began to look up, lifting his peg-top pants the higher to see fully his bright socks. His coat long and wide and leaf-green he opened like doors to see his high-up tawny pants and his pants he smoothed downward from the points of his collar, and he wore a luminous baby-pink satin shirt. At the end, he reached gently above his wide platter-shaped round hat, the color of a plum, and one finger touched at the feather, emerald green, blowing in the spring winds.

No matter how she looked, she could never look so fine as he did, and she was not sorry for that, she was pleased.

He took three jumps, one down and two up, and was by her side. "My name is Cash," he said.

He had a guinea pig in his pocket. They began to walk along. She stared on and on at him, as if he were doing some daring spectacular thing, instead of just walking beside her. It was not simply the city way he was dressed that made her look at him and see hope in its insolence looking back. It was not only the way he moved along kicking the flowers as if he could break through everything in the way and destroy anything in the world, that made her eyes grow bright. It might be, if he had not appeared the way he did appear that day she would never have looked so closely at him, but the time people come makes a difference.

They walked through the still leaves of the Natchez Trace, the light and the shade falling through trees about them, the white irises shining like candles on the banks and the new ferns shining like green stars up in the oak branches. They came out at Solomon's house, bottle trees and all. Livvie stopped and hung her head.

Cash began whistling a little tune. She did not know what it was, but she had heard it before from a distance, and she had a revelation. Cash was a field hand. He was a transformed field hand. Cash belonged to Solomon. But he had stepped out of his overalls into this. There in front of Solomon's house he laughed. He had a round head, a round face, all of him was young, and he flung his head up, rolled it against the mare's-tail sky in his round hat, and he could laugh just to see Solomon's house sitting there. Livvie looked at it, and there was Solomon's black hat hanging on the peg on the front door, the blackest thing in the world.

"I been to Natchez," Cash said, wagging his head around against the sky. "*I* taken a trip, *I* ready for Easter!"

How was it possible to look so fine before the harvest? Cash must have stolen the money, stolen it from Solomon. He stood in the path and lifted his spread hand high and brought it down again and again in his laughter. He kicked up his heels. A little chill went through her. It was as if Cash was bringing that strong hand down to beat a drum or to rain blows upon a man, such an abandon and menace were in his laugh. Frowning, she went closer to him and his swinging arm drew her in at once and the fright was crushed from her body, as a little match-flame might be smothered out by what it lighted. She gathered the folds of his coat behind him and fastened her red lips to his mouth, and she was dazzled by herself then, the way he had been dazzled at himself to begin with.

In that instant she felt something that could not be told—that Solomon's death was at hand, that he was the same to her as if he were dead now. She cried out, and uttering little cries turned and ran for the house.

At once Cash was coming, following after, he was running behind her. He came close, and half-way up the path he laughed and passed her. He even picked up a stone and sailed it into the bottle trees. She put her hands over her head, and sounds clattered through the bottle trees like cries of outrage. Cash stamped and plunged zigzag up the front steps and in at the door.

When she got there, he had stuck his hands in his pockets and was turning slowly about in the front room. The little guinea pig peeped out. Around Cash, the pinned-up palmettos looked as if a lazy green monkey had walked up and down and around the walls leaving green prints of his hands and feet.

She got through the room and his hands were still in his pockets, and she fell upon the closed door to the other room and pushed it open. She ran to Solomon's bed, calling "Solomon! Solomon!" The little shape of the old man never moved at all, wrapped under the quilt as if it were winter still.

"Solomon!" She pulled the quilt away, but there was another one under that, and she fell on her knees beside him. He made no sound except a sigh, and then she could hear in the silence the light springy steps of Cash walking and walking in the front room, and the ticking of Solomon's silver watch, which came from the bed. Old Solomon was far away in his sleep, his face looked small, relentless, and devout, as if he were walking somewhere where she could imagine the snow falling.

Then there was a noise like a hoof pawing the floor, and the door gave a creak, and Cash appeared beside her. When she looked up, Cash's face was so black it was bright, and so bright and bare of pity that it looked sweet to her. She stood up and held up her head. Cash was so powerful that his presence gave her strength even when she did not need any.

Under their eyes Solomon slept. People's faces tell of things and places not known to the one who looks at them while they sleep, and while Solomon slept under the eyes of Livvie and Cash his face told them like a mythical story that all his life he had built, little scrap by little scrap, respect. A beetle could not have been more laborious or more ingenious in the task of its destiny. When Solomon was young, as he was in his picture overhead, it was the infinite thing with him, and he could see no end to the respect he would contrive and keep in a house. He had built a lonely house, the way he would make a cage, but it grew to be the same with him as a great monumental pyramid and sometimes in his absorption of getting it erected he was like the builder-slaves of Egypt who forgot or never knew the origin and meaning of the thing to which they gave all the strength of their bodies and used up all their days. Livvie and Cash could see that as a man might rest from a life-labor he lay in his bed, and they could hear how, wrapped in his quilt, he sighed to himself comfortably in sleep, while in his dreams he might have been an ant, a beetle, a bird, an Egyptian, assembling and carrying on his back and building with his hands, or he might have been an old man of India or a swaddled baby, about to smile and brush all away.

Then without warning old Solomon's eyes flew wide open under the hedgelike brows. He was wide awake.

And instantly Cash raised his quick arm. A radiant sweat stood on his temples. But he did not bring his arm down—it stayed in the air, as if something might have taken hold.

It was not Livvie—she did not move. As if something said "Wait," she stood waiting. Even while her eyes burned under motionless lids, her lips parted in a stiff grimace, and with her arms stiff at her sides she stood above the prone old man and the panting young one, erect and apart.

Movement when it came came in Solomon's face. It was an old and strict face, a frail face, but behind it, like a covered light, came an animation that could play hide and seek, that would dart and escape, had always escaped. The mystery flickered in him, and invited from his eyes. It was that very mystery that Cash with his quick arm would have to strike, and that Livvie could not weep for. But Cash only stood holding his arm in the air, when the gentlest flick of his great strength, almost a puff of his breath, would have been enough, if he had known how to give it, to send the old man over the obstruction that kept him away from death.

If it could not be that the tiny illumination in the fragile and ancient face caused a crisis, a mystery in the room that would not permit a blow to fall, at least it was certain that Cash, throbbing in his Easter clothes, felt a pang of shame that the vigor of a man would come to such an end that he could not be struck without warning. He took down his hand and stepped back behind Livvie, like a round-eyed schoolboy on whose unsuspecting head the dunce cap has been set.

"Young ones can't wait," said Solomon.

Livvie shuddered violently, and then in a gush of tears she stooped for a glass of water and handed it to him, but he did not see her.

"So here come the young man Livvie wait for. Was no prevention. No prevention. Now I lay eyes on young man and it come to be somebody I know all the time, and been knowing since he were born in a cotton patch, and watched grow up year to year, Cash McCord, growed to size, growed up to come in my house in the end—ragged and barefoot."

Solomon gave a cough of distaste. Then he shut his eyes vigorously, and his lips began to move like a chanter's.

"When Livvie married, her husband were already somebody. He had paid great cost for his land. He spread sycamore leaves over the ground from wagon to door, day he brought her home, so her foot would not have to touch ground. He carried her through his door. Then he growed old and could not lift her, and she were still young."

Livvie's sobs followed his words like a soft melody repeating each thing as he stated it. His lips moved for a little without sound, or she cried too fervently, and unheard he might have been telling his whole life, and then he said, "God forgive Solomon for sins great and small. God forgive Solomon for carrying away too young girl for wife and keeping her away from her people and from all the young people would clamor for her back."

Then he lifted up his right hand toward Livvie where she stood by the bed and offered her his silver watch. He dangled it before her eyes, and she hushed crying; her tears stopped. For a moment the watch could be heard ticking as it always did, precisely in his proud hand. She lifted it away. Then he took hold of the quilt; then he was dead.

Livvie left Solomon dead and went out of the room. Stealthily, nearly without noise, Cash went beside her. He was like a shadow, but his shiny shoes moved over the floor in spangles, and the green downy feather shone like a light in his hat. As they reached the front room, he seized her deftly as a long black cat and dragged her hanging by the waist round and round him, while he turned in a circle, his face bent down to hers. The first moment, she kept one arm and its hand stiff and still, the one that held Solomon's watch. Then the fingers softly let go, all of her was limp, and the watch fell somewhere on the floor. It ticked away in the still room, and all at once there began outside the full song of a bird.

They moved around and around the room and into the brightness of the open door, then he stopped and shook her once. She rested in silence in his trembling arms, unprotesting as a bird on a nest. Outside the redbirds were flying and criss-crossing, the sun was in all the bottles on the prisoned trees, and the young peach was shining in the middle of them with the bursting light of spring.

QUESTIONS: *Livvie*

1. Of another of her stories, Eudora Welty wrote:

Above all I had no wish to sound mystical, but I did expect to sound mysterious now and then, if I could: this was a circumstantial realistic story in which the reality *was* mystery.

"Livvie," too, can be described as a "realistic story in which the reality *was* mystery." Which details in the story serve to make it both "realistic" and mysterious? Why does the story take place shortly before Easter? Why are Cash's clothes "luminous" and green and brown, and why is he described as "looking like a vision" (page 82)?

2. To a large extent the story is one of contrast, both explicit and implicit. What are some of the contrasting elements, and how do they reflect or illuminate the story's theme? Compare and contrast the four characters. Are any of their names significant? How?

3. Does Miss Welty say explicitly that Livvie is confined? Does Livvie feel confined? Do we feel that Livvie is confined? Explain.

4. Though there is a basic conflict between young Livvie and old Solomon, how does Miss Welty avoid a simple "good-bad" dichotomy?

5. Is the appearance of Miss Baby Marie an intrusion? Is she introduced merely for comic relief? Explain.

6. How are the bottle trees and Solomon's watch significant?

7. Compare the tone of "Livvie" with the tones of two other stories with a somewhat similar theme: "The Widow of Ephesus" and "Hautot and His Son." How would you characterize the tone of each of the three stories? How does it, in each case, help to illuminate the theme?

8. In the last two paragraphs of the story, which sentences most reflect Livvie's thought? Which sentences least reflect Livvie's thought? Explain.

A COLLECTION OF SHORT FICTION
Foreword

The modern short story is sometimes criticized for being neither short nor a story. Frank O'Connor complained that some short stories are monstrously long, and he cites James Joyce's *Ulysses*, William Faulkner's *As I Lay Dying*, and Angus Wilson's *Anglo-Saxon Attitudes* as really being, despite their length, short stories, because they deal with a brief period. A true novel, he says, deals with the effects of time on events and characters. Somerset Maugham has complained that some short stories are not really stories; authors influenced by Chekhov, he says, are clever at inventing characters but not at all clever at inventing stories to put them in, and the results are closer to character sketches than to stories.* The term "short story" (which, surprisingly, seems not to have been used before the last decade of the nineteenth century) needs some defining.

The stories of Ruth, Samson, Joseph, in the Old Testament, and the parables of Jesus in the New Testament, are sufficient evidence that brief narratives have existed for many centuries. The short tales comprising Boccaccio's *Decameron* and Chaucer's *Canterbury Tales* (the latter an amazing variety of narrative poems ranging from bawdy stories to legends of saints) are medieval examples of the ancient form. But, speaking generally, short narratives before the nineteenth century were either didactic pieces, with the narrative existing for the sake of a moral point, or they were "curious and striking" tales (to use Maugham's words for his favorite kind of story) recounted in order to entertain. The contemporary short story is rather different from both of these genres, which can be called the **parable** and the **anecdote.** Like the parable, the contemporary short story has a point, a meaning; but unlike the parable, it has a richness of surface as well as depth, so that it is interesting whether or not the reader goes on to ponder

---

* O'Connor's remarks are in *Writers at Work*, edited by Malcolm Cowley; Maugham's in *The Summing Up*.

"the meaning." The short story, like the anecdote, relates a happening, but where the happening in the anecdote is curious and the center of interest, the happening in the story often is less interesting in itself than as a manifestation of a character's state of mind.

The anecdotal story is what "story" means for most unsophisticated readers. It is an interesting happening or series of happenings. Desdemona "questioned me the story of my life," Othello says, "the battles, sieges, fortunes," and he complied by telling her:

> Of moving accidents by flood and field,
> Of hairbreadth 'scapes i' th' imminent deadly breach,
> Of being taken by the insolent foe
> And sold to slavery, of my redemption thence
> And portance in my travel's history.

The anecdotal story, the story of odd or involved happenings, survives, notably in the work of Maugham, and, usually on a much lower level, in the boy-meets-girl, boy-loses-girl, boy-gets-girl stories of slick magazines. But the anecdotal story, though sometimes excellently written, is quite different from most of the contemporary short stories in this book.

The anecdote is good entertainment, and good entertainment must not be lightly dismissed. But it has two elements within it that prevent it (unless it is something in addition to an anecdote) from taking high place among the world's literature. First, it cannot be reread with increasing or even continued pleasure. Even when it is well told, once we know the happening we may lose patience with the telling. Second, effective anecdotes are often highly implausible. Now, implausible anecdotes alleged to be true have a special impact by virtue of their alleged truth: they make us say to ourselves, "Truth is stranger than fiction." But the invented anecdote lacks this power; its unlikely coincidence, its unconvincing ironic situation, its surprise ending, are both untrue and unbelievable. It is entertaining but it is usually not especially meaningful. Leslie Stephen put it this way: "A marvelous event is interesting in real life, simply because we know that it happened. In a fiction we know that it did not happen; and therefore it is interesting only as far as it is explained."

The modern short story is not an anecdote and is not an abbreviated novel. If it were the latter, *Reader's Digest* condensations of novels would be short stories. But they aren't; they are only eviscerated novels. The novelist usually covers a long period of time, presenting not only a few individuals but also something of a society. He often tells of the development of several many-sided figures. In contrast, the short-story writer, having only a few pages, usually focuses on a single figure in a single episode, revealing his character rather than recording his development. Whereas the novel is narrative, the contemporary short story often seems less narrative than lyric and/or dramatic: in the short story we have a sense of a present mood or personality revealed, rather than the sense of a history reported. The revelation in a story is presented through incidents, of course, but the interest commonly resides in the character revealed through the incidents, rather than in the incidents themselves. Little "happens," in the sense that there is little rushing from place to place. What does "happen" is usually a mental reaction to an experience, and it is the mental reaction, rather than the external experience, that is the heart of the story. In older narratives the plot usually involves a conflict that is resolved, bringing about a change in the protagonist's condition; in contemporary stories the plot usually is designed to reveal a protagonist's state of mind. This de-emphasis of overt actions results in an affinity with the lyric and the drama.

Speaking roughly, in reading the old narratives—those, say in *The Arabian Nights* or *The Canterbury Tales*—we strongly sense the presence of a story-teller. But in the modern story the author, instead of making his presence felt as the narrator, has tended to disappear, and the reader is drawn into the story by being given the sense that he is *overhearing* people, rather than that he is hearing an author talk about people. By using an objective point of view, for example, an author can make himself unobtrusive, can force the reader to draw his own conclusions from what is seen and heard, and can (by recording much dialogue) push the story in the direction of a play. Similarly, by using a first-person point of view the author disappears, and the reader has the sense of being in the presence not of a storyteller but of a man undergoing the experiences related in the story. A selective omniscient point of view can also effectively bring the reader into the story; the author more or less effaces himself, and the reader sees and hears what a particular character or two see and hear. For example, in Joyce's "Clay" (page 184), we get most of the story either objectively or as it impinges on Maria's mind. Without editorial interpretation we accompany Maria, sharing her thoughts of her visit to Joe's ("What a nice evening they would have, all the children singing!"), her preparations for the visit, and the visit itself. When in the parlor game Maria is blindfolded and then touches the dish of clay, to the embarrassment of Joe's wife, Joyce does not tell us what has happened, but forces us to experience the event as Maria does: "There was a pause for a few seconds; . . . that was no play. Maria understood that it was wrong that time and so she had to do it over again." The absence of explicit editorial comment forces the reader to do his own thinking and to supply his own comment.

The de-emphasis on narrative in the contemporary short story is not an invention of the twentieth-century mind. It goes back at least to three important American writers of the early nineteenth century—Washington Irving, Nathaniel Hawthorne, and Edgar Allan Poe. In 1824 Irving wrote:

> I fancy much of what I value myself upon in writing, escapes the observation of the great mass of my readers: who are intent more upon the story than the way in which it is told. For my part I consider a story merely as a frame on which to stretch my materials. It is the play of thought, and sentiments and language; the weaving in of characters, lightly yet expressively delineated; the familiar and faithful exhibition of scenes in common life; and the half-concealed vein of humor that is often playing through the whole—these are among what I aim at, and upon which I felicitate myself in proportion as I think I succeed.

Hawthorne and Poe may seem stranger than Irving as forebears of the contemporary short story: both are known for their fantastic narratives (and in addition, Poe is known as the inventor of the detective story, a genre in which there is strong interest in curious happenings). But because Hawthorne's fantastic narratives are, as he said, highly allegorical, the reader's interest is pushed beyond the narrative to the moral significance. Poe's "arabesques," as he called his fanciful tales (in distinction from his detective tales of "ratiocination"), are aimed at revealing and arousing unusual mental states. The weird happenings and personages are symbolic representations of the mind or soul. In "The Fall of the House of Usher" the twins Roderick and Madeline probably represent complementary parts of a single personality, just as the house described in the poem within this story represents a person: the "banners yellow" are hair, the "two luminous windows" are eyes, the "fair palace door" of "pearl and ruby" is a mouth, and so on. But, it must be noted, in both Hawthorne and Poe we usually get what is commonly called the **tale** rather than the **short story:** we get short prose fiction dealing with the strange rather than the usual. (This distinction between the wondrous and the ordinary is discussed at some length in "Some Observations on the Novel," page 300.)

A paragraph from Poe's review (1842) of Hawthorne's *Twice-Told Tales*, though more useful in revealing Poe's theory of fiction than Hawthorne's, illuminates something of the kinship between the contemporary short story and the best short fiction of the earlier nineteenth century. In the review Poe has been explaining that because "unity of effect or impression" is essential, a tale (Poe doubtless uses "tale" to mean short fiction in general, rather than the special type just discussed) which can be read at a single sitting has an advantage over the novel.

A skilful artist has constructed a tale. He has not fashioned his thoughts to accommodate his incidents, but having deliberately conceived a certain single effect to be wrought, he then invents such incidents, he then combines such events, and discusses them in such tone as may best serve him in establishing this preconceived effect. If his very first sentence tend not to the outbringing of this effect, then in his very first step has he committed a blunder. In the whole composition there should be no word written of which the tendency, direct or indirect, is not to the one pre-established design. And by such means, with such care and skill, a picture is at length painted which leaves in the mind of him who contemplates it with a kindred art, a sense of the fullest satisfaction. The idea of the tale, its thesis, has been presented unblemished, because undisturbed—an end absolutely demanded, yet, in the novel, altogether unattainable.

Nothing that has been said here should be construed as suggesting that contemporary short stories are necessarily better than older short narratives. The object of these comments has not been to evaluate, but to call attention to the characteristics dominating most good contemporary brief fiction. Furthermore, it should not be thought that contemporary fiction is all of a piece; the preceding stories have already demonstrated its variety. The following are also varied; if the reader does not like one he need not despair; he need only (in Chaucer's words) "turne over the leef and chese another tale."

NATHANIEL HAWTHORNE (1804-1864)

Young Goodman Brown

Young Goodman Brown came forth at sunset into the street at Salem village; but put his head back, after crossing the threshold, to exchange a parting kiss with his young wife. And Faith, as the wife was aptly named, thrust her own pretty head into the street, letting the wind play with the pink ribbons of her cap while she called to Goodman Brown.

"Dearest heart," whispered she, softly and rather sadly, when her lips were close to his ear, "prithee put off your journey until sunrise and sleep in your own bed to-night. A lone woman is troubled with such dreams and such thoughts that she's afeard of herself sometimes. Pray tarry with me this night, dear husband, of all nights in the year."

"My love and my Faith," replied young Goodman Brown, "of all nights in the year, this one night must I tarry away from thee. My journey, as thou callest it, forth and back again, must needs be done 'twixt now and sunrise. What, my sweet, pretty wife, dost thou doubt me already, and we but three months married?"

"Then God bless you!" said Faith, with the pink ribbons; "and may you find all well when you come back."

"Amen!" cried Goodman Brown. "Say thy prayers, dear Faith, and go to bed at dusk, and no harm will come to thee."

So they parted; and the young man pursued his way until, being about to turn the corner by the meeting-house, he looked back and saw the head of Faith still peeping after him with a melancholy air, in spite of her pink ribbons.

"Poor little Faith!" thought he, for his heart smote him. "What a wretch am I to leave her on such an errand! She talks of dreams, too. Methought as she spoke there was trouble in her face, as if a dream had warned her what work is to be done to-night. But no, no; 't would kill her to think it. Well, she's a blessed angel on earth; and after this one night I'll cling to her skirts and follow her to heaven."

With this excellent resolve for the future, Goodman Brown felt himself justified in making more haste on his present evil purpose. He had taken a dreary road, darkened by all the gloomiest trees of the forest, which barely stood aside to let the narrow path creep through, and closed immediately behind. It was all as lonely as could be; and there is this peculiarity in such a solitude, that the traveller knows not who may be concealed by the innumerable trunks and the thick boughs overhead; so that with lonely footsteps he may yet be passing through an unseen multitude.

"There may be a devilish Indian behind every tree," said Goodman Brown to himself; and he glanced fearfully behind him as he added, "What if the devil himself should be at my very elbow!"

His head being turned back, he passed a crook of the road, and, looking forward again, beheld the figure of a man, in grave and decent attire, seated at the foot of an old tree. He arose at Goodman Brown's approach and walked onward side by side with him.

"You are late, Goodman Brown," said he. "The clock of the Old South was striking as I came through Boston, and that is full fifteen minutes agone."

"Faith kept me back a while," replied the young man, with a tremor in his voice, caused by the sudden appearance of his companion, though not wholly unexpected.

It was now deep dusk in the forest, and deepest in that part of it where these two were journeying. As nearly as could be discerned, the second traveller was about fifty years old, apparently in the same rank of life as Goodman Brown, and bearing a considerable resemblance to him, though perhaps more in expression than features. Still they might have been taken for father and son. And yet, though the elder person was as simply clad as the younger, and as simple in manner too, he had an indescribable air of one who knew the world, and who would not have felt abashed at the governor's dinner table or in King William's court, were it possible that his affairs should call him thither. But the only thing about him that could be fixed upon as remarkable was his staff, which bore the likeness of a great black snake, so curiously wrought that it might almost be seen to twist and wriggle itself like a living serpent. This, of course, must have been an ocular deception, assisted by the uncertain light.

"Come, Goodman Brown," cried his fellow-traveller, "this is a dull pace for the beginning of a journey. Take my staff, if you are so soon weary."

"Friend," said the other, exchanging his slow pace for a full stop "having kept covenant by meeting thee here, it is my purpose now to return whence I came. I have scruples touching the matter thou wot'st of."

"Sayest thou so?" replied he of the serpent, smiling apart. "Let us walk on, nevertheless, reasoning as we go; and if I convince thee not thou shalt turn back. We are but a little way in the forest yet."

"Too far! too far!" exclaimed the goodman, unconsciously resuming his walk. "My father never went into the woods on such an errand nor his father before him. We have been a race of honest men and good Christians since the days of the martyrs; and shall I be the first of the name of Brown that ever took this path and kept—"

"Such company, thou wouldst say," observed the elder person interpreting his pause. "Well said, Goodman Brown! I have been a well acquainted with your family as with ever a one among the Puritans; and that's no trifle to say. I helped your grandfather, the constable, when he lashed the Quaker woman so smartly through the streets of Salem; and it was I that brought your father a pitch-pine knot, kindled at my own hearth, to set fire to an Indian village, in King Philip's war. They were my good friends, both; and many a pleasant walk have we had along this path, and returned merrily after midnight. I would fain be friends with you for their sake."

"If it be as thou sayest," replied Goodman Brown, "I marvel they never spoke of these matters; or, verily, I marvel not, seeing that the least rumor of the sort would have driven them from New England

We are a people of prayer, and good works to boot, and abide no such wickedness."

"Wickedness or not," said the traveller with the twisted staff, "I have a very general acquaintance here in New England. The deacons of many a church have drunk the communion wine with me; the selectmen of divers towns make me their chairman; and a majority of the Great and General Court are firm supporters of my interest. The governor and I, too—But these are state secrets."

"Can this be so?" cried Goodman Brown, with a stare of amazement at his undisturbed companion. "Howbeit, I have nothing to do with the governor and council; they have their own ways, and are no rule for a simple husbandman like me. But, were I to go on with thee, how should I meet the eye of that good old man, our minister, at Salem village? Oh, his voice would make me tremble both Sabbath day and lecture day."

Thus far the elder traveller had listened with due gravity; but now burst into a fit of irrepressible mirth, shaking himself so violently that his snake-like staff actually seemed to wriggle in sympathy.

"Ha! ha! ha!" shouted he again and again; then composing himself, "Well, go on, Goodman Brown, go on; but, prithee, don't kill me with laughing."

"Well, then, to end the matter at once," said Goodman Brown, considerably nettled, "there is my wife, Faith. It would break her dear little heart; and I'd rather break my own."

"Nay, if that be the case," answered the other, "e'en go thy ways, Goodman Brown. I would not for twenty old women like the one hobbling before us that Faith should come to any harm."

As he spoke he pointed his staff at a female figure on the path, in whom Goodman Brown recognized a very pious and exemplary dame, who had taught him his catechism in youth, and was still his moral and spiritual adviser, jointly with the minister and Deacon Gookin.

"A marvel, truly, that Goody Cloyse should be so far in the wilderness at nightfall," said he. "But with your leave, friend, I shall take a cut through the woods until we have left this Christian woman behind. Being a stranger to you, she might ask whom I was consorting with and whither I was going."

"Be it so," said his fellow-traveller. "Betake you the woods, and let me keep the path."

Accordingly the young man turned aside, but took care to watch his companion, who advanced softly along the road until he had come within a staff's length of the old dame. She, meanwhile, was making the best of her way, with singular speed for so aged a woman, and mumbling some indistinct words—a prayer, doubtless—as she went.

The traveller put forth his staff and touched her withered neck with what seemed the serpent's tail.

"The devil!" screamed the pious old lady.

"Then Goody Cloyse knows her old friend?" observed the traveller, confronting her and leaning on his writhing stick.

"Ah, forsooth, and is it your worship indeed?" cried the good dame. "Yea, truly is it, and in the very image of my old gossip, Goodman Brown, the grandfather of the silly fellow that now is. But—would your worship believe it?—my broomstick hath strangely disappeared, stolen, as I suspect, by that unhanged witch, Goody Cory, and that, too, when I was all anointed with the juice of smallage, and cinquefoil, and wolf's bane—"

"Mingled with fine wheat and the fat of a new-born babe," said the shape of old Goodman Brown.

"Ah, your worship knows the recipe," cried the old lady, cackling aloud. "So, as I was saying, being all ready for the meeting, and no horse to ride on, I made up my mind to foot it; for they tell me there is a nice young man to be taken into communion to-night. But now your good worship will lend me your arm, and we shall be there in a twinkling."

"That can hardly be," answered her friend. "I may not spare you my arm, Goody Cloyse; but here is my staff, if you will."

So saying, he threw it down at her feet, where, perhaps, it assumed life, being one of the rods which its owner had formerly lent to the Egyptian magi. Of this fact, however, Goodman Brown could not take cognizance. He had cast up his eyes in astonishment, and, looking down again, beheld neither Goody Cloyse nor the serpentine staff, but his fellow-traveller alone, who waited for him as calmly as if nothing had happened.

"That old woman taught me my catechism," said the young man; and there was a world of meaning in this simple comment.

They continued to walk onward, while the elder traveller exhorted his companions to make good speed and persevere in the path, discoursing so aptly that his arguments seemed rather to spring up in the bosom of his auditor than to be suggested by himself. As they went, he plucked a branch of maple to serve for a walking stick, and began to strip it of the twigs and little boughs, which were wet with evening dew. The moment his fingers touched them they became strangely withered and dried up as with a week's sunshine. Thus the pair proceeded, at a good free pace, until suddenly, in a gloomy hollow of the road, Goodman Brown sat himself down on the stump of a tree and refused to go any farther.

"Friend," said he, stubbornly, "my mind is made up. Not another step will I budge on this errand. What if a wretched old woman do choose to go to the devil when I thought she was going to heaven: is that any reason why I should quit my dear Faith and go after her?"

"You will think better of this by and by," said his acquaintance, composedly. "Sit here and rest yourself a while; and when you feel like moving again, there is my staff to help you along."

Without more words, he threw his companion the maple stick, and was as speedily out of sight as if he had vanished into the deepening gloom. The young man sat a few moments by the roadside, applauding himself greatly, and thinking with how clear a conscience he should meet the minister in his morning walk, nor shrink from the eye of good old Deacon Gookin. And what calm sleep would be his that very night, which was to have been spent so wickedly, but so purely and sweetly now, in the arms of Faith! Amidst these pleasant and praiseworthy meditations, Goodman Brown heard the tramp of horses along the road, and deemed it advisable to conceal himself within the verge of the forest, conscious of the guilty purpose that had brought him thither, though now so happily turned from it.

On came the hoof tramps and the voices of the riders, two grave old voices, conversing soberly as they drew near. These mingled sounds appeared to pass along the road, within a few yards of the young man's hiding-place; but, owing doubtless to the depth of the gloom at that particular spot, neither the travellers nor their steeds were visible. Though their figures brushed the small boughs by the wayside, it could not be seen that they intercepted, even for a moment, the faint gleam from the strip of bright sky athwart which they must have passed. Goodman Brown alternately crouched and stood on tiptoe, pulling aside the branches and thrusting forth his head as far as he durst without discerning so much as a shadow. It vexed him the more, because he could have sworn, were such a thing possible, that he recognized the voices of the minister and Deacon Gookin, jogging along quietly, as they were wont to do, when bound to some ordination or ecclesiastical council. While yet within hearing, one of the riders stopped to pluck a switch.

"Of the two, reverend sir," said the voice like the deacon's, "I had rather miss an ordination dinner than to-night's meeting. They tell me that some of our community are to be here from Falmouth and beyond, and others from Connecticut and Rhode Island, besides several of the Indian powwows, who, after their fashion, know almost as much deviltry as the best of us. Moreover, there is a goodly young woman to be taken into communion."

"Mighty well, Deacon Gookin!" replied the solemn old tones of the minister. "Spur up, or we shall be late. Nothing can be done, you know, until I get on the ground."

The hoofs clattered again; and the voices, talking so strangely in the empty air, passed on through the forest, where no church had ever been gathered or solitary Christian prayed. Whither, then, could these holy men be journeying so deep into the heathen wilderness? Young Goodman Brown caught hold of a tree for support, being ready to sink down on the ground, faint and overburdened with the heavy sickness of his heart. He looked up to the sky, doubting whether there really was a heaven above him. Yet there was the blue arch, and the stars brightening in it.

"With heaven above and Faith below, I will yet stand firm against the devil!" cried Goodman Brown.

While he still gazed upward into the deep arch of the firmament and had lifted his hands to pray, a cloud, though no wind was stirring, hurried across the zenith and hid the brightening stars. The blue sky was still visible, except directly overhead, where this black mass of cloud was sweeping swiftly northward. Aloft in the air, as if from the depths of the cloud, came a confused and doubtful sound of voices. Once the listener fancied that he could distinguish the accents of towns-people of his own, men and women, both pious and ungodly, many of whom he had met at the communion table, and had seen others rioting at the tavern. The next moment, so indistinct were the sounds, he doubted whether he had heard aught but the murmur of the old forest, whispering without a wind. Then came a stronger swell of those familiar tones, heard daily in the sunshine at Salem village, but never until now from a cloud of night. There was one voice, of a young woman, uttering lamentations, yet with an uncertain sorrow, and entreating for some favor, which, perhaps, it would grieve her to obtain; and all the unseen multitude, both saints and sinners, seemed to encourage her onward.

"Faith!" shouted Goodman Brown, in a voice of agony and desperation; and the echoes of the forest mocked him, crying, "Faith! Faith!" as if bewildered wretches were seeking her all through the wilderness.

The cry of grief, rage, and terror was yet piercing the night, when the unhappy husband held his breath for a response. There was a scream, drowned immediately in a louder murmur of voices, fading into far-off laughter, as the dark cloud swept away, leaving the clear and silent sky above Goodman Brown. But something fluttered lightly down through the air and caught on the branch of a tree. The young man seized it, and beheld a pink ribbon.

"My Faith is gone!" cried he, after one stupefied moment. "There is no good on earth; and sin is but a name. Come, devil; for to thee is this world given."

And, maddened with despair, so that he laughed loud and long, did Goodman Brown grasp his staff and set forth again, at such a rate that he seemed to fly along the forest path rather than to walk or run. The road grew wilder and drearier and more faintly traced, and vanished at length, leaving him in the heart of the dark wilderness, still rushing onward with the instinct that guides mortal man to evil. The whole forest was peopled with frightful sounds—the creaking of the trees, the howling of wild beasts, and the yell of Indians; while sometimes the wind tolled like a distant church bell, and sometimes gave a broad roar around the traveller, as if all Nature were laughing him to scorn. But he was himself the chief horror of the scene, and shrank not from its other horrors.

"Ha! ha! ha!" roared Goodman Brown when the wind laughed at him. "Let us hear which will laugh loudest. Think not to frighten me with your deviltry. Come witch, come wizard, come Indian pow-wow, come devil himself, and here comes Goodman Brown. You may as well fear him as he fear you."

In truth, all through the haunted forest there could be nothing more frightful than the figure of Goodman Brown. On he flew among the black pines, brandishing his staff with frenzied gestures, now giving vent to an inspiration of horrid blasphemy, and now shouting forth such laughter as set all the echoes of the forest laughing like demons around him. The fiend in his own shape is less hideous than when he rages in the breast of man. Thus sped the demoniac on his course, until, quivering among the trees, he saw a red light before him, as when the felled trunks and branches of a clearing have been set on fire, and throw up their lurid blaze against the sky, at the hour of midnight. He paused, in a lull of the tempest that had driven him onward, and heard the swell of what seemed a hymn, rolling solemnly from a distance with the weight of many voices. He knew the tune; it was a familiar one in the choir of the village meeting-house. The verse died heavily away, and was lengthened by a chorus, not of human voices, but of all the sounds of the benighted wilderness pealing in awful harmony together. Goodman Brown cried out, and his cry was lost to his own ear by its unison with the cry of the desert.

In the interval of silence he stole forward until the light glared full upon his eyes. At one extremity of an open space, hemmed in by the dark wall of the forest, arose a rock, bearing some rude, natural resemblance either to an altar or a pulpit, and surrounded by four blazing pines, their tops aflame, their stems untouched, like candles at an evening meeting. The mass of foliage that had overgrown the summit of the rock was all on fire, blazing high into the night and fitfully illuminating the whole field. Each pendent twig and leafy festoon was in a blaze. As the red light arose and fell, a numerous congregation alternately shone forth, then disappeared in shadow, and again grew, as it were, out of the darkness, peopling the heart of the solitary woods at once.

"A grave and dark-clad company," quoth Goodman Brown.

In truth they were such. Among them, quivering to and fro between gloom and splendor, appeared faces that would be seen next day at the council board of the province, and others which, Sabbath after Sabbath, looked devoutly heavenward, and benignantly over the crowded pews, from the holiest pulpits in the land. Some affirm that the lady of the governor was there. At least there were high dames well known to her, and wives of honored husbands, and widows, a great multitude, and ancient maidens, all of excellent repute, and fair young girls, who trembled lest their mothers should espy them. Either the sudden gleams of light flashing over the obscure field bedazzled Goodman Brown, or he recognized a score of the church members of Salem village famous for their especial sanctity. Good old Deacon Gookin had arrived, and waited at the skirts of that venerable saint, his revered pastor. But, irreverently consorting with these grave, reputable, and pious people, these elders of the church, these chaste dames and dewy virgins, there were men of dissolute lives and women of spotted fame, wretches given over to all mean and filthy vice, and suspected even of horrid crimes. It was strange to see that the good shrank not from the wicked, nor were the sinners abashed by the saints. Scattered also among their pale-faced enemies were the Indian priests, or powwows, who had often scared their native forest with more hideous incantations than any known to English witchcraft.

"But where is Faith?" thought Goodman Brown; and, as hope came into his heart, he trembled.

Another verse of the hymn arose, a slow and mournful strain, such as the pious love, but joined to words which expressed all that our nature can conceive of sin, and darkly hinted at far more. Unfathomable to mere mortals is the lore of fiends. Verse after verse was sung; and still the chorus of the desert swelled between like the deepest tone of a mighty organ; and with the final peal of that dreadful anthem there came a sound, as if the roaring wind, the rushing streams, the howling beasts, and every other voice of the unconcerted wilderness were mingling and according with the voice of guilty man in homage to the prince of all. The four blazing pines threw up a loftier flame, and obscurely discovered shapes and visages of horror

n the smoke wreaths above the impious assembly. At the same moment the fire on the rock shot redly forth and formed a glowing arch
above its base, where now appeared a figure. With reverence be it
spoken, the figure bore no slight similitude, both in garb and manner,
to some grave divine of the New England churches.

"Bring forth the converts!" cried a voice that echoed through
the field and rolled into the forest.

At the word, Goodman Brown stepped forth from the shadow
of the trees and approached the congregation, with whom he felt a
loathful brotherhood by the sympathy of all that was wicked in his
heart. He could have well-nigh sworn that the shape of his own dead
father beckoned him to advance, looking downward from a smoke
wreath, while a woman, with dim features of despair, threw out her
hand to warn him back. Was it his mother? But he had no power
to retreat one step, nor to resist, even in thought, when the minister
and good old Deacon Gookin seized his arms and led him to the blazing rock. Thither came also the slender form of a veiled female, led
between Goody Cloyse, that pious teacher of the catechism, and
Martha Carrier, who had received the devil's promise to be queen of
hell. A rampant hag was she. And there stood the proselytes beneath
the canopy of fire.

"Welcome, my children," said the dark figure, "to the communion
of your race. Ye have found thus young your nature and your destiny.
My children, look behind you!"

They turned; and flashing forth, as it were, in a sheet of flame,
the fiend worshippers were seen; the smile of welcome gleamed darkly
on every visage.

"There," resumed the sable form, "are all whom ye have rever-
enced from youth. Ye deemed them holier than yourselves, and shrank
from your own sin, contrasting it with their lives of righteousness and
prayerful aspirations heavenward. Yet here are they all in my wor-
shipping assembly. This night it shall be granted you to know their
secret deeds: how hoary-bearded elders of the church have whispered
wanton words to the young maids of their households; how many a
woman, eager for widows' weeds, has given her husband a drink at
bedtime and let him sleep his last sleep in her bosom; how beardless
youths have made haste to inherit their fathers' wealth; and how fair
damsels—blush not, sweet ones—have dug little graves in the garden,
and bidden me, the sole guest, to an infant's funeral. By the sympathy
of your human hearts for sin ye shall scent out all the places—whether
in church, bed-chamber, street, field, or forest—where crime has been
committed, and shall exult to behold the whole earth one stain of
guilt, one mighty blood spot. Far more than this. It shall be yours

to penetrate, in every bosom, the deep mystery of sin, the fountain of all wicked arts, and which inexhaustibly supplies more evil impulse than human power—than my power at its utmost—can make manifest in deeds. And now, my children, look upon each other."

They did so; and, by the blaze of the hell-kindled torches, the wretched man beheld his Faith, and the wife her husband, trembling before that unhallowed altar.

"Lo, there ye stand, my children," said the figure, in a deep and solemn tone, almost sad with its despairing awfulness, as if his once angelic nature could yet mourn for our miserable race. "Depending upon one another's hearts, ye had still hoped that virtue were not all a dream. Now are ye undeceived. Evil is the nature of mankind. Evil must be your only happiness. Welcome again, my children, to the communion of your race."

"Welcome," repeated the fiend worshippers, in one cry of despair and triumph.

And there they stood, the only pair, as it seemed, who were yet hesitating on the verge of wickedness in this dark world. A basin was hollowed, naturally, in the rock. Did it contain water, reddened by the lurid light? or was it blood? or, perchance, a liquid flame? Herein did the shape of evil dip his hand and prepare to lay the mark of baptism upon their foreheads, that they might be partakers of the mystery of sin, more conscious of the secret guilt of others, both in deed and thought, than they could now be of their own. The husband cast one look at his pale wife, and Faith at him. What polluted wretches would the next glance show them to each other, shuddering alike at what they disclosed and what they saw!

"Faith! Faith!" cried the husband, "look up to heaven, and resist the wicked one."

Whether Faith obeyed he knew not. Hardly had he spoken when he found himself amid calm night and solitude, listening to a roar of the wind which died heavily away through the forest. He staggered against the rock, and felt it chill and damp; while a hanging twig, that had been all on fire, besprinkled his cheek with the coldest dew.

The next morning young Goodman Brown came slowly into the street of Salem village, staring around him like a bewildered man. The good old minister was taking a walk along the graveyard to get an appetite for breakfast and meditate his sermon, and bestowed a blessing, as he passed, on Goodman Brown. He shrank from the venerable saint as if to avoid an anathema. Old Deacon Gookin was at domestic worship, and the holy words of his prayer were heard through the open window. "What God doth the wizard pray to?" quoth Goodman Brown. Goody Cloyse, that excellent old Christian, stood in the early sunshine at her own lattice, catechizing a little girl who had brought her a pint of morning's milk. Goodman Brown snatched away the child as from the grasp of the fiend himself. Turning the corner by the meeting-house, he spied the head of Faith, with the pink ribbons, gazing anxiously forth, and bursting into such joy at sight of him that she skipped along the street and almost kissed her husband before the whole village. But Goodman Brown looked sternly and sadly into her face, and passed on without a greeting.

Had Goodman Brown fallen asleep in the forest and only dreamed a wild dream of a witch-meeting?

Be it so if you will; but, alas! it was a dream of evil omen for young Goodman Brown. A stern, a sad, a darkly meditative, a distrustful, if not a desperate man did he become from the night of that fearful dream. On the Sabbath day, when the congregation were singing a holy psalm, he could not listen because an anthem of sin rushed loudly upon his ear and drowned all the blessed strain. When the minister spoke from the pulpit with power and fervid eloquence, and, with his hand on the open Bible, of the sacred truths of our religion, and of saint-like lives and triumphant deaths, and of future bliss or misery unutterable, then did Goodman Brown turn pale, dreading lest the roof should thunder down upon the gray blasphemer and his hearers. Often, awaking suddenly at midnight, he shrank from the bosom of Faith; and at morning or eventide, when the family knelt down at prayer, he scowled and muttered to himself, and gazed sternly at his wife, and turned away. And when he had lived long, and was borne to his grave a hoary corpse, followed by Faith, an aged woman, and children and grandchildren, a goodly procession, besides neighbors not a few, they carved no hopeful verse upon his tombstone, for his dying hour was gloom.

NATHANIEL HAWTHORNE (1804-1864)

My Kinsman, Major Molineux

After the kings of Great Britain had assumed the right of appointing the colonial governors, the measures of the latter seldom met with the ready and generous approbation which had been paid to those of their predecessors, under the original charters. The people looked with most jealous scrutiny to the exercise of power which did not emanate from themselves, and they usually rewarded their rulers with slender gratitude for the compliances by which, in softening their instructions from beyond the sea, they had incurred the reprehension of those who gave them. The annals of Massachusetts Bay will inform us, that of six governors in the space of about forty years from the surrender of the old charter, under James II., two were imprisoned by a popular insurrection; a third, as Hutchinson inclines to believe, was driven from the province by the whizzing of a musket-ball; a fourth, in the opinion of the same historian, was hastened to his grave by continual bickerings with the House of Representatives; and the remaining two, as well as their successors, till the Revolution, were favored with few and brief intervals of peaceful sway. The inferior members of the court party, in times of high political excitement, led scarcely a more desirable life. These remarks may serve as a preface to the following adventures, which chanced upon a summer night, not far from a hundred years ago. The reader, in order to avoid a long and dry detail of colonial affairs, is requested to dispense with an account of the train of circumstances that had caused much temporary inflammation of the popular mind.

It was near nine o'clock of a moonlight evening, when a boat crossed the ferry with a single passenger, who had obtained his conveyance at that unusual hour by the promise of an extra fare. While he stood on the landing-place, searching in either pocket for the means of fulfilling his agreement, the ferryman lifted a lantern, by the aid of which, and the newly risen moon, he took a very accurate survey of the stranger's figure. He was a youth of barely eighteen years, evidently country-bred, and now, as it should seem, upon his first visit to town. He was clad in a coarse gray coat, well worn, but in excellent repair; his under garments were durably constructed of leather, and fitted tight to a pair of serviceable and well-shaped limbs; his stockings of blue yarn were the incontrovertible work of a mother or a sister; and on his head was a three-cornered hat, which in its better days had perhaps sheltered the graver brow of the lad's father. Under his left arm was a heavy cudgel formed of an oak sapling, and retaining a part of the hardened root; and his equipment was completed by a wallet, not so abundantly stocked as to incommode the vigorous shoulders on which it hung. Brown, curly hair, well-shaped features, and bright, cheerful eyes were nature's gifts, and worth all that art could have done for his adornment.

The youth, one of whose names was Robin, finally drew from his pocket the half of a little province bill of five shillings, which, in the depreciation in that sort of currency, did but satisfy the ferryman's demand, with the surplus of a sexangular piece of parchment, valued at three pence. He then walked forward into the town, with as light a step as if his day's journey had not already exceeded thirty miles, and with as eager an eye as if he were entering London city, instead of the little metropolis of a New England colony. Before Robin had proceeded far, however, it occurred to him that he knew not whither to direct his steps; so he paused, and looked up and down the narrow street, scrutinizing the small and mean wooden buildings that were scattered on either side.

"This low hovel cannot be my kinsman's dwelling," thought he, "nor yonder old house, where the moonlight enters at the broken casement; and truly I see none hereabouts that might be worthy of him. It would have been wise to inquire my way of the ferryman, and doubtless he would have gone with me, and earned a shilling from the Major for his pains. But the next man I meet will do as well."

He resumed his walk, and was glad to perceive that the street now became wider, and the houses more respectable in their appearance. He soon discerned a figure moving on moderately in advance, and hastened his steps to overtake it. As Robin drew nigh, he saw that the passenger was a man in years, with a full periwig of gray hair, a wide-skirted coat of dark cloth, and silk stockings rolled above his knees. He carried a long and polished cane, which he struck down perpendicularly before him at every step; and at regular intervals he uttered two successive hems, of a peculiarly solemn and sepulchral intonation. Having made these observations, Robin laid hold of the skirt of the old man's coat, just when the light from the open door and windows of a barber's shop fell upon both their figures.

"Good evening to you, honored sir," said he, making a low bow, and still retaining his hold of the skirt. "I pray you tell me whereabouts is the dwelling of my kinsman, Major Molineux."

The youth's question was uttered very loudly; and one of the barbers, whose razor was descending on a well-soaped chin, and another who was dressing a Ramillies wig, left their occupations, and came to the door. The citizen, in the mean time, turned a long-favored countenance upon Robin, and answered him in a tone of excessive anger and annoyance. His two sepulchral hems, however, broke into the very center of his rebuke, with most singular effect, like a thought of the cold grave obtruding among wrathful passions.

"Let go my garment, fellow! I tell you, I know not the man you speak of. What! I have authority, I have—hem, hem—authority; and if this be the respect you show for your betters, your feet shall be brought acquainted with the stocks by daylight, tomorrow morning!"

Robin released the old man's skirt, and hastened away, pursued by an ill-mannered roar of laughter from the barber's shop. He was at first considerably surprised by the result of his question, but, being a shrewd youth, soon thought himself able to account for the mystery.

"This is some country representative," was his conclusion, "who has never seen the inside of my kinsman's door, and lacks the breeding to answer a stranger civilly. The man is old, or verily—I might be tempted to turn back and smite him on the nose. Ah, Robin, Robin! even the barber's boys laugh at you for choosing such a guide! You will be wiser in time, friend Robin."

He now became entangled in a succession of crooked and narrow streets, which crossed each other, and meandered at no great distance from the water-side. The smell of tar was obvious to his nostrils, the masts of vessels pierced the moonlight above the tops of the buildings, and the numerous signs, which Robin paused to read, informed him that he was near the center of business. But the streets were empty, the shops were closed, and lights were visible only in the second stories of a few dwelling-houses. At length, on the corner of a narrow lane, through which he was passing, he beheld the broad countenance of a British hero swinging before the door of an inn, whence proceeded the voices of many guests. The casement of one of the lower windows was thrown back, and a very thin curtain permitted Robin to distinguish a party at supper, round a well-furnished table. The fragrance of the good cheer steamed forth into the outer air, and the youth could not fail to recollect that the last remnant of his travelling stock of provision had yielded to his morning appetite and that noon had found and left him dinnerless.

"Oh, that a parchment three-penny might give me a right to sit down at yonder table!" said Robin, with a sigh. "But the Major will make me welcome to the best of his victuals; so I will even step boldly in, and inquire my way to his dwelling."

He entered the tavern, and was guided by the murmur of voices and the fumes of tobacco to the public-room. It was a long and low apartment, with oaken walls, grown dark in the continual smoke, and a floor which was thickly sanded, but of no immaculate purity. A number of persons—the larger part of whom appeared to be mariners, or in some way connected with the sea—occupied the wooden benches, or leather-bottomed chairs, conversing on various matters, and occasionally lending their attention to some topic of general interest. Three or four little groups were draining as many bowls of punch, which the West India trade had long since made a familiar drink in the colony. Others, who had the appearance of men who lived by regular and laborious handicraft, preferred the insulated bliss of an unshared potation, and became more taciturn under its influence. Nearly all, in short, evinced a predilection for the Good Creature in some of its various shapes, for this is a vice to which, as Fast Day sermons of a hundred years ago will testify, we have a long hereditary claim. The only guests to whom Robin's sympathies inclined him were two or three sheepish countrymen, who were using the inn somewhat after the fashion of a Turkish caravansary; they had gotten themselves into the darkest corner of the room, and heedless of the Nicotian atmosphere, were supping on the bread of their own ovens, and the bacon cured in their own chimney-smoke. But though Robin felt a sort of brotherhood with these strangers, his eyes were attracted from them to a person who stood near the door, holding whispered conversation with a group of ill-dressed associates. His features were separately striking almost to grotesqueness, and the whole face left a deep impression on the memory. The forehead bulged out into a double prominence, with a vale between; the nose came boldly forth in an irregular curve, and its bridge was of more than a finger's breadth; the eyebrows were deep and shaggy, and the eyes glowed beneath them like fire in a cave.

While Robin deliberated of whom to inquire respecting his kinsman's dwelling, he was accosted by the innkeeper, a little man in a stained white apron, who had come to pay his professional welcome to the stranger. Being in the second generation from a French Protestant, he seemed to have inherited the courtesy of his parent nation; but no variety of circumstances was ever known to change his voice from the one shrill note in which he now addressed Robin.

"From the country, I presume, sir?" said he, with a profound bow. "Beg leave to congratulate you on your arrival, and trust you intend a long stay with us. Fine town here, sir, beautiful buildings, and much that may interest a stranger. May I hope for the honor of your commands in respect to supper?"

"The man sees a family likeness! the rogue has guessed that I am related to the Major!" thought Robin, who had hitherto experienced little superfluous civility.

All eyes were now turned on the country lad, standing at the door, in his worn three-cornered hat, gray coat, leather breeches, and blue yarn stockings, leaning on an oaken cudgel, and bearing a wallet on his back.

Robin replied to the courteous innkeeper, with such an assumption of confidence as befitted the Major's relative. "My honest friend," he said, "I shall make it a point to patronize your house on some occasion, when"—here he could not help lowering his voice—"when I may have more than a parchment three-pence in my pocket. My present business," continued he, speaking with lofty confidence, "is merely to inquire my way to the dwelling of my kinsman, Major Molineux."

There was a sudden and general movement in the room, which Robin interpreted as expressing the eagerness of each individual to become his guide. But the innkeeper turned his eyes to a written paper on the wall, which he read, or seemed to read, with occasional re-currences to the young man's figure.

"What have we here?" said he, breaking his speech into little dry fragments. " 'Left the house of the subscriber, bounden servant, Heze-kiah Mudge,—had on, when he went away, gray coat, leather breeches, master's third-best hat. One pound currency reward to whosoever shall lodge him in any jail of the providence.' Better trudge, boy; better trudge!"

Robin had begun to draw his hand towards the lighter end of the oak cudgel, but a strange hostility in every countenance induced him to relinquish his purpose of breaking the courteous innkeeper's head. As he turned to leave the room, he encountered a sneering glance from the bold-featured personage whom he had before noticed; and no sooner was he beyond the door, than he heard a general laugh, in which the innkeeper's voice might be distinguished, like the drop-ping of small stones into a kettle.

"Now, is it not strange," thought Robin, with his usual shrewd-ness,—"is it not strange that the confession of an empty pocket should outweigh the name of my kinsman, Major Molineux? Oh, if I had one of those grinning rascals in the woods, where I and my oak sapling grew up together, I would teach him that my arm is heavy though my purse be light!"

On turning the corner of the narrow lane, Robin found himself in a spacious street, with an unbroken line of lofty houses on each side, and a steepled building at the upper end, whence the ringing of a bell announced the hour of nine. The light of the moon, and the lamps from the numerous shop-windows, discovered people prom-enading on the pavement, and amongst them Robin had hoped to recognize his hitherto inscrutable relative. The result of his former inquiries made him unwilling to hazard another, in a scene of such publicity, and he determined to walk slowly and silently up the street, thrusting his face close to that of every elderly gentleman, in search of the Major's lineaments. In his progress, Robin encountered many gay and gallant figures. Embroidered garments of showy colors, enor-mous periwigs, gold-laced hats, and silver-hilted swords glided past him and dazzled his optics. Travelled youths, imitators of the Euro-pean fine gentlemen of the period, trod jauntily along, half dancing to the fashionable tunes which they hummed, and making poor Robin ashamed of his quiet and natural gait. At length, after many pauses to examine the gorgeous display of goods in the shop-windows, and after suffering some rebukes for the impertinence of his scrutiny into people's faces, the Major's kinsman found himself near the steepled building, still unsuccessful in his search. As yet, however, he had seen only one side of the thronged street; so Robin crossed, and continued the same sort of inquisition down the opposite pavement, with stronger hopes than the philosopher seeking an honest man, but with no better fortune. He had arrived about midway towards the lower end, from which his course began, when he overheard the approach of some one who struck down a cane on the flag-stones at every step, uttering at regular intervals, two sepulchral hems.

"Mercy on us!" quoth Robin, recognizing the sound.

Turning a corner, which chanced to be close at his right hand, he hastened to pursue his researches in some other part of the town. His patience now was wearing low, and he seemed to feel more fatigue from his rambles since he crossed the ferry, than from his journey of several days on the other side. Hunger also pleaded loudly within him, and Robin began to balance the propriety of demanding, violently, and with lifted cudgel, the necessary guidance from the first solitary passenger whom he should meet. While a resolution to this effect was gaining strength, he entered a street of mean appearance, on either side of which a row of ill-built houses was straggling towards the harbor. The moonlight fell upon no passenger along the whole extent, but in the third domicile which Robin passed there was a half-opened door, and his keen glance detected a woman's garment within.

"My luck may be better here," said he to himself.

Accordingly, he approached the door, and beheld it shut closer as he did so; yet an open space remained, sufficing for the fair occupant to observe the stranger, without a corresponding display on her part. All that Robin could discern was a strip of scarlet petticoat, and the occasional sparkle of an eye, as if the moonbeams were trembling on some bright thing.

"Pretty mistress," for I may call her so with a good conscience, thought the shrewd youth, since I know nothing to the contrary,—"my sweet pretty mistress, will you be kind enough to tell me whereabouts I must seek the dwelling of my kinsman, Major Molineux?"

Robin's voice was plaintive and winning, and the female, seeing nothing to be shunned in the handsome country youth, thrust open the door, and came forth into the moonlight. She was a dainty little figure, with a white neck, round arms, and a slender waist, at the extremity of which her scarlet petticoat jutted out over a hoop, as if she were standing in a balloon. Moreover, her face was oval and pretty, her hair dark beneath the little cap, and her bright eyes possessed a sly freedom, which triumphed over those of Robin.

"Major Molineux dwells here," said this fair woman.

Now, her voice was the sweetest Robin had heard that night, yet he could not help doubting whether that sweet voice spoke Gospel truth. He looked up and down the mean street, and then surveyed the house before which they stood. It was a small, dark edifice of two stories, the second of which projected over the lower floor, and the front apartment had the aspect of a shop for petty commodities.

"Now, truly, I am in luck," replied Robin, cunningly, "and so indeed is my kinsman, the Major, in having so pretty a housekeeper. But I prithee trouble him to step to the door; I will deliver him a message from his friends in the country, and then go back to my lodgings at the inn."

"Nay, the Major has been abed this hour or more," said the lady of the scarlet petticoat; "and it would be to little purpose to disturb him tonight, seeing his evening draught was of the strongest. But he is a kind-hearted man, and it would be as much as my life's worth to let a kinsman of his turn away from the door. You are the good old gentleman's very picture, and I could swear that was his rainy-weather hat. Also he has garments very much resembling those leather small-clothes. But come in, I pray, for I bid you hearty welcome in his name."

So saying, the fair and hospitable dame took our hero by the hand; and the touch was light, and the force was gentleness, and though Robin read in her eyes what he did not hear in her words, yet the slender-waisted woman in the scarlet petticoat proved stronger than the athletic country youth. She had drawn his half-willing footsteps nearly to the threshold, when the opening of a door in the neighborhood startled the Major's housekeeper, and, leaving the Major's kinsman, she vanished speedily into her own domicile. A heavy yawn preceded the appearance of a man, who, like the Moonshine of Pyramus and Thisbe, carried a lantern, needlessly aiding his sister luminary in the heavens. As he walked sleepily up the street, he turned his broad, dull face on Robin, and displayed a long staff, spiked at the end.

"Home, vagabond, home!" said the watchman, in accents that seemed to fall asleep as soon as they were uttered. "Home, or we'll set you in the stocks by peep of day!"

"This is the second hint of the kind," thought Robin. "I wish they would end my difficulties, by setting me there to-night."

Nevertheless, the youth felt an instinctive antipathy towards the guardian of midnight order, which at first prevented him from asking his usual question. But just when the man was about to vanish behind the corner, Robin resolved not to lose the opportunity, and shouted lustily after him,—

"I say, friend! will you guide me to the house of my kinsman, Major Molineux?"

The watchman made no reply, but turned the corner and was gone; yet Robin seemed to hear the sound of drowsy laughter stealing along the solitary street. At that moment, also, a pleasant titter saluted him from the open window above his head; he looked up, and caught the sparkle of a saucy eye; a round arm beckoned to him, and next he heard light footsteps descending the staircase within. But Robin, being of the household of a New England clergyman, was a good youth, as well as a shrewd one; so he resisted temptation, and fled away.

He now roamed desperately, and at random, through the town, almost ready to believe that a spell was on him, like that by which a wizard of his country had once kept three pursuers wandering, a whole winter night, within twenty paces of the cottage which they sought. The streets lay before him, strange and desolate, and the lights were extinguished in almost every house. Twice, however, little parties of men, among whom Robin distinguished individuals in outlandish attire, came hurrying along; but, though on both occasions, they paused to address him, such intercourse did not at all enlighten his perplexity. They did but utter a few words in some language of which Robin knew nothing, and perceiving his inability to answer, bestowed a curse upon him in plain English and hastened away. Finally, the lad determined to knock at the door of every mansion that might appear worthy to be occupied by his kinsman, trusting that perseverance would overcome the fatality that had hitherto thwarted him. Firm in this resolve, he was passing beneath the walls of a church, which formed the corner of two streets, when, as he turned into the shade of its steeple, he encountered a bulky stranger, muffled in a cloak. The man was proceeding with the speed of earnest business, but Robin planted himself full before him, holding the oak cudgel with both hands across his body as a bar to further passage.

"Halt, honest man, and answer me a question," said he, very resolutely. "Tell me, this instant, whereabouts is the dwelling of my kinsman, Major Molineux!"

"Keep your tongue between your teeth, fool, and let me pass!" said a deep, gruff voice, which Robin partly remembered. "Let me pass, or I'll strike you to the earth!"

"No, no, neighbor!" cried Robin, flourishing his cudgel and then thrusting its larger end close to the man's muffled face. "No, no, I'm not the fool you take me for, nor do you pass till I have an answer to my question. Whereabouts is the dwelling of my kinsman, Major Molineux?"

My Kinsman, Major Molineux 111

The stranger, instead of attempting to force his passage, stepped back into the moonlight, unmuffled his face, and stared full into that of Robin.

"Watch here an hour, and Major Molineux will pass by," said he.

Robin gazed with dismay and astonishment on the unprecedented physiognomy of the speaker. The forehead with its double prominence, the broad hooked nose, the shaggy eyebrows, and fiery eyes were those which he had noticed at the inn, but the man's complexion had undergone a singular, or, more properly, a twofold change. One side of the face blazed an intense red, while the other was black as midnight, the division line being in the broad bridge of the nose; and a mouth which seemed to extend from ear to ear with black or red, in contrast to the color of the cheek. The effect was as if two individual devils, a fiend of fire and a fiend of darkness, had united themselves to form this infernal visage. The stranger grinned in Robin's face, muffled his parti-colored features, and was out of sight in a moment.

"Strange things we travellers see!" ejaculated Robin.

He seated himself, however, upon the steps of the church-door, resolving to wait the appointed time for his kinsman. A few moments were consumed in philosophical speculations upon the species of man who had just left him; but having settled this point shrewdly, rationally, and satisfactorily, he was compelled to look elsewhere for his amusement. And first he threw his eyes along the street. It was of more respectable appearance than most of those into which he had wandered; and the moon, creating, like the imaginative power, a beautiful strangeness in familiar objects, gave something of romance to a scene that might not have possessed it in the light of day. The irregular and often quaint architecture of the houses, some of whose roofs were broken into numerous little peaks, while others ascended, steep and narrow, into a single point, and others again were square; the pure snow-white of some of their complexions, the aged darkness of others, and the thousand sparklings, reflected from bright substances in the walls of many; these matters engaged Robin's attention for a while, and then began to grow wearisome. Next he endeavored to define the forms of distant objects, starting away, with almost ghostly indistinctness, just as his eye appeared to grasp them; and finally he took a minute survey of an edifice which stood on the opposite side of the street, directly in front of the church-door, where he was stationed. It was a large, square mansion, distinguished from its neighbors by a balcony, which rested on tall pillars, and by an elaborate Gothic window, communicating therewith.

"Perhaps this is the very house I have been seeking," thought Robin.

Then he strove to speed away the time, by listening to a murmur which swept continually along the street, yet was scarcely audible, except to an unaccustomed ear like his; it was a low, dull, dreamy sound, compounded of many noises, each of which was at too great a distance to be separately heard. Robin marvelled at this snore of a sleeping town, and marvelled more whenever its continuity was broken by now and then a distant shout, apparently loud where it originated. But altogether it was a sleep-inspiring sound, and, to shake off its drowsy influence, Robin arose, and climbed a window-frame, that he might view the interior of the church. There the moonbeams came trembling in, and fell down upon the deserted pews, and extended along the quiet aisles. A fainter yet more awful radiance was hovering around the pulpit, and one solitary ray had dared to rest upon the open page of the great Bible. Had nature, in that deep hour, become a worshipper in the house which man had builded? Or was that heavenly light the visible sanctity of the place,—visible because no earthly and impure feet were within the walls? The scene made Robin's heart shiver with a sensation of loneliness stronger than he had ever felt in the remotest depths of his native woods; so he turned away and sat down again before the door. There were graves around the church, and now an uneasy thought obtruded into Robin's breast. What if the object of his search, which had been so often and so strangely thwarted, were all the time mouldering in his shroud? What if his kinsman should glide through yonder gate, and nod and smile to him in dimly passing by?

"Oh that any breathing thing were here with me!" said Robin.

Recalling his thoughts from this uncomfortable track, he sent them over forest, hill, and stream, and attempted to imagine how that evening of ambiguity and weariness had been spent by his father's household. He pictured them assembled at the door, beneath the tree, the great old tree, which had been spared for its huge twisted trunk and venerable shade, when a thousand leafy brethren fell. There, at the going down of the summer sun, it was his father's custom to perform domestic worship, that the neighbors might come and join with him like brothers of the family, and that the wayfaring man might pause to drink at that fountain, and keep his heart pure by freshening the memory of home. Robin distinguished the seat of every individual of the little audience; he saw the good man in the midst, holding the Scriptures in the golden light that fell from the western clouds; he beheld him close the book and all rise up to pray. He heard the old thanksgivings for daily mercies, the old supplications for their continuance, to which he had so often listened in weariness, but which were now among his dear remembrances. He perceived the slight inequality of his father's voice when he came to speak of the absent one; he noted how his mother turned her face to the broad and knotted trunk; how his elder brother scorned, because the beard was rough upon his upper lip, to permit his features to be moved; how the younger sister drew down a low hanging branch before her eyes; and how the little one of all, whose sports had hitherto broken the decorum of the scene, understood the prayer for her playmate, and burst into clamorous grief. Then he saw them go in at the door; and when Robin would have entered also, the latch tinkled into its place, and he was excluded from his home.

"Am I here, or there?" cried Robin, starting; for all at once, when his thoughts had become visible and audible in a dream, the long, wide, solitary street shone out before him.

He aroused himself, and endeavored to fix his attention steadily upon the large edifice which he had surveyed before. But still his mind kept vibrating between fancy and reality; by turns, the pillars of the balcony lengthened into the tall, bare stems of pines, dwindled down to human figures, settled again into their true shape and size, and then commenced a new succession of changes. For a single moment, when he deemed himself awake, he could have sworn that a visage—one which he seemed to remember, yet could not absolutely name as his kinsman's—was looking towards him from the Gothic window. A deeper sleep wrestled with and nearly overcame him, but fled at the sound of footsteps along the opposite pavement. Robin rubbed his eyes, discerned a man passing at the foot of the balcony, and addressed him in a loud, peevish, and lamentable cry.

"Hallo, friend! must I wait here all night for my kinsman, Major Molineux?"

The sleeping echoes awoke, and answered the voice; and the passenger, barely able to discern a figure sitting in the oblique shade of the steeple, traversed the street to obtain a nearer view. He was himself a gentleman in his prime, of open, intelligent, cheerful, and altogether prepossessing countenance. Perceiving a country youth, apparently homeless and without friends, he accosted him in a tone of real kindness, which had become strange to Robin's ears.

"Well, my good lad, why are you sitting here?" inquired he. "Can I be of service to you in any way?"

"I am afraid not, sir," replied Robin, despondingly; "yet I shall take it kindly, if you'll answer me a single question. I've been searching, half the night, for one Major Molineux; now, sir, is there really such a person in these parts, or am I dreaming?"

"Major Molineux! The name is not altogether strange to me,"

said the gentleman, smiling. "Have you any objection to telling me the nature of your business with him?"

Then Robin briefly related that his father was a clergyman, settled on a small salary, at a long distance back in the country, and that he and Major Molineux were brothers' children. The Major, having inherited riches, and acquired civil and military rank, had visited his cousin, in great pomp, a year or two before; had manifested much interest in Robin and an elder brother, and, being childless himself, had thrown out hints respecting the future establishment of one of them in life. The elder brother was destined to succeed to the farm which his father cultivated in the interval of sacred duties; it was therefore determined that Robin should profit by his kinsman's generous intentions, especially as he seemed to be rather the favorite, and was thought to possess other necessary endowments.

"For I have the name of being a shrewd youth," observed Robin, in this part of his story.

"I doubt not you deserve it," replied his new friend, goodnaturedly; "but pray proceed."

"Well, sir, being nearly eighteen years old, and well grown, as you see," continued Robin, drawing himself up to his full height, "I thought it high time to begin in the world. So my mother and sister put me in handsome trim, and my father gave me half the remnant of his last year's salary, and five days ago I started for this place, to pay the Major a visit. But, would you believe it, sir! I crossed the ferry a little after dark, and have yet found nobody that would show me the way to his dwelling; only, an hour or two since, I was told to wait here, and Major Molineux would pass by."

"Can you describe the man who told you this?" inquired the gentleman.

"Oh, he was a very ill-favored fellow, sir," replied Robin, "with two great bumps on his forehead, a hook nose, fiery eyes; and, what struck me as the strangest, his face was of two different colors. Do you happen to know such a man, sir?"

"Not intimately," answered the stranger, "but I chanced to meet him a little time previous to your stopping me. I believe you may trust his word, and that the Major will very shortly pass through this street. In the mean time, as I have a singular curiosity to witness your meeting, I will sit down here upon the steps and bear you company."

He seated himself accordingly, and soon engaged his companion in animated discourse. It was but of brief continuance, however, for a noise of shouting, which had long been remotely audible, drew so much nearer that Robin inquired its cause.

"What may be the meaning of this uproar?" asked he. "Truly, if your town be always as noisy, I shall find little sleep while I am an inhabitant."

"Why, indeed, friend Robin, there do appear to be three or four riotous fellows abroad to-night," replied the gentleman. "You must not expect all the stillness of your native woods here in our streets. But the watch will shortly be at the heels of these lads and"—

"Ay, and set them in the stocks by peep of day," interrupted Robin, recollecting his own encounter with the drowsy lantern-bearer. "But, dear sir, if I may trust my ears, an army of watchmen would never make head against such a multitude of rioters. There were at least a thousand voices went up to make that one shout."

"May not a man have several voices, Robin, as well as two complexions?" said his friend.

"Perhaps a man may; but Heaven forbid that a woman should!" responded the shrewd youth, thinking of the seductive tones of the Major's housekeeper.

The sounds of a trumpet in some neighboring street now became so evident and continual, that Robin's curiosity was strongly excited. In addition to the shouts, he heard frequent bursts from many instruments of discord, and a wild and confused laughter filled up the intervals. Robin rose from the steps, and looked wistfully towards a point whither people seemed to be hastening.

"Surely some prodigious merry-making is going on," exclaimed he. "I have laughed very little since I left home, sir, and should be sorry to lose an opportunity. Shall we step round the corner of that darkish house, and take our share of the fun?"

"Sit down again, sit down, good Robin," replied the gentleman, laying his hand on the skirt of the gray coat. "You forget that we must wait here for your kinsman; and there is reason to believe that he will pass by, in the course of a very few moments."

The near approach of the uproar had now disturbed the neighborhood; windows flew open on all sides; and many heads, in the attire of the pillow, and confused by sleep suddenly broken, were protruded to the gaze of whoever had leisure to observe them. Eager voices hailed each other from house to house, all demanding the explanation, which not a soul could give. Half-dressed men hurried towards the unknown commotion, stumbling as they went over the stone steps that thrust themselves into the narrow foot-walk. The shouts, the laughter, and the tuneless bray, the antipodes of music, came onwards with increasing din, till scattered individuals, and then denser bodies, began to appear round a corner at the distance of a hundred yards.

"Will you recognize your kinsman, if he passes in this crowd?" inquired the gentleman.

"Indeed, I can't warrant it, sir; but I'll take my stand here, and keep a bright lookout," answered Robin, descending to the outer edge of the pavement.

A mighty stream of people now emptied into the street, and came rolling slowly towards the church. A single horseman wheeled the corner in the midst of them, and close behind him came a band of fearful wind-instruments, sending forth a fresher discord now that no intervening buildings kept it from the ear. Then a redder light disturbed the moonbeams, and a dense multitude of torches shone along the street, concealing, by their glare, whatever object they illuminated. The single horseman, clad in a military dress, and bearing a drawn sword, rode onward as the leader, and, by his fierce and variegated countenance, appeared like war personified; the red of one cheek was an emblem of fire and sword; the blackness of the other betokened the mourning that attends them. In his train were wild figures in the Indian dress, and many fantastic shapes without a model, giving the whole march a visionary air, as if a dream had broken forth from some feverish brain, and were sweeping visibly through the midnight streets. A mass of people, inactive, except as applauding spectators, hemmed the procession in; and several women ran along the sidewalk, piercing the confusion of heavier sounds with their shrill voices of mirth or terror.

"The double-faced fellow has his eye upon me," muttered Robin, with an indefinite but an uncomfortable idea that he was himself to bear a part in the pageantry.

The leader turned himself in the saddle, and fixed his glance full upon the country youth, as the steed went slowly by. When Robin had freed his eyes from those fiery ones, the musicians were passing before him, and the torches were close at hand; but the unsteady brightness of the latter formed a veil which he could not penetrate. The rattling of wheels over the stones sometimes found its way to his ear, and confused traces of a human form appeared at intervals, and then melted into the vivid light. A moment more, and the leader thundered a command to halt: the trumpets vomited a horrid breath, and then held their peace; the shouts and laughter of the people died away, and there remained only a universal hum, allied to silence. Right before Robin's eyes was an uncovered cart. There the torches blazed the brightest, there the moon shone out like day, and there, in tar-and-feathery dignity, sat his kinsman, Major Molineux!

He was an elderly man, of large and majestic person, and strong, square features, betokening a steady soul; but steady as it was, his enemies had found means to shake it. His face was pale as death, and far more ghastly; the broad forehead was contracted in his agony, so that his eyebrows formed one grizzled line; his eyes were red and wild, and the foam hung white upon his quivering lip. His whole frame was agitated by a quick and continual tremor, which his pride strove to quell, even in those circumstances of overwhelming humiliation. But perhaps the bitterest pang of all was when his eyes met those of Robin; for he evidently knew him on the instant, as the youth stood witnessing the foul disgrace of a head grown gray in honor. They stared at each other in silence, and Robin's knees shook, and his hair bristled, with a mixture of pity and terror. Soon, however, a bewildering excitement began to seize upon his mind; the preceding adventures of the night, the unexpected appearance of the crowd, the torches, the confused din and the hush that followed, the specter of his kinsman reviled by that great multitude,—all this, and, more than all, a perception of tremendous ridicule in the whole scene, affected him with a sort of mental inebriety. At that moment a voice of sluggish merriment saluted Robin's ears; he turned instinctively, and just behind the corner of the church stood the lantern-bearer, rubbing his eyes, and drowsily enjoying the lad's amazement. Then he heard a peal of laughter like the ringing of silvery bells; a woman twitched his arm, a saucy eye met his, and he saw the lady of the scarlet petticoat. A sharp, dry cachinnation appealed to his memory, and, standing on tiptoe in the crowd, with his white apron over his head, he beheld the courteous little innkeeper. And lastly, there sailed over the heads of the multitude a great, broad laugh, broken in the midst of two sepulchral hems; thus, "Haw, haw, haw,—hem, hem,—haw, haw, haw, haw!"

The sound proceeded from the balcony of the opposite edifice and thither Robin turned his eyes. In front of the Gothic window stood the old citizen, wrapped in a wide gown, his gray periwig exchanged for a nightcap, which was thrust back from his forehead, and his silk stockings hanging about his legs. He supported himself on his polished cane in a fit of convulsive merriment, which manifested itself on his solemn old features like a funny inscription on a tombstone. Then Robin seemed to hear the voices of the barbers, of the guests of the inn, and of all who had made sport of him that night. The contagion was spreading among the multitude, when all at once, it seized upon Robin, and he sent forth a shout of laughter that echoed through the street,—every man shook his sides, every man emptied his lungs, but Robin's shout was the loudest there. The cloud-spirits peeped from their silvery islands, as the congregated mirth went roaring up the sky! The Man in the Moon heard the far bellow. "Oho," quoth he, "the old earth is frolicsome to-night!"

When there was a momentary calm in that tempestuous sea of sound, the leader gave the sign, the procession resumed its march. On they went, like fiends that throng in mockery around some dead potentate, mighty no more, but majestic still in his agony. On they went, in counterfeited pomp, in senseless uproar, in frenzied merriment, trampling all on an old man's heart. On swept the tumult, and left a silent street behind.

*   *   *   *   *

"Well, Robin, are you dreaming?" inquired the gentleman, laying his hand on the youth's shoulder.

Robin started, and withdrew his arm from the stone post to which he had instinctively clung, as the living stream rolled by him. His cheek was somewhat pale, and his eye not quite as lively as in the earlier part of the evening.

"Will you be kind enough to show me the way to the ferry?" said he, after a moment's pause.

"You have, then, adopted a new subject of inquiry?" observed his companion, with a smile.

"Why, yes, sir," replied Robin, rather dryly. "Thanks to you, and to my other friends, I have at last met my kinsman, and he will scarce desire to see my face again. I begin to grow weary of a town life, sir. Will you show me the way to the ferry?"

"No, my good friend Robin,—not to-night, at least," said the gentleman. "Some few days hence, if you wish it, I will speed you on your journey. Or, if you prefer to remain with us, perhaps, as you are a shrewd youth, you may rise in the world without the help of your kinsman, Major Molineux."

HERMAN MELVILLE (1819-1891)

Bartleby the Scrivener

A Story of Wall Street

I am a rather elderly man. The nature of my avocations for the last thirty years has brought me into more than ordinary contact with what would seem an interesting and somewhat singular set of men, of whom, as yet, nothing that I know of has ever been written—I mean the law-copyists, or scriveners. I have known very many of them, professionally and privately, and, if I please, could relate divers histories at which good-natured gentlemen might smile and sentimental souls might weep. But I waive the biographies of all other scriveners for a few passages in the life of Bartleby, who was a scrivener, the strangest I ever saw or heard of. While of other law-copyists I might write the complete life, of Bartleby nothing of that sort can be done. I believe that no materials exist for a full and satisfactory biography of this man. It is an irreparable loss to literature. Bartleby was one of those beings of whom nothing is ascertainable except from the original sources, and, in his case, those are very small. What my own astonished eyes saw of Bartleby, *that* is all I know of him, except, indeed, one vague report, which will appear in the sequel.

Ere introducing the scrivener as he first appeared to me, it is fit I make some mention of myself, my employees, my business, my chambers and general surroundings, because some such description is indispensable to an adequate understanding of the chief character about to be presented. *Imprimis*: I am a man who, from his youth upwards, has been filled with a profound conviction that the easiest way of life is the best. Hence, though I belong to a profession proverbially energetic and nervous even to turbulence at times, yet nothing of that sort have I ever suffered to invade my peace. I am one of those unambitious lawyers who never addresses a jury or in any way draws down public applause, but, in the cool tranquillity of a snug retreat, do a snug business among rich men's bonds, and mortgages, and title deeds. All who know me consider me an eminently *safe* man. The late John Jacob Astor, a personage little given to poetic enthusiasm, had no hesitation in pronouncing my first grand point to be prudence, my next, method. I do not speak it in vanity, but simply record the fact that I was not unemployed in my profession by the late John Jacob Astor, a name which, I admit, I love to repeat, for it hath a rounded and orbicular sound to it, and rings like unto bullion. I will freely add that I was not insensible to the late John Jacob Astor's good opinion.

Some time prior to the period at which this little history begins my avocations had been largely increased. The good old office, now extinct in the State of New York, of a Master in Chancery, had been conferred upon me. It was not a very arduous office, but very pleasantly remunerative. I seldom lose my temper, much more seldom indulge in dangerous indignation at wrongs and outrages, but I must be permitted to be rash here and declare that I consider the sudden and violent abrogation of the office of Master in Chancery, by the new Constitution, as a—premature act, inasmuch as I had counted upon a life lease of the profits, whereas I only received those of a few short years. But this is by the way.

My chambers were upstairs at No. — Wall Street. At one end they looked upon the white wall of the interior of a spacious skylight shaft, penetrating the building from top to bottom.

This view might have been considered rather tame than otherwise, deficient in what landscape painters call "life." But, if so, the view from the other end of my chambers offered at least a contrast, if nothing more. In that direction, my windows commanded an unobstructed view of a lofty brick wall, black by age and everlasting shade, which wall required no spyglass to bring out its lurking beauties, but, for the benefit of all nearsighted spectators, was pushed up to within ten feet of my windowpanes. Owing to the great height of the surrounding buildings, and my chambers' being on the second floor, the interval between this wall and mine not a little resembled a huge square cistern.

At the period just preceding the advent of Bartleby, I had two persons as copyists in my employment, and a promising lad as an office boy. First, Turkey; second, Nippers; third, Ginger Nut. These may seem names the like of which are not usually found in the Directory. In truth, they were nicknames, mutually conferred upon each other by my three clerks, and were deemed expressive of their respective persons or characters. Turkey was a short, pursy Englishman, of about my own age—that is, somewhere not far from sixty. In the morning, one might say, his face was of a fine florid hue, but after twelve o'clock meridian—his dinner hour—it blazed like a grate full of Christmas coals; and continued blazing—but, as it were, with a gradual wane—till six o'clock, P.M., or thereabouts; after which I saw no more of the proprietor of the face, which, gaining its meridian with the sun, seemed to set with it, to rise, culminate, and decline the following day, with the like regularity and undiminished glory. There are many singular coincidences I have known in the course of my life, not the least among which was the fact, that, exactly when Turkey displayed his fullest beams from his red and radiant countenance, just then, too, at that critical moment, began the daily period when I considered his business capacities as seriously disturbed for the remainder of the twenty-four hours. Not that he was absolutely idle or averse to business then; far from it. The difficulty was, he was apt to be altogether too energetic. There was a strange, inflamed, flurried, flighty recklessness of activity about him. He would be incautious in dipping his pen into his inkstand. All his blots upon my documents were dropped there after twelve o'clock, meridian. Indeed, not only would he be reckless and sadly given to making blots in the afternoon, but some days he went further and was rather noisy. At such times, too, his face flamed with augmented blazonry, as if cannel coal had been heaped on anthracite. He made an unpleasant racket with his chair; spilled his sandbox; in mending his pens, impatiently split them all to pieces and threw them on the floor in a sudden passion; stood up and leaned over his table, boxing his papers about in a most indecorous manner, very sad to behold in an elderly man like him. Nevertheless, as he was in many ways a most valuable person to me, and all the time before twelve o'clock, meridian, was the quickest, steadiest creature, too, accomplishing a great deal of work in a style not easily to be matched—for these reasons I was willing to overlook his eccentricities, though indeed, occasionally, I remonstrated with him. I did this very gently, however, because, though the civilest, nay, the blandest and most reverential of men in the morning, yet, in the afternoon he was disposed, upon provocation, to be slightly rash with his tongue—in fact, insolent. Now, valuing his morning services as I did, and resolved not to lose them—yet, at the same time, made uncomfortable by his inflamed ways after twelve o'clock—and being a man of peace, unwilling by my admonitions to call forth unseemly retorts from him, I took upon me one Saturday noon (he was always worse on Saturdays) to hint to him, very kindly, that perhaps, now that he was growing old, it might be well to abridge his labors; in short, he need not come to my chambers after twelve o'clock, but, dinner over, had best go home to his lodgings and rest himself till teatime. But no; he insisted upon his afternoon devotions. His countenance became intolerably fervid, as he oratorically assured me—gesticulating with a long ruler at the other end of the room—that if his services in the morning were useful, how indispensable, then, in the afternoon?

"With submission, sir," said Turkey, on this occasion, "I consider myself your right-hand man. In the morning I but marshal and deploy my columns, but in the afternoon I put myself at their head, and gallantly charge the foe, thus"—and he made a violent thrust with the ruler.

"But the bolts, Turkey," intimated I.

"True; but, with submission, sir, behold these hairs! I am getting old. Surely, sir, a blot or two of a warm afternoon is not to be severely urged against gray hairs. Old age—even if it blot the page—is honorable. With submission, sir, we *both* are getting old."

This appeal to my fellow feeling was hardly to be resisted. At all events, I saw that go he would not. So I made up my mind to let him stay, resolving, nevertheless, to see to it that, during the afternoon, he had to do with my less important papers.

Nippers, the second on my list, was a whiskered, sallow, and upon the whole rather piratical-looking young man of about five and twenty. I always deemed him the victim of two evil powers—ambition and indigestion. The ambition was evinced by a certain impatience of the duties of a mere copyist, an unwarrantable usurpation of strictly professional affairs, such as the original drawing up of legal documents. The indigestion seemed betokened in an occasional nervous testiness and grinning irritability, causing the teeth to audibly grind together over mistakes committed in copying; unnecessary maledictions, hissed rather than spoken, in the heat of business; and especially by a continual discontent with the height of the table where he worked. Though of a very ingenious mechanical turn, Nippers could never get this table to suit him. He put chips under it, blocks of various sorts, bits of pasteboard, and at last went so far as to attempt an exquisite adjustment by final pieces of folded blotting paper. But no invention would answer. If, for the sake of easing his back, he brought the table lid at a sharp angle well up towards his chin, and wrote there like a man using the steep roof of a Dutch house for his desk, then he declared that it stopped the circulation in his arms. If now he lowered the table to his waistbands and stooped over it in writing, then there was a sore aching in his back. In short, the truth of the matter was Nippers knew not what he wanted. Or, if he wanted anything, it was to be rid of a scrivener's table altogether. Among the manifestations of his diseased ambition was a fondness he had for receiving visits from certain ambiguous-looking fellows in seedy coats, whom he called his clients. Indeed, I was aware that not only was he, at times, considerable of a ward politician, but he occasionally did a little business at the Justices' courts, and was not unknown on the steps of the Tombs. I have good reason to believe, however, that one individual who called upon him at my chambers, and who, with a grand air, he insisted was his client, was no other than a dun, and the alleged title deed, a bill. But, with all his failings, and the annoyances he caused me, Nippers, like his compatriot Turkey, was a very useful man to me; wrote a neat, swift hand; and, when he chose, was not deficient in a gentlemanly sort of deportment. Added to this, he always dressed in a gentlemanly sort of way, and so, incidentally, reflected credit upon my chambers. Whereas, with respect to Turkey, I had much ado to keep him from being a reproach to me. His clothes were apt to look oily, and smell of eating houses. He wore his pantaloons very loose and baggy in summer. His coats were execrable, his hat not to be handled. But while the hat was a thing of indifference to me, inasmuch as his natural civility and deference, as a dependent Englishman, always led him to doff it the moment he entered the room, yet his coat was another matter. Concerning his coats, I reasoned with him, but with no effect. The truth was, I suppose, that a man with so small an income could not afford to sport such a lustrous face and a lustrous coat at one and the same time. As Nippers once observed, Turkey's money went chiefly for red ink. One winter day, I presented Turkey with a highly respectable-looking coat of my own—a padded gray coat of a most comfortable warmth, and which buttoned straight up from the knee to the neck. I thought Turkey would appreciate the favor and abate his rashness and obstreperousness of afternoons. But no; I verily believe that buttoning himself up in so downy and blanket-like a coat had a pernicious effect upon him—upon the same principle that too much oats are bad for horses. In fact, precisely as a rash, restive horse is said to feel his oats, so Turkey felt his coat. It made him insolent. He was a man whom prosperity harmed.

Though, concerning the self-indulgent habits of Turkey, I had my own private surmises, yet, touching Nippers, I was well persuaded that, whatever might be his faults in other respects, he was, at least, a temperate young man. But indeed, nature herself seemed to have been his vintner, and, at his birth, charged him so thoroughly with an irritable, brandylike disposition that all subsequent potations were needless. When I consider how, amid the stillness of my chambers, Nippers would sometimes impatiently rise from his seat, and, stooping over his table, spread his arms wide apart, seize the whole desk, and move it, and jerk it, with a grim, grinding motion on the floor, as if the table were a perverse voluntary agent, intent on thwarting and vexing him, I plainly perceive that, for Nippers, brandy-and-water were altogether superfluous.

It was fortunate for me that, owing to its peculiar cause—indigestion—the irritability and consequent nervousness of Nippers were mainly observable in the morning, while in the afternoon he was comparatively mild. So that, Turkey's paroxysms only coming on about twelve o'clock, I never had to do with their eccentricities at one time. Their fits relieved each other, like guards. When Nippers's was on, Turkey's was off; and vice versa. This was good natural arrangement under the circumstances.

Ginger Nut, the third on my list, was a lad some twelve years old. His father was a carman, ambitious of seeing his son on the bench instead of a cart before he died. So he sent him to my office, as student at law, errand boy, cleaner and sweeper, at the rate of one dollar a week. He had a little desk to himself, but he did not use it much. Upon inspection, the drawer exhibited a great array of the shells of various sorts of nuts. Indeed, to this quick-witted youth, the whole noble science of the law was contained in a nutshell. Not the least among the employments of Ginger Nut, as well as one which he discharged with the most alacrity, was his duty as cake and apple

purveyor for Turkey and Nippers. Copying law papers being proverbially a dry, husky sort of business, my two scriveners were fain to
moisten their mouths very often with Spitzenbergs, to be had at the
numerous stalls nigh the Custom House and Post Office. Also, they
sent Ginger Nut very frequently for that peculiar cake—small, flat,
round, and very spicy—after which he had been named by them. Of a
cold morning, when business was but dull, Turkey would gobble up
scores of these cakes, as if they were mere wafers—indeed, they sell
them at the rate of six or eight for a penny—the scrape of his pen
blending with the crunching of the crisp particles in his mouth. Of
all the fiery afternoon blunders and flurried rashnesses of Turkey was
his once moistening a ginger cake between his lips and clapping it on
to a mortgage for a seal. I came within an ace of dismissing him then.
But he mollified me by making an Oriental bow, and saying:

"With submission, sir, it was generous of me to find you in sta-
tionery on my own account."

Now my original business—that of a conveyancer and title hunter,
and drawer-up of recondite documents of all sorts—was considerably
increased by receiving the Master's office. There was now great work
for scriveners. Not only must I push the clerks already with me, but I
must have additional help.

In answer to my advertisement, a motionless young man one
morning stood upon my office threshold, the door being open, for it
was summer. I can see that figure now—pallidly neat, pitiably respectable, incurably forlorn! It was Bartleby.

After a few words touching his qualifications, I engaged him, glad
to have among my corps of copyists a man of so singularly sedate an
aspect, which I thought might operate beneficially upon the flighty
temper of Turkey and the fiery one of Nippers.

I should have stated before that ground-glass folding doors divided my premises into two parts, one of which was occupied by my
scriveners, the other by myself. According to my humor, I threw open
these doors or closed them. I resolved to assign Bartleby a corner by
the folding doors, but on my side of them, so as to have this quiet
man within easy call, in case any trifling thing was to be done. I placed
his desk close up to a small side window in that part of the room,
a window which originally had afforded a lateral view of certain
grimy back yards and bricks, but which, owing to subsequent erections,
commanded at present no view at all, though it gave some light. Within
three feet of the panes was a wall, and the light came down from
far above, between two lofty buildings, as from a very small opening
in a dome. Still further to a satisfactory arrangement, I procured a

high green folding screen, which might entirely isolate Bartleby from my sight, though not remove him from my voice. And thus, in a manner, privacy and society were conjoined.

At first, Bartleby did an extraordinary quantity of writing. As if long famishing for something to copy, he seemed to gorge himself on my documents. There was no pause for digestion. He ran a day and night line, copying by sunlight and by candlelight. I should have been quite delighted with his application, had he been cheerfully industrious. But he wrote on silently, palely, mechanically.

It is, of course, an indispensable part of a scrivener's business to verify the accuracy of his copy, word by word. Where there are two or more scriveners in an office, they assist each other in this examination, one reading from the copy, the other holding the original. It is a very dull, wearisome, and lethargic affair. I can readily imagine that, to some sanguine temperaments, it would be altogether intolerable. For example, I cannot credit that the mettlesome poet, Byron, would have contentedly sat down with Bartleby to examine a law document of, say five hundred pages, closely written in a crimpy hand.

Now and then, in the haste of business, it had been my habit to assist in comparing some brief document myself, calling Turkey or Nippers for this purpose. One object I had in placing Bartleby so handy to me behind the screen was to avail myself of his services on such trivial occasions. It was on the third day, I think, of his being with me, and before any necessity had arisen for having his own writing examined, that, being much hurried to complete a small affair I had in hand, I abruptly called to Bartleby. In my haste and natural expectancy of instant compliance, I sat with my head bent over the original on my desk, and my right hand sideways, and somewhat nervously extended with the copy, so that, immediately upon emerging from his retreat, Bartleby might snatch it and proceed to business without the least delay.

In this very attitude did I sit when I called to him, rapidly stating what it was I wanted him to do—namely, to examine a small paper with me. Imagine my surprise, nay, my consternation, when, without moving from his privacy, Bartleby, in a singularly mild, firm voice, replied, "I would prefer not to."

I sat awhile in perfect silence, rallying my stunned faculties. Immediately it occurred to me that my ears had deceived me, or Bartleby had entirely misunderstood my meaning. I repeated my request in the clearest tone I could assume; but in quite as clear a one came the previous reply, "I would prefer not to."

"Prefer not to," echoed I, rising in high excitement, and crossing the room with a stride. "What do you mean? Are you moon-struck?

I want you to help me compare this sheet here—take it," and I thrust it towards him.

"I would prefer not to," said he.

I looked at him steadfastly. His face was leanly composed; his gray eyes dimly calm. Not a wrinkle of agitation rippled him. Had there been the least uneasiness, anger, impatience or impertinence in his manner; in other words, had there been anything ordinarily human about him, doubtless I should have violently dismissed him from the premises. But as it was I should have as soon thought of turning my pale plaster-of-Paris bust of Cicero out of doors. I stood gazing at him awhile, as he went on with his own writing, and then reseated myself at my desk. This is very strange, thought I. What had one best do? But my business hurried me. I concluded to forget the matter for the present, reserving it for my future leisure. So calling Nippers from the other room, the paper was speedily examined.

A few days after this, Bartleby concluded four lengthy documents, being quadruplicates of a week's testimony taken before me in my High Court of Chancery. It became necessary to examine them. It was an important suit, and great accuracy was imperative. Having all things arranged, I called Turkey, Nippers and Ginger Nut, from the next room, meaning to place the four copies in the hands of my four clerks, while I should read from the original. Accordingly, Turkey, Nippers, and Ginger Nut had taken their seats in a row, each with his document in his hand, when I called to Bartleby to join this interesting group.

"Bartleby! quick, I am waiting."

I heard a slow scrape of his chair legs on the uncarpeted floor, and soon he appeared standing at the entrance of his hermitage.

"What is wanted?" said he, mildly.

"The copies, the copies," said I, hurriedly. "We are going to examine them. There"—and I held towards him the fourth quadruplicate.

"I would prefer not to," he said, and gently disappeared behind the screen.

For a few moments I was turned into a pillar of salt, standing at the head of my seated column of clerks. Recovering myself, I advanced towards the screen and demanded the reason for such extraordinary conduct.

"*Why* do you refuse?"

"I would prefer not to."

With any other man I should have flown outright into a dreadful passion, scorned all further words, and thrust him ignominiously from my presence. But there was something about Bartleby that not only strangely disarmed me, but, in a wonderful manner, touched and disconcerted me. I began to reason with him.

"These are your own copies we are about to examine. It is labor saving to you, because one examination will answer for your four papers. It is common usage. Every copyist is bound to help examine his copy. Is it not so? Will you not speak? Answer!"

"I prefer not to," he replied in a flutelike tone. It seemed to me that, while I had been addressing him, he carefully revolved every statement that I made; fully comprehended the meaning; could not gainsay the irresistible conclusion; but, at the same time, some paramount consideration prevailed with him to reply as he did.

"You are decided, then, not to comply with my request—a request made according to common usage and common sense?"

He briefly gave me to understand that on that point my judgment was sound. Yes: his decision was irreversible.

It is seldom the case that, when a man is browbeaten in some unprecedented and violently unreasonable way, he begins to stagger in his own plainest faith. He begins, as it were, vaguely to surmise that, wonderful as it may be, all the justice and all the reason is on the other side. Accordingly, if any disinterested persons are present, he turns to them for some reinforcement for his own faltering mind.

"Turkey," said I, "what do you think of this? Am I not right?"

"With submission, sir," said Turkey, in his blandest tone, "I think that you are."

"Nippers," said I, "what do *you* think of it?"

"I think I should kick him out of the office."

(The reader, of nice perceptions, will here perceive that, it being morning, Turkey's answer is couched in polite and tranquil terms, but Nippers replies in ill-tempered ones. Or, to repeat a previous sentence, Nippers's ugly mood was on duty, and Turkey's off.)

"Ginger Nut," said I, willing to enlist the smallest suffrage in my behalf, "what do *you* think of it?"

"I think, sir, he's a little *luny*," replied Ginger Nut, with a grin.

"You hear what they say," said I, turning towards the screen, "come forth and do your duty."

But he vouchsafed no reply. I pondered a moment in sore perplexity. But once more business hurried me. I determined again to postpone the consideration of this dilemma to my future leisure. With a little trouble we made out to examine the papers without Bartleby, though at every page or two Turkey deferentially dropped his opinion that this proceeding was quite out of the common; while Nippers, twitching in his chair with a dyspeptic nervousness, ground out between his set teeth occasional hissing maledictions against the stubborn oaf behind the screen. And for his (Nippers's) part, this was the first and the last time he would do another man's business without pay.

Meanwhile Bartleby sat in his hermitage, oblivious to everything but his own peculiar business there.

Some days passed, the scrivener being employed upon another lengthy work. His late remarkable conduct led me to regard his ways narrowly. I observed that he never went to dinner; indeed, that he never went anywhere. As yet I had never, of my personal knowledge, known him to be outside of my office. He was a perpetual sentry in the corner. At about eleven o'clock, though, in the morning, I noticed that Ginger Nut would advance towards the opening in Bartleby's screen, as if silently beckoned thither by a gesture invisible to me where I sat. The boy would then leave the office jingling a few pence, and reappear with a handful of gingernuts, which he delivered in the hermitage, receiving two of the cakes for his trouble.

He lives, then, on gingernuts, thought I; never eats a dinner, properly speaking; he must be a vegetarian, then; but no, he never eats even vegetables, he eats nothing but gingernuts. My mind then ran on in reveries concerning the probable effects upon the human constitution of living entirely on gingernuts. Gingernuts are so called because they contain ginger as one of their peculiar constituents, and the final flavoring one. Now, what was ginger? A hot, spicy thing. Was Bartleby hot and spicy? Not at all. Ginger, then, had no effect upon Bartleby. Probably he preferred it should have none.

Nothing so aggravates an earnest person as a passive resistance. If the individual so resisted be of a not inhumane temper, and the resisting one perfectly harmless in his passivity, then, in the better moods of the former, he will endeavor charitably to construe to his imagination what proves impossible to be solved by his judgment. Even so, for the most part, I regarded Bartleby and his ways. Poor fellow! thought I, he means no mischief; it is plain he intends no insolence; his aspect sufficiently evinces that his eccentricities are involuntary. He is useful to me. I can get along with him. If I turn him away, the chances are he will fall in with some less indulgent employer, and then he will be rudely treated, and perhaps driven forth miserably to starve. Yes. Here I can cheaply purchase a delicious self-approval. To befriend Bartleby, to humor him in his strange willfulness, will cost me little or nothing, while I lay up in my soul what will eventually prove a sweet morsel for my conscience. But this mood was not invariable with me. The passiveness of Bartleby sometimes irritated me. I felt strangely goaded on to encounter him in new opposition—to elicit some angry spark from him answerable to my own.

But, indeed, I might as well have essayed to strike fire with my knuckles against a bit of Windsor soap. But one afternoon the evil impulse in me mastered me, and the following little scene ensued:

"Bartleby," said I, "when those papers are all copied, I will compare them with you."

"I would prefer not to."

"How? Surely you do not mean to persist in that mulish vagary?"

No answer.

I threw open the folding doors near by, and, turning upon Turkey and Nippers, exclaimed:

"Bartleby a second time says he won't examine his papers. What do you think of it, Turkey?"

It was afternoon, be it remembered. Turkey sat glowing like a brass boiler, his bald head steaming, his hands reeling among his blotted papers.

"Think of it?" roared Turkey. "I think I'll just step behind his screen and black his eyes for him!"

So saying, Turkey rose to his feet and threw his arms into a pugilistic position. He was hurrying away to make good his promise when I detained him, alarmed at the effect of incautiously rousing Turkey's combativeness after dinner.

"Sit down, Turkey," said I, "and hear what Nippers has to say. What do you think of it, Nippers? Would I not be justified in immediately dismissing Bartleby?"

"Excuse me, that is for you to decide, sir. I think his conduct quite unusual, and indeed, unjust, as regards Turkey and myself. But it may only be a passing whim."

"Ah," exclaimed I, "you have strangely changed your mind, then —you speak very gently of him now."

"All beer," cried Turkey; "gentleness is effects of beer—Nippers and I dined together today. You see how gentle *I* am, sir. Shall I go and black his eyes?"

"You refer to Bartleby, I suppose. No, not today, Turkey," I replied; "pray, put up your fists."

I closed the doors and again advanced towards Bartleby. I felt additional incentives tempting me to my fate. I burned to be rebelled against again. I remembered that Bartleby never left the office.

"Bartleby," said I, "Ginger Nut is away; just step around to the Post Office, won't you? (it was but a three minutes' walk), and see if there is anything for me."

"I would prefer not to."

"You *will* not?"

"I *prefer* not."

I staggered to my desk and sat there in a deep study. My blind inveteracy returned. Was there any other thing in which I could procure myself to be ignominiously repulsed by this lean, penniless wight? —my hired clerk? What added thing is there, perfectly reasonable, that he will be sure to refuse to do?

"Bartleby!"

No answer.

"Bartleby," in a louder tone.

No answer.

"Bartleby," I roared.

Like a very ghost, agreeably to the laws of magical invocation, at the third summons he appeared at the entrance of his hermitage.

"Go to the next room, and tell Nippers to come to me."

"I prefer not to," he respectfully and slowly said, and mildly disappeared.

"Very good, Bartleby," said I, in a quiet sort of serenely severe self-possessed tone, intimating the unalterable purpose of some terrible retribution very close at hand. At the moment I half intended something of the kind. But upon the whole, as it was drawing towards my dinner hour, I thought it best to put on my hat and walk home for the day, suffering much from perplexity and distress of mind.

Shall I acknowledge it? The conclusion of this whole business was that it soon became a fixed fact of my chambers, that a pale young scrivener by the name of Bartleby had a desk there; that he copied for me at the usual rate of four cents a folio (one hundred words); but he was permanently exempt from examining the work done by him, that duty being transferred to Turkey and Nippers, out of compliment, doubtless, to their superior acuteness; moreover, said Bartleby was never, on any account, to be dispatched on the most trivial errand of any sort; and that even if entreated to take upon him such a matter, it was generally understood that he would "prefer not to"— in other words, that he would refuse point-blank.

As days passed on, I became considerably reconciled to Bartleby. His steadiness, his freedom from all dissipation, his incessant industry (except when he chose to throw himself into a standing reverie behind his screen), his great stillness, his unalterableness of demeanor under all circumstances, made him a valuable acquisition. One prime thing was this—*he was always there*—first in the morning, continually through the day, and the last at night. I had a singular confidence in his honesty. I felt my most precious papers perfectly safe in his hands. Sometimes, to be sure, I could not, for the very soul of me, avoid falling into sudden spasmodic passions with him. For it was exceeding difficult to bear in mind all the time those strange peculiarities, privileges, and unheard-of exemptions, forming the tacit stipulations on Bartleby's part under which he remained in my office. Now and then, in the eagerness of dispatching pressing business, I would inadvertently summon Bartleby, in a short, rapid tone, to put his finger, say, on the incipient tie of a bit of red tape with which I was about compressing some papers. Of course, from behind the screen the usual answer, "I prefer not to," was sure to come; and then, how could a human creature, with the common infirmities of our nature, refrain from bitterly exclaiming upon such perverseness—such unreasonableness. However, every added repulse of this sort which I received only tended to lessen the probability of my repeating the inadvertence.

Here it must be said that, according to the custom of most legal gentlemen occupying chambers in densely populated law buildings, there were several keys to my door. One was kept by a woman residing in the attic, which person weekly scrubbed and daily swept and dusted my apartments. Another was kept by Turkey for convenience' sake. The third I sometimes carried in my own pocket. The fourth I knew not who had.

Now, one Sunday morning I happened to go to Trinity Church, to hear a celebrated preacher, and finding myself rather early on the ground I thought I would walk round to my chambers for a while. Luckily I had my key with me, but upon applying it to the lock, I found it resisted by something inserted from the inside. Quite surprised, I called out, when to my consternation a key was turned from within, and, thrusting his lean visage at me, and holding the door ajar, the apparition of Bartleby appeared, in his shirt sleeves, and otherwise in a strangely tattered deshabille, saying quietly that he was sorry, but he was deeply engaged just then, and—preferred not admitting me at present. In a brief word or two, he moreover added, that perhaps I had better walk around the block two or three times, and by that time he would probably have concluded his affairs.

Now, the utterly unsurmised appearance of Bartleby, tenanting my law chambers of a Sunday morning, with his cadaverously gentlemanly *nonchalance*, yet withal firm and self-possessed, had such a strange effect upon me that incontinently I slunk away from my own door and did as desired. But not without sundry twinges of impotent rebellion against the mild effrontery of this unaccountable scrivener. Indeed, it was his wonderful mildness, chiefly, which not only disarmed me but unmanned me, as it were. For I consider that one, for the time, is sort of unmanned when he tranquilly permits his hired clerk to dictate to him and order him away from his own premises. Furthermore, I was full of uneasiness as to what Bartleby could possibly be doing in my office in his shirt sleeves, and in an otherwise dismantled condition, of a Sunday morning. Was anything amiss going on? Nay, that was out of the question. It was not to be thought of for a moment that Bartleby was an immoral person. But what could he be doing there?—copying? Nay again, whatever might be his eccentricities, Bartleby was an eminently decorous person. He would be the last man to sit down to his desk in any state approaching to nudity. Besides, it was Sunday; and there was something about Bartleby that forbade the supposition that he would by any secular occupation violate the proprieties of the day.

Nevertheless, my mind was not pacified, and, full of a restless curiosity, at last I returned to the door. Without hindrance I inserted my key, opened it, and entered. Bartleby was not to be seen. I looked round anxiously, peeped behind his screen, but it was very plain that he was gone. Upon more closely examining the place, I surmised that for an indefinite period Bartleby must have ate, dressed, and slept in my office, and that, too, without plate, mirror, or bed. The cushioned seat of a rickety old sofa in one corner bore that faint impress of a lean, reclining form. Rolled away under his desk I found a blanket; under the empty grate, a blacking box and brush; on a chair, a tin basin, with soap and a ragged towel; in a newspaper a few crumbs of gingernuts and a morsel of cheese. Yes, thought I, it is evident enough that Bartleby has been making his home here, keeping bachelor's hall all by himself. Immediately then the thought came sweeping across me, what miserable friendliness and loneliness are here revealed. His poverty is great, but his solitude, how horrible! Think of it. Of a Sunday, Wall Street is deserted as Petra, and every night of every day it is an emptiness. This building, too, which of weekdays hums with industry and life, at nightfall echoes with sheer vacancy, and all through Sunday is forlorn. And here Bartleby makes his home, sole spectator of a solitude which he has seen all populous—a sort of innocent and transformed Marius brooding among the ruins of Carthage!

For the first time in my life a feeling of overpowering stinging melancholy seized me. Before, I had never experienced aught but a not unpleasing sadness. The bond of a common humanity now drew me irresistibly to gloom. A fraternal melancholy! For both I and Bartleby were sons of Adam. I remembered the bright silks and sparkling faces I had seen that day, in gala trim, swanlike sailing down the Mississippi of Broadway; and I contrasted them with the pallid copyist, and thought to myself, Ah, happiness courts the light, so we deem the world is gay, but misery hides aloof, so we deem that misery there is none. These sad fancyings—chimeras, doubtless, of a sick and silly brain—led on to other and more special thoughts, concerning the eccentricities of Bartleby. Presentiments of strange discoveries hovered round me. The scrivener's pale form appeared to me laid out, among uncaring strangers in its shivering winding sheet.

Suddenly I was attracted by Bartleby's closed desk, the key in open sight left in the lock.

I mean no mischief, seek the gratification of no heartless curiosity, thought I; besides, the desk is mine, and its contents, too, so I will make bold to look within. Everything was methodically arranged, the papers smoothly placed. The pigeonholes were deep, and, removing the files of documents, I groped into their recesses. Presently I felt something there, and dragged it out. It was an old bandanna handkerchief, heavy and knotted. I opened it, and saw it was a savings bank.

I now recalled all the quiet mysteries which I had noted in the man. I remembered that he never spoke but to answer; that, though at intervals he had considerable time to himself, yet I had never seen him reading—no, not even a newspaper; that for long periods he would stand looking out, at his pale window behind the screen, upon the dead brick wall; I was quite sure he never visited any refectory or eating house, while his pale face clearly indicated that he never drank beer like Turkey, or tea and coffee even, like other men; that he never went anywhere in particular that I could learn; never went out for a walk, unless, indeed, that was the case at present; that he had declined telling who he was, or whence he came, or whether he had any relatives in the world; that though so thin and pale, he never complained of ill health. And more than all I remembered a certain unconscious air of pallid—how shall I call it?—of pallid haughtiness, say, or rather an austere reserve about him, which had positively awed me into my tame compliance with his eccentricities, when I had feared to ask him to do the slightest incidental thing for me, even though I might know, from his long-continued motionlessness, that behind his screen he must be standing in one of those dead-wall reveries of his.

Revolving all these things, and coupling them with the recently discovered fact that he made my office his constant abiding place and home, and not forgetful of his morbid moodiness—revolving all these things, a prudential feeling began to steal over me. My first emotions had been those of pure melancholy and sincerest pity; but just in proportion as the forlornness of Bartleby grew and grew to my imagination, did that same melancholy merge into fear, that pity into repulsion. So true it is, and so terrible too, that up to a certain point the thought or sight of misery enlists our best affections; but, in certain special cases, beyond that point it does not. They err who would assert that invariably this is owing to the inherent selfishness of the human heart.

It rather proceeds from a certain hopelessness of remedying excessive and organic ill. To a sensitive being, pity is not seldom pain. And when at last it is perceived that such pity cannot lead to effectual succor, common sense bids the soul be rid of it. What I saw that morning persuaded me that the scrivener was the victim of innate and incurable disorder. I might give alms to his body, but his body did not pain him—it was his soul that suffered, and his soul I could not reach.

I did not accomplish the purpose of going to Trinity Church that morning. Somehow, the things I had seen disqualified me for the time from churchgoing. I walked homeward, thinking what I would do with Bartleby. Finally, I resolved upon this—I would put certain calm questions to him the next morning, touching his history, etc., and if he declined to answer them openly and unreservedly (and I supposed he would prefer not), then to give him a twenty-dollar bill over and above whatever I might owe him, and tell him his services were no longer required; but that if in any other way I could assist him, I would be happy to do so, especially if he desired to return to his native place, wherever that might be, I would willingly help to defray the expenses. Moreover, if, after reaching home, he found himself at any time in want of aid, a letter from him would be sure of a reply.

The next morning came.

"Bartleby," said I, gently calling to him behind his screen.

No reply.

"Bartleby," said I, in a still gentler tone, "come here; I am not going to ask you to do anything you would prefer not to do—I simply wish to speak to you."

Upon this he noiselessly slid into view.

"Will you tell me, Bartleby, where you were born?"

"I would prefer not to."

"Will you tell me *anything* about yourself?"

"I would prefer not to."

"But what reasonable objection can you have to speak to me? I feel friendly towards you."

He did not look at me while I spoke, but kept his glance fixed upon my bust of Cicero, which, as I then sat, was directly behind me, some six inches above my head.

"What is your answer, Bartleby," said I, after waiting a considerable time for a reply, during which his countenance remained immovable, only there was the faintest conceivable tremor of the white attenuated mouth.

"At present I prefer to give no answer," he said, and retired into his hermitage.

It was rather weak in me I confess, but his manner, on this occasion, nettled me. Not only did there seem to lurk in it a certain calm disdain, but his perverseness seemed ungrateful, considering the undeniable good usage and indulgence he had received from me.

Again I sat ruminating what I should do. Mortified as I was at his behavior, and resolved as I had been to dismiss him when I entered my office, nevertheless I strangely felt something superstitious knocking at my heart, and forbidding me to carry out my purpose, and denouncing me for a villain if I dared to breathe one bitter word against this forlornest of mankind. At last, familiarly drawing my chair behind his screen, I sat down and said: "Bartleby, never mind, then, about revealing your history; but let me entreat you, as a friend, to comply as far as may be with the usages of this office. Say now, you will help to examine papers tomorrow or next day: in short, say now, that in a day or two you will begin to be a little reasonable:—say so, Bartleby."

"At present I would prefer not to be a little reasonable," was his mildly cadaverous reply.

Just then the folding doors opened and Nippers approached. He seemed suffering from an unusually bad night's rest, induced by severer indigestion than common. He overheard those final words of Bartleby.

"*Prefer not*, eh?" gritted Nippers—"I'd *prefer* him, if I were you, sir," addressing me—"I'd *prefer* him; I'd give him preferences, the stubborn mule! What is it, sir, pray, that he *prefers* not to do now?"

Bartleby moved not a limb.

"Mr. Nippers," said I, "I'd prefer that you would withdraw for the present."

Somehow, of late, I had got into the way of involuntarily using the word "prefer" upon all sorts of not exactly suitable occasions. And I trembled to think that my contact with the scrivener had already and seriously affected me in a mental way. And what further and deeper aberration might it not yet produce? This apprehension had not been without efficacy in determining me to summary measures.

As Nippers, looking very sour and sulky, was departing, Turkey blandly and deferentially approached.

"With submission, sir," said he, "yesterday I was thinking about Bartleby here, and I think that if he would but prefer to take a quart of good ale every day, it would do much towards mending him, and enabling him to assist in examining his papers."

"So you have got the word, too," said I, slightly excited.

"With submission, and word, sir?" asked Turkey, respectfully crowding himself into the contracted space behind the screen, and by so doing making me jostle the scrivener. "What word, sir?"

"I would prefer to be left alone here," said Bartleby, as if offended at being mobbed in his privacy.

"*That's* the word, Turkey," said I—"*that's* it."

"Oh, *prefer?* oh yes—queer word. I never use it myself. But, sir, as I was saying, if he would but prefer—"

"Turkey," interrupted I, "you will please withdraw."

"Oh certainly, sir, if you prefer that I should."

As he opened the folding door to retire, Nippers at his desk caught a glimpse of me, and asked whether I would prefer to have a certain paper copied on blue paper or white. He did not in the least roguishly accent the word prefer. It was plain that it involuntarily rolled from his tongue. I thought to myself, surely I must get rid of a demented man, who already has in some degree turned the tongues, if not the heads, of myself and clerks. But I thought it prudent not to break the dismission at once.

The next day I noticed that Bartleby did nothing but stand at his window in his dead-wall reverie. Upon asking him why he did not write, he said that he had decided upon doing no more writing.

"Why, how now? what next?" exclaimed I, "do no more writing?"

"No more."

"And what is the reason?"

"Do you not see the reason for yourself?" he indifferently replied.

I looked steadfastly at him, and perceived that his eyes looked dull and glazed. Instantly it occurred to me that his unexampled diligence in copying by his dim window for the first few weeks of his stay with me might have temporarily impaired his vision.

I was touched. I said something in condolence with him. I hinted that of course he did wisely in abstaining from writing for a while; and urged him to embrace that opportunity of taking wholesome exercise in the open air. This, however, he did not do. A few days after this, my other clerks being absent, and being in a great hurry to dispatch certain letters by the mail, I thought that, having nothing else earthly to do, Bartleby would surely be less inflexible than usual, and carry these letters to the Post Office. But he blankly declined. So, much to my inconvenience, I went myself.

Still added days went by. Whether Bartleby's eyes improved or not, I could not say. To all appearance, I thought they did. But when I asked him if they did, he vouchsafed no answer. At all events, he would do no copying. At last, in reply to my urgings, he informed me that he had permanently given up copying.

"What!" exclaimed I; "suppose your eyes should get entirely well —better than ever before—would you not copy then?"

"I have given up copying," he answered, and slid aside.

He remained as ever, a fixture in my chamber. Nay—if that were possible—he became still more of a fixture than before. What was to be done? He would do nothing in the office; why should he stay there? In plain fact, he had now become a millstone to me, not only useless as a necklace, but afflictive to bear. Yet I was sorry for him. I speak less than truth when I say that, on his own account, he occasioned me uneasiness. If he would but have named a single relative or friend, I would instantly have written and urged their taking the poor fellow away to some convenient retreat. But he seemed alone, absolutely alone in the universe. A bit of wreck in the mid-Atlantic. At length, necessities connected with my business tyrannized over all other considerations. Decently as I could, I told Bartleby that in six days' time he must unconditionally leave the office. I warned him to take measures, in the interval, for procuring some other abode. I offered to assist him in this endeavor, if he himself would but take the first step towards a removal. "And when you finally quit me, Bartleby," added I, "I shall see that you go not away entirely unprovided. Six days from this hour, remember."

At the expiration of that period, I peeped behind the screen, and lo! Bartleby was there.

I buttoned up my coat, balanced myself, advanced slowly towards him, touched his shoulder, and said, "The time has come; you must quit this place; I am sorry for you; here is money; but you must go."

"I would prefer not," he replied, with his back still towards me.

"You *must*."

He remained silent.

Now I had an unbounded confidence in this man's common honesty. He had frequently restored to me six-pences and shillings carelessly dropped upon the floor, for I am apt to be very reckless in such shirt-button affairs. The proceeding, then, which followed will not be deemed extraordinary.

"Bartleby," said I, "I owe you twelve dollars on account; here are thirty-two; the odd twenty are yours—Will you take it?" and I handed the bills towards him.

But he made no motion.

"I will leave them here, then," putting them under a weight on the table. Then taking my hat and cane and going to the door, I tranquilly turned and added—"After you have removed your things from these offices, Bartleby, you will of course lock the door—since everyone is now gone for the day but you—and if you please, slip your key underneath the mat, so that I may have it in the morning. I shall not see you again; so good-bye to you. If, hereafter, in your new place of abode, I can be of any service to you, do not fail to advise me by letter. Good-bye, Bartleby, and fare you well."

But he answered not a word; like the last column of some ruined temple, he remained standing mute and solitary in the middle of the otherwise deserted room.

As I walked home in a pensive mood, my vanity got the better of my pity. I could not but highly plume myself on my masterly management in getting rid of Bartleby. Masterly I call it, and such it must appear to any dispassionate thinker. The beauty of my procedure seemed to consist in its perfect quietness. There was no vulgar bullying, no bravado of any sort, no choleric hectoring and striding to and fro across the apartment, jerking out vehement commands for Bartleby to bundle himself off with his beggarly traps. Nothing of the kind. Without loudly bidding Bartleby depart—as an inferior genius might have done—I *assumed* the ground that depart he must, and upon that assumption built all I had to say. The more I thought over my procedure, the more I was charmed with it. Nevertheless, next morning, upon awakening, I had my doubts—I had somehow slept off the fumes of vanity. One of the coolest and wisest hours a man has is just after he awakes in the morning. My procedure seemed as sagacious as ever—but only in theory. How it would prove in practice—there was the rub. It was truly a beautiful thought to have assumed Bartleby's departure; but, after all, that assumption was simply my own, and none of Bartleby's. The great point was, not whether I had assumed that he would quit me, but whether he would prefer so to do. He was more a man of preferences than assumptions.

After breakfast, I walked downtown, arguing the probabilities pro and con. One moment I thought it would prove a miserable failure, and Bartleby would be found all alive at my office as usual; the next moment it seemed certain that I should find his chair empty. And so I kept veering about. At the corner of Broadway and Canal Street, I saw quite an excited group of people standing in earnest conversation.

"I'll take odds he doesn't," said a voice as I passed.

"Doesn't go?—done!" said I, "put up your money."

I was instinctively putting my hand in my pocket to produce my own, when I remembered that this was an election day. The words I had overheard bore no reference to Bartleby but to the success or nonsuccess of some candidate for the mayoralty. In my intent frame of mind, I had, as it were, imagined that all Broadway shared in my excitement, and were debating the same question with me. I passed on, very thankful that the uproar of the street screened my momentary absentmindedness.

As I had intended, I was earlier than usual at my office door. I stood listening for a moment. All was still. He must be gone. I tried the knob. The door was locked. Yes, my procedure had worked to a charm; he indeed must be vanished. Yet a certain melancholy mixed with this: I was almost sorry for my brilliant success. I was fumbling under the door mat for the key, which Bartleby was to have left there for me, when accidentally my knee knocked against a panel, producing a summoning sound, and in response a voice came to me from within—"Not yet; I am occupied."

It was Bartleby.

I was thunderstruck. For an instant I stood like the man who, pipe in mouth, was killed one cloudless afternoon long ago in Virginia by summer lightning; at his own warm open window he was killed, and remained leaning out there upon the dreamy afternoon, till someone touched him, when he fell.

"Not gone!" I murmured at last. But again obeying that wondrous ascendancy which the inscrutable scrivener had over me, and from which ascendancy, for all my chafing, I could not completely escape, I slowly went downstairs and out into the street, and while walking round the block considered what I should next do in this unheard-of perplexity. Turn the man out by an actual thrusting I could not; to drive him away by calling him hard names would not do; calling in the police was an unpleasant idea; and yet, permit him to enjoy his cadaverous triumph over me—this, too, I could not think of. What was to be done? or, if nothing could be done, was there anything further that I could *assume* in the matter? Yes, as before I had prospectively assumed that Bartleby would depart, so now I might retrospectively assume that departed he was. In the legitimate carrying out of this assumption I might enter my office in a great hurry, and, pretending not to see Bartleby at all, walk straight against him as if he were air. Such a proceeding would in a singular degree have the appearance of a home thrust. It was hardly possible that Bartleby could withstand such an application of the doctrine of assumptions. But upon second thoughts the success of the plan seemed rather dubious. I resolved to argue the matter over with him again.

"Bartleby," said I, entering the office, with a quietly severe expression, "I am seriously displeased. I am pained, Bartleby. I had thought better of you. I had imagined you of such a gentlemanly organization that in any delicate dilemma a slight hint would suffice —in short, an assumption. But it appears I am deceived. Why," I added, unaffectedly starting, "you have not even touched that money yet," pointing to it, just where I had left it the evening previous.

He answered nothing.

"Will you, or will you not, quit me?" I now demanded in a sudden passion, advancing close to him.

"I would prefer *not* to quit you," he replied, gently emphasizing the *not*.

"What earthly right have you to stay here? Do you pay any rent? Do you pay my taxes? Or is this property yours?"

He answered nothing.

"Are you ready to go on and write now? Are your eyes recovered? Could you copy a small paper for me this morning? or help examine a few lines? or step round to the Post Office? In a word, will you do anything at all to give a coloring to your refusal to depart the premises?"

He silently retired into his hermitage.

I was now in such a state of nervous resentment that I thought it but prudent to check myself at present from further demonstrations. Bartleby and I were alone. I remembered the tragedy of the unfortunate Adams and the still more unfortunate Colt in the solitary office of the latter; and how poor Colt, being dreadfully incensed by Adams, and imprudently permitting himself to get wildly excited, was at unawares hurried into his fatal act—an act which certainly no man could possibly deplore more than the actor himself. Often it had occurred to me in my ponderings upon the subject that had that altercation taken place in the public street, or at a private residence, it would not have terminated as it did. It was the circumstance of being alone in a solitary office, upstairs, of a building entirely unhallowed by humanizing domestic associations—an uncarpeted office, doubtless, of a dusty, haggard sort of appearance—this it must have been which greatly helped to enhance the irritable desperation of the hapless Colt.

But when this old Adam of resentment rose in me and tempted me concerning Bartleby, I grappled him and threw him. How? Why, simply by recalling the divine injunction: "A new commandment give I unto you, that ye love one another." Yes, this it was that saved me. Aside from higher considerations, charity often operates as a vastly wise and prudent principle—a great safeguard to its possessor. Men have committed murder for jealousy's sake, and anger's sake, and hatred's sake, and selfishness' sake, and spiritual pride's sake; but no man that ever I heard of ever committed a diabolical murder for sweet charity's sake. Mere self-interest, then, if no better motive can be enlisted, should, especially with high-tempered men, prompt all beings to charity and philanthropy. At any rate, upon the occasion in question, I strove to drown my exasperated feelings towards the scrivener by benevolently construing his conduct. Poor fellow, poor fellow! thought I, he don't mean anything, and besides, he has seen hard times, and ought to be indulged.

I endeavored, also, immediately to occupy myself, and at the same time to comfort my despondency. I tried to fancy that in the course of the morning, at such time as might prove agreeable to him, Bartleby, of his own free accord, would emerge from his hermitage and take up some decided line of march in the direction of the door. But no. Half-past twelve o'clock came; Turkey began to glow in the face, overturn his inkstand, and become generally obstreperous; Nippers abated down into quietude and courtesy; Ginger Nut munched his noon apple; and Bartleby remained standing at his window in one of his profoundest dead-wall reveries. Will it be credited? Ought I to acknowledge it? That afternoon I left the office without saying one further word to him.

Some days now passed during which, at leisure intervals, I looked a little into "Edwards on the Will," and "Priestley on Necessity." Under the circumstances, those books induced a salutary feeling. Gradually I slid into the persuasion that these troubles of mine touching the scrivener had been all predestinated from eternity, and Bartleby was billeted upon me for some mysterious purpose of an all-wise Providence, which it was not for a mere mortal like me to fathom. Yes, Bartleby, stay there behind your screen, thought I; I shall persecute you no more; you are harmless and noiseless as any of these old chairs; in short, I never feel so private as when I know you are here. At last I see it, I feel it; I penetrate to the predestinated purpose of my life. I am content. Others may have loftier parts to enact, but my mission in this world, Bartleby, is to furnish you with office room for such period as you may see fit to remain.

I believe that this wise and blessed frame of mind would have continued with me had it not been for the unsolicited and uncharitable remarks obtruded upon me by my professional friends who visited the rooms. But thus it often is that the constant friction of illiberal minds wears out at last the best resolves of the more generous. Though, to be sure, when I reflected upon it it was not strange that people entering my office should be struck by the peculiar aspect of the unaccountable Bartleby, and so be tempted to throw out some sinister observations concerning him. Sometimes an attorney having business with me, and calling at my office, and finding no one but the scrivener there, would undertake to obtain some sort of precise information from him touching my whereabouts; but without heeding his idle talk, Bartleby would remain standing immovable in the middle of the room.

So, after contemplating him in that position for a time, the attorney would depart no wiser than he came.

Also, when a reference was going on, and the room full of lawyers and witnesses, and business driving fast, some deeply-occupied legal gentleman present, seeing Bartleby wholly unemployed, would request him to run round to his (the legal gentleman's) office and fetch some papers for him. Thereupon Bartleby would tranquilly decline, and yet remain idle as before. Then the lawyer would give a great stare, and turn to me. And what could I say? At last I was made aware that all through the circle of my professional acquaintance a whisper of wonder was running round, having reference to the strange creature I kept at my office. This worried me very much. And as the idea came upon me of his possibly turning out a long-lived man, and keep occupying my chambers, and denying my authority; and perplexing my visitors; and scandalizing my professional reputation; and casting a general gloom over the premises; keeping soul and body together to the last upon his savings (for doubtless he spent but half a dime a day), and in the end perhaps outlive me, and claim possession of my office by right of his perpetual occupancy—as all these dark anticipations crowded upon me more and more, and my friends continually intruded their relentless remarks upon the apparition in my room, a great change was wrought in me. I resolved to gather all my faculties together and forever rid me of this intolerable incubus.

Ere revolving any complicated project, however, adapted to this end, I first simply suggested to Bartleby the propriety of his permanent departure. In a calm and serious tone, I commended the idea to his careful and mature consideration. But, having taken three days to meditate upon it, he apprised me that his original determination remained the same; in short, that he still preferred to abide with me.

What shall I do? I now said to myself, buttoning up my coat to the last button. What shall I do? what ought I to do? what does conscience say I *should* do with this man, or, rather, ghost. Rid myself of him, I must; go, he shall. But how? You will not thrust him, the poor, pale, passive mortal—you will not thrust such a helpless creature out of your door? you will not dishonor yourself by such cruelty? No, I will not, I cannot do that. Rather would I let him live and die here, and then mason up his remains in the wall. What, then, will you do? For all your coaxing, he will not budge. Bribes he leaves under your own paperweight on your table; in short, it is quite plain that he prefers to cling to you.

Then something severe, something unusual, must be done. What! surely you will not have him collared by a constable, and commit his innocent pallor to the common jail? And upon what ground could you procure such a thing to be done?—a vagrant, is he? What! he a vagrant, a wanderer, who refuses to budge? It is because he will *not* be a vagrant, then, that you seek to count him *as* a vagrant. That is too absurd. No visible means of support: there I have him. Wrong again: for indubitably he *does* support himself, and that is the only unanswerable proof that any man can show of his possessing the means so to do. No more, then. Since he will not quit me, I must quit him. I will change my offices; I will move elsewhere, and give him fair notice that if I find him on my new premises I will then proceed against him as a common trespasser.

Acting accordingly, next day I thus addressed him: "I find these chambers too far from the City Hall; the air is unwholesome. In a word, I propose to remove my offices next week, and shall no longer require your services. I tell you this now, in order that you may seek another place."

He made no reply, and nothing more was said.

On the appointed day I engaged carts and men, proceeded to my chambers, and, having but little furniture, everything was removed in a few hours. Throughout, the scrivener remained standing behind the screen, which I directed to be removed the last thing. It was withdrawn; and, being folded up like a huge folio, left him the motionless occupant of a naked room. I stood in the entry watching him a moment, while something from within me upbraided me.

I re-entered, with my hand in my pocket—and—and—my heart in my mouth.

"Goody-bye, Bartleby; I am going—good-bye; and God some way bless you; and take that," slipping something in his hand. But it dropped upon the floor, and then—strange to say—I tore myself from him whom I had so longed to be rid of.

Established in my new quarters, for a day or two I kept the door locked, and started at every footfall in the passages. When I returned to my rooms after my little absence, I would pause at the threshold for an instant and attentively listen ere applying my key. But these fears were needless. Bartleby never came nigh me.

I thought all was going well, when a perturbed-looking stranger visited me, inquiring whether I was the person who had recently occupied rooms at No. — Wall Street.

Full of forebodings, I replied that I was.

"Then, sir," said the stranger, who proved a lawyer, "you are responsible for the man you left there. He refuses to do any copying; he refuses to do anything; he says he prefers not to; and he refuses to quit the premises."

"I am very sorry, sir," said I, with assumed tranquillity, but an inward tremor, "but, really, the man you allude to is nothing to me —he is no relation or apprentice of mine, that you should hold me responsible for him."

"In mercy's name, who is he?"

"I certainly cannot inform you. I know nothing about him. Formerly I employed him as a copyist; but he has done nothing for me now for some time past."

"I shall settle him, then—good morning, sir."

Several days passed, and I heard nothing more; and, though I often felt a charitable prompting to call at the place and see poor Bartleby, yet a certain squeamishness, of I know not what, withheld me.

All is over with him, by this time, thought I at last, when, through another week, no further intelligence reached me. But, coming to my room the day after, I found several persons waiting at my door in a high state of nervous excitement.

"That's the man—here he comes," cried the foremost one, whom I recognized as the lawyer who had previously called upon me alone.

"You must take him away, sir, at once," cried a portly person among them, advancing upon me, and whom I knew to be the landlord of No. — Wall Street. "These gentlemen, my tenants, cannot stand it any longer; Mr. B——," pointing to the lawyer, "has turned him out of his room, and he now persists in haunting the building generally, sitting upon the banisters of the stairs by day, and sleeping in the entry by night. Everybody is concerned; clients are leaving the offices; some fears are entertained of a mob; something you must do, and that without delay."

Aghast at this torrent, I fell back before it, and would fain have locked myself in my new quarters. In vain I persisted that Bartleby was nothing to me—no more than to anyone else. In vain—I was the last person known to have anything to do with him, and they held me to the terrible account. Fearful, then, of being exposed in the papers (as one person present obscurely threatened), I considered the matter, and at length said that if the lawyer would give me a confidential interview with the scrivener, in his (the lawyer's) own room, I would, that afternoon, strive my best to rid them of the nuisance they complained of.

Going upstairs to my old haunt, there was Bartleby silently sitting upon the banister at the landing.

"What are you doing here, Bartleby?" said I.

"Sitting upon the banister," he mildly replied.

I motioned him into the lawyer's room, who then left us.

"Bartleby," said I, "are you aware that you are the cause of great tribulation to me, by persisting in occupying the entry after being dismissed from the office?"

No answer.

"Now one of two things must take place. Either you must do something, or something must be done to you. Now what sort of business would you like to engage in? Would you like to re-engage in copying for someone?"

"No; I would prefer not to make any change."

"Would you like a clerkship in a dry-goods store?"

"There is too much confinement about that. No, I would not like a clerkship; but I am not particular."

"Too much confinement," I cried; "why you keep yourself confined all the time!"

"I would prefer not to take a clerkship," he rejoined, as if to settle that little item at once.

"How would a bartender's business suit you? There is no trying of the eyesight in that."

"I would not like it at all; though, as I said before, I am not particular."

His unwonted wordiness inspirited me. I returned to the charge.

"Well, then, would you like to travel through the country collecting bills for the merchants? That would improve your health."

"No, I would prefer to be doing something else."

"How, then, would going as a companion to Europe, to entertain some young gentleman with your conversation—how would that suit you?"

"Not at all. It does not strike me that there is anything definite about that. I like to be stationary. But I am not particular."

"Stationary you shall be, then," I cried, now losing all patience, and, for the first time in all my exasperating connection with him, fairly flying into a passion. "If you do not go away from these premises before night, I shall feel bound—indeed, I *am* bound—to—to—to quit the premises myself!" I rather absurdly concluded, knowing not with what possible threat to try to frighten his immobility into compliance. Despairing of all further efforts, I was precipitately leaving him, when a final thought occurred to me—one which had not been wholly unindulged before.

"Bartleby," said I, in the kindest tone I could assume under such exciting circumstances, "will you go home with me now—not to my office, but my dwelling—and remain there till we can conclude upon some convenient arrangement for you at our leisure? Come, let us start now, right away."

"No; at present I would prefer not to make any change at all."

I answered nothing, but, effectually dodging everyone by the suddenness and rapidity of my flight, rushed from the building, ran up Wall Street towards Broadway, and, jumping into the first omnibus, was soon removed from pursuit. As soon as tranquillity returned, I distinctly perceived that I had now done all that I possibly could, both in respect to the demands of the landlord and his tenants, and with regard to my own desire and sense of duty, to benefit Bartleby, and shield him from rude persecution. I now strove to be entirely carefree and quiescent, and my conscience justified me in the attempt, though, indeed, it was not so successful as I could have wished. So fearful was I of being again hunted out by the incensed landlord and his exasperated tenants that, surrendering my business to Nippers for a few days, I drove about the upper part of the town and through the suburbs in my rockaway; crossed over to Jersey City and Hoboken, and paid fugitive visits to Manhattanville and Astoria. In fact, I almost lived in my rockaway for the time.

When again I entered my office, lo, a note from the landlord lay upon the desk. I opened it with trembling hands. It informed me that the writer had sent to the police, and had Bartleby removed to the Tombs as a vagrant. Moreover, since I knew more about him than anyone else, he wished me to appear at that place and make a suitable statement of the facts. These tidings had a conflicting effect upon me. At first I was indignant, but at last almost approved. The landlord's energetic, summary disposition had led him to adopt a procedure which I do not think I would have decided upon myself; and yet, as a last resort, under such peculiar circumstances, it seemed the only plan.

As I afterwards learned, the poor scrivener, when told that he must be conducted to the Tombs, offered not the slightest obstacle, but, in his pale, unmoving way, silently acquiesced.

Some of the compassionate and curious bystanders joined the party, and, headed by one of the constables arm in arm with Bartleby, the silent procession filed its way through all the noise, and heat, and joy of the roaring thoroughfares at noon.

The same day I received the note, I went to the Tombs, or, to speak more properly, the Halls of Justice. Seeking the right officer, I stated the purpose of my call, and was informed that the individual I described was indeed within. I then assured the functionary that Bartleby was a perfectly honest man, and greatly to be compassionated, however unaccountably eccentric. I narrated all I knew, and closed by suggesting the idea of letting him remain in as indulgent confinement as possible till something less harsh might be done—though, indeed, I hardly knew what. At all events, if nothing else could be decided upon, the almshouse must receive him. I then begged to have an interview.

Being under no disgraceful charge, and quite serene and harmless in all his ways, they had permitted him freely to wander about the prison, and, especially, in the inclosed grass-platted yards thereof. And so I found him there, standing all alone in the quietest of the yards, his face towards a high wall, while all around, from the narrow slits of the jail windows, I thought I saw peering out upon him the eyes of murderers and thieves.

"Bartleby!"

"I know you," he said, without looking round—"and I want nothing to say to you."

"It was not I that brought you here, Bartleby," said I, keenly pained at his implied suspicion. "And, to you, this should not be so vile a place. Nothing reproachful attaches to you by being here. And see, it is not so sad a place as one might think. Look, there is the sky, and here is the grass."

"I know where I am," he replied, but would say nothing more, and so I left him.

As I entered the corridor again, a broad meatlike man in an apron accosted me, and, jerking his thumb over his shoulder, said—"Is that your friend?"

"Yes."

"Does he want to starve? If he does, let him live on the prison fare, that's all."

"Who are you?" asked I, not knowing what to make of such an unofficially speaking person in such a place.

"I am the grubman. Such gentlemen as have friends here hire me to provide them with something good to eat."

"Is this so?" said I, turning to the turnkey.

He said it was.

"Well, then," said I, slipping some silver into the grubman's hands (for so they called him), "I want you to give particular attention to my friend there; let him have the best dinner you can get. And you must be as polite to him as possible."

"Introduce me, will you?" said the grubman, looking at me with an expression which seemed to say he was all impatience for an opportunity to give a specimen of his breeding.

Thinking it would prove of benefit to the scrivener, I acquiesced, and, asking the grubman his name, went up with him to Bartleby.

"Bartleby, this is a friend; you will find him very useful to you."

"Your sarvant, sir, your sarvant," said the grubman, making a low salutation behind his apron. "Hope you find it pleasant here, sir; nice grounds—cool apartments—hope you'll stay with us some time—try to make it agreeable. What will you have for dinner today?"

"I prefer not to dine today," said Bartleby, turning away. "It would disagree with me; I am unused to dinners." So saying, he slowly moved to the other side of the inclosure and took up a position fronting the dead-wall.

"How's this?" said the grubman, addressing me with a stare of astonishment. "He's odd, ain't he?"

"I think he is a little deranged," said I, sadly.

"Deranged? deranged is it? Well, now, upon my word, I thought that friend of yourn was a gentleman forger; they are always pale and genteel-like, them forgers. I can't help pity 'em—can't help, sir. Did you know Monroe Edwards?" he added, touchingly, and paused. Then, laying his hand piteously on my shoulder, sighed, "he died of consumption at Sing-Sing. So you weren't acquainted with Monroe?"

"No, I was never socially acquainted with any forgers. But I cannot stop longer. Look to my friend yonder. You will not lose by it. I will see you again."

Some few days after this, I again obtained admission to the Tombs, and went through the corridors in quest of Bartleby; but without finding him.

"I saw him coming from his cell not long ago," said a turnkey, "maybe he's gone to loiter in the yards."

So I went in that direction.

"Are you looking for the silent man?" said another turnkey, passing me. "Yonder he lies—sleeping in the yard there. 'Tis not twenty minutes since I saw him lie down."

The yard was entirely quiet. It was not accessible to the common prisoners. The surrounding walls, of amazing thickness, kept off all sounds behind them. The Egyptian character of the masonry weighed upon me with its gloom. But a soft imprisoned turf grew underfoot. The heart of the eternal pyramids, it seemed, wherein, by some strange magic, through the clefts, grass-seed, dropped by birds, had sprung.

Strangely huddled at the base of the wall, his knees drawn up and lying on his side, his head touching the cold stones, I saw the wasted Bartleby. But nothing stirred. I paused, then went close up to him, stooped over, and saw that his dim eyes were open; otherwise he seemed profoundly sleeping. Something prompted me to touch him. I felt his hand, when a tingling shiver ran up my arm and down my spine to my feet.

The round face of the grubman peered upon me now. "His dinner is ready. Won't he dine today, either? Or does he live without dining?"

"Lives without dining," said I, and closed the eyes.

"Eh!—He's asleep, ain't he?"

"With kings and counselors," murmured I.

*   *   *

There would seem little need for proceeding further in this history. Imagination will readily supply the meager recital of poor Bartleby's interment. But, ere parting with the reader, let me say that if this little narrative has sufficiently interested him to awaken curiosity as to who Bartleby was, and what manner of life he led prior to the present narrator's making his acquaintance, I can only reply that in such curiosity I fully share, but am wholly unable to gratify it. Yet here I hardly know whether I should divulge one little item of rumor which came to my ear a few months after the scrivener's decease. Upon what basis it rested, I could never ascertain, and hence how true it is I cannot now tell. But, inasmuch as this vague report has not been without a certain suggestive interest to me, however sad, it may prove the same with some others, and so I will briefly mention it. The report was this: that Bartleby had been a subordinate clerk in the Dead Letter Office at Washington, from which he had been suddenly removed by a change in the administration. When I think over this rumor, hardly can I express the emotions which seize me. Dead letters! does it not sound like dead men? Conceive a man by nature and misfortune prone to a pallid hopelessness, can any business seem more fitted to heighten it than that of continually handling these dead letters, and assorting them for the flames? For by the cartload they are annually burned. Sometimes from out the folded paper the pale clerk takes a ring—the finger it was meant for, perhaps, molders in the grave; a bank note sent in swiftest charity—he whom it would relieve nor eats nor hungers any more; pardon for those who died despairing; hope for those who died unhoping; good tidings for those who died stifled by unrelieved calamities. On errands of life, these letters speed to death.

Ah, Bartleby! Ah, humanity!

HENRY JAMES (1843-1916)

The Real Thing

I

When the porter's wife, who used to answer the house-bell, announced "A gentleman and a lady, sir," I had, as I often had in those days—the wish being father to the thought—an immediate vision of sitters. Sitters my visitors in this case proved to be; but not in the sense I should have preferred. There was nothing at first however to indicate that they mightn't have come for a portrait. The gentleman, a man of fifty, very high and very straight, with a moustache slightly grizzled and a dark gray walking-coat admirably fitted, both of which I noted professionally—I don't mean as a barber or yet as a tailor—would have struck me as a celebrity if celebrities often were striking. It was a truth of which I had for some time been conscious that a figure with a good deal of frontage was, as one might say, almost never a public institution. A glance at the lady helped to remind me of this paradoxical law: she also looked too distinguished to be a "personality." Moreover one would scarcely come across two variations together.

Neither of the pair immediately spoke—they only prolonged the preliminary gaze suggesting that each wished to give the other a chance. They were visibly shy; they stood there letting me take them in —which, as I afterwards perceived, was the most practical thing they could have done. In this way their embarrassment served their cause. I had seen people painfully reluctant to mention that they desired anything so gross as to be represented on canvas; but the scruples of my new friends appeared almost insurmountable. Yet the gentleman might have said "I should like a portrait of my wife," and the lady might have said "I should like a portrait of my husband." Perhaps they weren't husband and wife—this naturally would make the matter more delicate. Perhaps they wished to be done together—in which case they ought to have brought a third person to break the news.

"We come from Mr. Rivet," the lady finally said with a dim smile that had the effect of a moist sponge passed over a "sunk" piece of painting, as well as of a vague allusion to vanished beauty. She was as tall and straight, in her degree, as her companion, and with ten years less to carry. She looked as sad as a woman could look whose face was not charged with expression; that is her tinted oval mask showed waste as an exposed surface shows friction. The hand of time had played over her freely, but to an effect of elimination. She was slim and stiff, and so well-dressed, in dark blue cloth, with lappets and pockets and buttons, that it was clear she employed the same tailor as her husband. The couple had an indefinable air of prosperous thrift—they evidently got a good deal of luxury for their money. If I was to be one of their luxuries it would behoove me to consider my terms.

"Ah Claude Rivet recommended me?" I echoed; and I added that it was very kind of him, though I could reflect that, as he only painted landscape, this wasn't a sacrifice.

The lady looked very hard at the gentleman, and the gentleman looked round the room. Then staring at the floor a moment and stroking his moustache, he rested his pleasant eyes on me with the remark: "He said you were the right one."

"I try to be, when people want to sit."

"Yes, we should like to," said the lady anxiously.

"Do you mean together?"

My visitors exchanged a glance. "If you could do anything with *me* I suppose it would be double," the gentleman stammered.

"Oh yes, there's naturally a higher charge for two figures than for one."

"We should like to make it pay," the husband confessed.

"That's very good of you," I returned, appreciating so unwonted a sympathy—for I supposed he meant pay the artist.

A sense of strangeness seemed to dawn on the lady. "We mean for the illustrations—Mr. Rivet said you might put one in."

"Put in—an illustration?" I was equally confused.

"Sketch her off, you know," said the gentleman, coloring.

It was only then that I understood the service Claude Rivet had rendered me; he had told them how I worked in black-and-white, for magazines, for storybooks, for sketches of contemporary life, and consequently had copious employment for models. These things were true, but it was not less true—I may confess it now; whether because the aspiration was to lead to everything or to nothing I leave the reader to guess—that I couldn't get the honors, to say nothing of the emoluments, of a great painter of portraits out of my head. My "illustrations" were my pot-boilers; I looked to a different branch of art—far and away the most interesting it had always seemed to me—to perpetuate my fame. There was no shame in looking to it also to make my fortune; but that fortune was by so much further from being made from the moment my visitors wished to be "done" for nothing. I was disappointed; for in the pictorial sense I had immediately *seen* them. I had seized their type—I had already settled what I would do with it. Something that wouldn't absolutely have pleased them, I afterwards reflected.

"Ah you're—you're—a—?" I began as soon as I had mastered my surprise. I couldn't bring out the dingy word "models": it seemed so little to fit the case.

"We haven't had much practice," said the lady.

"We've got to *do* something, and we've thought that an artist in your line might perhaps make something of us," her husband threw off. He further mentioned that they didn't know many artists and that they had gone first, on the off-chance—he painted views of course, but sometimes put in figures; perhaps I remembered—to Mr. Rivet, whom they had met a few years before at a place in Norfolk where he was sketching.

"We used to sketch a little ourselves," the lady hinted.

"It's very awkward, but we absolutely *must* do something," her husband went on.

"Of course we're not so *very* young," she admitted with a wan smile.

With the remark that I might as well know something more about them the husband had handed me a card extracted from a neat new pocket-book—their appurtenances were all of the freshest—and inscribed with the words "Major Monarch." Impressive as these words were they didn't carry my knowledge much further; but my visitor presently added: "I've left the army and we've had the misfortune to lose our money. In fact our means are dreadfully small."

"It's awfully trying—a regular strain," said Mrs. Monarch.

They evidently wished to be discreet—to take care not to swagger because they were gentlefolk. I felt them willing to recognize this as something of a drawback, at the same time that I guessed at an underlying sense—their consolation in adversity—that they *had* their points. They certainly had; but these advantages struck me as preponderantly social; such for instance as would help to make a drawing-room look well. However, a drawing-room was always, or ought to be, a picture.

In consequence of his wife's allusion to their age Major Monarch observed: "Naturally it's more for the figure that we thought of going in. We can still hold ourselves up." On the instant I saw that the figure was indeed their strong point. His "naturally" didn't sound vain, but it lighted up the question. "*She* has the best one," he continued, nodding at his wife with a pleasant after-dinner absence of circumlocution. I could only reply, as if we were in fact sitting over our wine, that this didn't prevent his own from being very good; which led him in turn to make answer: "We thought that if you ever have to do people like us we might be something like it. *She* particularly—for a lady in a book, you know."

I was so amused by them that, to get more of it, I did my best to take their point of view; and though it was an embarrassment to find myself appraising physically, as if they were animals on hire or useful blacks, a pair whom I should have expected to meet only in one of the relations in which criticism is tacit, I looked at Mrs. Monarch judicially enough to be able to exclaim after a moment with conviction: "Oh yes, a lady in a book!" She was singularly like a bad illustration.

"We'll stand up, if you like," said the Major; and he raised himself before me with a really grand air.

I could take his measure at a glance—he was six feet two and a perfect gentleman. It would have paid any club in process of formation and in want of a stamp to engage him at a salary to stand in the principal window. What struck me at once was that in coming to me they had rather missed their vocation; they could surely have been turned to better account for advertising purposes. I couldn't of course see the thing in detail, but I could see them make somebody's fortune—I don't mean their own. There was something in them for a waistcoat-maker, an hotel-keeper or a soap-vendor. I could imagine "We always use it" pinned on their bosoms with the greatest effect; I had a vision of the brilliancy with which they would launch a table d'hôte.

Mrs. Monarch sat still, not from pride but from shyness, and presently her husband said to her: "Get up, my dear, and show how smart you are." She obeyed, but she had no need to get up to show it. She walked to the end of the studio and then came back blushing, her fluttered eyes on the partner of her appeal. I was reminded of an incident I had accidentally had a glimpse of in Paris—being with a friend there, a dramatist about to produce a play, when an actress came to him to ask to be entrusted with a part. She went through her paces before him, walked up and down as Mrs. Monarch was doing. Mrs. Monarch did it quite as well, but I abstained from applauding. It was very odd to see such people apply for such poor pay. She looked as if she had ten thousand a year. Her husband had used the word that described her: she was in the London current jargon essentially and typically "smart." Her figure was, in the same order of ideas, conspicuously and irreproachably "good." For a woman of her age her waist was surprisingly small; her elbow moreover had the orthodox crook. She held her head at the conventional angle, but why did she come to *me*? She ought to have tried on jackets at a big shop. I feared my visitors were not only destitute but "artistic"—which would be a great complication. When she sat down again I thanked her, observing that what a draughtsman most values in his model was the faculty of keeping quiet.

"Oh *she* can keep quiet," said Major Monarch. Then he added jocosely: "I've always kept her quiet."

"I'm not a nasty fidget, am I?" It was going to wring tears from me, I felt, the way she hid her head, ostrich-like, in the other broad bosom.

The owner of this expanse addressed his answer to me. "Perhaps it isn't out of place to mention—because we ought to be quite business-like, oughtn't we?—that when I married her she was known as the Beautiful Statue."

"Oh dear!" said Mrs. Monarch ruefully.

"Of course I should want a certain amount of expression," I rejoined.

"Of *course*!"—and I had never heard such unanimity.

"And then I suppose you know that you'll get awfully tired."

"Oh, we *never* get tired!" they eagerly cried.

"Have you had any kind of practice?"

They hesitated—they looked at each other. "We've been photographed—*immensely*," said Mrs. Monarch.

"She means the fellows have asked us themselves," added the Major.

"I see—because you're so good-looking."

"I don't know what they thought, but they were always after us."

"We always got our photographs for nothing," smiled Mrs. Monarch.

"We might have brought some, my dear," her husband remarked.

"I'm not sure we have any left. We've given quantities away," she explained to me.

"With our autographs and that sort of thing," said the Major.

"Are they to be got in the shops?" I enquired as a harmless pleasantry.

"Oh yes, *hers*—they used to be."

"Not now," said Mrs. Monarch with her eyes on the floor.

II

I could fancy the "sort of thing" they put on the presentation copies of their photographs, and I was sure they wrote a beautiful hand. It was odd how quickly I was sure of everything that concerned them. If they were now so poor as to have to earn shillings and pence they could never have had much of a margin. Their good looks had been their capital, and they had good-humoredly made the most of the career that this resource marked out for them. It was in their faces, the blankness, the deep intellectual repose of the twenty years of country-house visiting that had given them pleasant intonations. I could see the sunny drawing-rooms, sprinkled with periodicals she didn't read, in which Mrs. Monarch had continuously sat; I could see the wet shrubberies in which she had walked, equipped to admiration for either exercise. I could see the rich covers the Major had helped to shoot and the wonderful garments in which, late at night, he repaired to the smoking-room to talk about them. I could imagine their leggings and waterproofs, their knowing tweeds and rugs, their rolls of sticks and cases of tackle and neat umbrellas; and I could evoke the exact appearance of their servants and the compact variety of their luggage on the platforms of country stations.

They gave small tips, but they were liked; they didn't do anything themselves, but they were welcome. They looked so well everywhere; they gratified the general relish for stature, complexion and "form." They knew it without fatuity or vulgarity, and they respected themselves in consequence. They weren't superficial; they were thorough and kept themselves up—it had been their line. People with such a taste for activity had to have some line. I could feel how even in a dull house they could have been counted on for the joy of life. At present something had happened—it didn't matter what, their little income had grown less, it had grown least—and they had to do something for pocket-money. Their friends could like them, I made out, without liking to support them. There was something about them that represented credit—their clothes, their manners, their type; but if credit is a large empty pocket in which an occasional chink reverberates, the chink at least must be audible. What they wanted of me was to help to make it so. Fortunately they had no children—I soon divined that. They would also perhaps wish our relations to be kept secret: this was why it was "for the figure"—the reproduction of the face would betray them.

I liked them—I felt, quite as their friends must have done—they were so simple; and I had no objection to them if they would suit. But somehow with all their perfections I didn't easily believe in them. After all they were amateurs, and the ruling passion of my life was the detestation of the amateur. Combined with this was another perversity —an innate preference for the represented subject over the real one: the defect of the real one was so apt to be a lack of representation. I like things that appeared; then one was sure. Whether they *were* or not was a subordinate and almost always a profitless question. There were other considerations, the first of which was that I already had two or three recruits in use, notably a young person with big feet, in alpaca, from Kilburn, who for a couple of years had come to me regularly for my illustrations and with whom I was still—perhaps ignobly —satisfied. I frankly explained to my visitors how the case stood, but they had taken more precautions than I supposed. They had reasoned out their opportunity, for Claude Rivet had told them of the projected *édition de luxe* of one of the writers of our day—the rarest of the novelists—who, long neglected by the multitudinous vulgar and dearly prized by the attentive (need I mention Philip Vincent?) had had the happy fortune of seeing, late in life, the dawn and then the full light of a higher criticism; an estimate in which on the part of the public there was something really of expiation. The edition preparing, planned by a publisher of taste, was practically an act of high reparation; the wood-cuts with which it was to be enriched were the homage of English art to one of the most independent representatives of English letters. Major and Mrs. Monarch confessed to me they had hoped I might be able to work *them* into my branch of the enterprise. They knew I was to do the first of the books, "Rutland Ramsay," but I had to make clear to them that my participation in the rest of the affair—

this first book was to be a test—must depend on the satisfaction I should give. If this should be limited my employers would drop me with scarce common forms. It was therefore a crisis for me, and naturally I was making special preparations, looking about for new people, should they be necessary, and securing the best types. I admitted however that I should like to settle down to two or three good models who would do for everything.

"Should we have often to—a—put on special clothes?" Mrs. Monarch timidly demanded.

"Dear yes—that's half the business."

"And should we be expected to supply our own costumes?"

"Oh no; I've got a lot of things. A painter's models put on—or put off—anything he likes."

"And you mean—a—the same?"

"The same?"

Mrs. Monarch looked at her husband again.

"Oh she was just wondering," he explained, "if the costumes are in *general* use." I had to confess that they were, and I mentioned further that some of them—I had a lot of genuine greasy last-century things—had served their time, a hundred years ago, on living world-stained men and women; on figures not perhaps so far removed, in that vanished world, from *their* type, the Monarchs', *quoi!* of a breeched and bewigged age. "We'll put on anything that *fits*," said the Major.

"Oh I arrange that—they fit in the pictures."

"I'm afraid I should do better for the modern books. I'd come as you like," said Mrs. Monarch.

"She has got a lot of clothes at home: they might do for contemporary life," her husband continued.

"Oh I can fancy scenes in which you'd be quite natural." And indeed I could see the slipshod rearrangements of stale properties—the stories I tried to produce pictures for without the exasperation of reading them—whose sandy tracts the good lady might help to people. But I had to return to the fact that for this sort of work—the daily mechanical grind—I was already equipped: the people I was working with were fully adequate.

"We only thought we might be more like *some* characters," said Mrs. Monarch mildly, getting up.

Her husband also rose; he stood looking at me with a dim wistfulness that was touching in so fine a man. "Wouldn't it be rather a pull sometimes to have—a—to have—?" He hung fire; he wanted me to help him by phrasing what he meant. But I couldn't—I didn't know. So he brought it out awkwardly: "The *real* thing; a gentleman, you know, or a lady." I was quite ready to give a general assent—I admitted that there was a great deal in that. This encouraged Major Monarch to say, following up his appeal with an unacted gulp: "It's awfully hard —we've tried everything." The gulp was communicative; it proved too much for his wife. Before I knew it Mrs. Monarch had dropped again upon a divan and burst into tears. Her husband sat down beside her, holding one of her hands; whereupon she quickly dried her eyes with the other, while I felt embarrassed as she looked up at me. "There isn't a confounded job I haven't applied for—waited for—prayed for. You can fancy we'd be pretty bad first. Secretaryships and that sort of thing? You might as well ask for a peerage. I'd be *anything*—I'm strong; a messenger or a coalheaver. I'd put on a gold-laced cap and open carriage-doors in front of the haberdasher's; I'd hang about a station to carry portmanteaux; I'd be a postman. But they won't *look* at you; there are thousands as good as yourself already on the ground. *Gentlemen*, poor beggars, who've drunk their wine, who've kept their hunters!"

I was as reassuring as I knew how to be, and my visitors were presently on their feet again while, for the experiment, we agreed on an hour. We were discussing it when the door opened and Miss Churm came in with a wet umbrella. Miss Churm had to take the omnibus to Maida Vale and then walk half a mile. She looked a trifle blowsy and slightly splashed. I scarcely ever saw her come in without thinking afresh how odd it was that, being so little in herself, she should yet be so much in others. She was a meager little Miss Churm, but was such an ample heroine of romance. She was only a freckled cockney, but she could represent everything, from a fine lady to a shepherdess; she had the faculty as she might have had a fine voice or long hair. She couldn't spell and she loved beer, but she had two or three "points," and practice, and a knack, and mother-wit, and a whimsical sensibility, and love of the theater, and seven sisters, and not an ounce of respect, especially for the *h*. The first thing my visitors saw was that her umbrella was wet, and in their spotless perfection they visibly winced at it. The rain had come on since their arrival.

"I'm all in a soak; there *was* a mess of people in the 'bus. I wish you lived near a stytion," said Miss Churm. I requested her to get ready as quickly as possible, and she passed into the room in which she always changed her dress. But before going out she asked me what she was to get into this time.

"It's the Russian princess, don't you know?" I answered; "the one with the 'golden eyes,' in black velvet, for the long thing in the *Cheapside*."

"Golden eyes? I *say*!" cried Miss Churm, while my companions watched her with intensity as she withdrew. She always arranged herself, when she was late, before I could turn round; and I kept my visitors a little on purpose, so that they might get an idea, from seeing her, what would be expected of themselves. I mentioned that she was quite my notion of an excellent model—she was really very clever.

"Do you think she looks like a Russian princess?" Major Monarch asked with lurking alarm.

"When I make her, yes."

"Oh if you have to *make* her—!" he reasoned, not without point.

"That's the most you can ask. There are so many who are not makeable."

"Well now, *here's* a lady"—and with a persuasive smile he passed his arm into his wife's—"who's already made!"

"Oh I'm not a Russian princess," Mrs. Monarch protested a little coldly. I could see she had known some and didn't like them. There at once was a complication of a kind I never had to fear with Miss Churm.

This young lady came back in black velvet—the gown was rather rusty and very low on her lean shoulders—and with a Japanese fan in her red hands. I reminded her that in the scene I was doing she had to look over some one's head. "I forget whose it is; but it doesn't matter. Just look over a head."

"I'd rather look over a stove," said Miss Churm; and she took her station near the fire. She fell into position, settled herself into a tall attitude, gave a certain backward inclination to her head and a certain forward droop to her fan, and looked, at least to my prejudiced sense, distinguished and charming, foreign and dangerous. We left her looking so while I went downstairs with Major and Mrs. Monarch.

"I believe I could come about as near it as that," said Mrs. Monarch.

"Oh you think she's shabby, but you must allow for the alchemy of art."

However, they went off with an evident increase of comfort founded on their demonstrable advantage in being the real thing. I could fancy them shuddering over Miss Churm. She was very droll about them when I went back, for I told her what they wanted.

"Well, if *she* can sit I'll tyke to book-keeping," said my model.

"She's very ladylike," I replied as an innocent form of aggravation.

"So much the worse for *you*. That means she can't turn round."

"She'll do for the fashionable novels."

"Oh yes, she'll *do* for them!" my model humorously declared. "Ain't they bad enough without her?" I had often sociably denounced them to Miss Churm.

It was for the elucidation of a mystery in one of these works that I first tried Mrs. Monarch. Her husband came with her, to be useful if necessary—it was sufficiently clear that as a general thing he would prefer to come with her. At first I wondered if this were for "propriety's" sake—if he were going to be jealous and meddling. The idea was too tiresome, and if it had been confirmed it would speedily have brought our acquaintance to a close. But I soon saw there was nothing in it and that if he accompanied Mrs. Monarch it was—in addition to the chance of being wanted—simply because he had nothing else to do. When they were separate his occupation was gone and they never *had* been separate. I judged rightly that in their awkward situation their close union was their main comfort and that this union had no weak spot. It was a real marriage, an encouragement to the hesitating, a nut for pessimists to crack. Their address was humble—I remember afterwards thinking it had been the only thing about them that was really professional—and I could fancy the lamentable lodgings in which the Major would have been left alone. He could sit there more or less grimly with his wife—he couldn't sit there anyhow without her.

He had too much tact to try and make himself agreeable when he couldn't be useful; so when I was too absorbed in my work to talk he simply sat and waited. But I liked to hear him talk—it made my work, when not interrupting it, less mechanical, less special. To listen to him was to combine the excitement of going out with the economy of staying at home. There was only one hindrance—that I seemed not to know any of the people this brilliant couple had known. I think he wondered extremely, during the term of our intercourse, whom the deuce I *did* know. He hadn't a stray sixpence of an idea to fumble for, so we didn't spin it very fine; we confined ourselves to questions of leather and even of liquor—saddlers and breeches-makers and how to get excellent claret cheap—and matters like "good trains" and the habits of small game. His lore on these last subjects was astonishing—he managed to interweave the station-master with the ornithologist. When he couldn't talk about greater things he could talk cheerfully about smaller, and since I couldn't accompany him into reminiscences of the fashionable world he could lower the conversation without a visible effort to my level.

So earnest a desire to please was touching in a man who could so easily have knocked one down. He looked after the fire and had an opinion on the draught of the stove without my asking him, and I could see that he thought many of my arrangements not half knowing. I remember telling him that if I were only rich I'd offer him a salary to come and teach me how to live. Sometimes he gave a random sigh of which the essence might have been: "Give me even such a bare old barrack as *this*, and I'd do something with it!" When I wanted to use him he came alone; which was an illustration of the superior courage of women. His wife could bear her solitary second floor, and she was in general more discreet; showing by various small reserves that she was alive to the propriety of keeping our relations markedly professional —not letting them slide into sociability. She wished it to remain clear that she and the Major were employed, not cultivated, and if she approved of me as a superior, who could be kept in his place, she never thought me quite good enough for an equal.

She sat with great intensity, giving the whole of her mind to it, and was capable of remaining for an hour almost as motionless as before a photographer's lens. I could see she had been photographed often, but somehow the very habit that made her good for that purpose unfitted her for mine. At first I was extremely pleased with her lady-like air, and it was a satisfaction, on coming to follow her lines, to see how good they were and how far they could lead the pencil. But after a little skirmishing I began to find her too insurmountably stiff; do what I would with it my drawing looked like a photograph or a copy of a photograph. Her figure had no variety of expression—she herself had no sense of variety. You may say that this was my business and was only a question of placing her. Yet I placed her in every conceivable position and she managed to obliterate their differences. She was always a lady certainly, and into the bargain was always the same lady. She was the real thing, but always the same thing. There were moments when I rather writhed under the serenity of her confidence that she *was* the real thing. All her dealings with me and all her husband's were an implication that this was lucky for *me*. Meanwhile I found myself trying to invent types that approached her own, instead of making her own transform itself—in the clever way that was not impossible for instance to poor Miss Churm. Arrange as I would and take the precautions I would, she always came out, in my pictures, too tall—landing me in the dilemma of having represented a fascinating woman as seven feet high, which (out of respect perhaps to my own very much scantier inches) was far from my idea of such a personage.

The case was worse with the Major—nothing I could do would keep *him* down, so that he became useful only for the representation of brawny giants. I adored variety and range, I cherished human accidents, the illustrative note; I wanted to characterize closely, and the thing in the world I most hated was the danger of being ridden by a type. I had quarreled with some of my friends about it; I had parted company with them for maintaining that one *had* to be, and that if the type was beautiful—witness Raphael and Leonardo—the servitude was only a gain. I was neither Leonardo nor Raphael—I might only be a presumptuous young modern searcher; but I held that everything was to be sacrificed sooner than character. When they claimed that the obsessional form could easily *be* character I retorted, perhaps superficially, "Whose?" It couldn't be everybody's—it might end in being nobody's.

After I had drawn Mrs. Monarch a dozen times I felt surer even than before that the value of such a model as Miss Churm resided precisely in the fact that she had no positive stamp, combined of course with the other fact that what she did have was a curious and inexplicable talent for imitation. Her usual appearance was like a curtain which she could draw up at request for a capital performance. This performance was simply suggestive; but it was a word to the wise—it was vivid and pretty. Sometimes even I thought it, though she was plain herself, too insipidly pretty; I made it a reproach to her that the figures drawn from her were monotonously (*bêtement*, as we used to say) graceful. Nothing made her more angry; it was so much her pride to feel she could sit for characters that had nothing in common with each other. She would accuse me at such moments of taking away her "reputytion."

It suffered a certain shrinkage, this queer quantity, from the repeated visits of my new friends. Miss Churm was greatly in demand, never in want of employment, so I had no scruple in putting her off occasionally, to try them more at my ease. It was certainly amusing at first to do the real thing—it was amusing to do Major Monarch's trousers. They *were* the real thing, even if he did come out colossal. It was amusing to do his wife's back hair—it was so mathematically neat—and the particular "smart" tension of her tight stays. She lent herself especially to positions in which the face was somewhat averted or blurred; she abounded in ladylike back views and *profils perdus*. When she stood erect she took naturally one of the attitudes in which court-painters represent queens and princesses; so that I found myself wondering whether, to draw out this accomplishment, I couldn't get the editor of the *Cheapside* to publish a really royal romance, "A Tale of Buckingham Palace." Sometimes however the real thing and the make-believe came into contact; by which I mean that Miss Churm, keeping an appointment or coming to make one on days when I had much work in hand, encountered her invidious rivals. The encounter was not on their part, for they noticed her no more than if she had been the housemaid; not from intentional loftiness, but simply because as yet, professionally, they didn't know how to fraternize, as I could imagine they would have liked—or at least that the Major would. They couldn't talk about the omnibus—they always walked; and they didn't know what else to try—she wasn't interested in good rains or cheap claret. Besides, they must have felt—in the air—that he was amused at them, secretly derisive of their ever knowing how. She wasn't a person to conceal the limits of her faith if she had had a chance to show them. On the other hand Mrs. Monarch didn't think her tidy; for why else did she take pains to say to me—it was going out of the way, for Mrs. Monarch—that she didn't like dirty women?

One day when my young lady happened to be present with my other sitters—she even dropped in, when it was convenient, for a chat —I asked her to be so good as to lend a hand in getting tea, a service with which she was familiar and which was one of a class that, living as I did in a small way, with slender domestic resources, I often appealed to my models to render. They liked to lay hands on my property, to break the sitting, and sometimes the china—it made them feel Bohemian. The next time I saw Miss Churm after this incident she surprised me greatly by making a scene about it—she accused me of having wished to humiliate her. She hadn't resented the outrage at the time, but had seemed obliging and amused, enjoying the comedy of asking Mrs. Monarch, who sat vague and silent, whether she would have cream and sugar, and putting an exaggerated simper into the question. She had tried intonations—as if she too wished to pass for the real thing—till I was afraid my other visitors would take offense.

Oh they were determined not to do this, and their touching patience was the measure of their great need. They would sit by the hour, uncomplaining, till I was ready to use them; they would come back on the chance of being wanted and would walk away cheerfully if it failed. I used to go to the door with them to see in what magnificent order they retreated. I tried to find other employment for them— I introduced them to several artists. But they didn't "take," for reasons I could appreciate, and I became rather anxiously aware that after such disappointments they fell back upon me with a heavier weight. They did me the honor to think me most *their* form. They weren't romantic enough for the painters, and in those days there were few serious workers in black-and-white. Besides, they had an eye to the great job I had mentioned to them—they had secretly set their hearts on supplying the right essence for my pictorial vindication of our fine novelist. They knew that for this undertaking I should want no costume-effects, none of the frippery of past ages—that it was a case in which everything would be contemporary and satirical and presumably genteel. If I could work them into it their future would be assured, for the labor would of course be long and the occupation steady.

One day Mrs. Monarch came without her husband—she explained his absence by his having had to go to the City. While she sat there in her usual relaxed majesty there came at the door a knock which I immediately recognized as the subdued appeal of a model out of work. It was followed by the entrance of a young man whom I at once saw to be a foreigner and who proved in fact an Italian acquainted with no English word but my name, which he uttered in a way that made it seem to include all others. I hadn't then visited his country, nor was I proficient in his tongue; but as he was not so meanly constituted —what Italian is?—as to depend only on that member for expression he conveyed to me, in familiar but graceful mimicry, that he was in search of exactly the employment in which the lady before me was engaged. I was not struck with him at first, and while I continued to draw I dropped few signs of interest or encouragement. He stood his ground however—not importunately, but with a dumb dog-like fidelity in his eyes that amounted to innocent impudence, the manner of a devoted servant—he might have been in the house for years—unjustly suspected. Suddenly it struck me that this very attitude and expression made a picture; whereupon I told him to sit down and wait till I should be free. There was another picture in the way he obeyed me and I observed as I worked that there were others still in the way he looked wonderingly, with his head thrown back, about the high studio. He might have been crossing himself in Saint Peter's. Before I finished I said to myself "The fellow's a bankrupt orange-monger, but a treasure."

When Mrs. Monarch withdrew he passed across the room like a flash to open the door for her, standing there with the rapt pure gaze of the young Dante spellbound by the young Beatrice. As I never insisted, in such situations, on the blankness of the British domestic, I reflected that he had the making of a servant—and I needed one, but couldn't pay him to be only that—as well as of a model; in short I resolved to adopt my bright adventurer if he would agree to officiate in the double capacity. He jumped at my offer, and in the event my rashness—for I had really known nothing about him—wasn't brought home to me. He proved a sympathetic though a desultory ministrant, and had in a wonderful degree the *sentiment de la pose*. It was uncultivated, instinctive, a part of the happy instinct that had guided him to my door and helped him to spell out my name on the card nailed to it. He had had no other introduction to me than a guess, from the shape of my high north window, seen outside, that my place was a studio and that as a studio it would contain an artist. He had wandered to England in search of fortune, like other itinerants, and had embarked, with a partner and a small green handcart, on the sale of penny ices. The ices had melted away and the partner had dissolved in their train. My young man wore tight yellow trousers with reddish stripes and his name was Oronte. He was sallow but fair, and when I put him into ome old clothes of my own he looked like an Englishman. He was as good as Miss Churm, who could look, when requested, like an Italian.

IV

I thought Mrs. Monarch's face slightly convulsed when, on her coming back with her husband, she found Oronte installed. It was strange to have to recognize in a scrap of a lazzarone a competitor to her magnificent Major. It was she who scented danger first, for the Major was anecdotically unconscious. But Oronte gave us tea, with a hundred eager confusions—he had never been concerned in so queer a process—and I think she thought better of me for having at last an "establishment." They saw a couple of drawings that I had made of the establishment, and Mrs. Monarch hinted that it never would have struck her he had sat for them. "Now the drawings you make from *us*, they look exactly like us," she reminded me, smiling in triumph; and I recognized that this was indeed their defect. When I drew the Monarchs I couldn't anyhow get away from them—get into the character I wanted to represent; and I hadn't the least desire my model should be discoverable in my picture. Miss Churm never was, and Mrs. Monarch thought I hid her, very properly, because she was vulgar; whereas if she was lost it was only as the dead who go to heaven are lost—in the gain of an angel the more.

By this time I had got a certain start with "Rutland Ramsay," the first novel in the great projected series; that is I had produced a dozen drawings, several with the help of the Major and his wife, and I had sent them in for approval. My understanding with the publishers, as I have already hinted, had been that I was to be left to do my work, in this particular case, as I liked, with the whole book committed to me; but my connection with the rest of the series was only contingent. There were moments when, frankly, it *was* a comfort to have the real thing under one's hand; for there were characters in "Rutland Ramsay" that were very much like it. There were people presumably as erect as the Major and women of as good a fashion as Mrs. Monarch. There was a great deal of country-house life—treated, it is true, in a fine fanciful ironical generalized way—and there was a considerable implication of knickerbockers and kilts. There were certain things I had to settle at the outset; such things for instance as the exact appearance of the hero and the particular bloom and figure of the heroine. The author of course gave me a lead, but there was a margin for interpretation. I took the Monarchs into my confidence, I told them frankly what I was about, I mentioned my embarrassments and alternatives. "Oh, take *him*!" Mrs. Monarch murmured sweetly, looking at her husband; and "What could you want better than my wife?" the Major enquired with the comfortable candor that now prevailed between us

I wasn't obliged to answer these remarks—I was only obliged to place my sitters. I wasn't easy in mind, and I postponed a little timidly perhaps the solving of my question. The book was a large canvas, the other figures were numerous, and I worked off at first some of the episodes in which the hero and the heroine were not concerned. When once I had set *them* up I should have to stick to them—I couldn't make my young man seven feet high in one place and five feet nine in another. I inclined on the whole to the latter measurement, though the Major more than once reminded me that *he* looked about as young as any one. It was indeed quite possible to arrange him, for the figure, so that it would have been difficult to detect his age. After the spontaneous Oronte had been with me a month, and after I had given him to understand several times over that his native exuberance would presently constitute an insurmountable barrier to our further intercourse, I waked to a sense of his heroic capacity. He was only five feet seven, but the remaining inches were latent. I tried him almost secretly at first, for I was really rather afraid of the judgment my other models would pass on such a choice. If they regarded Miss Churm as little better than a snare what would they think of the representation by a person so little the real thing as an Italian streetvendor of a protagonist formed by a public school?

If I went a little in fear of them it wasn't because they bullied me, because they had got an oppressive foothold, but because in their really pathetic decorum and mysteriously permanent newness they counted on me so intensely. I was therefore very glad when Jack Hawley came home: he was always of such good counsel. He painted badly himself, but there was no one like him for putting his finger on the place. He had been absent from England for a year; he had been somewhere—I don't remember where—to get a fresh eye. I was in a good deal of dread of any such organ, but we were old friends; he had been away for months and a sense of emptiness was creeping into my life. I hadn't dodged a missile for a year.

He came back with a fresh eye, but with the same old black velvet blouse, and the first evening he spent in my studio we smoked cigarettes till the small hours. He had done no work himself, he had only got the eye; so the field was clear for the production of my little things. He wanted to see that I had produced for the *Cheapside*, but he was disappointed in the exhibition. That at least seemed the meaning of two or three comprehensive groans which, as he lounged on my big divan, his leg folded under him, looking at my latest drawings, issued from his lips with the smoke of the cigarette.

"What's the matter with you?" I asked.

"What's the matter with *you*?"

"Nothing save that I'm mystified."

"You are indeed. You're quite off the hinge. What's the meaning of this new fad?" And he tossed me, with visible irreverence, a drawing in which I happened to have depicted both my elegant models. I asked if he didn't think it good, and he replied that it struck him as execrable, given the sort of thing I had always represented myself to him as wishing to arrive at; but I let that pass—I was so anxious to see exactly what he meant. The two figures in the picture looked colossal, but I supposed this was *not* what he meant, inasmuch as, for aught he knew to the contrary, I might have been trying for some such effect. I maintained that I was working exactly in the same way as when he last had done me the honor to tell me I might do something some day. "Well, there's a screw loose somewhere," he answered; "wait a bit and I'll discover it." I depended upon him to do so: where else was the fresh eye? But he produced at last nothing more luminous than "I don't know—I don't like your types." This was lame for a critic who had never consented to discuss with me anything but the question of execution, the direction of strokes and the mystery of values.

"In the drawings you've been looking at I think my types are very handsome."

"Oh they won't do!"

"I've been working with new models."

"I see you have. *They* won't do."

"Are you very sure of that?"

"Absolutely—they're stupid."

"You mean I am—for I ought to get round that."

"You *can't*—with such people. Who are they?"

I told him, so far as was necessary, and he concluded heartlessly: "Ce sont des gens qu'il faut mettre à la porte."

"You've never seen them; they're awfully good"—I flew to their defense.

"Not seen them? Why all this recent work of yours drops to pieces with them. It's all I want to see of them."

"No one else has said anything against it—the *Cheapside* people are pleased."

"Every one else is an ass, and the *Cheapside* people the biggest asses of all. Come, don't pretend at this time of day to have pretty illusions about the public, especially about publishers and editors. It's not for *such* animals you work—it's for those who know, *coloro che sanno*; so keep straight for *me* if you can't keep straight for yourself. There was a certain sort of thing you used to try for—and a very good thing it was. But this twaddle isn't *in* it." When I talked with Hawley later about "Rutland Ramsay" and its possible successors he declared that I must get back into my boat again or I should go to the bottom. His voice in short was the voice of warning.

I noted the warning, but I didn't turn my friends out of doors. They bored me a good deal; but the very fact that they bored me admonished me not to sacrifice them—if there was anything to be done with them—simply to irritation. As I look back at this phase they seem to me to have pervaded my life not a little. I have a vision of them as most of the time in my studio, seated against the wall on an old velvet bench to be out of the way, and resembling the while a pair of patient courtiers in a royal ante-chamber. I'm convinced that during the coldest weeks of the winter they held their ground because it saved them fire. Their newness was losing its gloss, and it was impossible not to feel them objects of charity. Whenever Miss Churm arrived they went away, and after I was fairly launched in "Rutland Ramsay" Miss Churm arrived pretty often. They managed to express to me tacitly that they supposed I wanted her for the low life of the book, and I let them suppose it, since they had attempted to study the work—it was lying about the studio—without discovering that it dealt only with the highest circles. They had dipped into the most brilliant of our novelists without deciphering many passages. I still took an hour from them, now and again, in spite of Jack Hawley's warning: it would be time enough to dismiss them, if dismissal should be necessary, when the rigor of the season was over. Hawley had made their acquaintance —he had met them at my fireside—and thought them a ridiculous pair. Learning that he was a painter they tried to approach him, to show him too that they were the real thing; but he looked at them, across the big room, as if they were miles away: they were a compendium of everything he most objected to in the social system of his country. Such people as that, all convention and patent-leather, with ejaculations that stopped conversation, had no business in a studio. A studio was a place to learn to see, and how could you see through a pair of feather-beds?

The main inconvenience I suffered at their hands was that at first I was shy of letting it break upon them that my artful little servant had begun to sit to me for "Rutland Ramsay." They knew I had been odd enough—they were prepared by this time to allow oddity to artists— to pick a foreign vagabond out of the streets when I might have had a person with whiskers and credentials; but it was some time before they learned how high I rated his accomplishments. They found him in an attitude more than once, but they never doubted I was doing him as an organ-grinder. There were several things they never guessed, and one of them was that for a striking scene in the novel, in which a footman briefly figured, it occurred to me to make use of Major Monarch as the menial. I kept putting this off, I didn't like to ask him to don the livery —besides the difficulty of finding a livery to fit him. At last, one day late in the winter, when I was at work on the despised Oronte, who caught one's idea on the wing, and was in the glow of feeling myself go very straight, they came in, the Major and his wife, with their society laugh about nothing (there was less and less to laugh at); came in like country-callers—they always reminded me of that—who have walked across the park after church and are presently persuaded to stay to luncheon. Luncheon was over, but they could stay to tea—I knew they wanted it. The fit was on me, however, and I couldn't let my ardor cool and my work wait, with the fading daylight, while my model prepared it. So I asked Mrs. Monarch if she would mind laying it out—a request which for an instant brought all the blood to her face. Her eyes were on her husband's for a second, and some mute telegraphy passed between them. Their folly was over the next instant; his cheerful shrewdness put an end to it. So far from pitying their wounded pride, I must add, I was moved to give it as complete a lesson as I could. They bustled about together and got out the cups and saucers and made the kettle boil. I know they felt as if they were waiting on my servant, and when the tea was prepared I said: ":He'll have a cup, please—he's tired." Mrs. Monarch brought him one where he stood, and he took it from her as if he had been a gentleman at a party squeezing a crush-hat with an elbow.

Then it came over me that she had made a great effort for me— made it with a kind of nobleness—and that I owed her a compensation. Each time I saw her after this I wondered what the compensation could be. I couldn't go on doing the wrong thing to oblige them. Oh it *was* the wrong thing, the stamp of the work for which they sat—Hawley was not the only person to say it now. I sent in a large number of the drawings I had made for "Rutland Ramsay," and I received a warning that was more to the point than Hawley's. The artistic adviser of the house for which I was working was of opinion that many of my illustrations were not what had been looked for. Most of these illustrations were the subjects in which the Monarchs had figured. Without going into the question of what *had* been looked for, I had to face the fact that at this rate I shouldn't get the other books to do. I hurled myself in despair on Miss Churm—I put her through all her paces. I not only adopted Oronte publicly as my hero, but one morning when the Major looked in to see if I didn't require him to finish a *Cheapside* figure for which he had begun to sit the week before, I told him I had changed my mind—I'd do the drawing from my man. At this my visitor turned pale and stood looking at me. "Is *he* your idea of an English gentleman?" he asked.

I was disappointed, I was nervous, I wanted to get on with my work; so I replied with irritation: "Oh my dear Major—I can't be ruined for *you!*"

It was a horrid speech, but he stood another moment—after which, without a word, he quitted the studio. I drew a long breath, for I said to myself that I shouldn't see him again. I hadn't told him definitely that I was in danger of having my work rejected, but I was vexed at his not having felt the catastrophe in the air, read with me the moral of our fruitless collaboration, the lesson that in the deceptive atmosphere of art even the highest respectability may fail of being plastic.

I didn't owe my friends money, but I did see them again. They reappeared together three days later, and, given all the other facts, there was something tragic in that one. It was a clear proof they could find nothing else in life to do. They had threshed the matter out in a dismal conference—they had digested the bad news that they were not in for the series. If they weren't useful to me even for the *Cheapside* their function seemed difficult to determine, and I could only judge at first that they had come, forgivingly, decorously, to take a last leave. This made me rejoice in secret that I had little leisure for a scene; for I had placed both my other models in position together and I was pegging away at a drawing from which I hoped to derive glory. It had been suggested by the passage in which Rutland Ramsay, drawing up a chair to Artemisia's piano stool, says extraordinary things to her while she ostensibly fingers out a difficult piece of music. I had done Miss Churm at the piano before—it was an attitude in which she knew how to take on an absolutely poetic grace. I wished the two figures to "compose" together with intensity, and my little Italian had entered perfectly into my conception. The pair were vividly before me, the piano had been pulled out; it was a charming show of blended youth and murmured love, which I had only to catch and keep. My visitors stood and looked at it, and I was friendly to them over my shoulder.

They made no response, but I was used to silent company and went on with my work, only a little disconcerted—even though exhilarated by the sense that *this* was at least the ideal thing—at not having got rid of them after all. Presently I heard Mrs. Monarch's sweet voice beside or rather above me: "I wish her hair were a little better done." I looked up and she was staring with a strange fixedness at Miss Churm, whose back was turned to her. "Do you mind my just touching it?" she went on—a question which made me spring up for an instant as with the instinctive fear that she might do the young lady a harm.

But she quieted me with a glance I shall never forget—I confess I should like to have been able to paint *that*—and went for a moment to my model. She spoke to her softly, laying a hand on her shoulder and bending over her; and as the girl, understanding, gratefully assented, she disposed her rough curls, with a few quick passes, in such a way as to make Miss Churm's head twice as charming. It was one of the most heroic personal services I've ever seen rendered. Then Mrs. Monarch turned away with a low sigh and, looking about her as if for something to do, stooped to the floor with a noble humility and picked up a dirty rag that had dropped out of my paint-box.

The Major meanwhile had also been looking for something to do, and, wandering to the other end of the studio, saw before him my breakfast-things neglected, unremoved. "I say, can't I be useful *here*?" he called out to me with an irrepressible quaver. I assented with a laugh that I fear was awkward, and for the next ten minutes, while I worked, I heard the light clatter of china and the tinkle of spoons and glass. Mrs. Monarch assisted her husband—they washed up my crockery, they put it away. They wandered off into my little scullery, and I afterwards found that they had cleaned my knives and that my slender stock of plate had an unprecedented surface. When it came over me, the latent eloquence of what they were doing, I confess that my drawing was blurred for a moment—the picture swam. They had accepted their failure, but they couldn't accept their fate. They had bowed their heads in bewilderment to the perverse and cruel law in virtue of which the real thing could be so much less precious than the unreal; but they didn't want to starve. If my servants were my models, then my models might be my servants. They would reverse the parts—the others would sit for the ladies and gentlemen and *they* would do the work. They would still be in the studio—it was an intense dumb appeal to me not to turn them out. "Take us on," they wanted to say—"we'll do *anything*."

My pencil dropped from my hand; my sitting was spoiled and I got rid of my sitters, who were also evidently rather mystified and awestruck. Then, alone with the Major and his wife I had a most uncomfortable moment. He put their prayer into a single sentence: "I say, you know—just let *us* do for you, can't you?" I couldn't—it was dreadful to see them emptying my slops; but I pretended I could, to oblige them, for about a week. Then I gave them a sum of money to go away, and I never saw them again. I obtained the remaining books, but my friend Hawley repeats that Major and Mrs. Monarch did me a permanent harm, got me into false ways. If it be true I'm content to have paid the price—for the memory.

HENRY JAMES (1843-1916)

The Tree of Knowledge

It was one of the secret opinions, such as we all have, of Peter Brench that his main success in life would have consisted in his never having committed himself about the work, as it was called, of his friend Morgan Mallow. This was a subject on which it was, to the best of his belief, impossible with veracity to quote him, and it was nowhere on record that he had, in the connection, on any occasion and in any embarrassment, either lied or spoken the truth. Such a triumph had its honor even for a man of other triumphs—a man who had reached fifty, who had escaped marriage, who had lived within his means, who had been in love with Mrs. Mallow for years without breathing it, and who, last but not least, had judged himself once for all. He had so judged himself in fact that he felt an extreme and general humility to be his proper portion; yet there was nothing that made him think so well of his parts as the course he had steered so often through the shallows just mentioned. It became thus a real wonder that the friends in whom he had most confidence were just those with whom he had most reserves. He couldn't tell Mrs. Mallow—or at least he supposed, excellent man, he couldn't—that she was the one beautiful reason he had never married; any more than he could tell her husband that the sight of the multiplied marbles in that gentleman's studio was an affliction of which even time had never blunted the edge. His victory, however, as I have intimated, in regard to these productions, was not simply in his not having let it out that he deplored them; it was, remarkably, in his not having kept it in by anything else.

The whole situation, among these good people, was verily a marvel, and there was probably not such another for a long way from the spot that engages us—the point at which the soft declivity of Hampstead began at that time to confess in broken accents to Saint John's Wood. He despised Mallow's statues and adored Mallow's wife, and yet was distinctly fond of Mallow, to whom, in turn, he was equally dear. Mrs. Mallow rejoiced in the statues—though she preferred, when pressed, the busts; and if she was visibly attached to Peter Brench it was because of his affection for Morgan. Each loved the other moreover for the love borne in each case to Lancelot, whom the Mallows respectively cherished as their only child and whom the friend of their fireside identified as the third—but decidedly the handsomest—of his godsons. Already in the old years it had come to that—that no one, for such a relation, could possibly have occurred to any of them, even to the baby itself, but Peter. There was luckily a certain independence, of the pecuniary sort, all round: the Master could never otherwise have spent his solemn *Wanderjahre* in Florence and Rome, and continued by the Thames as well as by the Arno and the Tiber to add unpurchased group to group and model, for what was too apt to prove in the event mere love, fancy-heads of celebrities either too busy or too buried—too much of the age or too little of it—to sit. Neither could Peter, lounging in almost daily, have found time to keep the whole complicated tradition so alive by his presence. He was massive but mild, the depositary of these mysteries—large and loose and ruddy and curly, with deep tones, deep eyes, deep pockets, to say nothing of the habit of long pipes, soft hats and brownish greyish weather-faded clothes, apparently always the same.

He had "written," it was known, but had never spoken, never spoken in particular of that; and he had the air (since, as was believed, he continued to write) of keeping it up in order to have something more—as if he hadn't at the worst enough—to be silent about. Whatever his air, at any rate, Peter's occasional unmentioned prose and verse were quite truly the result of an impulse to maintain the purity of his taste by establishing still more firmly the right relation of fame to feebleness. The little green door of his domain was in a garden-wall on which the discolored stucco made patches, and in the small detached villa behind it everything was old, the furniture, the servants, the books, the prints, the immemorial habits and the new improvements. The Mallows, at Carrara Lodge, were within ten minutes, and the studio there was on their little land, to which they had added, in their happy faith, for building it. This was the good fortune, if it was not the ill, of her having brought him in marriage a portion that put them in a manner at their ease and enabled them thus, on their side, to keep it up. And they did keep it up—they always had—the infatuated sculptor and his wife, for whom nature had refined on the impossible by relieving them of the sense of the difficult. Morgan had at all events everything of the sculptor but the spirit of Phidias—the brown velvet, the becoming *beretto*, the "plastic" presence, the fine fingers, the beautiful accent in Italian and the old Italian factotum. He seemed to make up for everything when he addressed Egidio with the "tu" and waved him to turn one of the rotary pedestals of which the place was full. They were tremendous Italians at Carrara Lodge, and the secret of the part played by this fact in Peter's life was in a large degree that it gave him, sturdy Briton as he was, just the amount of "going abroad" he could bear. The Mallows were all his Italy, but it was in a measure for Italy he liked them. His one worry was that

Lance—to which they had shortened his godson—was, in spite of a public school, perhaps a shade too Italian. Morgan meanwhile looked like somebody's flattering idea of somebody's own person as expressed in the great room provided at the Uffizi Museum for the general illustration of that idea by eminent hands. The Master's sole regret that he hadn't been born rather to the brush than to the chisel sprang from his wish that he might have contributed to that collection.

It appeared with time at any rate to be to the brush that Lance had been born; for Mrs. Mallow, one day when the boy was turning twenty, broke it to their friend, who shared, to the last delicate morsel, their problems and pains, that it seemed as if nothing would really do but that he should embrace the career. It had been impossible longer to remain blind to the fact that he was gaining no glory at Cambridge, where Brench's own college had for a year tempered its tone to him as for Brench's own sake. Therefore why renew the vain form of preparing him for the impossible? The impossible—it had become clear—was that he should be anything but an artist.

"Oh dear, dear!" said poor Peter.

"Don't you believe in it?" asked Mrs. Mallow, who still, at more than forty, had her violet velvet eyes, her creamy satin skin and her silken chestnut hair.

"Believe in what?"

"Why in Lance's passion."

"I don't know what you mean by 'believing in it.' I've never been unaware, certainly, of his disposition, from his earliest time, to daub and draw; but I confess I've hoped it would burn out."

"But why should it," she sweetly smiled, "with his wonderful heredity? Passion is passion—though of course indeed *you*, dear Peter, know nothing of that. Has the Master's ever burned out?"

Peter looked off a little and, in his familiar formless way, kept up for a moment, a sound between a smothered whistle and a subdued hum. "Do you think he's going to be another Master?"

She seemed scarce prepared to go that length, yet she had on the whole a marvellous trust. "I know what you mean by that. Will it be a career to incur the jealousies and provoke the machinations that have been at times almost too much for his father? Well—say it may be, since nothing but clap-trap, in these dreadful days, *can*, it would seem, make its way, and since, with the curse of refinement and distinction, one may easily find one's self begging one's bread. Put it at the worst —say he *has* the misfortune to wing his flight further than the vulgar taste of his stupid countrymen can follow. Think, all the same, of the happiness—the same the Master has had. He'll *know*."

Peter looked rueful. "Ah but *what* will he know?"

"Quiet joy!" cried Mrs. Mallow, quite impatient and turning away.

II

He had of course before long to meet the boy himself on it and to hear that practically everything was settled. Lance was not to go up again, but to go instead to Paris where, since the die was cast, he would find the best advantages. Peter had always felt he must be taken as he was, but had never perhaps found him so much of that pattern as on this occasion. "You chuck Cambridge then altogether? Doesn't that seem rather a pity?"

Lance would have been like his father, to his friend's sense, had he had less humor, and like his mother had he had more beauty. Yet it was a good middle way for Peter that, in the modern manner, he was, to the eye, rather the young stockbroker than the young artist. The youth reasoned that it was a question of time—there was such a mill to go through, such an awful lot to learn. He had talked with fellows and had judged. "One has got, today," he said, "don't you see? to know."

His interlocutor, at this, gave a groan. "Oh hang it, *don't* know!"

Lance wondered. " 'Don't'? Then what's the use—?"

"The use of what?"

"Why of anything. Don't you think I've talent?"

Peter smoked away for a little in silence; then went on: "It isn't knowledge, it's ignorance that—as we've been beautifully told—is bliss."

"Don't you think I've talent?" Lance repeated.

Peter, with his trick of queer kind demonstrations, passed his arm round his godson and held him a moment. "How do I know?"

"Oh," said the boy, "if it's your own ignorance you're defending—!"

Again, for a pause, on the sofa, his godfather smoked. "It isn't. I've the misfortune to be omniscient."

"Oh well," Lance laughed again, "if you know *too* much—!"

"That's what I do, and it's why I'm so wretched."

Lance's gaiety grew. "Wretched? Come, I say!"

"But I forgot," his companion went on—"you're not to know about that. It would indeed for you too make the too much. Only I'll tell you what I'll do." And Peter got up from the sofa. "If you'll go up again I'll pay your way at Cambridge."

Lance stared, a little rueful in spite of being still more amused. "Oh Peter! You disapprove so of Paris?"

"Well, I'm afraid of it."

"Ah I see!"

"No, you don't see—yet. But you will—that is you would. And you mustn't."

The young man thought more gravely. "But one's innocence, already—!"

"Is considerably damaged? Ah that won't matter," Peter persisted—"we'll patch it up here."

"Here? Then you want me to stay at home?"

Peter almost confessed to it. "Well, we're so right—we four together—just as we are. We're so safe. Come, don't spoil it."

The boy, who had turned to gravity, turned from this, on the real pressure in his friend's tone, to consternation. "Then what's a fellow to be?"

"My particular care. Come, old man"—and Peter now fairly pleaded—"I'll look out for you."

Lance, who had remained on the sofa with his legs out and his hands in his pockets, watched him with eyes that showed suspicion. Then he got up. "You think there's something the matter with me—that I can't make a success."

"Well, what do you call a success?"

Lance thought again. "Why the best sort, I suppose, is to please one's self. Isn't that the sort that, in spite of cabals and things, is—in his own peculiar line—the Master's?"

There were so much too many things in this question to be answered at once that they practically checked the discussion, which became particularly difficult in the light of such renewed proof that, though the young man's innocence might, in the course of his studies, as he contended, somewhat have shrunken, the finer essence of it still remained. That was indeed exactly what Peter had assumed and what above all he desired; yet perversely enough it gave him a chill. The boy believed in the cabals and things, believed in the peculiar line, believed, to be brief, in the Master. What happened a month or two later wasn't that he went up again at the expense of his godfather, but that a fortnight after he had got settled in Paris this personage sent him fifty pounds.

He had meanwhile at home, this personage, made up his mind to the worst; and what that might be had never yet grown quite so vivid to him as when, on his presenting himself one Sunday night, as he never failed to do, for supper, the mistress of Carrara Lodge met him with an appeal as to—of all things in the world—the wealth of the Canadians. She was earnest, she was even excited. "Are many of them *really* rich?"

He had to confess he knew nothing about them, but he often thought afterwards of that evening. The room in which they sat was adorned with sundry specimens of the Master's genius, which had the merit of being, as Mrs. Mallow herself frequently suggested, of an unusually convenient size. They were indeed of dimensions not customary in the products of the chisel, and they had the singularity that, if the objects and features intended to be small looked too large, the objects and features intended to be large looked too small. The Master's idea, either in respect to this matter or to any other, had in almost any case, even after years, remained undiscoverable to Peter Brench. The creations that so failed to reveal it stood about on pedestals and brackets, on tables and shelves, a little staring white population, heroic, idyllic, allegoric, mythic, symbolic, in which "scale" had so strayed and lost itself that the public square and the chimney-piece seemed to have changed places, the monumental being all diminutive and the diminutive all monumental; branches at any rate, markedly, of a family in which stature was rather oddly irrespective of function, age and sex. They formed, like the Mallows themselves, poor Brench's own family—having at least to such a degree the note of familiarity. The occasion was one of those he had long ago learnt to know and to name—short flickers of the faint flame, soft gusts of a kinder air. Twice a year regularly the Master believed in his fortune, in addition to believing all the year round in his genius. This time it was to be made by a bereaved couple from Toronto, who had given him the handsomest order for a tomb to three lost children, each of whom they desired to see, in the composition, emblematically and characteristically represented.

Such was naturally the moral of Mrs. Mallow's question: if their wealth was to be assumed, it was clear, from the nature of their admiration, as well as from mysterious hints thrown out (they were a little odd!) as to other possibilities of the same mortuary sort, that their further patronage might be; and not less evident that should the Master become at all known in those climes nothing would be more inevitable than a run of Canadian custom. Peter had been present before at runs of custom, colonial and domestic—present at each of those of which the aggregation had left so few gaps in the marble company round him; but it was his habit never at these junctures to prick the bubble in advance. The fond illusion, while it lasted, eased the wound of elections never won, the long ache of medals and diplomas carried off, on every change, by every one but the Master; it moreover lighted the lamp that would glimmer through the next eclipse. They lived, however, after all—as it was always beautiful to see—at a height scarce susceptible to ups and downs. They strained a point at times charmingly, strained it to admit that the public was here and there not too bad to buy; but they would have been nowhere without their attitude that the Master was always too good to sell. They were at all events deliciously formed, Peter often said to himself, for their fate; the Master had a vanity, his wife had a loyalty, of which success, depriving these things of innocence, would have diminished the merit and the grace. Any one could be charming under a charm, and as he looked about him at a world of prosperity more void of proportion even than the Master's museum he wondered if he knew another pair that so completely escaped vulgarity.

"What a pity Lance isn't with us to rejoice!" Mrs. Mallow on this occasion sighed at supper.

"We'll drink to the health of the absent," her husband replied, filling his friend's glass and his own and giving a drop to their companion; "but we must hope he's preparing himself for a happiness much less like this of ours this evening—excusable as I grant it to be! —than like the comfort we have always (whatever has happened or has not happened) been able to trust ourselves to enjoy. The comfort," the Master explained, leaning back in the pleasant lamplight and firelight, holding up his glass and looking round at his marble family, quartered more or less, a monstrous brood, in every room—"the comfort of art in itself!"

Peter looked a little shyly at his wine. "Well—I don't care what you may call it when a fellow doesn't—but Lance must learn to *sell*, you know. I drink to his acquisition of the secret of a base popularity!"

"Oh, yes, *he* must sell," the boy's mother, who was still more, however, this seemed to give out, the Master's wife, rather artlessly allowed.

"Ah," the sculptor after a moment confidently pronounced, "Lance *will*. Don't be afraid. He'll have learnt."

"Which is exactly what Peter," Mrs. Mallow gaily returned— "why in the world were you so perverse, Peter?—wouldn't when he told him hear of."

Peter, when this lady looked at him with accusatory affection— a grace on her part not infrequent—could never find a word; but the Master, who was always all amenity and tact, helped him out now as he had often helped him before. "That's his old idea, you know—on which we've so often differed: his theory that the artist should be all impulse and instinct. *I* go in of course for a certain amount of school. Not too much—but a due proportion. There's where his protest came in," he continued to explain to his wife, "as against what *might*, don't you see? be in question for Lance."

"Ah well"—and Mrs. Mallow turned the violet eyes across the

table at the subject of this discourse—"he's sure to have meant of course nothing but good. Only that wouldn't have prevented him, if Lance *had* taken his advice, from being in effect horribly cruel."

They had a sociable way of talking of him to his face as if he had been in the clay or—at most—in the plaster, and the Master was unfailingly generous. He might have been waving Egidio to make him revolve. "Ah but poor Peter wasn't so wrong as to what it may after all come to that he *will* learn."

"Oh but nothing artistically bad," she urged—still, for poor Peter, arch and dewy.

"Why just the little French tricks," said the Master: on which their friend had to pretend to admit, when pressed by Mrs. Mallow, that these aesthetic vices had been the objects of his dread.

III

"I know now," Lance said to him the next year, "why you were so much against it." He had come back supposedly for a mere interval and was looking about him at Carrara Lodge, where indeed he had already on two or three occasions since his expatriation briefly reappeared. This had the air of a longer holiday. "Something rather awful has happened to me. It *isn't* so very good to know."

"I'm bound to say high spirits don't show in your face," Peter was rather ruefully forced to confess. "Still, are you very sure you do know?"

"Well, I at least know about as much as I can bear." These remarks were exchanged in Peter's den, and the young man, smoking cigarettes, stood before the fire with his back against the mantel. Something of his bloom seemed really to have left him.

Poor Peter wondered. "You're clear then as to what in particular I wanted you not to go for?"

"In particular?" Lance thought. "It seems to me that in particular there can have been only one thing."

They stood for a little sounding each other. "Are you quite sure?"

"Quite sure I'm a beastly duffer? Quite—by this time."

"Oh!"—and Peter turned away as if almost with relief.

"It's *that* that isn't pleasant to find out."

"Oh I don't care for 'that,' " said Peter, presently coming round again. "I mean I personally don't."

"Yet I hope you can understand a little that I myself should!"

"Well, what do you mean by it?" Peter sceptically asked.

And on this Lance had to explain—how the upshot of his studies in Paris had inexorably proved a mere deep doubt of his means. These studies had so waked him up that a new light was in his eyes; but

The Tree of Knowledge 179

what the new light did was really to show him too much. "Do you know what's the matter with me? I'm too horribly intelligent. Paris was really the last place for me. I've learnt what I can't do."

Poor Peter stared—it was a staggerer; but even after they had had, on the subject, a longish talk in which the boy brought out to the full the hard truth of his lesson, his friend betrayed less pleasure than usually breaks into a face to the happy tune of "I told you so!" Poor Peter himself made now indeed so little a point of having told him so that Lance broke ground in a different place a day or two after. "What was it then that—before I went—you were afraid I should find out?" This, however, Peter refused to tell him—on the ground that if he hadn't yet guessed perhaps he never would, and that in any case nothing at all for either of them was to be gained by giving the thing a name. Lance eyed him on this an instant with the bold curiosity of youth—with the air indeed of having in his mind two or three names, of which one or other would be right. Peter nevertheless, turning his back again, offered no encouragement, and when they parted afresh it was with some show of impatience on the side of the boy. Accordingly on their next encounter Peter saw at a glance that he had now, in the interval, divined and that, to sound his note, he was only waiting till they should find themselves alone. This he had soon arranged and he then broke straight out. "Do you know your conundrum has been keeping me awake? But in the watches of the night the answer came over me—so that, upon my honor, I quite laughed out. Had you been supposing I had to go to Paris to learn *that*?" Even now, to see him still so sublimely on his guard, Peter's young friend had to laugh afresh. "You won't give a sign till you're sure? Beautiful old Peter!" But Lance at last produced it. "Why, hang it, the truth about the Master."

It made between them for some minutes a lively passage, full of wonder for each at the wonder of the other. "Then how long have you understood—"

"The true value of his work? I understood it," Lance recalled, "as soon as I began to understand anything. But I didn't begin fully to do that, I admit, till I got *là-bas*."

"Dear, dear!"—Peter gasped with retrospective dread.

"But for what have you taken me? I'm a hopeless muff—that I *had* to have rubbed in. But I'm not such a muff as the Master!" Lance declared.

"Then why did you never tell me—?"

"That I hadn't, after all"—the boy took him up—"remained such an idiot? Just because I never dreamed *you* knew. But I beg your pardon. I only wanted to spare you. And what I don't now understand is how the deuce then for so long you've managed to keep bottled."

Peter produced his explanation, but only after some delay and with a gravity not void of embarrassment. "It was for your mother."

"Oh!" said Lance.

"And that's the great thing now—since the murder *is* out. I want a promise from you. I mean"—and Peter almost feverishly followed it up—"a vow from you, solemn and such as you owe me here on the spot, that you'll sacrifice anything rather than let her ever guess—"

"That *I've* guessed?"—Lance took it in. "I see." He evidently after a moment had taken in much. "But what is it you've in mind that I may have a chance to sacrifice?"

"Oh one has always something."

Lance looked at him hard. "Do you mean that *you've* had—?" The look he received back, however, so put the question by that he found soon enough another. "Are you really sure my mother doesn't know?"

Peter, after renewed reflection, was really sure. "If she does she's too wonderful."

"But aren't we all too wonderful?"

"Yes," Peter granted—"but in different ways. The thing's so desperately important because your father's little public consists only, as you know then," Peter developed—"well, of how many?"

"First of all," the Master's son risked, "of himself. And last of all too. I don't quite see of whom else."

Peter had an approach to impatience. "Of your mother, I say— *always*."

Lance cast it all up. "You absolutely feel that?"

"Absolutely."

"Well then with yourself that makes three."

"Oh *me*!"—and Peter, with a wag of his kind old head, modestly excused himself. "The number's at any rate small enough for any individual dropping out to be too dreadfully missed. Therefore, to put it in a nutshell, take care, my boy—that's all—that *you're* not!"

"I've got to keep on humbugging?" Lance wailed.

"It's just to warn you of the danger of your failing of that that I've seized this opportunity."

"And what do you regard in particular," the young man asked, "as the danger?"

"Why this certainty: that the moment your mother, who feels so strongly, should suspect your secret—well," said Peter desperately, "the fat would be on the fire."

Lance for a moment seemed to stare at the blaze, "She'd throw me over?"

"She'd throw *him* over."

"And come round to us?"

Peter, before he answered, turned away. "Come round to *you*." But he had said enough to indicate—and, as he evidently trusted, to avert—the horrid contingency.

IV

Within six months again, none the less, his fear was on more occasions than one all before him. Lance had returned to Paris for another trial; then had reappeared at home and had had, with his father, for the first time in his life, one of the scenes that strike sparks. He described it with much expression to Peter, touching whom (since they had never done so before) it was the sign of a new reserve on the part of the pair at Carrara Lodge that they at present failed, on a matter of intimate interest, to open themselves—if not in joy then in sorrow—to their good friend. This produced perhaps practically between the parties a shade of alienation and a slight intermission of commerce—marked mainly indeed by the fact that to talk at his ease with his old playmate Lance had in general to come to see him. The closest if not quite the gayest relation they had yet known together was thus ushered in. The difficulty for poor Lance was a tension at home—begotten by the fact that his father wished him to be at least the sort of success he himself had been. He hadn't "chucked" Paris—though nothing appeared more vivid to him than that Paris had chucked him: he would go back again because of the fascination in trying, in seeing, in sounding the depths—in learning one's lesson, briefly, even if the lesson were simply that of one's impotence in the presence of one's larger vision. But what did the Master, all aloft in his senseless fluency, know of impotence, and what vision—to be called such—had he in all his blind life ever had? Lance, heated and indignant, frankly appealed to his godparent on this score.

His father, it appeared, had come down on him for having, after so long, nothing to show, and hoped that on his next return this deficiency would be repaired. *The* thing, the Master complacently set forth was—for any artist, however inferior to himself—at least to "do" something. "What can you do? That's all I ask!" *He* had certainly done enough, and there was no mistake about what he had to show. Lance had tears in his eyes when it came thus to letting his old friend know how great the strain might be on the "sacrifice" asked of him. It wasn't so easy to continue humbugging—as from son to parent—after feeling one's self despised for not grovelling in mediocrity. Yet a noble duplicity was what, as they intimately faced the situation, Peter went on requiring; and it was still for a time what his young friend, bitter and sore, managed loyally to comfort him with. Fifty pounds more than once again, it was true, rewarded both in London and in Paris the young friend's loyalty; none the less sensibly, doubtless, at the moment, that the money was a direct advance on a decent sum for which Peter had long since privately prearranged an ultimate function. Whether by these arts or others, at all events, Lance's just resentment was kept for a season—but only for a season—at bay. The day arrived when he warned his companion that he could hold out—or hold in—no longer. Carrara Lodge had had to listen to another lecture delivered from a great height—an infliction really heavier at last than, without striking back or in some way letting the Master have the truth, flesh and blood could bear.

"And what I don't see is," Lance observed with a certain irritated eye for what was after all, if it came to that, owing to himself too; "what I don't see is, upon my honor, how *you*, as things are going, can keep the game up."

"Oh the game for me is only to hold my tongue," said placid Peter. "And I have my reason."

"Still my mother?"

Peter showed a queer face as he had often shown it before—that is by turning it straight away. "What will you have? I haven't ceased to like her."

"She's beautiful—she's a dear of course," Lance allowed; "but what is she to you, after all, and what is it to you that, as to anything whatever, she should or she shouldn't?"

Peter, who had turned red, hung fire a little. "Well—it's all simply what I make of it."

· There was now, however, in his young friend a strange, an adopted insistence. "What are you after all to *her*?"

"Oh nothing. But that's another matter."

"She cares only for my father," said Lance the Parisian.

"Naturally—and that's just why."

"Why you've wish to spare her?"

"Because she cares so tremendously much."

Lance took a turn about the room, but with his eyes still on his host. "How awfully—always—you must have liked her!"

"Awfully. Always," said Peter Brench.

The young man continued for a moment to muse—then stopped again in front of him. "Do you know how much she cares?" Their eyes met on it, but Peter, as if his own found something new in Lance's, appeared to hesitate, for the first time in an age, to say he

The Tree of Knowledge 183

did know. "*I've* only just found out," said Lance. "She came to my room last night, after being present, in silence and only with her eyes on me, at what I had had to take from him; she came—and she was with me an extraordinary hour."

He had paused again and they had again for a while sounded each other. Then something—and it made him suddenly turn pale—came to Peter. "She *does* know?"

"She does know. She let it all out to me—so as to demand of me no more than 'that,' as she said, of which she herself had been capable. She has always, always known," said Lance without pity.

Peter was silent a long time; during which his companion might have heard him gently breathe, and on touching him might have felt within him the vibration of a long low sound suppressed. By the time he spoke at last he had taken everything in. "Then I do see how tremendously much."

"Isn't it wonderful?" Lance asked.

"Wonderful," Peter mused.

"So that if your original effort to keep me from Paris was to keep me from knowledge—!" Lance exclaimed as if with a sufficient indication of this futility.

It might have been at the futility Peter appeared for a little to gaze. "I think it must have been—without my quite at the time knowing it—to keep *me!*" he replied at last as he turned away.

JAMES JOYCE (1882-1941)

Clay

The matron had given her leave to go out as soon as the women's tea was over and Maria looked forward to her evening out. The kitchen was spick and span: the cook said you could see yourself in the big copper boilers. The fire was nice and bright and on one of the side-tables were four very big barmbracks. These barmbracks seemed uncut; but if you went closer you would see that they had been cut into long thick even slices and were ready to be handed round at tea. Maria had cut them herself.

Maria was a very, very small person indeed but she had a very long nose and a very long chin. She talked a little through her nose, always soothingly: "Yes, *my dear*," and "No, *my dear*." She was always sent for when the women quarreled over their tubs and always succeeded in making peace. One day the matron had said to her:

"Maria, you are a veritable peacemaker!"

And the sub-matron and two of the Board ladies had heard the compliment. And Ginger Mooney was always saying what she wouldn't do to the dummy who had charge of the irons if it wasn't for Maria. Everyone was so fond of Maria.

The women would have their tea at six o'clock and she would be able to get away before seven. From Ballsbridge to the Pillar, twenty minutes; from the Pillar to Drumcondra, twenty minutes; and twenty minutes to buy the things. She would be there before eight. She took out her purse with the silver clasps and read again the words A *Present from Belfast*. She was very fond of that purse because Joe had brought it to her five years before when he and Alphy had gone to Belfast on a Whit-Monday trip. In the purse were two half-crowns and some coppers. She would have five shillings clear after paying train fare. What a nice evening they would have, all the children singing! Only she hoped that Joe wouldn't come in drunk. He was so different when he took any drink.

Often he had wanted her to go and live with them; but she would have felt herself in the way (though Joe's wife was ever so nice with her) and she had become accustomed to the life of the laundry. Joe was a good fellow. She had nursed him and Alphy too; and Joe used often say:

"Mamma is mamma but Maria is my proper mother."

After the break-up at home the boys had got her that position in the *Dublin by Lamplight* laundry, and she liked it. She used to have such a bad opinion of Protestants but now she thought they were very nice people, a little quiet and serious, but still very nice people to live with. Then she had her plants in the conservatory and she liked looking after them. She had lovely ferns and wax-plants and, whenever anyone came to visit her, she always gave the visitor one or two slips from her conservatory. There was one thing she didn't like and that was the tracts on the walls; but the matron was such a nice person to deal with, so genteel.

When the cook told her everything was ready she went into the women's room and began to pull the big bell. In a few minutes the women began to come in by twos and threes, wiping their steaming hands in their petticoats and pulling down the sleeves of their blouses over their red steaming arms. They settled down before their huge mugs which the cook and the dummy filled up with hot tea, already mixed with milk and sugar in huge tin cans. Maria superintended the distribution of the barmbrack and saw that every woman got her four slices. There was a great deal of laughing and joking during the meal. Lizzie Fleming said Maria was sure to get the ring and, though Fleming had said that for so many Hallow Eves, Maria had to laugh and say she didn't want any ring or man either; and when she laughed her gray-green eyes sparkled with disappointed shyness and the tip of her nose nearly met the tip of her chin. Then Ginger Mooney lifted up her mug of tea and proposed Maria's health while all the other women clattered with their mugs on the table, and said she was sorry she hadn't a sup of porter to drink it in. And Maria laughed again till the tip of her nose nearly met the tip of her chin and till her minute body nearly shook itself asunder because she knew that Mooney meant well though, of course, she had the notions of a common woman.

But wasn't Maria glad when the women had finished their tea and the cook and the dummy had begun to clear away the tea things! She went into her little bedroom and, remembering that the next morning was a mass morning, changed the hand of the alarm from seven to six. Then she took off her working skirt and her house-boots and laid her best skirt out on the bed and her tiny dress-boots beside the foot of the bed. She changed her blouse too and, as she stood before the mirror, she thought of how she used to dress for mass on Sunday morning when she was a young girl; and she looked with quaint affection at the diminutive body which she had so often adorned. In spite of its years she found it a nice tidy little body.

When she got outside the streets were shining with rain and she was glad of her old brown waterproof. The tram was full and she had to sit on the little stool at the end of the car, facing all the people, with her toes barely touching the floor. She arranged in her mind all she was going to do and thought how much better it was to be independent and to have your own money in your pocket. She hoped they would have a nice evening. She was sure they would but she could not help thinking what a pity it was Alphy and Joe were not speaking. They were always falling out now but when they were boys together they used to be the best of friends: but such was life.

She got out of her tram at the Pillar and ferreted her way quickly among the crowds. She went into Downes's cake-shop but the shop was so full of people that it was a long time before she could get herself attended to. She bought a dozen of mixed penny cakes, and at last came out of the shop laden with a big bag. Then she thought what else would she buy: she wanted to buy something really nice. They would be sure to have plenty of apples and nuts. It was hard to know what to buy and all she could think of was cake. She decided to buy some plumcake but Downes's plumcake had not enough almond icing on top of it so she went over to a shop in Henry Street. Here she was a long time in suiting herself and the stylish young lady behind the counter, who was evidently a little annoyed by her, asked her was it wedding cake she wanted to buy. That made Maria blush and smile at the young lady; but the young lady took it all very seriously and finally cut a thick slice of plumcake, parceled it up and said:

"Two-and-four, please."

She thought she would have to stand in the Drumcondra tram because none of the young men seemed to notice her but an elderly gentleman made room for her. He was a stout gentleman and he wore a brown hard hat; he had a square red face and a grayish mustache. Maria thought he was a colonel-looking gentleman and she reflected how much more polite he was than the young men who simply stared straight before them. The gentleman began to chat with her about Hallow Eve and the rainy weather. He supposed the bag was full of good things for the little ones and said it was only right that the youngsters should enjoy themselves while they were young. Maria agreed with him and favored him with demure nods and hems. He was very nice with her, and when she was getting out at the Canal Bridge she thanked him and bowed, and he bowed to her and raised his hat and smiled agreeably; and while she was going up along the terrace, bending her tiny head under the rain, she thought how easy it was to know a gentleman even when he has a drop taken.

Everybody said: "O, here's Maria!" when she came to Joe's house. Joe was there, having come home from business, and all the children had their Sunday dresses on. There were two big girls in from next door and games were going on. Maria gave the bag of cakes to the eldest boy, Alphy, to divide and Mrs. Donnelly said it was too good of her to bring such a big bag of cakes and made all the children say:

"Thanks, Maria."

But Maria said she had brought something special for papa and mamma, something they would be sure to like, and she began to look for her plumcake. She tried in Downes's bag and then in the pockets of her waterproof and then on the hallstand but nowhere could she find it. Then she asked all the children had any of them eaten it—by mistake, of course—but the children all said no and looked as if they did not like to eat cakes if they were to be accused of stealing. Everybody had a solution for the mystery and Mrs. Donnelly said it was plain that Maria had left it behind her in the tram. Maria, remembering how confused the gentleman with the grayish mustache had made her, colored with shame and vexation and disappointment. At the thought of the failure of her little surprise and of the two and four-pence she had thrown away for nothing she nearly cried outright.

But Joe said it didn't matter and made her sit down by the fire. He was very nice with her. He told her all that went on in his office, repeating for her a smart answer which he had made to the manager. Maria did not understand why Joe laughed so much over the answer he had made but she said that the manager must have been a very overbearing person to deal with. Joe said he wasn't so bad when you knew how to take him, that he was a decent sort so long as you didn't rub him the wrong way. Mrs. Donnelly played the piano for the children and they danced and sang. Then the two next-door girls handed round the nuts. Nobody could find the nutcrackers and Joe was nearly getting cross over it and asked how did they expect Maria to crack nuts without a nutcracker. But Maria said she didn't like nuts and that they weren't to bother about her. Then Joe asked would she take a bottle of stout and Mrs. Donnelly said there was port wine too in the house if she would prefer that. Maria said she would rather they didn't ask her to take anything: but Joe insisted.

So Maria let him have his way and they sat by the fire talking over old times and Maria thought she would put in a good word for Alphy. But Joe cried that God might strike him stone dead if ever he spoke a word to his brother again and Maria said she was sorry she had mentioned the matter. Mrs. Donnelly told her husband it was a great shame for him to speak that way of his own flesh and blood but Joe said that Alphy was no brother of his and there was nearly being a row on the head of it. But Joe said he would not lose his temper on account of the night it was and asked his wife to open some more stout. The two next-door girls had arranged some Hallow Eve games and soon everything was merry again. Maria was delighted to see the children so merry and Joe and his wife in such good spirits. The next-door girls put some saucers on the table and then led the children up to the table, blindfold. One got the prayer book and the other three got the water; and when one of the next-door girls got the ring Mrs. Donnelly shook her finger at the blushing girl as much as to say: O, I know all about it! They insisted then on blindfolding Maria and leading her up to the table to see what she would get; and, while they were putting on the bandage, Maria laughed and laughed again till the tip of her nose nearly met the tip of her chin.

They led her up to the table amid laughing and joking and she put her hand out in the air as she was told to do. She moved her hand about here and there in the air and descended on one of the saucers. She felt a soft wet substance with her fingers and was surprised that nobody spoke or took off her bandage. There was a pause for a few seconds; and then a great deal of scuffling and whispering. Somebody said something about the garden, and at last Mrs. Donnelly said something very cross to one of the next-door girls and told her to throw it out at once: that was no play. Maria understood that it was wrong that time and so she had to do it over again: and this time she got the prayer book.

After that Mrs. Donnelly played Miss McCloud's Reel for the children and Joe made Maria take a glass of wine. Soon they were all quite merry again and Mrs. Donnelly said Maria would enter a convent before the year was out because she had got the prayer book. Maria had never seen Joe so nice to her as he was that night, so full of pleasant talk and reminiscences. She said they were all very good to her.

At last the children grew tired and sleepy and Joe asked Maria would she not sing some little song before she went, one of the old songs. Mrs. Donnelly said: *"Do, please, Maria!"* and so Maria had to get up and stand beside the piano. Mrs. Donnelly bade the children be quiet and listen to Maria's song. Then she played the prelude and said *"Now, Maria!"* and Maria, blushing very much, began to sing in a tiny quavering voice. She sang *I Dreamt that I Dwelt*, and when she came to the second verse she sang again:

> *I dreamt that I dwelt in marble halls*
> *With vassals and serfs at my side,*
> *And of all who assembled within those walls*
> *That I was the hope and the pride.*
>
> *I had riches too great to count, could boast*
> *Of a high ancestral name,*
> *But I also dreamt, which pleased me most,*
> *That you loved me still the same.*

But no one tried to show her her mistake; and when she had ended her song Joe was very much moved.* He said that there was no time like the long ago and no music for him like poor old Balfe, whatever other people might say; and his eyes filled up so much with tears that he could not find what he was looking for and in the end he had to ask his wife to tell him where the corkscrew was.

* Maria's song is from Balfe's opera *The Bohemian Girl*. Her "mistake" is that she sings the first verse twice, omitting the second and third stanzas:

> *I dreamt that suitors sought my hand*
> *That knights on bended knee,*
> *And with vows no maiden heart could withstand,*
> *They pledged their faith to me.*
>
> *And I dreamt that one of that noble band*
> *Came forth my heart to claim,*
> *But I also dreamt, which charmed me most,*
> *That you loved me still the same.*   (Editors' note)

JAMES JOYCE (1882-1941)

Araby

North Richmond Street, being blind, was a quiet street except at the hour when the Christian Brothers' School set the boys free. An uninhabited house of two storeys stood at the blind end, detached from its neighbors in a square ground. The other houses of the street, conscious of decent lives within them, gazed at one another with brown imperturbable faces.

The former tenant of our house, a priest, had died in the back drawing-room. Air, musty from having been long enclosed, hung in all the rooms, and the waste room behind the kitchen was littered with old useless papers. Among these I found a few paper-covered books, the pages of which were curled and damp: *The Abbot*, by Walter Scott, *The Devout Communicant* and *The Memoirs of Vidocq*. I liked the last best because its leaves were yellow. The wild garden behind the house contained a central apple-tree and a few straggling bushes under one of which I found the late tenant's rusty bicycle-pump. He had been a very charitable priest; in his will he had left all his money to institutions and the furniture of his house to his sister.

When the short days of winter came dusk fell before we had well eaten our dinners. When we met in the street the houses had grown somber. The space of sky above us was the color of ever-changing violet and towards it the lamps of the street lifted their feeble lanterns. The cold air stung us and we played till our bodies glowed. Our shouts echoed in the silent street. The career of our play brought us through the dark muddy lanes behind the houses where we ran the gauntlet of the rough tribes from the cottages, to the back doors of the dark dripping gardens where odors arose from the ashpits, to the dark odorous stables where a coachman smoothed and combed the horse or shook music from the buckled harness. When we returned to the street light from the kitchen windows had filled the areas. If my uncle was seen turning the corner we hid in the shadow until we had seen him safely housed. Or if Mangan's sister came out on the doorstep to call her brother in to his tea we watched her from our shadow peer up and down the street. We waited to see whether she would remain or go in and, if she remained, we left our shadow and walked up to Mangan's steps resignedly. She was waiting for us, her figure defined by the light from the half-opened door. Her brother always teased her before he obeyed and I stood by the railings looking at her. Her dress swung as she moved her body and the soft rope of her hair tossed from side to side.

Every morning I lay on the floor in the front parlor watching her door. The blind was pulled down to within an inch of the sash so that I could not be seen. When she came out on the doorstep my heart leaped. I ran to the hall, seized my books and followed her. I kept her brown figure always in my eye and, when we came near the point at which our ways diverged, I quickened my pace and passed her. This happened morning after morning. I had never spoken to her, except for a few casual words, and yet her name was like a summons to all my foolish blood.

Her image accompanied me even in places the most hostile to romance. On Saturday evenings when my aunt went marketing I had to go to carry some of the parcels. We walked through the flaring streets, jostled by drunken men and bargaining women, amid the curses of laborers, the shrill litanies of shop-boys who stood on guard by the barrels of pigs' cheeks, the nasal chanting of street-singers, who sang a *come-all-you* about O'Donovan Rossa, or a ballad about the troubles in our native land. These noises converged in a single sensation of life for me: I imagined that I bore my chalice safely through a throng of foes. Her name sprang to my lips at moments in strange prayers and praises which I myself did not understand. My eyes were often full of tears (I could not tell why) and at times a flood from my heart seemed to pour itself out into my bosom. I thought little of the future. I did not know whether I would ever speak to her or not or, if I spoke to her, how I could tell her of my confused adoration. But my body was like a harp and her words and gestures were like fingers running upon the wires.

One evening I went into the back drawing-room in which the priest had died. It was a dark rainy evening and there was no sound in the house. Through one of the broken panes I heard the rain impinge upon the earth, the fine incessant needles of water playing in the sodden beds. Some distant lamp or lighted window gleamed below me. I was thankful that I could see so little. All my senses seemed to desire to veil themselves and, feeling that I was about to slip from them, I pressed the palms of my hands together until they trembled, murmuring: "O love! O love!" many times.

At last she spoke to me. When she addressed the first words to me I was so confused that I did not know what to answer. She asked me was I going to *Araby*. I forgot whether I answered yes or no. It would be a splendid bazaar, she said she would love to go.

"And why can't you?" I asked.

While she spoke she turned a silver bracelet round and round her wrist. She could not go, she said, because there would be a retreat that week in her convent. Her brother and two other boys were fighting for their caps and I was alone at the railings. She held one of the spikes, bowing her head towards me. The light from the lamp opposite our door caught the white curve of her neck, lit up her hair that rested there and, falling, lit up the hand upon the railing. It fell over one side of her dress and caught the white border of a petticoat, just visible as she stood at ease.

"It's well for you," she said.

"If I go," I said, "I will bring you something."

What innumerable follies laid waste my waking and sleeping thoughts after that evening! I wished to annihilate the tedious intervening days. I chafed against the work of school. At night in my bedroom and by day in the classroom her image came between me and the page I strove to read. The syllables of the word *Araby* were called to me through the silence in which my soul luxuriated and cast an Eastern enchantment over me. I asked for leave to go to the bazaar on Saturday night. My aunt was surprised and hoped it was not some Freemason affair. I answered few questions in class. I watched my master's face pass from amiability to sternness; he hoped I was not beginning to idle. I could not call my wandering thoughts together. I had hardly any patience with the serious work of life which, now that it stood between me and my desire, seemed to me child's play, ugly monotonous child's play.

On Saturday morning I reminded my uncle that I wished to go to the bazaar in the evening. He was fussing at the hallstand, looking for the hat-brush, and answered me curtly:

"Yes, boy, I know."

As he was in the hall I could not go into the front parlor and lie at the window. I left the house in bad humor and walked slowly towards the school. The air was pitilessly raw and already my heart misgave me.

When I came home to dinner my uncle had not yet been home. Still it was early. I sat staring at the clock for some time and, when its ticking began to irritate me, I left the room. I mounted the staircase and gained the upper part of the house. The high cold empty gloomy rooms liberated me and I went from room to room singing. From the front window I saw my companions playing below in the street. Their cries reached me weakened and indistinct and, leaning my forehead against the cool glass, I looked over at the dark house where she lived. I may have stood there for an hour, seeing nothing but the brown-clad figure cast by my imagination, touched discreetly by the lamplight at the curved neck, at the hand upon the railings and at the border below the dress.

When I came downstairs again I found Mrs. Mercer sitting at the fire. She was an old garrulous woman, a pawnbroker's widow, who collected used stamps for some pious purpose. I had to endure the gossip of the tea-table. The meal was prolonged beyond an hour and still my uncle did not come. Mrs. Mercer stood up to go: she was sorry she couldn't wait any longer, but it was after eight o'clock and she did not like to be out late, as the night air was bad for her. When she had gone I began to walk up and down the room, clenching my fists. My aunt said:

"I'm afraid you may put off your bazaar for this night of Our Lord."

At nine o'clock I heard my uncle's latchkey in the halldoor. I heard him talking to himself and heard the hallstand rocking when it had received the weight of his overcoat. I could interpret these signs. When he was midway through his dinner I asked him to give me the money to go to the bazaar. He had forgotten.

"The people are in bed and after their first sleep now," he said.

I did not smile. My aunt said to him energetically:

"Can't you give him the money and let him go? You've kept him late enough as it is."

My uncle said he was very sorry he had forgotten. He said he believed in the old saying: "All work and no play makes Jack a dull boy." He asked me where I was going and, when I had told him a second time he asked me did I know *The Arab's Farewell to His Steed*. When I left the kitchen he was about to recite the opening lines of the piece to my aunt.

I held a florin tightly in my hand as I strode down Buckingham Street towards the station. The sight of the streets thronged with buyers and glaring with gas recalled to me the purpose of my journey. I took my seat in a third-class carriage of a deserted train. After an intolerable delay the train moved out of the station slowly. It crept onward among ruinous houses and over the twinkling river. At Westland Row Station a crowd of people pressed to the carriage doors; but the porters moved them back, saying that it was a special train for the bazaar. I remained alone in the bare carriage. In a few minutes the train drew up beside an improvised wooden platform. I passed out on to the road and saw by the lighted dial of a clock that it was ten minutes to ten. In front of me was a large building which displayed the magical name.

I could not find any sixpenny entrance and, fearing that the bazaar would be closed, I passed in quickly through a turnstile, handing a shilling to a weary-looking man. I found myself in a big hall girdled at half its height by a gallery. Nearly all the stalls were closed and the greater part of the hall was in darkness. I recognized a silence like that which pervades a church after a service. I walked into the center of the bazaar timidly. A few people were gathered about the stalls which were still open. Before a curtain, over which the words *Café Chantant* were written in colored lamps, two men were counting money on a salver. I listened to the fall of the coins.

Remembering with difficulty why I had come I went over to one of the stalls and examined porcelain vases and flowered tea-sets. At the door of the stall a young lady was talking and laughing with two young gentlemen. I remarked their English accents and listened vaguely to their conversation.

"O, I never said such a thing!"

"O, but you did!"

"O, but I didn't!"

"Didn't she say that?"

"Yes. I heard her."

"O, there's a . . . fib!"

Observing me the young lady came over and asked me did I wish to buy anything. The tone of her voice was not encouraging; she seemed to have spoken to me out of a sense of duty. I looked humbly at the great jars that stood like eastern guards at either side of the dark entrance to the stall and murmured:

"No, thank you."

The young lady changed the position of one of the vases and went back to the two young men. They began to talk of the same subject. Once or twice the young lady glanced at me over her shoulder.

I lingered before her stall, though I knew my stay was useless, to make my interest in her wares seem the more real. Then I turned away slowly and walked down the middle of the bazaar. I allowed the two pennies to fall against the sixpence in my pocket. I heard a voice call from one end of the gallery that the light was out. The upper part of the hall was now completely dark.

Gazing up into the darkness I saw myself as a creature driven and derided by vanity; and my eyes burned with anguish and anger.

D. H. LAWRENCE (1885-1930)

The Horse Dealer's Daughter

"Well, Mabel, and what are you going to do with yourself?" asked Joe, with foolish flippancy. He felt quite safe himself. Without listening for an answer, he turned aside, worked a grain of tobacco to the tip of his tongue and spat it out. He did not care about anything, since he felt safe himself.

The three brothers and the sister sat round the desolate breakfast table, attempting some sort of desultory consultation. The morning's post had given the final tap to the family fortune, and all was over. The dreary dining-room itself, with its heavy mahogany furniture, looked as if it were waiting to be done away with.

But the consultation amounted to nothing. There was a strange air of ineffectuality about the three men, as they sprawled at table, smoking and reflecting vaguely on their own condition. The girl was alone, a rather short, sullen-looking young woman of twenty-seven. She did not share the same life as her brothers. She would have been good-looking, save for the impassive fixity of her face, "bull-dog," as her brothers called it.

There was a confused tramping of horses' feet outside. The three men all sprawled round in their chairs to watch. Beyond the dark holly-bushes that separated the strip of lawn from the highroad, they could see a cavalcade of shire horses swinging out of their own yard, being taken for exercise. This was the last time. These were the last horses that would go through their hands. The young men watched with critical, callous look. They were all frightened at the collapse of their lives, and the sense of disaster in which they were involved left them no inner freedom.

Yet they were three fine, well-set fellows enough. Joe, the eldest, was a man of thirty-three, broad and handsome in a hot, flushed way. His face was red, he twisted his black moustache over a thick finger, his eyes were shallow and restless. He had a sensual way of uncovering his teeth when he laughed, and his bearing was stupid. Now he watched the horses with a glazed look of helplessness in his eyes, a certain stupor of downfall.

The great draught-horses swung past. They were tied head to tail, four of them, and they heaved along to where a lane branched off from the highroad, planting their great hoofs floutingly in the fine black mud, swinging their great rounded haunches sumptuously, and trotting a few sudden steps as they were led into the lane, round the corner. Every movement showed a massive, slumbrous strength, and a stupidity which held them in subjection. The groom at the head looked back, jerking the leading rope. And the cavalcade moved out of sight up the lane, the tail of the last horse, bobbed up tight and stiff, held out taut from the swinging great haunches as they rocked behind the hedges in a motion-like sleep.

Joe watched with glazed hopeless eyes. The horses were almost like his own body to him. He felt he was done for now. Luckily he was engaged to a woman as old as himself, and therefore her father, who was steward of a neighboring estate, would provide him with a job. He would marry and go into harness. His life was over, he would be a subject animal now.

He turned uneasily aside, the retreating steps of the horses echoing in his ears. Then, with foolish restlessness, he reached for the scraps of bacon-rind from the plates, and making a faint whistling sound, flung them to the terrier that lay against the fender. He watched the dog swallow them, and waited till the creature looked into his eyes. Then a faint grin came on his face, and in a high, foolish voice he said:

"You won't get much more bacon, shall you, you little bitch?"

The dog faintly and dismally wagged its tail, then lowered its haunches, circled round, and lay down again.

There was another helpless silence at the table. Joe sprawled uneasily in his seat, not willing to go till the family conclave was dissolved. Fred Henry, the second brother, was erect, clean-limbed, alert. He had watched the passing of the horses with more sang-froid. If he was an animal, like Joe, he was an animal which controls, not one which is controlled. He was master of any horse, and he carried himself with a well-tempered air of mastery. But he was not master of the situations of life. He pushed his coarse brown moustache upwards, off his lip, and glanced irritably at his sister, who sat impassive and inscrutable.

"You'll go and stop with Lucy for a bit, shan't you?" he asked. The girl did not answer.

"I don't see what else you can do," persisted Fred Henry.

"Go as a skivvy," Joe interpolated laconically.

The girl did not move a muscle.

"If I was her, I should go in for training for a nurse," said Malcolm, the youngest of them all. He was the baby of the family, a young man of twenty-two, with a fresh, jaunty *museau*.

But Mabel did not take any notice of him. They had talked at her and round her for so many years, that she hardly heard them at all.

The marble clock on the mantelpiece softly chimed the half-hour, the dog rose uneasily from the hearthrug and looked at the party at the breakfast table. But still they sat on in ineffectual conclave.

"Oh, all right," said Joe suddenly, apropos of nothing. "I'll get a move on."

He pushed back his chair, straddled his knees with a downward jerk, to get them free, in horsey fashion, and went to the fire. Still he did not go out of the room; he was curious to know what the others would do or say. He began to charge his pipe, looking down at the dog and saying, in a high, affected voice:

"Going wi' me? Going wi' me are ter? Tha'rt goin' further tha that counts on just now, dost hear?"

The dog faintly wagged its tail, the man stuck out his jaw and covered his pipe with his hands, and puffed intently, losing himself in the tobacco, looking down all the while at the dog with an absent brown eye. The dog looked at him in mournful distrust. Joe stood with his knees stuck out, in real horsey fashion.

"Have you had a letter from Lucy?" Fred Henry asked of his sister.

"Last week," came the neutral reply.

"And what does she say?"

There was no answer.

"Does she *ask* you to go and stop there?" persisted Fred Henry.

"She says I can if I like."

"Well, then, you'd better. Tell her you'll come on Monday."

This was received in silence.

"That's what you'll do then, is it?" said Fred Henry, in some exasperation.

But she made no answer. There was a silence of futility and irritation in the room. Malcolm grinned fatuously.

"You'll have to make up your mind between now and next Wednesday," said Joe loudly, "or else find yourself lodgings on the curbstone."

The face of the young woman darkened, but she sat on immutable.

"Here's Jack Fergusson!" exclaimed Malcolm, who was looking aimlessly out of the window.

"Where?" exclaimed Joe, loudly.

"Just gone past."

"Coming in?"

Malcolm craned his neck to see the gate.

"Yes," he said.

There was a silence. Mabel sat on like one condemned, at the head of the table. Then a whistle was heard from the kitchen. The dog got up and barked sharply. Joe opened the door and shouted:

"Come on."

After a moment a young man entered. He was muffled up in overcoat and a purple woolen scarf, and his tweed cap, which he did not remove, was pulled down on his head. He was of medium height, his face was rather long and pale, his eyes looked tired.

"Hello, Jack! Well, Jack!" exclaimed Malcolm and Joe. Fred Henry merely said, "Jack."

"What's doing?" asked the newcomer, evidently addressing Fred Henry.

"Same. We've got to be out by Wednesday. Got a cold?"

"I have—got it bad, too."

"Why don't you stop in?"

"*Me* stop in? When I can't stand on my legs, perhaps I shall have a chance." The young man spoke huskily. He had a slight Scotch accent.

"It's a knock-out, isn't it," said Joe, boisterously, "if a doctor goes round croaking with a cold. Looks bad for the patients, doesn't it?"

The young doctor looked at him slowly.

"Anything the matter with *you*, then?" he asked sarcastically.

"Not as I know of. Damn your eyes, I hope not. Why?"

"I thought you were very concerned about the patients, wondered if you might be one yourself."

"Damn it, no, I've never been patient to no flaming doctor, and hope I never shall be," returned Joe.

At this point Mabel rose from the table, and they all seemed to become aware of her existence. She began putting the dishes together. The young doctor looked at her, but did not address her. He had not greeted her. She went out of the room with the tray, her face impassive and unchanged.

"When are you off then, all of you?" asked the doctor.

"I'm catching the eleven-forty," replied Malcolm. "Are you goin' down wi' th' trap, Joe?"

"Yes, I've told you I'm going down wi' th' trap, haven't I?"

"We'd better be getting her in then. So long, Jack, if I don't see you before I go," said Malcolm, shaking hands.

He went out, followed by Joe, who seemed to have his tail between his legs.

"Well, this is the devil's own," exclaimed the doctor, when he was left alone with Fred Henry. "Going before Wednesday, are you?"

"That's the orders," replied the other.

"Where, to Northampton?"

"That's it."

"The devil!" exclaimed Fergusson, with quiet chagrin.

And there was silence between the two.

"All settled up, are you?" asked Fergusson.

"About."

There was another pause.

"Well, I shall miss yer, Freddy, boy," said the young doctor.

"And I shall miss thee, Jack," returned the other.

"Miss you like hell," mused the doctor.

Fred Henry turned aside. There was nothing to say. Mabel came in again, to finish clearing the table.

"What are *you* going to do, then, Miss Pervin?" asked Fergusson. "Going to your sister's, are you?"

Mabel looked at him with her steady, dangerous eyes, that always made him uncomfortable, unsettling his superficial ease.

"No," she said.

"Well, what in the name of fortune *are* you going to do? Say what you mean to do," cried Fred Henry, with futile intensity.

But she only averted her head, and continued her work. She folded the white table-cloth, and put on the chenille cloth.

"The sulkiest bitch that ever trod!" muttered her brother.

But she finished her task with perfectly impassive face, the young doctor watching her interestedly all the while. Then she went out.

Fred Henry stared after her, clenching his lips, his blue eyes fixing in sharp antagonism, as he made a grimace of sour exasperation.

"You could bray her into bits, and that's all you'd get out of her," he said in a small, narrowed tone.

The doctor smiled faintly.

"What's she *going* to do, then?" he asked.

"Strike me if I know!" returned the other.

There was a pause. Then the doctor stirred.

"I'll be seeing you to-night, shall I?" he said to his friend.

"Ay—where's it to be? Are we going over to Jessdale?"

"I don't know. I've got such a cold on me. I'll come round to the Moon and Stars, anyway."

"Let Lizzie and May miss their night for once, eh?"

"That's it—if I feel as I do now."

"All's one—"

The two young men went through the passage and down to the back door together. The house was large, but it was servantless now, and desolate. At the back was a small bricked house-yard, and beyond that a big square, graveled fine and red, and having stables on two sides. Sloping, dank, winter-dark fields stretched away on the open sides.

But the stables were empty. Joseph Pervin, the father of the family, had been a man of no education, who had become a fairly large horse dealer. The stables had been full of horses, there was a great turmoil and come-and-go of horses and of dealers and grooms. Then the kitchen was full of servants. But of late things had declined. The old man had married a second time, to retrieve his fortunes. Now he was dead and everything was gone to the dogs, there was nothing but debt and threatening.

For months, Mabel had been servantless in the big house, keeping the home together in penury for her ineffectual brothers. She had kept house for ten years. But previously it was with unstinted means. Then, however brutal and coarse everything was, the sense of money had kept her proud, confident. The men might be foul-mouthed, the women in the kitchen might have bad reputations, her brothers might have illegitimate children. But so long as there was money, the girl felt herself established, and brutally proud, reserved.

No company came to the house, save dealers and coarse men. Mabel had no associates of her own sex, after her sister went away. But she did not mind. She went regularly to church, she attended to her father. And she lived in the memory of her mother, who had died when she was fourteen, and whom she had loved. She had loved her father, too, in a different way, depending upon him, and feeling secure in him, until at the age of fifty-four he married again. And then she had set hard against him. Now he had died and left them all hopelessly in debt.

She had suffered badly during the period of poverty. Nothing, however, could shake the curious sullen, animal pride that dominated each member of the family. Now, for Mabel, the end had come. Still she would not cast about her. She would follow her own way just the same. She would always hold the keys of her own situation. Mindless and persistent, she endured from day to day. Why should she think? Why should she answer anybody? It was enough that this was the end, and there was no way out. She need not pass any more darkly along the main street of the small town, avoiding every eye. She need not demean herself any more, going into the shops and buying the cheapest food. This was at an end. She thought of nobody, not even of herself. Mindless and persistent, she seemed in a sort of ecstasy to be coming nearer to her fulfilment, her own glorification, approaching her dead mother, who was glorified.

In the afternoon she took a little bag, with shears and sponge and a small scrubbing brush, and went out. It was a gray, wintry day, with saddened, dark green fields and an atmosphere blackened by the smoke of foundries not far off. She went quickly, darkly along the causeway, heeding nobody, through the town to the churchyard.

There she always felt secure, as if no one could see her, although as a matter of fact she was exposed to the stare of every one who passed along under the churchyard wall. Nevertheless, once under the shadow of the great looming church, among the graves, she felt immune from the world, reserved within the thick churchyard wall as in another country.

Carefully she clipped the grass from the grave, and arranged the pinky white, small chrysanthemums in the tin cross. When this was done, she took an empty jar from a neighboring grave, brought water, and carefully, most scrupulously sponged the marble headstone and the coping-stone.

It gave her sincere satisfaction to do this. She felt in immediate contact with the world of her mother. She took minute pains, went through the park in a state bordering on pure happiness, as if in performing this task she came into a subtle, intimate connection with her mother. For the life she followed here in the world was far less real than the world of death she inherited from her mother.

The doctor's house was just by the church. Fergusson, being a mere hired assistant, was slave to the countryside. As he hurried now to attend to the outpatients in the surgery, glancing across the graveyard with his quick eyes, he saw the girl at her task at the grave. She seemed so intent and remote, it was like looking into another world. Some mystical element was touched in him. He slowed down as he walked, watching her as if spellbound.

She lifted her eyes, feeling him looking. Their eyes met. And each looked away again at once, each feeling, in some way, found out by the other. He lifted his cap and passed on down the road. There remained distinct in his consciousness, like a vision, the memory of her face, lifted from the tombstone in the churchyard, and looking at him with slow, large, portentous eyes. It *was* portentous, her face. It seemed to mesmerize him. There was a heavy power in her eyes which laid hold of his whole being, as if he had drunk some powerful drug. He had been feeling weak and done before. Now the life came back into him, he felt delivered from his own fretted, daily self.

He finished his duties at the surgery as quickly as might be, hastily filling up the bottle of the waiting people with cheap drugs. Then, in perpetual haste, he set off again to visit several cases in another part of his round, before teatime. At all times he preferred to walk if he could, but particularly when he was not well. He fancied the motion restored him.

The Horse Dealer's Daughter 201

The afternoon was falling. It was gray, deadened, and wintry, with a slow, moist, heavy coldness sinking in and deadening all the faculties. But why should he think or notice? He hastily climbed the hill and turned across the dark green fields, following the black cinder-track. In the distance, across a shallow dip in the country, the small town was clustered like smouldering ash, a tower, a spire, a heap of low, raw, extinct houses. And on the nearest fringe of the town, sloping into the dip, was Oldmeadow, the Pervins' house. He could see the stables and the outbuildings distinctly, as they lay towards him on the slope. Well, he would not go there many more times! Another resource would be lost to him, another place gone: the only company he cared for in the alien, ugly little town he was losing. Nothing but work, drudgery, constant hastening from dwelling to dwelling among the colliers and the iron-workers. It wore him out, but at the same time he had a craving for it. It was a stimulant to him to be in the homes of the working people, moving as it were through the inner-most body of their life. His nerves were excited and gratified. He could come so near, into the very lives of the rough, inarticulate, powerfully emotional men and women. He grumbled, he said he hated the hellish hole. But as a matter of fact it excited him, the contact with the rough, strongly-feeling people was a stimulant applied direct to his nerves.

Below Oldmeadow, in the green, shallow, soddened hollow of fields, lay a square, deep pond. Roving across the landscape, the doctor's quick eye detected a figure in black passing through the gate of the field, down towards the pond. He looked again. It would be Mabel Pervin. His mind suddenly became alive and attentive.

Why was she going down there? He pulled up on the path on the slope above, and stood staring. He could just make sure of the small black figure moving in the hollow of the failing day. He seemed to see her in the midst of such obscurity, that he was like a clairvoyant, seeing rather with the mind's eye than with ordinary sight. Yet he could see her positively enough, while he kept his eye attentive. He felt, if he looked away from her, in the thick, ugly falling dusk, he would lose her altogether.

He followed her minutely as she moved, direct and intent, like something transmitted rather than stirring in voluntary activity, straight down the field towards the pond. There she stood on the bank for a moment. She never raised her head. Then she waded slowly into the water.

He stood motionless as the small black figure walked slowly and deliberately towards the center of the pond, very slowly, gradually moving deeper into the motionless water, and still moving forward as the water got up to her breast. Then he could see her no more in the dusk of the dead afternoon.

"There!" he exclaimed. "Would you believe it?"

And he hastened straight down, running over the wet, soddened fields, pushing through the hedges, down into the depression of callous wintry obscurity. It took him several minutes to come to the pond. He stood on the bank, breathing heavily. He could see nothing. His eyes seemed to penetrate the dead water. Yes, perhaps that was the dark shadow of her black clothing beneath the surface of the water.

He slowly ventured into the pond. The bottom was deep, soft clay, he sank in, and the water clasped dead cold round his legs. As he stirred he could smell the cold, rotten clay that fouled up into the water. It was objectionable in his lungs. Still, repelled and yet not heeding, he moved deeper into the pond. The cold water rose over his thighs, over his loins, upon his abdomen. The lower part of his body was all sunk in the hideous cold element. And the bottom was so deeply soft and uncertain he was afraid of pitching with his mouth underneath. He could not swim, and was afraid.

He crouched a little, spreading his hands under the water and moving them round, trying to feel for her. The dead cold pond swayed upon his chest. He moved again, a little deeper, and again, with his hands underneath, he felt all around under the water. And he touched her clothing. But it evaded his fingers. He made a desperate effort to grasp it.

And so doing he lost his balance and went under, horribly, suffocating in the foul earthy water, struggling madly for a few moments. At last, after what seemed an eternity, he got his footing, rose again into the air and looked around. He gasped, and knew he was in the world. Then he looked at the water. She had risen near him. He grasped her clothing, and drawing her nearer, turned to take his way to land again.

He went very slowly, carefully, absorbed in the slow progress. He rose higher, climbing out of the pond. The water was now only about his legs; he was thankful, full of relief to be out of the clutches of the pond. He lifted her and staggered on to the bank, out of the horror of wet, gray clay.

He laid her down on the bank. She was quite unconscious and running with water. He made the water come from her mouth, he worked to restore her. He did not have to work very long before he could feel the breathing begin again in her; she was breathing naturally. He worked a little longer. He could feel her live beneath his hands; she was coming back. He wiped her face, wrapped her in his overcoat, looked round into the dim, dark gray world, then lifted her and staggered down the bank and across the fields.

It seemed an unthinkably long way, and his burden so heavy he felt he would never get to the house. But at last he was in the stable-yard, and then in the house-yard. He opened the door and went into the house. In the kitchen he laid her down on the hearthrug, and called. The house was empty. But the fire was burning in the grate.

Then again he kneeled to attend to her. She was breathing regularly, her eyes were wide open and as if conscious, but there seemed something missing in her look. She was conscious in herself, but unconscious of her surroundings.

He ran upstairs, took blankets from a bed, and put them before the fire to warm. Then he removed her saturated, earthy-smelling clothing, rubbed her dry with a towel, and wrapped her naked in the blankets. Then he went into the dining-room, to look for spirits. There was a little whisky. He drank a gulp himself, and put some into her mouth.

The effect was instantaneous. She looked full into his face, as if she had been seeing him for some time, and yet had only just become conscious of him.

"Dr. Fergusson?" she said.

"What?" he answered.

He was divesting himself of his coat, intending to find some dry clothing upstairs. He could not bear the smell of the dead, clayey water, and he was mortally afraid of his own health.

"What did I do?" she asked.

"Walked into the pond," he replied. He had begun to shudder like one sick, and could hardly attend to her. Her eyes remained full on him, he seemed to be going dark in his mind, looking back at her helplessly. The shuddering became quieter in him, his life came back in him, dark and unknowing, but strong again.

"Was I out of my mind?" she asked, while her eyes were fixed on him all the time.

"Maybe, for the moment," he replied. He felt quiet, because his strength had come back. The strange fretful strain had left him.

"Am I out of my mind now?" she asked.

"Are you?" he reflected a moment. "No," he answered truthfully, "I don't see that you are." He turned his face aside. He was afraid now, because he felt dazed, and felt dimly that her power was stronger than his, in this issue. And she continued to look at him fixedly all the time. "Can you tell me where I shall find some dry things to put on?" he asked.

"Did you dive into the pond for me?" she asked.

"No," he answered. "I walked in. But I went in overhead as well."

There was silence for a moment. He hesitated. He very much wanted to go upstairs to get into dry clothing. But there was another desire in him. And she seemed to hold him. His will seemed to have gone to sleep, and left him, standing there slack before her. But he felt warm inside himself. He did not shudder at all, though his clothes were sodden on him.

"Why did you?" she asked.

"Because I didn't want you to do such a foolish thing," he said.

"It wasn't foolish," she said, still gazing at him as she lay on the floor, with a sofa cushion under her head. "It was the right thing to do. I knew best, then." *(Nothing to live for) (Now he knew right)*

"I'll go and shift these wet things," he said. But still he had not the power to move out of her presence, until she sent him. It was as if she had the life of his body in her hands, and he could not extricate himself. Or perhaps he did not want to.

Suddenly she sat up. Then she became aware of her own immediate condition. She felt the blankets about her, she knew her own limbs. For a moment it seemed as if her reason were going. She looked round, with wild eye, as if seeking something. He stood still with fear. She saw her clothing lying scattered.

"Who undressed me?" she asked, her eyes resting full and inevitable on his face.

"I did," he replied, "to bring you round."

For some moments she sat and gazed at him awfully, her lips parted.

"Do you love me, then?" she asked. *she knows she loves him at this point*

He only stood and stared at her, fascinated. His soul seemed to melt. *FIRE, WARM, LOVE!*

She shuffled forward on her knees, and put her arms round him, round his legs, as he stood there, pressing her breasts against his knees and thighs, clutching him with strange, convulsive certainty, pressing his thighs against her, drawing him to her face, her throat, as she looked up at him with flaring, humble eyes of transfiguration, triumphant in first possession. *clue of desire, shyness of 1st love*

"You love me," she murmured, in strange transport, yearning and triumphant and confident. "You love me. I know you love me, I know."

And she was passionately kissing his knees, through the wet clothing, passionately and indiscriminately kissing his knees, his legs, as if unaware of everything.

He looked down at the tangled wet hair, the wild, bare, animal shoulders. He was amazed, bewildered, and afraid. He had never

animal pride coming thru.

thought of loving her. He had never wanted to love her. When he rescued her and restored her, he was a doctor, and she was a patient. He had had no single personal thought of her. Nay, this introduction of the personal element was very distasteful to him, a violation of his professional honor. It was horrible to have her there embracing his knees. It was horrible. He revolted from it, violently. And yet—and yet —he had not the power to break away.

She looked at him again, with the same supplication of powerful love, and that same transcendent, frightening light of triumph. In view of the delicate flame which seemed to come from her face like a light, he was powerless. And yet he had never intended to love her. He had never intended. And something stubborn in him could not give way.

"You love me," she repeated, in a murmur of deep, rhapsodic assurance. "You love me."

Her hands were drawing him, drawing him down to her. He was afraid, even a little horrified. For he had, really, no intention of loving her. Yet her hands were drawing him towards her. He put out his hand quickly to steady himself, and grasped her bare shoulder. A flame seemed to burn the hand that grasped her soft shoulder. He had no intention of loving her: his whole will was against his yielding. It was horrible. And yet wonderful was the touch of her shoulders, beautiful the shining of her face. Was she perhaps mad? He had a horror of yielding to her. Yet something in him ached also.

He had been staring away at the door, away from her. But his hand remained on her shoulder. She had gone suddenly very still. He looked down at her. Her eyes were now wide with fear, with doubt, the light was dying from her face, a shadow of terrible grayness was returning. He could not bear the touch of her eyes' question upon him, and the look of death behind the question.

With an inward groan he gave way, and let his heart yield towards her. A sudden gentle smile came on his face. And her eyes, which never left his face, slowly, slowly filled with tears. He watched the strange water rise in her eyes, like some slow fountain coming up. And his heart seemed to burn and melt away in his breast.

He could not bear to look at her any more. He dropped on his knees and caught her head with his arms and pressed her face against his throat. She was very still. His heart, which seemed to have broken, was burning with a kind of agony in his breast. And he felt her slow, hot tears wetting his throat. But he could not move.

He felt the hot tears wet his neck and the hollows of his neck, and he remained motionless, suspended through one of man's eternities. Only now it had become indispensable to him to have her face pressed close to him; he could never let her go again. He could never let her head go away from the close clutch of his arm. He wanted to remain like that for ever, with his heart hurting him in a pain that was also life to him. Without knowing, he was looking down on her damp, soft brown hair.

Then, as it were suddenly, he smelt the horrid stagnant smell of that water. And at the same moment she drew away from him and looked at him. Her eyes were wistful and unfathomable. He was afraid of them, and he fell to kissing her, not knowing what he was doing. He wanted her eyes not to have that terrible, wistful, unfathomable look.

When she turned her face to him again, a faint delicate flush was glowing, and there was again dawning that terrible shining of joy in her eyes, which really terrified him, and yet which he now wanted to see, because he feared the look of doubt still more.

"You love me?" she said, rather faltering. *able to ask him*

"Yes." The word cost him a painful effort. Not because it wasn't true. But because it was too newly true, the *saying* seemed to tear open again his newly-torn heart. And he hardly wanted it to be true, even now.

She lifted her face to him, and he bent forward and kissed her on the mouth, gently, with the one kiss that is an eternal pledge. And as he kissed her his heart strained again in his breast. He never intended to love her. But now it was over. He had crossed over the gulf to her, and all that he had left behind had shriveled and become void.

After the kiss, her eyes again slowly filled with tears. She sat still, away from him, with her face drooped aside, and her hands folded in her lap. The tears fell very slowly. There was complete silence. He too sat there motionless and silent on the hearthrug. The strange pain of his heart that was broken seemed to consume him. That he should love her? That this was love! That he should be ripped open in this way! Him, a doctor! How they would all jeer if they knew! It was agony to him to think they might know.

In the curious naked pain of the thought he looked again to her. She was sitting there drooped into a muse. He saw a tear fall, and his heart flared hot. He saw for the first time that one of her shoulders was quite uncovered, one arm bare, he could see one of her small breasts; dimly, because it had become almost dark in the room.

"Why are you crying?" he asked, in an altered voice.

She looked up at him, and behind her tears the consciousness of her situation for the first time brought a dark look of shame to her eyes.

"I'm not crying, really," she said, watching him half frightened.

The Horse Dealer's Daughter 207

He reached his hand, and softly closed it on her bare arm.

"I love you! I love you!" he said in a soft, low vibrating voice, unlike himself.

She shrank, and dropped her head. The soft, penetrating grip of his hand on her arm distressed her. She looked up at him.

"I want to go," she said. "I want to go and get you some dry things."

"Why?" he said. "I'm all right."

"But I want to go," she said. "And I want you to change your things."

He released her arm, and she wrapped herself in the blanket, looking at him rather frightened. And still she did not rise.

"Kiss me," she said wistfully.

He kissed her, but briefly, half in anger.

Then, after a second, she rose nervously, all mixed up in the blanket. He watched her in her confusion, as she tried to extricate herself and wrap herself up so that she could walk. He watched her relentlessly, as she knew. And as she went, the blanket trailing, and as he saw a glimpse of her feet and her white leg, he tried to remember her as she was when he had wrapped her in the blanket. But then he didn't want to remember, because she had been nothing to him then, and his nature revolted from remembering her as she was when she was nothing to him.

A tumbling, muffled noise from within the dark house startled him. Then he heard her voice:—"There are clothes." He rose and went to the foot of the stairs, and gathered up the garments she had thrown down. Then he came back to the fire, to rub himself down and dress. He grinned at his own appearance when he had finished.

The fire was sinking, so he put on coal. The house was now quite dark, save for the light of a street-lamp that shone in faintly from beyond the holly trees. He lit the gas with matches he found on the mantelpiece. Then he emptied the pockets of his own clothes, and threw all his wet things in a heap into the scullery. After which he gathered up her sodden clothes, gently, and put them in a separate heap on the copper-top in the scullery.

It was six o'clock on the clock. His own watch had stopped. He ought to go back to the surgery. He waited, and still she did not come down. So he went to the foot of the stairs and called:

"I shall have to go."

Almost immediately he heard her coming down. She had on her best dress of black voile, and her hair was tidy, but still damp. She looked at him—and in spite of herself, smiled.

"I don't like you in those clothes," she said.

208 D. H. LAWRENCE

"Do I look a sight?" he answered.

They were shy of one another.

"I'll make you some tea," she said.

"No, I must go."

"Must you?" And she looked at him again with the wide, strained, doubtful eyes. And again, from the pain of his breast, he knew how he loved her. He went and bent to kiss her, gently, passionately, with his heart's painful kiss.

"And my hair smells so horrible," she murmured in distraction. "And I'm so awful, I'm so awful! Oh, no, I'm too awful." And she broke into bitter, heart-broken sobbing. "You can't want to love me, I'm horrible."

"Don't be silly, don't be silly," he said, trying to comfort her, kissing her, holding her in his arms. "I want you, I want to marry you, we're going to be married, quickly, quickly—tomorrow if I can."

But she only sobbed terribly, and cried:

"I feel awful. I feel awful. I feel I'm horrible to you."

"No, I want you, I want you," was all he answered, blindly, with that terrible intonation which frightened her almost more than her horror lest he should *not* want her.

KATHERINE ANNE PORTER (1890-   )

The Jilting of Granny Weatherall

She flicked her wrist neatly out of Doctor Harry's pudgy careful fingers and pulled the sheet up to her chin. The brat ought to be in knee breeches. Doctoring around the country with spectacles on his nose! "Get along now, take your schoolbooks and go. There's nothing wrong with me."

Doctor Harry spread a warm paw like a cushion on her forehead where the forked green vein danced and made her eyelids twitch. "Now, now, be a good girl, and we'll have you up in no time."

"That's no way to speak to a woman nearly eighty years old just because she's down. I'd have you respect your elders, young man."

"Well, Missy, excuse me." Doctor Harry patted her cheek. "But I've got to warn you, haven't I? You're a marvel, but you must be careful or you're going to be good and sorry."

"Don't tell me what I'm going to be. I'm on my feet now, morally speaking. It's Cornelia. I had to go to bed to get rid of her."

Her bones felt loose, and floated around in her skin, and Doctor Harry floated like a balloon around the foot of the bed. He floated and pulled down his waistcoat and swung his glasses on a cord. "Well, stay where you are, it certainly can't hurt you."

"Get along and doctor your sick," said Granny Weatherall. "Leave a well woman alone. I'll call for you when I want you. . . . Where were you forty years ago when I pulled through milk-leg and double pneumonia? You weren't even born. Don't let Cornelia lead you on," she shouted, because Doctor Harry appeared to float up to the ceiling and out. "I pay my own bills, and I don't throw my money away on nonsense!"

She meant to wave good-by, but it was too much trouble. Her eyes closed of themselves, it was like a dark curtain drawn around the bed. The pillow rose and floated under her, pleasant as a hammock in a light wind. She listened to the leaves rustling outside the window. No, somebody was swishing newspapers: no, Cornelia and Doctor Harry were whispering together. She leaped broad awake, thinking they whispered in her ear.

"She was never like this, *never* like this!" "Well, what can we expect?" "Yes, eighty years old. . . ."

Well, and what if she was? She still had ears. It was like Cornelia to whisper around doors. She always kept things secret in such a public way. She was always being tactful and kind. Cornelia was dutiful; that was the trouble with her. Dutiful and good: "So good and dutiful," said Granny, "that I'd like to spank her." She saw herself spanking Cornelia and making a fine job of it.

"What'd you say, Mother?"

Granny felt her face tying up in hard knots.

"Can't a body think, I'd like to know?"

"I thought you might want something."

"I do. I want a lot of things. First off, go away and don't whisper."

She lay and drowsed, hoping in her sleep that the children would keep out and let her rest a minute. It had been a long day. Not that she was tired. It was always pleasant to snatch a minute now and then. There was always so much to be done, let me see: tomorrow.

Tomorrow was far away and there was nothing to trouble about. Things were finished somehow when the time came; thank God there was always a little margin over for peace: then a person could spread out the plan of life and tuck in the edges orderly. It was good to have everything clean and folded away, with the hair brushes and tonic bottles sitting straight on the white embroidered linen: the day started without fuss and the pantry shelves laid out with rows of jelly glasses and brown jugs and white stone-china jars with blue whirligigs and words painted on them: coffee, tea, sugar, ginger, cinnamon, allspice: and the bronze clock with the lion on top nicely dusted off. The dust that lion could collect in twenty-four hours! The box in the attic with all those letters tied up, well, she'd have to go through that tomorrow. All those letters—George's letters and John's letters and her letters to them both—lying around for the children to find afterwards made her uneasy. Yes, that would be tomorrow's business. No use to let them know how silly she had been once.

While she was rummaging around she found death in her mind and it felt clammy and unfamiliar. She had spent so much time preparing for death there was no need for bringing it up again. Let it take care of itself now. When she was sixty she had felt very old, finished, and went around making farewell trips to see her children and grandchildren, with a secret in her mind: This is the very last of your mother, children! Then she made her will and came down with a long fever. That was all just a notion like a lot of other things, but it was lucky too, for she had once for all got over the idea of dying for a long time. Now she couldn't be worried. She hoped she had better sense now. Her father had lived to be one hundred and two years old and had drunk a noggin of strong hot toddy on his last birthday. He told the reporters it was his daily habit, and he owed his long life to that. He had made quite a scandal and was very pleased about it. She believed she'd just plague Cornelia a little.

"Cornelia! Cornelia!" No footsteps, but a sudden hand on her cheek. "Bless you, where have you been?"

"Here, mother."

"Well, Cornelia, I want a noggin of hot toddy."

"Are you cold, darling?"

"I'm chilly, Cornelia. Lying in bed stops the circulation. I must have told you that a thousand times."

Well, she could just hear Cornelia telling her husband that Mother was getting a little childish and they'd have to humor her. The thing that most annoyed her was that Cornelia thought she was deaf, dumb, and blind. Little hasty glances and tiny gestures tossed around her and over her head saying, "Don't cross her, let her have her way, she's eighty years old," and she sitting there as if she lived in a thin glass cage. Sometimes Granny almost made up her mind to pack up and move back to her own house where nobody could remind her every minute that she was old. Wait, wait, Cornelia, till your own children whisper behind your back!

In her day she had kept a better house and had got more work done. She wasn't too old yet for Lydia to be driving eighty miles for advice when one of the children jumped the track, and Jimmy still dropped in and talked things over: "Now, Mammy, you've a good business head, I want to know what you think of this? . . ." Old.

Cornelia couldn't change the furniture around without asking. Little things, little things! They had been so sweet when they were little. Granny wished the old days were back again with the children young and everything to be done over. It had been a hard pull, but not too much for her. When she thought of all the food she had cooked, and all the clothes she had cut and sewed, and all the gardens she had made —well, the children showed it. There they were, made out of her, and they couldn't get away from that. Sometimes she wanted to see John again and point to them and say, Well, I didn't do so badly, did I? But that would have to wait. That was for tomorrow. She used to think of him as a man, but now all the children were older than their father, and he would be a child beside her if she saw him now. It seemed strange and there was something wrong in the idea. Why, he couldn't possibly recognize her. She had fenced in a hundred acres once, digging the post holes herself and clamping the wires with just a negro boy to help. That changed a woman. John would be looking for a young woman with the peaked Spanish comb in her hair and the painted fan. Digging post holes changed a woman. Riding country roads in the winter when women had their babies was another thing: sitting up nights with sick horses and sick negroes and sick children and hardly ever losing one. John, I hardly ever lost one of them! John would see that in a minute, that would be something he could understand, she wouldn't have to explain anything!

It made her feel like rolling up her sleeves and putting the whole place to rights again. No matter if Cornelia was determined to be everywhere at once, there were a great many things left undone on this place. She would start tomorrow and do them. It was good to be strong enough for everything, even if all you made melted and changed and slipped under your hands, so that by the time you finished you almost forgot what you were working for. What was it I set out to do? she asked herself intently, but she could not remember. A fog rose over the valley, she saw it marching across the creek swallowing the trees and moving up the hill like an army of ghosts. Soon it would be at the near edge of the orchard, and then it was time to go in and light the lamps. Come in, children, don't stay out in the night air.

Lighting the lamps had been beautiful. The children huddled up to her and breathed like little calves waiting at the bars in the twilight. Their eyes followed the match and watched the flame rise and settle in a blue curve, then they moved away from her. The lamp was lit, they didn't have to be scared and hang on to mother any more. Never, never, never more. God, for all my life I thank Thee. Without Thee, my God, I could never have done it. Hail, Mary, full of grace.

I want you to pick all the fruit this year and see that nothing is wasted. There's always someone who can use it. Don't let good things rot for want of using. You waste life when you waste good food. Don't let things get lost. It's bitter to lose things. Now, don't let me get to thinking, not when I am tired and taking a little nap before supper. . . .

The pillow rose about her shoulders and pressed against her heart and the memory was being squeezed out of it: oh, push down the pillow, somebody: it would smother her if she tried to hold it. Such a fresh breeze blowing and such a green day with no threats in it. But he had not come, just the same. What does a woman do when she has put on the white veil and set out the white cake for a man and he doesn't come? She tried to remember. No, I swear he never harmed me but in that. He never harmed me but in that . . . and what if he did? There was the day, the day, but a whirl of dark smoke rose and covered it, crept up and over into the bright field where everything was planted so carefully in orderly rows. That was hell, she knew hell when she saw it. For sixty years she had prayed against remembering him and against losing her soul in the deep pit of hell, and now the two things were mingled in one and the thought of him was a smoky cloud from hell that moved and crept in her head when she had just got rid of Doctor Harry and was trying to rest a minute. Wounded vanity, Ellen, said a sharp voice in the top of her mind. Don't let your wounded vanity get the upper hand of you. Plenty of girls get jilted. You were jilted, weren't you? Then stand up to it. Her eyelids wavered and let in streamers of blue-gray light like tissue paper over her eyes. She must get up and pull the shades down or she'd never sleep. She was in bed again and the shades were not down. How could that happen? Better turn over, hide from the light, sleeping in the light gave you nightmares. "Mother, how do you feel now?" and a stinging wetness on her forehead. But I don't like having my face washed in cold water!

Hapsy? George? Lydia? Jimmy? No, Cornelia, and her features were swollen and full of little puddles. "They're coming, darling, they'll all be here soon." Go wash your face, child, you look funny.

Instead of obeying, Cornelia knelt down and put her head on the pillow. She seemed to be talking but there was no sound. "Well, are you tongue-tied? Whose birthday is it? Are you going to give a party?"

Cornelia's mouth moved urgently in strange shapes. "Don't do that, you bother me, daughter."

"Oh, no, Mother. Oh, no. . . ."

Nonsense. It was strange about children. They disputed your every word. "No what, Cornelia?"

"Here's Doctor Harry."

"I won't see that boy again. He just left five minutes ago."

"That was this morning, Mother. It's night now. Here's the nurse."

"This is Doctor Harry, Mrs. Weatherall. I never saw you look so young and happy!"

"Ah, I'll never be young again—but I'd be happy if they'd let me lie in peace and get rested."

She thought she spoke up loudly, but no one answered. A warm weight on her forehead, a warm bracelet on her wrist, and a breeze went on whispering, trying to tell her something. A shuffle of leaves in the everlasting hand of God. He blew on them and they danced and rattled. "Mother, don't mind, we're going to give you a little hypodermic." "Look here, daughter, how do ants get in this bed? I saw sugar ants yesterday." Did you send for Hapsy too?

It was Hapsy she really wanted. She had to go a long way back through a great many rooms to find Hapsy standing with a baby on her arm. She seemed to herself to be Hapsy also, and the baby on Hapsy's arm was Hapsy and himself and herself, all at once, and there was no surprise in the meeting. Then Hapsy melted from within and turned flimsy as gray gauze and the baby was a gauzy shadow, and Hapsy came up close and said, "I thought you'd never come," and looked at her very searchingly and said, "You haven't changed a bit!" They leaned forward to kiss, when Cornelia began whispering from a long way off, "Oh, is there anything you want to tell me? Is there anything I can do for you?"

Yes, she had changed her mind after sixty years and she would like to see George. I want you to find George. Find him and be sure to tell him I forgot him. I want him to know I had my husband just the same and my children and my house like any other woman. A good house too and a good husband that I loved and fine children out of him. Better than I hoped for even. Tell him I was given back everything he took away and more. Oh, no, oh, God, no, there was something else besides the house and the man and the children. Oh, surely they were not all? What was it? Something not given back. . . . Her breath crowded down under her ribs and grew into a monstrous frightening shape with cutting edges; it bored up into her head, and the agony was unbelievable: Yes, John, get the doctor now, no more talk, my time has come.

When this one was born it should be the last. The last. It should have been born first, for it was the one she had truly wanted. Everything came in good time. Nothing left out, left over. She was strong, in three days she would be as well as ever. Better. A woman needed milk in her to have her full health.

"Mother, do you hear me?"

"I've been telling you—"

"Mother, Father Connolly's here."

"I went to Holy Communion only last week. Tell him I'm not so sinful as all that."

"Father just wants to speak to you."

He could speak as much as he pleased. It was like him to drop in and inquire about her soul as if it were a teething baby, and then stay on for a cup of tea and a round of cards and gossip. He always had a funny story of some sort, usually about an Irishman who made his little mistakes and confessed them, and the point lay in some absurd thing he would blurt out in the confessional showing his struggles between native piety and original sin. Granny felt easy about her soul. Cornelia, where are your manners? Give Father Connolly a chair. She had her secret comfortable understanding with a few favorite saints who cleared a straight road to God for her. All as surely signed and sealed as the papers for the new Forty Acres. Forever . . . heirs and assigns forever. Since the day the wedding cake was not cut, but thrown out and wasted. The whole bottom dropped out of the world, and there she was blind and sweating with nothing under her feet and the walls falling away. His hand had caught her under the breast, she had not fallen, there was the freshly polished floor with the green rug on it, just as before. He had cursed like a sailor's parrot and said, "I'll kill him for you." Don't lay a hand on him, for my sake leave something to God. "Now, Ellen, you must believe what I tell you. . . ."

So there was nothing, nothing to worry about any more, except sometimes in the night one of the children screamed in a nightmare, and they both hustled out shaking and hunting for the matches and calling, "There, wait a minute, here we are!" John, get the doctor now, Hapsy's time has come. But there was Hapsy standing by the bed in a white cap. "Cornelia, tell Hapsy to take off her cap. I can't see her plain."

Her eyes opened very wide and the room stood out like a picture she had seen somewhere. Dark colors with the shadows rising towards the ceiling in long angles. The tall black dresser gleamed with nothing on it but John's picture, enlarged from a little one, with John's eyes very black when they should have been blue. You never saw him, so how do you know how he looked? But the man insisted the copy was perfect, it was very rich and handsome. For a picture, yes, but it's not my husband. The table by the bed had a linen cover and a candle and a crucifix. The light was blue from Cornelia's silk lampshades. No sort of light at all, just frippery. You had to live forty years with kerosene lamps to appreciate honest electricity. She felt very strong and she saw Doctor Harry with a rosy nimbus around him.

"You look like a saint, Doctor Harry, and I vow that's as near as you'll ever come to it."

"She's saying something."

"I heard you, Cornelia. What's all this carrying-on?"

"Father Connolly's saying—"

Cornelia's voice staggered and bumped like a cart in a bad road. It rounded corners and turned back again and arrived nowhere. Granny stepped up in the cart very lightly and reached for the reins, but a man sat beside her and she knew him by his hands, driving the cart. She did not look in his face, for she knew without seeing, but looked instead down the road where the trees leaned over and bowed to each other and a thousand birds were singing a Mass. She felt like singing too, but she put her hand in the bosom of her dress and pulled out a rosary, and Father Connolly murmured Latin in a very solemn voice and tickled her feet. My God, will you stop that nonsense? I'm a married woman. What if he did run away and leave me to face the priest by myself? I found another a whole world better. I wouldn't have exchanged my husband for anybody except St. Michael himself, and you may tell him that for me with a thank you in the bargain.

Light flashed on her closed eyelids, and a deep roaring shook her. Cornelia, is that lightning? I hear thunder. There's going to be a storm. Close all the windows. Call the children in. . . . "Mother, here we are, all of us." "Is that you, Hapsy?" "Oh, no, I'm Lydia. We drove as fast as we could." Their faces drifted above her, drifted away. The rosary fell out of her hands and Lydia put it back. Jimmy tried to help, their hands fumbled together, and Granny closed two fingers around Jimmy's thumb. Beads wouldn't do, it must be something alive. She was so amazed her thoughts ran round and round. So, my dear Lord, this is my death and I wasn't even thinking about it. My children have come to see me die. But I can't, it's not time. Oh, I always hated surprises. I wanted to give Cornelia the amethyst set—Cornelia, you're to have the amethyst set, but Hapsy's to wear it when she wants, and, Doctor Harry, do shut up. Nobody sent for you. Oh, my dear Lord, do wait a minute. I meant to do something about the Forty Acres, Jimmy doesn't need it and Lydia will later on, with that worthless husband of hers. I meant to finish the altar cloth and send six bottles of wine to Sister Borgia for her dyspepsia. I want to send six bottles of wine to Sister Borgia, Father Connolly, now don't let me forget.

Cornelia's voice made short turns and tilted over and crashed. "Oh, Mother, oh, Mother, oh, Mother. . . ."

"I'm not going, Cornelia. I'm taken by surprise. I can't go."

You'll see Hapsy again. What about her? "I thought you'd never come." Granny made a long journey outward, looking for Hapsy.

What if I don't find her? What then? Her heart sank down and down, there was no bottom to death, she couldn't come to the end of it. The blue light from Cornelia's lampshade drew into a tiny point in the center of her brain, it flickered and winked like an eye, quietly it fluttered and dwindled. Granny lay curled down within herself, amazed and watchful, staring at the point of light that was herself; her body was now only a deeper mass of shadow in an endless darkness and this darkness would curl around the light and swallow it up. God, give a sign!

For the second time there was no sign. Again no bridegroom and the priest in the house. She could not remember any other sorrow because this grief wiped them all away. Oh, no, there's nothing more cruel than this—I'll never forgive it. She stretched herself with a deep breath and blew out the light.

JAMES THURBER (1894-1961)

The Secret Life of Walter Mitty

"We're going through!" The Commander's voice was like thin ice breaking. He wore his full-dress uniform, with the heavily braided white cap pulled down rakishly over one cold gray eye. "We can't make it, sir. It's spoiling for a hurricane, if you ask me." "I'm not asking you, Lieutenant Berg," said the Commander. "Throw on the power lights! Rev her up to 8,500! We're going through!" The pounding of the cylinders increased; ta-pocketa-pocketa-pocketa-*pocketa-pocketa*. The Commander stared at the ice forming on the pilot window. He walked over and twisted a row of complicated dials. "Switch on No. 8 auxiliary!" he shouted. "Switch on No. 8 auxiliary!" repeated Lieutenant Berg. "Full strength in No. 3 turret!" shouted the Commander. "Full strength in No. 3 turret!" The crew, bending to their various tasks in the huge, hurtling eight-engined Navy hydroplane, looked at each other and grinned. "The Old Man'll get us through," they said to one another. "The Old Man ain't afraid of Hell!" . . .

"Not so fast! You're driving too fast!" said Mrs. Mitty. "What are you driving so fast for?"

"Hmm?" said Walter Mitty. He looked at his wife, in the seat beside him, with shocked astonishment. She seemed grossly unfamiliar, like a strange woman who had yelled at him in a crowd. "You were up to fifty-five," she said. "You know I don't like to go more than forty. You were up to fifty-five." Walter Mitty drove on toward Waterbury in silence, the roaring of the SN202 through the worst storm in twenty years of Navy flying fading in the remote, intimate airways of his mind. "You're tensed up again," said Mrs. Mitty. "It's one of your days. I wish you'd let Dr. Renshaw look you over."

Walter Mitty stopped the car in front of the building where his wife went to have her hair done. "Remember to get those overshoes while I'm having my hair done," she said. "I don't need overshoes," said Mitty. She put her mirror back into her bag. "We've been all through that," she said, getting out of the car. "You're not a young man any longer." He raced the engine a little. "Why don't you wear your gloves? Have you lost your gloves?" Walter Mitty reached in a pocket and brought out the gloves. He put them on, but after she had turned and gone into the building and he had driven on to a red light, he took them off again. "Pick it up, brother!" snapped a cop as the light changed, and Mitty hastily pulled on his gloves and lurched ahead. He drove around the streets aimlessly for a time, and then he drove past the hospital on his way to the parking lot.

. . . "It's the millionaire banker, Wellington McMillan," said the pretty nurse. "Yes?" said Walter Mitty, removing his gloves slowly. "Who has the case?" "Dr. Renshaw and Dr. Benbow, but there are two specialists here, Dr. Remington from New York and Dr. Pritchard-Mitford from London. He flew over." A door opened down a long, cool corridor and Dr. Renshaw came out. He looked distraught and haggard. "Hello, Mitty," he said. "We're having the devil's own time with McMillan, the millionaire banker and close personal friend of Roosevelt. Obstreosis of the ductal tract. Tertiary. Wish you'd take a look at him." "Glad to," said Mitty.

In the operating room there were whispered introductions: "Dr. Remington, Dr. Mitty. Dr. Pritchard-Mitford, Dr. Mitty." "I've read your book on streptothricosis," said Pritchard-Mitford, shaking hands. "A brilliant performance, sir." "Thank you," said Walter Mitty. "Didn't know you were in the States, Mitty," grumbled Remington. "Coals to Newcastle, bringing Mitford and me up here for a tertiary." "You are very kind," said Mitty. A huge, complicated machine, connected to the operating table, with many tubes and wires, began at this moment to go pocketa-pocketa-pocketa. "The new anaesthetizer is giving away!" shouted an interne. "There is no one in the East who knows how to fix it!" "Quiet, man!" said Mitty, in a low, cool voice. He sprang to the machine, which was now going pocketa-pocketa-queep-pocketa-queep. He began fingering delicately a row of glistening dials. "Give me a fountain pen!" he snapped. Someone handed him a fountain pen. He pulled a faulty piston out of the machine and inserted the pen in its place. "That will hold for ten minutes," he said.

"Get on with the operation." A nurse hurried over and whispered to Renshaw, and Mitty saw the man turn pale. "Coreopsis has set in," said Renshaw nervously. "If you would take over, Mitty?" Mitty looked at him and at the craven figure of Benbow, who drank, and at the grave, uncertain faces of the two great specialists. "If you wish," he said. They slipped a white gown on him; he adjusted a mask and drew on thin gloves; nurses handed him shining . . .

"Back it up, Mac! Look out for that Buick!" Walter Mitty jammed on the brakes. "Wrong lane, Mac," said the parking-lot attendant, looking at Mitty closely. "Gee. Yeh," muttered Mitty. He began cautiously to back out of the lane marked "Exit Only." "Leave her sit there," said the attendant. "I'll put her away." Mitty got out of the car. "Hey, better leave the key." "Oh," said Mitty, handing the man the ignition key. The attendant vaulted into the car, backed it up with insolent skill, and put it where it belonged.

They're so damn cocky, thought Walter Mitty, walking along Main Street; they think they know everything. Once he had tried to take his chains off, outside New Milford, and he had got them wound around the axles. A man had had to come out in a wrecking car and unwind them, a young, grinning garage man. Since then Mrs. Mitty always made him drive to a garage to have the chains taken off. The next time, he thought, I'll wear my right arm in a sling; they won't grin at me then. I'll have my right arm in a sling and they'll see I couldn't possibly take the chains off myself. He kicked at the slush on the sidewalk. "Overshoes," he said to himself, and he began looking for a shoe store.

When he came out into the street again, with the overshoes in a box under his arm, Walter Mitty began to wonder what the other thing was his wife had told him to get. She had told him, twice before they set out from their house for Waterbury. In a way he hated these weekly trips to town—he was always getting something wrong. Kleenex, he thought, Squibb's, razor blades? No. Toothpaste, toothbrush, bicarbonate, carborundum, initiative and referendum? He gave it up. But she would remember it. "Where's the what's-its-name?" she would ask. "Don't tell me you forgot the what's-its-name." A newsboy went by shouting something about the Waterbury trial.

. . . "Perhaps this will refresh your memory." The District Attorney suddenly thrust a heavy automatic at the quiet figure on the witness stand. "Have you ever seen this before?" Walter Mitty took the gun and examined it expertly. "This is my Webley-Vickers 50.80," he said calmly. An excited buzz ran around the courtroom. The judge rapped for order. "You are a crack shot with any sort of firearms, I believe?" said the District Attorney, insinuatingly. "Objection!" shouted Mitty's attorney. "We have shown that the defendant could not have fired the shot. We have shown that he wore his right arm in a sling on the night of the fourteenth of July." Walter Mitty raised his hand briefly and the bickering attorneys were stilled. "With any known make of gun," he said evenly, "I could have killed Gregory Fitzhurst at three hundred feet *with my left hand*." Pandemonium broke loose in the courtroom. A woman's scream rose above the bedlam and suddenly a lovely, dark-haired girl was in Walter Mitty's arms. The District Attorney struck at her savagely. Without rising from his chair, Mitty let the man have it on the point of the chin. "You miserable cur!" . . .

"Puppy biscuit," said Walter Mitty. He stopped walking and the buildings of Waterbury rose up out of the misty courtroom and surrounded him again. A woman who was passing laughed. "He said 'Puppy biscuit,'" she said to her companion. "That man said 'Puppy biscuit' to himself." Walter Mitty hurried on. He went into an A. & P., not the first one he came to but a smaller one farther up the street. "I want some biscuit for small, young dogs," he said to the clerk. "Any special brand, sir?" The greatest pistol shot in the world thought a moment. "It says 'Puppies Bark for It' on the box," said Walter Mitty.

His wife would be through at the hairdresser's in fifteen minutes, Mitty saw in looking at his watch, unless they had trouble drying it; sometimes they had trouble drying it. She didn't like to get to the hotel first; she would want him to be there waiting for her as usual. He found a big leather chair in the lobby, facing a window, and he put the overshoes and the puppy biscuit on the floor beside it. He picked up an old copy of *Liberty* and sank down into the chair. "Can Germany Conquer the World through the Air?" Walter Mitty looked at the pictures of bombing planes and of ruined streets.

. . . "The cannonading has got the wind up in young Raleigh, sir," said the sergeant. Captain Mitty looked up at him through tousled hair. "Get him to bed," he said wearily, "with the others. I'll fly alone." "But you can't, sir," said the sergeant anxiously. "It takes two men to handle that bomber and the Archies are pounding hell out of the air. Von Richtman's circus is between here and Saulier." "Somebody's got to get that ammunition dump," said Mitty. "I'm going over. Spot of brandy?" He poured a drink for the sergeant and one for himself. War thundered and whined around the dugout and battered at the door. There was a rending of wood and splinters flew through the room. "A bit of a near thing," said Captain Mitty carelessly. "The box barrage is closing in," said the sergeant. "We only live once, sergeant," said Mitty, with his faint, fleeting smile. "Or do we?" He poured another brandy and tossed it off. "I never see a man could hold his brandy like you, sir," said the sergeant. "Begging your pardon, sir." Captain Mitty stood up and strapped on his huge Webley-Vickers automatic. "It's forty kilometers through hell, sir," said the sergeant. Mitty finished one last brandy. "After all," he said softly, "what isn't?" The pounding of the cannon increased; there was the rat-tat-tatting of machine guns, and from somewhere came the menacing pocketa-pocketa-pocketa of the new flame-throwers. Walter Mitty walked to the door of the dugout humming "*Après de Ma Blonde*." He turned and waved to the sergeant. "Cheerio!" he said. . . .

Something struck his shoulder. "I've been looking all over this hotel for you," said Mrs. Mitty. "Why do you have to hide in this old chair? How did you expect me to find you?" "Things close in," said Walter Mitty vaguely. "What?" Mrs. Mitty said. "Did you get the what's-its-name? The puppy biscuit? What's in that box?" "Overshoes," said Mitty. "Couldn't you have put them on in the store?" "I was thinking," said Walter Mitty. "Does it ever occur to you that I am sometimes thinking?" She looked at him. "I'm going to take your temperature when I get you home," she said.

They went out through the revolving doors that made a faintly derisive whistling sound when you pushed them. It was two blocks to the parking lot. At the drugstore on the corner she said, "Wait here for me. I forgot something. I won't be a minute." She was more than a minute. Walter Mitty lighted a cigarette. It began to rain, rain with sleet in it. He stood up against the wall of the drugstore, smoking. . . . He put his shoulders back and his heels together. "To hell with the handkerchief," said Walter Mitty scornfully. He took one last drag on his cigarette and snapped it away. Then, with that faint, fleeting smile playing about his lips, he faced the firing squad; erect and motionless, proud and disdainful, Walter Mitty the Undefeated, inscrutable to the last.

ERNEST HEMINGWAY (1899-1961)

The Short Happy Life of Francis Macomber

It was now lunch time and they were all sitting under the double green fly of the dining tent pretending that nothing had happened.

"Will you have lime juice or lemon squash?" Macomber asked.

"I'll have a gimlet," Robert Wilson told him.

"I'll have a gimlet too. I need something," Macomber's wife said.

"I suppose it's the thing to do," Macomber agreed. "Tell him to make three gimlets."

The mess boy had started them already, lifting the bottles out of the canvas cooling bags that sweated wet in the wind that blew through the trees that shaded the tents.

"What had I ought to give them?" Macomber asked.

"A quid would be plenty," Wilson told him. "You don't want to spoil them."

"Will the headman distribute it?"

"Absolutely."

Francis Macomber had, half an hour before, been carried to his tent from the edge of the camp in triumph on the arms and shoulders of the cook, the personal boys, the skinner and the porters. The gun-bearers had taken no part in the demonstration. When the native boys put him down at the door of his tent, he had shaken all their hands, received their congratulations, and then gone into the tent and sat on the bed until his wife came in. She did not speak to him when she came in and he left the tent at once to wash his face and hands in the port-able wash basin outside and go over to the dining tent to sit in a comfortable canvas chair in the breeze and the shade.

"You've got your lion," Robert Wilson said to him, "and a damned fine one too."

Mrs. Macomber looked at Wilson quickly. She was an extremely handsome and well-kept woman of the beauty and social position which had, five years before, commanded five thousand dollars as the price of endorsing, with photographs, a beauty product which she had never used. She had been married to Francis Macomber for eleven years.

"He is a good lion, isn't he?" Macomber said. His wife looked at him now. She looked at both these men as though she had never seen them before.

One, Wilson, the white hunter, she knew she had never truly seen before. He was about middle height with sandy hair, a stubby mustache, a very red face and extremely cold blue eyes with faint white wrinkles at the corners that grooved merrily when he smiled. He smiled at her now and she looked away from his face at the way his shoulders sloped in the loose tunic he wore with the four big cartridges held in loops where the left breast pocket should have been, at his big brown hands, his old slacks, his very dirty boots and back to his red face again. She noticed where the baked red of his face stopped in a white line that marked the circle left by his Stetson hat that hung now from one of the pegs of the tent pole.

"Well, here's to the lion," Robert Wilson said. He smiled at her again and, not smiling, she looked curiously at her husband.

Francis Macomber was very tall, very well built if you did not mind that length of bone, dark, his hair cropped like an oarsman, rather thin-lipped, and was considered handsome. He was dressed in the same sort of safari clothes that Wilson wore except that his were new, he was thirty-five years old, kept himself very fit, was good at court games, had a number of big-game fishing records, and had just shown himself, very publicly, to be a coward.

"Here's to the lion," he said. "I can't ever thank you for what you did."

Margaret, his wife, looked away from him and back to Wilson.

"Let's not talk about the lion," she said.

Wilson looked over at her without smiling and now she smiled at him.

"It's been a very strange day," she said. "Hadn't you ought to put your hat on even under the canvas at noon? You told me that, you know."

"Might put it on," said Wilson.

"You know you have a very red face, Mr. Wilson," she told him and smiled again.

"Drink," said Wilson.

"I don't think so," she said. "Francis drinks a great deal, but his face is never red."

"It's red today," Macomber tried a joke.

"No," said Margaret. "It's mine that's red today. But Mr. Wilson's is always red."

"Must be racial," said Wilson. "I say, you wouldn't like to drop my beauty as a topic, would you?"

"I've just started on it."

"Let's chuck it," said Wilson.

"Conversation is going to be so difficult," Margaret said.

"Don't be silly, Margot," her husband said.

"No difficulty," Wilson said. "Got a damn fine lion."

Margot looked at them both and they both saw that she was going to cry. Wilson had seen it coming for a long time and he dreaded it. Macomber was past dreading it.

"I wish it hadn't happened. Oh, I wish it hadn't happened," she said and started for her tent. She made no noise of crying but they could see that her shoulders were shaking under the rose-colored, sun-proofed shirt she wore.

"Women upset," said Wilson to the tall man. "Amounts to nothing. Strain on the nerves and one thing'n another."

"No," said Macomber. "I suppose that I rate that for the rest of my life now."

"Nonsense. Let's have a spot of the giant killer," said Wilson. "Forget the whole thing. Nothing to it anyway."

"We might try," said Macomber. "I won't forget what you did for me though."

"Nothing," said Wilson. "All nonsense."

So they sat there in the shade where the camp was pitched under some wide-topped acacia trees with a boulder-strewn cliff behind them, and a stretch of grass that ran to the bank of a boulder-filled stream in front with forest beyond it, and drank their just-cool lime drinks and avoided one another's eyes while the boys set the table for lunch. Wilson could tell that the boys all knew about it now and when he saw Macomber's personal boy looking curiously at his master while he was putting dishes on the table he snapped at him in Swahili. The boy turned away with his face blank.

"What were you telling him?" Macomber asked.

"Nothing. Told him to look alive or I'd see he got about fifteen of the best."

"What's that? Lashes?"

"It's quite illegal," Wilson said. "You're supposed to fine them."

"Do you still have them whipped?"

"Oh, yes. They could raise a row if they chose to complain. But they don't. They prefer it to the fines."

"How strange!" said Macomber.

"Not strange, really," Wilson said. "Which would you rather do? Take a good birching or lose your pay?"

Then he felt embarrassed at asking it and before Macomber could answer he went on, "We all take a beating every day, you know, one way or another."

This was no better. "Good God," he thought. "I am a diplomat, aren't I?"

"Yes, we take a beating," said Macomber, still not looking at him. "I'm awfully sorry about that lion business. It doesn't have to go any further, does it? I mean no one will hear about it, will they?"

"You mean will I tell it at the Mathaiga Club?" Wilson looked at him now coldly. He had not expected this. So he's a bloody four-letter man as well as a bloody coward, he thought. I rather liked him too until today. But how is one to know about an American?

"No," said Wilson. "I'm a professional hunter. We never talk about our clients. You can be quite easy on that. It's supposed to be bad form to ask us not to talk though."

He had decided now that to break would be much easier. He would eat, then, by himself and could read a book with his meals. They would eat by themselves. He would see them through the safari on a very formal basis—what was it the French called it? Distinguished consideration—and it would be a damn sight easier than having to go through this emotional trash. He'd insult him and make a good clean break. Then he could read a book with his meals and he'd still be drinking their whisky. That was the phrase for it when a safari went bad. You ran into another white hunter and you asked, "How is everything going?" and he answered, "Oh, I'm still drinking their whisky," and you knew everything had gone to pot.

"I'm sorry," Macomber said and looked at him with his American face that would stay adolescent until it became middle-aged, and Wilson noted his crew-cropped hair, fine eyes only faintly shifty, good nose, thin lips and handsome jaw. "I'm sorry I didn't realize that. There are lots of things I don't know."

So what could he do, Wilson thought. He was all ready to break it off quickly and neatly and here the beggar was apologizing after he had just insulted him. He made one more attempt. "Don't worry about me talking," he said. "I have a living to make. You know in Africa no woman ever misses her lion and no white man ever bolts."

"I bolted like a rabbit," Macomber said.

Now what in hell were you going to do about a man who talked like that, Wilson wondered.

Wilson looked at Macomber with his flat, blue, machine-gunner's eyes and the other smiled back at him. He had a pleasant smile if you did not notice how his eyes showed when he was hurt.

"Maybe I can fix it up on buffalo," he said. "We're after them next, aren't we?"

"In the morning if you like," Wilson told him. Perhaps he had been wrong. This was certainly the way to take it. You most certainly could not tell a damned thing about an American. He was all for Macomber again. If you could forget the morning. But, of course, you couldn't. The morning had been about as bad as they come.

"Here comes the Memsahib," he said. She was walking over from her tent looking refreshed and cheerful and quite lovely. She had a very perfect oval face, so perfect that you expected her to be stupid. But she wasn't stupid, Wilson thought, no, not stupid.

"How is the beautiful red-faced Mr. Wilson? Are you feeling better, Francis, my pearl?"

"Oh, much," said Macomber.

"I've dropped the whole thing," she said, sitting down at the table. "What importance is there to whether Francis is any good at killing lions? That's not his trade. That's Mr. Wilson's trade. Mr. Wilson is really very impressive killing anything. You do kill anything, don't you?"

"Oh, anything," said Wilson. "Simply anything." They are, he thought, the hardest in the world; the hardest, the cruelest, the most predatory and the most attractive and their men have softened or gone to pieces nervously as they have hardened. Or is it that they pick men they can handle? They can't know that much at the age they marry, he thought. He was grateful that he had gone through his education on American women before now because this was a very attractive one.

"We're going after buff in the morning," he told her.

"I'm coming," she said.

"No, you're not."

"Oh, yes, I am. Mayn't I, Francis?"

"Why not stay in camp?"

"Not for anything," she said. "I wouldn't miss something like today for anything."

When she left, Wilson was thinking, when she went off to cry, she seemed a hell of a fine woman. She seemed to understand, to realize, to be hurt for him and for herself and to know how things really stood. She is away for twenty minutes and now she is back, simply enamelled in that American female cruelty. They are the damnedest women. Really the damnedest.

"We'll put on another show for you tomorrow," Francis Macomber said.

"You're not coming," Wilson said.

"You're very mistaken," she told him. "And I want *so* to see you perform again. You were lovely this morning. That is if blowing things' heads off is lovely."

"Here's the lunch," said Wilson. "You're very merry, aren't you?"

"Why not? I didn't come here to be dull."

"Well, it hasn't been dull," Wilson said. He could see the boulders in the river and the high bank beyond with the trees and he remembered the morning.

"Oh, no," she said. "It's been charming. And tomorrow. You don't know how I look forward to tomorrow."

"That's eland he's offering you," Wilson said.

"They're the big cowy things that jump like hares, aren't they?"

"I suppose that describes them," Wilson said.

"It's very good meat," Macomber said.

"Did you shoot it, Francis?" she asked.

"Yes."

"They're not dangerous, are they?"

"Only if they fall on you," Wilson told her.

"I'm so glad."

"Why not let up on the bitchery just a little, Margot," Macomber said, cutting the eland steak and putting some mashed potato, gravy and carrot on the down-turned fork that tined through the piece of meat.

"I suppose I could," she said, "since you put it so prettily."

"Tonight we'll have champagne for the lion," Wilson said. "It's a bit too hot at noon."

"Oh, the lion," Margot said. "I'd forgotten the lion!"

So, Robert Wilson thought to himself, she *is* giving him a ride, isn't she? Or do you suppose that's her idea of putting up a good show? How should a woman act when she discovers her husband is a bloody coward? She's damn cruel but they're all cruel. They govern, of course, and to govern one has to be cruel sometimes. Still, I've seen enough of their damn terrorism.

"Have some more eland," he said to her politely.

That afternoon, late, Wilson and Macomber went out in the motor car with the native driver and the two gun-bearers. Mrs. Macomber stayed in the camp. It was too hot to go out, she said, and she was going with them in the early morning. As they drove off Wilson saw her standing under the big tree, looking pretty rather than beautiful in her faintly rosy khaki, her dark hair drawn back off her forehead and gathered in a knot low on her neck, her face as fresh, he thought, as though she were in England. She waved to them as the car went off through the swale of high grass and curved around through the trees into the small hills of orchard bush.

In the orchard bush they found a herd of impala, and leaving the car they stalked one old ram with long, wide-spread horns and Macomber killed it with a very creditable shot that knocked the buck down at a good two hundred yards and sent the herd off bounding wildly and leaping over one another's backs in long, leg-drawn-up leaps as unbelievable and as floating as those one makes sometimes in dreams.

"That was a good shot," Wilson said. "They're a small target."

"Is it a worth-while head?" Macomber asked.

"It's excellent," Wilson told him. "You shoot like that and you'll have no trouble."

"Do you think we'll find buffalo tomorrow?"

"There's a good chance of it. They feed out early in the morning and with luck we may catch them in the open."

"I'd like to clear away that lion business," Macomber said. "It's not very pleasant to have your wife see you do something like that."

I should think it would be even more unpleasant to do it, Wilson thought, wife or no wife, or to talk about it having done it. But he said, "I wouldn't think about that any more. Any one could be upset by his first lion. That's all over."

But that night after dinner and a whisky and soda by the fire before going to bed, as Francis Macomber lay on his cot with the mosquito bar over him and listened to the night noises it was not all over. It was neither all over nor was it beginning. It was there exactly as it happened with some parts of it indelibly emphasized and he was miserably ashamed at it. But more than shame he felt cold, hollow fear in him. The fear was still there like a cold slimy hollow in all the emptiness where once his confidence had been and it made him feel sick. It was still there with him now.

It had started the night before when he had wakened and heard the lion roaring somewhere up along the river. It was a deep sound and at the end there were sort of coughing grunts that made him seem just outside the tent, and when Francis Macomber woke in the night to hear it he was afraid. He could hear his wife breathing quietly, asleep. There was no one to tell he was afraid, nor to be afraid with him, and, lying alone, he did not know the Somali proverb that says a brave man is always frightened three times by a lion; when he first sees his track, when he first hears him roar and when he first confronts him. Then while they were eating breakfast by lantern light out in the dining tent, before the sun was up, the lion roared again and Francis thought he was just at the edge of camp.

"Sounds like an old-timer," Robert Wilson said, looking up from his kippers and coffee. "Listen to him cough."

"Is he very close?"

"A mile or so up the stream."

"Will we see him?"

"We'll have a look."

"Does his roaring carry that far? It sounds as though he were right in camp."

"Carries a hell of a long way," said Robert Wilson. "It's strange the way it carries. Hope he's a shootable cat. The boys said there was a very big one about here."

"If I get a shot, where should I hit him," Macomber asked, "to stop him?"

"In the shoulders," Wilson said. "In the neck if you can make it. Shoot for bone. Break him down."

"I hope I can place it properly," Macomber said.

"You shoot very well," Wilson told him. "Take your time. Make sure of him. The first one in is the one that counts."

"What range will it be?"

"Can't tell. Lion has something to say about that. Won't shoot unless it's close enough so you can make sure."

"At under a hundred yards?" Macomber asked.

Wilson looked at him quickly.

"Hundred's about right. Might have to take him a bit under. Shouldn't chance a shot at much over that. A hundred's a decent range. You can hit him wherever you want at that. Here comes the Memsahib."

"Good morning," she said. "Are we going after that lion?"

"As soon as you deal with your breakfast," Wilson said. "How are you feeling?"

"Marvellous," she said. "I'm very excited."

"I'll just go and see that everything is ready," Wilson went off. As he left the lion roared again.

"Noisy beggar," Wilson said. "We'll put a stop to that."

"What's the matter, Francis?" his wife asked him.

"Nothing," Macomber said.

"Yes, there is," she said. "What are you upset about?"

"Nothing," he said.

"Tell me," she looked at him. "Don't you feel well?"

"It's that damned roaring," he said. "It's been going on all night, you know."

"Why didn't you wake me," she said. "I'd love to have heard it."

"I've got to kill the damned thing," Macomber said, miserably.

"Well, that's what you're out here for, isn't it?"

"Yes. But I'm nervous. Hearing the thing roar gets on my nerves."

"Well then, as Wilson said, kill him and stop his roaring."

"Yes, darling," said Francis Macomber. "It sounds easy, doesn't it?"

"You're not afraid, are you?"

"Of course not. But I'm nervous from hearing him roar all night."

"You'll kill him marvellously," she said. "I know you will. I'm awfully anxious to see it."

"Finish your breakfast and we'll be starting."

"It's not light yet," she said. "This is a ridiculous hour."

Just then the lion roared in a deep-chested moaning, suddenly guttural, ascending vibration that seemed to shake the air and ended in a sigh and a heavy, deep-chested grunt.

"He sounds almost here," Macomber's wife said.

"My God," said Macomber. "I hate that damned noise."

"It's very impressive."

"Impressive. It's frightful."

Robert Wilson came up then carrying his short, ugly, shockingly big-bored .505 Gibbs and grinning.

"Come on," he said. "Your gun-bearer has your Springfield and the big gun. Everything's in the car. Have you solids?"

"Yes."

"I'm ready," Mrs. Macomber said.

"Must make him stop that racket," Wilson said. "You get in front. The Memsahib can sit back here with me."

They climbed into the motor car and, in the gray first daylight, moved off up the river through the trees. Macomber opened the breech of his rifle and saw he had metal-cased bullets, shut the bolt and put the rifle on safety. He saw his hand was trembling. He felt in his pocket for more cartridges and moved his fingers over the cartridges in the loops of his tunic front. He turned back to where Wilson sat in the rear seat of the doorless, box-bodied motor car beside his wife, them both grinning with excitement, and Wilson leaned forward and whispered,

"See the birds dropping. Means the old boy has left his kill."

On the far bank of the stream Macomber could see, above the trees, vultures circling and plummeting down.

"Chances are he'll come to drink along here," Wilson whispered. "Before he goes to lay up. Keep an eye out."

They were driving slowly along the high bank of the stream which here cut deeply to its boulder-filled bed, and they wound in and out through big trees as they drove. Macomber was watching the opposite bank when he felt Wilson take hold of his arm. The car stopped.

"There he is," he heard the whisper. "Ahead and to the right. Get out and take him. He's a marvellous lion."

Macomber saw the lion now. He was standing almost broadside, his great head up and turned toward them. The early morning breeze that blew toward them was just stirring his dark mane, and the lion looked huge, silhouetted on the rise of bank in the gray morning light, his shoulders heavy, his barrel of a body bulking smoothly.

"How far is he?" asked Macomber, raising his rifle.

"About seventy-five. Get out and take him."

"Why not shoot from where I am?"

"You don't shoot them from cars," he heard Wilson saying in his ear. "Get out. He's not going to stay there all day."

Macomber stepped out of the curved opening at the side of the front seat, onto the step and down onto the ground. The lion still stood looking majestically and coolly toward this object that his eyes only showed in silhouette, bulking like some super-rhino. There was no man smell carried toward him and he watched the object, moving his great head a little from side to side. Then watching the object, not afraid, but hesitating before going down the bank to drink with such a thing opposite him, he saw a man figure detach itself from it and he turned his heavy head and swung away toward the cover of the trees as he heard a cracking crash and felt the slam of a .30–06 220-grain solid bullet that bit his flank and ripped in sudden hot scalding nausea through his stomach. He trotted, heavy, big-footed, swinging wounded full-bellied, through the trees toward the tall grass and cover, and the crash came again to go past him ripping the air apart. Then it crashed again and he felt the blow as it hit his lower ribs and ripped on through, blood sudden hot and frothy in his mouth, and he galloped toward the high grass where he could crouch and not be seen and make them bring the crashing thing close enough so he could make a rush and get the man that held it.

Macomber had not thought how the lion felt as he got out of the car. He only knew his hands were shaking and as he walked away from the car it was almost impossible for him to make his legs move. They were stiff in the thighs, but he could feel the muscles fluttering. He raised the rifle, sighted on the junction of the lion's head and shoulders and pulled the trigger. Nothing happened though he pulled until he thought his finger would break. Then he knew he had the safety on and as he lowered the rifle to move the safety over he moved another frozen pace forward, and the lion seeing his silhouette now clear of the silhouette of the car, turned and started off at a trot, and, as Macomber fired, he heard a whunk that meant that the bullet was home; but the lion kept on going. Macomber shot again and every one saw the bullet throw a spout of dirt beyond the trotting lion. He shot again, remembering to lower his aim, and they all heard the bullet hit, and the lion went into a gallop and was in the tall grass before he had the bolt pushed forward.

Macomber stood there feeling sick at his stomach, his hands that held the Springfield still cocked, shaking, and his wife and Robert Wilson were standing by him. Beside him too were the two gun-bearers chattering in Wakamba.

"I hit him," Macomber said. "I hit him twice."

"You gun-shot him and you hit him somewhere forward," Wilson said without enthusiasm. The gun-bearers looked very grave. They were silent now.

"You may have killed him," Wilson went on. "We'll have to wait a while before we go in to find out."

"What do you mean?"

"Let him get sick before we follow him up."

"Oh," said Macomber.

"He's a hell of a fine lion," Wilson said cheerfully. "He's gotten into a bad place though."

"Why is it bad?"

"Can't see him until you're on him."

"Oh," said Macomber.

"Come on," said Wilson. "The Memsahib can stay here in the car. We'll go to have a look at the blood spoor."

"Stay here, Margot," Macomber said to his wife. His mouth was very dry and it was hard for him to talk.

"Why?" she asked.

"Wilson says to."

"We're going to have a look," Wilson said. "You stay here. You can see even better from here."

"All right."

Wilson spoke in Swahili to the driver. He nodded and said, "Yes, Bwana."

Then they went down the steep bank and across the stream, climbing over and around the boulders and up the other bank, pulling up by some projecting roots, and along it until they found where the lion had been trotting when Macomber first shot. There was dark blood on the short grass that the gun-bearers pointed out with grass stems, and that ran away behind the river bank trees.

"What do we do?" asked Macomber.

"Not much choice," said Wilson. "We can't bring the car over. Bank's too steep. We'll let him stiffen up a bit and then you and I'll go in and have a look for him."

"Can't we set the grass on fire?" Macomber asked.

"Too green."

"Can't we send beaters?"

Wilson looked at him appraisingly. "Of course we can," he said. "But it's just a touch murderous. You see we know the lion's wounded. You can drive an unwounded lion—he'll move on ahead of a noise—but a wounded lion's going to charge. You can't see him until you're right on him. He'll make himself perfectly flat in cover you wouldn't think would hide a hare. You can't very well send boys in there to that sort of a show. Somebody bound to get mauled."

"What about the gun-bearers?"

"Oh, they'll go with us. It's their *shauri*. You see, they signed on for it. They don't look too happy though, do they?"

"I don't want to go in there," said Macomber. It was out before he knew he'd said it.

"Neither do I," said Wilson very cheerily. "Really no choice though." Then, as an afterthought, he glanced at Macomber and saw suddenly how he was trembling and the pitiful look on his face.

"You don't have to go in, of course," he said. "That's what I'm hired for, you know. That's why I'm so expensive."

"You mean you'd go in by yourself? Why not leave him there?"

Robert Wilson, whose entire occupation had been with the lion and the problem he presented, and who had not been thinking about Macomber except to note that he was rather windy, suddenly felt as though he had opened the wrong door in a hotel and seen something shameful.

"What do you mean?"

"Why not just leave him?"

"You mean pretend to ourselves he hasn't been hit?"

"No. Just drop it."

"It isn't done."

"Why not?"

"For one thing, he's certain to be suffering. For another, some one else might run onto him."

"I see."

"But you don't have to have anything to do with it."

"I'd like to," Macomber said. "I'm just scared, you know."

"I'll go ahead when we go in," Wilson said, "with Kongoni tracking. You keep behind me and a little to one side. Chances are we'll hear him growl. If we see him we'll both shoot. Don't worry about anything. I'll keep you backed up. As a matter of fact, you know, perhaps you'd better not go. It might be much better. Why don't you go over and join the Memsahib while I just get it over with?"

"No, I want to go."

"All right," said Wilson. "But don't go in if you don't want to. This is my *shauri* now, you know."

"I want to go," said Macomber.

They sat under a tree and smoked.

"Want to go back and speak to the Memsahib while we're waiting?" Wilson asked.

"No."

"I'll just step back and tell her to be patient."

"Good," said Macomber. He sat there, sweating under his arms, his mouth dry, his stomach hollow feeling, wanting to find courage to tell Wilson to go on and finish off the lion without him. He could not know that Wilson was furious because he had not noticed the state he was in earlier and sent him back to his wife. While he sat there Wilson came up. "I have your big gun," he said. "Take it. We've given him time, I think. Come on."

Macomber took the big gun and Wilson said:

"Keep behind me and about five yards to the right and do exactly as I tell you." Then he spoke in Swahili to the two gun-bearers who looked the picture of gloom.

"Let's go," he said.

"Could I have a drink of water?" Macomber asked. Wilson spoke to the older gun-bearer, who wore a canteen on his belt, and the man unbuckled it, unscrewed the top and handed it to Macomber, who took it noticing how heavy it seemed and how hairy and shoddy the felt covering was in his hand. He raised it to drink and looked ahead at the high grass with the flat-topped trees behind it. A breeze was blowing toward them and the grass rippled gently in the wind. He looked at the gun-bearer and he could see the gun-bearer was suffering too with fear.

Thirty-five yards into the grass the big lion lay flattened out along the ground. His ears were back and his only movement was a slight twitching up and down of his long, black-tufted tail. He had turned at bay as soon as he had reached this cover and he was sick with the wound through his full belly, and weakening with the wound through his lungs that brought a thin foamy red to his mouth each time he breathed. His flanks were wet and hot and flies were on the little openings the solid bullets had made in his tawny hide, and his big yellow eyes, narrowed with hate, looked straight ahead, only blinking when the pain came as he breathed, and his claws dug in the softbaked earth. All of him, pain, sickness, hatred and all of his remaining strength, was tightening into an absolute concentration for a rush. He could hear the men talking and he waited, gathering all of himself into this preparation for a charge as soon as the men would come into the grass. As he heard their voices his tail stiffened to twitch up and down, and, as they came into the edge of the grass, he made a coughing grunt and charged.

Kongoni, the old gun-bearer, in the lead watching the blood spoor, Wilson watching the grass for any movement, his big gun ready, the second gun-bearer looking ahead and listening, Macomber close to Wilson, his rifle cocked, they had just moved into the grass when Macomber heard the blood-choked coughing grunt, and saw the swishing rush in the grass. The next thing he knew he was running; running wildly, in panic in the open, running toward the stream.

He heard the *ca-ra-wong!* of Wilson's big rifle, and again in a second crashing *carawong!* and turning saw the lion, horrible-looking now, with half his head seeming to be gone, crawling toward Wilson in the edge of the tall grass while the red-faced man worked the bolt on the short ugly rifle and aimed carefully as another blasting *cara-*

wong! came from the muzzle, and the crawling, heavy, yellow bulk of the lion stiffened and the huge, mutilated head slid forward and Macomber, standing by himself in the clearing where he had run, holding a loaded rifle, while two black men and a white man looked back at him in contempt, knew the lion was dead. He came toward Wilson, his tallness all seeming a naked reproach, and Wilson looked at him and said:

"Want to take pictures?"

"No," he said.

That was all any one had said until they reached the motor car. Then Wilson had said:

"Hell of a fine lion. Boys will skin him out. We might as well stay here in the shade."

Macomber's wife had not looked at him nor he at her and he had sat by her in the back seat with Wilson sitting in the front seat. Once he had reached over and taken his wife's hand without looking at her and she had removed her hand from his. Looking across the stream to where the gun-bearers were skinning out the lion he could see that she had been able to see the whole thing. While they sat there his wife had reached forward and put her hand on Wilson's shoulder. He turned and she had leaned forward over the low seat and kissed him on the mouth.

"Oh, I say," said Wilson, going redder than his natural baked color.

"Mr. Robert Wilson," she said. "The beautiful red-faced Mr. Robert Wilson."

Then she sat down beside Macomber again and looked away across the stream to where the lion lay, with uplifted, white-muscled, tendon-marked naked forearms, and white bloating belly, as the black men fleshed away the skin. Finally the gun-bearers brought the skin over, wet and heavy, and climbed in behind with it, rolling it up before they got in, and the motor car started. No one had said anything more until they were back in camp.

That was the story of the lion. Macomber did not know how the lion had felt before he started his rush, nor during it when the unbelievable smash of the .505 with a muzzle velocity of two tons had hit him in the mouth, nor what kept him coming after that, when the second ripping crash had smashed his hind quarters and he had come crawling on toward the crashing, blasting thing that had destroyed him. Wilson knew something about it and only expressed it by saying, "Damned fine lion," but Macomber did not know how Wilson felt about things either. He did not know how his wife felt except that she was through with him.

His wife had been through with him before but it never lasted.

He was very wealthy, and would be much wealthier, and he knew she would not leave him ever now. That was one of the few things that he really knew. He knew about that, about motor cycles—that was earliest—about motor cars, about duck-shooting, about fishing, trout, salmon and big-sea, about sex in books, many books, too many books, about all court games, about dogs, not much about horses, about hanging on to his money, about most of the other things his world dealt in, and about his wife not leaving him. His wife had been a great beauty and she was still a great beauty in Africa, but she was not a great enough beauty any more at home to be able to leave him and better herself and she knew it and he knew it. She had missed the chance to leave him and he knew it. If he had been better with women she would probably have started to worry about him getting another new, beautiful wife; but she knew too much about him to worry about him either. Also, he had always had a great tolerance which seemed the nicest thing about him if it were not the most sinister.

All in all they were known as a comparatively happily married couple, one of those whose disruption is often rumored but never occurs, and as the society columnist put it, they were adding more than a spice of *adventure* to their much envied and ever-enduring *Romance* by a *Safari* in what was known as *Darkest Africa* until the Martin Johnsons lighted it on so many silver screens where they were pursuing *Old Simba* the lion, the buffalo, *Tembo* the elephant and as well collecting specimens for the Museum of Natural History. This same columnist had reported them *on the verge* at least three times in the past and they had been. But they always made it up. They had a sound basis of union. Margot was too beautiful for Macomber to divorce her and Macomber had too much money for Margot ever to leave him.

It was now about three o'clock in the morning and Francis Macomber, who had been asleep a little while after he had stopped thinking about the lion, wakened and then slept again, woke suddenly, frightened in a dream of the bloody-headed lion standing over him, and listening while his heart pounded, he realized that his wife was not in the other cot in the tent. He lay awake with that knowledge for two hours.

At the end of that time his wife came into the tent, lifted her mosquito bar and crawled cozily into bed.

"Where have you been?" Macomber asked in the darkness.

"Hello," she said. "Are you awake?"

"Where have you been?"

"I just went out to get a breath of air."

"You did, like hell."

"What do you want me to say, darling?"

"Where have you been?"

"Out to get a breath of air."

"That's a new name for it. You *are* a bitch."

"Well, you're a coward."

"All right," he said. "What of it?"

"Nothing as far as I'm concerned. But please let's not talk, darling, because I'm very sleepy."

"You think that I'll take anything."

"I know you will, sweet."

"Well, I won't."

"Please, darling, let's not talk. I'm so very sleepy."

"There wasn't going to be any of that. You promised there wouldn't be."

"Well, there is now," she said sweetly.

"You said if we made this trip that there would be none of that. You promised."

"Yes, darling. That's the way I meant it to be. But the trip was spoiled yesterday. We don't have to talk about it, do we?"

"You don't wait long when you have an advantage, do you?"

"Please let's not talk. I'm so sleepy, darling."

"I'm going to talk."

"Don't mind me then, because I'm going to sleep." And she did.

At breakfast they were all three at the table before daylight and Francis Macomber found that, of all the many men that he had hated, he hated Robert Wilson the most.

"Sleep well?" Wilson asked in his throaty voice, filling a pipe.

"Did you?"

"Topping," the white hunter told him.

You bastard, thought Macomber, you insolent bastard.

So she woke him when she came in, Wilson thought, looking at them both with his flat, cold eyes. Well, why doesn't he keep his wife where she belongs? What does he think I am, a bloody plaster saint? Let him keep her where she belongs. It's his own fault.

"Do you think we'll find buffalo?" Margot asked, pushing away a dish of apricots.

"Chance of it," Wilson said and smiled at her. "Why don't you stay in camp?"

"Not for anything," she told him.

"Why not order her to stay in camp?" Wilson said to Macomber.

"You order her," said Macomber coldly.

"Let's not have any ordering, nor," turning to Macomber, "any silliness, Francis," Margot said quite pleasantly.

"Are you ready to start?" Macomber asked.

The Short Happy Life of Francis Macomber 237

"Any time," Wilson told him. "Do you want the Memsahib to go?"

"Does it make any difference whether I do or not?"

The hell with it, thought Robert Wilson. The utter complete hell with it. So this is what it's going to be like. Well, this is what it's going to be like, then.

"Makes no difference," he said.

"You're sure you wouldn't like to stay in camp with her yourself and let me go out and hunt the buffalo?" Macomber asked.

"Can't do that," said Wilson. "Wouldn't talk rot if I were you."

"I'm not talking rot. I'm disgusted."

"Bad word, disgusted."

"Francis, will you please try to speak sensibly?" his wife said.

"I speak too damned sensibly," Macomber said. "Did you ever eat such filthy food?"

"Something wrong with the food?" asked Wilson quietly.

"No more than with everything else."

"I'd pull yourself together, laddybuck," Wilson said very quietly. "There's a boy waits at table that understands a little English."

"The hell with him."

Wilson stood up and puffing on his pipe strolled away, speaking a few words in Swahili to one of the gun-bearers who was standing waiting for him. Macomber and his wife sat on at the table. He was staring at his coffee cup.

"If you make a scene I'll leave you, darling," Margot said quietly.

"No, you won't."

"You can try it and see."

"You won't leave me."

"No," she said. "I won't leave you and you'll behave yourself."

"Behave myself? That's a way to talk. Behave myself."

"Yes. Behave yourself."

"Why don't *you* try behaving?"

"I've tried it so long. So very long."

"I hate that red-faced swine," Macomber said. "I loathe the sight of him."

"He's really *very* nice."

"Oh, *shut up*," Macomber almost shouted. Just then the car came up and stopped in front of the dining tent and the driver and the two gun-bearers got out. Wilson walked over and looked at the husband and wife sitting there at the table.

"Going shooting?" he asked.

"Yes," said Macomber, standing up. "Yes."

"Better bring a woolly. It will be cool in the car," Wilson said.

"I'll get my leather jacket," Margot said.

"The boy has it," Wilson told her. He climbed into the front with the driver and Francis Macomber and his wife sat, not speaking, in the back seat.

Hope the silly beggar doesn't take a notion to blow the back of my head off, Wilson thought to himself. Women *are* a nuisance on safari.

The car was grinding down to cross the river at a pebbly ford in the gray daylight and then climbed, angling up the steep bank, where Wilson had ordered a way shovelled out the day before so they could reach the parklike wooded rolling country on the far side.

It was a good morning, Wilson thought. There was a heavy dew and as the wheels went through the grass and low bushes he could smell the odor of the crushed fronds. It was an odor like verbena and he liked this early morning smell of the dew, the crushed bracken and the look of the tree trunks showing black through the early morning mist, as the car made its way through the untracked, parklike country. He had put the two in the back seat out of his mind now and was thinking about buffalo. The buffalo that he was after stayed in the day-time in a thick swamp where it was impossible to get a shot, but in the night they fed out into an open stretch of country and if he could come between them and their swamp with the car, Macomber would have a good chance at them in the open. He did not want to hunt buff with Macomber in thick cover. He did not want to hunt buff or anything else with Macomber at all, but he was a professional hunter and he had hunted with some rare ones in his time. If they got buff today there would only be rhino to come and the poor man would have gone through his dangerous game and things might pick up. He'd have nothing more to do with the woman and Macomber would get over that too. He must have gone through plenty of that before by the look of things. Poor beggar. He must have a way of getting over it. Well, it was the poor sod's own bloody fault.

He, Robert Wilson, carried a double size cot on safari to accommodate any windfalls he might receive. He had hunted for a certain clientele, the international, fast, sporting set, where the women did not feel they were getting their money's worth unless they had shared that cot with the white hunter. He despised them when he was away from them although he liked some of them well enough at the time, but he made his living by them; and their standards were his standards as long as they were hiring him.

They were his standards in all except the shooting. He had his own standards about the killing and they could live up to them or get some one else to hunt them. He knew, too, that they all respected him for this. This Macomber was an odd one though. Damned if he wasn't. Now the wife. Well, the wife. Yes, the wife. Hm, the wife. Well he'd dropped all that. He looked around at them. Macomber sat grim and furious. Margot smiled at him. She looked younger today, more innocent and fresher and not so professionally beautiful. What's in her heart God knows, Wilson thought. She hadn't talked much last night. At that it was a pleasure to see her.

The motor car climbed up a slight rise and went on through the trees and then out into a grassy prairie-like opening and kept in the shelter of the trees along the edge, the driver going slowly and Wilson looking carefully out across the prairie and all along its far side. He stopped the car and studied the opening with his field glasses. Then he motioned to the driver to go on and the car moved slowly along, the driver avoiding wart-hog holes and driving around the mud castles ants had built. Then, looking across the opening, Wilson suddenly turned and said,

"By God, there they are!"

And looking where he pointed, while the car jumped forward and Wilson spoke in rapid Swahili to the driver, Macomber saw three huge, black animals looking almost cylindrical in their long heaviness, like big black tank cars, moving at a gallop across the far edge of the open prairie. They moved at a stiff-necked, stiff bodied gallop and he could see the upswept wide black horns on their heads as they galloped heads out; the heads not moving.

"They're three old bulls," Wilson said. "We'll cut them off before they get to the swamp."

The car was going a wild forty-five miles an hour across the open and as Macomber watched, the buffalo got bigger and bigger until he could see the gray, hairless, scabby look of one huge bull and how his neck was a part of his shoulders and the shiny black of his horns as he galloped a little behind the others that were strung out in that steady plunging gait; and then, the car swaying as though it had just jumped a road, they drew up close and he could see the plunging hugeness of the bull, and the dust in his sparsely haired hide, the wide boss of horn and his outstretched wide-nostrilled muzzle, and he was raising his rifle when Wilson shouted, "Not from the car, you fool!" and he had no fear, only hatred of Wilson, while the brakes clamped on and the car skidded, plowing sideways to an almost stop and Wilson was out on one side and he on the other, stumbling as his feet hit the still speeding-by of the earth, and then he was shooting at the bull as he moved away, hearing the bullets whunk into him, emptying his rifle at him as he moved steadily away, finally remembering to get his shots forward into the shoulder, and as he fumbled to re-load, he saw the bull was down. Down on his knees, his big head tossing, and seeing the other two still galloping he shot at the leader and hit him. He shot again and missed and he heard the *carawonging* roar as Wilson shot and saw the leading bull slide forward onto his nose.

"Get that other," Wilson said. "Now you're shooting!"

But the other bull was moving steadily at the same gallop and he missed, throwing a spout of dirt, and Wilson missed and the dust rose in a cloud and Wilson shouted, "Come on. He's too far!" and grabbed his arm and they were in the car again, Macomber and Wilson hanging on the sides and rocketing swayingly over the uneven ground, drawing up on the steady, plunging, heavy-necked, straight-moving gallop of the bull.

They were behind him and Macomber was filling his rifle, dropping shells onto the ground, jamming it, clearing the jam, then they were almost up with the bull when Wilson yelled "Stop," and the car skidded so that it almost swung over and Macomber fell forward onto his feet, slammed his bolt forward and fired as far forward as he could aim into the galloping, rounded black back, aimed and shot again, then again, then again, and the bullets, all of them hitting, had no effect on the buffalo that he could see. Then Wilson shot, the roar deafening him, and he could see the bull stagger. Macomber shot again, aiming carefully, and down he came, onto his knees.

"All right," Wilson said. "Nice work. That's the three."

Macomber felt a drunken elation.

"How many times did you shoot?" he asked.

"Just three," Wilson said. "You killed the first bull. The biggest one. I helped you finish the other two. Afraid they might have got into cover. You had them killed. I was just mopping up a little. You shot damn well."

"Let's go to the car," said Macomber. "I want a drink."

"Got to finish off that buff first," Wilson told him. The buffalo was on his knees and he jerked his head furiously and bellowed in pig-eyed, roaring rage as they came toward him.

"Watch he doesn't get up," Wilson said. Then, "Get a little broadside and take him in the neck just behind the ear."

Macomber aimed carefully at the center of the huge, jerking, rage-driven neck and shot. At the shot the head dropped forward.

"That does it," said Wilson. "Got the spine. They're a hell of a looking thing, aren't they?"

"Let's get the drink," said Macomber. In his life he had never felt so good.

In the car Macomber's wife sat very white faced. "You were marvellous, darling," she said to Macomber. "What a ride."

"Was it rough?" Wilson asked.

"It was frightful. I've never been more frightened in my life."

"Let's all have a drink," Macomber said.

"By all means," said Wilson. "Give it to the Memsahib." She drank the neat whisky from the flask and shuddered a little when she swallowed. She handed the flask to Macomber who handed it to Wilson.

"It was frightfully exciting," she said. "It's given me a dreadful headache. I didn't know you were allowed to shoot them from cars though."

"No one shot from cars," said Wilson coldly.

"I mean chase them from cars."

"Wouldn't ordinarily," Wilson said. "Seemed sporting enough to me though while we were doing it. Taking more chance driving that way across the plain full of holes and one thing and another than hunting on foot. Buffalo could have charged us each time we shot if he liked. Gave him every chance. Wouldn't mention it to any one though. It's illegal if that's what you mean."

"It seemed very unfair to me," Margot said, "chasing those big helpless things in a motor car."

"Did it?" said Wilson.

"What would happen if they heard about it in Nairobi?"

"I'd lose my licence for one thing. Other unpleasantnesses," Wilson said, taking a drink from the flask. "I'd be out of business."

"Really?"

"Yes, really."

"Well," said Macomber, and he smiled for the first time all day. "Now she has something on you."

"You have such a pretty way of putting things, Francis," Margot Macomber said. Wilson looked at them both. If a four-letter man marries a five-letter woman, he was thinking, what number of letters would their children be? What he said was, "We lost a gun-bearer. Did you notice it?"

"My God, no," Macomber said.

"Here he comes," Wilson said. "He's all right. He must have fallen off when we left the first bull."

Approaching them was the middle-aged gun-bearer, limping along in his knitted cap, khaki tunic, shorts and rubber sandals, gloomy-faced and disgusted looking. As he came up he called out to Wilson in Swahili and they all saw the change in the white hunter's face.

"What does he say?" asked Margot.

"He says the first bull got up and went into the bush," Wilson said with no expression in his voice.

"Oh," said Macomber blankly.

"Then it's going to be just like the lion," said Margot, full of anticipation.

"It's not going to be a damned bit like the lion," Wilson told her. "Did you want another drink, Macomber?"

"Thanks, yes," Macomber said. He expected the feeling he had had about the lion to come back but it did not. For the first time in his life he really felt wholly without fear. Instead of fear he had a feeling of definite elation.

"We'll go and have a look at the second bull," Wilson said. "I'll tell the driver to put the car in the shade."

"What are you going to do?" asked Margaret Macomber.

"Take a look at the buff," Wilson said.

"I'll come."

"Come along."

The three of them walked over to where the second buffalo bulked blackly in the open, head forward on the grass, the massive horns swung wide.

"He's a very good head," Wilson said. "That's close to a fifty-inch spread."

Macomber was looking at him with delight.

"He's hateful looking," said Margot. "Can't we go into the shade?"

"Of course," Wilson said. "Look," he said to Macomber, and pointed. "See that patch of bush?"

"Yes."

"That's where the first bull went in. The gun-bearer said when he fell off the bull was down. He was watching us helling along and the other two buff galloping. When he looked up there was the bull up and looking at him. Gun-bearer ran like hell and the bull went off slowly into that bush."

"Can we go in after him now?" asked Macomber eagerly.

Wilson looked at him appraisingly. Damned if this isn't a strange one, he thought. Yesterday he's scared sick and today he's a ruddy fire eater.

"No, we'll give him a while."

"Let's please go into the shade," Margot said. Her face was white and she looked ill.

They made their way to the car where it stood under a single, wide-spreading tree and all climbed in.

"Chances are he's dead in there," Wilson remarked. "After a little we'll have a look."

Macomber felt a wild unreasonable happiness that he had never known before.

"By God, that was a chase," he said. "I've never felt any such feeling. Wasn't it marvellous, Margot?"

"I hated it."

"Why?"

"I hated it," she said bitterly. "I loathed it."

"You know I don't think I'd ever be afraid of anything again," Macomber said to Wilson. "Something happened in me after we first saw the buff and started after him. Like a dam bursting. It was pure excitement."

"Cleans out your liver," said Wilson. "Damn funny things happen to people."

Macomber's face was shining. "You know something did happen to me," he said. "I feel absolutely different."

His wife said nothing and eyed him strangely. She was sitting far back in the seat and Macomber was sitting forward talking to Wilson who turned sideways talking over the back of the front seat.

"You know, I'd like to try another lion," Macomber said. "I'm really not afraid of them now. After all, what can they do to you?"

"That's it," said Wilson. "Worst one can do is kill you. How does it go? Shakespeare. Damned good. See if I can remember. Oh, damned good. Used to quote it to myself at one time. Let's see. 'By my troth, I care not; a man can die but once; we owe God a death and let it go which way it will he that dies this year is quit for the next.' Damned fine, eh?"

He was very embarrassed, having brought out this thing he had lived by, but he had seen men come of age before and it always moved him. It was not a matter of their twenty-first birthday.

It had taken a strange chance of hunting, a sudden precipitation into action without opportunity for worrying beforehand, to bring this about with Macomber, but regardless of how it had happened it had most certainly happened. Look at the beggar now, Wilson thought. It's that some of them stay little boys so long, Wilson thought. Sometimes all their lives. Their figures stay boyish when they're fifty. The great American boy-men. Damned strange people. But he liked this Macomber now. Damned strange fellow. Probably meant the end of cuckoldry too. Well, that would be a damned good thing. Damned good thing. Beggar had probably been afraid all his life. Don't know what started it. But over now. Hadn't had time to be afraid with the buff. That and being angry too. Motor car too. Motor cars made it familiar. Be a damn fire eater now. He'd seen it in the war work the same way. More of a change than any loss of virginity. Fear gone like an operation. Something else grew in its place. Main thing a man had. Made him into a man. Women knew it too. No bloody fear.

From the far corner of the seat Margaret Macomber looked at the two of them. There was no change in Wilson. She saw Wilson as she had seen him the day before when she had first realized what his great talent was. But she saw the change in Francis Macomber now.

"Do you have that feeling of happiness about what's going to happen?" Macomber asked, still exploring his new wealth.

"You're not supposed to mention it," Wilson said, looking in the other's face. "Much more fashionable to say you're scared. Mind you, you'll be scared too, plenty of times."

"But you *have* a feeling of happiness about action to come?"

"Yes," said Wilson. "There's that. Doesn't do to talk too much about all this. Talk the whole thing away. No pleasure in anything if you mouth it up too much."

"You're both talking rot," said Margot. "Just because you've chased some helpless animals in a motor car you talk like heroes."

"Sorry," said Wilson. "I have been gassing too much." She's worried about it already, he thought.

"If you don't know what we're talking about why not keep out of it?" Macomber asked his wife.

"You've gotten awfully brave, awfully suddenly," his wife said contemptuously, but her contempt was not secure. She was very afraid of something.

Macomber laughed, a very natural hearty laugh. "You know I *have*," he said. "I really have."

"Isn't it sort of late?" Margot said bitterly. Because she had done the best she could for many years back and the way they were together now was no one person's fault.

"Not for me," said Macomber.

Margot said nothing but sat back in the corner of the seat.

"Do you think we've given him time enough?" Macomber asked Wilson cheerfully.

"We might have a look," Wilson said. "Have you any solids left?"

"The gun-bearer has some."

Wilson called in Swahili and the older gun-bearer, who was skinning out one of the heads, straightened up, pulled a box of solids out of his pocket and brought them over to Macomber, who filled his magazine and put the remaining shells in his pocket.

"You might as well shoot the Springfield," Wilson said. "You're used to it. We'll leave the Mannlicher in the car with the Memsahib. Your gun-bearer can carry your heavy gun. I've this damned cannon. Now let me tell you about them."

He had saved this until the last because he did not want to worry Macomber. "When a buff comes he comes with his head high and thrust straight out. The boss of the horns covers any sort of a brain shot. The only shot is straight into the nose. The only other shot is into his chest or, if you're to one side, into the neck or the shoulders. After they've been hit once they take a hell of a lot of killing. Don't try anything fancy. Take the easiest shot there is. They've finished skinning out that head now. Should we get started?"

He called to the gun-bearers, who came up wiping their hands, and the older one got into the back.

"I'll only take Kongoni," Wilson said. "The other can watch to keep the birds away."

As the car moved slowly across the open space toward the island of brushy trees that ran in a tongue of foliage along a dry water course that cut the open swale, Macomber felt his heart pounding and his mouth was dry again, but it was excitement, not fear.

"Here's where he went in," Wilson said. Then to the gun-bearer in Swahili, "Take the blood spoor."

The car was parallel to the patch of bush. Macomber, Wilson and the gun-bearer got down. Macomber, looking back, saw his wife, with the rifle by her side, looking at him. He waved to her and she did not wave back.

The brush was very thick ahead and the ground was dry. The middle-aged gun-bearer was sweating heavily and Wilson had his hat down over his eyes and his red neck showed just ahead of Macomber. Suddenly the gun-bearer said something in Swahili to Wilson and ran forward.

"He's dead in there," Wilson said. "Good work," and he turned to grip Macomber's hand and as they shook hands, grinning at each other, the gun-bearer shouted wildly and they saw him coming out of the bush sideways, fast as a crab, and the bull coming, nose out, mouth tight closed, blood dripping, massive head straight out, coming in a charge, his little pig eyes bloodshot as he looked at them. Wilson, who was ahead was kneeling shooting, and Macomber, as he fired, unhearing his shot in the roaring of Wilson's gun, saw fragments like slate burst from the huge boss of the horns, and the head jerked, he shot again at the wide nostrils and saw the horns jolt again and fragments fly, and he did not see Wilson now and, aiming carefully, shot again with the buffalo's huge bulk almost on him and his rifle almost level with the on-coming head, nose cut, and he could see the little wicked eyes and the head started to lower and he felt a sudden white-hot, blinding flash explode inside his head and that was all he ever felt.

Wilson had ducked to one side to get in a shoulder shot. Macomber had stood solid and shot for the nose, shooting a touch high each time and hitting the heavy horns, splintering and chipping them like hitting a slate roof, and Mrs. Macomber, in the car, had shot at the buffalo with the 6.5 Mannlicher as it seemed about to gore Macomber and had hit her husband about two inches up and a little to one side of the base of his skull.

Francis Macomber lay now face down, not two yards from where the buffalo lay on his side and his wife knelt over him with Wilson beside her.

"I wouldn't turn him over," Wilson said.

The woman was crying hysterically.

"I'd get back in the car," Wilson said. "Where's the rifle?"

She shook her head, her face contorted. The gun-bearer picked up the rifle.

"Leave it as it is," said Wilson. Then, "Go get Abdulla so that he may witness the manner of the accident."

He knelt down, took a handkerchief from his pocket, and spread it over Francis Macomber's crew-cropped head where it lay. The blood sank into the dry, loose earth.

Wilson stood up and saw the buffalo on his side, his legs out, his thinly-haired belly crawling with ticks. "Hell of a good bull," his brain registered automatically. "A good fifty inches, or better. Better." He called to the driver and told him to spread a blanket over the body and stay by it. Then he walked over to the motor car where the woman sat crying in the corner.

"That was a pretty thing to do," he said in a toneless voice. "He *would* have left you too."

"Stop it," she said.

"Of course it's an accident," he said. "I know that."

"Stop it," she said.

"Don't worry," he said. "There will be a certain amount of unpleasantness but I will have some photographs taken that will be very useful at the inquest. There's the testimony of the gun-bearers and the driver too. You're perfectly all right."

"Stop it," she said.

"There's a hell of a lot to be done," he said. "And I'll have to send a truck off to the lake to wireless for a plane to take the three of us into Nairobi. Why didn't you poison him? That's what they do in England."

"Stop it. Stop it. Stop it," the woman cried.

The Short Happy Life of Francis Macomber 247

Wilson looked at her with his flat blue eyes.

"I'm through now," he said. "I was a little angry. I'd begun to like your husband."

"Oh, please stop it," she said. "Please, please stop it."

"That's better," Wilson said. "Please is much better. Now I'll stop."

EUDORA WELTY (1909-   )

A Worn Path

It was December—a bright frozen day in the early morning. Far out in the country there was an old Negro woman with her head tied in a red rag, coming along a path through the pinewoods. Her name was Phoenix Jackson. She was very old and small and she walked slowly in the dark pine shadows, moving a little from side to side in her steps, with the balanced heaviness and lightness of a pendulum in a grandfather clock. She carried a thin, small cane made from an umbrella, and with this she kept tapping the frozen earth in front of her. This made a grave and persistent noise in the still air, that seemed meditative, like the chirping of a solitary little bird.

She wore a dark striped dress reaching down to her shoetops, and an equally long apron of bleached sugar sacks, with a full pocket; all neat and tidy, but every time she took a step she might have fallen over her shoe-laces, which dragged from her unlaced shoes. She looked straight ahead. Her eyes were blue with age. Her skin had a pattern all its own of numberless branching wrinkles and as though a whole little tree stood in the middle of her forehead, but a golden color ran underneath, and the two knobs of her cheeks were illuminated by a yellow burning under the dark. Under the red rag her hair came down on her neck in the frailest of ringlets, still black, and with an odor like copper.

Now and then there was a quivering in the thicket. Old Phoenix said, "Out of my way, all you foxes, owls, beetles, jack rabbits, coons, and wild animals! . . . Keep out from under these feet, little bobwhites. . . . Keep the big wild hogs out of my path. Don't let none of those come running my direction. I got a long way." Under her small black-freckled hand her cane, limber as a buggy whip, would switch at the brush as if to rouse up any hiding things.

On she went. The woods were deep and still. The sun made the pine needles almost too bright to look at, up where the wind rocked.

The cones dropped as light as feathers. Down in the hollow was the mourning dove—it was not too late for him.

The path ran up a hill. "Seem like there is chains about my feet, time I get this far," she said, in the voice of argument old people keep to use with themselves. "Something always take a hold on this hill—pleads I should stay."

After she got to the top she turned and gave a full, severe look behind her where she had come. "Up through pines," she said at length. "Now down through oaks."

Her eyes opened their widest and she started down gently. But before she got to the bottom of the hill a bush caught her dress.

Her fingers were busy and intent, but her skirts were full and long, so that before she could pull them free in one place they were caught in another. It was not possible to allow the dress to tear. "I in the thorny bush," she said. "Thorns, you doing your appointed work. Never want to let folks pass—no sir. Old eyes thought you was a pretty little *green* bush."

Finally, trembling all over, she stood free, and after a moment dared to stoop for her cane.

"Sun so high!" she cried, leaning back and looking, while the thick tears went over her eyes. "The time getting all gone here."

At the foot of this hill was a place where a log was laid across the creek.

"Now comes the trial," said Phoenix.

Putting her right foot out, she mounted the log and shut her eyes. Lifting her skirt, levelling her cane fiercely before her, like a festival figure in some parade, she began to march across. Then she opened her eyes and she was safe on the other side.

"I wasn't as old as I thought," she said.

But she sat down to rest. She spread her skirts on the bank around her and folded her hands over her knees. Up above her was a tree in a pearly cloud of mistletoe. She did not dare to close her eyes, and when a little boy brought her a little plate with a slice of marble-cake on it she spoke to him. "That would be acceptable," she said. But when she went to take it there was just her own hand in the air.

So she left that tree, and had to go through a barbed-wire fence. There she had to creep and crawl, spreading her knees and stretching her fingers like a baby trying to climb the steps. But she talked loudly to herself: she could not let her dress be torn now, so late in the day, and she could not pay for having her arm or her leg sawed off if she got caught fast where she was.

At last she was safe through the fence and risen up out in the clearing. Big dead trees, like black men with one arm, were standing in the purple stalks of the withered cotton field. There sat a buzzard.

"Who you watching?"

In the furrow she made her way along.

"Glad this not the season for bulls," she said, looking sideways, "and the good Lord made his snakes to curl up and sleep in the winter. A pleasure I don't see no two-headed snake coming around that tree, where it come once. It took a while to get by him, back in the summer."

She passed through the old cotton and went into a field of dead corn. It whispered and shook, and was taller than her head. "Through the maze now," she said, for there was no path.

Then there was something tall, black, and skinny there, moving before her.

At first she took it for a man. It could have been a man dancing in the field. But she stood still and listened, and it did not make a sound. It was as silent as a ghost.

"Ghost," she said sharply, "who be you the ghost of? For I have heard of nary death close by."

But there was no answer, only the ragged dancing in the wind.

She shut her eyes, reached out her hand, and touched a sleeve. She found a coat and inside that an emptiness, cold as ice.

"You scarecrow," she said. Her face lighted. "I ought to be shut up for good," she said with laughter. "My senses is gone. I too old. I the oldest people I ever know. Dance, old scarecrow," she said, "while I dancing with you."

She kicked her foot over the furrow, and with mouth drawn down shook her head once or twice in a little strutting way. Some husks blew down and whirled in streamers about her skirts.

Then she went on, parting her way from side to side with the cane, through the whispering field. At last she came to the end, to a wagon track, where the silver grass blew between the red ruts. The quail were walking around like pullets, seeming all dainty and unseen.

"Walk pretty," she said. "This the easy place. This the easy going."

She followed the track, swaying through the quiet bare fields, through the little strings of trees silver in their dead leaves, past cabins silver from weather, with the doors and windows boarded shut, all like old women under a spell sitting there. "I walking in their sleep," she said, nodding her head vigorously.

In a ravine she went where a spring was silently flowing through a hollow log. Old Phoenix bent and drank. "Sweetgum makes the water sweet," she said, and drank more. "Nobody knows who made this well, for it was here when I was born."

The track crossed a swampy part where the moss hung as white as lace from every limb. "Sleep on, alligators, and blow your bubbles." Then the track went into the road.

Deep, deep the road went down between the high green-colored banks. Overhead the live-oaks met, and it was as dark as a cave.

A black dog with a lolling tongue came up out of the weeds by the ditch. She was meditating, and not ready, and when he came at her she only hit him a little with her cane. Over she went in the ditch, like a little puff of milk-weed.

Down there, her senses drifted away. A dream visited her, and she reached her hand up, but nothing reached down and gave her a pull. So she lay there and presently went to talking. "Old woman," she said to herself, "that black dog come up out of the weeds to stall you off, and now there he sitting on his fine tail, smiling at you."

A white man finally came along and found her—a hunter, a young man, with his dog on a chain.

"Well, Granny!" he laughed. "What are you doing there?"

"Lying on my back like a June-bug waiting to be turned over, mister," she said, reaching up her hand.

He lifted her up, gave her a swing in the air, and set her down, "Anything broken, Granny?"

"No sir, them old dead weeds is springy enough," said Phoenix, when she had got her breath. "I thank you for your trouble."

"Where do you live, Granny?" he asked, while the two dogs were growling at each other.

"Away back yonder, sir, behind the ridge. You can't even see it from here."

"On your way home?"

"No, sir, I going to town."

"Why, that's too far! That's as far as I walk when I come out myself, and I get something for my trouble." He patted the stuffed bag he carried, and there hung down a little closed claw. It was one of the bobwhites, with its beak hooked bitterly to show it was dead. "Now you go on home, Granny!"

"I bound to go to town, mister," said Phoenix. "The time come around."

He gave another laugh, filling the whole landscape. "I know you colored people! Wouldn't miss going to town to see Santa Claus!"

But something held Old Phoenix very still. The deep lines in her face went into a fierce and different radiation. Without warning she had seen with her own eyes a flashing nickel fall out of the man's pocket on to the ground.

"How old are you, Granny?" he was saying.

"There is no telling, mister," she said, "no telling."

Then she gave a little cry and clapped her hands, and said, "Git on away from here, dog! Look! Look at that dog!" She laughed as if in admiration. "He ain't scared of nobody. He a big black dog." She whispered, "Sick him!"

"Watch me get rid of that cur," said the man. "Sick him, Pete! Sick him!"

Phoenix heard the dogs fighting and heard the man running and throwing sticks. She even heard a gunshot. But she was slowly bending forward by that time, further and further forward, the lids stretched down over her eyes, as if she were doing this in her sleep. Her chin was lowered almost to her knees. The yellow palm of her hand came out from the fold of her apron. Her fingers slid down and along the ground under the piece of money with the grace and care they would have in lifting an egg from under a sitting hen. Then she slowly straightened up, she stood erect, and the nickel was in her apron pocket. A bird flew by. Her lips moved. "God watching me the whole time. I come to stealing."

The man came back, and his own dog panted about them. "Well, I scared him off that time," he said, and then he laughed and lifted his gun and pointed it at Phoenix.

She stood straight and faced him.

"Doesn't the gun scare you?" he said, still pointing it.

"No, sir, I seen plenty go off closer by, in my day, and for less than what I done," she said, holding utterly still.

He smiled, and shouldered the gun. "Well, Granny," he said, "you must be a hundred years old, and scared of nothing. I'd give you a dime if I had any money with me. But you take my advice and stay home, and nothing will happen to you."

"I bound to go on my way, mister," said Phoenix. She inclined her head in the red rag. Then they went in different directions, but she could hear the gun shooting again and again over the hill.

She walked on. The shadows hung from the oak trees to the road like curtains. Then she smelled wood-smoke, and smelled the river, and she saw a steeple and the cabins on their steep steps. Dozens of little black children whirled around her. There ahead was Natchez shining. Bells were ringing. She walked on.

In the paved city it was Christmas time. There were red and green electric lights strung and crisscrossed everywhere, and all turned on in the daytime. Old Phoenix would have been lost if she had not distrusted her eyesight and depended on her feet to know where to take her.

She paused quietly on the sidewalk, where people were passing by. A lady came along in the crowd, carrying an armful of red-, green-, and silver-wrapped presents; she gave off perfume like the red roses in hot summer, and Phoenix stopped her.

"Please, missy, will you lace up my shoe?" She held up her foot.

"What do you want, Grandma?"

"See my shoe," said Phoenix. "Do all right for out in the country, but wouldn't look right to go in a big building."

"Stand still then, Grandma," said the lady. She put her packages down carefully on the sidewalk beside her and laced and tied both shoes tightly.

"Can't lace 'em with a cane," said Phoenix. "Thank you, missy. I doesn't mind asking a nice lady to tie up my shoe when I gets out on the street."

Moving slowly and from side to side, she went into the stone building and into a tower of steps, where she walked up and around and around until her feet knew to stop.

She entered a door, and there she saw nailed up on the wall the document that had been stamped with the gold seal and framed in the gold frame which matched the dream that was hung up in her head.

"Here I be," she said. There was a fixed and ceremonial stiffness over her body.

"A charity case, I suppose," said an attendant who sat at the desk before her.

But Phoenix only looked above her head. There was sweat on her face; the wrinkles shone like a bright net.

"Speak up, Grandma," the women said. "What's your name? We must have your history, you know. Have you been here before? What seems to be the trouble with you?"

Old Phoenix only gave a twitch to her face as if a fly were bothering her.

"Are you deaf?" cried the attendant.

But then the nurse came in.

"Oh, that's just old Aunt Phoenix," she said. "She doesn't come for herself—she has a little grandson. She makes these trips just as regular as clockwork. She lives away back off the Old Natchez Trace." She bent down. "Well, Aunt Phoenix, why don't you just take a seat? We won't keep you standing after your long trip." She pointed.

The old woman sat down, bolt upright in the chair.

"Now, how is the boy?" asked the nurse.

Old Phoenix did not speak.

"I said, how is the boy?"

But Phoenix only waited and stared straight ahead, her face very solemn and withdrawn into rigidity.

"Is his throat any better?" asked the nurse. "Aunt Phoenix, don't you hear me? Is your grandson's throat any better since the last time you came for the medicine?"

With her hands on her knees, the old woman waited, silent, erect and motionless, just as if she were in armour.

"You mustn't take up our time this way, Aunt Phoenix," the nurse said. "Tell us quickly about your grandson, and get it over. He isn't dead, is he?"

At last there came a flicker and then a flame of comprehension across her face, and she spoke.

"My grandson. It was my memory had left me. There I sat and forgot why I made my long trip."

"Forgot?" The nurse frowned. "After you came so far?"

Then Phoenix was like an old woman begging a dignified forgiveness for waking up frightened in the night. "I never did go to school —I was too old at the Surrender," she said in a soft voice. "I'm an old woman without an education. It was my memory fail me. My little grandson, he is just the same, and I forgot it in the coming."

"Throat never heals, does it?" said the nurse, speaking in a loud, sure voice to Old Phoenix. By now she had a card with something written on it, a little list. "Yes. Swallowed lye. When was it—January —two—three years ago—"

Phoenix spoke unasked now. "No, missy, he not dead, he just the same. Every little while his throat begin to close up again, and he not able to swallow. He not get his breath. He not able to help himself. So the time come around, and I go on another trip for the soothing-medicine."

"All right. The doctor said as long as you came to get it you could have it," said the nurse. "But it's an obstinate case."

"My little grandson, he sit up there in the house all wrapped up, waiting by himself," Phoenix went on. "We is the only two left in the world. He suffer and it don't seem to put him back at all. He got a sweet look. He going to last. He wear a little patch quilt and peep out, holding his mouth open like a little bird. I remembers so plain now. I not going to forget him again, no, the whole enduring time. I could tell him from all the others in creation."

"All right." The nurse was trying to hush her now. She brought her a bottle of medicine. "Charity," she said, making a check mark in a book.

Old Phoenix held the bottle close to her eyes and then carefully put it into her pocket.

"I thank you," she said.

"It's Christmas time, Grandma," said the attendant. "Could I give you a few pennies out of my purse?"

"Five pennies is a nickel," said Phoenix stiffly.

"Here's a nickel," said the attendant.

Phoenix rose carefully and held out her hand. She received the nickel and then fished the other nickel out of her pocket and laid it beside the new one. She stared at her palm closely, with her head on one side.

Then she gave a tap with her cane on the floor.

"This is what come to me to do," she said. "I going to the store and buy my child a little windmill they sells, made out of paper. He going to find it hard to believe there such a thing in the world. I'll march myself back where he waiting, holding it straight up in this hand."

She lifted her free hand, gave a little nod, turned round, and walked out of the doctor's office. Then her slow step began on the stairs, going down.

ALBERT CAMUS (1913-1960)

The Guest

Translated by Justin O'Brien

The schoolmaster was watching the two men climb toward him. One was on horseback, the other on foot. They had not yet tackled the abrupt rise leading to the schoolhouse built on the hillside. They were toiling onward, making slow progress in the snow, among the stones, on the vast expanse of the high, deserted plateau. From time to time the horse stumbled. Without hearing anything yet, he could see the breath issuing from the horse's nostrils. One of the men, at least, knew the region. They were following the trail although it had disappeared days ago under a layer of dirty white snow. The schoolmaster calculated that it would take them half an hour to get onto the hill. It was cold; he went back into the school to get a sweater.

He crossed the empty, frigid classroom. On the blackboard the four rivers of France, drawn with four different colored chalks, had been flowing toward their estuaries for the past three days. Snow had suddenly fallen in mid-October after eight months of drought without the transition of rain, and the twenty pupils, more or less, who lived in the villages scattered over the plateau had stopped coming. With fair weather they would return. Daru now heated only the single room that was his lodging, adjoining the classroom and giving also onto the plateau to the east. Like the class windows, his window looked to the south too. On that side the school was a few kilometers from the point where the plateau began to slope toward the south. In clear weather could be seen the purple mass of the mountain range where the gap opened onto the desert.

Somewhat warmed, Daru returned to the window from which he had first seen the two men. They were no longer visible. Hence they must have tackled the rise. The sky was not so dark, for the snow had stopped falling during the night. The morning had opened with a dirty light which had scarcely become brighter as the ceiling of clouds lifted. At two in the afternoon it seemed as if the day were merely beginning. But still this was better than those three days when the thick snow was falling amidst unbroken darkness with little gusts of wind that rattled the double door of the classroom. Then Daru had spent long hours in his room, leaving it only to go to the shed and feed the chickens or get some coal. Fortunately the delivery truck from Tadjid, the nearest village to the north, had brought his supplies two days before the blizzard. It would return in forty-eight hours.

Besides, he had enough to resist a siege, for the little room was cluttered with bags of wheat that the administration left as a stock to distribute to those of his pupils whose families had suffered from the drought. Actually they had all been victims because they were all poor. Every day Daru would distribute a ration to the children. They had missed it, he knew, during these bad days. Possibly one of the fathers or big brothers would come this afternoon and he could supply them with grain. It was just a matter of carrying them over to the next harvest. Now shiploads of wheat were arriving from France and the worst was over. But it would be hard to forget that poverty, that army of ragged ghosts wandering in the sunlight, the plateaus burned to a cinder month after month, the earth shriveled up little by little, literally scorched, every stone bursting into dust under one's foot. The sheep had died then by thousands and even a few men, here and there, sometimes without anyone's knowing.

In contrast with such poverty, he who lived almost like a monk in his remote schoolhouse, nonetheless satisfied with the little he had and with the rough life, had felt like a lord with his whitewashed walls, his narrow couch, his unpainted shelves, his well, and his weekly provision of water and food. And suddenly this snow, without warning, without the foretaste of rain. This is the way the region was, cruel to live in, even without men—who didn't help matters either. But Daru had been born here. Everywhere else, he felt exiled.

He stepped out onto the terrace in front of the schoolhouse. The two men were now halfway up the slope. He recognized the horseman as Balducci, the old gendarme he had known for a long time. Balducci was holding on the end of a rope an Arab who was walking behind him with hands bound and head lowered. The gendarme waved a greeting to which Daru did not reply, lost as he was in contemplation of the Arab dressed in a faded blue jellaba, his feet in sandals but covered with socks of heavy raw wool, his head surmounted by a narrow, short *chèche*. They were approaching. Balducci was holding back his horse in order not to hurt the Arab, and the group was advancing slowly.

Within earshot, Balducci shouted: "One hour to do the three kilometers from El Ameur!" Daru did not answer. Short and square in his thick sweater, he watched them climb. Not once had the Arab raised his head. "Hello," said Daru when they got up onto the terrace. "Come in and warm up." Balducci painfully got down from his horse without letting go of the rope. From under his bristling mustache he smiled at the schoolmaster. His little dark eyes, deep-set under a tanned forehead, and his mouth surrounded with wrinkles made him look attentive and studious. Daru took the bridle, led the horse to the shed, and came back to the two men, who were now waiting for him in the school. He led them into his room. "I am going to heat up the classroom," he said. "We'll be more comfortable there." When he entered the room again, Balducci was on the couch. He had undone the rope tying him to the Arab, who had squatted near the stove. His hands still bound, the *chèche* pushed back on his head, he was looking toward the window. At first Daru noticed only his huge lips, fat, smooth, almost Negroid; yet his nose was straight, his eyes were dark and full of fever. The *chèche* revealed an obstinate forehead and, under the weathered skin now rather discolored by the cold, the whole face had a restless and rebellious look that struck Daru when the Arab, turning his face toward him, looked him straight in the eyes. "Go into the other room," said the schoolmaster, "and I'll make you some mint tea." "Thanks," Balducci said. "What a chore! How I long for retirement." And addressing his prisoner in Arabic: "Come on, you." The Arab got up and, slowly, holding his bound wrists in front of him, went into the classroom.

With the tea, Daru brought a chair. But Balducci was already enthroned on the nearest pupil's desk and the Arab had squatted against the teacher's platform facing the stove, which stood between the desk and the window. When he held out the glass of tea to the prisoner, Daru hesitated at the sight of his bound hands. "He might perhaps be untied." "Sure," said Balducci. "That was for the trip." He started to get to his feet. But Daru, setting the glass on the floor, had knelt beside the Arab. Without saying anything, the Arab watched him with his feverish eyes. Once his hands were free, he rubbed his swollen wrists against each other, took the glass of tea, and sucked up the burning liquid in swift little sips.

"Good," said Daru. "And where are you headed?"

Balducci withdrew his mustache from the tea. "Here, son."

"Odd pupils! And you're spending the night?"

"No. I'm going back to El Ameur. And you will deliver this fellow to Tinguit. He is expected at police headquarters."

Balducci was looking at Daru with a friendly little smile.

"What's this story?" asked the schoolmaster. "Are you pulling my leg?"

"No, son. Those are the orders."

"The orders? I'm not . . ." Daru hesitated, not wanting to hurt the old Corsican. "I mean, that's not my job."

"What! What's the meaning of that? In wartime people do all kinds of jobs."

"Then I'll wait for the declaration of war!"

Balducci nodded.

"O.K. But the orders exist and they concern you too. Things are brewing, it appears. There is talk of a forthcoming revolt. We are mobilized, in a way."

Daru still had his obstinate look.

"Listen, son," Balducci said. "I like you and you must understand. There's only a dozen of us at El Ameur to patrol throughout the whole territory of a small department and I must get back in a hurry. I was told to hand this guy over to you and return without delay. He couldn't be kept there. His village was beginning to stir; they wanted to take him back. You must take him to Tinguit tomorrow before the day is over. Twenty kilometers shouldn't faze a husky fellow like you. After that, all will be over. You'll come back to your pupils and your comfortable life."

Behind the wall the horse could be heard snorting and pawing the earth. Daru was looking out the window. Decidedly, the weather was clearing and the light was increasing over the snowy plateau. When all the snow was melted, the sun would take over again and once more would burn the fields of stone. For days, still, the unchanging sky would shed its dry light on the solitary expanse where nothing had any connection with man.

"After all," he said, turning around toward Balducci, "what did he do?" And, before the gendarme had opened his mouth, he asked: "Does he speak French?"

"No, not a word. We had been looking for him for a month, but they were hiding him. He killed his cousin."

"Is he against us?"

"I don't think so. But you can never be sure."

"Why did he kill?"

"A family squabble, I think. One owed the other grain, it seems. It's not at all clear. In short, he killed his cousin with a billhook. You know, like a sheep, *kreezk!*"

Balducci made the gesture of drawing a blade across his throat and the Arab, his attention attracted, watched him with a sort of anxiety. Daru felt a sudden wrath against the man, against all men with their rotten spite, their tireless hates, their blood lust.

But the kettle was singing on the stove. He served Balducci more tea, hesitated, then served the Arab again, who, a second time, drank avidly. His raised arms made the jellaba fall open and the schoolmaster saw his thin, muscular chest.

"Thanks, kid," Balducci said. "And now, I'm off."

He got up and went toward the Arab, taking a small rope from his pocket.

"What are you doing?" Daru asked dryly.

Balducci, disconcerted, showed him the rope.

"Don't bother."

The old gendarme hesitated. "It's up to you. Of course, you are armed?"

"I have my shotgun."

"Where?"

"In the trunk."

"You ought to have it near your bed."

"Why? I have nothing to fear."

"You're crazy, son. If there's an uprising, no one is safe, we're all in the same boat."

"I'll defend myself. I'll have time to see them coming."

Balducci began to laugh, then suddenly the mustache covered the white teeth. "You'll have time? O.K. That's just what I was saying. You have always been a little cracked. That's why I like you, my son was like that."

At the same time he took out his revolver and put it on the desk.

"Keep it; I don't need two weapons from here to El Ameur."

The revolver shone against the black paint of the table. When the gendarme turned toward him, the schoolmaster caught the smell of leather and horseflesh.

"Listen, Balducci," Daru said suddenly, "every bit of this disgusts me, and first of all your fellow here. But I won't hand him over. Fight, yes, if I have to. But not that."

The old gendarme stood in front of him and looked at him severely.

"You're being a fool," he said slowly. "I don't like it either. You don't get used to putting a rope on a man even after years of it, and you're even ashamed—yes, ashamed. But you can't let them have their way."

"I won't hand him over," Daru said again.

"It's an order, son, and I repeat it."

"That's right. Repeat to them what I've said to you: I won't hand him over."

Balducci made a visible effort to reflect. He looked at the Arab and at Daru. At last he decided.

"No, I won't tell them anything. If you want to drop us, go ahead; I'll not denounce you. I have an order to deliver the prisoner and I'm doing so. And now you'll just sign this paper for me."

"There's no need. I'll not deny that you left him with me."

"Don't be mean with me. I know you'll tell the truth. You're from hereabouts and you are a man. But you must sign, that's the rule."

Daru opened his drawer, took out a little square bottle of purple ink, the red wooden penholder with the "sergeant-major" pen he used for making models of penmanship, and signed. The gendarme carefully folded the paper and put it into his wallet. Then he moved toward the door.

"I'll see you off," Daru said.

"No," said Balducci. "There's no use being polite. You insulted me."

He looked at the Arab, motionless in the same spot, sniffed peevishly, and turned away toward the door. "Good-by, son," he said. The door shut behind him. Balducci appeared suddenly outside the window and then disappeared. His footsteps were muffled by the snow. The horse stirred on the other side of the wall and several chickens fluttered in fright. A moment later Balducci reappeared outside the window leading the horse by the bridle. He walked toward the little rise without turning around and disappeared from sight with the horse following him. A big stone could be heard bouncing down. Daru walked back toward the prisoner, who, without stirring, never took his eyes off him. "Wait," the schoolmaster said in Arabic and went toward the bedroom. As he was going through the door, he had a second thought, went to the desk, took the revolver, and stuck it in his pocket. Then, without looking back, he went into his room.

For some time he lay on his couch watching the sky gradually close over, listening to the silence. It was this silence that had seemed painful to him during the first days here, after the war. He had requested a post in the little town at the base of the foothills separating the upper plateaus from the desert. There, rocky walls, green and black to the north, pink and lavender to the south, marked the frontier of eternal summer. He had been named to a post farther north, on the plateau itself. In the beginning, the solitude and the silence had been hard for him on these wastelands peopled only by stones. Occasionally, furrows suggested cultivation, but they had been dug to uncover a certain kind of stone good for building. The only plowing here was to harvest rocks. Elsewhere a thin layer of soil accumulated in the hollows would be scraped out to enrich paltry village gardens. This is the way it was: bare rock covered three quarters of the region. Towns sprang up, flourished, then disappeared; men came by, loved one another or fought bitterly, then died. No one in this desert, neither he nor his guest, mattered. And yet, outside this desert neither of them, Daru knew, could have really lived.

When he got up, no noise came from the classroom. He was amazed at the unmixed joy he derived from the mere thought that the Arab might have fled and that he would be alone with no decision to make. But the prisoner was there. He had merely stretched out between the stove and the desk. With eyes open, he was staring at the ceiling. In that position, his thick lips were particularly noticeable, giving him a pouting look. "Come," said Daru. The Arab got up and followed him. In the bedroom, the schoolmaster pointed to a chair near the table under the window. The Arab sat down without taking his eyes off Daru.

"Are you hungry?"

"Yes," the prisoner said.

Daru set the table for two. He took flour and oil, shaped a cake in a frying-pan, and lighted the little stove that functioned on bottled gas. While the cake was cooking, he went out to the shed to get cheese, eggs, dates, and condensed milk. When the cake was done he set it on the window sill to cool, heated some condensed milk diluted with water, and beat up the eggs into an omelette. In one of his motions he knocked against the revolver stuck in his right pocket. He set the bowl down, went into the classroom, and put the revolver in his desk drawer. When he came back to the room, night was falling. He put on the light and served the Arab. "Eat," he said. The Arab took a piece of the cake, lifted it eagerly to his mouth, and stopped short.

"And you?" he asked.

"After you. I'll eat too."

The thick lips opened slightly. The Arab hesitated, then bit into the cake determinedly.

The meal over, the Arab looked at the schoolmaster. "Are you the judge?"

"No, I'm simply keeping you until tomorrow."

"Why do you eat with me?"

"I'm hungry."

The Arab fell silent. Daru got up and went out. He brought back a folding bed from the shed, set it up between the table and the stove, perpendicular to his own bed. From a large suitcase which, upright in a corner, served as a shelf for papers, he took two blankets and arranged them on the camp bed. Then he stopped, felt useless, and sat down on his bed. There was nothing more to do or to get ready. He had to look at this man. He looked at him, therefore, trying to imagine his face bursting with rage. He couldn't do so. He could see nothing but the dark yet shining eyes and the animal mouth.

"Why did you kill him?" he asked in a voice whose hostile tone surprised him.

The Arab looked away. "He ran away. I ran after him."

He raised his eyes to Daru again and they were full of a sort of woeful interrogation. "Now what will they do to me?"

"Are you afraid?"

He stiffened, turning his eyes away.

"Are you sorry?"

The Arab stared at him openmouthed. Obviously he did not understand. Daru's annoyance was growing. At the same time he felt awkward and self-conscious with his big body wedged between the two beds.

"Lie down there," he said impatiently. "That's your bed."

The Arab didn't move. He called to Daru:

"Tell me!"

The schoolmaster looked at him.

"Is the gendarme coming back tomorrow?"

"I don't know."

"Are you coming with us?"

"I don't know. Why?"

The prisoner got up and stretched out on top of the blankets, his feet toward the window. The light from the electric bulb shone straight into his eyes and he closed them at once.

"Why?" Daru repeated, standing beside the bed.

The Arab opened his eyes under the blinding light and looked at him, trying not to blink.

"Come with us," he said.

In the middle of the night, Daru was still not asleep. He had gone to bed after undressing completely; he generally slept naked. But when he suddenly realized that he had nothing on, he hesitated. He felt vulnerable and the temptation came to him to put his clothes back on. Then he shrugged his shoulders; after all, he wasn't a child and, if need be, he could break his adversary in two. From his bed he could observe him, lying on his back, still motionless with his eyes closed under the harsh light. When Daru turned out the light, the darkness seemed to coagulate all of a sudden. Little by little, the night came back to life in the window where the starless sky was stirring gently. The schoolmaster soon made out the body lying at his feet. The Arab still did not move, but his eyes seemed open. A faint wind was prowling around the schoolhouse. Perhaps it would drive away the clouds and the sun would reappear.

During the night the wind increased. The hens fluttered a little and then were silent. The Arab turned over on his side with his back to Daru, who thought he heard him moan. Then he listened for his guest's breathing, become heavier and more regular. He listened to that breath so close to him and mused without being able to go to sleep. In this room where he had been sleeping alone for a year, this presence bothered him. But it bothered him also by imposing on him a sort of brotherhood he knew well but refused to accept in the present circumstances. Men who share the same rooms, soldiers or prisoners, develop a strange alliance as if, having cast off their armor with their clothing, they fraternized every evening, over and above their differences, in the ancient community of dream and fatigue. But Daru shook himself; he didn't like such musings, and it was essential to sleep.

A little later, however, when the Arab stirred slightly, the schoolmaster was still not asleep. When the prisoner made a second move, he stiffened, on the alert. The Arab was lifting himself slowly on his arms with almost the motion of a sleepwalker. Seated upright in bed, he waited motionless without turning his head toward Daru, as if he were listening attentively. Daru did not stir; it had just occurred to him that the revolver was still in the drawer of his desk. It was better to act at once. Yet he continued to observe the prisoner, who, with the same slithery motion, put his feet on the ground, waited again, then began to stand up slowly. Daru was about to call out to him when the Arab began to walk, in a quite natural but extraordinary silent way. He was

The Guest 263

heading toward the door at the end of the room that opened into the shed. He lifted the latch with precaution and went out, pushing the door behind him but without shutting it. Daru had not stirred. "He is running away," he merely thought. "Good riddance!" Yet he listened attentively. The hens were not fluttering; the guest must be on the plateau. A faint sound of water reached him, and he didn't know what it was until the Arab again stood framed in the doorway, closed the door carefully, and came back to bed without a sound. Then Daru turned his back on him and fell asleep. Still later he seemed, from the depths of his sleep, to hear furtive steps around the schoolhouse. "I'm dreaming! I'm dreaming!" he repeated to himself. And he went on sleeping.

When he awoke, the sky was clear; the loose window let in a cold, pure air. The Arab was asleep, hunched up under the blankets now, his mouth open, utterly relaxed. But when Daru shook him, he started dreadfully, staring at Daru with wild eyes as if he had never seen him and such a frightened expression that the schoolmaster stepped back. "Don't be afraid. It's me. You must eat." The Arab nodded his head and said yes. Calm had returned to his face, but his expression was vacant and listless.

The coffee was ready. They drank it seated together on the folding bed as they munched their pieces of the cake. Then Daru led the Arab under the shed and showed him the faucet where he washed. He went back into the room, folded the blankets and the bed, made his own bed and put the room in order. Then he went through the classroom and out onto the terrace. The sun was already rising in the blue sky; a soft, bright light was bathing the deserted plateau. On the ridge the snow was melting in spots. The stones were about to reappear. Crouched on the edge of the plateau, the schoolmaster looked at the deserted expanse. He thought of Balducci. He had hurt him, for he had sent him off in a way as if he didn't want to be associated with him. He could still hear the gendarme's farewell and, without knowing why, he felt strangely empty and vulnerable. At that moment, from the other side of the schoolhouse, the prisoner coughed. Daru listened to him almost despite himself and then, furious, threw a pebble that whistled through the air before sinking into the snow. That man's stupid crime revolted him, but to hand him over was contrary to honor. Merely thinking of it made him smart with humiliation. And he cursed at one and the same time his own people who had sent him this Arab and the Arab too who had dared to kill and not managed to get away. Daru got up, walked in a circle on the terrace, waited motionless, and then went back into the schoolhouse.

The Arab, leaning over the cement floor of the shed, was washing his teeth with two fingers. Daru looked at him and said: "Come." He went back into the room ahead of the prisoner. He slipped a hunting-jacket on over his sweater and put on walking-shoes. Standing, he waited until the Arab had put on his *chèche* and sandals. They went into the classroom and the schoolmaster pointed to the exit, saying: "Go ahead." The fellow didn't budge. "I'm coming," said Daru. The Arab went out. Daru went back into the room and made a package of pieces of rusk, dates, and sugar. In the classroom, before going out, he hesitated a second in front of his desk, then crossed the threshold and locked the door. "That's the way," he said. He started toward the east, followed by the prisoner. But, a short distance from the schoolhouse, he thought he heard a slight sound behind them. He retraced his steps and examined the surroundings of the house; there was no one there. The Arab watched him without seeming to understand. "Come on," said Daru.

They walked for an hour and rested beside a sharp peak of lime-stone. The snow was melting faster and faster and the sun was drink-ing up the puddles at once, rapidly cleaning the plateau, which gradu-ally dried and vibrated like the air itself. When they resumed walking, the ground rang under their feet. From time to time a bird rent the space in front of them with a joyful cry. Daru breathed in deeply the fresh morning light. He felt a sort of rapture before the vast familiar expanse, now almost entirely yellow under its dome of blue sky. They walked an hour more, descending toward the south. They reached a level height made up of crumbly rocks. From there on, the plateau sloped down, eastward toward a low plain where there were a few spindly trees and, to the south, toward outcroppings of rock that gave the landscape a chaotic look.

Daru surveyed the two directions. There was nothing but the sky on the horizon. Not a man could be seen. He turned toward the Arab, who was looking at him blankly. Daru held out the package to him. "Take it," he said. "There are dates, bread, and sugar. You can hold out for two days. Here are a thousand francs too." The Arab took the package and the money but kept his full hands at chest level as if he didn't know what to do with what was being given him. "Now look," the schoolmaster said as he pointed in the direction of the east, "there's the way to Tinguit. You have a two-hour walk. At Tinguit you'll find the administration and the police. They are expecting you." The Arab looked toward the east, still holding the package and the money against his chest. Daru took his elbow and turned him rather roughly toward the south. At the foot of the height on which they stood could be seen a faint path. "That's the trail across the plateau. In a day's walk from here you'll find pasturelands and the first nomads. They'll take you in and shelter you according to their law." The Arab had now turned toward Daru and a sort of panic was visible in his expression. "Listen," he said. Daru shook his head: "No, be quiet. Now I'm leaving you." He turned his back on him, took two long steps in the direction of the school, looked hesitantly at the motionless Arab, and started off again. For a few minutes he heard nothing but his own step resounding on the cold ground and did not turn his head. A moment later, however, he turned around. The Arab was still there on the edge of the hill, his arms hanging now, and he was looking at the schoolmaster. Daru felt something rise in his throat. But he swore with impatience, waved vaguely, and started off again. He had already gone some distance when he again stopped and looked. There was no longer anyone on the hill.

Daru hesitated. The sun was now rather high in the sky and was beginning to beat down on his head. The schoolmaster retracted his steps, at first somewhat uncertainly, then with decision. When he reached the little hill, he was bathed in sweat. He climbed it as fast as he could and stopped, out of breath, at the top. The rock-fields to the south stood out sharply against the blue sky, but on the plain to the east a steamy heat was already rising. And in that slight haze, Daru, with heavy heart, made out the Arab walking slowly on the road to prison.

A little later, standing before the window of the classroom, the schoolmaster was watching the clear light bathing the whole surface of the plateau, but he hardly saw it. Behind him on the blackboard, among the winding French rivers, sprawled the clumsily chalked-up words he had just read: "You handed over our brother. You will pay for this." Daru looked at the sky, the plateau, and, beyond, the invisible lands stretching all the way to the sea. In this vast landscape he had loved so much, he was alone.

LAWRENCE SARGENT HALL (1915-   )

The Ledge

On Christmas morning before sunup the fisherman embraced his warm wife and left his close bed. She did not want him to go. It was Christmas morning. He was a big, raw man, with too much strength, whose delight in winter was to hunt the sea ducks that flew in to feed by the outer ledges, bare at low tide.

As his bare feet touched the cold floor and the frosty air struck his nude flesh, he might have changed his mind in the dark of this special day. It was a home day, which made it seem natural to think of the outer ledges merely as some place he had shot ducks in the past. But he had promised his son, thirteen, and his nephew, fifteen, who came from inland. That was why he had given them his present of an automatic shotgun each the night before, on Christmas Eve. Rough man though he was known to be, and no spoiler of boys, he kept his promises when he understood what they meant. And to the boys, as to him, home meant where you came for rest after you had had your Christmas fill of action and excitement.

His legs astride, his arms raised, the fisherman stretched as high as he could in the dim privacy of his bedroom. Above the snug murmur of his wife's protest he heard the wind in the pines and knew it was easterly as the boys had hoped and he had surmised the night before. Conditions would be ideal, and when they were, anybody ought to take advantage of them. The birds would be flying. The boys would get a man's sport their first time outside on the ledges.

His son at thirteen, small but steady and experienced, was fierce to grow up in hunting, to graduate from sheltered waters and the blinds along the shores of the inner bay. His nephew at fifteen, an overgrown farm boy, had a farm boy's love of the sea, though he could not swim a stroke and was often sick in choppy weather. That was the reason his father, the fisherman's brother, was a farmer and chose to sleep in on the holiday morning at his brother's house. Many of the ones the farmer had grown up with were regularly seasick and could not swim, but they were unafraid of the water. They could not have dreamed of being anything but fishermen. The fisherman himself could swim like a seal and was never sick, and he would sooner die than be anything else.

He dressed in the cold and dark, and woke the boys gruffly. They tumbled out of bed, their instincts instantly awake while their thoughts still fumbled slumbrously. The fisherman's wife in the adjacent bedroom heard them apparently trying to find their clothes, mumbling sleepily and happily to each other, while her husband went down to the hot kitchen to fry eggs—sunny-side up, she knew, because that was how they all liked them.

Always in winter she hated to have them go outside, the weather was so treacherous and there were so few others out in case of trouble. To the fisherman these were no more than woman's fears, to be taken for granted and laughed off. When they were first married they fought miserably every fall because she was after him constantly to put his boat up until spring. The fishing was all outside in winter, and though prices were high the storms made the rate of attrition high on gear. Nevertheless he did well. So she could do nothing with him.

People thought him a hard man, and gave him the reputation of being all out for himself because he was inclined to brag and be disdainful. If it was true, and his own brother was one of those who strongly felt it was, they lived better than others, and his brother had small right to criticize. There had been times when in her loneliness she had yearned to leave him for another man. But it would have been dangerous. So over the years she had learned to shut her mind to his hard-driving, and take what comfort she might from his unsympathetic competence. Only once or twice, perhaps, had she gone so far as to dwell guiltily on what it would be like to be a widow.

The thought that her boy, possibly because he was small, would not be insensitive like his father, and the rattle of dishes and smell of frying bacon downstairs in the kitchen shut off from the rest of the chilly house, restored the cozy feeling she had had before she was alone in bed. She heard them after a while go out and shut the back door.

Under her window she heard the snow grind drily beneath their boots, and her husband's sharp, exasperated commands to the boys. She shivered slightly in the envelope of her own warmth. She listened to the noise of her son and nephew talking elatedly. Twice she caught the glimmer of their lights on the white ceiling above the window as they went down the path to the shore. There would be frost on the skiff and freezing suds at the water's edge. She herself used to go gunning when she was younger; now, it seemed to her, anyone going out like that on Christmas morning had to be incurably male. They would none of them think about her until they returned and piled the birds they had shot on top of the sink for her to dress.

Ripping into the quiet pre-dawn cold she heard the hot snarl of the outboard taking them out to the boat. It died as abruptly as it had burst into life. Two or three or four or five minutes later the big engine broke into a warm reassuring roar. He had the best of equipment, and he kept it in the best of condition. She closed her eyes. It would not be too long before the others would be up for Christmas. The summer drone of the exhaust deepened. Then gradually it faded in the wind until it was lost at sea, or she slept.

The engine had started immediately in spite of the temperature. This put the fisherman in a good mood. He was proud of his boat. Together he and the two boys heaved the skiff and outboard onto the stern and secured it athwartships. His son went forward along the deck, iridescent in the ray of the light the nephew shone through the windshield, and cast the mooring pennant loose into darkness. The fisherman swung to starboard, glanced at his compass, and headed seaward down the obscure bay.

268 LAWRENCE SARGENT HALL

There would be just enough visibility by the time they reached the headland to navigate the crooked channel between the islands. It was the only nasty stretch of water. The fisherman had done it often in fog or at night—he always swore he could go anywhere in the bay blindfolded—but there was no sense in taking chances if you didn't have to. From the mouth of the channel he could lay a straight course for Brown Cow Island, anchor the boat out of sight behind it, and from the skiff set their tollers off Devil's Hump three hundred yards to seaward. By then the tide would be clearing the ledge and they could land and be ready to shoot around half-tide.

It was early, it was Christmas, and it was farther out than most hunters cared to go in this season of the closing year, so that he felt sure no one would be taking possession ahead of them. He had shot thousands of ducks there in his day. The Hump was by far the best hunting. Only thing was you had to plan for the right conditions because you didn't have too much time. About four hours was all, and you had to get it before three in the afternoon when the birds left and went out to sea ahead of nightfall.

They had it figured exactly right for today. The ledge would not be going under until after the gunning was over, and they would be home for supper in good season. With a little luck the boys would have a skiff-load of birds to show for their first time outside. Well beyond the legal limit, which was no matter. You took what you could get in this life, or the next man made out and you didn't.

The fisherman had never failed to make out gunning from Devil's Hump. And this trip, he had a hunch, would be above ordinary. The easterly wind would come up just stiff enough, the tide was right, and it was going to storm by tomorrow morning so the birds would be moving. Things were perfect.

The old fierceness was in his bones. Keeping a weather eye to the murk out front and a hand on the wheel, he reached over and cuffed both boys playfully as they stood together close to the heat of the exhaust pipe running up through the center of the house. They poked back at him and shouted above the drumming engine, making bets as they always did on who would shoot the most birds. This trip they had the thrill of new guns, the best money could buy, and a man's hunting ground. The black retriever wagged at them and barked. He was too old and arthritic to be allowed in December water, but he was jaunty anyway at being brought along.

Groping in his pocket for his pipe the fisherman suddenly had his high spirits rocked by the discovery that he had left his tobacco at home. He swore. Anticipation of a day out with nothing to smoke made him incredulous. He searched his clothes, and then he searched them again, unable to believe the tobacco was not somewhere. When the boys inquired what was wrong he spoke angrily to them, blaming them for being in some devious way at fault. They were instantly crestfallen and willing to put back after the tobacco, though they could appreciate what it meant only through his irritation. But he bitterly refused. That would throw everything out of phase. He was a man who did things the way he set out to do.

He clamped his pipe between his teeth, and twice more during the next few minutes he ransacked his clothes in disbelief. He was no stoic. For one relaxed moment he considered putting about and gunning somewhere nearer home. Instead he held his course and sucked the empty pipe, consoling himself with the reflection that at least he had whiskey enough if it got too uncomfortable on the ledge. Peremptorily he made the boys check to make certain the bottle was really in the knapsack with lunches where he thought he had taken care to put it. When they reassured him he despised his fate a little less.

The fisherman's judgment was as usual accurate. By the time they were abreast of the headland there was sufficient light so that he could wind his way among the reefs without slackening speed. At last he turned his bows toward open ocean, and as the winter dawn filtered upward through long layers of smoky cloud on the eastern rim his spirits rose again with it.

He opened the throttle, steadied on his course, and settled down to the two-hour run. The wind was stronger but seemed less cold coming from the sea. The boys had withdrawn from the fisherman and were talking together while they watched the sky through the windows. The boat churned solidly through a light chop, flinging spray off her flaring bows. Astern the headland thinned rapidly till it lay like a blackened sill on the grey water. No other boats were abroad.

The boys fondled their new guns, sighted along the barrels, worked the mechanisms, compared notes, boasted, and gave each other contradictory advice. The fisherman got their attention once and pointed at the horizon. They peered through the windows and saw what looked like a black scum floating on top of gently agitated water. It wheeled and tilted, rippled, curled, then rose, strung itself out and became a huge raft of ducks escaping over the sea. A good sign.

The boys rushed out and leaned over the washboards in the wind and spray to see the flock curl below the horizon. Then they went and hovered around the hot engine, bewailing their lot. If only they had been already set out and waiting. Maybe these ducks would be crazy enough to return later and be slaughtered. Ducks were known to be foolish.

In due course and right on schedule they anchored at mid-morning in the lee of Brown Cow Island. They put the skiff overboard and loaded it with guns, knapsacks, and tollers. The boys showed their eagerness by being clumsy. The fisherman showed his in bad temper and abuse which they silently accepted in the absorbed tolerance of being boys. No doubt they laid it to lack of tobacco.

By outboard they rounded the island and pointed due east in the direction of a ridge of foam which could be seen whitening the surface three hundred yards away. They set the decoys in a broad, straddling vee opening wide into the ocean. The fisherman warned them not to get their hands wet, and when they did he made them carry on with red and painful fingers, in order to teach them. Once the last toller was bobbing among his fellows, brisk and alluring, they got their numbed fingers inside their oilskins and hugged their warm crotches. In the meantime the fisherman had turned the skiff toward the patch of foam where as if by magic, like a black glossy rib of earth, the ledge had broken through the belly of the sea.

Carefully they inhabited their slippery nub of the North American continent, while the unresting Atlantic swelled and swirled as it had for eons round the indomitable edges. They hauled the skiff after them, established themselves as comfortably as they could in a shallow sump on top, lay on their sides a foot or so above the water, and waited, guns in hand.

In time the fisherman took a thermos bottle from the knapsack and they drank steaming coffee, and waited for the nodding decoys to lure in the first flight to the rock. Eventually the boys got hungry and restless. The fisherman let them open the picnic lunch and eat one sandwich apiece, which they both shared with the dog. Having no tobacco the fisherman himself would not eat.

Actually the day was relatively mild, and they were warm enough at present in their woolen clothes and socks underneath oilskins and hip boots. After a while, however, the boys began to feel cramped. Their nerves were agonized by inactivity. The nephew complained and was severely told by the fisherman—who pointed to the dog, crouched unmoving except for his white-rimmed eyes—that part of doing a man's hunting was learning how to wait. But he was beginning to have misgivings of his own. This could be one of those days where all the right conditions masked an incalculable flaw.

If the fisherman had been alone, as he often was, stopping off when the necessary coincidence of tide and time occurred on his way home from hauling trawls, and had plenty of tobacco, he would not have fidgeted. The boys' being nervous made him nervous. He growled at them again. When it came it was likely to come all at once, and then in a few moments be over. He warned them not to slack off, never to slack off, to be always ready. Under his rebuke they kept their tortured peace, though they could not help shifting and twisting until he lost what patience he had left and bullied them into lying still. A duck could see an eyelid twitch. If the dog could go without moving so could they.

"Here it comes!" the fisherman said tersely at last.

The boys quivered with quick relief. The flock came in downwind, quartering slightly, myriad, black, and swift.

"Beautiful—" breathed the fisherman's son.

"All right," said the fisherman, intense and precise. "Aim at singles in the thickest part of the flock. Wait for me to fire and then don't stop shooting till your gun's empty." He rolled up onto his left elbow and spread his legs to brace himself. The flock bore down, arrowy and vibrant, then a hundred yards beyond the decoys it veered off.

"They're going away!" the boys cried, sighting in.

"Not yet!" snapped the fisherman. "They're coming round."

The flock changed shape, folded over itself, and drove into the wind in a tight arc. "Thousands—" the boys hissed through their teeth. All at once a whistling storm of black and white broke over the decoys.

"Now!" the fisherman shouted. "Perfect!" And he opened fire at the flock just as it hung suspended in momentary chaos above the tollers. The three pulled at their triggers and the birds splashed into the water, until the last report went off unheard, the last smoking shell flew unheeded over their shoulders, and the last of the routed flock scattered diminishing, diminishing, diminishing in every direction.

Exultantly the boys dropped their guns, jumped up and scrambled for the skiff.

"I'll handle that skiff!" the fisherman shouted at them. They stopped. Gripping the painter and balancing himself he eased the skiff into the water stern first and held the bow hard against the side of the rock shelf the skiff had rested on. "You stay here," he said to his nephew. "No sense in all three of us going in the boat."

The boy on the reef gazed at the grey water rising and falling hypnotically along the glistening edge. It had dropped about a foot since their arrival. "I want to go with you," he said in a sullen tone, his eyes on the streaming eddies.

"You want to do what I tell you if you want to gun with me," answered the fisherman harshly. The boy couldn't swim, and he wasn't going to have him climbing in and out of the skiff any more than necessary. Besides he was too big.

The fisherman took his son in the skiff and cruised round and round among the decoys picking up dead birds. Meanwhile the other boy stared unmoving after them from the highest part of the ledge. Before they had quite finished gathering the dead birds, the fisherman cut the outboard and dropped to his knees in the skiff. "Down!" he yelled. "Get down!" About a dozen birds came tolling in. "Shoot—shoot!" his son hollered from the bottom of the boat to the boy on the ledge.

The dog, who had been running back and forth whining, sank to his belly, his muzzle on his forepaws. But the boy on the ledge never stirred. The ducks took late alarm at the skiff, swerved aside and into the air, passing with a whirr no more than fifty feet over the head of the boy, who remained on the ledge like a statue, without his gun, watching the two crouching in the boat.

The fisherman's son climbed onto the ledge and held the painter. The bottom of the skiff was covered with feathery black and white bodies with feet upturned and necks lolling. He was jubilant. "We got twenty-seven!" he told his cousin. "How's that? Nine apiece. Boy—" he added, "what a cool Christmas!"

The fisherman pulled the skiff onto its shelf and all three went and lay down again in anticipation of the next flight. The son, reloading, patted his shotgun affectionately. "I'm going to get me ten next time," he said. Then he asked his cousin, "Whatsamatter—didn't you see the strays?"

"Yeah," the boy said.

"How come you didn't shoot at 'em?"

"Didn't feel like it," replied the boy, still with a trace of sullenness.

"You stupid or something?" The fisherman's son was astounded. "What a highlander!" But the fisherman, though he said nothing, knew that the older boy had had an attack of ledge fever.

"Cripes!" his son kept at it. "I'd at least of tried."

"Shut up," the fisherman finally told him, "and leave him be."

At slack water three more flocks came in, one right after the other, and when it was over, the skiff was half full of clean, dead birds. During the subsequent lull they broke out the lunch and ate it all and finished the hot coffee. For a while the fisherman sucked away on his cold pipe. Then he had himself a swig of whiskey.

The boys passed the time contentedly jabbering about who shot the most—there were ninety-two all told—which of their friends they would show the biggest ones to, how many each could eat at a meal provided they didn't have to eat any vegetables. Now and then they heard sporadic distant gunfire on the mainland, at its nearest point about two miles to the north. Once far off they saw a fishing boat making in the direction of home.

At length the fisherman got a hand inside his oilskins and produced his watch.

"Do we have to go now?" asked his son.

"Not just yet," he replied. "Pretty soon." Everything had been perfect. As good as he had ever had it. Because he was getting tired of the boys' chatter he got up, heavily in his hip boots, and stretched. The tide had turned and was coming in, the sky was more ashen, and the wind had freshened enough so that whitecaps were beginning to blossom. It would be a good hour before they had to leave the ledge and pick up the tollers. However, he guessed they would leave a little early. On account of the rising wind he doubted there would be much more shooting. He stepped carefully along the back of the ledge, to work his kinks out. It was also getting a little colder.

The whiskey had begun to warm him, but he was unprepared for the sudden blaze that flashed upward inside him from belly to head. He was standing looking at the shelf where the skiff was. Only the foolish skiff was not there!

For the second time that day the fisherman felt the deep vacuity of disbelief. He gaped, seeing nothing but the flat shelf of rock. He whirled, started toward the boys, slipped, recovered himself, fetched a complete circle, and stared at the unimaginably empty shelf. Its emptiness made him feel as if everything he had done that day so far, his life, he had dreamed. What could have happened? The tide was still nearly a foot below. There had been no sea to speak of. The skiff could hardly have slid off by itself. For the life of him, consciously careful as he inveterately was, he could not now remember hauling it up the last time. Perhaps in the heat of hunting, he had left it to the boy. Perhaps he could not remember which was the last time.

"Christ—" he exclaimed loudly, without realizing it because he was so entranced by the invisible event.

"What's wrong, Dad?" asked his son, getting to his feet.

The fishermen went blind with uncontainable rage. "Get back down there where you belong!" he screamed. He scarcely noticed the boy sink back in amazement. In a frenzy he ran along the ledge thinking the skiff might have been drawn up at another place, though he knew better. There was no other place.

He stumbled, half falling, back to the boys who were gawking at him in consternation, as though he had gone insane. "God damn it!" he yelled savagely, grabbing both of them and yanking them to their knees. "Get on your feet!"

"What's wrong?" his son repeated in a stifled voice.

"Never mind what's wrong," he snarled. "Look for the skiff—it's adrift!" When they peered around he gripped their shoulders, brutally facing them about. "Down wind—" He slammed his fist against his thigh. "Jesus!" he cried, struck to madness at their stupidity.

At last he sighted the skiff himself, magically bobbing along the grim sea like a toller, a quarter of a mile to leeward on a direct course for home. The impulse to strip himself naked was succeeded instantly by a queer calm. He simply sat down on the ledge and forgot everything except the marvellous mystery.

As his awareness partially returned he glanced toward the boys. They were still observing the skiff speechlessly. Then he was gazing into the clear young eyes of his son.

"Dad," asked the boy steadily, "what do we do now?"

That brought the fisherman upright. "The first thing we have to do," he heard himself saying with infinite tenderness as if he were making love, "is think."

"Could you swim it?" asked his son.

He shook his head and smiled at them. They smiled quickly back, too quickly. "A hundred yards maybe, in this water. I wish I could," he added. It was the most intimate and pitiful thing he had ever said. He walked in circles round them, trying to break the stall his mind was left in.

He gauged the level of the water. To the eye it was quite stationary, six inches from the shelf at this second. The fisherman did not have to mark it on the side of the rock against the passing of time to prove to his reason that it was rising, always rising. Already it was over the brink of reason, beyond the margins of thought—a senseless measurement. No sense to it.

All his life the fisherman had tried to lick the element of time, by getting up earlier and going to bed later, owning a faster boat, planning more than the day would hold, and tackling just one other job before the deadline fell. If, as on rare occasions he had the grand illusion, he ever really had beaten the game, he would need to call on all his reserves of practice and cunning now.

He sized up the scant but unforgivable three hundred yards to Brown Cow Island. Another hundred yards behind it his boat rode at anchor, where, had he been aboard, he could have cut in a fathometer to plumb the profound and occult seas, or a ship-to-shore radio on which in an interminably short time he would have heard his wife's voice talking to him over the air about homecoming.

"Couldn't we wave something so somebody would see us?" his nephew suggested.

The fisherman spun round. "Load your guns!" he ordered. They loaded as if the air had suddenly gone frantic with birds. "I'll fire once and count to five. Then you fire. Count to five. That way they won't just think it's only somebody gunning ducks. We'll keep doing that."

"We've only got just two-and-a-half boxes left," said his son.

The fisherman nodded, understanding that from beginning to end their situation was purely mathematical, like the ticking of the alarm clock in his silent bedroom. Then he fired. The dog, who had been keeping watch over the decoys, leaped forward and yelped in confusion. They all counted off, fired the first five rounds by threes and reloaded. The fisherman scanned first the horizon, then the contracting borders of the ledge, which was the sole place the water appeared to be climbing. Soon it would be over the shelf.

They counted off and fired the second five rounds. "We'll hold off a while on the last one," the fisherman told the boys. He sat down and pondered what a trivial thing was a skiff. This one he and the boy had knocked together in a day. Was a gun, manufactured for killing.

His son tallied up the remaining shells, grouping them symmetrically in threes on the rock when the wet box fell apart. "Two short," he announced. They reloaded and laid the guns on their knees.

Behind thickening clouds they could not see the sun going down. The water, coming up, was growing blacker. The fisherman thought he might have told his wife they would be home before dark since it was Christmas day. He realized he had forgotten about its being any particular day. The tide would not be high until two hours after sunset. When they did not get in by nightfall, and could not be raised by radio, she might send somebody to hunt for them right away. He rejected this arithmetic immediately, with a sickening shock, recollecting it was a two-and-a-half hour run at best. Then it occurred to him that she might send somebody on the mainland who was nearer. She would think he had engine trouble.

He rose and searched the shoreline, barely visible. Then his glance dropped to the toy shoreline at the edges of the reef. The shrinking ledge, so sinister from a boat, grew dearer minute by minute as though the whole wide world he gazed on from horizon to horizon balanced on its contracting rim. He checked the water level and found the shelf awash.

Some of what went through his mind the fisherman told to the boys. They accepted it without comment. If he caught their eyes they looked away to spare him or because they were not yet old enough to face what they saw. Mostly they watched the rising water. The fisherman was unable to initiate a word of encouragement. He wanted one of them to ask him whether somebody would reach them ahead of the tide. He would have found it possible to say yes. But they did not inquire.

The fisherman was not sure how much, at their age, they were able to imagine. Both of them had seen from the docks drowned bodies put ashore out of boats. Sometimes they grasped things, and sometimes not. He supposed they might be longing for the comfort of their mothers, and was astonished, as much as he was capable of any astonishment except the supreme one, to discover himself wishing he had not left his wife's dark, close, naked bed that morning.

"Is it time to shoot now?" asked his nephew.

"Pretty soon," he said, as if he were putting off making good on a promise. "Not yet."

His own boy cried softly for a brief moment, like a man, his face averted in an effort neither to give or show pain.

"Before school starts," the fisherman said, wonderfully detached, "we'll go to town and I'll buy you boys anything you want."

With great difficulty, in a dull tone as though he did not in the least desire it, his son said after a pause, "I'd like one of those new thirty-horse outboards."

"All right," said the fisherman. And to his nephew, "How about you?"

The nephew shook his head desolately. "I don't want anything," he said.

After another pause the fisherman's son said, "Yes he does, Dad. He wants one too."

"All right—" the fisherman said again, and said no more.

The dog whined in uncertainty and licked the boys' faces where they sat together. Each threw an arm over his back and hugged him. Three strays flew in and sat companionably down among the stiff-necked decoys. The dog crouched, obedient to his training. The boys observed them listlessly. Presently, sensing something untoward, the ducks took off, splashing the wave tops with feet and wingtips, into the dusky waste.

The sea began to make up in the mounting wind, and the wind bore a new and deathly chill. The fisherman, scouring the somber, dwindling shadow of the mainland for a sign, hoped it would not snow. But it did. First a few flakes, then a flurry, then storming past horizontally. The fisherman took one long, bewildered look at Brown Cow Island three hundred yards dead to leeward, and got to his feet.

Then it shut in, as if what was happening on the ledge was too private even for the last wan light of the expiring day.

"Last round," the fisherman said austerely.

The boys rose and shouldered their tacit guns. The fisherman fired into the flying snow. He counted methodically to five. His son fired and counted. His nephew. All three fired and counted. Four rounds.

"You've got one left, Dad," his son said.

The fisherman hesitated another second, then he fired the final shell. Its pathetic report, like the spat of a popgun, whipped away on the wind and was instantly blanketed in falling snow.

Night fell all in a moment to meet the ascending sea. They were now barely able to make one another out through driving snowflakes, dim as ghosts in their yellow oilskins. The fisherman heard a sea break and glanced down where his feet were. They seemed to be wound in a snowy sheet. Gently he took the boys by the shoulders and pushed them in front of him, feeling with his feet along the shallow sump to the place where it triangulated into a sharp crevice at the highest point of the ledge. "Face ahead," he told them. "Put the guns down."

"I'd like to hold mine, Dad," begged his son.

"Put it down," said the fisherman. "The tide won't hurt it. Now brace your feet against both sides and stay there."

They felt the dog, who was pitch black, running up and down in perplexity between their straddled legs. "Dad," said his son, "what about the pooch?"

If he had called the dog by name it would have been too personal. The fisherman would have wept. As it was he had all he could do to keep from laughing. He bent his knees, and when he touched the dog hoisted him under one arm. The dog's belly was soaking wet.

So they waited, marooned in their consciousness, surrounded by a monstrous tidal space which was slowly, slowly closing them out. In this space the periwinkle beneath the fisherman's boots was king. While hovering airborne in his mind he had an inward glimpse of his house as curiously separate, like a June mirage.

Snow, rocks, seas, wind the fisherman had lived by all his life. Now he thought he had never comprehended what they were, and he hated them. Though they had not changed. He was deadly chilled. He set out to ask the boys if they were cold. There was no sense. He thought of the whiskey, and sidled backward, still holding the awkward dog, till he located the bottle under water with his toe. He picked it up squeamishly as though afraid of getting his sleeve wet, worked his way forward and bent over his son. "Drink it," he said, holding the bottle against the boy's ribs. The boy tipped his head back, drank, coughed hotly, then vomited.

"I can't," he told his father wretchedly.

"Try—try—" the fisherman pleaded, as if it meant the difference between life and death.

The boy obediently drank, and again he vomited hotly. He shook his head against his father's chest and passed the bottle forward to his cousin, who drank and vomited also. Passing the bottle back, the boys dropped it in the frigid water between them.

When the waves reached his knees the fisherman set the warm dog loose and said to his son, "Turn around and get up on my shoulders." The boy obeyed. The fisherman opened his oilskin jacket and twisted his hands behind him through his suspenders, clamping the boy's booted ankles with his elbows.

"What about the dog?" the boy asked.

"He'll make his own way all right," the fisherman said. "He can take the cold water." His knees were trembling. Every instinct shrieked for gymnastics. He ground his teeth and braced like a colossus against the sides of the submerged crevice.

The dog, having lived faithfully as though one of them for eleven years, swam a few minutes in and out around the fisherman's legs, not knowing what was happening, and left them without a whimper. He would swim and swim at random by himself, round and round in the blinding night, and when he had swum routinely through the paralyzing water all he could, he would simply, in one incomprehensible moment, drown. Almost the fisherman, waiting out infinity, envied him his pattern.

Freezing seas swept by, flooding inexorably up and up as the earth sank away imperceptibly beneath them. The boy called out once to his cousin. There was no answer. The fisherman, marvelling on a terror without voice, was dumbly glad when the boy did not call again. His own boots were long full of water. With no sensation left in his straddling legs he dared not move them. So long as the seas came sidewise against his hips, and then sidewise against his shoulders, he might balance—no telling how long. The upper half of him was what felt frozen. His legs, disengaged from his nerves and his will, he came to regard quite scientifically. They were the absurd, precarious axis around which reeled and surged universal tumult. The waves would come on and on; he could not visualize how many tossing reinforcements lurked in the night beyond—inexhaustible numbers, and he wept in supernatural fury at each because it was higher, till he transcended hate and took them, swaying like a convert, one by one as they lunged against him and away aimlessly into their own undisputed, wild realm.

From his hips upward the fisherman stretched to his utmost as a man does whose spirit reaches out of dead sleep. The boy's head, none too high, must be at least seven feet above the ledge. Though growing larger every minute, it was a small light life. The fisherman meant to hold it there, if need be, through a thousand tides.

By and by the boy, slumped on the head of his father, asked, "Is it over your boots, Dad?"

"Not yet," the fisherman said. Then through his teeth he added, "If I fall—kick your boots off—swim for it—downwind—to the island. . . ."

"You . . .?" the boy finally asked.

The fisherman nodded against the boy's belly. "—Won't see each other," he said.

The boy did for the fisherman the greatest thing that can be done. He may have been too young for perfect terror, but he was old enough to know there were things beyond the power of any man. All he could do he did, by trusting his father to do all he could, and asking nothing more.

The fisherman, rocked to his soul by a sea, held his eyes shut upon the interminable night.

"Is it time now?" the boy said.

The fisherman could hardly speak. "Not yet," he said. "Not just yet. . . ."

As the land mass pivoted toward sunlight the day after Christmas, a tiny fleet of small craft converged off shore like iron filing to a magnet. At daybreak they found the skiff floating unscathed off the headland, half full of ducks and snow. The shooting *had* been good, as someone hearing on the nearby mainland the previous afternoon had supposed. Two hours afterward they found the unharmed boat adrift five miles at sea. At high noon they found the fisherman at ebb tide, his right foot jammed cruelly into a glacial crevice of the ledge beside three shotguns, his hands tangled behind him in his suspenders, and under his right elbow a rubber boot with a sock and a live starfish in it. After dragging unlit depths all day for the boys, they towed the fisherman home in his own boat at sundown, and in the frost of evening, mute with discovering purgatory, laid him on his wharf for his wife to see.

She, somehow, standing on the dock as in her frequent dream, gazing at the fisherman pure as crystal on the icy boards, a small rubber boot still frozen under one clenched arm, saw him exaggerated beyond remorse or grief, absolved of his mortality.

A Good Man Is Hard to Find

The grandmother didn't want to go to Florida. She wanted to visit some of her connections in east Tennessee and she was seizing at every chance to change Bailey's mind. Bailey was the son she lived with, her only boy. He was sitting on the edge of his chair at the table, bent over the orange sports section of the *Journal*. "Now look here, Bailey," she said, "see here, read this," and she stood with one hand on her thin hip and the other rattling the newspaper at his bald head. "Here this fellow that calls himself The Misfit is aloose from the Federal Pen and headed toward Florida and you read here what it says he did to these people. Just you read it. I wouldn't take my children in any direction with a criminal like that aloose in it. I couldn't answer to my conscience if I did."

Bailey didn't look up from his reading so she wheeled around then and faced the children's mother, a young woman in slacks, whose face was as broad and innocent as a cabbage and was tied round with a green head-kerchief that had two points on the top like rabbit's ears. She was sitting on the sofa, feeding the baby his apricots out of a jar. "The children have been to Florida before," the old lady said. "You all ought to take them somewhere else for a change so they would see different parts of the world and be broad. They never have been to east Tennessee."

The children's mother didn't seem to hear her but the eight-year-old boy, John Wesley, a stocky child with glasses, said, "If you don't want to go to Florida, why dontcha stay at home?" He and the little girl, June Star, were reading the funny papers on the floor.

"She wouldn't stay at home to be queen for a day," June Star said without raising her yellow head.

"Yes and what would you do if this fellow, The Misfit, caught you?" the grandmother asked.

"I'd smack his face," John Wesley said.

"She wouldn't stay at home for a million bucks," June Star said. "Afraid she'd miss something. She has to go everywhere we go."

"All right, Miss," the grandmother said. "Just remember that the next time you want me to curl your hair."

June Star said her hair was naturally curly.

The next morning the grandmother was the first one in the car, ready to go. She had her big black valise that looked like the head of a hippopotamus in one corner, and underneath it she was hiding a basket with Pitty Sing, the cat, in it. She didn't intend for the cat to be left alone in the house for three days because he would miss her too much and she was afraid he might brush against one of the gas burners and accidentally asphyxiate himself. Her son, Bailey, didn't like to arrive at a motel with a cat.

She sat in the middle of the back seat with John Wesley and June Star on either side of her. Bailey and the children's mother and the baby sat in the front and they left Atlanta at eight forty-five with the mileage on the car at 55890. The grandmother wrote this down because she thought it would be interesting to say how many miles they had been when they got back. It took them twenty minutes to reach the outskirts of the city.

The old lady settled herself comfortably, removing her white cotton gloves and putting them up with her purse on the shelf in front of the back window. The children's mother still had on slacks and still had her head tied up in a green kerchief, but the grandmother had on a navy blue straw sailor hat with a bunch of white violets on the brim and a navy blue dress with a small white dot in the print. Her collar and cuffs were white organdy trimmed with lace and at her neckline she had pinned a purple spray of cloth violets containing a sachet. In case of an accident, anyone seeing her dead on the highway would know at once that she was a lady.

She said she thought it was going to be a good day for driving, neither too hot nor too cold, and she cautioned Bailey that the speed limit was fifty-five miles an hour and that the patrolmen hid themselves behind billboards and small clumps of trees and sped out after you before you had a chance to slow down. She pointed out interesting details of the scenery: Stone Mountain; the blue granite that in some places came up to both sides of the highway; the brilliant red clay banks slightly streaked with purple; and the various crops that made rows of green lace-work on the ground. The trees were full of silver-white sunlight and the meanest of them sparkled. The children were reading comic magazines and their mother had gone back to sleep.

"Let's go through Georgia fast so we won't have to look at it much," John Wesley said.

"If I were a little boy," said the grandmother, "I wouldn't talk about my native state that way. Tennessee has the mountains and Georgia has the hills."

"Tennessee is just a hillbilly dumping ground," John Wesley said, "and Georgia is a lousy state too."

"You said it," June Star said.

"In my time," said the grandmother, folding her thin veined fingers, "children were more respectful of their native states and their parents and everything else. People did right then. Oh look at the

cute little pickaninny!" she said and pointed to a Negro child standing in the door of a shack. "Wouldn't that make a picture, now?" she
asked and they all turned and looked at the little Negro out of the
back window. He waved.

"He didn't have any britches on," June said.

"He probably didn't have any," the grandmother explained. "Little
niggers in the country don't have things like we do. If I could paint,
I'd paint that picture," she said.

The children exchanged comic books.

The grandmother offered to hold the baby and the children's
mother passed him over the front seat to her. She set him on her
knee and bounced him and told him about the things they were passing. She rolled her eyes and screwed up her mouth and stuck her
leathery thin face into his smooth bland one. Occasionally he gave
her a faraway smile. They passed a large cotton field with five or six
graves fenced in the middle of it, like a small island. "Look at the
graveyard!" the grandmother said, pointing it out. "That was the old
family burying ground. That belonged to the plantation."

"Where's the plantation?" John Wesley asked.

"Gone With the Wind," said the grandmother. "Ha. Ha."

When the children finished all the comic books they had brought,
they opened the lunch and ate it. The grandmother ate a peanut butter
sandwich and an olive and would not let the children throw the box
and the paper napkins out the window. When there was nothing else
to do they played a game by choosing a cloud and making the other
two guess what shape it suggested. John Wesley took one the shape
of a cow and June Star guessed a cow and John Wesley said, no, an
automobile, and June Star said he didn't play fair, and they began
to slap each other over the grandmother.

The grandmother said she would tell them a story if they would
keep quiet. When she told a story, she rolled her eyes and waved her
head and was very dramatic. She said once when she was a maiden lady
she had been courted by a Mr. Edgar Atkins Teagarden from Jasper,
Georgia. She said he was a very good-looking man and a gentleman
and that he brought her a watermelon every Saturday afternoon with
his initials cut in it, E. A. T. Well, one Saturday, she said, Mr. Teagarden brought the watermelon and there was nobody at home and
he left it on the front porch and returned in his buggy to Jasper, but
she never got the watermelon, she said, because a nigger boy ate it
when he saw the initials, E. A. T.! This story tickled John Wesley's
funny bone and he giggled and giggled but June Star didn't think
it was any good. She said she wouldn't marry a man that just brought
her a watermelon on Saturday. The grandmother said she would have

done well to marry Mr. Teagarden because he was a gentleman and had bought Coca-Cola stock when it first came out and that he had died only a few years ago, a very wealthy man.

They stopped at The Tower for barbecued sandwiches. The Tower was a part stucco and part wood filling station and dance hall set in a clearing outside of Timothy. A fat man named Red Sammy Butts ran it and there were signs stuck here and there on the building and for miles up and down the highway saying, TRY RED SAMMY'S FAMOUS BARBECUE. NONE LIKE FAMOUS RED SAMMY'S! RED SAM! THE FAT BOY WITH THE HAPPY LAUGH. A VETERAN! RED SAMMY'S YOUR MAN!

Red Sammy was lying on the bare ground outside The Tower with his head under a truck while a gray monkey about a foot high, chained to a small chinaberry tree, chattered nearby. The monkey sprang back into the tree and got on the highest limb as soon as he saw the children jump out of the car and run toward him.

Inside, The Tower was a long dark room with a counter at one end and tables at the other and dancing space in the middle. They all sat down at a broad table next to the nickelodeon and Red Sam's wife, a tall burnt-brown woman with hair and eyes lighter than her skin, came and took their order. The children's mother put a dime in the machine and played "The Tennessee Waltz," and the grandmother said that tune always made her want to dance. She asked Bailey if he would like to dance but he only glared at her. He didn't have a naturally sunny disposition like she did and trips made him nervous. The grandmother's brown eyes were very bright. She swayed her head from side to side and pretended she was dancing in her chair. June Star said play something she could tap to so the children's mother put in another dime and played a fast number and June Star stepped out onto the dance floor and did her tap routine.

"Ain't she cute?" Red Sam's wife said, leaning over the counter. "Would you like to come be my little girl?"

"No I certainly wouldn't," June Star said. "I wouldn't live in a broken-down place like this for a million bucks!" and she ran back to the table.

"Ain't she cute?" the woman repeated, stretching her mouth politely.

"Aren't you ashamed?" hissed the grandmother.

Red Sam came in and told his wife to quit lounging on the counter and hurry with these people's order. His khaki trousers reached just to his hip bones and his stomach hung over them like a sack of meal swaying under his shirt. He came over and sat down at a table nearby and let out a combination sigh and yodel. "You can't win," he said. "You can't win," and he wiped his sweating red face off with a gray handkerchief. "These days you don't know who to trust," he said. "Ain't that the truth?"

"People are certainly not nice like they used to be," said the grandmother.

"Two fellers come in here last week," Red Sammy said, "driving a Chrysler. It was a old beat-up car but it was a good one and these boys looked all right to me. Said they worked at the mill and you know I let them fellers charge the gas they bought? Now why did I do that?"

"Because you're a good man!" the grandmother said at once.

"Yes'm, I suppose so," Red Sam said as if he were struck with the answer.

His wife brought the orders, carrying the five plates all at once without a tray, two in each hand and one balanced on her arm. "It isn't a soul in this green world of God's that you can trust," she said. "And I don't count anybody out of that, not nobody," she repeated, looking at Red Sammy.

"Did you read about that criminal, The Misfit, that's escaped?" asked the grandmother.

"I wouldn't be a bit surprised if he didn't attact this place right here," said the woman. "If he hears about it being here, I wouldn't be none surprised to see him. If he hears it's two cent in the cash register, I wouldn't be a tall surprised if he . . ."

"That'll do," Red Sam said. "Go bring these people their Co'Colas," and the woman went off to get the rest of the order.

"A good man is hard to find," Red Sammy said. "Everything is getting terrible. I remember the day you could go off and leave your screen door unlatched. Not no more."

He and the grandmother discussed better times. The old lady said that in her opinion Europe was entirely to blame for the way things were now. She said the way Europe acted you would think we were made of money and Red Sam said it was no use talking about it, she was exactly right. The children ran outside into the white sunlight and looked at the monkey in the lacy chinaberry tree. He was busy catching fleas on himself and biting each one carefully between his teeth as if it were a delicacy.

They drove off again into the hot afternoon. The grandmother took cat naps and woke up every few minutes with her own snoring. Outside of Toombsboro she woke up and recalled an old plantation that she had visited in this neighborhood once when she was a young lady. She said the house had six white columns across the front and that there was an avenue of oaks leading up to it and two little wooden trellis arbors on either side in front where you sat down with your suitor after a stroll in the garden. She recalled exactly which road to turn off to get to it. She knew that Bailey would not be willing to lose any time looking at an old house, but the more she talked about it, the more she wanted to see it once again and find out if the little twin arbors were still standing. "There was a secret panel in this house," she said craftily, not telling the truth but wishing that she were, "and the story went that all the family silver was hidden in it when Sherman came through but it was never found . . ."

"Hey!" John Wesley said. "Let's go see it! We'll find it! We'll poke all the woodwork and find it! Who lives there? Where do you turn off at? Hey Pop, can't we turn off there?"

"We never have seen a house with a secret panel!" June Star shrieked. "Let's go to the house with the secret panel! Hey, Pop, can't we go see the house with the secret panel!"

"It's not far from here, I know," the grandmother said. "It wouldn't take over twenty minutes."

Bailey was looking straight ahead. His jaw was as rigid as a horseshoe. "No," he said.

The children began to yell and scream that they wanted to see the house with the secret panel. John Wesley kicked the back of the front seat and June Star hung over her mother's shoulder and whined desperately into her ear that they never had any fun even on their vacation, and that they could never do what THEY wanted to do. The baby began to scream and John Wesley kicked the back of the seat so hard that his father could feel the blows in his kidney.

"All right!" he shouted, and drew the car to a stop at the side of the road. "Will you all shut up? Will you all just shut up for one second? If you don't shut up, we won't go anywhere."

"It would be very educational for them," the grandmother murmured.

"All right," Bailey said, "but get this: this is the only time we're going to stop for anything like this. This is the one and only time."

"The dirt road that you have to turn down is about a mile back," the grandmother directed. "I marked it when we passed."

"A dirt road," Bailey groaned.

After they had turned around and were headed toward the dirt road, the grandmother recalled other points about the house, the beautiful glass over the front doorway and the candle-lamp in the hall. John Wesley said that the secret panel was probably in the fireplace.

"You can't go inside this house," Bailey said. "You don't know who lives there."

"While you all talk to the people in front, I'll run around behind and get in a window," John Wesley suggested.

"We'll all stay in the car," his mother said.

They turned onto the dirt road and the car raced roughly along in a swirl of pink dust. The grandmother recalled the times when there were no paved roads and thirty miles was a day's journey. The dirt road was hilly and there were sudden washes in it and sharp curves on dangerous embankments. All at once they would be on a hill, looking down over the blue tops of trees for miles around, then the next minute, they would be in a red depression with the dust-coated trees looking down on them.

"This place had better turn up in a minute," Bailey said, "or I'm going to turn around."

The road looked as if no one had traveled on it in months.

"It's not much farther," the grandmother said and just as she said it, a horrible thought came to her. The thought was so embarrassing that she turned red in the face and her eyes dilated and her feet jumped up, upsetting her valise in the corner. The instant the valise moved, the newspaper top she had over the basket under it rose with a snarl and Pitty Sing, the cat, sprang onto Bailey's shoulder.

The children were thrown to the floor and their mother, clutching the baby, was thrown out the door onto the ground, the old lady was thrown into the front seat. The car turned over once and landed right-side-up in a gulch on the side of the road. Bailey remained in the driver's seat with the cat—gray-striped with a broad white face and an orange nose—clinging to his neck like a caterpillar.

As soon as the children saw they could move their arms and legs, they scrambled out of the car, shouting, "We've had an ACCIDENT!" The grandmother was curled up under the dashboard, hoping she was injured so that Bailey's wrath would not come down on her all at once. The horrible thought she had had before the accident was that the house she had remembered so vividly was not in Georgia but in Tennessee.

Bailey removed the cat from his neck with both hands and flung it out the window against the side of a pine tree. Then he got out of the car and started looking for the children's mother. She was sitting against the side of the red gutted ditch, holding the screaming baby, but she only had a cut down her face and a broken shoulder. "We've had an ACCIDENT!" the children screamed in a frenzy of delight.

"But nobody's killed," June Star said with disappointment as the grandmother limped out of the car, her hat still pinned to her head but the broken front brim standing up at a jaunty angle and the violet spray hanging off the side. They all sat down in the ditch, except the children, to recover from the shock. They were all shaking.

"Maybe a car will come along," said the children's mother hoarsely.

"I believe I have injured an organ," said the grandmother, pressing her side, but no one answered her. Bailey's teeth were clattering. He had on a yellow sport shirt with bright blue parrots designed in it and his face was as yellow as the shirt. The grandmother decided that she would not mention that the house was in Tennessee.

The road was about ten feet above and they could see only the tops of the trees on the other side of it. Behind the ditch they were sitting in there were more woods, tall and dark and deep. In a few minutes they saw a car some distance away on top of a hill, coming slowly as if the occupants were watching them. The grandmother stood up and waved both arms dramatically to attract their attention. The car continued to come on slowly, disappeared around a bend and appeared again, moving even slower, on top of the hill they had gone over. It was a big black battered hearse-like automobile. There were three men in it.

It came to a stop just over them and for some minutes, the driver looked down with a steady expressionless gaze to where they were sitting, and didn't speak. Then he turned his head and muttered something to the other two and they got out. One was a fat boy in black trousers and a red sweat shirt with a silver stallion embossed on the front of it. He moved around on the right side of them and stood staring, his mouth partly open in a kind of loose grin. The other had on khaki pants and a blue striped coat and a gray hat pulled down very low, hiding most of his face. He came around slowly on the left side. Neither spoke.

The driver got out of the car and stood by the side of it, looking down at them. He was an older man than the other two. His hair was just beginning to gray and he wore silver-rimmed spectacles that gave him a scholarly look. He had a long creased face and didn't have on any shirt or undershirt. He had on blue jeans that were too tight for him and was holding a black hat and a gun. The two boys also had guns.

"We've had an ACCIDENT!" the children screamed.

The grandmother had the peculiar feeling that the bespectacled man was somone she knew. His face was as familiar to her as if she had known him all her life but she could not recall who he was. He moved away from the car and began to come down the embankment, placing his feet carefully so that he wouldn't slip. He had on tan and white shoes and no socks, and his ankles were red and thin. "Good afternoon," he said. "I see you all had you a little spill."

"We turned over twice!" said the grandmother.

"Oncet," he corrected. "We seen it happen. Try their car and see will it run, Hiram," he said quietly to the boy with the gray hat.

"What you got that gun for?" John Wesley asked. "Whatcha gonna do with that gun?"

"Lady," the man said to the children's mother, "would you mind calling them children to sit down by you? Children make me nervous. I want all you all to sit down right together there where you're at."

"What are you telling us what to do for?" June Star asked.

Behind them the line of woods gaped like a dark open mouth. "Come here," said their mother.

"Look here now," Bailey began suddenly, "we're in a predicament! We're in . . ."

The grandmother shrieked. She scrambled to her feet and stood staring. "You're The Misfit!" she said. "I recognized you at once."

"Yes'm," the man said, smiling slightly as if he were pleased in spite of himself to be known, "but it would have been better for all of you, lady, if you hadn't of reckernized me."

Bailey turned his head sharply and said something to his mother that shocked even the children. The old lady began to cry and The Misfit reddened.

"Lady," he said, "don't you get upset. Sometimes a man says things he don't mean. I don't reckon he meant to talk to you thataway."

"You wouldn't shoot a lady, would you?" the grandmother said and removed a clean handkerchief from her cuff and began to slap at her eyes with it.

The Misfit pointed the toe of his shoe into the ground and made a little hole and then covered it up again. "I would hate to have to," he said.

"Listen," the grandmother almost screamed, "I know you're a good man. You don't look a bit like you have common blood. I know you must come from nice people!"

"Yes mam," he said, "finest people in the world." When he smiled he showed a row of strong white teeth. "God never made a finer woman than my mother and my daddy's heart was pure gold," he said. The boy with the red sweat shirt had come around behind them and was standing with his gun at his hip. The Misfit squatted down on the ground. "Watch them children, Bobby Lee," he said. "You know they make me nervous." He looked at the six of them huddled together in front of him and he seemed to be embarrassed as if he couldn't think of anything to say. "Ain't a cloud in the sky," he remarked, looking up at it. "Don't see no sun but don't see no cloud neither."

"Yes, it's a beautiful day," said the grandmother. "Listen," she said, "you shouldn't call yourself The Misfit because I know you're a good man at heart. I can just look at you and tell."

A Good Man Is Hard to Find 289

"Hush!" Bailey yelled. "Hush! Everybody shut up and let me handle this!" He was squatting in the position of a runner about to sprint forward but he didn't move.

"I pre-chate that, lady," The Misfit said and drew a little circle in the ground with the butt of his gun.

"It'll take a half a hour to fix this here car," Hiram called, looking over the raised hood of it.

"Well, first you and Bobby Lee get him and that little boy to step over yonder with you," The Misfit said, pointing to Bailey and John Wesley. "The boys want to ask you something," he said to Bailey. "Would you mind stepping back in them woods there with them?"

"Listen," Bailey began, "we're in a terrible predicament. Nobody realizes what this is," and his voice cracked. His eyes were as blue and intense as the parrots in his shirt and he remained perfectly still.

The grandmother reached up to adjust her hat brim as if she were going to the woods with him but it came off in her hand. She stood staring at it and after a second she let it fall on the ground. Hiram pulled Bailey up by the arm as if he were assisting an old man. John Wesley caught hold of his father's hand and Bobby Lee followed. They went off toward the woods and just as they reached the dark edge, Bailey turned and supporting himself against a gray naked pine trunk, he shouted, "I'll be back in a minute, Mamma, wait on me!"

"Come back this instant!" his mother shrilled but they all disappeared into the woods.

"Bailey Boy!" the grandmother called in a tragic voice but she found she was looking at The Misfit squatting on the ground in front of her. "I just know you're a good man," she said desperately. "You're not a bit common!"

"Nome, I ain't a good man," The Misfit said after a second as if he had considered her statement carefully, "but I ain't the worst in the world neither. My daddy said I was different breed of dog from my brothers and sisters. 'You know,' Daddy said, 'it's some that can live their whole life out without asking about it and it's others has to know why it is, and this boy is one of the latters. He's going to be into everything!' " He put on his black hat and looked up suddenly and then away deep into the woods as if he were embarrassed again. "I'm sorry I don't have on a shirt before you ladies," he said, hunching his shoulders slightly. "We buried our clothes that we had on when we escaped and we're just making do until we can get better. We borrowed these from some folks we met," he explained.

"That's perfectly all right," the grandmother said. "Maybe Bailey has an extra shirt in his suitcase."

"I'll look and see terrectly," The Misfit said.

"Where are they taking him?" the children's mother screamed.

"Daddy was a card himself," The Misfit said. "You couldn't put anything over on him. He never got in trouble with the Authorities though. Just had the knack of handling them."

"You could be honest too if you'd only try," said the grandmother. "Think how wonderful it would be to settle down and live a comfortable life and not have to think about somebody chasing you all the time."

The Misfit kept scratching in the ground with the butt of his gun as if he were thinking about it. "Yes'm, somebody is always after you," he murmured.

The grandmother noticed how thin his shoulder blades were just behind his hat because she was standing up looking down on him. "Do you ever pray?" she asked.

He shook his head. All she saw was the black hat wiggle between his shoulder blades. "Nome," he said.

There was a pistol shot from the woods, followed closely by another. Then silence. The old lady's head jerked around. She could hear the wind move through the tree tops like a long satisfied insuck of breath. "Bailey Boy!" she called.

"I was a gospel singer for a while," The Misfit said. "I been most everything. Been in the arm service, both land and sea, at home and abroad, been twict married, been an undertaker, been with the railroads, plowed Mother Earth, been in a tornado, seen a man burnt alive oncet," and he looked up at the children's mother and the little girl who were sitting close together, their faces white and their eyes glassy; "I even seen a woman flogged," he said.

"Pray, pray," the grandmother began, "pray, pray . . ."

"I never was a bad boy that I remember of," The Misfit said in an almost dreamy voice, "but somewheres along the line I done something wrong and got sent to the penitentiary. I was buried alive," and he looked up and held her attention to him by a steady stare.

"That's when you should have started to pray," she said. "What did you do to get sent to the penitentiary that first time?"

"Turn to the right, it was a wall," The Misfit said, looking up again at the cloudless sky. "Turn to the left, it was a wall. Look up it was a ceiling, look down it was a floor. I forgot what I done, lady. I set there and set there, trying to remember what it was I done and I ain't recalled it to this day. Oncet in a while, I would think it was coming to me, but it never come."

"Maybe they put you in by mistake," the old lady said vaguely.

"Nome," he said. "It wasn't no mistake. They had the papers on me."

"You must have stolen something," she said.

The Misfit sneered slightly. "Nobody had nothing I wanted," he said. "It was a head-doctor at the penitentiary said what I had done was kill my daddy but I know that for a lie. My daddy died in nineteen ought nineteen of the epidemic flu and I never had a thing to do with it. He was buried in the Mount Hopewell Baptist churchyard and you can go there and see for yourself."

"If you would pray," the old lady said, "Jesus would help you."

"That's right," The Misfit said.

"Well then, why don't you pray?" she asked trembling with delight suddenly.

"I don't want no hep," he said. "I'm doing all right by myself."

Bobby Lee and Hiram came ambling back from the woods. Bobby Lee was dragging a yellow shirt with bright blue parrots in it.

"Throw me that shirt, Bobby Lee," The Misfit said. The shirt came flying at him and landed on his shoulder and he put it on. The grandmother couldn't name what the shirt reminded her of. "No, lady," The Misfit said while he was buttoning it up. "I found out the crime don't matter. You can do one thing or you can do another, kill a man or take a tire off his car, because sooner or later you're going to forget what it was you done and just be punished for it."

The children's mother had begun to make heaving noises as if she couldn't get her breath. "Lady," he asked, "would you and that little girl like to step off yonder with Bobby Lee and Hiram and join your husband?"

"Yes, thank you," the mother said faintly. Her left arm dangled helplessly and she was holding the baby, who had gone to sleep, in the other. "Hep that lady up, Hiram," The Misfit said as she struggled to climb out of the ditch, "and Bobby Lee, you hold onto that little girl's hand."

"I don't want to hold hands with him," June Star said. "He reminds me of a pig."

The fat boy blushed and laughed and caught her by the arm and pulled her off into the woods after Hiram and her mother.

Alone with The Misfit, the grandmother found that she had lost her voice. There was not a cloud in the sky nor any sun. There was nothing around her but woods. She wanted to tell him that he must pray. She opened and closed her mouth several times before anything came out. Finally she found herself saying, "Jesus, Jesus," meaning Jesus will help you, but the way she was saying it, it sounded as if she might be cursing.

"Yes'm," The Misfit said as if he agreed. "Jesus thown everything off balance. It was the same case with Him as with me except He hadn't committed any crime and they could prove I had committed one because they had the papers on me. Of course," he said, "they never shown me my papers. That's why I sign myself now. I said long ago, you get you a signature and sign everything you do and keep a copy of it. Then you'll know what you done and you can hold up the crime to the punishment and see do they match and in the end you'll have something to prove you ain't been treated right. I call myself The Misfit," he said, "because I can't make what all I done wrong fit what all I gone through in punishment."

There was a piercing scream from the woods, followed closely by a pistol report. "Does it seem right to you, lady, that one is punished a heap and another ain't punished at all?"

"Jesus!" the old lady cried. "You've got good blood! I know you wouldn't shoot a lady! I know you come from nice people! Pray! Jesus, you ought not to shoot a lady. I'll give you all the money I've got!"

"Lady," The Misfit said, looking beyond her far into the woods, "there never was a body that give the undertaker a tip."

There were two more pistol reports and the grandmother raised her head like a parched old turkey hen crying for water and called, "Bailey Boy, Bailey Boy!" as if her heart would break.

"Jesus was the only One that ever raised the dead," The Misfit continued, "and He shouldn't have done it. He thown everything off balance. If He did what He said, then it's nothing for you to do but thow away everything and follow Him, and if He didn't, then it's nothing for you to do but enjoy the few minutes you got left the best way you can—by killing somebody or burning down his house or doing some other meanness to him. No pleasure but meanness," he said and his voice had become almost a snarl.

"Maybe He didn't raise the dead," the old lady mumbled, not knowing what she was saying and feeling so dizzy that she sank down in the ditch with her legs twisted under her.

"I wasn't there so I can't say He didn't," The Misfit said. "I wisht I had of been there," he said, hitting the ground with his fist. "It ain't right I wasn't there because if I had of been there I would of known. Listen lady," he said in a high voice, "if I had of been there I would of known and I wouldn't be like I am now." His voice seemed about to crack and the grandmother's head cleared for an instant. She saw the man's face twisted close to her own as if he were going to cry and she murmured, "Why you're one of my babies. You're one of my own children!" She reached out and touched him on the shoulder. The Misfit sprang back as if a snake had bitten him and shot her three times through the chest. Then he put his gun down on the ground and took off his glasses and began to clean them.

Hiram and Bobby Lee returned from the woods and stood over the ditch, looking down at the grandmother who half sat and half lay in a puddle of blood with her legs crossed under her like a child's and her face smiling up at the cloudless sky.

Without his glasses, The Misfit's eyes were red-rimmed and pale and defenseless-looking. "Take her off and thow her where you thown the others," he said, picking up the cat that was rubbing itself against his leg.

"She was a talker, wasn't she?" Bobby Lee said, sliding down the ditch with a yodel.

"She would of been a good woman," The Misfit said, "if it had been somebody there to shoot her every minute of her life."

"Some fun!" Bobby Lee said.

"Shut up, Bobby Lee," The Misfit said. "It's no real pleasure in life."

JOHN UPDIKE (1932-   )

A & P

In walks these three girls in nothing but bathing suits. I'm in the third checkout slot, with my back to the door, so I don't see them until they're over by the bread. The one that caught my eye first was the one in the plaid green two-piece. She was a chunky kid, with a good tan and a sweet broad soft-looking can with those two crescents of white just under it, where the sun never seems to hit, at the top of the backs of her legs. I stood there with my hand on a box of HiHo crackers trying to remember if I rang it up or not. I ring it up again and the customer starts giving me hell. She's one of these cash-register-watchers, a witch about fifty with rouge on her cheekbones and no eyebrows, and I know it made her day to trip me up. She'd been watching cash registers for fifty years and probably never seen a mistake before.

By the time I got her feathers smoothed and her goodies into a bag—she gives me a little snort in passing, if she'd been born at the right time they would have burned her over in Salem—by the time I get her on her way the girls had circled around the bread and were coming back, without a pushcart, back my way along the counters, in the aisle between the checkouts and the Special bins. They didn't even have shoes on. There was this chunky one, with the two-piece—it was bright green and the seams on the bra were still sharp and her belly was still pretty pale so I guessed she just got it (the suit)—there was this one, with one of those chubby berry-faces, the lips all bunched together under her nose, this one, and a tall one, with black hair that hadn't quite frizzed right, and one of these sunburns right across under the eyes, and a chin that was too long—you know, the kind of girl other girls think is very "striking" and "attractive" but never quite makes it, as they very well know, which is why they like her so much— and then the third one, that wasn't quite so tall. She was the queen. She kind of led them, the other two peeking around and making their shoulders round. She didn't look around, not this queen, she just walked straight on slowly, on these long white prima-donna legs. She came down a little hard on her heels, as if she didn't walk in her bare feet that much, putting down her heels and then letting the weight move along to her toes as if she was testing the floor with every step, putting a little deliberate extra action into it. You never know for sure how girls' minds work (do you really think it's a mind in there or just a little buzz like a bee in a glass jar?) but you got the idea she had talked the other two into coming in here with her, and now she was showing them how to do it, walk slow and hold yourself straight.

She had on a kind of dirty-pink—beige maybe, I don't know— bathing suit with a little nubble all over it and, what got me, the straps were down. They were off her shoulders looped loose around the cool tops of her arms, and I guess as a result the suit had slipped a little on her, so all around the top of the cloth there was this shining rim. If it hadn't been there you wouldn't have known there could have been anything whiter than those shoulders. With the straps pushed off, there was nothing between the top of the suit and the top of her head except just *her*, this clean bare plane of the top of her chest down from the shoulder bones like a dented sheet of metal tilted in the light. I mean, it was more than pretty.

She had sort of oaky hair that the sun and salt had bleached, done up in a bun that was unravelling, and a kind of prim face. Walking into the A & P with your straps down, I suppose it's the only kind of face you *can* have. She held her head so high her neck, coming up out of those white shoulders, looked kind of stretched, but I didn't mind. The longer her neck was, the more of her there was.

She must have felt in the corner of her eye me and over my shoulder Stokesie in the second slot watching, but she didn't tip. Not this queen. She kept her eyes moving across the racks, and stopped, and turned so slow it made my stomach rub the inside of my apron, and buzzed to the other two, who kind of huddled against her for relief, and then they all three of them went up the cat-and-dog-food- breakfast-cereal-macaroni-rice-raisins-seasonings-spreads-spaghetti-soft- drinks-crackers-and-cookies aisle. From the third slot I look straight up this aisle to the meat counter, and I watched them all the way. The fat one with the tan sort of fumbled with the cookies, but on second thought she put the package back. The sheep pushing their carts down the aisle—the girls were walking against the usual traffic (not that we have one-way signs or anything)—were pretty hilarious. You could see them, when Queenie's white shoulders dawned on them, kind of jerk, or hop, or hiccup, but their eyes snapped back to their own baskets and on they pushed. I bet you could set off dynamite in an A & P and the people would by and large keep reaching and checking oatmeal off their lists and muttering "Let me see, there was a third thing, began with A, asparagus, no, ah, yes, applesauce!" or whatever it is they do mutter. But there was no doubt, this jiggled them. A few houseslaves in pin curlers even look around after pushing their carts past to make sure what they had seen was correct.

You know, it's one thing to have a girl in a bathing suit down on the beach, where what with the glare nobody can look at each other much anyway, and another thing in the cool of the A & P, under the fluorescent lights, against all those stacked packages, with her feet paddling along naked over our checker-board green-and-cream rubber-tile floor.

"Oh Daddy," Stokesie said beside me. "I feel so faint."

"Darling," I said. "Hold me tight." Stokesie's married, with two babies chalked up on his fuselage already, but as far as I can tell that's the only difference. He's twenty-two, and I was nineteen this April.

"Is it done?" he asks, the responsible married man finding his voice. I forgot to say he thinks he's going to be manager some sunny day, maybe in 1990 when it's called the Great Alexandrov and Petrooshki Tea Company or something.

What he meant was, our town is five miles from a beach, with a big summer colony out on the Point, but we're right in the middle of town, and the women generally put on a shirt or shorts or something before they get out of the car into the street. And anyway these are usually women with six children and varicose veins mapping their legs and nobody, including them, could care less. As I say, we're right in the middle of town, and if you stand at our front doors you can see two banks and the Congregational church and the newspaper store and three real-estate offices and about twenty-seven old freeloaders tearing up Central Street because the sewer broke again. It's not as if we're on the Cape; we're north of Boston and there's people in this town haven't seen the ocean for twenty years.

The girls had reached the meat counter and were asking McMahon something. He pointed, they pointed, and they shuffled out of sight behind a pyramid of Diet Delight peaches. All that was left for us to see was old McMahon patting his mouth and looking after them sizing up their joints. Poor kids, I began to feel sorry for them, they couldn't help it.

Now here comes the sad part of the story, at least my family says it's sad, but I don't think it's so sad myself. The store's pretty empty, it being Thursday afternoon, so there was nothing much to do except lean on the register and wait for the girls to show up again. The whole store was like a pinball machine and I didn't know which tunnel they'd come out of. After a while they come around out of the far aisle, around the light bulbs, records at discount of the Caribbean Six or Tony Martin Sings or some such gunk you wonder they waste the wax on, sixpacks of candy bars, and plastic toys done up in cellophane that fall apart when a kid looks at them anyway. Around they come, Queenie still leading the way, and holding a little gray jar in her hand. Slots Three through Seven are unmanned and I could see her wondering between Stokes and me, but Stokesie with his usual luck draws an old party in baggy gray pants who stumbles up with four giant cans of pineapple juice (what do these bums *do* with all that pineapple juice? I've often asked myself) so the girls come to me. Queenie puts down the jar and I take it into my fingers icy cold. Kingfish Fancy Herring Snacks in Pure Sour Cream: 49¢. Now her hands are empty, not a ring or a bracelet, bare as God made them, and I wonder where the money's coming from. Still with that prim look she lifts a folded dollar bill out of the hollow at the center of her nubbled pink top. The jar went heavy in my hand. Really, I thought that was so cute.

Then everybody's luck begins to run out. Lengel comes in from haggling with a truck full of cabbages on the lot and is about to scuttle into the door marked MANAGER behind which he hides all day when the girls touch his eye. Lengel's pretty dreary, teaches Sunday school and the rest, but he doesn't miss that much. He comes over and says, "Girls, this isn't the beach."

Queenie blushes, though maybe it's just a brush of sunburn I was noticing for the first time, now that she was so close. "My mother asked me to pick up a jar of herring snacks." Her voice kind of startled me, the way voices do when you see the people first, coming out so flat and dumb yet kind of tony, too, the way it ticked over "pick up" and "snacks." All of a sudden I slid right down her voice into her living room. Her father and the other men were standing around in ice-cream coats and bow ties and the women were in sandals picking up herring snacks on toothpicks off a big glass plate and they were all holding drinks the color of water with olives and sprigs of mint in them. When my parents have somebody over they get lemonade and if it's a real racy affair Schlitz in tall glasses with "They'll Do It Every Time" cartoons stencilled on.

"That's all right," Lengel said. "But this isn't the beach." His repeating this struck me as funny, as if it had just occurred to him, and he had been thinking all these years the A & P was a great big dune and he was the head lifeguard. He didn't like my smiling—as I say he doesn't miss much—but he concentrates on giving the girls that sad Sunday-school-superintendent stare.

Queenie's blush is no sunburn now, and the plump one in plaid, that I liked better from the back—a really sweet can—pipes up, "We weren't doing any shopping. We just came in for the one thing."

"That makes no difference," Lengel tells her, and I could see from the way his eyes went that he hadn't noticed she was wearing a two-piece before. "We want you decently dressed when you come in here."

"We *are* decent," Queenie says suddenly, her lower lip pushing, getting sore now that she remembers her place, a place from which the crowd that runs the A & P must look pretty crummy. Fancy Herring Snacks flashed in her very blue eyes.

"Girls, I don't want to argue with you. After this come in here with your shoulders covered. It's our policy." He turns his back. That's policy for you. Policy is what the kingpins want. What the others want is juvenile delinquency.

All this while, the customers had been showing up with their carts but, you know, sheep, seeing a scene, they had all bunched up on Stokesie, who shook open a paper bag as gently as peeling a peach, not wanting to miss a word. I could feel in the silence everybody getting nervous, most of all Lengel, who asks me, "Sammy, have you rung up this purchase?"

I thought and said "No" but it wasn't about that I was thinking. I go through the punches, 4, 9, GROC, TOT—it's more complicated than you think, and after you do it often enough, it begins to make a little song, that you hear words to, in my case "Hello (*bing*) there, you (*gung*) hap-py *pee*-pul (*splat*)!"—the *splat* being the drawer flying out. I uncrease the bill, tenderly as you may imagine, it just having come from between the two smoothest scoops of vanilla I had ever known were there, and pass a half and a penny into her narrow pink palm, and nestle the herrings in a bag and twist its neck and hand it over, all the time thinking.

The girls, and who'd blame them, are in a hurry to get out, so I say "I quit" to Lengel quick enough for them to hear, hoping they'll stop and watch me, their unsuspected hero. They keep right on going, into the electric eye; the door flies open and they flicker across the lot to their car, Queenie and Plaid and Big Tall Goony-Goony (not that as raw material she was so bad), leaving me with Lengel and a kink in his eyebrow.

"Did you say something, Sammy?"

"I said I quit."

"I thought you did."

"You didn't have to embarrass them."

"It was they who were embarrassing us."

I started to say something that came out "Fiddle-de-doo." It's a saying of my grandmother's, and I know she would have been pleased.

"I don't think you know what you're saying," Lengel said.

"I know you don't," I said. "But I do." I pull the bow at the back of my apron and start shrugging it off my shoulders. A couple customers that had been heading for my slot begin to knock against each other, like scared pigs in a chute.

Lengel sighs and begins to look very patient and old and gray. He's been a friend of my parents for years. "Sammy, you don't want to do this to your Mom and Dad," he tells me. It's true, I don't. But it seems to me that once you begin a gesture it's fatal not to go through with it. I fold the apron, "Sammy" stitched in red on the pocket, and put it on the counter, and drop the bow tie on top of it. The bow tie is theirs, if you've ever wondered. "You'll feel this for the rest of your life," Lengel says, and I know that's true, too, but remembering how he made that pretty girl blush makes me so scrunchy inside I punch the No Sale tab and the machine whirs "pee-pul" and the drawer splats out. One advantage to this scene taking place in summer, I can follow this up with a clean exit, there's no fumbling around getting your coat and galoshes, I just saunter into the electric eye in my white shirt that my mother ironed the night before, and the door heaves itself open, and outside the sunshine is skating around on the asphalt.

I look around for my girls, but they're gone, of course. There wasn't anybody but some young married screaming with her children about some candy they didn't get by the door of a powder-blue Falcon station wagon. Looking back in the big windows, over the bags of peat moss and aluminum lawn furniture stacked on the pavement, I could see Lengel in my place in the slot, checking the sheep through. His face was dark gray and his back stiff, as if he'd just had an injection of iron, and my stomach kind of fell as I felt how hard the world was going to be to me hereafter.

Some Observations on the Novel

Most of what has been said about short stories (*e.g.*, on probability, narrative point of view, style) is relevant to the novel. And just as the short story of the last hundred years or so is rather different from earlier short fiction (see page 90), the novel—though here we must say of the last few hundred years—is different from earlier long fiction.

The ancient epic is at best a distant cousin to the novel, for though a narrative, the epic is in verse, and deals with godlike men and even with gods themselves. One has only to think of the *Odyssey* or the *Iliad* or the *Aeneid* or *Beowulf* or *Paradise Lost* to recall that epic does not deal with the sort of people one meets in *Tom Jones, David Copperfield, Crime and Punishment, The Return of the Native, The Portrait of a Lady, The Sun Also Rises,* or *The Stranger.*

The romance is perhaps a closer relative to the novel. Ancient romances were even in prose. But the hallmark of the romance, whether the romance is by a Greek sophist (Longus' *Daphnis and Chloe*) or by a medieval English poet (Chaucer's "The Knight's Tale") or by an American (Hawthorne's *The House of the Seven Gables*), is a presentation of the remote or the marvelous, rather than the local and the ordinary. The distinction is the same as that between the tale and the short story. "Tale" has the suggestion of a yarn, of unreality or of wondrous reality. (A case can be made for excluding Hawthorne's "Young Goodman Brown" from a collection of short stories on the ground that its remoteness and its allegorical implications mark it as a tale rather than a short story. This is not to say it is inferior to a story, but only different.) In his preface to *The House of the Seven Gables* Hawthorne himself distinguishes between the romance and the novel: "The latter form of composition is presumed to aim at a very minute fidelity, not merely to the possible, but to the probable and ordinary course of man's experience. The former—while, as a work of art, it must rigidly subject itself to laws, and while it sins unpardonably so far as it may swerve aside from the truth of the human heart—has fairly a right to present that truth under circumstances, to a great extent, of the writer's own choosing or creation." In his preface to *The Marble Faun* Hawthorne explains that he chose "Italy as the site of his Romance" because it afforded him "a sort of poetic or fairy precinct, where actualities would not be so terribly insisted upon as they are . . . in America."

"Actualities . . . insisted upon." That, in addition to prose and length, is the hallmark of the novel. The novel is a sort of long newspaper story; the very word "novel" comes from an Italian word meaning a little new thing, and is related to the French word that gives us "news." (It is noteworthy that the French cognate of Hawthorne's "actualities," *actualités*, means "news" or "current events," and *vues d'actualités* are newsreels.) It is no accident that many novelists have been newspapermen: Defoe, Dickens, Crane, Dreiser, Joyce, Hemingway, Camus—the list could be almost infinitely extended. And this connection with reportage perhaps helps to account for the relatively low esteem in which the novel is occasionally held: a course in the novel to some does not seem quite up to a course in poetry, and people who read novels but not poetry are not likely to claim an interest in "literature." Poetry is, allegedly, about beautiful thoughts, but novels are just about people.

Take Defoe's *Robinson Crusoe*. Though it is set in a far-off place, and thus might easily have been a romance, in Defoe's day it was close to current events, for it is a fictionalized version of events that had recently made news—Alexander Selkirk's life on the island of Juan Fernandez. And the story is not about marvelous happenings, but about a man's struggle for survival in dismal surroundings. Crusoe is armed not with Arthur's Excalibur or with Gawain's supposedly magic girdle, nor does he struggle as does Arthur with a Demon Cat and with a giant of St. Michael's Mount or as does Gawain with a Green Knight who survives decapitation; he has a carpenter's chest of tools and he struggles against commonplace nature. This chest was "much more valuable than a ship-loading of gold would have been at that time." The world of romance contains splendid castles and enchanted forests, but Crusoe's world contains not much more than a plot of ground, some animals and vegetables, and Friday. "I fancied I could make all but the wheel [of a wheelbarrow Crusoe needed], but that I had no notion of, neither did I know how to go about it; besides, I had no possible way to make the iron gudgeons for the spindle or axis of the wheel to run in, so I gave it over." The book, in short, emphasizes not the strange, but (given the initial situation) the usual, the commonsensical, the probable. The world of *Robinson Crusoe* is hardly different from the world we meet in the beginning of almost any novel:

We were in study hall when the headmaster walked in, followed by a new boy not wearing a school uniform, and by a janitor carrying a large desk. Those who were sleeping awoke, and we all stood up as though interrupting our work.

Gustave Flaubert, *Madame Bovary*

My father's family name being Pirrip, and my christian name Philip, my infant tongue could make of both names nothing longer or more explicit than Pip. So I called myself Pip, and came to be called Pip.

I give Pirrip as my father's family name, on the authority of his tombstone and my sister—Mrs. Joe Gargery, who married the blacksmith.

Charles Dickens, *Great Expectations*

In beginning the life story of my hero, Alexey Fyodorovich Karamazov, I find myself in somewhat of a quandary. Namely, although I call Alexey Fyodorovich my hero, I myself know that he is by no means a great man, and hence I foresee such unavoidable questions as these: "What is so remarkable about your Alexey Fyodorovich, that you have chosen him as your hero? What has he accomplished? What is he known for, and by whom? Why should I, the reader, spend time learning the facts of his life?"

Fyodor Dostoyevsky, *The Brothers Karamazov*

If you really want to hear about it, the first thing you'll probably want to know is where I was born, and what my lousy childhood was like, and how my parents were occupied and all before they had me, and all that David Copperfield kind of crap, but I don't feel like going into it, if you want to know the truth.

J. D. Salinger, *The Catcher in the Rye*

Boys are playing basketball around a telephone pole with a backboard bolted to it. Legs, shouts. The scrape and snap of Keds on loose alley pebbles seems to catapult their voices high into the moist March air blue above the wires. Rabbit Angstrom, coming up the alley in a business suit, stops and watches, though he's twenty-six and six three.

John Updike, *Rabbit, Run*

Sleepy boys in a school room; the brother of the wife of a blacksmith named Joe Gargery; a hero who "is by no means a great man"; a boy who in boy's language seems reluctant to talk of his "lousy childhood"; boys wearing Keds, playing in an alley, watched by a man who is "twenty-six and six three." In all of these passages, and in the openings of most other novels, we are confronted with current biography. (The so-called historical novel, it might be mentioned, is not a novel but the twentieth-century version of the romance, the adult version of the fairy tale.) In contrast to these beginnings, look at the beginning of one of Chaucer's great romances:

> Whilom°, as olde stories tellen us,   *once*
> Ther was a duc that highte° Theseus;   *was named*
> Of Atthenes he was lord and governour,
> And in his tyme swich° a conquerour,   *such*
> That gretter was ther noon under the sonne.

"Whilom." "Olde stories." "Gretter was ther noon under the sonne." We are in a timeless past, in which unusual people dwell. But the novel is almost always set in the present or very recent past (Updike even casts the whole novel in the present tense: "Boys are playing. . . . Rabbit Angstrom . . . stops and watches") and it deals with ordinary people. It so often deals with ordinary people, and presents them, apparently, in so ordinary a fashion that we sometimes wonder what is the point of it. Although the romance is often "escape" literature, it usually is didactic, holding up to us images of noble and ignoble behavior, revealing the rewards of courage and the power of love. In the preface to *The Marble Faun*, for instance, Hawthorne says he "proposed to himself merely to write a fanciful story, evolving a thoughtful moral, and did not propose attempting a portraiture of Italian manners and character." But portraiture is what the novelist gives us. Intent on revealing the world of real men and women going about their daily work and play, he does not simplify his characters into representatives of vices and virtues as does the romancer who wishes to evolve a thoughtful moral, but gives abundant detail—some of it apparently irrelevant. The innumerable details add up to a long book, although there need not be many physical happenings. The novel tells a story, of course, but the story is not only what people overtly do but also about what they think (*i.e.*, their mental doings) and about the society in which they are immersed and by which they are in part shaped. In the much-quoted preface to *Pierre and Jean*, Maupassant puts it this way:

> The skill of the novelist's plan will not reside in emotional effects, in attractive writing, in a striking beginning or a moving dénouement, but in the artful building up of solid details from which the essential meaning of the work will emerge.

As we read a novel we feel we are seeing not the "higher reality" or the "inner reality" so often mentioned by students of the arts, but the real reality.

    The short story, too, is detailed, but commonly it reveals only a single character at a moment of crisis, whereas the novel commonly traces the development of an individual, a group of people, a world.

The novelist, of course, has an attitude toward his world; he is not compiling an almanac but telling an invented story, making a work of art, and he therefore selects and shapes his material. One way of selecting and shaping the material is through the chosen point of view: we do not get everything in nineteenth-century England, but only everything that Pip remembers or chooses to set down about his experiences, and what he sets down is colored by his personality. "I remember Mr. Hubble as a tough high-shouldered stooping old man, of a saw-dusty fragrance, with his legs extraordinarily wide apart: so that in my short days I always saw some miles of open country between them when I met him coming up the lane." In any case, the coherence in a novel seems inclusive rather than exclusive. The novelist usually conveys the sense that he, as distinct from his characters, is—in the words of Christopher Isherwood's *The Berlin Stories*—"a camera with its shutter open, quite passive, recording not thinking. Recording the man shaving at the windows opposite and the woman in the kimono washing her hair. Some day, all of this will have to be developed, carefully fixed, printed."

It is not merely that the novel gives us details. *Gulliver's Travels* has plenty of details about people six inches tall and people sixty feet tall, and about a flying island and rational horses. But these things are recognized as fanciful inventions, though they do turn our mind toward the real world. *Gulliver* is a satire that holds up to us a picture of a fantastic world by which, paradoxically, we come to see the real world a little more clearly. The diminutive stature of the Lilliputians is an amusing and potent metaphor for the littleness of man, the flying island for abstract thinkers who have lost touch with reality, and so on. But the novelist who wants to show us the littleness of man invents not Lilliput but a world of normal-sized people who do little things and have little thoughts. Take Voltaire's *Candide* as a second example of a book that is prose fiction but not a novel. There are plenty of details, and even (as in *Gulliver*) references to events that were recent history. But the historical references are like raisins in a cake rather than like yeast; they do not permeate the whole. The details are often heaped up and incongruously juxtaposed to provoke laughter rather than credibility (the Portuguese governor's name is Don Fernando d'Ibaraa y Figueora y Mascarenes y Lampourdos y Souza; the old lady repeatedly reminds us that she has only half of a backside). The world of *Candide* is a world in which the main characters, participating in coincidence after coincidence, survive innumerable disasters—including shipwreck, earthquake, hanging, sword thrusts, and capture by cannibals. It is a world in which things happen at so breakneck a speed (think of the Marx Brothers wrecking all they touch; or think of animated cartoons in which a cat is chasing a mouse, swallows a fire-cracker, is blown high into the air, and a moment later is chasing the mouse again) that in a sense nothing much *really* happens. It is a world in which a character threatened with "re-killing" can say to Candide, "You can kill me again, if you like, but while I live, you shall never marry my sister." What we have in *Candide*, of course, is not a novel but a *conte philosophique*, improbable prose fiction used as a vehicle to convey a philosophic attitude. *Candide* is not a coherent image of reality but a comic rejection of one philosophic view of reality. It is not a novel; it is a fable and a parody.

Having spent so much time saying that the novel is not the epic or romance or fable, it must be mentioned that a work may hover on the borderlines of these forms. In so far as *Moby-Dick* narrates with abundant realistic detail the experiences of a whaler ("This book," Dorothy Parker has said, "taught me more about whales than I ever wanted to know") it is a novel; but in its evocation of mystery—Queequeg, the prophecies, Ishmael's miraculous rescue from the sea filled with sharks who "glided by as if with padlocks on their mouths" —it is a romance with strong symbolic implications.

The point is that although a reader of a long piece of prose fiction can complain that he did not get what he paid for, he should find out what he did get, rather than damn it for not being what it isn't. Bishop Butler's famous remark is relevant to literary criticism: "Everything is what it is and not another thing."

POETRY

Narrative Poetry: Popular Ballads • Lyric Poetry • The Speaking Tone of Voice • Figurative Language: Simile, Metaphor, Personification, Apostrophe, Imagery, Symbolism • Irony and Paradox • Rhythm • The Sonnet • Poets at Work

Seven

NARRATIVE POETRY: POPULAR BALLADS

European literature begins with Homer's *Iliad* and *Odyssey*, which means that it begins with stories in verse. In non-literate societies men got their stories from story-tellers who relied on memory rather than on the written word; the memorized stories were often poems, partly because (in Sir Philip Sidney's words) "verse far exceedeth prose in the knitting up of the memory." Even in literate societies, few people could read or write until the invention of the printing press at the close of the fifteenth century. While the printing press did not immediately destroy oral verse narratives, as the centuries passed, an increasingly large reading public developed which preferred prose narratives.

Among the great verse narratives are the English and Scottish **popular ballads,** some of the best of which are attributed to the fifteenth century, though they were not recorded until much later. These anonymous stories in song acquired their distinctive flavor by being passed down orally from generation to generation, each singer consciously or unconsciously modifying his inheritance. It is not known who made up the popular ballads; often they were made up partly out of earlier ballads by singers as bold as Kipling's cockney:

> When 'Omer smote 'is blooming lyre,
> He'd 'eard men sing by land an' sea;
> An' what he thought 'e might require,
> 'E went an' took—the same as me!

Most ballad singers probably were composers only by accident; they intended to transmit what they had heard, but their memories were sometimes faulty and their imaginations active. The modifications effected by oral transmission generally give a ballad three noticeable qualities. First, it is impersonal; even if there is an "I" who sings the tale, he is usually characterless. Second, the ballad—like the nursery rhyme, the counting-out rhyme ("one potato, two potato"), and other oral literature—is filled with repetition, sometimes of lines, sometimes of words. Consider, for example, "Go saddle me the black, the black,/ Go saddle me the brown," or "O wha is this has done this deid,/ This ill deid don to me?" Sometimes, in fact, the story is told by repeating lines with only a few significant variations. This **incremental repetition** (repetition with slight variations advancing the narrative) is the heart of "Edward," on page 314. Furthermore, **stock epithets** are repeated from ballad to ballad: "true love," "milk-white steed," "golden hair." Oddly, these clichés do not bore us but by their impersonality often lend a simplicity that effectively contrasts with the violence of the tale. Third, because the ballads are transmitted orally, residing in the memory rather than on the printed page, weak stanzas have often dropped out, leaving a series of sharp scenes, frequently with dialogue:

> The king sits in Dumferling toune,
>   Drinking the blude-reid wine:
> "O whar will I get guid sailor,
>   To sail this schip of mine?"

Because ballads were sung rather than printed, and because singers made alterations, there is no one version of a ballad that is the "correct" one. The versions printed here have become such favorites that they are almost regarded as definitive, but the reader should consult a collection of ballads (*e.g., The Viking Book of Folk Ballads*, ed. Albert B. Friedman [1958]) to get some idea of the wide variety.

Popular ballads have been much imitated by professional poets, especially since the late eighteenth century. Three such **literary ballads** are Auden's "O what is that sound" (p. 446), Keats's "La Belle Dame sans Merci" (p. 424), and Coleridge's "The Rime of the Ancient Mariner." In a literary ballad the story element is often infused with multiple meanings, with insistent symbolic implications. Ambiguity is often found in the popular ballad also, but it is of a rather different sort. Whether it is due to the loss of stanzas or to the creator's unconcern with some elements of the narrative, the ambiguity of the popular ballad commonly lies in the narrative itself rather than in the significance of the narrative.

ANONYMOUS

Sir Patrick Spence

The king sits in Dumferling toune,
    Drinking the blude-reid wine:
"O whar will I get guid sailor,
    To sail this schip of mine?"

5 Up and spak an eldern knicht,
    Sat at the kings richt kne:
"Sir Patrick Spence is the best sailor,
    That sails upon the se."

The king has written a braid letter,
10   And signed it wi' his hand,
And sent it to Sir Patrick Spence,
    Was walking on the sand.

The first line that Sir Patrick red,
    A loud lauch° lauched he;   *laugh*
15 The next line that Sir Patrick red,
    The teir blinded his ee.

"O wha is this has done this deid,
    This ill deid don to me,
To send me out this time o' the yeir,
20   To sail upon the se?!

"Mak hast, mak hast, my mirry men all,
    Our guid schip sails the morne:"
"O say na sae, my master deir,
    For I feir a deadlie storme.

25 "Late late yestreen I saw the new moone,
    Wi' the auld moone in hir arme,
And I feir, I feir, my deir master,
    That we will cum to harme."

O our Scots nobles wer richt laith°   *loath*
30   To weet their cork-heild schoone°;   *cork-heeled shoes*
Bot lang owre° a' the play wer playd,   *ere*
    Thair hats they swam aboone°.   *above*

O lang, lang may their ladies sit,
    Wi' thair fans into their hand,
35 Or eir° they se Sir Patrick Spence   *ere*
    Cum sailing to the land.

O lang, lang may the ladies stand,
    Wi' thair gold kems in their hair,
Waiting for their ain deir lords,
40   For they'll se thame na mair.

Have owre°, have owre to Aberdour,   *half over*
    It's fiftie fadom deip,
And thair lies guid Sir Patrick Spence,
    Wi' the Scots lords at his feit.

QUESTIONS: *Sir Patrick Spence*

1. The shipwreck occurs between lines 29 and 32, but it is not described. Does the omission stimulate the reader to imagine the details of the wreck? Or does the omission suggest that the poem is not so much about a shipwreck as it is about kinds of behavior? Explain. What do lines 33-40 contribute?

2. Might lines 17-18 warrant the inference that the "eldern knicht" (line 5) is Sir Patrick's enemy?

3. Explain lines 13-16.

4. In place of lines 37-40, another version of this ballad has the following stanza:

The ladies crack't their fingers white,
    The maidens tore their hair,
A' for the sake o' their true loves,
    For them they ne'er saw mair.

Why is one more effective than the other?

5. In the other version, the stanza that is here the final one (lines 41-44) precedes the stanzas about the ladies (lines 33-40). Which stanza makes a better conclusion? Why?

ANONYMOUS

The Three Ravens

There were three ravens sat on a tree,
    Downe a downe, hay down, hay downe
There were three ravens sat on a tree,
    With a downe
5   There were three ravens sat on a tree,
They were as blacke as they might be,
    With a downe derrie, derrie, derrie, downe, downe.

The one of them said to his mate,
"Where shall we our breakfast take?"

10 "Down in yonder greene field,
There lies a knight slain under his shield.

"His hounds they lie downe at his feete,
So well they can their master keepe.

"His haukes they flie so eagerly,
15 There's no fowle dare him come nie."

pregnant

As great with yong as she might goe.
Downe there comes a fallow° doe,   *brown*

She lift up his bloudy hed,
And kist his wounds that were so red.

20 She got him up upon her backe,
And carried him to earthen lake°.   *pit*

She buried him before the prime°,   *about nine* A.M.
She was dead herselfe ere even-song time.

God send every gentleman
25 Such haukes, such hounds, and such a leman°.   *sweetheart*

The "doe" (line 16), often taken as a suggestive description of the knight's beloved, is probably a vestige of the folk belief that an animal may be an enchanted human being.

QUESTIONS: *The Three Ravens*

1. The hounds and the hawks are loyal followers of the knight, as is the doe. How do the references to the hounds and hawks in some degree prepare us for the doe? Is preparation necessary? Why?

2. Why does the poet include the ravens? Do they confuse a poem on loyalty, or do they provide an effective contrast? Do the ravens help to give a fuller, more realistic picture of life? Explain.

3. Are the final two lines an intrusive comment? Explain.

ANONYMOUS

The Twa Corbies

As I was walking all alane,
I heard twa corbies° making a mane°;   *two ravens; lament*
The tane° unto the t' other say,   *one*
"Where sall we gang° and dine to-day?"   *shall we go*

5 "In behint yon auld fail dyke°,   *old turf wall*
I wot° there lies a new-slain knight;   *know*
And naebody kens° that he lies there,   *knows*
But his hawk, his hound, and lady fair.

"His hound is to the hunting gane,
10 His hawk, to fetch the wild-fowl hame,
His lady's ta'en another mate,
So we may mak our dinner sweet.

"Ye'll sit on his white hause-bane°,   *neck bone*
And I'll pike out his bonny blue een°.   *eyes*

¹⁵ Wi' ae° locks o' his gowden° hair ~~mehe nest~~ *with one; golden*
We'll theek° our nest when it grows bare. *thatch*

"Mony a one for him makes mane,
But nane sall ken whare he is gane;
O'er his white banes, when they are bare,
²⁰ The wind sall blaw for evermair."

QUESTIONS: *The Twa Corbies*

1. The story in this poem is implied (in the second and third stanzas) rather than made explicit. What is it? Is it the worse for being implicit? Explain.
2. How do lines 9-10 reinforce or parallel the basic story?
3. Hair is usually "gowden" in ballads. What does this conventional detail tell us about the knight's age? Why is his age significant?
4. What does the fourth stanza (especially lines 15-16) contribute to the poem?
5. Animals cannot speak; is the poem therefore an absurdity? Explain.
6. How accurate is the observation that this ballad is a "cynical variation" of "The Three Ravens"?

ANONYMOUS

Edward

"Why dois your brand° sae° drap wi' bluid, *sword; so*
        Edward, Edward?
Why dois your brand sae drap wi' bluid?
        And why sae sad gang° yee, O?" *go*
⁵ "O, I hae killed my hauke sae guid,
        Mither, mither,
O, I hae killed my hauke sae guid,
        And I had nae mair bot hee, O."

"Your haukis bluid was nevir sae reid,
¹⁰   Edward, Edward,
Your haukis bluid was nevir sae reid,
        My deir son I tell thee, O."
"O, I hae killed my reid-roan steid,
        Mither, mither,
¹⁵ O, I hae killed my reid-roan steid,
        That erst° was sa fair and frie°, O." *once; spirited*

"Your steid was auld, and ye hae gat mair,
        Edward, Edward,

Your steid was auld, and ye hae gat mair,
20   Sum other dule° ye drie°, O."   *grief; suffer*
"O, I hae killed my fadir deir,
        Mither, mither,
O, I hae killed my fadir deir,
    Alas, and wae is mee, O!"

25 "And whatten penance wul ye drie for that,
        Edward, Edward?
And whatten penance wul ye drie for that?
    My deir son, now tell me, O."
"Ile set my feit in yonder boat,
30   Mither, mither,
Ile set my feit in yonder boat,
    And Ile fare ovir the sea, O."

"And what wul ye doe wi' your towirs and your ha'°,   *hall*
        Edward, Edward,
35 And what wul ye doe wi' your towirs and your ha',
    That were sae fair to see, O?"
"Ile let thame stand tul they doun fa'°,
        Mither, mither,
Ile let thame stand tul they doun fa',
40   For here nevir mair maun° I bee, O."   *must*

"And what wul ye leive to your bairns° and your wife,   *children*
        Edward, Edward?
And what wul ye leive to your bairns and your wife,
    When ye gang ovir the sea, O?"
45 "The warldis° room, late° them beg thrae° life,   *world's; let;*
        Mither, mither,   *through*
The warldis room, late them beg thrae life,
    For thame nevir mair wul I see, O."

"And what wul ye leive to your ain mither deir,
50   Edward, Edward?
And what wul ye leive to your ain mither deir?
    My deir son, now tell me, O."
"The curse of hell frae me sall ye beir,
        Mither, mither,
55 The curse of hell frae me sall ye beir,
    Sic° counseils ye gave to me, O."   *such*

QUESTIONS: *Edward*

1. The poem consists of two parts. How does the structure of
the first part parallel that of the second?

2. What might have been the mother's motives? Would the
story be improved if we knew the motives behind her "counseils"?
Explain.

3. Can Edward's statements about his wife and children be explained?

4. What do the refrains ("Edward, Edward" and "Mither, mither") contribute to the poem?

5. Line 21 offers a surprise, but it is topped by the surprise in the final four lines. Can the poem be re-read with pleasure once the surprises are known? Explain.

Many ballads, like the next one, deal with supernatural happenings. "The Demon Lover" exists in many versions, and is often titled "The House Carpenter" or "James Harris," though in the versions printed here the man is unnamed. The gist of the various versions is along these lines: James Harris and Jane Reynolds had exchanged vows of marriage. He was impressed as a sailor, and when three years later he was reported dead, the girl married a carpenter. Four years after the marriage James's spirit visited Jane, assured her he was a shipowner, and enticed her to leave her family. Destruction followed.

The first version below is from the eighteenth century, the second from the twentieth century.

ANONYMOUS

The Demon Lover (*an early version*)

"O where have you been, my long, long love,
    This long seven years and mair?"
"O I'm come to seek my former vows
    Ye granted me before."

5 "O hold your tongue of your former vows,
    For they will breed sad strife;
O hold your tongue of your former vows,
    For I am become a wife."

He turned him right and round about,
10   And the tear blinded his ee:
"I wad never hae trodden on Irish ground,
    If it had not been for thee.

"I might hae had a king's daughter,
    Far, far beyond the sea;
15 I might have had a king's daughter,
    Had it not been for love o thee."

"If ye might have had a king's daughter,
    Yer sel ye had to blame;
Ye might have taken the king's daughter,
20   For ye kend° that I was nane.   *knew*

"If I was to leave my husband dear,
    And my two babes also,
O what have you to take me to,
    If with you I should go?"

25 "I hae seven ships upon the sea—
    The eighth brought me to land—
With four-and-twenty bold mariners,
    And music on every hand."

She has taken up her two little babes,
30   Kissed them baith cheek and chin:
"O fair ye weel, my ain two babes,
    For I'll never see you again."

She set her foot upon the ship,
    No mariners could she behold;
35 But the sails were o the taffetie,
    And the masts o the beaten gold.

They had not sailed a league, a league,
    A league but barely three,
When dismal grew his countenance,
40   And drumlie° grew his ee.   *gloomy*

They had not sailed a league, a league,
    A league but barely three,
Until she espied his cloven foot,
    And she wept right bitterlie.

45 "O hold your tongue of your weeping," says he,
    "Of your weeping now let me be;
I will show you how the lilies grow
    On the banks of Italy."

"O what hills are yon, yon pleasant hills,
50   That the sun shines sweetly on?"
"O yon are the hills of heaven," he said,
    "Where you will never win°."   *gain, get to*

"O whaten mountain is yon," she said,
    "All so dreary wi frost and snow?"
55 "O yon is the mountain of hell," he cried,
    "Where you and I will go."

He strack the tap-mast wi his hand,
    The fore-mast wi his knee,
And he brake that gallant ship in twain,
60   And sank her in the sea.

1. What is the first hint that supernatural forces are at work?
2. What does the "cloven foot" (line 43) signify? Is the spirit motivated by malice? By love? By both?
3. Read the modern American version below, recorded in the South, and then compare the effectiveness of the final stanza of each poem.

ANONYMOUS

The Demon Lover (*a late version*)

"Well met, well met," said an old true love,
"Well met, well met," said he;
"I'm just returning from the salt, salt sea,
And it's all for the love of thee."

5 "Come in, come in, my old true love,
And have a seat with me.
It's been three-fourths of a long, long year
Since together we have been."

"Well I can't come in or I can't sit down,
10 For I haven't but a moment's time.
They say you're married to a house carpenter,
And your heart will never be mine.

"Now it's I could have married a king's daughter dear;
I'm sure she'd a married me;
15 But I've forsaken her crowns of gold,
And it's all for the love of thee.

"Now will you forsaken your house carpenter
And go along with me?
I'll take you where the grass grows green
20 On the banks of the deep blue sea."

She picked up her little babe,
And kisses gave it three.
Says, "Stay right here, my darling little babe,
And keep our poppa company."

25 Well he hadn't been on ship but about two weeks—
I'm sure it was not three—
Till his true love begin to weep and mourn
And to weep most bitterly.

Says, "Are you weeping for my silver or my gold?"
30 Says, "Are you weeping for my store?
Are you weeping for that house carpenter
Whose face you'll never see any more?"

"No, it's I'm not a-weeping for your silver or your gold,
   Or neither for your store;
35 I am weeping for my darling little babe
   Whose face I'll never see any more."

   Well he hadn't been on ship but about three weeks—
   I'm sure it was not four—
   Till they sprung a leak in the bottom of the ship
40 And sunk for to rise no more.

ANONYMOUS

De Titanic

   De rich folks 'cided to take a trip
   On de fines' ship dat was ever built.
   De cap'n presuaded dese peoples to think
   Dis Titanic too safe to sink.

5 *Chorus* Out on dat ocean,
            De great wide ocean,
            De Titanic, out on de ocean,
            Sinkin' down!

   De ship lef' de harbor at a rapid speed,
10 'Twuz carryin' everythin' dat de peoples need.
   She sailed six-hundred miles away,
   Met an icebug in her way.

   De ship lef' de harbor, 'twuz runnin' fas'.
   'Twuz her fus' trip an' her las'.
15 Way out on dat ocean wide
   An icebug ripped her in de side.

   Up come Bill from de bottom flo'
   Said de water wuz runnin' in de boiler do'.
   Go back, Bill, an' shut yo' mouth,
20 Got forty-eight pumps to keep de water out!

   Jus' about den de cap'n looked aroun',
   He seed de Titanic wuz a-sinkin' down.
   He give orders to de mens aroun':
   "Get yo' life-boats an' let 'em down !"

25 De mens standin' roun' like heroes brave,
   Nothin' but de wimin an' de chillun to save;
   De wimin an' de chillun a-wipin' dere eyes,
   Kissin' dere husbands an' friends good-bye.

On de fifteenth day of May nineteen-twelve,
30 De ship wrecked by an icebug out in de ocean dwell.
De people wuz thinkin' o' Jesus o' Nazaree,
While de band played "Nearer My God to Thee!"

On her maiden voyage in 1912, the *Titanic* struck an iceberg and sank. Almost at once Southern Negroes were composing, selling, and buying songs about the disaster, and during the First World War these songs were especially popular among Negro troops sailing for France. (For another treatment of the sinking of the *Titanic*, see Thomas Hardy's "The Convergence of the Twain," page 429.)

QUESTIONS: *De Titanic*

1. If the pronunciations were "corrected" (*e.g.*, line 9, "The ship left the harbor at a rapid speed"), would any of the poem's effect be lost? Or are the mispronunciations an important part of the poem's total effect? What does the misnomer "icebug" (lines 12, 16, 30) suggest that "iceberg" lacks?

2. What characteristics of older ballads are in this modern one?

Eight

LYRIC POETRY

The preceding chapter suggested that narrative poetry is not as dominant as it was before the age of printing. Today when we think of poetry we are less likely to think of the *Aeneid*, of *Paradise Lost*, or of the ballads, than of lyric poems, pieces that seem to be emotional or reflective soliloquies, such as Wordsworth's "I wandered lonely as a cloud" (page 409). Wordsworth, it is true, narrates a happening (he wandered and came across some daffodils) and describes a scene (the daffodils were "fluttering and dancing in the breeze"). But the poem is about the speaker's emotional response to the flowers he happened upon: when he recalls them his "heart with pleasure fills,/And dances with the daffodils." The recollection of an emotion, which causes a new emotion, is in fact at the root of Wordsworth's theory of poetry. In his Preface to the second edition (1800) of *Lyrical Ballads* he wrote:

> I have said that poetry is the spontaneous overflow of powerful feelings: it takes its origin from emotion recollected in tranquillity; the emotion is contemplated till, by a species of reaction, the tranquillity gradually disappears, and an emotion, kindred to that which was before the subject of contemplation, is gradually produced, and does itself actually exist in the mind. In this mood successful composition generally begins, and in a mood similar to this it is carried on; but the emotion, of whatever kind, and in whatever degree, from various causes, is qualified by various pleasures, so that in describing any passions whatsoever, which are voluntarily described, the mind will, upon the whole, be in a state of enjoyment.

Though Wordsworth wrote some narrative and dramatic poetry, he was most often successful with lyric poetry, and this is probably the sort to which his theory chiefly applies. For the Greeks a **lyric** was a song accompanied by a lyre, but by Wordsworth's time it had its present meaning of a poem that, neither narrative (*i.e.,* telling a story) nor strictly dramatic (*i.e.*, performed by actors), is an emotional or reflective soliloquy.

Speaking roughly, we can say that while the narrative is set in the past, telling what happened, the lyric is set in the present, catching a speaker in a moment of expression; but a lyric can, of course, glance backward or forward, as in this song from Shakespeare's *Measure for Measure*:

> Take, O take those lips away,
>   That so sweetly were forsworn;
> And those eyes, the break of day,
>   Lights that do mislead the morn:
> But my kisses bring again,
>   Bring again,
> Seals of love, but seal'd in vain,
>   Seal'd in vain.

Lyrics are sometimes differentiated among themselves. For example, if a lyric is melancholy or mournfully contemplative, especially if it laments a death, it may be called an **elegy** (though before Gray's famous "Elegy," the word often denoted a personal poem written in pairs of lines, on whatever theme). If a lyric is rather long, elaborate, and on a lofty theme (*e.g.*, immortality, a hero's victory), it may be called an **ode**. Greek odes were choral pieces, more or less hymns of praise in elaborate stanzas, but in Rome, Horace (65-8 B.C.) applied the word to quieter pieces, usually in stanzas of four lines, celebrating love, patriotism, or simple Roman morality. Distinctions among lyrics are often vague, and one man's ode may be another man's elegy. Still, when a writer uses one of these words in his title, he is inviting the reader to recall the tradition in which he is working. Of the poet's link to tradition T. S. Eliot said:

> No poet, no artist of any art, has his complete meaning alone. His significance, his appreciation is the appreciation of his relation to the dead poets and artists. You cannot value him alone; you must set him, for contrast and comparison, among the dead.

Although the lyric is often ostensibly addressed to someone ("Take, O take those lips away"), the reader often feels that the speaker is really talking to himself. He is not, say, in the presence of his lady; rather, his heart is overflowing (the reader senses) and he pretends to address her. A comment by John Stuart Mill on poetry is especially true of the lyric:

> Eloquence is *heard*, poetry is *over*heard. Eloquence supposes an audience; the peculiarity of poetry appears to us to lie in the poet's

utter unconsciousness of a listener. Poetry is feeling confessing itself to itself, in moments of solitude.

The sense of "feeling confessing itself to itself, in moments of solitude," is strong and clear in this short cowboy song:

The Colorado Trail

Eyes like the morning star,
Cheek like a rose,
Laura was a pretty girl,
God Almighty knows.

Weep all ye little rains,
Wail winds wail,
All along, along, along
The Colorado trail.

Here is another anonymous lyric, this one sung by coal miners whose most constant companions during their long hours below the surface of the earth were mules that dragged carts of coal:

My Sweetheart's the Mule in the Mines

My sweetheart's the mule in the mines,
I drive her without any lines,
On the bumper I sit,
I chew and I spit,
All over my sweetheart's behind.

One other anonymous poem:

Western Wind

Western wind, when wilt thou blow,
The small rain down can rain?
Christ, if my love were in my arms,
And I in my bed again!

QUESTIONS: *Western Wind*

1. What is the tone of the speaker's voice in the first two lines? Angry? Impatient? Supplicating? Be as precise as possible. What is the tone in the next two lines?

2. In England the west wind, warmed by the Gulf Stream, rises in the spring. What associations link the wind and rain of lines 1 and 2 with lines 3 and 4?

3. Ought we to have been told why the lovers are separated? Explain.

4. Is the cry in line 3 blasphemous and/or licentious? Explain.

WILLIAM SHAKESPEARE (1564-1616)

Spring

When daisies pied and violets blue
    And lady-smocks° all silver white   *also called cuckooflowers*
And cuckoo-buds° of yellow hue   *buttercups*
    Do paint the meadows with delight,
5 The cuckoo then, on every tree,
Mocks married men; for thus sings he,
                "Cuckoo,
Cuckoo, cuckoo!" O word of fear,
Unpleasing to a married ear!

10 When shepherds pipe on oaten straws°,   *musical instruments*
    And merry larks are ploughmen's clocks.
When turtles tread°, and rooks, and daws,   *turtledoves mate*
    And maidens bleach their summer smocks,
The cuckoo then, on every tree,
15 Mocks married men; for thus sings he,
                "Cuckoo,
Cuckoo, cuckoo!" O word of fear,
Unpleasing to a married ear!

WILLIAM SHAKESPEARE (1564-1616)

Winter

When icicles hang by the wall,
    And Dick the shepherd blows his nail°,   *breathes on his finger-*
And Tom bears logs into the hall,   *nails to warm them*
    And milk comes frozen home in pail,
5 When blood is nipped, and ways° be foul,   *roads*
Then nightly sings the staring owl,
                "Tu-whit, tu-who!"

A merry note,
While greasy Joan doth keel° the pot.   *cool, by skimming*

10 When all aloud the wind doth blow,
     And coughing drowns the parson's saw°,   *wise saying*
   And birds sit brooding in the snow,
     And Marian's nose looks red and raw, 𝒯𝑜𝑚'𝑠 𝑤𝑖𝑓𝑒
   When roasted crabs° hiss in the bowl,   *crab apples*
15 Then nightly sings the staring owl,
          "Tu-whit, tu-who!"

A merry note,
While greasy Joan doth keel the pot.

"Spring" and "Winter" are sung at the end of *Love's Labors Lost*. Because the cuckoo lays its eggs in other birds' nests, its name (based on its cry during the mating season) gave rise to the word "cuckold."

QUESTIONS: *Spring* and *Winter*

   1. Why is the cuckoo appropriate to spring? The owl to winter?
   2. Did you expect a poem on spring to bring in infidelity? Is the poem bitter? Explain.
   3. Does "Winter" describe only the hardships of the season, or does it communicate also the joys?

WALT WHITMAN (*1819-1892*)

A Noiseless Patient Spider

A noiseless patient spider,
I mark'd where on a little promontory it stood isolated,
Mark'd how to explore the vacant vast surrounding,
It launch'd forth filament, filament, filament, out of itself,
5 Ever unreeling them, ever tirelessly speeding them.

And you O my soul where you stand,
Surrounded, detached, in measureless oceans of space,
Ceaselessly musing, venturing, throwing, seeking the spheres to
     connect them,
Till the bridge you will need be form'd, till the ductile anchor
     hold,
10 Till the gossamer thread you fling catch somewhere, O my soul.

QUESTIONS: *A Noiseless Patient Spider*

   1. Does "promontory" (line 2), in the context of the poem, have suggestions beyond the literal meaning? How are the suggestions in "launch'd" (line 4) and "unreeling" (line 5) continued in the second stanza?

2. How are the varying lengths of lines 1, 4, and 8 relevant to their ideas?

3. Is the second stanza a complete sentence? Why? The poem is unrhymed. What is the effect of the near-rhyme (hold : soul) in the last two lines?

ROBERT FROST (1874-1963)

Stopping by Woods on a Snowy Evening

Whose woods these are I think I know.
His house is in the village though;
He will not see me stopping here
To watch his woods fill up with snow.

5 My little horse must think it queer
To stop without a farmhouse near
Between the woods and frozen lake
The darkest evening of the year.

He gives his harness bells a shake
10 To ask if there is some mistake.
The only other sound's the sweep
Of easy wind and downy flake.

The woods are lovely, dark and deep.
But I have promises to keep,
15 And miles to go before I sleep,
And miles to go before I sleep.

QUESTIONS: *Stopping by Woods*

1. Line 5 originally read: "The steaming horses think it queer." Line 7 read: "Between a forest and a lake." Evaluate the changes.

2. The rhyming words in the first stanza can be indicated by *aaba*; the second stanza picks up the *b* rhyme: *bbcb*. Indicate the rhymes for the third stanza. For the fourth. Why is it appropriate that the rhyme scheme differ in the fourth stanza?

3. Hearing that the poem had been interpreted as a "death poem," Frost said, "I never intended that, but I did have the feeling it was loaded with ulteriority." What "ulteriority" is implicit? How is the time of day and year significant? How does the horse's attitude make a contrast with the man's?

SAMUEL JOHNSON (1709-1784)

On the Death of Mr. Robert Levet

Condemned to Hope's delusive mine,
    As on we toil from day to day,
By sudden blasts, or slow decline,
    Our social comforts drop away.

5 Well tried through many a varying year,
    See Levet to the grave descend,
Officious°, innocent, sincere,   *obliging*
    Of every friendless name the friend.

Yet still he fills Affection's eye,
10   Obscurely wise and coarsely kind;
Nor, lettered Arrogance, deny
    Thy praise to merit unrefined.

When fainting Nature called for aid,
    And hovering Death prepared the blow,
15 His vigorous remedy displayed
    The power of art without the show.

In Misery's darkest caverns known,
    His useful care was ever nigh,
Where hopeless Anguish poured his groan,
20   And lonely Want retired to die.

No summons mocked by chill delay,
    No petty gain disdained by pride;
The modest wants of every day
    The toil of every day supplied.

25 His virtues walked their narrow round,
    Nor made a pause, nor left a void;
And sure the Eternal Master found
    The single talent well employed.

The busy day, the peaceful night,
30   Unfelt, uncounted, glided by;
His frame was firm, his powers were bright,
    Though now his eightieth year was nigh.

Then with no throbbing, fiery pain,
    No cold gradations of decay,
35 Death broke at once the vital chain,
    And freed his soul the nearest way.

James Boswell describes Johnson's close friend Levet as "an obscure practiser in physick amongst the lower people." Levet, an unlicensed physician, paid house calls to the indigent, unlike most of his professional superiors.

1. How is the figure of the mine (line 1) continued in other stanzas?

2. Are lines 9-12 out of place in a poem commemorating the death of a friend? Explain.

3. Lines 27-28 allude to Jesus' parable of the talents, in Matthew 25:14-30. How does Johnson add a twist to the parable?

4. Why is it appropriate that Levet's death was quick and easy?

5. Does the lack of personal expression of grief suggest insincerity? Explain.

JOHN KEATS (1795-1821)

Ode on a Grecian Urn

I

Thou still unravished bride of quietness,
    Thou foster-child of silence and slow time,
Sylvan historian, who canst thus express
    A flowery tale more sweetly than our rhyme:
5 What leaf-fringed legend haunts about thy shape
    Of deities or mortals, or of both,
       In Tempe or the dales of Arcady?
    What men or gods are these? What maidens loth?
What mad pursuit? What struggle to escape?
10   What pipes and timbrels? What wild ecstasy?

II

Heard melodies are sweet, but those unheard
    Are sweeter; therefore, ye soft pipes, play on;
Not to the sensual° ear, but, more endeared,   *sensuous*
    Pipe to the spirit ditties of no tone:
15 Fair youth, beneath the trees, thou canst not leave
    Thy song, nor ever can those trees be bare;
       Bold Lover, never, never canst thou kiss,
    Though winning near the goal—yet, do not grieve;
       She cannot fade, though thou hast not thy bliss,
20   For ever wilt thou love, and she be fair!

III

Ah, happy, happy boughs! that cannot shed
    Your leaves, nor ever bid the Spring adieu;
And, happy melodist, unwearied,
    For ever piping songs for ever new;
25 More happy love! more happy, happy love!

For ever warm and still to be enjoyed,
    For ever panting, and for ever young;
All breathing human passion far above,
    That leaves a heart high-sorrowful and cloyed,
30   A burning forehead, and a parching tongue.

IV

Who are these coming to the sacrifice?
    To what green altar, O mysterious priest,
Lead'st thou that heifer lowing at the skies,
    And all her silken flanks with garlands drest?
35 What little town by river or sea shore,
    Or mountain-built with peaceful citadel,
        Is emptied of this folk, this pious morn?
And, little town, thy streets for evermore
    Will silent be; and not a soul to tell
40   Why thou art desolate, can e'er return.

V

O Attic shape! Fair attitude! with brede°   *design*
    Of marble men and maidens overwrought,
With forest branches and the trodden weed;
    Thou, silent form, dost tease us out of thought
45 As doth eternity: Cold Pastoral!
When old age shall this generation waste,
        Thou shalt remain, in midst of other woe
    Than ours, a friend to man, to whom thou say'st,
"Beauty is truth, truth beauty,—that is all
50   Ye know on earth, and all ye need to know."

QUESTIONS: *Ode on a Grecian Urn*

1. Why "sylvan" historian (line 3)? As the poem continues, what evidence is there that the urn cannot "express" (line 3) a tale so sweetly as the speaker said?

2. What is the meaning of lines 11-14?

3. Is the town (lines 35-40) depicted on the urn, or does the speaker imagine it? How does the description (especially lines 38-40) modify the earlier attitude toward the urn?

4. What might the urn stand for in the first three stanzas? In the third stanza is the speaker caught up in the urn's world or is he sharply aware of his own?

5. Does "tease us out of thought" (line 44) mean "draw us into a realm of imaginative experience superior to that of reason," or "draw us into futile and frustrating questions"? Or both, or neither? What are the suggestions in "Cold Pastoral" (line 45)?

6. T. S. Eliot said of "Beauty is truth, truth beauty" (line 49) : "On re-reading the whole Ode, this line strikes me as a serious blemish on a beautiful poem, and the reason must be either that I fail to understand it, or that it is a statement which is untrue. . . . The statement of Keats seems to me meaningless: or perhaps the fact that it is grammatically meaningless conceals another meaning from me." Do lines 49-50 perhaps mean that imagination, stimulated by the urn, achieves a realm richer than the daily world? Or perhaps that art, the highest earthly wisdom, suggests there is a realm wherein earthly troubles are resolved?

There is a further problem: although here we have the last two lines in quotation marks, attributing them to the urn, Keat's own punctuation is uncertain. Many have held that the last line and a half are the speaker's reply to the urn's assertion that "Beauty is truth, truth beauty." The speaker of the poem (one argument goes), aware of the sorrows and surfeits of life in this world (lines 29-30), rejects the urn's short-sighted assertion that only beauty exists. To hold this interpretation, one must say that the speaker's last remark is addressed to the figures on the urn ("Ye" is plural), and one must more or less ignore "*on* earth" (line 50). Or is the speaker of the last line and a half—if the speaker is not the urn—turning (as another interpretation holds) to address people in general?

Nine

THE SPEAKING TONE OF VOICE

Everything written is as good as it is dramatic. . . . [A poem is] heard as sung or spoken by a person in a scene—in character, in a setting. By whom, where and when is the question. By a dreamer of the better world out in a storm in Autumn; by a lover under a window at night.

Robert Frost, Preface, *A Way Out*

If we fall into the habit of saying "Shakespeare says 'Take, O take those lips away,' " or "Keats says 'Heard melodies are sweet, but those unheard are sweeter,' " we neglect the important truth in Frost's comment: a poem is written by an author, but it is spoken by an invented speaker. The author counterfeits the speech of a person in a particular situation. The anonymous author of "Edward" (page 314) invents the speeches of a murderer and his mother; the anonymous author of "Western Wind" (page 323) invents the speech of an unhappy lover who longs for the spring; Robert Frost in "Stopping by Woods" (page 326) invents the speech of a man who, sitting in a horse-drawn sleigh, is surveying woods that are "lovely, dark and deep." Had the setting in Frost's poem been different—say, a snowbound cabin—the speaker of the poem would have said something different.

The speaker's voice, of course, often has the ring of the author's own voice, and to make a distinction between speaker and author may at times seem perverse. Robert Burns, for example, sometimes lets us know that the poem is spoken by "Rob"; he may address his wife by name; beneath the title "To a Mouse" he writes, "On Turning Up Her Nest With the Plow, November, 1785," and beneath the title "To a Mountain Daisy" he writes, "On Turning One Down With the Plow in April, 1786." Still, even in these allegedly autobiographical poems, it may be convenient to distinguish between author and speaker; the speaker is Burns the lover, or Burns the meditative man, or Burns the compassionate man, not simply Robert Burns the poet. Here are two poems by Burns; in the first the lover speaks, in the second, we hear a different speaker.

ROBERT BURNS (1759-1796)

Mary Morison

O Mary, at thy window be,
    It is the wished, the trysted hour!
Those smiles and glances let me see,
    That make the miser's treasure poor:
5 How blithely wad I bide the stour°,   *endure the struggle*
    A weary slave frae sun to sun,
Could I the rich reward secure,
    The lovely Mary Morison.

Yestreen, when to the trembling string
10   The dance gaed through the lighted ha',
To thee my fancy took its wing,
    I sat, but neither heard nor saw:
Though this was fair, and that was braw°,   *handsome*
    And yon the toast of a' the town,
15 I sighed, and said amang them a',
    "Ye are na Mary Morison."

O Mary, canst thou wreck his peace,
    Wha for thy sake wad gladly die?
Or canst thou break that heart of his,
20   Whase only faut is loving thee?
If love for love thou wilt na gie°,   *give*
    At least be pity to me shown!
A thought ungentle canna be
    The thought o' Mary Morison.

ROBERT BURNS (1759-1796)

John Anderson My Jo

John Anderson my jo°, John   *joy, sweetheart*
    When we were first acquent,
Your locks were like the raven,
    Your bonnie brow was brent°;   *smooth*
5 But now your brow is beld, John,
    Your locks are like the snaw,
But blessings on your frosty pow°,   *head*
    John Anderson my jo!

John Anderson my jo, John
10   We clamb the hill thegither,
And monie a cantie° day, John   *happy*
    We've had wi' ane anither:
Now we maun° totter down, John   *must*
    And hand in hand we'll go,
15 And sleep thegither at the foot,
    John Anderson my jo!

QUESTIONS: *Mary Morison* and *John Anderson*

1. Is the speaker addressing Mary Morison?
2. In "Mary Morison," how convincing are the assertions of the
first stanza (that her smiles and glances are more valuable than great
wealth; that he would willingly be a "weary slave" if only he could
win her)? How does the third stanza enlarge our conception of the
speaker's personality? For example, do lines 21-22 introduce an aspect
not present earlier?
3. In "John Anderson My Jo," the speaker cannot be identified
with Burns, but do we feel that there is in the poem anything of the
particular accent of an old lady? Why?

Although all poems are "dramatic" in Frost's sense of being
uttered by a speaker in a situation, and although most short poems
are monologues, the term **dramatic monologue** is reserved for those
poems in which a single character—not the poet—is speaking at a
critical moment to a person or persons whose presence we strongly
feel. The *locus classicus* is the following poem.

ROBERT BROWNING (1812-1889)

My Last Duchess
Ferrara°   *town in Italy*

That's my last Duchess painted on the wall,
Looking as if she were alive. I call
That piece a wonder, now; Frà Pandolf's° hands   *a fictitious*
Worked busily a day, and there she stands.   *painter*
5 Will't please you sit and look at her? I said
"Frà Pandolf" by design, for never read
Strangers like you that pictured countenance,
The depth and passion of its earnest glance,
But to myself they turned (since none puts by
10 The curtain I have drawn for you, but I)
And seemed as they would ask me, if they durst,

How such a glance came there; so, not the first
Are you to turn and ask thus. Sir, 'twas not
Her husband's presence only, called that spot
15 Of joy into the Duchess' cheek; perhaps
Frà Pandolf chanced to say "Her mantle laps
Over my Lady's wrist too much," or, "Paint
Must never hope to reproduce the faint
Half-flush that dies along her throat." Such stuff
20 Was courtesy, she thought, and cause enough
For calling up that spot of joy. She had
A heart—how shall I say?—too soon made glad,
Too easily impressed; she liked whate'er
She looked on, and her looks went everywhere.
25 Sir, 'twas all one! My favor at her breast,
The dropping of the daylight in the west,
The bough of cherries some officious fool
Broke in the orchard for her, the white mule
She rode with round the terrace—all and each
30 Would draw from her alike the approving speech,
Or blush, at least. She thanked men—good! but thanked
Somehow—I know not how—as if she ranked
My gift of a nine-hundred-years-old name
With anybody's gift. Who'd stoop to blame
35 This sort of trifling? Even had you skill
In speech—(which I have not) —to make your will
Quite clear to such an one, and say, "Just this
Or that in you disgusts me; here you miss,
Or there exceed the mark"—and if she let
40 Herself be lessoned so, nor plainly set
Her wits to yours, forsooth, and made excuse,
—E'en then would be some stooping; and I choose
Never to stoop. Oh, Sir, she smiled, no doubt,
Whene'er I passed her; but who passed without
45 Much the same smile? This grew; I gave commands;
Then all smiles stopped together. There she stands
As if alive. Will't please you rise? We'll meet
The company below, then. I repeat,
The Count your master's known munificence
50 Is ample warrant that no just pretence
Of mine for dowry will be disallowed;
Though his fair daughter's self, as I avowed
At starting, is my object. Nay, we'll go
Together down, Sir. Notice Neptune, though,
55 Taming a sea-horse, thought a rarity,
Which Claus of Innsbruck° cast in bronze for me!   *a fictitious
                                                        sculptor*

QUESTIONS: *My Last Duchess*

1. Who is speaking to whom? On what occasion?

2. What words or lines especially convey the speaker's arrogance? What is our attitude toward the speaker? Loathing? Fascination? Respect? Explain.

3. The time and place are Renaissance Italy; how do they affect our attitude toward the duke? What would be the effect if the poem were set in the twentieth century?

4. Why does this poem sound more like talk and less like song than Burns's "John Anderson"?

5. Years after writing this poem, Browning explained that the duke's "commands" (line 45) were "that she should be put to death, or he might have had her shut up in a convent." Should the poem have been more explicit? Does Browning's later uncertainty indicate that the poem is badly thought out? Suppose we did not have Browning's comment on line 45; could the line then mean only that he commanded her to stop smiling and that she obeyed? Explain.

6. Evaluate the theory that the duke's speech—especially in view of the last two lines—constitutes an indirect threat to the duke's next wife.

7. Elizabeth Barrett (not yet Mrs. Browning) wrote to Robert Browning that it was not "by the dramatic medium that poets teach most impressively. . . . It is too difficult for the common reader to analyze, and to discern between the vivid and the earnest." She went on, urging him to teach "in the directest and most impressive way, the mask thrown off." What teaching, if any, is in this poem? If there is any teaching here, would it be more impressive if Browning had not used the mask of a Renaissance duke? Explain.

DICTION. From the whole of language, one consciously or unconsciously selects certain words and grammatical constructions; this selection constitutes one's **diction**. It is partly by the diction that we come to know the speaker of a poem. "Amang" and "frae sun to sun" tell us that the speaker of "Mary Morison" is a Scot. In "My Last Duchess" such words as "countenance," "munificence," and "disallowed"—none of which is conceivable in Burns's poem—help us form our impression of the duke. Of course, some words are used in both poems: "I said," "and," "smile[s]," "glance[s]," etc. The fact remains, however, that although a large part of language is shared by all speakers, some parts of language are used only by certain speakers.

Like some words, some grammatical constructions are used only by certain kinds of speakers. Consider these two passages:

> In Adam's fall
> We sinned all.
>
> (from *The New England Primer*)

> Of Man's first disobedience, and the fruit
> Of that forbidden tree whose mortal taste
> Brought death into the World, and all our woe,
> With loss of Eden, till one greater Man
> Restore us, and regain the blissful seat,
> Sing, Heavenly Muse, that, on the secret top
> Of Oreb, or of Sinai, didst inspire
> That shepherd who first taught the chosen seed
> In the beginning how the heavens and earth
> Rose out of Chaos. . . .
>
> (Milton, from *Paradise Lost*)

There is an enormous difference in the diction of these two passages. Milton, speaking as an inspired poet who regards his theme as "a great argument," appropriately uses words and grammatical constructions somewhat removed from common life. Hence, while the anonymous author of the primer speaks directly of "Adam's fall," Milton speaks allusively of the fall, calling it "Man's first disobedience." Milton's sentence is nothing that any Englishman ever said in conversation; its genitive beginning, its length (the sentence continues for six lines beyond the quoted passage), and its postponement of the main verb until the sixth line mark it as the utterance of a poet working in the tradition of Latin poetry. The primer's statement, by its choice of words as well as by its brevity, suggests a far less sophisticated speaker.

TONE. A speaker has attitudes toward himself, his subject, and his audience, and (consciously or unconsciously) he chooses his words, pitch, and modulation accordingly; all these add up to his **tone**. In written literature, tone must be detected without the aid of the ear; the reader must understand by the selection and sequence of words the way (*i.e.*, playfully, angrily, confidentially, ironically, etc.) in which they are meant to be heard. The reader must catch what Frost calls "the speaking tone of voice somehow entangled in the words and fastened to the page for the ear of the imagination." * Some examples will clarify what is meant by "the speaking tone of voice." Innumera-

* This discussion concentrates on the speaker's tone. But one can also talk of the author's tone, that is, of the author's attitude toward his invented speaker. The speaker's tone might, for example, be angry, but the author's tone (as detected by the reader) might be humorous. For further comment on the author's tone, see p. 74.

ble poems present a young man urging a young lady to wake up and enjoy the beauty of a spring morning. But such a young man may speak impatiently, or tenderly, or politely, or cozily. In a song from Shakespeare's *Cymbeline* there is the line "My lady sweet, arise"; in Robert Herrick's "Corinna's Going A-Maying," "Get up, sweet slug-a-bed." In "My lady sweet, arise," we detect a somewhat formal tone, as is entirely proper in the context (a minstrel is serenading a princess at the request of a royal wooer). In "Get up, sweet slug-a-bed," we detect, at least in context, a cozy, intimate, playful tone (the speaker is presumably addressing an intimate friend). One might paraphrase either line as "Wake up, lady," but this restatement distorts both lines because it obliterates the distinctions in diction, tone, and speaker. That paraphrase enervates can easily be seen by comparing Macbeth's

> Where got'st thou that goose look?

with a late seventeenth-century alteration:

> What means thy change of countenance?

The following poem was written by Robert Herrick, but the speaker is not the impatient young man who said (in "Corinna") "Get up, sweet slug-a-bed," though Herrick also wrote that line.

ROBERT HERRICK (1591-1674)

To the Virgins, to Make Much of Time

Gather ye rosebuds while ye may,
  Old Time is still a-flying;
And this same flower that smiles today,
  Tomorrow will be dying.

5 The glorious lamp of heaven, the sun,
  The higher he's a-getting,
The sooner will his race be run,
  And nearer he's to setting.

That age is best which is the first,
10   When youth and blood are warmer;
But being spent, the worse, and worst
  Times, still succeed the former.

Then be not coy, but use your time;
  And while ye may, go marry:
15 For having lost but once your prime,
  You may for ever tarry.

Carpe diem (Latin: "seize the day") is the theme. But if we want to get the full force of the poem, we must understand who is talking to whom. Look, for example, at "Old Time" in line 2. Time is "old," of course, in the sense of having been around a long while, but doesn't "old" in this context suggest also easy familiarity, almost affection? We visit the old school, and our friend is old George. Time is destructive, yes, and the speaker urges the young maidens to make the most of their spring, but the speaker is neither bitter nor importunate; rather, he seems to be the wise old man, the counselor, the man who has made his peace with time, and is giving advice to the young. Time moves rapidly in the poem (the rosebud of line 1 is already a flower in line 3), but the speaker is unhurried; in line 5 he has leisure to explain that the glorious lamp of heaven is the sun.

THE VOICE OF THE SATIRIST. The writer of **satire**, in one way or another, ridicules an aspect or several aspects of human behavior, seeking to arouse in the reader some degree of amused contempt for the object. The line between satire and comedy is not always distinct, but the satirist is always critical, however urbane in tone. By cleverly holding up foibles or vices for the world's derision, satire (Alexander Pope claimed) "heals with morals what it hurts with wit." The laughter of comedy is an end in itself; the laughter of satire is a weapon against the world: "The intellectual dagger," Frank O'Connor called satire, "opposing the real dagger." Jonathan Swift, of whom O'Connor is speaking, insisted that his satires were not malice but medicine:

> His satire points at no defect
> But what all mortals may correct. . . .
> He spared a hump or crooked nose,
> Whose owners set not up for beaux.

But Swift, although he claimed that satire is therapeutic, also saw its futility: "Satire is a sort of glass wherein beholders do generally discover everybody's face but their own."

Sometimes the satirist speaks out directly as defender of public morals, abusively but wittily chopping off heads. Byron, for example, writes:

> Prepare for rhyme—I'll publish, right or wrong:
> Fools are my theme, let Satire be my song.

But sometimes the satirist chooses to invent a speaker far removed from himself, just as Browning chose to invent a Renaissance duke. The satirist may, for example, invent a callous brigadier-general or a pompous judge who unconsciously annihilates himself. E. E. Cummings has a wittily constructed satire in which the speaker is an unusual combination of the satirist and the invented victim:

E. E. CUMMINGS (1894-1962)

next to of course god america i

"next to of course god america i
love you land of the pilgrims' and so forth oh
say can you see by the dawn's early my
country 'tis of centuries come and go
5 and are no more what of it we should worry
in every language even deafanddumb
thy sons acclaim your glorious name by gorry
by jingo by gee by gosh by gum
why talk of beauty what could be more beaut-
10 iful than these heroic happy dead
who rushed like lions to the roaring slaughter
they did not stop to think they died instead
then shall the voice of liberty be mute?"

He spoke. And drank rapidly a glass of water

Cummings might have written, in the voice of a solid citizen or a good poet, a direct attack on chauvinistic windbags; instead, he chose to invent a windbag whose rhetoric punctures itself. Yet the last line tells that we are really hearing someone who is recounting what the windbag said; that is, the speaker of all the lines but the last is a sort of combination of the chauvinist *and* the satiric observer of the chauvinist. (When Cummings himself recited these lines there was mockery in his voice.) Only in the final line of the poem does the author seem to speak entirely on his own, and even here he adopts a matter-of-fact pose that is far more potent than **invective** (direct abuse) would be. Yet the last line is not totally free of explicit hostility. It might, for example, have run, "He spoke. And poured slowly a glass of water." Why does this version lack the punch of Cummings'? And what is implied by the absence of a final period in line 14?

WALTER DE LA MARE (1873-1956)

An Epitaph

Here lies a most beautiful lady:
Light of step and heart was she;
I think she was the most beautiful lady
That ever was in the West Country.
But beauty vanishes; beauty passes;
However rare—rare it be;
And when I crumble, who will remember
This lady of the West Country?

THE SPEAKING TONE OF VOICE 339

1. Comment on the speaker of this poem.

2. Does the simple language lack dignity? In popular ballads a disyllable at the end of a line has the stress in the second syllable, as "sailor" in "Sir Patrick Spence" (page 311). What effect is gained here by rhyming "Country" and "she" and "be"?

3. What is the effect of the abundant pauses in the poem?

4. Do the last two lines introduce a new idea, or deepen the implications of earlier lines? Explain.

WILLIAM BUTLER YEATS (1865-1939)

No Second Troy

Why should I blame her that she filled my days
With misery, or that she would of late
Have taught to ignorant men most violent ways,
Or hurled the little streets upon the great,
5 Had they but courage equal to desire?
What could have made her peaceful with a mind
That nobleness made simple as a fire,
With beauty like a tightened bow, a kind
That is not natural in an age like this,
10 Being high and solitary and most stern?
Why, what could she have done, being what she is?
Was there another Troy for her to burn?

QUESTIONS: *No Second Troy*

1. The poem is about Maud Gonne, a beautiful Irishwoman who devoted most of her life to exhorting the Irish to rebel against the English. To whom is she compared in this poem?

2. What is the tone of lines 1-5? Forgiving? Angry? Bitter? What is the speaker's tone at the end of the poem?

3. Paraphrase line 4. How does it convey the speaker's attitude? Comment on the appropriateness of the comparisons in lines 7-8.

GERARD MANLEY HOPKINS (1844-1889)

Spring and Fall: To a Young Child

Márgarét, are you gríeving
Over Goldengrove unleaving?
Leáves, líke the things of man, you
With your fresh thoughts care for, can you?

5 Áh! ás the heart grows older
It will come to such sights colder
By and by, nor spare a sigh
Though worlds of wanwood leafmeal lie;
And yet you wíll weep and know why.
10 Now no matter, child, the name:
Sórrow's spríngs áre the same.
Nor mouth had, no nor mind, expressed
What heart heard of, ghost guessed:
It ís the blight man was born for,
15 It is Margaret you mourn for.

QUESTIONS: *Spring and Fall*

1. What is the speaker's age? His tone? What is the relevance of the title to the speaker and to Margaret? What meanings are in "Fall"?

2. What is meant by Margaret's "fresh thoughts" (line 4)? Paraphrase lines 3-4 and lines 12-13.

3. "Wanwood" and "leafmeal" are neologisms coined by Hopkins. What are their suggestions?

4. Why is it not contradictory for the speaker to say that Margaret weeps for herself (line 15) after saying that she weeps for "Goldengrove unleaving" (line 2)?

JOHN UPDIKE (1932-   )

Youth's Progress

Dick Schneider of Wisconsin . . . was elected
"Greek God" for an interfraternity ball.
                                        —*Life*

When I was born, my mother taped my ears
So they lay flat. When I had aged ten years,
My teeth were firmly braced and much improved.
Two years went by; my tonsils were removed.

5 At fourteen, I began to comb my hair
A fancy way. Though nothing much was there,
I shaved my upper lip—next year, my chin.
At seventeen, the freckles left my skin.

Just turned nineteen, a nicely molded lad,
10 I said goodbye to Sis and Mother; Dad
Drove me to Wisconsin and set me loose.
At twenty-one, I was elected Zeus.

1. Suppose the first two lines ran thus:

> To keep them flat, my mother taped my ears;
> And then, at last, when I had aged ten years. . . .

How does the revision destroy the special tone of voice in the original two lines? (Note that in the revision there is a heavy pause at the end of the first line.) Why, in the second line of the revision, is "at last" false to the "tone" or "voice" in the rest of the poem?

2. What is the speaker's attitude toward himself? What is the poet's attitude toward the speaker?

3. The poem is in pairs of rhyming lines. Why does the poet divide it into three stanzas?

ARTHUR FREEMAN (1938-   )

Cut Laurels

Among the last acts of the lady in the park
whose face is crumpled as a cabbage, and whose pinched eyes
glint like oysters in the settling dark,
has been in perfect silence to have gazed

5 past the unpardonable children churning turf,
the lovers tangled on the benches, the brisk prams
and chipper nannies, to the tarnished rump
of the benign brass stallion of a king of France

for thirty minutes; for three hundred years
10 rider and horse have seemed about to part,
such pedestalled impatience paws the air.
But execution is the tease of art,

and rather, the old lady it will be,
shouldering her sackcloth, who must rise,
15 resigned to living, and lag home to sleep
and die, as, ultimately, you and I.

QUESTIONS: *Cut Laurels*

1. The poem moves in preoccupation from "the lady in the park" to "you and I." How does it justify this movement? How does the change of tense in the verbs assist?

2. What tone does the poem establish toward (*a*) the old woman, (*b*) the children, nannies, etc., and (*c*) the statue? What implication *re* sympathy can we derive? Is the concept of "sympathy" germane to the poem?

3. Elucidate the connotations of words like "last acts" (line 1), "perfect" (line 4), "execution" (line 12), "ultimately" (line 16), and the title itself. Do these aid in agreeing upon a single "point" of the poem?

MARIANNE MOORE (1887-   )

Silence

My father used to say,
"Superior people never make long visits,
have to be shown Longfellow's grave
or the glass flowers at Harvard.
5 Self-reliant like the cat—
that takes its prey to privacy,
the mouse's limp tail hanging like a shoelace from its mouth—
they sometimes enjoy solitude,
and can be robbed of speech
10 by speech which has delighted them.
The deepest feeling always shows itself in silence;
not in silence, but restraint."
Nor was he insincere in saying, "Make my house your inn."
Inns are not residences.

QUESTIONS: *Silence*

1. How does the first line affect the tone of the rest of the poem?

2. Evaluate the opinion that the comparison in lines 5-8 is needlessly expanded. Paraphrase lines 9-10 and relate them to lines 5-8.

3. In the last line, why "residences" instead of "homes"?

4. What is the connection between the last two lines and the rest of the poem?

THOMAS GRAY (1716-1771)

Ode on the Death of a Favorite Cat Drowned in a Tub of Gold-Fishes

'Twas on a lofty vase's side,
Where China's gayest art had dyed
    The azure flowers that blow;
Demurest of the tabby kind,
5 The pensive Selima reclined,
    Gazed on the lake below.

Her conscious tail her joy declared;
The fair round face, the snowy beard,
   The velvet of her paws,
10 Her coat, that with the tortoise vies,
Her ears of jet, and emerald eyes,
   She saw; and purred applause.

Still had she gazed; but midst the tide
Two angel forms were seen to glide,
15   The Genii° of the stream: *guardian spirits*
Their scaly armor's Tyrian hue
Through richest purple to the view
   Betrayed a golden gleam.

The hapless nymph with wonder saw:
20 A whisker first, and then a claw,
   With many an ardent wish,
She stretched in vain to reach the prize.
What female heart can gold despise?
   What cat's averse to fish?

25 Presumptuous maid! with looks intent
Again she stretched, again she bent,
   Nor knew the gulf between.
(Malignant Fate sat by, and smiled.)
The slipp'ry verge her feet beguiled;
30   She tumbled headlong in.

Eight times emerging from the flood
She mewed to ev'ry wat'ry god,
   Some speedy aid to send.
No dolphin* came, no Nereid stirred:
35 Nor cruel Tom, nor Susan heard.
   A fav'rite has no friend!

From hence, ye beauties, undeceived,
Know, one false step is ne'er retrieved,
   And be with caution bold.
40 Not all that tempts your wand'ring eyes
And heedless hearts is lawful prize;
   Nor all that glisters, gold.

QUESTIONS: *On the Death of a Favorite Cat*

1. **A mock heroic** poem does not mock the heroic but mocks a trivial subject by treating it in the elevated terms normally reserved for heroic subjects. Its elevated diction (*e.g.*, "lake" in line 6, for a tub of water) produces a comic effect. What examples are here? What comic juxtapositions? What is the tone of the poem?

* Legend held that Arion, a Greek musician, was saved by a dolphin.

2. Is this a satire on cats? What does the cat come to represent?

3. Explain the paradox in line 36. Is the explicit moralizing (*e.g.*, line 36, lines 37-42) offensive? Explain.

4. Dr. Johnson said of this poem: "The poem *On the Cat* was doubtless by its author considered as a trifle, but it is not a happy trifle. . . . The sixth stanza contains a melancholy truth, that 'a favorite has no friend'; but the last ends in a pointed sentence of no relation to the purpose: if *what glistered* had been *gold*, the cat would not have gone into the water; and if she had, would not less have been drowned." Evaluate Johnson's comment.

EZRA POUND (*1885-*   )

From Hugh Selwyn Mauberley

II

The age demanded an image
Of its accelerated grimace,
Something for the modern stage,
Not, at any rate, an Attic grace;

5 Not, not certainly, the obscure reveries
Of the inward gaze;
Better mendacities
Than the classics in paraphrase!

The "age demanded" chiefly a mould in plaster,
10 Made with no loss of time,
A prose kinema, not, not assuredly, alabaster
Or the "sculpture" of rhyme.

This poem is from a sequence of poems entitled "Hugh Selwyn Mauberley" (1919). The setting is London after World War I.

QUESTIONS: *The age demanded*

1. What quality do the first two lines attribute to the age?

2. What aspects of the present age is the speaker condemning? Is the implication in "accelerated" (line 2) picked up later in the poem?

3. How is "kinema" in line 11 related both to the preceding line and to the succeeding line?

4. Why is "age demanded" (line 9) in quotation marks?

5. What effect is gained by the repetitions and variations in "Not, at any rate" (line 4), "Not, not certainly" (line 5), and "not, not assuredly" (line 11)?

6. Ezra Pound (in *Literary Essays*) says, "Satire reminds one that certain things are not worth while. It draws one to consider time wasted." Does Pound's remark apply to his own poem? Explain.

JOHN MILLINGTON SYNGE (1871-1909)

The Curse

To a sister of an enemy of the author's
who disapproved of "The Playboy"

Lord, confound this surly sister,
Blight her brow with blotch and blister,
Cramp her larynx, lung, and liver,
In her guts a galling give her.

5 Let her live to earn her dinners
In Mountjoy with seedy sinners:
Lord, this judgment quickly bring,
And I'm Your servant, J. M. Synge.

The dedication alludes to Synge's comedy, *The Playboy of the Western World*. "Mountjoy" in line 6 is a prison in Dublin.

QUESTIONS: *The Curse*

1. What qualities in this poem make it resemble a charm or a spell?

2. Is "The Curse" an example of invective? What is the first hint of comedy?

3. In a draft of the poem, the next-to-last line runs: "Lord these torments quickly bring." Is the revision better? Why?

Ten

FIGURATIVE LANGUAGE:

Simile, Metaphor, Personification, Apostrophe

Hippolyta. 'Tis strange, my Theseus, that these lovers speak of.
Theseus. More strange than true. I never may believe
These antique fables, nor these fairy toys.
Lovers and madmen have such seething brains,
Such shaping fantasies, that apprehend
More than cool reason ever comprehends.
The lunatic, the lover, and the poet,
Are of imagination all compact.
One sees more devils than vast hell can hold,
That is the madman. The lover, all as frantic,
Sees Helen's beauty in a brow of Egypt.
The poet's eye, in a fine frenzy rolling,
Doth glance from heaven to earth, from earth to heaven;
And as imagination bodies forth
The forms of things unknown, the poet's pen
Turns them to shapes, and gives to airy nothing
A local habitation and a name.
Such tricks hath strong imagination,
That, if it would but apprehend some joy,
It comprehends the bringer of that joy;
Or in the night, imagining some fear,
How easy is a bush suppos'd a bear!

A Midsummer Night's Dream, V. i. 1-22

Theseus was neither the first nor the last to suggest that poets, like lunatics and lovers, freely employ their imagination. Terms such as "poetic license" and "poetic justice" imply that poets are free to depict a never-never land. One has only to leaf through any anthology of poetry to encounter numerous statements that are, from a logical point of view, lunacies. Here are a few:

347

Look like th' innocent flower,
But be the serpent under 't.   (Shakespeare)

Each outcry from the hunted hare
A fiber from the brain does tear.   (William Blake)

Every thread of summer is at last unwoven.   (Wallace Stevens)

On a literal level such assertions are nonsense (so, too, is Theseus' notion that reason is cool). But of course they are not to be taken literally; rather, they employ **figures of speech**—departures from logical usage that are aimed at gaining special effects. Consider the lunacies that Robert Burns heaps up here:

ROBERT BURNS (1759-1796)

A Red, Red Rose

O, my luve is like a red, red rose,
    That's newly sprung in June.
O, my luve is like the melodie,
    That's sweetly played in tune.

5 As fair art thou, my bonnie lass,
    So deep in luve am I,
And I will luve thee still, my dear,
    Till a'° the seas gang° dry.   *all; go*

Till a' the seas gang dry, my dear,
10   And the rocks melt wi' the sun!
And I will luve thee still, my dear,
    While the sands o' life shall run.

And fare thee weel, my only luve,
    And fare thee weel awhile!
15 And I will come again, my luve,
    Though it were ten thousand mile!

To the charge that these lines are lunacies or untruths, at least two replies can be made. First, it might be said that the speaker is not really making assertions about a girl; he is saying he feels a certain way. His words, it can be argued, are not assertions about external reality, but expressions of his state of mind, just as a tune one whistles asserts nothing about external reality but expresses the whistler's state of mind. In this view, the non-logical language of poetry (like groans of pain and exclamations of joy) is an expression of emotion; its further aim, if it has one, is to induce in the hearer an emotion. Second, and more to the point here, it can be said that non-logical language does indeed make assertions about external reality, and even gives the reader an insight into this reality that logical language cannot. For example, the opening comparison in Burns's poem brings before our eyes the lady's beauty in a way that the reasonable assertion "She is beautiful" does not. She is fragrant; her skin is perhaps like a rose in texture and (in some measure) color; she will not keep her beauty long. The poet, that is, has communicated a state of mind, and has even discovered some things (both in the beloved and in the lover's own feelings) that interest us. His discovery is not world-shaking; it is less important than the discovery of America, or the discovery that the meek are blessed, but it *is* a discovery and it provides the reader with the feeling, "Yes, that's right. I hadn't quite thought of it that way, but that's right." A poem, Robert Frost said, "assumes direction with the first line laid down, . . . runs a course of lucky events, and ends in a clarification of life—not necessarily a great clarification, such as sects and cults are founded on, but in a momentary stay against confusion." What is clarified? In another paragraph Frost provides an answer: "For me the initial delight is in the surprise of remembering something I didn't know I knew." John Keats has a similar statement: "Poetry . . . should strike the Reader as a wording of his own highest thoughts, and appear almost a Remembrance."

SIMILE. In a **simile** items from different classes are explicitly compared by a connective such as "like," "as," or "than," or by a verb such as "appears" or "seems." (If the objects compared are from the same class, *e.g.*, "New York is like London," no simile is present.)

How like a marriage is the season of clouds.　　(James Merrill)

It is a beauteous evening, calm and free.
The holy time is quiet as a Nun,
Breathless with adoration.　　(Wordsworth)

How sharper than a serpent's tooth it is
To have a thankless child.　　(Shakespeare)

Seems he a dove? His feathers are but borrowed.　　(Shakespeare)

The following poem develops the simile to unusual length.

RICHARD WILBUR (1921-　　)
Mind

Mind in its purest play is like some bat
That beats about in caverns all alone,
Contriving by a kind of senseless wit
Not to conclude against a wall of stone.

5 It has no need to falter or explore;
Darkly it knows what obstacles are there,
And so may weave and flitter, dip and soar
In perfect courses through the blackest air.

And has this simile a like perfection?
10 The mind is like a bat. Precisely. Save
That in the very happiest intellection
A graceful error may correct the cave.

METAPHOR. A **metaphor** asserts the identity, without a connective such as "like" or a verb such as "appears," of terms that are literally incompatible.

She is the rose, the glory of the day.   (Spenser)

O western orb sailing the heaven.   (Whitman)

Notice how in the last example only one of the terms ("orb") is stated; the other ("ship") is implied in "sailing." In the following poem, Keats's excitement on reading Chapman's translation of Homer is communicated first through a metaphor and then through a simile.

JOHN KEATS (1795-1821)

On First Looking into Chapman's Homer

Much have I traveled in the realms of gold,
And many goodly states and kingdoms seen;
Round many western islands have I been
Which bards in fealty to Apollo hold.
5 Oft of one wide expanse have I been told
That deep-browed Homer ruled as his demesne;
Yet did I never breathe its pure serene
Till I heard Chapman speak out loud and bold:

Then felt I like some watcher of the skies
10 When a new planet swims into his ken;
Or like stout Cortez when with eagle eyes
He stared at the Pacific—and all his men
Looked at each other with a wild surmise—
Silent, upon a peak in Darien.

QUESTIONS: *On First Looking into Chapman's Homer*

1. In line 1, what does "realms of gold" stand for? Chapman was an Elizabethan; how does this fact add relevance to the metaphor in the first line?

2. Does the simile in line 9 introduce a totally new idea, or is it somewhat connected to the opening metaphor?

Two types of metaphor deserve special mention. In **synecdoche**, the whole is replaced by the part, or the part by the whole. For example, "bread," in "Give us this day our daily bread," replaces the whole class of edibles; and in Shakespeare's "Unpleasing to a married ear" (page 324), "ear" stands for the whole man and, in fact, for all married men. In **metonymy**, something is named that replaces something closely related to it. For example, James Shirley names certain objects, using them to replace social classes to which they are related:

> Scepter and crown must tumble down
> And in the dust be equal made
> With the poor crooked scythe and spade

PERSONIFICATION. The attribution of human feelings or characteristics to abstractions or to inanimate objects is called **personification**.

> But Time did beckon to the flowers, and they
> By noon most cunningly did steal away.   (Herbert)

Herbert attributes a human gesture to Time and shrewdness to flowers. Of all figures, personification most surely gives to airy nothings a local habitation and a name:

> There's Wrath who has learnt every trick of guerilla warfare,
> The shamming dead, the night-raid, the feinted retreat.
>   (Auden)

> Hope, thou bold taster of delight.   (Crashaw)

The figure was specially popular in the eighteenth century; Dr. Johnson's elegy, "On the Death of Mr. Robert Levet" (page 327) uses it throughout.

APOSTROPHE. Crashaw's personification, "Hope, thou bold taster of delight," is also an example of the figure called **apostrophe**, an address to a person or thing not literally listening. Wordsworth begins a sonnet by apostrophizing Milton:

> Milton, thou shouldst be living at this hour,

and Shelley begins an ode by apostrophizing a skylark:

> Hail to thee, blithe Spirit!

Here is a poem largely built on apostrophe:

Simile, Metaphor, Personification, Apostrophe 351

EDMUND WALLER (1606-1687)

Song

Go, lovely rose,
Tell her that wastes her time and me,
  That now she knows,
When I resemble her to thee,
5   How sweet and fair she seems to be.

Tell her that's young,
And shuns to have her graces spied,
  That hadst thou sprung
In deserts where no men abide,
10   Thou must have uncommended died.

Small is the worth
Of beauty from the light retired:
  Bid her come forth,
Suffer her self to be desired,
15   And not blush so to be admired.

Then die, that she
The common fate of all things rare
  May read in thee,
How small a part of time they share,
20   That are so wondrous sweet and fair.

What conclusions, then, can we draw about figurative language? First, **figurative language**, with its literally incompatible terms, forces the reader to attend to the connotations (suggestions, associations) rather than to the denotations (dictionary definitions) of one of the terms. Second, although figurative language is said to differ from ordinary discourse, it is found in ordinary discourse as well as in literature. "It rained cats and dogs," "War is hell," "Don't be a pig," "Mr. Know-all," and other tired figures comprise part of our daily utterances. But through repeated use these (and most of the figures we use) have lost whatever impact they once had and are only a shade removed from expressions which, though once figurative, have become literal: the *eye* of a needle, a *branch* office, the *face* of a clock. Third, good figurative language is usually (*a*) concrete, (*b*) condensed, and (*c*) interesting. The concreteness lends precision and vividness; when Keats writes that he felt "like some watcher of the skies/When a new planet swims into his ken," he more sharply characterizes his feelings than if he had said, "I felt excited." His simile isolates for us a precise kind of excitement, and the metaphoric "swims" vividly brings up the oceanic aspect of the sky. The second of these three qualities, condensation, can be seen by attempting to paraphrase some of the figures.

A paraphrase will commonly use more words than the original and it will have less impact—as the gradual coming of night usually has less impact on us than a sudden darkening of the sky, or as a prolonged push has less impact than a sudden blow. (Whether or not Richard Wilbur's "Mind," on page 349, illustrates the principle of condensation is worth discussing.) The third quality, interest, is largely dependent on the previous two: the successful figure often makes us open our eyes wider and take notice. Keats's "deep-browed Homer" arouses our interest in Homer as "thoughtful Homer" or "meditative Homer" does not. Similarly, when W. B. Yeats says (page 366):

> An aged man is but a paltry thing,
> A tattered coat upon a stick, unless
> Soul clap its hands and sing, and louder sing
> For every tatter in its mortal dress,

the metaphoric identification of an old man with a scarecrow jolts us out of all our usual unthinking attitudes about old men as kind, happy folk content to have passed from youth into age.

Finally, two points must be made: first, figurative language is not a *sine qua non* in poetry, and second, a poem that seems to contain no figures may in fact be one extended figure. Let us take the first point first. The anonymous ballad "Edward" (page 314) contains no figures; Shakespeare's "Winter" (page 324) contains only a few inconspicuous figures, yet surely these are poems and no one would say that more figures would make them better poems. Here is another poem that employs no figures, the epigraph to Robert Frost's *Collected Poems*:

ROBERT FROST (1874-1963)

The Pasture

I'm going out to clean the pasture spring;
I'll only stop to rake leaves away
(And wait to watch the water clear, I may):
I sha'n't be gone long.—You come too.

I'm going out to fetch the little calf
That's standing by the mother. It's so young,
It totters when she licks it with her tongue.
I sha'n't be gone long.—You come too.

There is nothing here that cannot be taken literally; a man might have said this to someone, and there is not a word in it that is illogical. Yet surely it is a poem. Now for the second point, that an entire poem may be an extended figure. By placing "The Pasture" at the opening of his *Collected Poems,* Frost allows us to read it as a figure; the invitation to accompany the speaker on a trip to the pasture can easily be read as an invitation to accompany the poet on a trip to the poet's world—his poems.

EMILY DICKINSON (*1830-1886*)

Because I Could Not Stop for Death

Because I could not stop for Death—
He kindly stopped for me—
The Carriage held but just Ourselves—
And Immortality.

5 We slowly drove—He knew no haste
And I had put away
My labor and my leisure too,
For His Civility—

We passed the School, where Children strove
10 At Recess—in the Ring—
We passed the Fields of Gazing Grain—
We passed the Setting Sun—

Or rather—He passed Us—
The Dews drew quivering and chill—
15 For only Gossamer, my Gown—
My Tippet—only Tulle—

We paused before a House that seemed
A Swelling of the Ground—
The Roof was scarcely visible—
20 The Cornice—in the Ground—

Since then—'tis Centuries—and yet
Feels shorter than the Day
I first surmised the Horses Heads
Were toward Eternity—

QUESTIONS: *Because I Could Not Stop for Death*

1. Characterize death as it appears in lines 1-8.

2. What is the significance of the details and their arrangement in the third stanza? Why "strove" rather than "played" (line 9)? What meanings does "Ring" (line 10) have? Is "Gazing Grain" better than "Golden Grain"?

3. What is the "House" in the fifth stanza? Does this stanza introduce an aspect of death not present—or present only very faintly —in the rest of the poem? Explain.

4. Evaluate this statement about the poem (from Yvor Winters'

Here is a poem that stands on the border between metaphor and symbol. With half our mind we say, "Well, clearly the seed and flower are metaphors, standing for . . ." but suddenly we are caught, and are not quite sure how to go on.

JON SWAN (1929-   )
The Opening

Seed said to flower:
    You are too rich and wide.
    You spend too soon and loosely
    That grave and spacious beauty
5   I keep secret, inside.
    You will die of your pride.

Flower said to seed:
    Each opens, gladly
    Or in defeat. Clenched, close,
10   You hold a hidden rose
    That will break you to be
    Free of your dark modesty.

WALLACE STEVENS (1879-1955)
Anecdote of the Jar

I placed a jar in Tennessee,
And round it was, upon a hill.
It made the slovenly wilderness
Surround that hill.

5   The wilderness rose up to it,
And sprawled around, no longer wild.
The jar was round upon the ground
And tall and of a port in air.

It took dominion everywhere.
10   The jar was gray and bare.
It did not give of bird or bush,
Like nothing else in Tennessee.

---

accompanying attitude and feelings (which may work mainly in one or in both directions) from one object to another. If I began to think and feel about a man, in certain respects, as I did about my father, and to treat him as I treated my father, then he becomes a father symbol for me. Analogously, in fictional contexts, when we transfer trains of thought and the related attitudes and feelings from one object to another, a symbol is established." *Poetic Discourse* (Berkeley: University of California Press, 1958, p. 138).

Stevens, asked for an interpretation of another poem, said (in *The Explicator*, November, 1948): "Things that have their origin in the imagination or in the emotions (poems) . . . very often take on a form that is ambiguous or uncertain. It is not possible to attach a single, rational meaning to such things without destroying the imaginative or emotional ambiguity or uncertainty that is inherent in them and that is why poets do not like to explain. That the meanings given by others are sometimes meanings not intended by the poet or that were never present in his mind does not impair them as meanings."

QUESTIONS: *Anecdote of the Jar*

1. What is the meaning of line 8? Check "port" in a dictionary.

2. Does the poem suggest that the jar organizes slovenly nature, or that the jar impoverishes abundant nature? Or both, or neither? Is the jar a symbol of the imagination, or of the arts, or of man's material progress?

ALFRED, LORD TENNYSON (1809-1892)

The Kraken

Below the thunders of the upper deep,
Far, far beneath in the abysmal sea,
His ancient, dreamless, uninvaded sleep
The Kraken* sleepeth: faintest sunlights flee
5 About his shadowy sides; above him swell
Huge sponges of millennial growth and height;
And far away into the sickly light,
From many a wondrous grot and secret cell
Unnumber'd and enormous polypi
10 Winnow with giant arms the slumbering green.
There hath he lain for ages, and will lie
Battening upon huge sea-worms in his sleep,
Until the latter fire shall heat the deep;
Then once by man and angels to be seen,
15 In roaring he shall rise and on the surface die.

QUESTIONS: *The Kraken*

1. What does "millennial" (line 6) mean? What religious suggestions are in "latter fire" (line 13) and "he shall rise" (line 15)? In view of the last three lines, do the first ten lines take on the suggestion of a weird underwater Eden? Explain.

* The kraken is a fabulous Scandinavian sea monster.

2. What effect is gained by the repeated "and's" in lines 6-9?

3. The last line has more syllables than the previous lines; what effect is thus gained?

4. What is the speaker's tone?

When Coleridge published "Kubla Khan" in 1816, he prefixed it with the following explanatory note:

> The following fragment is here published at the request of a poet of great and deserved celebrity, and, as far as the author's own opinions are concerned, rather as a psychological curiosity, than on the ground of any supposed *poetic* merits.
>
> In the summer of the year 1797, the author, then in ill health, had retired to a lonely farmhouse between Porlock and Linton, on the Exmoor confines of Somerset and Devonshire. In consequence of a slight indisposition, an anodyne had been prescribed, from the effects of which he fell asleep in his chair at the moment that he was reading the following sentence, or words of the same substance, in *Purchas's Pilgrimage*: "Here the Khan Kubla commanded a palace to be built, and a stately garden thereunto. And thus ten miles of fertile ground were inclosed with a wall." The author continued for about three hours in a profound sleep, at least of the external senses, during which time he has the most vivid confidence that he could not have composed less than from two to three hundred lines; if that indeed can be called composition in which all the images rose up before him as *things*, with a parallel production of the correspondent expressions, without any sensation or consciousness of effort. On awaking he appeared to himself to have a distinct recollection of the whole, and taking his pen, ink, and paper, instantly and eagerly wrote down the lines that are here preserved. At this moment he was unfortunately called out by a person on business from Porlock, and detained by him above an hour, and on his return to his room, found, to his no small surprise and mortification, that though he still retained some vague and dim recollection of the general purport of the vision, yet, with the exception of some eight or ten scattered lines and images, all the rest had passed away like the images on the surface of a stream into which a stone has been cast, but, alas! without the after restoration of the latter!

Then all the charm

Is broken—all that phantom world so fair
Vanishes, and a thousand circlets spread,
And each misshape[s] the other. Stay awhile,
Poor youth! who scarcely dar'st lift up thine eyes—
The stream will soon renew its smoothness, soon

The visions will return! And lo, he stays,
And soon the fragments dim of lovely forms
Come trembling back, unite, and now once more
The pool becomes a mirror.
       [From Coleridge's *The Picture; or, the Lover's Resolution*,
                                                          lines 91-100]

Yet from the still surviving recollections in his mind, the author has frequently purposed to finish for himself what had been originally, as it were, given to him. Σαμερον αδιον ασω [to-day I shall sing more sweetly]: but the tomorrow is yet to come.

SAMUEL TAYLOR COLERIDGE (1772-1834)

Kubla Khan

OR, A VISION IN A DREAM. A FRAGMENT.

In Xanadu did Kubla Khan
A stately pleasure-dome decree:
Where Alph, the sacred river, ran
Through caverns measureless to man
5   Down to a sunless sea.
So twice five miles of fertile ground
With walls and towers were girdled round:
And here were gardens bright with sinuous rills,
Where blossomed many an incense-bearing tree;
10 And here were forests ancient as the hills,
Enfolding sunny spots of greenery.
But oh! that deep romantic chasm which slanted
Down the green hill athwart a cedarn cover!
A savage place! as holy and enchanted
15 As e'er beneath a waning moon was haunted
By woman wailing for her demon-lover!
And from this chasm, with ceaseless turmoil seething,
As if this earth in fast thick pants were breathing
A mighty fountain momently was forced;
20 Amid whose swift half-intermitted burst
Huge fragments vaulted like rebounding hail,
Or chaffy grain beneath the thresher's flail:
And 'mid these dancing rocks at once and ever
It flung up momently the sacred river.
25 Five miles meandering with a mazy motion
Through wood and dale the sacred river ran,

Then reached the caverns measureless to man,
And sank in tumult to a lifeless ocean:
And 'mid this tumult Kubla heard from far
30 Ancestral voices prophesying war!

    The shadow of the dome of pleasure
    Floated midway on the waves;
    Where was heard the mingled measure
    From the fountain and the caves.
35 It was a miracle of rare device,
A sunny pleasure-dome with caves of ice!
    A damsel with a dulcimer
    In a vision once I saw:
    It was an Abyssinian maid,
40   And on her dulcimer she played,
    Singing of Mount Abora.
    Could I revive within me
    Her symphony and song,
    To such a deep delight 'twould win me,
45 That with music loud and long,
I would build that dome in air,
That sunny dome! those caves of ice!
And all who heard should see them there,
And all should cry, Beware! Beware!
50 His flashing eyes, his floating hair!
Weave a circle round him thrice,
And close your eyes with holy dread,
For he on honey-dew hath fed,
And drunk the milk of Paradise.

QUESTIONS: *Kubla Khan*

1. Coleridge changed the "palace" of his source into a "dome"
line 2). What are the relevant associations of "dome"?

2. What pairs of contrasts (*e.g.*, underground river, fountain)
o you find? What do they contribute to the poem?

3. If Coleridge had not said that the poem is a fragment, might
: seem to us to be a complete poem, the first thirty-six lines describ-
ng the creative imagination, and the remainder lamenting the loss of
oetic power?

WILLIAM BUTLER YEATS (1865-1939)

Sailing to Byzantium

I

That is no country for old men. The young
In one another's arms, birds in the trees
—Those dying generations—at their song,
The salmon-falls, the mackerel-crowded seas,
5 Fish, flesh, or fowl, commend all summer long
Whatever is begotten, born, and dies.
Caught in that sensual music all neglect
Monuments of unageing intellect.

II

An aged man is but a paltry thing,
10 A tattered coat upon a stick, unless
Soul clap its hands and sing, and louder sing
For every tatter in its mortal dress,
Nor is there singing school but studying
Monuments of its own magnificence;
15 And therefore I have sailed the seas and come
To the holy city of Byzantium.

III

O sages standing in God's holy fire
As in the gold mosaic of a wall,
Come from the holy fire, perne° in a gyre,   *whirl down*
20 And be the singing-masters of my soul.
Consume my heart away; sick with desire
And fastened to a dying animal
It knows not what it is; and gather me
Into the artifice of eternity.

IV

25 Once out of nature I shall never take
My bodily form from any natural thing,
But such a form as Grecian goldsmiths make
Of hammered gold and gold enameling
To keep a drowsy Emperor awake;
30 Or set upon a golden bough to sing
To lords and ladies of Byzantium
Of what is past, or passing, or to come.

Byzantium was the ancient city on whose site Constantinople (now
Istanbul) was built. The capital of the Eastern Roman Empire (330 to
1453) and the "holy city" of the Greek Orthodox Church, its culture

noted for mysticism, the preservation of ancient learning, and exquisitely refined symbolic art. In short, its culture (as Yeats saw it)
was wise and passionless. In A Vision, his prose treatment of his complex mystical system, Yeats says:

> I think that in early Byzantium, maybe never before or since
> in recorded history, religious, aesthetic and practical life were
> one, that architect and artificers—though not, it may be, poets, for
> language had been the instrument of controversy and must have
> grown abstract—spoke to the multitude and the few alike. The
> painter, the mosaic worker, the worker in gold and silver, the
> illuminator of sacred books, were almost impersonal, almost per-
> haps without the consciousness of individual design, absorbed in
> their subject matter and that the vision of the whole people. They
> could copy out of old Gospel books those pictures that seemed as
> sacred as the text, and yet weave all into a vast design, the work of
> many that seemed the work of one, that made building, picture,
> pattern, metal-work of rail and lamp, seem but a single image.

QUESTIONS: *Sailing to Byzantium*

1. Re-read the first two stanzas. To what does "That" (line 1)
refer? Is the description in lines 2-8 contemptuous? Why does the
speaker go to Byzantium? What is meant by lines 9-12?

2. What are the "Monuments of unageing intellect" (line 8)?

3. How does "animal" (line 22) look back to the first stanza
and ahead to the fourth stanza?

4. What, if anything, does the golden bird (lines 27-30) stand
for? How does it make a contrast to the birds of line 2?

5. What idea is common to the final line of each stanza? Why?

Twelve

IRONY AND PARADOX

There is a kind of discourse which, though non-literal, need not use similes, metaphors, apostrophes, personification, or symbols. A speaker, without using these figures, may say things that are not to be taken literally. He may, in short, employ **irony**. In Greek comedy the *eiron* was the sly underdog who, by dissembling inferiority, outwitted his opponent. As Aristotle put it, irony (employed by the *eiron*) is a "pretense tending toward the under-side" of truth. Later, Cicero somewhat altered the meaning of the word: he defined it as saying one thing and meaning another (*aliud dicere ac sentias*), and he held that Socrates, who feigned ignorance and let his opponents entrap themselves in their own arguments, was the ironist par excellence. In **verbal irony**, as the term is now used, what is stated is in some degree negated by what is suggested. A classic example is Lady Macbeth's order to get ready for King Duncan's visit: "He that's coming/Must be provided for." The words seem to say that she and Macbeth must busy themselves with household preparations so that the king may be received in appropriate style, but this suggestion of hospitality is undercut by an opposite meaning: preparations must be made for the murder of the king. Two other examples of verbal irony are Rosalind's observation (in *As You Like It*) that:

Men have died from time to time;

and the lover's assertion (in Marvell's "To His Coy Mistress") that:

The grave's a fine and private place,
But none, I think, do there embrace.

Under Marvell's cautious words we detect a wryness; the **understatement** masks yet reveals a deep-felt awareness of mortality and the barrenness of the grave. The self-mockery in this understatement proclaims modesty, but suggests assurance. The speaker here, like most ironists, is both playful and serious at once. Irony packs a great deal into a few words.*

Overstatement (hyperbole) as well as understatement is ironic when it contains a contradictory suggestion:

> For Brutus is an honorable man;
> So are they all, all honorable men.

Similarly, Alexander Pope damns the proud not with faint praise but with encouragement to be yet more proud:

> Go, wiser thou! and, in thy scale of sense,
> Weigh thy opinion against Providence. . . .
> Snatch from His hand the balance of the rod,
> Re-judge His justice, be the God of God.

The sense of contradiction that is inherent in verbal irony is also inherent in a paradox. **Paradox** has several meanings for philosophers, but we need only be concerned with its meaning of an apparent contradiction. In Gerard Manley Hopkins' "Spring and Fall" (page 340), there is an apparent contradiction in the assertions that Margaret is weeping for the woods (line 2), and for herself (line 15), but the contradiction is not real: both the woods and Margaret are parts of the nature blighted by Adam's sin. Other paradoxes are:

> The child is father of the man   (Wordsworth)

and (on the soldiers who died to preserve the British Empire):

> The saviors come not home tonight;
>   Themselves they could not save;   (Housman)

and:

> One short sleep past, we wake eternally,
> And Death shall be no more; Death thou shalt die.   (Donne)

Donne's lines are a reminder that paradox is not only an instrument of the poet. Christianity embodies several paradoxes: God became man; through the death on the cross, man can obtain eternal life; man does not live fully until he dies.

Some critics have put a high premium on ironic and paradoxical poetry. Briefly, the argument runs that great poetry recognizes the complexity of experience, and that irony and paradox are ways of doing justice to this complexity. I. A. Richards uses "irony" to denote

---

* A word of caution: We have been talking about verbal irony, not **irony of situation**. Like ironic words, ironic situations have in them an element of contrast. A clown whose heart is breaking must make his audience laugh; an author's worst book is his only financial success; a fool solves a problem that vexes the wise.

"The bringing in of the opposite, the complementary impulses," and suggests (in *The Principles of Literary Criticism*) that irony in this sense is a characteristic of poetry of "the highest order." R. P. Warren (in *Selected Essays*), explaining the importance of Shakespeare's use of the bawdy Mercutio in *Romeo and Juliet*, says that "the poet wishes to indicate that his vision has been earned, that it can survive reference to the complexities and contradictions of experience. And irony is one such device of reference." It is dubious that all poets must always bring in the opposite and must indicate that their vision has been earned. But it is certain that much poetry is ironic and paradoxical.

SAMUEL JOHNSON (1709-1784)

A Short Song of Congratulation

Long-expected one and twenty
　　Ling'ring year at last is flown,
Pomp and pleasure, pride and plenty,
　　Great Sir John, are all your own.

5　Loosened from the minor's tether;
　　Free to mortgage or to sell,
Wild as wind, and light as feather
　　Bid the slaves of thrift farewell.

Call the Bettys, Kates, and Jennys
10　Every name that laughs at care,
Lavish of your grandsire's guineas,
　　Show the spirit of an heir.

All that prey on vice and folly
　　Joy to see their quarry fly,
15　Here the gamester light and jolly
　　There the lender grave and sly.

Wealth, Sir John, was made to wander,
　　Let it wander as it will;
See the jockey, see the pander,
20　Bid them come, and take their fill.

When the bonny blade carouses,
　　Pockets full, and spirits high,
What are acres? What are houses?
　　Only dirt, or° wet or dry.　　　　　　　　　　　*either*

25　If the guardian or the mother
　　Tell the woes of willful waste,
Scorn their counsel and their pother,
　　You can hang or drown at last.

1. Why in line 4 is Sir John called "great"?

2. At what point is it clear that the speaker is not congratulating Sir John?

3. What alternative other than selling or mortgaging (line 6) has Sir John? For the speaker, what indeed are "acres" if not "only dirt, or wet or dry"?

4. Does "fly" (line 14) mean flee? Why should those who prey on vice and folly "joy to see their quarry fly"?

5. What, aside from the alliteration, would be lost if "grandsire's" in line 11 were "father's"?

JOHN CROWE RANSOM (1888-   )

Bells for John Whiteside's Daughter

There was such speed in her little body,
And such lightness in her footfall,
It is no wonder her brown study
Astonishes us all.

5 Her wars were bruited in our high window.
We looked among orchard trees and beyond
Where she took arms against her shadow,
Or harried unto the pond

The lazy geese, like a snow cloud
10 Dripping their snow on the green grass,
Tricking and stopping, sleepy and proud,
Who cried in goose, Alas,

For the tireless heart within the little
Lady with rod that made them rise
15 From their noon apple-dreams and scuttle
Goose-fashion under the skies!

But now go the bells, and we are ready,
In one house we are sternly stopped
To say we are vexed at her brown study,
20 Lying so primly propped.

QUESTIONS: *Bells for John Whiteside's Daughter*

1. What is the literal meaning of "a brown study" in line 3? For what is it an understatement here? What is meant (line 5) by "her wars"? What are the literal and figurative suggestions of "took arms against her shadow" in line 7?

2. Why is "tireless heart" (line 13) ironic?

3. In line 17 the speaker says "we are ready." Ready for what? What word in a later line indicates that he is not "ready"?

ANDREW MARVELL (1621-1678)

To His Coy Mistress

Had we but world enough, and time,
This coyness, lady, were no crime.
We would sit down, and think which way
To walk, and pass our long love's day.
5 Thou by the Indian Ganges' side
Should'st rubies find: I by the tide
Of Humber would complain°. I would   *write love poems*
Love you ten years before the Flood,
And you should, if you please, refuse
10 Till the conversion of the Jews.
My vegetable° love should grow   *i.e., unconsciously growing*
Vaster than empires, and more slow.
An hundred years should go to praise
Thine eyes, and on thy forehead gaze:
15 Two hundred to adore each breast:
But thirty thousand to the rest.
An age at least to every part,
And the last age should show your heart.
For, lady, you deserve this state,
20 Nor would I love at lower rate.
     But at my back I always hear
Time's winged chariot hurrying near;
And yonder all before us lie
Deserts of vast eternity.
25 Thy beauty shall no more be found,
Nor in thy marble vault shall sound
My echoing song; then worms shall try
That long preserved virginity,
And your quaint honor turn to dust,
30 And into ashes all my lust.
The grave's a fine and private place,
But none, I think, do there embrace.
     Now therefore, while the youthful hue
Sits on thy skin like morning dew,
35 And while thy willing soul transpires
At every pore with instant fires,
Now let us sport us while we may;
And now, like am'rous birds of prey,

Rather at once our time devour,
40 Than languish in his slow-chapt power,
Let us roll all our strength, and all
Our sweetness, up into one ball;
And tear our pleasures with rough strife
Thorough° the iron gates of life.   *through*
45 Thus, though we cannot make our sun
Stand still, yet we will make him run.

QUESTIONS: *To His Coy Mistress*

1. Are the assertions in lines 1-20 so inflated that we detect behind them a playfully ironic tone? Explain. Why does the speaker in line 8 say he would love "ten years before the Flood," rather than merely "since the Flood"?

2. Explain lines 21-24. Why is time behind the speaker, and eternity in front of him? Is this "eternity" the same as the period discussed in lines 1-20? Discuss the change in the speaker's tone after line 20?

3. Do you agree with the comment (page 368) on lines 31-32? What more can be said about these lines, in context?

4. Why "am'rous birds of prey" (line 38) rather than the conventional doves? Is the idea of preying continued in the poem?

5. What is meant by "slow-chapt" (line 40)? Consult a dictionary for various meanings of "chap." In the seventeenth century a cannonball was simply called a "ball." Could lines 42-44 suggest a cannonball ripping through a city's fortifications?

6. Is there any verbal irony in lines 33-46? Explain the last two lines, and characterize the speaker's tone. Are they anticlimactic?

7. The poem is organized in the form of an argument. Trace the steps.

JOHN DONNE (1572-1631)

The Flea

Mark but this flea, and mark in this
How little that which thou deny'st me is;
It sucked me first, and now sucks thee,
And in this flea our two bloods mingled be;
5 Thou know'st that this cannot be said
A sin, nor shame, nor loss of maidenhead;
   Yet this enjoys before it woo,
   And pampered swells with one blood made of two,
   And this, alas, is more than we would do.

10 Oh stay, three lives in one flea spare,
   Where we almost, yea, more than married are.
   This flea is you and I, and this
   Our marriage bed and marriage temple is;
   Though parents grudge, and you, we are met
15 And cloistered in these living walls of jet.
      Though use° make you apt to kill me,   *custom*
      Let not to that, self-murder added be,
      And sacrilege, three sins in killing three.

   Cruel and sudden, hast thou since
20 Purpled thy nail in blood of innocence?
   Wherein could this flea guilty be,
   Except in that drop which it sucked from thee?
   Yet thou triumph'st and say'st that thou
   Find'st not thyself, nor me the weaker now.
25   'Tis true. Then learn how false fears be:
      Just so much honor, when thou yield'st to me,
      Will waste, as this flea's death took life from thee.

QUESTIONS: *The Flea*

   1. In the first stanza the speaker argues that because the blood
of the lovers is mixed in the flea, it would be "little," or no consequence, for the woman to give herself sexually to the speaker. What
evidence is there in the poem that he does not really think that a
sexual union is of no importance?
   2. What is hyperbolic about line 10? Why does the speaker overstate the matter in the second stanza? How does the overstatement
serve to diminish the subject?
   3. What has the lady done between the second and third stanzas?
In line 25 the speaker says that the lady's view is "true." Has he
changed his mind during the course of the poem, or has he been
leading up to this point?

JOHN DONNE (1572-1631)

Holy Sonnet XIV

Batter my heart, three-personed God; for you
As yet but knock, breathe, shine, and seek to mend;
That I may rise and stand, o'erthrow me, and bend
Your force, to break, blow, burn, and make me new.
5 I, like an usurped town, to another due,
Labor to admit you, but oh, to no end,
Reason, your viceroy in me, me should defend,

But is captived, and proves weak or untrue.
Yet dearly I love you, and would be loved fain,
But am betrothed unto your enemy:
Divorce me, untie, or break that knot again,
Take me to you, imprison me, for I
Except you enthrall me, never shall be free,
Nor ever chaste, except you ravish me.

QUESTIONS: *Holy Sonnet XIV*

1. Explain the paradoxes in lines 1, 3, 13, 14.

2. In lines 1-4 what is God implicitly compared to (considering specially lines 2 and 4)? How does this comparison lead into the comparison that dominates lines 5-8? What words in lines 9-12 are specially related to the earlier lines?

3. What is gained by piling up verbs in lines 2-4?

4. Are sexual references necessarily irreverent in a religious poem? Donne, incidentally, was an Anglican priest.

Thirteen

RHYTHM

EZRA POUND (1885-   )

Immorality

Sing we for love and idleness,
Naught else is worth the having.

Though I have been in many a land,
There is naught else in living.

And I would rather have my sweet,
Though rose-leaves die of grieving,

Than do high deeds in Hungary
To pass all men's believing.

A good poem. To begin with, it sings; as Pound has said, "Poetry withers and dries out when it leaves music, or at least imagined music, too far behind it. Poets who are not interested in music are, or become, bad poets." The ballads in a preceding chapter, it must be remembered, are songs, and other poetry too is sung, especially by children. A child reciting a counting-out rhyme, or singing on his way home from school, is enjoying poetry:

Pease-porridge hot,
  Pease-porridge cold,
Pease-porridge in the pot
  Nine days old.

Nothing very important is being said, but for generations children have enjoyed the music of these lines, and adults, too, have recalled them with pleasure—though few people know what pease-porridge is.

The "music"—the catchiness of certain sounds—should not be underestimated. Here are some lines chanted by the witches in *Macbeth*:

Double, double, toil and trouble;
Fire burn and cauldron bubble.

nis is rather far from words that mean approximately the same
ing: "Twice, twice, work and care;/Fire ignite, and pot boil." The
fference is more in the sounds than in the instructions. What is lost
 the paraphrase is the magic, the incantation, which resides in
 borate repetitions of sounds and stresses.

Rhythm (most simply, in English poetry, stresses at regular in-
rvals) has a power of its own. A highly pronounced rhythm is com-
on in such forms of poetry as charms, college yells, and lullabies;
l of them (like the witches' speech) are aimed at inducing a special
fect magically. It is not surprising that *carmen*, the Latin word for
rse or song, is also the Latin word for charm, and the word from
hich "charm" is derived.

> Rain, rain, go away;
> Come again another day.

> Block that kick! Block that kick! Block that kick!

> Rock a-bye baby, on the tree top,
> When the wind blows, the cradle will rock.

ere are the first two stanzas of a medieval lullaby:

> Lullay, my child, and wepe no more,
>   Slepe and be now still.
> The kind of bliss thy fader is
>   As it was his will.

> The endris° night I saw a sight,   *other*
>   A maid a cradell kepe,
> And ever she sang and seid among:
>   "Lullay, my child, and slepe."

In much poetry rhythm is only half-heard, but its omnipresence
 suggested by the fact that when poetry is printed it is customary to
egin each line with a capital letter. Prose (from Latin *prorsus*, "for-
ard," "straight on") keeps running across the paper until the right-
and margin is reached, and then, merely because the paper has given
ut, the writer or printer starts again at the left, with a small letter.
ut verse (Latin *versus*, "a turning") often ends well short of the
ight-hand margin, and the next line begins at the left—usually with
 capital—not because paper has run out but because the rhythmic
attern begins again. Lines of poetry are continually reminding us
hat they have a pattern.

Before turning to some other highly rhythmic pieces, a word of
aution: a mechanical, unvarying rhythm may be good to put the baby
o sleep, but it can be deadly to readers who wish to keep awake. A
oet varies his rhythm according to his purpose; he ought not to be

so regular that he is (in W. H. Auden's words) an "accentual pest." In competent hands, rhythm contributes to meaning; it says something. The rhythm in the lines from *Macbeth*, for example, helps suggest the strong binding power of magic. Again Ezra Pound has a relevant comment: "Rhythm *must* have meaning. It can't be merely a careless dash off, with no grip and no real hold to the words and sense, a tumty tum tumty tum tum ta." Consider this description of Hell from *Paradise Lost*:

    Rócks, cáves, lákes, féns, bógs, déns, ănd shádes ŏf déath.

Milton immediately follows one heavy stress with another (in contrast to the iambic feet—alternating unstressed and stressed syllables —that are the norm in the poem), helping to communicate the "meaning"—the impressive monotony of Hell. As a second example, consider the function of the rhythm in two lines by Alexander Pope:

    Whĕn Ájăx stríves sŏme róck's vást wéight tŏ thrów,

    Thĕ líne tŏo lábŏrs, ănd thĕ wórds móve slów.

The heavier stresses (again marked by /) do not merely alternate with the lighter ones (marked ˘); rather, the great weight of the rock is suggested by three consecutive stressed words, "rock's vast weight," and the great effort involved in moving it is suggested by another three consecutive stresses, "line too labors," and by yet another three, "words move slow." Note, also, the abundant pauses within the lines. In the first line, for example, unless one's speech is slovenly, one must pause at least slightly after "Ajax," "strives," "rock's," "vast," "weight," and "throw." The grating sounds in "Ajax" and "rock's" do their work, too, and so do the explosive t's. When Pope wishes to suggest lightness, he reverses his procedure and he groups *un*stressed syllables:

    Not so, when swift Camilla scours the plain,

    Flíes o'ĕr th' ŭnbéndĭng córn, ănd skíms ălŏng thĕ máin.

This last line has twelve syllables, and is thus longer than the line about Ajax, but the addition of "along" helps to communicate lightness and swiftness because in this line (it can be argued) neither of its syllables is strongly stressed. If "along" is omitted, the line still makes grammatical sense and becomes more "regular," but it also becomes less imitative of lightness.

    The very regularity of a line may be meaningful too. Shakespeare begins a sonnet thus:

    Whĕn Í dŏ cóunt thĕ clóck thăt télls thĕ tíme.

is line about a mechanism runs with appropriate regularity. (It is
rth noting, too, that "count the *c*lock" and "*t*ells the *t*ime" empha-
e the regularity by the repetition of sounds and syntax.) But notice
at Shakespeare does in the middle of the next line:

And see the brave day sunk in hideous night.

llowing are some poems in which the strongly felt pulsations are
ghly important.

WILLIAM CARLOS WILLIAMS (1883-1963)

The Dance

In Breughel's great picture, The Kermess,
the dancers go round, they go round and
around, the squeal and the blare and the
tweedle of bagpipes, a bugle and fiddles
5 tipping their bellies (round as the thick-
sided glasses whose wash they impound)
their hips and their bellies off balance
to turn them. Kicking and rolling about
the Fair Grounds, swinging their butts, those
10 shanks must be sound to bear up under such
rollicking measures, prance as they dance
in Breughel's great picture, The Kermess.

QUESTIONS: *The Dance*

1. Read the poem aloud several times, and decide where the
eavy stresses fall. Mark the heavily stressed syllables (/), the lightly
ressed ones (`), and the unstressed ones (ˇ). Are all the lines identi-
l? What effect is thus gained, especially when read aloud? What
es the parenthetical statement (lines 5-6) do to the rhythm? Does
final syllable often receive a heavy stress here? Are there noticeable
auses at the ends of the lines? What is the consequence? Are the
ancers waltzing?

2. What syllables rhyme or are repeated (*e.g.*, "round" in lines
and 5, and "-pound" in line 6; "-ing" in lines 5, 8, 9, 11)? What
fect do they have? Does the poem contain much assonance and
onsonance? Is there any onomatopoeia? (See pages 386-87 for defini-
ons of these terms.)

3. How does the absence at the beginning of each line of the
ustomary capital contribute to the meaning? Why is the last line the
ame as the first?

THEODORE ROETHKE (1908-1963)

My Papa's Waltz

The whiskey on your breath
Could make a small boy dizzy;
But I hung on like death:
Such waltzing was not easy.

5 We romped until the pans
Slid from the kitchen shelf;
My mother's countenance
Could not unfrown itself.

The hand that held my wrist
10 Was battered on one knuckle;
At every step you missed
My right ear scraped a buckle.

You beat time on my head
With a palm caked hard by dirt,
15 Then waltzed me off to bed
Still clinging to your shirt.

QUESTIONS: *My Papa's Waltz*

1. Is the rhythm more regular than in Williams' "The Dance"?
Do the syntactical pauses vary much from stanza to stanza? Be specific.
Would you say that the rhythm suggests lightness? Why?

2. Does the rhythm parallel, or ironically contrast with, the
episode described? Was the dance a graceful waltz? Explain.

3. Is the stress on "Slid" (line 6) expected? Are the stresses in
lines 13-14 functional? Explain.

WILLIAM SHAKESPEARE (1564-1616)

Fear No More the Heat o' th' Sun

Guiderius: Fear no more the heat o' th' sun*
                  Nor the furious winter's rages;
              Thou thy worldly task hast done,
                  Home art gone, and ta'en thy wages;
              Golden lads and girls all must,   5
              As chimney-sweepers, come to dust.

* These lines, from *Cymbeline*, are spoken by two brothers, over the body of
their sister, who they think is dead.

viragus:	Fear no more the frown o' th' great,
	Thou art past the tyrant's stroke;
	Care no more to clothe and eat,
	To thee the reed is as the oak:
	The scepter, learning, physic°, must	*medicine, i.e.,*
	All follow this and come to dust.	*the physician*

10

uiderius:	Fear no more the lightning flash,
viragus:	Nor the all-dreaded thunder-stone°;	*thunderbolt*
uiderius:	Fear not slander, censure rash;

15

rviragus:	Thou hast finished joy and moan:
oth:	All lovers young, all lovers must
	Consign to thee° and come to dust.	*sign the contract*
		along with you

| *uiderius:* | No exorciser harm thee! |
| *rviragus:* | Nor no witchcraft charm thee! |

20

uiderius:	Ghost unlaid° forbear thee!	*wandering ghost*
rviragus:	Nothing ill come near thee!
oth:	Quiet consummation have,
	And renowned be thy grave.

QUESTIONS: *Fear No More the Heat o' th' Sun*

1. Characterize the tone of lines 19-24. How and why does it differ from the tone of the earlier lines?

2. What effect is gained by repeating "Fear no more" in lines , 7, 13? Note, too, "Fear not" in line 15. In English poetry it is unusual for a poem to begin many lines with a stressed syllable. How many such lines are in this poem? What is the effect?

3. What are the connotations in "golden" (line 5)?

4. What figure of speech is used in line 11?

GEORGE HERBERT (1593-1633)

Discipline

Throw away thy rod,
Throw away thy wrath.
   O my God,
Take the gentle path.

⁵ For my heart's desire
Unto thine is bent;
  I aspire
To a full consent.

  Not a word or look
¹⁰ I affect to own,
   But by book,
And thy book alone.

  Though I fail, I weep.
Though I halt in pace,
¹⁵ Yet I creep
To the throne of grace.

  Then let wrath remove;
Love will do the deed,
   For with love
²⁰ Stony hearts will bleed.

  Love is swift of foot,
Love's a man of war,
   And can shoot,
And can hit from far.

²⁵ Who can 'scape his bow?
That which wrought on thee,
   Brought thee low,
Needs must work on me.

  Throw away thy rod.
³⁰ Though man frailties hath,
   Thou art God.
Throw away thy wrath.

QUESTIONS: *Discipline*

1. What is the effect of the short third line in each stanza? Is the line prolonged in reading?

2. Is the poem "disciplined"? What do the lengths of the lines and the emphatic rhymes contribute?

3. Explain the paradox (lines 19-28) that love is warlike. What figure of speech is used in lines 21-24? Explain lines 26-27. Would "Love" be a better title than "Discipline"? Why?

4. Compare the tone of the last stanza with that of the first. Would the poem be more effective if the last stanza were identical with the first? Why?

5. The Christian usually petitions God rather than commands Him. Is this poem offensively imperious? Explain.

Some Principles of Versification

The technical vocabulary of **prosody** (the study of the principles verse structure, including meter, rhyme and other sound effects, and ınzaic patterns) is large. An understanding of these terms will not ɾn anyone into a poet, but it will enable one to discuss some aspects poetry more efficiently. A knowledge of them, like a knowledge of ɔst other technical terms (*e.g.,* "misplaced modifier," "woofer," utomatic transmission") allows for quick and accurate communica- ɔn. It saves time if you can tell your car dealer that you want an tomatic transmission; it wastes time if you have to say you want a ɾ "where I don't have to push that little rod—you know, the one at on old cars comes out of the floor but on newer ones is on the ɛering wheel—back and forth to make the car really get going." ɪe following are the chief terms of prosody.

Most English poetry has a pattern of **stressed** (**accented**) sounds, ɪd this pattern is the **meter** (from the Greek word for "measure"). though in Old English poetry (poetry written in England before the orman-French Conquest in 1066) a line may have any number of ɪstressed syllables in addition to four stressed syllables, most poetry ɾitten in England since the Conquest not only has a fixed number of ɾesses in a line but also a fixed number of unstressed syllables before after each stressed one. (One really ought not to talk of "unstressed" "unaccented" syllables, since to utter a syllable—however lightly—is give it some stress. But the fact is that "unstressed" or "unaccented" ɛ parts of the established terminology of versification.)

In a line of poetry the **foot** is the basic unit of measurement. It is ɪ rare occasions a single stressed syllable; but generally a foot con- ɪts of two or three syllables, one of which is stressed. (Stress is in- ɪcated by / ; lack of stress by ˇ .) The repetition of feet, then, pro- ɪces a pattern of stresses throughout the poem.

TWO CAUTIONS:

1. A poem will seldom contain only one kind of foot throughout; significant variations usually occur, but one kind of foot is dominant.

2. In reading a poem one pays attention to the sense as well as to the metrical pattern. By paying attention to the sense one often finds that the stress falls on a word that according to the metrical pattern would be unstressed. Or a word that according to the pattern would be stressed may be seen to be unstressed. Further- more, by reading for sense one finds that not all stresses are equally heavy; some are almost as light as unstressed syllables, and

sometimes there is a **hovering stress,** that is, the stress is equally distributed over two adjacent syllables. To repeat: one reads for sense, allowing the syntax to help indicate the stresses.

The most common feet in English poetry are:

iamb (adjective: **iambic**): one unstressed syllable followed by one stressed syllable. The iamb, said to be the most common pattern in English speech, is surely the most common in English poetry. It is called a **rising meter,** the foot rising toward the stress. The following example has five iambic feet:

Ĭ sáw | thĕ ský | dĕscénd | ĭng bláck | ănd whíte.   (Robert Lowell)

trochee (**trochaic**): one stressed syllable followed by one unstressed; a **falling meter,** the foot falling away from the stress.

Lét hĕr | líve tŏ | eárn hĕr | dínnĕrs.   (J. M. Synge)

anapest (**anapestic**): two unstressed syllables followed by one stressed; a rising meter.

Thĕre ăre mán | y̆ whŏ sáy | thăt ă dóg | hăs hĭs dáy.
                                                    (Dylan Thomas)

dactyl (**dactylic**): one stressed syllable followed by two unstressed; a falling meter. This tri-syllabic foot, like the anapest, is common in light verse, or verse suggesting joy, but its use is not limited to such material. Thomas Hood's sentimental "The Bridge of Sighs" begins:

Táke hĕr ŭp | téndĕrly̆.   (Hood)

spondee (**spondaic**): two stressed syllables; most often used as a substitute for an iamb or trochee; it neither rises nor falls.

Smárt lád, | tŏ slíp | bĕtímes | ă̆wáy.   (A. E. Housman)

Because the **pyrrhic** foot (two unstressed syllables) lacks a stress, it is often not considered a legitimate foot in English.

A metrical line consists of one or more feet and is named for the number of feet in it. The following names are used:

monometer:	one foot	**pentameter:**	five feet
dimeter:	two feet	**hexameter:**	six feet
trimeter	three feet	**heptameter:**	seven feet
tetrameter:	four feet	**octameter:**	eight feet

A line is scanned for the kind and number of feet in it, and the
scansion tells you if it is, say, anapestic trimeter (three anapests):

Ăs Ĭ cáme | tŏ thĕ édge | ŏf thĕ wóods.   (Frost)

Another example, this time iambic pentameter:

Sĭnce bráss, nŏr stóne, nŏr eárth, nŏr bóundlĕss séa. (Shakespeare)

A line ending with a stress has a **masculine ending**; a line ending with
an extra unstressed syllable has a **feminine ending**. The lines above by
Synge and Hood have feminine endings; those by Lowell, Thomas,
Housman, Frost, and Shakespeare have masculine endings. The **caesura**
(usually indicated by the symbol //) is a slight pause within the line. It
need not be indicated by punctuation, and it does not affect the
metrical count:

> Awake, my St. John! // leave all meaner things
> To low ambition, // and the pride of kings.
> Let us // (since Life can little more supply
> Than just to look about us // and to die)
> Expatiate free // o'er all this scene of Man;
> A mighty maze! // but not without a plan;
> A wild, // where weeds and flowers promiscuous shoot;
> Or garden, // tempting with forbidden fruit.   (Pope)

The varying position of the caesura helps to give Pope's lines an
informality that plays against the formality of the pairs of rhyming
lines.

An **end-stopped line** concludes with a distinct syntactical pause, but
a **run-on line** has its sense carried over into the next line without
syntactical pause. (The running-on of a line is called **enjambment**.)
In the following passage, only the first is a run-on line:

> Yet if we look more closely we shall find
> Most have the seeds of judgment in their mind:
> Nature affords at least a glimmering light;
> The lines, though touched but faintly, are drawn right.   (Pope)

Meter produces **rhythm,** recurrences at equal intervals, but rhythm
(from a Greek word meaning "flow") is usually applied to larger units
than feet. Often it depends most obviously on pauses. Thus, a poem
with run-on lines will have a different rhythm from a poem with end-
stopped lines, even though both are in the same meter. And prose,
though it is unmetrical, can thus have rhythm, too. In addition to
being affected by syntactical pause, rhythm is affected by pauses due

to consonant clusters and the length of words. Polysyllabic words establish a different rhythm from monosyllabic words, even in metrically identical lines. One can say, then, that rhythm is altered by shifts in meter, syntax, and the length and ease of pronunciation. But even with no such shift, even if a line is repeated verbatim, a reader may sense a change in rhythm. The rhythm of the final line of a poem, for example, may well differ from that of the line before, even though in all other respects the lines are identical, as in Frost's "Stopping by Woods," which concludes by repeating "And miles to go before I sleep" (page 326). One may simply sense that this final line ought to be spoken, say, more slowly.

Though rhythm is basic to poetry, **rhyme** is not. Rhyme is the repetition of the identical or similar stressed sound or sounds. It is, presumably, pleasant in itself; it suggests order; and it also may be related to meaning, for it brings two words sharply together, often implying a relationship, as, for example, Pope's "throne" and "alone." **Perfect** or **exact rhymes** occur when differing consonant-sounds are followed by identical stressed vowel-sounds, and the following sounds, if any, are identical (foe: toe; meet: fleet; buffer: rougher). Note that perfect rhyme involves identity of sound, not of spelling. "Fix" and "sticks," like "buffer" and "rougher," are perfect rhymes.

Half-rhyme (or **slant-rhyme, approximate-rhyme, near-rhyme, off-rhyme**): only the final consonant-sounds of the rhyming words are identical; the stressed vowel-sounds as well as the initial consonant-sounds, if any, differ (soul: oil; mirth: forth; trolley: bully). **Eye-rhyme** is not really rhyme; it merely looks like rhyme (cough: bough: rough). **Masculine rhyme:** the final syllables are stressed and, after their differing initial consonant-sounds, are identical in sound (stark: mark; support: retort). **Feminine rhyme** (or **double-rhyme**): stressed rhyming syllables are followed by identical unstressed syllables (revival: arrival; flatter: batter). **Triple-rhyme:** a kind of feminine rhyme in which identical stressed vowel-sounds are followed by two identical unstressed syllables (machinery: scenery; tenderly: slenderly). **End-rhyme** (or **terminal-rhyme**) has the rhyming word at the end of the line. **Internal rhyme** has at least one of the rhyming words within the line (Wilde's "Each narrow *cell* in which we *dwell*"). **Alliteration** is sometimes defined as the repetition of initial sounds ("All the *aw*ful *au*guries" or "Bring me my *b*ow of *b*urning gold"), sometimes as the prominent repetition of a consonant ("*a*fter *li*fe's *fi*tful *fe*ver"). **Assonance:** identical vowel-sounds preceded and followed by differing consonant-sounds, in words in proximity. Whereas "tide" and "hide" are rhymes, "tide" and "mine" are assonantal. **Consonance:** identical consonant-sounds and differing vowel-sounds in words in proximity

il: feel; rough: roof; pitter: patter). Sometimes consonance is more
sely defined merely as the repetition of a consonant (fai*l*: pee*l*).
omatopoeia is said to occur when the sound of a word echoes or
ggests the meaning of a word. "Hiss" and "buzz" are onomatopoetic.
ere is a mistaken tendency to see onomatopoeia everywhere, for
mple, in "thunder" and "horror." Many words sometimes thought
be onomatopoetic are not clearly imitative of the thing they denote;
ey merely contain some sounds which—when we know what the
rd means—seem to have some resemblance to the thing they denote.
nnyson's lines from "Come down, O maid" are usually cited as an
mple of onomatopoeia:

> The moan of doves in immemorial elms
> And murmuring of innumerable bees.

t John Crowe Ransom has pointed out that if many of the sounds
"murmuring of innumerable bees" are reproduced in a line of
ferent meaning—"murdering of innumerable beeves"—the sugges-
eness is lost.

Lines of poetry are commonly arranged in a rhythmical unit called
stanza (from an Italian word meaning a "room" or "stopping-
ace"). Usually all the stanzas in a poem have the same rhyme
ttern. A stanza is sometimes called a **verse,** though "verse" may also
ean a single line of poetry. (In discussing stanzas, rhymes are in-
cated by identical letters. Thus, *abab* indicates that the first and third
es rhyme with each other, while the second and fourth lines are
ked by a different rhyme. x is used to denote an unrhymed line.)
ommon stanzaic forms in English poetry are the following:

uplet: stanza of two lines, usually, but not necessarily with end-
ymes. "Couplet" is also used for a pair of rhyming lines. The **octo-
llabic couplet** is iambic or trochaic tetrameter:

> Had we but world enough, and time,
> This coyness, lady, were no crime.   (Marvell)

roic couplet: a rhyming couplet of iambic pentameter, often
losed," *i.e.*, containing a complete thought, there being a fairly
eavy pause at the end of the first line and a still heavier one at the
d of the second. Commonly, there is a parallel or an antithesis
ithin a line, or between the two lines. It is called heroic because in
ngland, especially in the eighteenth century, it was much used for
roic (epic) poems.

> Some foreign writers, some our own despise;
> The ancients only, or the moderns, prize.   (Pope)

SOME PRINCIPLES OF VERSIFICATION 387

triplet (or **tercet**): a three-line stanza, usually with one rhyme.

> Whenas in silks my Julia goes
> Then, then (methinks) how sweetly flows
> That liquefaction of her clothes. (Herrick)

quatrain: a four-line stanza, rhymed or unrhymed. The **heroic** (or **elegiac**) **quatrain** is iambic pentameter, rhyming *abab*. The **ballad stanza** is a quatrain alternating iambic tetrameter with iambic trimeter lines, usually rhyming *abxb*. Sometimes it is followed by a **refrain**, a line or lines repeated several times.

sonnet: a fourteen-line poem. For further details and for examples, see pages 392-400.

A good deal of English poetry is unrhymed, much of it in **blank verse,** *i.e.,* unrhymed iambic pentameter. Introduced into English poetry by Surrey in the middle of the sixteenth century, late in the century it became the standard medium (especially in the hands of Marlowe and Shakespeare) of English drama. In the seventeenth century, Milton used it for *Paradise Lost,* and it has continued to be used in both dramatic and non-dramatic literature. For an example see the passage from Shakespeare on page 347. A passage of blank verse that has a rhetorical unity is sometimes called a **verse paragraph.**

The second kind of unrhymed poetry fairly common in English, especially in the twentieth century, is **free verse** (or *vers libre*), *i.e.,* rhythmical lines varying in length, adhering to no fixed metrical pattern and usually unrhymed. The pattern is often largely based on repetition and parallel grammatical structure. Though such a form may appear unrestrained, as T. S. Eliot (a practitioner) has said, "No *vers* is *libre* for the man who wants to do a good job." Whitman's "A Noiseless Patient Spider" (page 325) is an example; Arnold's "Dover Beach" (page 355) is another example, though less typical because it uses rhyme.

The previous pages are a somewhat tedious account of versification. Here is a more entertaining one.

GEORGE MAC BETH (1932-   )

What Metre Is

> it is a matter
> of counting (five
> syllables in the first line, four
> in the second) and

5   so on. Or we can change to
    seven words in the first line
    six in the second. Is
    that arbitrary?

    Prose is another possibility. There could be three
10 sentences in the stanza. This would be an example of
    that.

    Which (on the other hand)
    we could lay out
    by a letter count, as (this by the way is
15 free verse, without metre)

    "pro
    se is another possib
    ility. There could be th
    ree sent
20 ences in the st
    anza. This would be an exam
    ple of that." I mean

    it is a matter
    of mathematics. Intervals between
25 the words, three to
    a line is the
    rule here. It results

    in the same as
    having words, four to
30 a line. In the

    mind of the poet,
    though, it makes a
    difference. White spaces
    (now it is
35 two spaces) are

    just articulation,
    space, words
    (now it
    is one)

40 mean
    something
    (now
    it
    is
45 words) and

no it is
not
music either. Internal
rhyming (though sometimes
50 the kernel of new ideas) is
a matter of timing.

The same is true for
rhythm, the beat
(two to a line
55 it is here)

only becomes like a rhythm when
as here it moves with a regular
dactyl or two to a line. If

slow now spondees
60 make lines move, stiff

rhythm is metre (in dactyls again) but

rhythm is usually not
like this. In a word

it can escalate
65 drop

do as it pleases
move freely
(look out, I'm coming)

stop
70 at a stop

and so on. Assonance
that semblance
(except in Owen)
a, when

75 it works, echo
of awkwardness is O.K.

but not for me: nor is lively
alliteration
leaping
80 long lean and allusive
through low lines. It

becomes a matter
of going back
to metre, ending w

85 ith its mos
t irrit
ating (perhaps) manif
estation thi
s inarticul

90 ate mechanical stu
tter. It is the voi
ce of the type-wr
iter. It is the abdic
ation of insp

95 iration. I li
ke it. It i
s the logica

l exp
ression o
100 f itsel
f.

Fourteen

THE SONNET

Assist me some extemporal god of rime, for I am sure I shall
turn sonneter. Devise, wit; write, pen; for I am for whole
volumes in folio.

> Don Armado, in Shakespeare's *Love's Labors Lost*, I. ii

Don Armado, described as one who "draweth out the thread of
his verbosity finer than the staple of his argument," was not the only
Renaissance man seeking to fill large volumes with sonnets. For the
Elizabethan, a **sonnet** was any short song-like poem (Italian, *sonnetto*,
a song; from Latin *sonus*, a sound), but the word has come to denote
a lyric of fourteen lines (rarely, a few more or less) whose meter, if
the poem is in English, is prevailingly iambic pentameter. Though the
form developed in thirteenth-century Italy, it was a fourteenth-century
Italian, Francis Petrarch (1304-1374), who was the chief influence on
English sonneteers, and then not until two hundred years after his
death. A few sonnets (in the modern sense of the word) were written
in England in the middle of the sixteenth century, but the great
English vogue of sonneteering was delayed until the final decade of
the century, when about two thousand were published, and uncounted
thousands circulated in manuscript. Often these were not isolated
sonnets but were parts of "sequences," clusters of sonnets. The lover's
joy might be a staple for part of a sequence; his grief for another part;
his renewed hope for yet another. Not surprisingly, Shakespeare's
sequence of 154 sonnets (published in 1609, but probably written in
the 1590's) is a good deal richer than those of his contemporaries. To
the basic theme of love he added, among other things, the themes of
friendship, honor, duty, lust.

The rhyme scheme of the **Petrarchan** (or **Italian**) sonnet is organized into an **octave** (the first eight lines) and a **sestet** (the last six):
usually it rhymes *abbaabba cdecde*, but the sestet often has variations.

Petrarch's sonnets and in those of many of his imitators, there is "turn" with the beginning of the ninth line; for example, a generali- tion in the octave may be illustrated by a particularization in the stet. The sestet is something of a restatement of the octave, or a mment on it. But, whether from indifference or inability, this nice sposition of parts is not always observed by English writers, and it dangerous to generalize about the perfection of the Italian structure a lyric vehicle. Milton in particular had a tendency to run straight beyond the octave; rather than saying he composed faulty Petrar- an sonnets, scholars say he composed Miltonic sonnets.

The **Shakespearean** (or **English**) sonnet has the fourteen lines of e Petrarchan, but organizes them into three quatrains (four lines ch) and a couplet (pair of lines): *abab cdcd efef gg*. The couplet s frequently been the *pons asinorum* of English sonneteers (even casionally of Shakespeare): often it seems a needless appendage, ten it seems too snappy a close; less often it seems just right.

Why poets choose to imprison themselves in fourteen tightly ymed lines is something of a mystery. Tradition has a great deal to with it: the form, having been handled successfully by major poets, ands as a challenge. In writing a sonnet a poet gains a little of the thority of Petrarch, of Shakespeare, of Milton, of Wordsworth, and other masters who showed that the sonnet is not merely a trick. A cond reason perhaps resides in the very tightness of the rhymes, hich can help as well as hinder. Many poets have felt, along with ichard Wilbur (in *Mid-Century American Poets*, ed. John Ciardi), at the need for a rhyme has suggested

> . . . arbitrary connections of which the mind may take advantage if it likes. For example, if one has to rhyme with *tide*, a great number of rhyme-words at once come to mind (ride, bide, shied, confide, Akenside, etc.). Most of these, in combination with *tide*, will probably suggest nothing apropos, but one of them may reveal precisely what one wanted to say. If none of them does, *tide* must be dispensed with. Rhyme, austerely used, may be a stimulus to discovery and a stretcher of the attention.

At the top of the next page is a sonnet calling attention to another dvantage of the form.*

In addition to those that follow here, other sonnets will be found on pages 39, 350, 358, 374, 404, 405, 410, 411, 424, 431.

Nuns Fret Not at Their Convent's Narrow Room

Nuns fret not at their convent's narrow room;
And hermits are contented with their cells;
And students with their pensive citadels;
Maids at the wheel, the weaver at his loom,
5 Sit blithe and happy; bees that soar for bloom,
High as the highest Peak of Furness-fells,
Will murmur by the hour in foxglove bells:
In truth the prison, unto which we doom
Ourselves, no prison is: and hence for me,
10 In sundry moods, 'twas pastime to be bound
Within the Sonnet's scanty plot of ground;
Pleased if some Souls (for such there needs must be)
Who have felt the weight of too much liberty,
Should find brief solace there, as I have found.

WILLIAM SHAKESPEARE (1564-1616)

Sonnet 55

Not marble nor the gilded monuments
Of princes shall outlive this pow'rful rhyme;
But you shall shine more bright in these contents
Than unswept stone, besmeared with sluttish time.
5 When wasteful war shall statues overturn,
And broils root out the work of masonry,
Nor Mars his sword nor war's quick fire shall burn
The living record of your memory.
'Gainst death and all oblivious enmity
10 Shall you pace forth; your praise shall still find room
Even in the eyes of all posterity
That wear this world out to the ending doom.
    So, till the Judgment that° yourself arise,   *when*
    You live in this, and dwell in lovers'° eyes.   *admirers'*

QUESTIONS: *Sonnet 55*

1. Explain "sluttish time" (line 4). What prepares the reader for the image?

2. What verb is omitted from line 7? What effect is thus gained?

3. What effect is gained by the enjambment in lines 9, 10, 11? By the abundant monosyllables and long vowels in lines 10-12? Scan

line 10; what is the tone of "Shall you pace forth"? How does the meter contribute to the tone?

4. Does "all oblivious enmity" (line 9) mean "all enmity that brings oblivion"; or should it be hyphenated ("all-oblivious enmity"), as many editors suggest?

5. Why "eyes" instead of "ears" in line 11? How does it strengthen the assertions of the earlier quatrains?

6. Is the couplet tacked on? Explain.

WILLIAM SHAKESPEARE (1564-1616)

Sonnet 73

That time of year thou mayst in me behold
When yellow leaves, or none, or few, do hang
Upon those boughs which shake against the cold,
Bare ruined choirs where late the sweet birds sang.
5 In me thou see'st the twilight of such day
As after sunset fadeth in the west,
Which by-and-by black night doth take away,
Death's second self that seals up all in rest.
In me thou see'st the glowing of such fire
10 That on the ashes of his youth doth lie,
As the deathbed whereupon it must expire,
Consumed with that which it was nourished by.
    This thou perceiv'st, which makes thy love more strong,
    To love that well which thou must leave ere long.

QUESTIONS: *Sonnet 73*

1. To what does the speaker metaphorically compare himself in the first quatrain? In the second? In the third? Is there a unifying theme beneath all these metaphors? What, if anything, would be lost if the quatrains were put in a different order?

2. In each quatrain the speaker depersonalizes himself by various metaphors. How does the last line of the couplet carry the depersonalization further?

3. Explain the fourth line, which is a metaphor engendered by the previous metaphor. Look up "choirs" in a dictionary. What do the birds contribute to the poem? In the second and third quatrains do the basic figures engender other figures? Explain.

4. Why is night called death's twin in line 8? Explain the paradox in line 12. Is the figure in lines 9-12 an apt one?

5. What is the tone of the couplet?

Sonnet 146

Poor soul, the center of my sinful earth,
My sinful earth these rebel pow'rs that thee array,
Why dost thou pine within and suffer dearth,
Painting thy outward walls so costly gay?
5 Why so large cost°, having so short a lease,   *expense*
Dost thou upon thy fading mansions spend?
Shall worms, inheritors of this excess,
Eat up thy charge? Is this thy body's end?
Then, soul, live thou upon thy servant's loss,
10 And let that pine to aggravate thy store;
Buy terms divine° in selling hours of dross;   *buy ages of*
Within be fed, without be rich no more.   *immortality*
   So shalt thou feed on Death, that feeds on men,
   And death once dead, there's no more dying then.

QUESTIONS: *Sonnet 146*

1. In line 2, "My sinful earth" is doubtless a printer's error. Among suggested emendations are "Thrall to," "Fooled by," "Rebuke these," "Leagued with," "Feeding." Which do you prefer? Why?

2. What is the tone of the first two lines? Where in the poem does the thought take its chief turn? What is the tone of the couplet?

3. What does "array" (line 2) mean?

4. Explain the paradox in lines 13-14.

5. In a poem on the relation between the body and the soul, is battle imagery surprising? Commercial imagery (lines 5-12)? What other imagery is in the poem? Is the sonnet a dull preachment? If not, why not?

MICHAEL DRAYTON (1563-1631)
Since There's No Help

Since there's no help, come let us kiss and part;
Nay, I have done, you get no more of me,
And I am glad, yea glad with all my heart
That thus so cleanly I myself can free;
5 Shake hands for ever, cancel all our vows,
And when we meet at any time again,
Be it not seen in either of our brows
That we one jot of former love retain.
Now at the last gasp of Love's latest breath,

10 When, his pulse failing, Passion speechless lies,
    When Faith is kneeling by his bed of death,
    And Innocence is closing up his eyes,
       Now if thou wouldst, when all have given him over,
       From death to life thou mightst him yet recover.

QUESTIONS: *Since There's No Help*

1. Which lines explicitly refute the assertion of line 1? Explain the inconsistency.

2. What is the tone of lines 1-8? What words especially establish this tone? What is the tone in lines 9-14? What is the significance of the shift from "you" (line 2) to "thou" (line 13)?

3. What figure of speech is used in lines 9-14? Is it effective and appropriate? Why?

4. What is the effect of the feminine rhyme of the couplet?

JOHN MILTON (1608-1674)

When I Consider How My Light Is Spent

When I consider how my light is spent,
Ere half my days in this dark world and wide,
And that one talent which is death to hide
Lodged with me useless, though my soul more bent
5 To serve therewith my Maker, and present
My true account, lest He returning chide,
"Doth God exact day-labor, light denied?"
I fondly° ask. But Patience, to prevent   *foolishly*
That murmur, soon replies, "God doth not need
10 Either man's work or his own gifts; who best
Bear his mild yoke, they serve him best. His state
Is kingly: thousands° at his bidding speed   *thousands of*
And post o'er land and ocean without rest;   *angels*
They also serve who only stand and wait."

"Light" denotes Milton's vision; he became totally blind about 1651, and perhaps wrote this sonnet then or shortly thereafter. But "light," in the context of Milton's life and of the poem, may also suggest spiritual, intellectual, and poetic illumination.

QUESTIONS: *When I Consider How My Light Is Spent*

1. Does "and wide" (line 2) merely fill out the line, or does it contribute something? Explain.

2. Lines 3-4 allude to Jesus' parable of the talents (Matthew 25:14-30). Explain the passage. Do the words of Patience contradict Jesus' parable?

3. What characteristics are implicitly attributed to God in lines 6-7? Why is "day-labor" more effective than, say, "my labor"?

4. Where is the turn? What characteristics are attributed to God after the turn?

5. Compare the tone of the first and the last sentences. How does the length of each of these sentences contribute to the tone?

JOHN MILTON (1608-1674)

Methought I Saw My Late Espoused Saint

Methought I saw my late espoused Saint
Brought to me like Alcestis from the grave,
Whom Jove's great son to her glad husband gave,
Rescued from death by force though pale and faint.
5 Mine as whom washt from spot of childbed taint,
Purification in the old Law did save,
And such, as yet once more I trust to have
Full sight of her in Heaven without restraint,
Came vested all in white, pure as her mind:
10 Her face was veiled, yet to my fancied sight,
Love, sweetness, goodness, in her person shined
So clear, as in no face with more delight.
But O as to embrace me she inclined
I waked, she fled, and day brought back my night.

Lines 1-4 compare Milton's deceased wife, now in heaven ("late espoused Saint"), with the mythical Alcestis, Admetus' queen, whom Hercules rescued from death's door. Alcestis was presented veiled to Admetus. The comparison in lines 5-9 is between Milton's wife and a Hebrew woman ritually cleansed after childbirth (see Leviticus 12). Perhaps the points of similarity in lines 5-9 are a white-robed woman, weak, pale, and purified. If the poem is about Milton's first wife, who died in childbirth, the passage has an added force: his wife, who had not survived the period ordained in Leviticus, appeared *as though* she had.

QUESTIONS: *Methought I Saw My Late Espoused Saint*
1. Is the poem sentimental? Or embarrassingly personal? Explain.
2. Where is the turn?

3. What is the effect of the two pauses within the last line? Of the ten monosyllables in this line? Of the five verbs in the last two lines? Contrast the tone of the last line with that of the first. In line 14, does "night" suggest anything other than blindness?

WILFRED OWEN (1893-1918)

Anthem for Doomed Youth

What passing-bells for these who die as cattle?
　　Only the monstrous anger of the guns.
　　Only the stuttering rifles' rapid rattle
Can pattern out their hasty orisons.
5 No mockeries for them; no prayers nor bells,
Nor any voice of mourning save the choirs,—
The shrill, demented choirs of wailing shells;
And bugles calling for them from sad shires.

What candles may be held to speed them all?
10 　　Not in the hands of boys, but in their eyes
Shall shine the holy glimmers of good-byes.
　　The pallor of girls' brows shall be their pall;
Their flowers the tenderness of patient minds,
And each slow dusk a drawing-down of blinds.

QUESTIONS: *Anthem for Doomed Youth*

　1. In lines 3 and 4 what sound effects seem to be intended?

　2. What is implied in "mockeries" in line 5?

　3. Explain lines 10-14.

　4. Does the poem suffer from lack of understatement? For example, is "shrill, demented" (in line 7) a mistake? And "monstrous" in line 2?

X. J. KENNEDY (1929-　　)

Nothing in Heaven Functions as It Ought

Nothing in Heaven functions as it ought:
Peter's bifocals, blindly sat on, crack;
His gates lurch wide with the cackle of a cock,
Not with a hush of gold as Milton had thought;
5 Gangs of the slaughtered innocents keep huffing
The nimbus off the Venerable Bede
Like that of a dandelion gone to seed;
The beatific choir keep breaking up, coughing.

But Hell, sweet Hell hath no freewheeling part:
10 None takes his own sweet time, nor quickens pace.
Ask anyone, "How come you here, poor heart?"
And he will slot a quarter through his face—
There'll be an instant click—a tear will start
Imprinted with an abstract of his case.

Milton (in *Paradise Lost*, VII, 205-07) wrote: "Heaven opened wide/Her ever-during gates, harmonious sound/On golden hinges moving. . . ." For an account of the slaughter of the innocents, see Matthew 2:16. The Venerable Bede (673-735) was an English theologian and historian.

QUESTIONS: *Nothing in Heaven Functions as It Ought*

1. Sum up the argument of the octave, and that of the sestet. What qualities are attributed to Heaven? What to Hell?

2. What advantage to this poem (if any) is the sonnet form?

3. What irregularities of rhyme, rhythm, and meter are evident in this sonnet? What connection is there between the occurrence of these irregularities and what is being said?

JOHN CROWE RANSOM (1888-   )

Piazza Piece

—I am a gentleman in a dustcoat trying
To make you hear. Your ears are soft and small
And listen to an old man not at all,
They want the young men's whispering and sighing.
5 But see the roses on your trellis dying
And hear the spectral singing of the moon;
For I must have my lovely lady soon,
I am a gentleman in a dustcoat trying.

—I am a lady young in beauty waiting
10 Until my truelove comes, and then we kiss.
But what gray man among the vines is this
Whose words are dry and faint as in a dream?
Back from my trellis, Sir, before I scream!
I am a lady young in beauty waiting.

1. Who speaks the octave? What words especially characterize him? Characterize the speaker of the sestet.

2. In lines 9-10, she is waiting for her "truelove." Comment on the suggestions in this word. In line 14 she is still "waiting." For whom does she think she is waiting? For whom does the reader know she is waiting? How?

3. The first and last lines of the octave are identical, and so are the first and last lines of the sestet. What does this indicate about the degree to which the speakers communicate to each other?

Fifteen

POETS AT WORK

It is not inspiration that exhausts one, but Art.   (W. B. Yeats)

The theory that the poet, inspired by a divine wind, composes effortlessly is nicely put in this poem.

ROBERT HERRICK (1591-1674)
Not Every Day Fit for Verse

'Tis not ev'ry day that I
Fitted am to prophesy.
No, but when the spirit fills
The fantastic pannicles
Full of fire, then I write
As the godhead doth indite.
Thus enraged, my lines are hurled,
Like the Sibyl's, through the world.
Look how next the holy fire
Either slakes, or doth retire;
So the fancy cools, till when
That brave spirit comes again.

Perhaps Herrick really did compose this way. But most poets have found that to inspiration they must add hard conscious intellection, what Yeats calls "Art." It is useful to remember that "art" comes from Latin *ars*, meaning "skill," and that it is related to "artifice" and "artificial"; cunning and craftsmanship as well as inspiration have their place in poetry. In "Adam's Curse" Yeats suggests that although a poem must seem to be the product of a moment, it may in fact be the product of hours of revisions:

> . . . a line will take us hours maybe;
> Yet if it does not seem a moment's thought,
> Our stitching and unstitching has been naught.

There is a good deal of evidence—some of it being the numerous drafts of Yeat's own poems—to support his assertion that poets un-stitch and re-stitch. But the purpose of this chapter is not to demonstrate that poets work; rather, it is to let the reader in some degree see poems in process. We cannot get into the poet's head, but we can catch glimpses of what comes out of his head at various moments. These glimpses give us a way of seeing the finished poem more clearly. The alterations provide us with a focus; we can, for example, see more clearly the rightness of Frost's description of a dead moth—"Like a white piece of rigid satin cloth"—when we see that he earlier described it as "Like a white piece of lifeless satin cloth." The change is small, but, as Mark Twain said, the difference between the right word and the almost right one is the difference between lightning and the lightning-bug.

Robert Frost has said that of his own poems his favorites are those that came all at once. "The Silken Tent" is such a poem.* It is the sort of which he said, "Here is a poem that is a triumphal intention, that bore right through and dismissed itself."

* The holograph of Robert Frost's "The Silken Tent" (on page 404) is reproduced by courtesy of the Lockwood Memorial Library, State University of New York at Buffalo.

The Silken Tent

In Praise of your Poise
in a field
She is as on the town a silken tent
At midday when a sunny summer breeze
Has dried the dew and all its ropes relent,
So that in guys it gently sways at ease,

And its supporting central cedar pole,
to
That is its summit pointing heavenward
And signifies the sureness of the soul,
naught
Seems to owe nothing to any single cord,

But strictly held by none, is loosely bound
By countless silken ties of love and thought
To everything on earth the compass round,
And only by one's going slightly taut
In the capriciousness of of summer air,
Is of the slightest bondage made aware.

ROBERT FROST (1874-1963)

The Silken Tent

She is as in a field a silken tent
At midday when a sunny summer breeze
Has dried the dew and all its ropes relent,
So that in guys it gently sways at ease,
5 And its supporting central cedar pole,
That is its pinnacle to heavenward
And signifies the sureness of the soul,
Seems to owe naught to any single cord,
But strictly held by none, is loosely bound
10 By countless silken ties of love and thought
To everything on earth the compass round,
And only by one's going slightly taut
In the capriciousness of summer air
Is of the slightest bondage made aware.

ut even the creative act that produced this poem had its second
houghts, as the revisions in the manuscript show (see the opposite
age). He altered the title; in line 1 he altered "on the lawn" to "in a
eld"; in line 6, "summit pointing" to "pinnacle to"; and in line 8,
nothing" to "naught." How do these changes affect the poem?

Some of Frost's other poems, such as "Design," no less triumphal
o the reader, took more labor. "Design" was first published in 1936,
ut an early version, called "In White," survives in a letter dated
4 January 1912. "In White," not included in Frost's *Complete Poems*,
s reprinted below with his permission.

ROBERT FROST (1874-1963)

In White

A dented spider like a snow drop white
On a white Heal-all°, holding up a moth   *a flower,*
Like a white piece of lifeless satin cloth—   *normally blue*
Saw ever curious eye so strange a sight?—
5 Portent in little, assorted death and blight
Like the ingredients of a witches' broth?—
The beady spider, the flower like a froth,
And the moth carried like a paper kite.

What had that flower to do with being white,
10 The blue prunella every child's delight.
What brought the kindred spider to that height?
(Make we no thesis of the miller's° plight.)   *moth's*
What but design of darkness and of night?
Design, design! Do I use the word aright?

Design

I found a dimpled spider, fat and white,
On a white heal-all, holding up a moth
Like a white piece of rigid satin cloth—
Assorted characters of death and blight
5 Mixed ready to begin the morning right,
Like the ingredients of a witches' broth—
A snow-drop spider, a flower like froth,
And dead wings carried like a paper kite.

What had that flower to do with being white,
10 The wayside blue and innocent heal-all?
What brought the kindred spider to that height,
Then steered the white moth thither in the night?
What but design of darkness to appall?—
If design govern in a thing so small.

Synge wrote several versions of "Is It a Month" in 1907, and there is some uncertainty about which version is the final one, but there is no doubt that what we call "A" is earlier than "B."

JOHN MILLINGTON SYNGE (1871-1909)

Is It a Month (*version A*)

Is it a month since I and you
Watched stars rising from Glen Dubh,
Underneath
~~Since beneath~~ that hazel bough
Long we kissed from throat to brow,
5 Since your fingers, neck, and chin
Made the bars that fenced me in,
~~While your voice in twilight's key~~
~~Wrought my spirit's ecstasy~~
Till Paradise seemed but a wreck
10 Near your bosom, brow, and neck,
       wilder
And stars grew ~~older~~, growing wise,
In the splendour of your eyes!

                    brow
Since we kissed from ~~ear~~ to ear
       ~~*While*~~
Till ~~Till~~ the weazels wandered near,
15 And the wet and withered leaves
Blew about your cap and sleeves,
Till
~~And~~ the moon sank tired through the ledge
Of the wet and windy hedge?
              starry
  ~~And we took the slushy lane~~   *stet.*
20 ~~Back to Dublin town again.~~   *stet.*

Is It a Month (*version B*)

Is it a month since I and you
In the starlight of Glen Dubh
Stretched beneath a hazel bough
Kissed from ear and throat to brow,
5 Since your fingers, neck, and chin
Made the bars that fenced me in,
Till Paradise seemed but a wreck
Near your bosom, brow, and neck,
And stars grew wilder, growing wise,
10 In the splendour of your eyes!
Since the weasel wandered near
Whilst we kissed from ear to ear

And the wet and withered leaves
Blew about your cap and sleeves,
15 Till the moon sank tired through the ledge
Of the wet and windy hedge?
And we took the starry lane
Back to Dublin town again.

James Joyce's *Pomes Penyeach* (1927) sold for a shilling (*i.e.*, 12 pence) and contained 13 poems. Because in Dublin a "tilly" is the thirteenth item in a baker's dozen, Joyce called the extra poem "Tilly." The date of "Tilly" is uncertain, but an early version, entitled "Ruminants" (see frontispiece), is probably of 1904. Most of the changes are small but important; the large change in the last stanza, however, turns "Tilly" not only into a better poem than "Ruminants" but also into a quite different one.

JAMES JOYCE (1882-1941)

Ruminants

He travels after the wintry sun,
Driving the cattle along the straight red road;
Calling to them in a voice they know,
He drives the cattle above Cabra.

5 His voice tells them home is not far.
They low and make soft music with their hoofs.
He drives them without labor before him,
Steam pluming their foreheads.

Herdsman, careful of the herd,
10 Tonight sleep well by the fire
When the herd too is asleep
And the door made fast.

Tilly

He travels after a winter sun,
Urging the cattle along a cold red road,
Calling to them, a voice they know,
He drives his beasts above Cabra.

5 The voice tells them home is warm.
They moo and make brute music with their hoofs.
He drives them with a flowering branch before him,
Smoke pluming their foreheads.

Boor, bond of the herd,
10 Tonight stretch full by the fire!
I bleed by the black stream
For my torn bough!

On 15 April 1802, William Wordsworth and his sister, Dorothy, took a walk, during which they saw some daffodils near a lake. Dorothy recorded the experience in her journal, and this entry affords us something close to the raw material out of which Wordsworth's poem, "I Wandered Lonely as a Cloud," was made. The entry is not, of course, Wordsworth's own experience; Dorothy's experience was not William's, and Dorothy's words cannot exactly reproduce even her own experience. (It should be noted, incidentally, that Dorothy's description is not entirely "factual"; her daffodils rest their heads, glance, dance, etc.) Still, the entry gives us something of the phenomena that stirred in Wordsworth an emotion, and for Wordsworth poetry was made out of "emotion recollected in tranquillity." In 1804, two years after the walk, presumably he recollected and contemplated the emotion, and wrote "I Wandered Lonely as a Cloud."

Wordsworth first published the poem in 1807, but the version printed below (which is the one everyone knows) is that of 1815. The differences between the first and second versions are these: in the first version lines 7-12 are lacking; line 4 has "dancing" instead of "golden"; line 5 has "Along" instead of "Beside"; line 6 has "Ten thousand" instead of "Fluttering and"; line 16 has "laughing" instead of "jocund."

DOROTHY WORDSWORTH (1771-1855)

From Journals, 15 April 1802

It was a threatening, misty morning, but mild. We set off after dinner from Eusemere. Mrs. Clarkson went a short way with us, but turned back. The wind was furious, and we thought we must have returned. We first rested in the large boat-house, then under a furze bush opposite Mr. Clarkson's. Saw the plough going in the field. The wind seized our breath. The Lake was rough. . . . When we were in the woods beyond Gowbarrow Park we saw a few daffodils close to the water-side. We fancied that the lake had floated the seeds ashore, and that the little colony had so sprung up. But as we went along there were more and yet more; and at last, under the boughs of the trees, we saw that there was a long belt of them along the shore, about the breadth of a country turnpike road. I never saw daffodils so beautiful. They grew among the mossy stones about and about them; some rested their heads upon these stones as on a pillow for weariness; and the rest tossed and reeled and danced, and seemed as if they verily laughed with the wind, that blew upon them over the lake; they looked so gay, ever glancing, ever changing. This wind blew directly over the lake to them. There was here and there a little knot, and a few stragglers a few yards higher up; but they were so few as not to disturb the simplicity, unity, and life of that one busy highway. We rested again and again. The bays were stormy, and we heard the waves at different distances, and in the middle of the water, like the sea. Rain came on—we were wet when we reached Luff's, but we called in.

WILLIAM WORDSWORTH (1770-1850)

I Wandered Lonely as a Cloud

I wandered lonely as a cloud
That floats on high o'er vales and hills,
When all at once I saw a crowd,
A host, of golden daffodils,
5 Beside the lake, beneath the trees,
Fluttering and dancing in the breeze.

Continuous as the stars that shine
And twinkle on the milky way,
They stretched in never-ending line
10 Along the margin of a bay;
Ten thousand saw I at a glance,
Tossing their heads in sprightly dance.

The waves beside them danced, but they
Outdid the sparkling waves in glee;
15 A poet could not but be gay,
In such a jocund company;
I gazed—and gazed—but little thought
What wealth the show to me had brought:

For oft, when on my couch I lie
20 In vacant or in pensive mood,
They flash upon that inward eye
Which is the bliss of solitude;
And then my heart with pleasure fills,
And dances with the daffodils.

According to Greek mythology, Zeus fell in love with Leda, disguised himself as a swan, and ravished her. Among the offspring of this union were Helen and Clytemnestra. Paris abducted Helen, causing the Greeks to raze Troy; Clytemnestra, wife of Agamemnon, murdered her husband on his triumphant return to Greece. Yeats saw political significance in the myth of beauty and war engendered by a god, but, as he tells us, when he was composing "Leda and the Swan" the political significance evaporated:

> After the individualistic, demagogic movements, founded by Hobbes and popularized by the Encyclopaedists and the French Revolution, we have a soil so exhausted that it cannot grow that crop again for centuries. Then I thought "Nothing is now possible but some movement, or birth from above, preceded by some violent annunciation." My fancy began to play with Leda and the Swan for metaphor, and I began this poem, but as I wrote, bird and lady took such possession of the scene that all politics went out of it.

The first version below is from a manuscript dated 18 September 1923; the second version was printed in a magazine, August 1924; the third version is Yeats's final one, first published in 1928.

WILLIAM BUTLER YEATS (1865-1939)

Leda and the Swan (*an early version*)

Now can the swooping godhead have his will
Yet hovers, though her helpless thighs are pressed
By the webbed toes; and that all powerful bill
Has suddenly bowed her face upon his breast.
5 How can those terrified vague fingers push
The feathered glory from her loosening thighs?
All the stretched body's laid in that white rush
And feels the strange heart beating where it lies.
A shudder in the loins engenders there
10 The broken wall, the burning roof and Tower
And Agamemnon dead. . . .
                              Being so caught up
Did nothing pass before her in the air?
Did she put on his knowledge with his power
Before the indifferent beak could let her drop?

Leda and the Swan (*a later version*)

A rush, a sudden wheel, and hovering still
The bird descends, and her frail thighs are pressed
By the webbed toes, and that all-powerful bill
Has laid her helpless face upon his breast.
5 How can those terrified vague fingers push
The feathered glory from her loosening thighs!
All the stretched body's laid on the white rush
And feels the strange heart beating where it lies;
A shudder in the loins engenders there
10 The broken wall, the burning roof and tower
And Agamemnon dead.
                              Being so caught up,
So mastered by the brute blood of the air,
Did she put on his knowledge with his power
Before the indifferent beak could let her drop?

Leda and the Swan (*the final version*)

A sudden blow: the great wings beating still
Above the staggering girl, her thighs caressed
By the dark webs, her nape caught in his bill,
He holds her helpless breast upon his breast.

5 How can those terrified vague fingers push
The feathered glory from her loosening thighs?
And how can body, laid in that white rush,
But feel the strange heart beating where it lies?

A shudder in the loins engenders there
10 The broken wall, the burning roof and tower
And Agamemnon dead.
                              Being so caught up,
So mastered by the brute blood of the air,
Did she put on his knowledge with his power
Before the indifferent beak could let her drop?

A COLLECTION OF POEMS

SIR THOMAS WYATT (1503?-1542)

They Flee from Me

They flee from me that sometime did me seek
With naked foot stalking in my chamber.
I have seen them gentle, tame, and meek
That now are wild and do not remember
5 That sometime they put themselves in danger
To take bread at my hand; and now they range
Busily seeking with a continual change.

Thankèd be Fortune, it hath been otherwise
Twenty times better; but once in special,
10 In thin array after a pleasant guise,
When her loose gown from her shoulders did fall,
And she me caught in her arms long and small;°   *narrow*
And therewithall sweetly did me kiss,
And softly said, "Dear heart, how like you this?"

15 It was no dream; I lay broad waking.
But all is turned thorough my gentleness
Into a strange fashion of forsaking;
And I have leave to go of her goodness,
And she also to use newfangleness.
20 But since that I so kindely° am served,   (1) *naturally* (2) *kindly*
I would fain know what she hath deserved.   (ironic)

JOHN DONNE (1572-1631)

A Valediction: Forbidding Mourning

As virtuous men pass mildly away,
   And whisper to their souls, to go,
Whilst some of their sad friends do say,
   "The breath goes now," and some say, "No":

5 So let us melt, and make no noise.
   No tear-floods, nor sigh-tempests move.
'Twere profanation of our joys
   To tell the laity our love.

Moving of the earth° brings harms and fears,   *an earthquake*
10   Men reckon what it did and meant;
But trepidation of the spheres,
   Though greater far, is innocent.*

Dull sublunary° lovers' love   *under the moon, i.e.,*
   (Whose soul is sense) cannot admit   *earthly*
15 Absence, because it doth remove
   Those things which elemented it.

But we, by a love so much refined
   That our selves know not what it is,
Inter-assured of the mind,
20   Care less, eyes, lips, and hands to miss.

Our two souls therefore, which are one,
   Though I must go, endure not yet
A breach, but an expansion,
   Like gold to airy thinness beat.

25 If they be two, they are two so
   As stiff twin compasses° are two: *i.e., a carpenter's*
Thy soul, the fixed foot, makes no show   *compass*
   To move, but doth, if the other do.

And though it in the center sit,
30   Yet when the other far doth roam,
It leans, and hearkens after it,
   And grows erect, as that comes home.

Such wilt thou be to me, who must
   Like the other foot, obliquely run:
35 Thy firmness makes my circle just,
   And makes me end where I begun.

* But the movement of the heavenly spheres (in Ptolemaic astronomy), though
far greater, is harmless.

The Blossom

Little think'st thou, poor flower,
Whom I have watched six or seven days,
And seen thy birth, and seen what every hour
Gave to thy growth, thee to this height to raise,
5   And now dost laugh and triumph on this bough,
Little think'st thou
That it will freeze anon, and that I shall
Tomorrow find thee fall'n, or not at all.

Little think'st thou, poor heart,
10   That labor'st yet to nestle thee,
And think'st by hovering here to get a part
In a forbidden or forbidding tree,
And hop'st her stiffness by long siege to bow,
Little think'st thou,
15   That thou tomorrow, ere that Sun° doth wake,   *i.e., his lady*
Must with this sun, and me, a journey take.

But thou, which lov'st to be
Subtle to plague thyself, wilt say:
"Alas! if you must go, what's that to me?
20   Here lies my business, and here I will stay:
You go to friends, whose love and means present
Various content°   *satisfaction*
To your eyes, ears, and tongue, and every part.
If then your body go, what need you a heart?"

25   Well then, stay here; but know,
When thou hast stayed and done thy most,
A naked thinking heart, that makes no show,
Is, to a woman, but a kind of ghost;
How shall she know my heart; or, having none,
30   Know thee for one?
Practice may make her know some other part,
But take my word, she doth not know a heart.
Meet me at London, then,
Twenty days hence, and thou shalt see
35   Me fresher, and more fat, by being with men,
Than if I had stayed still with her and thee.
For God's sake, if you can, be you so too:
I would give you
There, to another friend, whom we shall find
40   As glad to have my body, as my mind.

BEN JONSON (1573-1637)
The Hour-Glass

Consider this small dust, here in the glass,
    By atoms moved.
Could you believe that this the body was
    Of one that loved;
And in his mistress' flame playing like a fly,
Was turned to cinders by her eye?
Yes; and in death, as life, unblest,
    To have 't expressed,
Even ashes of lovers find no rest.

BEN JONSON (1573-1637)
To Heaven

Good and great God! can I not think of Thee,
But it must straight my melancholy be?
Is it interpreted in me disease
That, laden with my sins, I seek for ease?
5 Oh be Thou witness, that the reins dost know
And hearts of all, if I be sad for show;
And judge me after, if I dare pretend
To aught but grace, or aim at other end.
As Thou art all, so be Thou all to me,
10 First, midst, and last, converted One and Three!
My faith, my hope, my love; and in this state,
My judge, my witness, and my advocate.
Where have I been this while exiled from Thee,
And whither rapt, now Thou but stoop'st to me?
15 Dwell, dwell here still! Oh, being everywhere,
How can I doubt to find Thee ever here?
I know my state, both full of shame and scorn,
Conceived in sin, and unto labor born,
Standing with fear, and must with horror fall,
20 And destined unto judgment, after all.
I feel my griefs too, and there scarce is ground
Upon my flesh t' inflict another wound.
Yet dare I not complain or wish for death,
With holy Paul°, lest it be thought the breath   *see Romans 7:24*
25 Of discontent; or that these pray'rs be
For weariness of life, not love of Thee.

ROBERT HERRICK (1591-1674)

Corinna's Going A-Maying

Get up, get up, for shame; the blooming morn
Upon her wings presents the god unshorn.*
    See how Aurora throws her fair
    Fresh-quilted colors through the air.
5   Get up, sweet slug-a-bed, and see
    The dew bespangling herb and tree.
Each flower has wept, and bowed toward the East,
Above an hour since; yet you not dressed,
    Nay! not so much as out of bed?
10   When all the birds have matins said
    And sung their thankful hymns, 'tis sin,
    Nay, profanation to keep in,
Whenas a thousand virgins on this day
Spring, sooner than the lark, to fetch in May.

15 Rise! and put on your foliage, and be seen
To come forth, like the springtime, fresh and green,
    And sweet as Flora. Take no care
    For jewels for your gown, or hair;
    Fear not, the leaves will strew
20   Gems in abundance upon you;
Besides, the childhood of the day has kept,
Against° you come, some orient pearls unwept;   *until*
    Come, and receive them while the light
    Hangs on the dewlocks of the night,
25   And Titan° on the eastern hill   *the sun*
    Retires himself or else stands still
Till you come forth. Wash, dress, be brief in praying!
Few beads° are best, when once we go a-Maying.   *rosary beads*
Come, my Corinna, come; and, coming, mark
30 How each field turns a street, each street a park
    Made green and trimmed with trees. See how
    Devotion gives each house a bough
    Or branch; each porch, each door, ere this
    An ark, a tabernacle, is,
35 Made up of white-thorn, neatly interwove;
As if here were those cooler shades of love.
    Can such delights be in the street
    And open fields, and we not see't?
    Come, we'll abroad; and let's obey
40   The proclamation made for May,
And sin no more, as we have done, by staying;
But, my Corinna, come, let's go a-Maying.

* Apollo, the sun god, whose uncut locks are rays.

There's not a budding boy or girl this day
But is got up, and gone to bring in May.
45   A deal of youth, ere this, is come
      Back, and with white-thorn laden home.
      Some have despatched their cakes and cream,
      Before that we have left to dream;
And some have wept and wooed and plighted troth,
50 And chose their priest, ere we can cast off sloth.
      Many a green-gown° has been given,   *grass-stained gown*
      Many a kiss, both odd and even;
      Many a glance, too, has been sent
      From out the eye, love's firmament;
55 Many a jest told of the keys' betraying
This night, and locks picked, yet we're not a-Maying.

Come, let us go while we are in our prime,
And take the harmless folly of the time.
      We shall grow old apace, and die
60   Before we know our liberty.
      Our life is short, and our days run
      As fast away as does the sun;
And, as a vapor or a drop of rain,
Once lost, can ne'er be found again,
65   So, when or you or I are made
      A fable, song, or fleeting shade,
      All love, all liking, all delight,
      Lies drowned with us in endless night.
Then while time serves, and we are but decaying,
70 Come, my Corinna, come, let's go a-Maying.

JONATHAN SWIFT (1667-1745)

A Satirical Elegy on the Death
of a Late Famous General

      His Grace°! impossible! what, dead!   *Duke of Marlborough*
      Of old age too, and in his bed!
      And could that Mighty Warrior fall?
      And so inglorious, after all!
5 Well, since he's gone, no matter how,
      The last loud trump must wake him now:
      And, trust me, as the noise grows stronger,
      He'd wish to sleep a little longer.
      And could he be indeed so old
10 As by the newspapers we're told?
      Threescore, I think, is pretty high;
      'Twas time in conscience he should die.

This world he cumbered long enough;
He burnt his candle to the snuff;
15 And that's the reason, some folks think,
He left behind *so great a s...k.*
Behold his funeral appears,
Nor widow's sighs, nor orphan's tears,
Wont at such times each heart to pierce,
20 Attend the progress of his hearse.
But what of that, his friends may say,
He had those honors in his day.
True to his profit and his pride,
He made them weep before he died.

25   Come hither, all ye empty things,
Ye bubbles raised by breath of Kings;
Who float upon the tide of state,
Come hither, and behold your fate.
Let pride be taught by this rebuke,
30 How very mean a thing's a Duke;
From all his ill-got honors flung,
Turned to that dirt from whence he sprung.

JONATHAN SWIFT (1667-1745)

On Stella's Birthday

Stella* this day is thirty-four
(We shan't dispute a year or more)—
However, Stella, be not troubled,
Although thy size and years are doubled,
5 Since first I saw thee at sixteen,
The brightest virgin on the green,
So little is thy form declined,
Made up so largely in thy mind.
Oh, would it please the gods, to split
10 Thy beauty, size, and years, and wit,
No age could furnish out a pair
Of nymphs so graceful, wise, and fair,
With half the luster of your eyes,
With half your wit, your years, and size.
15 And then, before it grew too late,
How should I beg of gentle Fate
(That either nymph might have her swain)
To split my Worship** too in twain.

* Hester Johnson, Swift's protégée and intimate friend.
** Swift, who as Dean of St. Patrick's, was addressed as "Your Worship."

JONATHAN SWIFT (1667-1745)

A Description of the Morning

Now hardly here and there an hackney-coach
Appearing, showed the ruddy morn's approach.
Now Betty from her master's bed had flown,
And softly stole to discompose her own.
5 The slipshod 'prentice from his master's door,
Had pared the dirt, and sprinkled round the floor.
Now Moll had whirled her mop with dext'rous airs,
Prepared to scrub the entry and the stairs.
The youth with broomy stumps began to trace
10 The kennel° edge, where wheels had worn the place.   *gutter*
The small-coal man was heard with cadence deep,
'Till drowned in shriller notes of chimney sweep,
Duns at his lordship's gate began to meet,
And brickdust° Moll had screamed through half a street.   *(used*
15 The turnkey now his flock returning sees,   *for scouring)*
Duly let out a-nights to steal for fees.
The watchful bailiffs take their silent stands;
And schoolboys lag with satchels in their hands.

ALEXANDER POPE (1688-1744)

Epistle to Miss Blount on Her Leaving
the Town after the Coronation†

As some fond virgin, whom her mother's care
Drags from the Town to wholesome country air,
Just when she learns to roll a melting eye,
And hear a spark°, yet think no danger nigh;   *beau*
5 From the dear man unwilling she must sever,
Yet takes one kiss before she parts forever:
Thus from the world fair Zephalinda flew,
Saw others happy, and with sighs withdrew;
Not that their pleasures caused her discontent,
10 She sighed not that they stayed, but that she went.
    She went, to plain-work°, and to purling brooks,   *sewing*
Old-fashioned halls, dull aunts, and croaking rooks;
She went from op'ra, park, assembly, play,
To morning-walks, and prayers three hours a day;

The poem is addressed to Teresa Blount (call Zephalinda in line 7), who
t London after the coronation of George I in 1714. Parthenia (line 46) is
: sister Martha.

15 To part her time 'twixt reading and bohea°,   *tea*
   To muse, and spill her solitary tea,
   Or o'er cold coffee trifle with the spoon,
   Count the slow clock, and dine exact at noon;
   Divert her eyes with pictures in the fire,
20 Hum half a tune, tell stories to the squire;
   Up to her godly garret after seven,
   There starve and pray, for that's the way to heaven.
       Some squire, perhaps, you take delight to rack,
   Whose game is whisk, whose treat a toast in sack;
25 Who visits with a gun, presents you birds,
   Then gives a smacking buss, and cries—"No words!"
   Or with his hound comes hollowing from the stable,
   Makes love with nods and knees beneath a table;
   Whose laughs are hearty, though his jests are coarse,
30 And loves you best of all things—but his horse.
       In some fair evening, on your elbow laid,
   You dream of Triumphs° in the rural shade;   *public celebrations*
   In pensive thought recall the fancied scene,
   See Coronations rise on every green;
35 Before you pass the imaginary sights
   Of lords, and earls, and dukes, and gartered knights,
   While the spread fan o'ershades your closing eyes;
   Then give one flirt, and all the vision flies.
   Thus vanish scepters, coronets, and balls,
40 And leave you in lone woods, or empty walls.
       So when your slave, at some dear idle time
   (Not plagued with headaches, or the want of rhyme),
   Stands in the streets, abstracted from the crew,
   And while he seems to study, thinks of you;
45 Just when his fancy points your sprightly eyes,
   Or sees the blush of soft Parthenia rise,
   Gay° pats my shoulder, and you vanish quite,   *Pope's friend,*
   Streets, chairs, and coxcombs rush upon my sight;   *John Gay*
   Vexed to be still in town, I knit my brow,
50 Look sour, and hum a tune—as you may now.

WILLIAM BLAKE (1757-1827)

The Echoing Green

The Sun does arise,
And make happy the skies;
The merry bells ring
To welcome the Spring;
5 The skylark and thrush,
The birds of the bush,
Sing louder around
To the bells' cheerful sound,
While our sports shall be seen
10 On the Echoing Green.
Old John, with white hair,
Does laugh away care,
Sitting under the oak,
Among the old folk.
15 They laugh at our play,
And soon they all say:
"Such, such were the joys
When we all, girls and boys,
In our youth time were seen
20 On the Echoing Green."

Till the little ones, weary,
No more can be merry;
The sun does descend,
And our sports have an end.
25 Round the laps of their mothers
Many sisters and brothers,
Like birds in their nest,
Are ready for rest,
And sport no more seen
30 On the darkening Green.

WILLIAM BLAKE (1757-1827)

The Lamb

Little Lamb, who made thee?
Dost thou know who made thee?
Gave thee life, and bid thee feed
By the stream and o'er the mead;
5 Gave thee clothing of delight,
Softest clothing, wooly, bright;

Gave thee such a tender voice,
Making all the vales rejoice?
  Little Lamb, who made thee?
10 Dost thou know who made thee?

  Little Lamb, I'll tell thee,
  Little Lamb, I'll tell thee:
He is callèd by thy name,
For he calls himself a Lamb.
15 He is meek, and he is mild;
He became a little child.
I a child, and thou a lamb,
We are callèd by his name.
  Little Lamb, God bless thee!
20 Little Lamb, God bless thee!

WILLIAM BLAKE (1757-1827)

The Tyger

Tyger! Tyger! burning bright
In the forest of the night,
What immortal hand or eye
Could frame thy fearful symmetry?

5 In what distant deeps or skies
Burnt the fire of thine eyes?
On what wings dare he aspire?
What the hand dare seize the fire?

And what shoulder, and what art,
10 Could twist the sinews of thy heart?
And, when thy heart began to beat,
What dread hand? and what dread feet?

What the hammer? what the chain?
In what furnace was thy brain?
15 What the anvil? what dread grasp
Dare its deadly terrors clasp?

When the stars threw down their spears,
And watered heaven with their tears,
Did he smile his work to see?
20 Did he who made the lamb make thee?

Tyger! Tyger! burning bright
In the forests of the night,
What immortal hand or eye,
Dare frame thy fearful symmetry?

WILLIAM WORDSWORTH (1770-1850)

The Solitary Reaper

Behold her, single in the field,
Yon solitary Highland Lass!
Reaping and singing by herself;
Stop here, or gently pass!
5 Alone she cuts and binds the grain,
And sings a melancholy strain;
O listen! for the Vale profound
Is overflowing with the sound.

No Nightingale did ever chant
10 More welcome notes to weary bands
Of travellers in some shady haunt,
Among Arabian sands:
A voice so thrilling ne'er was heard
In spring-time from the Cuckoo-bird,
15 Breaking the silence of the seas
Among the farthest Hebrides.

Will no one tell me what she sings?—
Perhaps the plaintive numbers flow
For old, unhappy, far-off things,
20 And battles long ago:
Or is it some more humble lay,
Familiar matter of today?
Some natural sorrow, loss, or pain,
That has been, and may be again?

25 Whate'er the theme, the maiden sang
As if her song could have no ending;
I saw her singing at her work,
And o'er the sickle bending;—
I listened, motionless and still;
30 And, as I mounted up the hill,
The music in my heart I bore
Long after it was heard no more.

WILLIAM WORDSWORTH (1770-1850)

Composed upon Westminster Bridge, September 3, 1802

Earth has not anything to show more fair:
Dull would he be of soul who could pass by
A sight so touching in its majesty:
This city now doth, like a garment, wear
5 The beauty of the morning; silent, bare,
Ships, towers, domes, theaters, and temples lie
Open unto the fields, and to the sky;
All bright and glittering in the smokeless air.
Never did sun more beautifully steep
10 In his first splendor, valley, rock, or hill;
Ne'er saw I, never felt, a calm so deep!
The river glideth at his own sweet will:
Dear God! the very houses seem asleep;
And all that mighty heart is lying still!

JOHN KEATS (1795-1821)

La Belle Dame sans Merci

O what can ail thee, knight-at-arms,
    Alone and palely loitering?
The sedge has withered from the lake,
    And no birds sing.

5 O what can ail thee, knight-at-arms,
    So haggard and so woe-begone?
The squirrel's granary is full,
    And the harvest's done.

I see a lily on thy brow,
10   With anguish moist and fever dew,
And on thy cheeks a fading rose
    Fast withereth too.

"I met a lady in the meads,
    Full beautiful—a faery's child,
15 Her hair was long, her foot was light,
    And her eyes were wild.

"I made a garland for her head,
    And bracelets too, and fragrant zone°;   *belt of flowers*
She looked at me as she did love,
20   And made sweet moan.

"I set her on my pacing steed,
    And nothing else saw all day long,
For sidelong would she bend and sing
    A faery's song.

25 "She found me roots of relish sweet,
    And honey wild, and manna dew,
And sure in language strange she said
    'I love thee true.'

"She took me to her elfin grot,
30   And there she wept and sighed full sore,
And there I shut her wild wild eyes
    With kisses four.

"And there she lulled me asleep,
    And there I dreamed—Ah! woe betide!
35 The latest dream I ever dreamed
    On the cold hill side.

"I saw pale kings and princes too,
    Pale warriors, death-pale were they all;
They cried, 'La Belle Dame sans Merci°   *the beautiful pitiless lady*
40   Hath thee in thrall!'

"I saw their starved lips in the gloam
    With horrid warning gaped wide,
And I awoke, and found me here,
    On the cold hill's side.

45 "And this is why I sojourn here,
    Alone and palely loitering,
Though the sedge has withered from the lake,
    And no birds sing."

JOHN KEATS (1795-1821)

To Autumn

I

Season of mists and mellow fruitfulness,
    Close bosom-friend of the maturing sun;
Conspiring with him how to load and bless
    With fruit the vines that round the thatch-eaves run;
5 To bend with apples the mossed cottage-trees,
    And fill all fruit with ripeness to the core;
        To swell the gourd, and plump the hazel shells
    With a sweet kernel; to set budding more,
    And still more, later flowers for the bees,
10   Until they think warm days will never cease,
        For summer has o'er-brimmed their clammy cells.

Who hath not seen thee oft amid thy store?
 Sometimes whoever seeks abroad may find
Thee sitting careless on a granary floor,
₁₅ Thy hair soft-lifted by the winnowing wind;
Or on a half-reaped furrow sound asleep,
  Drowsed with the fume of poppies, while thy hook
   Spares the next swath and all its twined flowers:
And sometime like a gleaner thou dost keep
₂₀ Steady thy laden head across a brook;
 Or by a cider-press, with patient look,
  Thou watchest the last oozings hours by hours.

Where are the songs of Spring? Ay, where are they?
 Think not of them, thou hast thy music too,—
₂₅ While barred clouds bloom the soft-dying day,
 And touch the stubble-plains with rosy hue;
Then in a wailful choir the small gnats mourn
  Among the river sallows, borne aloft
   Or sinking as the light wind lives or dies;
₃₀ And full-grown lambs loud bleat from hilly bourn;
 Hedge-crickets sing; and now with treble soft
 The red-breast whistles from a garden-croft;
  And gathering swallows twitter in the skies.

RALPH WALDO EMERSON (*1803-1882*)

Days

Daughters of Time, the hypocritic Days,
Muffled and dumb like barefoot dervishes,
And marching single in an endless file,
Bring diadems and fagots in their hands.
₅ To each they offer gifts after his will,
Bread, kingdoms, stars, and sky that holds them all.
I, in my pleached garden, watched the pomp,
Forgot my morning wishes, hastily
Took a few herbs and apples, and the Day
₁₀ Turned and departed silent. I, too late,
Under her solemn fillet saw the scorn.

ALFRED, LORD TENNYSON (1809-1892)

Ulysses

It little profits that an idle king,
By this still hearth, among these barren crags,
Matched with an aged wife, I mete and dole
Unequal laws unto a savage race,
5 That hoard, and sleep, and feed, and know not me.
I cannot rest from travel; I will drink
Life to the lees. All times I have enjoyed
Greatly, have suffered greatly, both with those
That loved me, and alone; on shore, and when
10 Thro' scudding drifts the rainy Hyades
Vext the dim sea. I am become a name;
For always roaming with a hungry heart
Much have I seen and known,—cities of men
And manners, climates, councils, governments,
15 Myself not least, but honored of them all,—
And drunk delight of battle with my peers,
Far on the ringing plains of windy Troy.
I am a part of all that I have met;
Yet all experience is an arch wherethro'
20 Gleams that untravelled world whose margin fades
For ever and for ever when I move.
How dull it is to pause, to make an end,
To rust unburnished, not to shine in use!
As tho' to breathe were life! Life piled on life
25 Were all too little, and of one to me
Little remains; but every hour is saved
From that eternal silence, something more,
A bringer of new things; and vile it were
For some three suns to store and hoard myself,
30 And this gray spirit yearning in desire
To follow knowledge like a sinking star,
Beyond the utmost bound of human thought.

This is my son, mine own Telemachus,
To whom I leave the scepter and the isle,—
35 Well-loved of me, discerning to fulfill
This labor, by slow prudence to make mild
A rugged people, and thro' soft degrees
Subdue them to the useful and the good.
Most blameless is he, centered in the sphere
40 Of common duties, decent not to fail
In offices of tenderness, and pay
Meet adoration to my household gods,
When I am gone. He works his work, I mine.

There lies the port; the vessel puffs her sail;
45 There gloom the dark, broad seas. My mariners,
Souls that have toiled, and wrought, and thought with me,—
That ever with a frolic welcome took
The thunder and the sunshine, and opposed
Free hearts, free foreheads,—you and I are old;
50 Old age hath yet his honor and his toil.
Death closes all; but something ere the end,
Some work of noble note, may yet be done,
Not unbecoming men that strove with Gods.
The lights begin to twinkle from the rocks;
55 The long day wanes; the slow moon climbs; the deep
Moans round with many voices. Come, my friends.
'T is not too late to seek a newer world.
Push off, and sitting well in order smite
The sounding furrows; for my purpose holds
60 To sail beyond the sunset, and the baths
Of all the western stars, until I die.
It may be that the gulfs will wash us down;
It may be we shall touch the Happy Isles,
And see the great Achilles, whom we knew.
65 Tho' much is taken, much abides; and tho'
We are not now that strength which in old days
Moved earth and heaven, that which we are, we are.
One equal temper of heroic hearts,
Made weak by time and fate, but strong in will
70 To strive, to seek, to find, and not to yield.

EMILY DICKINSON (1830-1886)

The Soul Selects Her Own Society

The Soul selects her own Society—
Then—shuts the Door—
To her divine Majority—
Present no more—

5 Unmoved—she notes the Chariots—pausing—
At her low Gate—
Unmoved—an Emperor be kneeling
Upon her Mat—

I've known her—from an ample nation—
10 Choose One—
Then—close the Valves of her attention—
Like Stone—

THOMAS HARDY (1840-1928)

The Convergence of the Twain

(*Lines on the loss of the "Titanic"*)

I

In a solitude of the sea
Deep from human vanity,
And the Pride of Life that planned her, stilly couches she.

II

Steel chambers, late the pyres
Of her salamandrine fires,
Cold currents thrid°, and turn to rhythmic tidal lyres.   *thread*

III

Over the mirrors meant
To glass the opulent
The sea-worm crawls—grotesque, slimed, dumb, indifferent.

IV

Jewels in joy designed
To ravish the sensuous mind
Lie lightless, all their sparkles bleared and black and blind.

V

Dim moon-eyed fishes near
Gaze at the gilded gear
And query: "What does this vaingloriousness down here?"

VI

Well: while was fashioning
This creature of cleaving wing,
The Immanent Will that stirs and urges everything

VII

Prepared a sinister mate
For her—so gaily great—
A Shape of Ice, for the time far and dissociate.

VIII

And as the smart ship grew
In stature, grace, and hue,
In shadowy silent distance grew the Iceberg too.

IX

Alien they seemed to be:
No mortal eye could see
The intimate welding of their later history,

X

Or sign that they were bent
By paths coincident
30 On being anon twin halves of one august event,

XI

Till the Spinner of the Years
Said "Now!" And each one hears,
And consummation comes, and jars two hemispheres.

THOMAS HARDY (1840-1928)

Channel Firing

That night your great guns, unawares,
Shook all our coffins as we lay,
And broke the chancel window-squares,
We thought it was the Judgment-day

5 And sat upright. While drearisome
Arose the howl of wakened hounds:
The mouse let fall the altar-crumb,
The worms drew back into the mounds,

The glebe cow drooled. Till God called, "No;
10 It's gunnery practice out at sea
Just as before you went below;
The world is as it used to be:

"All nations striving strong to make
Red war yet redder. Mad as hatters
15 They do no more for Christès sake
Than you who are helpless in such matters.

"That this is not the judgment-hour
For some of them's a blessed thing,
For if it were they'd have to scour
20 Hell's floor for so much threatening . . .

"Ha, ha. It will be warmer when
I blow the trumpet (if indeed
I ever do; for you are men,
And rest eternal sorely need)."

25 So down we lay again. "I wonder,
Will the world ever saner be,"
Said one, "than when He sent us under
In our indifferent century!"

And many a skeleton shook his head.
30 "Instead of preaching forty year,"
My neighbor Parson Thirdly said,
"I wish I had stuck to pipes and beer."

Again the guns disturbed the hour,
Roaring their readiness to avenge,
35 As far inland as Stourton Tower,
And Camelot, and starlit Stonehenge.

GERARD MANLEY HOPKINS (1844-1889)
Thou Art Indeed Just, Lord

*Justus quidem tu es, Domine, si disputem tecum: verumta-
men justa loquar ad te: Quare via impiorum prosperatur? etc.*
(Jeremiah 12:1, translated in lines 1-3)

Thou art indeed just, Lord, if I contend
With thee; but, sir, so what I plead is just.
Why do sinners' ways prosper? and why must
Disappointment all I endeavor end?
5 Wert thou my enemy, O thou my friend,
How wouldst thou worse, I wonder, than thou dost
Defeat, thwart me? Oh, the sots and thralls of lust
Do in spare hours more thrive than I that spend,
Sir, life upon thy cause. See, banks and brakes
10 Now, leavèd how thick! lacèd they are again
With fretty chervil, look, and fresh wind shakes
Them; birds build—but not I build; no, but strain,
Time's eunuch, and not breed one work that wakes
Mine, O thou lord of life, send my roots rain.

A. E. HOUSMAN (1859-1936)
Eight O'Clock

He stood, and heard the steeple
    Sprinkle the quarters on the morning town.
One, two, three, four, to market-place and people
    It tossed them down.

Strapped, noosed, nighing his hour,
    He stood and counted them and cursed his luck;
And then the clock collected in the tower
    Its strength, and struck.

A. E. HOUSMAN (1859-1936)

Shropshire Lad #31

On Wenlock Edge* the wood's in trouble;
    His forest fleece the Wrekin heaves;
The gale, it plies the saplings double,
    And thick on Severn snow the leaves.

5 'Twould blow like this through holt and hanger°   *wood and thicket*
    When Uricon the city stood:
'Tis the old wind in the old anger,
    But then it threshed another wood.

Then, 'twas before my time, the Roman
10   At yonder heaving hill would stare:
The blood that warms an English yeoman,
    The thoughts that hurt him, they were there.

There, like the wind through woods in riot,
    Through him the gale of life blew high;
15 The tree of man was never quiet:
    Then 'twas the Roman, now 'tis I.

The gale, it plies the saplings double,
    It blows so hard, 'twill soon be gone:
To-day the Roman and his trouble
20   Are ashes under Uricon.

ROBERT FROST (1874-1963)

Come In

As I came to the edge of the woods,
Thrush music—hark!
Now if it was dusk outside,
Inside it was dark.

---

* Wenlock Edge is a range of hills southeast of Shrewsbury; the Wrekin (line 2) is an extinct volcano, and the Severn (line 4) a river. Uricon (line 6) or Uriconium, an ancient Roman city also southeast of Shrewsbury, was burned by the Saxons in 584, and only ruins are left.

⁵ Too dark in the woods for a bird
By sleight of wing
To better its perch for the night,
Though it still could sing.

The last of the light of the sun
¹⁰ That had died in the west
Still lived for one song more
In a thrush's breast.

Far in the pillared dark
Thrush music went—
¹⁵ Almost like a call to come in
To the dark and lament.

But no, I was out for stars:
I would not come in.
I meant not even if asked,
²⁰ And I hadn't been.

ROBERT FROST (1874-1963)

The Most of It

He thought he kept the universe alone;
For all the voice in answer he could wake
Was but the mocking echo of his own
From some tree-hidden cliff across the lake.
⁵ Some morning from the boulder-broken beach
He would cry out on life, that what it wants
Is not its own love back in copy speech,
But counter-love, original response.
And nothing ever came of what he cried
¹⁰ Unless it was the embodiment that crashed
In the cliff's talus on the other side,
And then in the far distant water splashed,
But after a time allowed for it to swim,
Instead of proving human when it neared
¹⁵ And someone else additional to him,
As a great buck it powerfully appeared,
Pushing the crumpled water up ahead,
And landed pouring like a waterfall,
And stumbled through the rocks with horny tread,
²⁰ And forced the underbrush—and that was all.

WALLACE STEVENS (1879-1955)

Peter Quince at the Clavier *

I

Just as my fingers on these keys
Make music, so the selfsame sounds
On my spirit make a music, too.

Music is feeling, then, not sound;
5 And thus it is that what I feel,
Here in this room, desiring you,

Thinking of your blue-shadowed silk,
Is music. It   like the strain
Waked in the elders by Susanna.**

10 Of a green evening, clear and warm,
She bathed in her still garden, while
The red-eyed elders watching, felt

The basses of their beings throb
In witching chords, and their thin blood
15 Pulse pizzicati of Hosanna.

II

In the green water, clear and warm,
Susanna lay.
She searched
The touch of springs,
20 And found
Concealed imaginings.
She sighed,
For so much melody.

Upon the bank, she stood
25 In the cool
Of spent emotions.
She felt, among the leaves,
The dew
Of old devotions.

* Peter Quince is a clownish carpenter in A *Midsummer Night's Dream*.
** According to the History of Susanna (Apocrypha, and Douay Bible, Daniel 13), two Hebrew elders lusted after the beautiful and virtuous Susanna. They hid in her garden, watched her bathe, sought to seduce her, and then when her maids came in response to her cries, they accused Susanna of unchastity. Because the elders were judges, their charges were believed and Susanna was sentenced to death. When the prophet Daniel disproved the charges, the elders were executed instead of Susanna.

She walked upon the grass,
Still quavering.
The winds were like her maids,
On timid feet,
Fetching her woven scarves,
Yet wavering.

A breath upon her hand
Muted the night.
She turned—
A cymbal crashed,
And roaring horns.

III

Soon, with a noise like tambourines,
Came her attendant Byzantines.

They wondered why Susanna cried
Against the elders by her side;

And as they whispered, the refrain
Was like a willow swept by rain.

Anon, their lamps' uplifted flame
Revealed Susanna and her shame.

And then, the simpering Byzantines
Fled, with a noise like tambourines.

IV

Beauty is momentary in the mind—
The fitful tracing of a portal;
But in the flesh it is immortal.

The body dies; the body's beauty lives.
So evenings die, in their green going,
A wave, interminably flowing.
So gardens die, their meek breath scenting
The cowl of winter, done repenting.
So maidens die, to the auroral
Celebration of a maiden's choral.

Susanna's music touched the bawdy strings
Of those white elders; but, escaping,
Left only Death's ironic scraping.
Now, in its immortality, it plays
On the clear viol of her memory,
And makes a constant sacrament of praise.

WALLACE STEVENS (1879-1955)

Of Modern Poetry

The poem of the mind in the act of finding
What will suffice. It has not always had
To find: the scene was set; it repeated what
Was in the script.
5   Then the theatre was changed
To something else. Its past was a souvenir.
It has to be living, to learn the speech of the place.
It has to face the men of the time and to meet
The women of the time. It has to think about war
10 And it has to find what will suffice. It has
To construct a new stage. It has to be on that stage
And, like an insatiable actor, slowly and
With meditation, speak words that in the ear,
In the delicatest ear of the mind, repeat,
15 Exactly, that which it wants to hear, at the sound
Of which, an invisible audience listens,
Not to the play, but to itself, expressed
In an emotion as of two people, as of two
Emotions becoming one. The actor is
20 A metaphysician in the dark, twanging
An instrument, twanging a wiry string that gives
Sounds passing through sudden rightnesses, wholly
Containing the mind, below which it cannot descend,
Beyond which it has no will to rise.
25   It must
Be the finding of a satisfaction, and may
Be of a man skating, a woman dancing, a woman
Combing. The poem of the act of the mind.

MARIANNE MOORE (1887-)

Poetry*

I, too, dislike it: there are things that are important beyond all this fiddle.
   Reading it, however, with a perfect contempt for it, one discovers in
     it after all, a place for the genuine.
      Hands that can grasp, eyes
      that can dilate, hair that can rise
        if it must, these things are important not because a

* In a note to this poem, Miss Moore says that the quotation in lines 17-18
is derived from *The Diaries of Leo Tolstoy*; the quotation in lines 21-22 from
W. B. Yeats's *Ideas of Good and Evil*.
   A comment in *Predilections*, Miss Moore's volume of literary essays, affords

high-sounding interpretation can be put upon them but because they are
   useful. When they become so derivative as to become unintelligible,
   the same thing may be said for all of us, that we
      do not admire what
      we cannot understand: the bat
         holding on upside down or in quest of something to

eat, elephants pushing, a wild horse taking a roll, a tireless wolf under
   a tree, the immovable critic twitching his skin like a horse that feels a flea,
                                                                    the base-
   ball fan, the statistician—
      nor is it valid
         to discriminate against "business documents and

school-books"; all these phenomena are important. One must make a distinction
   however: when dragged into prominence by half poets, the result is not poetry,
   nor till the poet among us can be
      "literalists of
      the imagination"—above
         insolence and triviality and can present

for inspection, "imaginary gardens with real toads in them," shall we have
   it. In the meantime, if you demand on the one hand,
   the raw material of poetry in
      all its rawness and
      that which is on the other hand
         genuine, you are interested in poetry.

EDWIN MUIR (1887-1959)
The Enchanted Knight

Lulled by La Belle Dame Sans Merci° he lies   *see page 424*
   In the bare wood below the blackening hill.
The plough drives nearer now, the shadow flies
   Past him across the plain, but he lies still.

5 Long since the rust its gardens here has planned,
   Flowering his armor like an autumn field.
From his sharp breast-plate to his iron hand
   A spider's web is stretched, a phantom shield.

---

some insight into her style: "My own fondness for the unaccepted rhyme
derives, I think, from an instinctive effort to ensure naturalness. Even elate
and fearsome rightness like Shakespeare's is only preserved from the offense of
being 'poetic' by his well-nested effects of helpless naturalness."

When footsteps pound the turf beside his ear
10   Armies pass through his dream in endless line,
And one by one his ancient friends appear;
    They pass all day, but he can make no sign.

When a bird cries within the silent grove
The long-lost voice goes by, he makes to rise
15 And follow, but his cold limbs never move,
    And on the turf unstirred his shadow lies.

But if a withered leaf should drift
    Across his face and rest, the dread drops start
Chill on his forehead. Now he tries to lift
20   The insulting weight that stays and breaks his heart.

T. S. ELIOT (1888-1965)

The Love Song of J. Alfred Prufrock

> S'io credesse che mia risposta fosse
> A persona che mai tornasse al mondo,
> Questa fiamma staria senza piu scosse.
> Ma perciocche giammai di questo fondo
> Non torno vivo alcun, s'i'odo il vero,
> Senza tema d'infamia ti rispondo.*

Let us go then, you and I,
When the evening is spread out against the sky
Like a patient etherised upon a table;
Let us go, through certain half-deserted streets,
5 The muttering retreats
Of restless nights in one-night cheap hotels
And sawdust restaurants with oyster-shells:

---

* In Dante's *Inferno* XXVII: 61-66, a damned soul, who had sought absolution before committing a crime, addresses Dante, thinking that his words will never reach the earth: "If I believed that my answer were to a person who could ever return to the world, this flame would no longer quiver. But because no one ever returned from this depth, if what I hear is true, without fear of infamy, I answer you."

Explanations of allusions in the poem may be helpful. "Works and days" (line 29) is the title of a poem on farm life by Hesiod (eighth century B.C.); "dying fall" (line 52) echoes *Twelfth Night* I.i.4; lines 81-83 allude to John the Baptist (see Matthew 14:1-11); line 92 echoes lines 41-42 of Marvell's "To His Coy Mistress" (see page 372); for "Lazarus" (line 94) see Luke 16 and John 11; lines 112-117 allude to Polonius and perhaps to other figures in *Hamlet*; "full of high sentence" (line 117) comes from Chaucer's description of the Clerk of Oxford in *The Canterbury Tales*. (Editors' note)

Streets that follow like a tedious argument
Of insidious intent
10 To lead you to an overwhelming question . . .
Oh, do not ask, "What is it?"
Let us go and make our visit.

In the room the women come and go
Talking of Michelangelo.

15 The yellow fog that rubs its back upon the window-panes,
The yellow smoke that rubs its muzzle on the window-panes
Licked its tongue into the corners of the evening,
Lingered upon the pools that stand in drains,
Let fall upon its back the soot that falls from chimneys,
20 Slipped by the terrace, made a sudden leap,
And seeing that it was a soft October night,
Curled once about the house, and fell asleep.

And indeed there will be time
For the yellow smoke that slides along the street,
25 Rubbing its back upon the window-panes;
There will be time, there will be time
To prepare a face to meet the faces that you meet;
There will be time to murder and create,
And time for all the works and days of hands
30 That lift and drop a question on your plate;
Time for you and time for me,
And time yet for a hundred indecisions,
And for a hundred visions and revisions,
Before the taking of a toast and tea.

35 In the room the women come and go
Talking of Michelangelo.

And indeed there will be time
To wonder, "Do I dare?" and, "Do I dare?"
Time to turn back and descend the stair,
40 With a bald spot in the middle of my hair—
[They will say: "How his hair is growing thin!"]
My morning coat, my collar mounting firmly to the chin,
My necktie rich and modest, but asserted by a simple pin—
[They will say: "But how his arms and legs are thin!"]
45 Do I dare
Disturb the universe?
In a minute there is time
For decisions and revisions which a minute will reverse.

For I have known them all already, known them all:—
50 Have known the evenings, mornings, afternoons,

I have measured out my life with coffee spoons;
I know the voices dying with a dying fall
Beneath the music from a farther room.
    So how should I presume?

55 And I have known the eyes already, known them all—
The eyes that fix you in a formulated phrase,
And when I am formulated, sprawling on a pin,
When I am pinned and wriggling on the wall,
Then how should I begin
60 To spit out all the butt-ends of my days and ways?
    And how should I presume?

And I have known the arms already, known them all—
Arms that are braceleted and white and bare
[But in the lamplight, downed with light brown hair!]
65 Is it perfume from a dress
That makes me so digress?
Arms that lie along a table, or wrap about a shawl.
    And should I then presume?
    And how should I begin?

                .   .   .   .   .

70 Shall I say, I have gone at dusk through narrow streets
And watched the smoke that rises from the pipes
Of lonely men in shirt-sleeves, leaning out of windows? . . .

I should have been a pair of ragged claws
Scuttling across the floors of silent seas.

                .   .   .   .   .

75 And the afternoon, the evening, sleeps so peacefully!
Smoothed by long fingers,
Asleep . . . tired . . . or it malingers,
Stretched on the floor, here beside you and me.
Should I, after tea and cakes and ices,
80 Have the strength to force the moment to its crisis?
But though I have wept and fasted, wept and prayed,
Though I have seen my head [grown slightly bald]-brought in
        upon a platter,
I am no prophet—and here's no great matter;
I have seen the moment of my greatness flicker,
85 And I have seen the eternal Footman hold my coat, and snicker,
And in short, I was afraid.

And would it have been worth it, after all,
After the cups, the marmalade, the tea,
Among the porcelain, among some talk of you and me,
90 Would it have been worth while,

To have bitten off the matter with a smile,
To have squeezed the universe into a ball
To roll it toward some overwhelming question,
To say: "I am Lazarus, come from the dead,
95 Come back to tell you all, I shall tell you all"
If one, settling a pillow by her head,
    Should say: "That is not what I meant at all.
    That is not it, at all."

And would it have been worth it, after all,
100 Would it have been worth while,
After the sunsets and the dooryards and the sprinkled streets,
After the novels, after the teacups, after the skirts that trail along
    the floor—
And this, and so much more?—
It is impossible to say just what I mean!
105 But as if a magic lantern threw the nerves in patterns on a screen:
Would it have been worth while
If one, settling a pillow or throwing off a shawl,
And turning toward the window, should say:
    "That is not it at all,
110   That is not what I meant, at all."

    .   .   .   .   .

No! I am not Prince Hamlet, nor was meant to be;
Am an attendant lord, one that will do
To swell a progress, start a scene or two,
Advise the prince; no doubt, an easy tool,
115 Deferential, glad to be of use,
Politic, cautious, and meticulous;
Full of high sentence, but a bit obtuse;
At times, indeed, almost ridiculous—
Almost, at times, the Fool.

120 I grow old . . . I grow old . . .
I shall wear the bottoms of my trousers rolled.

Shall I part my hair behind? Do I dare to eat a peach?
I shall wear white flannel trousers, and walk upon the beach.
I have heard the mermaids singing, each to each.

125 I do not think that they will sing to me.

I have seen them riding seaward on the waves
Combing the white hair of the waves blown back
When the wind blows the water white and black.

We have lingered in the chambers of the sea
130 By sea-girls wreathed with seaweed red and brown
Till human voices wake us, and we drown.

T. S. ELIOT (1888-1965)

Journey of the Magi

"A cold coming we had of it,
Just the worst time of the year
For a journey, and such a long journey:
The ways deep and the weather sharp,
5   The very dead of winter." *
And the camels galled, sore-footed, refractory,
Lying down in the melting snow.
There were times we regretted
The summer palaces on slopes, the terraces,
10   And the silken girls bringing sherbet.
Then the camel men cursing and grumbling
And running away, and wanting their liquor and women,
And the night-fires going out, and the lack of shelters,
And the cities hostile and the towns unfriendly
15   And the villages dirty and charging high prices:
A hard time we had of it.
At the end we preferred to travel all night,
Sleeping in snatches,
With the voices singing in our ears, saying
20   That this was all folly.

Then at dawn we came down to a temperate valley,
Wet, below the snow line, smelling of vegetation;
With a running stream and a water-mill beating the darkness,
And three trees on the low sky,
25   And an old white horse galloped away in the meadow.
Then we came to a tavern with vine-leaves over the lintel,
Six hands at an open door dicing for pieces of silver,
And feet kicking the empty wine-skins.
But there was no information, and so we continued
30   And arrived at evening, not a moment too soon
Finding the place; it was (you may say) satisfactory.

All this was a long time ago, I remember,
And I would do it again, but set down
This set down

* For the Journey of the Magi, see Matthew 2. Lines 1-5 are in quotation
marks because they are adapted from a sermon on the Nativity by Lancelot
Andrewes (1555-1626). For line 24, see Matthew 27:38, for line 25, see
Revelation 6:2 and 19:11. Perhaps, too, the white horse that gallops away is
partly derived from G. K. Chesterton's *The Ballad of the White Horse*, in
which the disappearance of the horse represents the disappearance of paganism
at the advent of Christianity. The vine (line 26) is often associated with
Christ; see, for example, John 15. Line 27 may allude to Matthew 27:3-6, 35.
(Editors' note)

35 This: were we led all that way for
    Birth or Death? There was a Birth, certainly,
    We had evidence and no doubt. I had seen birth and death,
    But had thought they were different; this Birth was
    Hard and bitter agony for us, like Death, our death.
40 We returned to our places, these Kingdoms,
    But no longer at ease here, in the old dispensation,
    With an alien people clutching their gods.
    I should be glad of another death.

ARCHIBALD MACLEISH (1892-   )

Ars Poetica

A poem should be palpable and mute
As a globed fruit,

Dumb
As old medallions to the thumb,

5 Silent as the sleeve-worn stone
Of casement ledges where the moss has grown—

A poem should be wordless
As the flight of birds.

                    *

A poem should be motionless in time
10 As the moon climbs,

Leaving, as the moon releases
Twig by twig the night-entangled trees,

Leaving, as the moon behind the winter leaves,
Memory by memory the mind—

15 A poem should be motionless in time
As the moon climbs.

                    *

A poem should be equal to:
Not true.

For all the history of grief
20 An empty doorway and a maple leaf.

For love
The leaning grasses and two lights above the sea—

A poem should not mean
But be.

The War Against the Trees

The man who sold his lawn to standard oil
Joked with his neighbors come to watch the show
While the bulldozers, drunk with gasoline,
Tested the virtue of the soil
5   Under the branchy sky
By overthrowing first the privet-row.

Forsythia-forays and hydrangea-raids
Were but preliminaries to a war
Against the great-grandfathers of the town,
10 So freshly lopped and maimed.
They struck and struck again,
And with each elm a century went down.

All day the hireling engines charged the trees,
Subverting them by hacking underground
15 In grub-dominions, where dark summer's mole
Rampages through his halls,
Till a northern seizure shook
Those crowns, forcing the giants to their knees.

I saw the ghosts of children at their games
20 Racing beyond their childhood in the shade,
And while the green world turned its death-foxed page
And a red wagon wheeled,
I watched them disappear
Into the suburbs of their grievous age.

25 Ripped from the craters much too big for hearts
The club-roots bared their amputated coils,
Raw gorgons matted blind, whose pocks and scars
Cried Moon! on a corner lot
One witness-moment, caught
30 In the rear-view mirrors of the passing cars.

w. h. auden (1907-   )

Musée des Beaux Arts

About suffering they were never wrong,
The Old Masters: how well they understood
Its human position; how it takes place
While someone else is eating or opening a window or just walking
   dully along;
5   How, when the aged are reverently, passionately waiting

For the miraculous birth, there always must be
Children who did not specially want it to happen, skating
On a pond at the edge of the wood:
They never forgot
10 That even the dreadful martyrdom must run its course
Anyhow in a corner, some untidy spot
Where the dogs go on with their doggy life and the torturer's
    horse
Scratches its innocent behind on a tree.

In Brueghel's *Icarus*, for instance: how everything turns away
15 Quite leisurely from the disaster; the ploughman may
Have heard the splash, the forsaken cry,
But for him it was not an important failure; the sun shone
As it had to on the white legs disappearing into the green
Water; and the expensive delicate ship that must have seen
20 Something amazing, a boy falling out of the sky,
Had somewhere to get to and sailed calmly on.

w. h. auden (1907-   )

The Unknown Citizen

*(To JS/07/M/378
This Marble Monument
Is Erected by the State)*

He was found by the Bureau of Statistics to be
One against whom there was no official complaint,
And all the reports on his conduct agree
That, in the modern sense of an old-fashioned word, he was a
    saint,
5 For in everything he did he served the Greater Community.
Except for the War till the day he retired
He worked in a factory and never got fired,
But satisfied his employers, Fudge Motors Inc.
Yet he wasn't a scab or odd in his views,
10 For his Union reports that he paid his dues,
(Our report on his Union shows it was sound)
And our Social Psychology workers found
That he was popular with his mates and liked a drink.
The Press are convinced that he bought a paper every day
15 And that his reactions to advertisements were normal in every way.
Policies taken out in his name prove that he was fully insured,
And his Health-card shows he was once in hospital but left it
    cured.

Both Producers Research and High-Grade Living declare
He was fully sensible to the advantages of the Instalment Plan
20 And had everything necessary to the Modern Man,
A phonograph, a radio, a car and a frigidaire.
Our researchers into Public Opinion are content
That he held the proper opinions for the time of year;
When there was peace, he was for peace; when there was war,
    he went.
25 He was married and added five children to the population,
Which our Eugenist says was the right number for a parent of his
    generation,
And our teachers report that he never interfered with their
    education.
Was he free? Was he happy? The question is absurd:
Had anything been wrong, we should certainly have heard.

W. H. AUDEN (1907-   )

O What Is That Sound Which So Thrills the Ear

O what is that sound which so thrills the ear
    Down in the valley drumming, drumming?
Only the scarlet soldiers, dear,
    The soldiers coming.

5 O what is that light I see flashing so clear
    Over the distance brightly, brightly?
Only the sun on their weapons, dear,
    As they step lightly.

O what are they doing with all that gear,
10   What are they doing this morning, this morning?
Only their usual maneuvers, dear,
    Or perhaps a warning.

O why have they left the road down there,
    Why are they suddenly wheeling, wheeling?
15 Perhaps a change in their orders, dear.
    Why are you kneeling?

O haven't they stopped for the doctor's care,
    Haven't they reined their horses, their horses?
Why, they are none of them wounded, dear,
20   None of these forces.

O is it the parson they want, with white hair,
    Is it the parson, is it, is it?
No, they are passing his gateway, dear,
    Without a visit.

25 O it must be the farmer who lives so near.
   It must be the farmer so cunning, so cunning?
   They have passed the farmyard already, dear,
      And now they are running.

   O where are you going? Stay with me here!
30   Were the vows you swore, deceiving, deceiving?
   No, I promised to love you, dear,
      But I must be leaving.

   O it's broken the lock and splintered the door,
      O it's the gate where they're turning, turning;
35 Their boots are heavy on the floor
      And their eyes are burning.

THEODORE ROETHKE (1908-1963)

Elegy for Jane

(*My student, thrown by a horse*)

I remember the neckcurls, limp and damp as tendrils;
And her quick look, a sidelong pickerel smile;
And how, once startled into talk, the light syllables leaped for
   her,
And she balanced in the delight of her thought,
5 A wren, happy, tail into the wind,
Her song trembling the twigs and small branches.
The shade sang with her;
The leaves, their whispers turned to kissing,
And the mould sang in the bleached valleys under the rose.

10 Oh, when she was sad, she cast herself down into such a pure
      depth,
Even a father could not find her:
Scraping her cheek against straw,
Stirring the clearest water.

My sparrow, you are not here,
15 Waiting like a fern, making a spiney shadow.
The sides of wet stones cannot console me,
Nor the moss, wound with the last light.

If only I could nudge you from this sleep,
My maimed darling, my skittery pigeon.
20 Over this damp grave I speak the words of my love:
I, with no rights in this matter,
Neither father nor lover.

DYLAN THOMAS (1914-1953)

After the Funeral

(*In memory of Ann Jones*)

After the funeral, mule praises, brays,
Windshake of sailshaped ears, muffle-toed tap
Tap happily of one peg in the thick
Grave's foot, blinds down the lids, the teeth in black,
5 The spittled eyes, the salt ponds in the sleeves,
Morning smack of the spade that wakes up sleep,
Shakes a desolate boy who slits his throat
In the dark of the coffin and sheds dry leaves,
That breaks one bone to light with a judgment clout,
10 After the feast of tear-stuffed time and thistles
In a room with a stuffed fox and a stale fern,
I stand, for this memorial's sake, alone
In the snivelling hours with dead, humped Ann
Whose hooded, fountain heart once fell in puddles
15 Round the parched worlds of Wales and drowned each sun
(Though this for her is a monstrous image blindly
Magnified out of praise; her death was a still drop;
She would not have me sinking in the holy
Flood of her heart's fame; she would lie dumb and deep
20 And need no druid of her broken body).
But I, Ann's bard on a raised hearth, call all
The seas to service that her wood-tongued virtue
Babble like a bellbuoy over the hymning heads,
Bow down the walls of the ferned and foxy woods
25 That her love sing and swing through a brown chapel,
Bless her bent spirit with four, crossing birds.
Her flesh was meek as milk, but this skyward statue
With the wild breast and blessed and giant skull
Is carved from her in a room with a wet window
30 In a fiercely mourning house in a crooked year
I know her scrubbed and sour humble hands
Lie with religion in their cramp, her threadbare
Whisper in a damp word, her wits drilled hollow,
Her fist of a face died clenched on a round pain;
35 And sculptured Ann is seventy years of stone.
These cloud-sopped, marble hands, this monumental
Argument of the hewn voice, gesture and psalm,
Storm me forever over her grave until
The stuffed lung of the fox twitch and cry Love
40 And the strutting fern lay seeds on the black sill.

DYLAN THOMAS (1914-1953)

Fern Hill

Now as I was young and easy under the apple boughs
About the lilting house and happy as the grass was green,
   The night above the dingle starry,
     Time let me hail and climb
5   Golden in the heydays of his eyes,
And honored among wagons I was prince of the apple towns
And once below a time I lordly had the trees and leaves
     Trail with daisies and barley
   Down the rivers of the windfall light.

10 And as I was green and carefree, famous among the barns
About the happy yard and singing as the farm was home,
   In the sun that is young once only,
     Time let me play and be
   Golden in the mercy of his means,
15 And green and golden I was huntsman and herdsman, the calves
Sang to my horn, the foxes on the hills barked clear and cold,
     And the sabbath rang slowly
   In the pebbles of the holy streams.

All the sun long it was running, it was lovely, the hay
20 Fields high as the house, the tunes from the chimneys, it was air
   And playing, lovely and watery
     And fire green as grass.
   And nightly under the simple stars
As I rode to sleep the owls were bearing the farm away,
25 All the moon long I heard, blessed among stables, the nightjars
   Flying with the ricks, and the horses
     Flashing into the dark.

And then to awake, and the farm, like a wanderer white
With the dew, come back, the cock on his shoulder: it was all
30 Shining, it was Adam and maiden,
     The sky gathered again
   And the sun grew round that very day.
So it must have been after the birth of the simple light
In the first, spinning place, the spellbound horses walking warm
35 Out of the whinnying green stable
     On to the fields of praise.

And honored among foxes and pheasants by the gay house
Under the new made clouds and happy as the heart was long,
   In the sun born over and over,
40   I ran my heedless ways,
   My wishes raced through the house high hay
And nothing I cared, at my sky blue trades, that time allows

In all his tuneful turning so few and such morning songs
   Before the children green and golden
45   Follow him out of grace,

Nothing I cared, in the lamb white days, that time would take me
Up to the swallow thronged loft by the shadow of my hand,
   In the moon that is always rising,
     Nor that riding to sleep
50 I should hear him fly with the high fields
And wake to the farm forever fled from the childless land.
Oh as I was young and easy in the mercy of his means,
   Time held me green and dying
   Though I sang in my chains like the sea.

JOHN MALCOLM BRINNIN (1916-   )

Nuns at Eve

On St. Martin's evening green
Imaginary diamond, between
The vestry buttress and the convent wall,
Solemn as sea-birds in a sanctuary,
5 Under the statue of the Virgin they play baseball.
They are all named Mary,
Sister Mary, Mary Anthony, or Mary Rose,
And when the softball flies
In the shadow of the cross
10 The little chaplet of the Virgin's hands
Contains their soft excitements like a house.

A flying habit traces
The unprecedented rounding of the bases
By Sister Mary Agatha, who thanks God
15 For the easy triple and turns her eyes toward home;
As *Mary, Mother, Help Me* echoes in her head,
Mild cries from the proud team
Encourage her, and the obliging sun,
Dazzling the pitcher's box
20 With the last celestial light upon
The gold-spiked halo of the Virgin in her niche,
Leads Sister Mary John to a wild pitch.
Prayer wins the game.
As Sister Mary Agatha comes sailing home
25 Through infield dusk, like birds fan-wise
In the vague cloisters of slow-rising mist,
Winners and losers gather in to praise
The fleetness of a bride of Christ.

Flushed and humble, Agatha collects the bats
30 And balls, while at her belt
Catcher's and pitcher's mitts
—Brute fingers, toes and gross lopsided heads—
Fumble the ropes of her long swinging beads.

ROBERT LOWELL (1917-   )

The Quaker Graveyard in Nantucket

(For Warren Winslow, Dead at Sea)*

*Let man have dominion over the fishes of the sea and the
fowls of the air and the beasts and the whole earth, and every
creeping creature that moveth upon the earth.*

I

A brackish reach of shoal off Madaket,—
The sea was still breaking violently and night
Had steamed into our North Atlantic Fleet,
When the drowned sailor clutched the drag-net. Light
5 Flashed from his matted head and marble feet,
He grappled at the net
With the coiled, hurdling muscles of his thighs:
The corpse was bloodless, a botch of reds and whites,
Its open, staring eyes
10 Were lustreless dead-lights
Or cabin-windows on a stranded hulk
Heavy with sand. We weight the body, close
Its eyes and heave it seaward whence it came,
Where the heel-headed dogfish barks its nose
15 On Ahab's void and forehead; and the name
Is blocked in yellow chalk.

* Warren Winslow, the author's cousin, was drowned at sea during World
War II. The epigraph ("Let man . . .") comes from Genesis 1:26, and much
of the imagery of the shipwreck in the first dozen lines of the poem comes
from the first chapter of Thoreau's *Cape Cod*. "Madaket" (line 1; properly
Maddaket) is a harbor on the west end of the island of Nantucket. "Ahab"
(line 15) is the captain of the whaler *Pequod* (line 31) in Melville's *Moby-
Dick*; when the *Pequod* sank, it dragged down with it a hawk caught on the
mast-head from which flew a red flag (line 105). "Sconset" (line 33; properly Siasconset) is a town on eastern Nantucket. *"Clamavimus"* (line 78),
"we have cried out," suggests "Out of the depths have I cried unto thee,"
in Psalms 130:1, King James Version (Psalms 129:1, Douay Version).
"Leviathan" (line 87) is several times mentioned in the Bible; usually it
denotes the crocodile, but in Psalms 104:26 (Psalms 103:26, Douay Version)

Sailors, who pitch this portent at the sea
Where dreadnaughts shall confess
Its hell-bent deity,
20 When you are powerless
To sand-bag this Atlantic bulwark, faced
By the earth-shaker, green, unwearied, chaste
In his steel scales: ask for no Orphean lute
To pluck life back. The guns of the steeled fleet
25 Recoil and then repeat
The hoarse salute.

II

Whenever winds are moving and their breath
Heaves at the roped-in bulwarks of this pier,
The terns and sea-gulls tremble at your death
30 In these home waters. Sailor, can you hear
The Pequod's sea wings, beating landward, fall
Headlong and break on our Atlantic wall
Off Sconset, where the yawing S-boats splash
The bellbuoy, with ballooning spinnakers,
35 As the entangled, screeching mainsheet clears
The blocks: off Madaket, where lubbers lash
The heavy surf and throw their long lead squids
For blue-fish? Sea-gulls blink their heavy lids
Seaward. The winds' wings beat upon the stones,
40 Cousin, and scream for you and the claws rush
At the sea's throat and wring it in the slush
Of this old Quaker graveyard where the bones
Cry out in the long night for the hurt beast
Bobbing by Ahab's whaleboats in the East.

---

it denotes the whale. "Wood's Hole" (line 91; properly Woods Hole) is a town on Cape Cod; "Martha's Vineyard" (line 92) is an island south of Cape Cod. "Jehoshaphat" (line 94) in Joel 3:2 is said to be the place where God will judge the heathen nations; Lowell says of it: "The valley of judgment. The world, according to some prophets and scientists, will end in fire." "Jonas Messias" (line 106) refers to Jonah, called the Messiah because his three days in the whale's belly anticipate the three days before Christ's resurrection. "Our Lady of Walsingham" (line 106) was a famous English shrine near the sea. The author says of the passage: "Our Lady of Walsingham is an adaptation of several paragraphs from E. I. Watkin's *Catholic Art and Culture*. The Virgin is a symbol of contemplation." "Shiloah" (line 114; or Shiloh) is a sacred town in Palestine. *"Non est species . . ."* (line 122), a quotation from Isaiah 53:2, is translated thus in the Douay Version: "There is no beauty in him, nor comeliness." "Sion" (line 124; or Zion) is a hill in Jerusalem, or Jerusalem itself. For the "rainbow" (line 143) see Genesis 9:13. (Editors' note)

45 All you recovered from Poseidon died
   With you, my cousin, and the harrowed brine
   Is fruitless on the blue beard of the god,
   Stretching beyond us to the castles in Spain,
   Nantucket's westward haven. To Cape Cod
50 Guns, cradled on the tide,
   Blast the eelgrass about a waterclock
   Of bilge and backwash, roil the salt and sand
   Lashing earth's scaffold, rock
   Our warships in the hand
55 Of the great God, where time's contrition blues
   Whatever it was these Quaker sailors lost
   In the mad scramble of their lives. They died
   When time was open-eyed,
   Wooden and childish; only bones abide
60 There, in the nowhere, where their boats were tossed
   Sky-high, where mariners had fabled news
   Of IS, the whited monster. What it cost
   Them is their secret. In the sperm-whale's slick
   I see the Quakers drown and hear their cry:
65 "If God himself had not been on our side,
   If God himself had not been on our side,
   When the Atlantic rose against us, why,
   Then it had swallowed us up quick."

IV

   This is the end of the whaleroad and the whale
70 Who spewed Nantucket bones on the thrashed swell
   And stirred the troubled waters to whirlpools
   To send the Pequod packing off to hell:
   This is the end of them, three-quarters fools,
   Snatching at straws to sail
75 Seaward and seaward on the turntail whale,
   Spouting out blood and water as it rolls,
   Sick as a dog to these Atlantic shoals:
   Clamavimus, O depths. Let the sea-gulls wail
   For water, for the deep where the high tide
80 Mutters to its hurt self, mutters and ebbs.
   Waves wallow in their wash, go out and out,
   Leave only the death-rattle of the crabs,
   The beach increasing, its enormous snout
   Sucking the ocean's side.
85 This is the end of running on the waves;
   We are poured out like water. Who will dance
   The mast-lashed master of the Leviathans
   Up from this field of Quakers in their unstoned graves?

When the whale's viscera go and the roll
90 Of its corruption overruns this world
Beyond tree-swept Nantucket and Wood's Hole
And Martha's Vineyard, Sailor, will your sword
Whistle and fall and sink into the fat?
In the great ash-pit of Jehoshaphat
95 The bones cry for the blood of the white whale,
The fat flukes arch and whack about its ears,
The death-lance churns into the sanctuary, tears
The gun-blue swingle, heaving like a flail,
And hacks the coiling life out: it works and drags
100 And rips the sperm-whale's midriff into rags,
Gobbets of blubber spill to wind and weather,
Sailor, and gulls go round the stoven timbers
Where the morning stars sing out together
And thunder shakes the white surf and dismembers
105 The red flag hammered in the mast-head. Hide,
Our steel, Jonas Messias, in Thy side.

VI

Our Lady of Walsingham

There once the penitents took off their shoes
And then walked barefoot the remaining mile;
And the small trees, a stream and hedgerows file
110 Slowly along the munching English lane,
Like cows to the old shrine, until you lose
Track of your dragging pain.
The stream flows down under the druid tree,
Shiloah's whirlpools gurgle and make glad
115 The castle of God. Sailor, you were glad
And whistled Sion by that stream. But see:

Our Lady, too small for her canopy,
Sits near the altar. There's no comeliness
At all or charm in that expressionless
120 Face with its heavy eyelids. As before,
This face, for centuries a memory,
Non est species, neque decor,
Expressionless, expresses God: it goes
Past castled Sion. She knows what God knows,
125 Not Calvary's Cross nor crib at Bethlehem
Now, and the world shall come to Walsingham.

VII

The empty winds are creaking and the oak
Splatters and splatters on the cenotaph,

The boughs are trembling and a gaff
Bobs on the untimely stroke
Of the greased wash exploding on a shoal-bell
In the old mouth of the Atlantic. It's well;
Atlantic, you are fouled with the blue sailors,
Sea-monsters, upward angel, downward fish:
Unmarried and corroding, spare of flesh
Mart once of supercilious, wing'd clippers,
Atlantic, where your bell-trap guts its spoil
You could cut the brackish winds with a knife
Here in Nantucket, and cast up the time
When the Lord God formed man from the sea's slime
And breathed into his face the breath of life,
And blue-lung'd combers lumbered to the kill.
The Lord survives the rainbow of His will.

ROBERT LOWELL (1917-   )

Mr. Edwards and the Spider*

I saw the spiders marching through the air,
Swimming from tree to tree that mildewed day
    In latter August when the hay
    Came creaking to the barn. But where
5   The wind is westerly,
Where gnarled November makes the spiders fly
Into the apparitions of the sky,
They purpose nothing but their ease and die
Urgently beating east to sunrise and the sea;

10 What are we in the hands of the great God?
    It was in vain you set up thorn and briar
        In battle array against the fire
        And treason crackling in your blood;
        For the wild thorns grow tame
15 And will do nothing to oppose the flame;
    Your lacerations tell the losing game
    You play against a sickness past your cure.
How will the hands be strong? How will the heart endure?

Jonathan Edwards (1703-1758), New England theologian, was born in
Windsor, Connecticut. As a boy he wrote a detailed treatise on flying spiders;
as a man he preached a sermon in which he asserted that "the God that holds
you over the pit of hell, much as one holds a spider or some loathsome insect
over the fire, abhors you." Hawley (line 38) was Edwards' uncle, Joseph (or
Josiah) Hawley, who committed suicide. (Editors' note)

A very little thing, a little worm,
20 Or hourglass-blazoned spider, it is said,
    Can kill a tiger. Will the dead
    Hold up his mirror and affirm
        To the four winds the smell
    And flash of his authority? It's well
25 If God who holds you to the pit of hell,
    Much as one holds a spider, will destroy,
Baffle and dissipate your soul. As a small boy

    On Windsor March, I saw the spider die
    When thrown into the bowels of fierce fire:
30   There's no long struggle, no desire
    To get up on its feet and fly—
        It stretches out its feet
    And dies. This is the sinner's last retreat;
    Yes, and no strength exerted on the heat
35 Then sinews the abolished will, when sick
And full of burning, it will whistle on a brick.

    But who can plumb the sinking of that soul?
    Josiah Hawley, picture yourself cast
        Into a brick-kiln where the blast
40   Fans your quick vitals to a coal—
        If measured by a glass,
    How long would it seem burning! Let there pass
    A minute, ten, ten trillion; but the blaze
    Is infinite, eternal: this is death,
To die and know it. This is the Black Widow, death.

SYLVIA PLATH (1932-1963)

Daddy

You do not do, you do not do
Any more, black shoe
In which I have lived like a foot
For thirty years, poor and white,
5 Barely daring to breathe or Achoo.

Daddy, I have had to kill you.
You died before I had time—
Marble-heavy, a bag full of God,
Ghastly statue with one grey toe
10 Big as a Frisco seal

And a head in the freakish Atlantic
Where it pours bean green over blue
In the waters off beautiful Nauset.

I used to pray to recover you.
15 Ach, du.

In the German tongue, in the Polish town
Scraped flat by the roller
Of wars, wars, wars.
But the name of the town is common.
20 My Polack friend

Says there are a dozen or two.
So I never could tell where you
Put your foot, your root,
I never could talk to you.
25 The tongue stuck in my jaw.

It stuck in a barb wire snare.
Ich, ich, ich, ich,
I could hardly speak.
I thought every German was you.
30 And the language obscene

An engine, an engine
Chuffing me off like a Jew.
A Jew to Dachau, Auschwitz, Belsen.
I began to talk like a Jew.
35 I think I may well be a Jew.

The snows of the Tyrol, the clear beer of Vienna
Are not very pure or true.
With my gypsy ancestress and my weird luck
And my Taroc pack and my Taroc pack
40 I may be a bit of a Jew.

I have always been scared of *you*,
With your Luftwaffe, your gobbledygoo.
And your neat moustache
And your Aryan eye, bright blue,
45 Panzer-man, panzer-man, O You—

Not God but a swastika
So black no sky could squeak through.
Every woman adores a Fascist,
The boot in the face, the brute
50 Brute heart of a brute like you.

You stand at the blackboard, daddy,
In the picture I have of you,
A cleft in your chin instead of your foot
But no less a devil for that, no not
55 Any less the black man who

Bit my pretty red heart in two.
I was ten when they buried you.
At twenty I tried to die
And get back, back, back to you.
60 I thought even the bones would do.

But they pulled me out of the sack,
And they stuck me together with glue,
And then I knew what to do.
I made a model of you,
65 A man in black with a Meinkampf look

And a love of the rack and the screw.
And I said I do, I do.
So daddy, I'm finally through.
The black telephone's off at the root,
70 The voices just can't worm through.

If I've killed one man, I've killed two—
The vampire who said he was you
And drank my blood for a year,
Seven years, if you want to know.
75 Daddy, you can lie back now.

There's a stake in your fat black heart
And the villagers never liked you.
They are dancing and stamping on you.
They always *knew* it was you.
80 Daddy, daddy, you bastard, I'm through.

DRAMA

Some Elements of Drama • Tragedy • Comedy
Two Plays for Further Study

Sixteen

SOME ELEMENTS OF DRAMA

The earlier parts of this book have dealt with narrative, whether in prose or verse, and with what can roughly be called song or lyric; a third literary type (to use a traditional system of classification) is drama, consisting of plays written for the theater.* In a play, the author has receded from his creation; the words are communicated by actors who impersonate the characters. Of course both story and song have their dramatic aspects. The author of a story usually includes **dialogue** (conversation) in which the characters are heard directly rather than through the voice of the narrator; and the narrator himself may be an invented character. Similarly, the author of a lyric poem invents a speaker and a situation. The distinguishing characteristic of a play, then, is not invented speakers or dialogue, but impersonation by actors.

Here is a brief play, a tenth-century imitation (*i.e.*, representation or re-creation) of the New Testament narrative of the discovery that the crucified Christ had arisen from the tomb.** Three priests represent the three Marys who visited the tomb. They go to a place representing the tomb, and find an angel (a fourth priest, dressed in white, holding a palm branch), who by displaying a cloth in which the cross had previously been wrapped, shows that Christ has arisen. The bits of dialogue (based closely on Matthew 28:1-7 and Mark 16:1-8) had

---

* **Drama,** unfortunately, has acquired too many meanings. It can denote (as above) the whole body of work written for the theater, or a single play, or a serious but untragic play, or (as in "Life is full of drama") events that contain conflict, tension, surprise.
** This play, known as *Quem Quaeritis* (Latin: "whom do you seek") is of great historical importance, for it is commonly considered the earliest extant European play after the end of the Roman drama. The few lines were amplified in the following centuries, and extended dramas of events in the Old and New Testaments gradually developed. Still later, secular subjects were dramatized, but the Biblical plays survived even into Shakespeare's boyhood.

461

developed in the ninth century, but it is the tenth-century Latin account by Ethelwold, Bishop of Winchester, that gives us the stage
directions for the play. What follows is a translation of Ethelwold,*
run together with a translation of the play:

ANONYMOUS

Quem Quaeritis

While the third lesson is being chanted, let four brethren vest
themselves. Let one of these, vested in an alb, enter as though to
take part in the service, and let him approach the sepulcher without attracting attention and sit there quietly with a palm in his
hand. While the third respond is chanted, let the remaining three
follow, and let them all, vested in copes, bearing in their hands
thuribles with incense, and stepping delicately as those who seek
something, approach the sepulcher. These things are done in
imitation of the angel sitting in the monument, and the women
with spices coming to anoint the body of Jesus. When therefore
he who sits there beholds the three approach him like folk lost
and seeking something, let him begin in a dulcet voice of medium
pitch to sing:

Whom do you seek in the sepulcher, O followers of Christ?

And when he has sung it to the end, let the three reply in unison:

Jesus of Nazareth who was crucified, O celestial one!

So he:

He is not here, He has risen as He foretold.
Go, announce that He is risen from the dead.

At the word of this bidding let those three turn to the choir and
say:

Alleluia! The Lord is risen today,
The strong lion, Christ the Son of God! Unto God give thanks,
eia!

This said, let the one, still sitting there and as if recalling them,
say the anthem:

Come, and see the place where the Lord was laid,
Alleluia! Alleluia!

And saying this, let him rise, and lift the veil, and show them the

* The translation is by E. K. Chambers, *The Medieval Stage*, II, 14-15 (Oxford, 1903).

place bare of the cross, but only the cloths laid there in which the cross was wrapped:

> Go quickly, and tell the disciples that the Lord is risen. Alleluia Alleluia!

And when they have seen this, let them set down the thuribles which they bare in that same sepulcher, and take the cloth, and hold it up in the face of the clergy, and as if to demonstrate that the Lord has risen and is no longer wrapped therein, let them sing the anthem:

> The Lord is risen from the sepulcher,
> Who for us was hanged on the cross, alleluia!

and lay the cloth upon the altar. When the anthem is done, let the prior, sharing in their gladness at the triumph of our King, in that, having vanquished death, He rose again, begin the hymn *Te Deum laudamus*. And this begun, all the bells chime out together.

All the elements of a play are here: an action (the movement om doubt to joyful certainty) imitated by impersonators (priests). Note, too, that the impersonation is aided by scenery ("the place are of the cross"), properties (the angel's palm branch), costumes copes and an alb), and gestures ("stepping delicately as those who :ek something"). Even sound effects are used: "all the bells chime ut together."

Before looking at a longer and more complex play, a few words hould be said about **plot**. Although plot is sometimes equated with he gist of the narrative—the story—it is sometimes reserved to denote he writer's arrangement of the happenings in the story. Thus, two lays might have the same story (*e.g.*, the life of Joan of Arc) but heir plots would be different if the writers arranged their episodes lifferently. For example, if one playwright has a scene in the English amp followed by a scene in the French camp, and the other playwright everses the order, the plots are different.

Handbooks on the drama often suggest that a plot (arrangement of happenings) should have a **rising action**, a **climax**, and a **falling action**. This sort of plot can be diagrammed as a pyramid, the tension ising through complications or **crises** to a climax, at which point the ate of the **protagonist** (chief character) is firmly established; the :limax is the apex, and the tension allegedly slackens as we witness he **dénouement** (unknotting). Shakespeare sometimes used a pyramidal structure, placing his climax neatly in the middle of what seems to us to be the third of five acts.* Roughly the first half of *Romeo and Juliet*, for example, shows Romeo winning Juliet, but when in III.i he kills her cousin Tybalt, Romeo sets in motion (it is often said) the second half of the play, the losing of Juliet and of his own life. Similarly, in *Julius Caesar*, Brutus rises in the first half of the play, reaching his height in III.i, with the death of Caesar; but later in this scene he gives Marc Antony permission to speak at Caesar's funeral and thus he sets in motion his own fall, which occupies the second half of the play. In *Macbeth*, the protagonist attains his height in III.i ("Thou hast it now: King"), but he soon perceives that he is going downhill:

> I am in blood
> Stepped in so far, that, should I wade no more,
> Returning were as tedious as go o'er.

In *Hamlet*, the protagonist proves to his own satisfaction Claudius' guilt (by the play within the play) in III.ii, but almost immediately he begins to worsen his position, by failing to kill Claudius when he is an easy target (III.iii) and by contaminating himself with the murder of Polonius (III.iv).

There is, of course, no law that demands such a structure, and a hunt for the pyramid usually causes the hunter to overlook all the crises but the middle one. William Butler Yeats once suggestively diagrammed a good plot not as a pyramid but as a line moving diagonally upward, punctuated by several crises. Perhaps it is sufficient to say that a good plot has its moments of tension, but that the location of these will vary with the play. They are the product of **conflict**, but it should be noted that not all conflict produces tension; there is conflict but no tension in a ball game when the score is 10-0 and the visiting pitcher comes to bat in the ninth inning with two out and none on base.

---

* An **act** is a main division in a drama or opera. Act divisions probably stem from Roman theory and derive ultimately from the Greek practice of separating episodes in a play by choral interludes, but Greek (and probably Roman) plays were performed without interruption, for the choral interludes were part of the plays themselves. Elizabethan plays, too, may have been performed without breaks; the division of Elizabethan plays into five acts is usually the work of editors rather than of authors. Frequently an act division today (commonly indicated by lowering the curtain and turning up the house-lights) denotes change in locale and lapse of time. A **scene** is a smaller unit, either: (i) a division with no change of locale or abrupt shift of time, or (ii) a division consisting of an actor or group of actors on the stage; according to the second definition, the departure or entrance of an actor changes the composition of the group and thus introduces a new scene. (In an entirely different sense, the scene is the locale where a work is set.)

Regardless of how a plot is diagrammed, the **exposition** is that rt which tells the audience what it has to know about the past, the tecedent action. The two gossiping servants who tell each other at after a year away in Paris the young master is coming home to-orrow with a new wife are giving the audience the exposition. The position in Shakespeare's *The Tempest* is almost ruthlessly direct: ospero tells his naïve daughter "I should inform thee farther," and r about one hundred and fifty lines he proceeds to tell her why she on an almost uninhabited island. Prospero's harangue is punctuated · his daughter's professions of attention, but the Elizabethans (and e Greeks) sometimes tossed out all pretense at dialogue, and began th a *prologue*, like the one spoken by the Chorus at the outset of omeo and Juliet:

> Two households, both alike in dignity
>> In fair Verona, where we lay our scene,
> From ancient grudge break to new mutiny,
>> Where civil blood makes civil hands unclean.
> From forth the fatal loins of these two foes
>> A pair of star-crossed lovers take their life. . . .

n the other hand, the exposition may extend far into the play, being ven in dribs and drabs. Occasionally the **soliloquy** (speech of a char-·ter alone on the stage, revealing his thoughts) or the **aside** (speech . the presence of others, but unheard by them) is used to do the b of putting the audience in possession of the essential facts.

Exposition has been discussed as though it simply consists of in-·rming the audience about events; but exposition can do much more. can give us an understanding of the characters who themselves are .lking about other characters, it can evoke a mood, and it can generate ·nsion. The first scene in *Julius Caesar*, in which the tribunes drive 1e commoners from the stage, is less important for the details it gives s about Caesar and Pompey than for its picture of a fickle mob, a 1ob which will later applaud the death of Caesar and then turn and rive the assassins out of Rome. When we summarize the opening act f a play, and treat it as "mere exposition," we are probably losing ·hat is in fact dramatic in it. Similarly, a synopsis of the whole play annot help but be false to the play, for it omits the effect of scenery, ·estures, and tone of voice, and it fails to see that what a deed *is* ·epends in part on who does it and how and why. Voltaire's infamous .immary of *Hamlet* nicely shows that the summary is not the play:

> It is a vulgar and barbarous play, which would not be tolerated by the lowest rabble of France or Italy. Hamlet goes crazy in the second act, and his mistress goes crazy in the third. The prince,

pretending to kill a rat, kills his mistress' father, and the heroine throws herself into the river. A grave is dug on the stage, and gravediggers make puns worthy of themselves, holding skulls in their hands; Hamlet replies to their loathsome vulgarities with equally disgusting extravagances. Meanwhile, another of the actors conquers Poland. Hamlet, his mother, and his step-father carouse on the stage; at the table there is singing, quarreling, fighting, and killing. One would think this play the creation of a drunken savage.

This is an amusing summary of *Hamlet*, but it is not *Hamlet*. Take the statement that Hamlet, "pretending to kill a rat, kills his mistress' father." Hamlet, after exchanging bitter words with his mother, so frightens her that she calls for help; Polonius, concealed behind the arras, calls out, and Hamlet stabs him through the arras, saying "How now? A rat? Dead for a ducat, dead!" Voltaire's summary has entirely omitted Hamlet's agitated mind and his momentary sense of triumph over deceit. Hamlet's action is a revelation of a state of mind, a revelation of character. To summarize the deed without reference to the mind of the doer is to travesty it. Whatever Hamlet is doing in this turbulent scene, he is not "pretending to kill a rat."

Because a play is not simply words but words spoken with accompanying gestures by performers who are usually costumed and in a particular setting, it may be argued that to read a play (rather than to see and hear it) is to falsify it. Drama is not literature, some people hold, but theater. However, there are replies: a play can be literature as well as theater, and the reader of a play can perhaps enact in the theater of his mind a more effective play than the one put on by imperfect actors ("The best in this kind are but shadows," Shakespeare's Duke Theseus says) in front of an audience that coughs and whispers. This mental enactment is aided by abundant stage direction in many contemporary plays. In O'Neill's *Desire Under the Elms*, for example, about four hundred words (describing the set and the gestures of some of the characters) precede the first speech. This speech consists of two words, "God! Purty!" and it is followed by two hundred words of further description. O'Neill informs the reader that the elms over the house have "a sinister maternity," that Eben, twenty-five years old, "finds himself trapped but inwardly unsubdued," that Simeon is thirty-nine, that Peter is thirty-seven, and so forth. (In the theater, not every actor can communicate by his words, gestures, and make-up that he is twenty-five or thirty-nine or thirty-seven.) Bernard Shaw sometimes outdid O'Neill in writing for the reader: many of his plays have enormous prefaces, and some (like *Candida*) have unactable stage directions: "They embrace. But they do not know the secret in the poet's heart." Furthermore, the author's dialogue rarely reaches the stage intact; in addition to interpreting, directors cut and reshape scenes, so that it is often accurate to say we get Gielgud's or Olivier's rather than Shakespeare's *Hamlet*.

Finally (to reverse our tactics), even if it be granted that a good performance reveals qualities in a play that a reading misses, half a loaf is better than none. You may never get a chance to see Synge's *Riders to the Sea*, but why not experience at least a good part of it in a reading?

JOHN MILLINGTON SYNGE (1871-1909)

Riders to the Sea

PERSONS IN THE PLAY

Maurya, an old woman
Bartley, her son
Cathleen, her daughter
Nora, a younger daughter
Men and Women

SCENE. *An Island off the West of Ireland.*

Cottage kitchen, with nets, oil-skins, spinning wheel, some new boards standing by the wall, etc. Cathleen, a girl of about twenty, finishes kneading cake, and puts it down in the pot-oven by the fire; then wipes her hands, and begins to spin at the wheel. Nora, a young girl, puts her head in at the door.

Nora(*in a low voice*). Where is she?
Cathleen. She's lying down, God help her, and may be sleeping, if she's able.

Nora comes in softly, and takes a bundle from under her shawl.

Cathleen (*spinning the wheel rapidly*). What is it you have?
Nora. The young priest is after bringing them. It's a shirt and a plain stocking were got off a drowned man in Donegal.

Cathleen stops her wheel with a sudden movement, and leans out to listen.

Nora. We're to find out if it's Michael's they are, some time herself will be down looking by the sea.
Cathleen. How would they be Michael's, Nora. How would he go the length of that way to the far north?
Nora. The young priest says he's known the like of it. "If it's Michael's they are," says he, "you can tell herself he's got a clean burial by

the grace of God, and if they're not his, let no one say a word about them, for she'll be getting her death," says he, "with crying and lamenting."

The door which Nora half closed is blown open by a gust of wind.

Cathleen (*looking out anxiously*). Did you ask him would he stop Bartley going this day with the horses to the Galway fair?

Nora. "I won't stop him," says he, "but let you not be afraid. Herself does be saying prayers half through the night, and the Almighty God won't leave her destitute," says he, "with no son living."

Cathleen. Is the sea bad by the white rocks, Nora?

Nora. Middling bad, God help us. There's a great roaring in the west, and it's worse it'll be getting when the tide's turned to the wind.

She goes over to the table with the bundle.

Shall I open it now?

Cathleen. Maybe she'd wake up on us, and come in before we'd done. (*Coming to the table.*) It's a long time we'll be, and the two of us crying.

Nora (*goes to the inner door and listens*). She's moving about on the bed. She'll be coming in a minute.

Cathleen. Give me the ladder, and I'll put them up in the turf-loft, the way she won't know of them at all, and maybe when the tide turns she'll be going down to see would he be floating from the east.

They put the ladder against the gable of the chimney; Cathleen goes up a few steps and hides the bundle in the turf-loft. Maurya comes from the inner room.

Maurya (*looking up at Cathleen and speaking querulously*). Isn't it turf enough you have for this day and evening?

Cathleen. There's a cake baking at the fire for a short space (*throwing down the turf*) and Bartley will want it when the tide turns if he goes to Connemara.

Nora picks up the turf and puts it round the pot-oven.

Maurya (*sitting down on a stool at the fire*). He won't go this day with the wind rising from the south and west. He won't go this day, for the young priest will stop him surely.

Nora. He'll not stop him, mother, and I heard Eamon Simon and Stephen Pheety and Colum Shawn saying he would go.

Maurya. Where is he itself?

Nora. He went down to see would there be another boat sailing in the week, and I'm thinking it won't be long till he's here now, for the tide's turning at the green head, and the hooker's[1] tacking from the east.

[1] Sailing boat.

Cathleen. I hear some one passing the big stones.

Nora (looking out). He's coming now, and he in a hurry.

Bartley (comes in and looks round the room. Speaking sadly and quietly). Where is the bit of new rope, Cathleen, was bought in Connemara?

Cathleen (coming down). Give it to him, Nora; it's on a nail by the white boards. I hung it up this morning, for the pig with the black feet was eating it.

Nora (giving him a rope). Is that it, Bartley?

Maurya. You'd do right to leave that rope, Bartley, hanging by the boards. *(Bartley takes the rope.)* It will be wanting in this place, I'm telling you, if Michael is washed up to-morrow morning, or the next morning, or any morning in the week, for it's a deep grave we'll make him by the grace of God.

Bartley (beginning to work with the rope). I've no halter the way I can ride down on the mare, and I must go now quickly. This is the one boat going for two weeks or beyond it, and the fair will be a good fair for horses I heard them saying below.

Maurya. It's a hard thing they'll be saying below if the body is washed up and there's no man in it to make the coffin, and I after giving a big price for the finest white boards you'd find in Connemara.

She looks round at the boards.

Bartley. How would it be washed up, and we after looking each day for nine days, and a strong wind blowing a while back from the west and south?

Maurya. If it wasn't found itself, that wind is raising the sea, and there was a star up against the moon, and it rising in the night. If it was a hundred horses, or a thousand horses you had itself, what is the price of a thousand horses against a son where there is one son only?

Bartley (working at the halter, to Cathleen). Let you go down each day, and see the sheep aren't jumping in on the rye, and if the jobber comes you can sell the pig with the black feet if there is a good price going.

Maurya. How would the like of her get a good price for a pig?

Bartley (to Cathleen). If the west wind holds with the last bit of the moon let you and Nora get up weed enough for another cock for the kelp.[2] It's hard set we'll be from this day with no one in it but one man to work.

Maurya. It's hard set we'll be surely the day you're drownd'd with the rest. What way will I live and the girls with me, and I an old woman looking for the grave?

Bartley lays down the halter, takes off his old coat, and puts on a newer one of the same flannel.

[2] Seaweed (used for manure).

Bartley (*to Nora*). Is she coming to the pier?

Nora (*looking out*). She's passing the green head and letting fall her sails.

Bartley (*getting his purse and tobacco*). I'll have half an hour to go down, and you'll see me coming again in two days, or in three days, or maybe in four days if the wind is bad.

Maurya (*turning round to the fire, and putting her shawl over her head*). Isn't it a hard and cruel man won't hear a word from an old woman, and she holding him from the sea?

Cathleen. It's the life of a young man to be going on the sea, and who would listen to an old woman with one thing and she saying it over?

Bartley (*taking the halter*). I must go now quickly. I'll ride down on the red mare, and the gray pony'll run behind me. . . . The blessing of God on you.

He goes out.

Maurya (*crying out as he is in the door*). He's gone now, God spare us, and we'll not see him again. He's gone now, and when the black night is falling I'll have no son left me in the world.

Cathleen. Why wouldn't you give him your blessing and he looking round in the door? Isn't it sorrow enough is on every one in this house without your sending him out with an unlucky word behind him, and a hard word in his ear?

Maurya takes up the tongs and begins raking the fire aimlessly without looking round.

Nora (*turning towards her*). You're taking away the turf from the cake.

Cathleen (*crying out*). The Son of God forgive us, Nora, we're after forgetting his bit of bread.

She comes over to the fire.

Nora. And it's destroyed he'll be going till dark night, and he after eating nothing since the sun went up.

Cathleen (*turning the cake out of the oven*). It's destroyed he'll be, surely. There's no sense left on any person in a house where an old woman will be talking for ever.

Maurya sways herself on her stool.

Cathleen (*cutting off some of the bread and rolling it in a cloth; to Maurya*). Let you go down now to the spring well and give him this and he passing. You'll see him then and the dark word will be broken, and you can say "God speed you," the way he'll be easy in his mind.

Maurya (*taking the bread*). Will I be in it as soon as himself?

Cathleen. If you go now quickly.

Maurya (standing up unsteadily). It's hard set I am to walk.

Cathleen (looking at her anxiously). Give her the stick, Nora, or maybe she'll slip on the big stones.

Nora. What stick?

Cathleen. The stick Michael brought from Connemara.

Maurya (taking a stick Nora gives her). In the big world the old people do be leaving things after them for their sons and children, but in this place it is the young men do be leaving things behind for them that do be old.

She goes out slowly. Nora goes over to the ladder.

Cathleen. Wait, Nora, maybe she'd turn back quickly. She's that sorry, God help her, you wouldn't know the thing she'd do.

Nora. Is she gone round by the bush?

Cathleen (looking out). She's gone now. Throw it down quickly, for the Lord knows when she'll be out of it again.

Nora (getting the bundle from the loft). The young priest said he'd be passing to-morrow, and we might go down and speak to him below if it's Michael's they are surely.

Cathleen (taking the bundle). Did he say what way they were found?

Nora (coming down). "There were two men," says he, "and they rowing round with poteen[3] before the cocks crowed, and the oar of one of them caught the body, and they passing the black cliffs of the north."

Cathleen (trying to open the bundle). Give me a knife, Nora, the strings perished with the salt water, and there's a black knot on it you wouldn't loosen in a week.

Nora (giving her a knife). I've heard tell it was a long way to Donegal.

Cathleen (cutting the string). It is surely. There was a man in here a while ago—the man sold us that knife—and he said if you set off walking from the rock beyond, it would be seven days you'd be in Donegal.

Nora. And what time would a man take, and he floating?

Cathleen opens the bundle and takes out a bit of a stocking. They look at them eagerly.

Cathleen (in a low voice). The Lord spare us, Nora! isn't it a queer hard thing to say if it's his they are surely?

Nora. I'll get his shirt off the hook the way we can put the one flannel on the other. (*She looks through some clothes hanging in the corner.*) It's not with them, Cathleen, and where will it be?

Cathleen. I'm thinking Bartley put it on him in the morning, for his own shirt was heavy with the salt in it (*pointing to the corner*). There's a bit of a sleeve was of the same stuff. Give me that and it will do.

[3] Illegal whiskey.

Nora brings it to her and they compare the flannel.

Cathleen. It's the same stuff Nora; but if it is itself aren't there great rolls of it in the shops of Galway, and isn't it many another man may have a shirt of it as well as Michael himself?

Nora (who has taken up the stocking and counted the stitches, crying out). It's Michael, Cathleen, it's Michael; God spare his soul, and what will herself say when she hears this story, and Bartley on the sea?

Cathleen (taking the stocking). It's a plain stocking.

Nora. It's the second one of the third pair I knitted, and I put up three score stitches, and I dropped four of them.

Cathleen (counts the stitches). It's that number is in it (*crying out*). Ah, Nora, isn't it a bitter thing to think of him floating that way to the far north, and no one to keen[4] him but the black hags that do be flying on the sea?

Nora (swinging herself round, and throwing out her arms on the clothes). And isn't it a pitiful thing when there is nothing left of a man who was a great rower and fisher, but a bit of an old shirt and a plain stocking?

Cathleen (after an instant). Tell me is herself coming, Nora? I hear a little sound on the path.

Nora (looking out). She is, Cathleen. She's coming up to the door.

Cathleen. Put these things away before she'll come in. Maybe it's easier she'll be after giving her blessing to Bartley, and we won't let on we've heard anything the time he's on the sea.

Nora (helping Cathleen to close the bundle). We'll put them here in the corner.

They put them into a hole in the chimney corner. Cathleen goes back to the spinning-wheel.

Nora. Will she see it was crying I was?

Cathleen. Keep your back to the door the way the light'll not be on you.

Nora sits down at the chimney corner, with her back to the door. Maurya comes in very slowly, without looking at the girls, and goes over to her stool at the other side of the fire. The cloth with the bread is still in her hand. The girls look at each other, and Nora points to the bundle of bread.

Cathleen (after spinning for a moment). You didn't give him his bit of bread?

Maurya begins to keen softly, without turning round.

Cathleen. Did you see him riding down?

[4] Lament.

Maurya goes on keening.

Cathleen (*a little impatiently*). God forgive you; isn't it a better thing to raise your voice and tell what you seen, than to be making lamentation for a thing that's done? Did you see Bartley, I'm saying to you.

Maurya (*with a weak voice*). My heart's broken from this day.

Cathleen (*as before*). Did you see Bartley?

Maurya. I seen the fearfulest thing.

Cathleen (*leaves her wheel and looks out*). God forgive you; he's riding the mare now over the green head, and the gray pony behind him.

Maurya (*starts, so that her shawl falls back from her head and shows her white tossed hair. With a frightened voice*). The gray pony behind him.

Cathleen (*coming to the fire*). What is it ails you, at all?

Maurya (*speaking very slowly*). I've seen the fearfulest thing any person has seen, since the day Bride Dara seen the dead man with the child in his arms.

Cathleen and Nora. Uah.

They crouch down in front of the old woman at the fire.

Nora. Tell us what it is you seen.

Maurya. I went down to the spring well, and I stood there saying a prayer to myself. Then Bartley came along, and he riding on the red mare with the gray pony behind him. (*She puts up her hands, as if to hide something from her eyes.*) The Son of God spare us, Nora!

Cathleen. What is it you seen.

Maurya. I seen Michael himself.

Cathleen (*speaking softly*). You did not, mother; it wasn't Michael you seen, for his body is after being found in the far north, and he's got a clean burial by the grace of God.

Maurya (*a little defiantly*). I'm after seeing him this day, and he riding and galloping. Bartley came first on the red mare; and I tried to say "God speed you," but something choked the words in my throat. He went by quickly; and "the blessing of God on you," says he, and I could say nothing. I looked up then, and I crying, at the gray pony, and there was Michael upon it—with fine clothes on him, and new shoes on his feet.

Cathleen (*begins to keen*). It's destroyed we are from this day. It's destroyed, surely.

Nora. Didn't the young priest say the Almighty God wouldn't leave her destitute with no son living?

Maurya (*in a low voice, but clearly*). It's little the like of him knows of the sea. . . . Bartley will be lost now, and let you call in Eamon and make me a good coffin out of the white boards, for I won't live after them. I've had a husband, and a husband's father, and six sons in this house—six fine men, though it was a hard birth I had with every one of them and they coming to the world—and some of them were found and some of them were not found, but they're gone now the lot of them.... There were Stephen, and Shawn, were lost in the great wind, and found after in the Bay of Gregory of the Golden Mouth, and carried up the two of them on the one plank, and in by that door.

She pauses for a moment, the girls start as if they heard something through the door that is half open behind them.

Nora (*in a whisper*). Did you hear that, Cathleen? Did you hear a noise in the north-east?

Cathleen (*in a whisper*). There's some one after crying out by the seashore.

Maurya (*continues without hearing anything*). There was Sheamus and his father, and his own father again, were lost in a dark night, and not a stick or sign was seen of them when the sun went up. There was Patch after was drowned out of a curagh[5] that turned over. I was sitting here with Bartley, and he a baby, lying on my two knees, and I seen two women, and three women, and four women coming in, and they crossing themselves, and not saying a word. I looked out then, and there were men coming after them, and they holding a thing in the half of a red sail, and water dripping out of it—it was a dry day, Nora—and leaving a track to the door.

She pauses again with her hand stretched out towards the door. It opens softly and old women begin to come in, crossing themselves on the threshold, and kneeling down in front of the stage with red petticoats over their heads.

Maurya (*half in a dream, to Cathleen*). It is Patch, or Michael, or what it is at all?

Cathleen. Michael is after being found in the far north, and when he is found there how could he be here in this place?

Maurya. There does be a power of young men floating round in the sea, and what way would they know if it was Michael they had, or another man like him, for when a man is nine days in the sea, and the wind blowing, it's hard set his own mother would be to say what man was it.

Cathleen. It's Michael, God spare him, for they're after sending us a bit of his clothes from the far north.

She reaches out and hands Maurya the clothes that belonged to Michael. Maurya stands up slowly and takes them in her hand. Nora looks out.

[5] Unstable vessel of tarred canvas on a wood frame; canoe.

Nora. They're carrying a thing among them and there's water dripping out of it and leaving a track by the big stones.

Cathleen (in a whisper to the women who have come in). Is it Bartley it is?

One of the women. It is surely, God rest his soul.

> *Two younger women come in and pull out the table. Then men carry in the body of Bartley, laid on a plank, with a bit of sail over it, and lay it on the table.*

Cathleen (to the women, as they are doing so). What way was he drowned?

One of the women. The gray pony knocked him into the sea, and he was washed out where there is a great surf on the white rocks.

> *Maurya has gone over and knelt down at the head of the table. The women are keening softly and swaying themselves with a slow movement. Cathleen and Nora kneel at the other end of the table. The men kneel near the door.*

Maurya (raising her head and speaking as if she did not see the people around her). They're all gone now, and there isn't anything more the sea can do to me. . . . I'll have no call now to be up crying and praying when the wind breaks from the south, and you can hear the surf is in the east, and the surf is in the west, making a great stir with the two noises, and they hitting one on the other. I'll have no call now to be going down and getting Holy Water in the dark nights after Samhain,[6] and I won't care what way the sea is when the other women will be keening. (*To Nora.*) Give me the Holy Water, Nora, there's a small sup still on the dresser.

> *Nora gives it to her.*

Maurya (drops Michael's clothes across Bartley's feet, and sprinkles the Holy Water over him). It isn't that I haven't prayed for you, Bartley, to the Almighty God. It isn't that I haven't said prayers in the dark night till you wouldn't know what I'ld be saying; but it's a great rest I'll have now, and it's time surely. It's a great rest I'll have now, and great sleeping in the long nights after Samhain, if it's only a bit of wet flour we do have to eat, and maybe a fish that would be stinking.

> *She kneels down again, crossing herself, and saying prayers under her breath.*

Cathleen (to an old man). Maybe yourself and Eamon would make a coffin when the sun rises. We have fine white boards herself bought, God help her, thinking Michael would be found, and I have a new cake you can eat while you'll be working.

[6] 1 November, All Saints' Day.

The old man (*looking at the boards*). Are there nails with them?

Cathleen. There are not, Colum; we didn't think of the nails.

Another man. It's a great wonder she wouldn't think of the nails, and all the coffins she's seen made already.

Cathleen. It's getting old she is, and broken.

> *Maurya stands up again very slowly and spreads out the pieces of Michael's clothes beside the body, sprinkling them with the last of the Holy Water.*

Nora (*in a whisper to Cathleen*). She's quiet now and easy; but the day Michael was drowned you could hear her crying out from this to the spring well. It's fonder she was of Michael, and would any one have thought that?

Cathleen (*slowly and clearly*). An old woman will be soon tired with anything she will do, and isn't it nine days herself is after crying and keening, and making great sorrow in the house?

Maurya (*puts the empty cup mouth downwards on the table, and lays her hands together on Bartley's feet*). They're all together this time, and the end is come. May the Almighty God have mercy on Bartley's soul, and on Michael's soul, and on the souls of Sheamus and Patch, and Stephen and Shawn (*bending her head*); and may He have mercy on my soul, Nora, and on the soul of every one is left living in the world.

> *She pauses, and the keen rises a little more loudly from the women, then sinks away.*

Maurya (*continuing*). Michael has a clean burial in the far north, by the grace of the Almighty God. Bartley will have a fine coffin out of the white boards, and a deep grave surely. What more can we want than that? No man at all can be living for ever, and we must be satisfied.

> *She kneels down again and the curtain falls slowly.*

Synge first visited the Aran Islands (three rocky places off the west coast of Ireland, inhabited by Gaelic-speaking fishermen) in the summer of 1898. From this visit and subsequent ones he derived the material for *The Aran Islands,* an account of life there, full of observations and bits of folklore he had picked up. In it one can find something of the origins of *Riders to the Sea:* there are descriptions of bringing horses across the sound, including an account of an old woman who had a vision of her drowned son riding on a horse; there is a reference to a coffin untimely made out of boards prepared for another person; and there is a reference to a body that floated ashore some weeks after the man drowned. In writing the play Synge chose among the innumerable things he saw and heard, selecting (as any artist does) from the welter or chaos of experience to put together a unified story. A summary of the play's story would run along these lines: an old woman named Maurya, who has lost her husband and five sons to the sea—one very recently—learns that a fifth drowned man has been found, and almost simultaneously she learns of the death of her sixth son. This summary of the story proceeds chronologically, but the play does not. The play begins with a daughter, Cathleen, kneading a cake, setting it in the oven, and then spinning at a wheel. Another daughter enters and speaks the first line, asking about some third woman, who we later come to understand is Maurya. The next few speeches are about "a shirt and a plain stocking were got off a drowned man in Donegal," and we learn that these remnants may belong to someone named Michael. In another moment we learn that Michael and the woman (still referred to only as "she") are closely related. With the eighth speech yet another important character is named, Bartley, who intends to take horses to the Galway fair. And so we are introduced to the characters, with oblique references, and bit by bit we put together the relationships. The playwright's *arrangement of the story*, rather than a strictly chronological arrangement, is (for many critics) Synge's **plot**.

In a play, gesture no less than dialogue is a means of communication. What Cathleen *says* is important, but so too is what she *does*. Her actions, described in the first stage direction, tell us a good deal about the islanders' laborious existence. She finishes one task, kneading the dough, and turns to another, spinning. Synge tells us in another stage direction that during the first few lines she turns the wheel "rapidly," but when Nora mentions the clothing that has been found, "Cathleen stops her wheel with a sudden movement, and leans out to listen." She stops turning the wheel, of course, in order to concentrate on Nora's words, but the abrupt halting of the wheel also is part of the dramatist's way of saying that Michael no longer lives: his thread of life has been spun and untimely cut. A moment later there is another stage direction that has symbolic implications: "The door which Nora half closed is blown open by a gust of wind," suggesting (no less than the abundant talk of the bad weather) the periodic intrusion of powerful natural forces upon the lives of the islanders.

One need not compare *Riders to the Sea* (in which everything is related to everything else) with *The Aran Islands* (in which we have a wonderful grab bag of scarcely related details) to see that the careful arrangement of physical happenings and dialogue gives us more than a slice of life, more than a picture of a certain kind of Irish life. Synge's art extends beyond his plot to his language. The islanders spoke Gaelic, and Synge claimed that his English was close to a translation of their language; but the speeches—as distinct from the words —are Synge's, just as Macbeth's "I am in blood/Stepped in so far, that, should I wade no more,/Returning were as tedious as go o'er" is Shakespeare's creation although the individual words are pretty much the property of any literate American or Englishman. The speeches Synge creates, no less than his plot, belong to the world of art, though the speeches and the events are made up of the materials of Aran life.

Synge chose the peasant idiom because it seemed to him to have beauty and even grandeur, while at the same time it was rooted in men who lived an elemental existence. He saw no need to choose between beauty and truth: beauty without truth led writers of the late nineteenth century (he believed) to highly wrought yet trivial or even meaningless verse; and truth without beauty to dull pictures of man's insignificance. It is partly by making "every speech . . . as fully flavored as a nut or apple" that Synge produced a work that (although it deals with multiple deaths) is not depressing but is, like every work of art, stimulating: "Let you go down each day, and see the sheep aren't jumping in on the rye, and if the jobber comes you can sell the pig with the black feet if there is a good price going." Even the speeches on the inevitable end of man have, while they call attention to man's ignominious remains, richness and dignity: "And isn't it a pitiful thing when there is nothing left of a man who was a great rower and fisher, but a bit of an old shirt and a plain stocking?" Throughout the play this artful use of language communicates a picture of heroism and humbleness that is reassuring as well as grievous, nowhere more so than in Maurya's final speech, which calls attention to the hardness of life and the inevitability of death in such a way as almost to offer a kind of reassurance.

What is *Riders to the Sea* about? It is, of course, "about" people named Maurya, Bartley, etc., and it is about the life of Irish islanders— particularly the women—of 1900 and earlier. But clearly it is about something more, it adds up to a vision of existence. If we turn to *The Aran Islands* we find there a passage about "the maternal feeling" that has some relevance to *Riders to the Sea*:

> The maternal feeling is so powerful on these islands that it gives a life of torment to the women. Their sons grow up to be banished as soon as they are of age, or to live here in continual danger on the sea; their daughters go away also, or are worn out in their youth with bearing children that grow up to harass them in their own turn a little later.

But just as Synge shaped a plot and invented speeches that make the play more than a rendition of *The Aran Islands* in dialogue, so too he shaped a theme distinct from that of the book. What is this theme? Life proceeds from the sea, and is nourished by the sea, but the sea is also a source of death: "It's the life of a young man to be going on the sea," Cathleen says, suggesting something of man's inevitable struggle against the enormous impersonal forces of nature. "They're all gone now, and there isn't anything more the sea can do to me," Maurya says a little later, suggesting something of man's inevitable defeat in this struggle and of man's ability to triumph—in a way—by a clarity of vision. And finally Maurya says, in the last speech of the play: "Michael has a clean burial in the far north, by the grace of the Almighty God. Bartley will have a fine coffin out of the white boards, and a deep grave surely. What more can we want than that? No man at all can be living for ever, and we must be satisfied." Michael has a clean burial—but we know that the loss is grievous. Bartley will have a fine coffin—but the coffin was not meant for him, and we may recall two of Maurya's earlier speeches, when Bartley was alive: "It's hard set we'll be surely the day you're drownd'd with the rest. What way will I live and the girls with me, and I an old woman looking for the grave?" And: "In the big world the old people do be leaving things after them for their sons and children, but in this place it is the young men do be leaving things behind for them that do be old." At the end of the play, the young men are all gone, the last of them "knocked . . . into the sea" by a gray pony, but, paradoxically, Maurya's final speech reveals a majesty she lacked in the early part of the play when, a little better off, she spoke "querulously" and raked the fire "aimlessly." In the most important sense, then, the action of the play is this movement of Maurya's mind, rather than the physical doings of men and women who enter, cut open a bundle, bring in a corpse, etc. The word *drama* is from the Greek verb *dran*, to do, to accomplish; in *Riders to the Sea* the thing accomplished is not only the identification of Michael's clothing and the death of Bartley, but the shift in Maurya's mind. Early in the play the priest (Nora says) suggested that Michael may have had "a clean burial by the grace of God"; midway in the play Cathleen says it is "a bitter thing to think of him floating that way to the far north, and no one to keen him but the black hags that do be flying on the sea." Finally, after the death of Bartley, Maurya derives some comfort from the thought that "Bartley will have a fine coffin out of the white boards," and Michael "a clean burial in the far north." But we distinguish between Maurya's view, born out of suffering, and the simple faith of "the young priest" (his youth is insisted on); she has been "hard set," known despair, seen the worst that can happen ("They're all gone now, and there isn't anything more the sea can do to me"), and now from the vantage point of one stripped of all that one has cherished she can utter with dignity the most terrible facts of life.

This is not to say that the play has a message. Synge abhorred didactic drama, and in a preface to another play insisted that "the drama, like the symphony, does not teach or prove anything." It offers us "pleasure and excitement," rather than solutions that inevitably become old-fashioned. The best plays, he said in a characteristically homely figure, "can no more go out of fashion than the blackberries on the hedges."

QUESTIONS: *Riders to the Sea*

1. What is revealed about Maurya's state of mind by her speech (p. 468): "He won't go this day with the wind rising from the south and west. He won't go this day, for the young priest will stop him surely." Why is her reference to the need for the rope (p. 469) one of the strongest arguments she can propose for Bartley's staying?

2. Note the references to the bread (or cake). Why are they in the play? And why the emphasis upon the rope?

3. What is implied by Maurya's vision (p. 473) of Michael "with fine clothes on him, and new shoes on his feet"?

4. Trace the foreshadowing of Bartley's death.

5. Nora and Cathleen hear someone (p. 474) calling out by the seashore. Why doesn't Maurya hear the noise? Why does Synge not have a stage direction calling for a cry?

6. Does the fact that Maurya has forgotten the coffin-nails indicate (as Cathleen says, p. 476) that she is "broken"?

Seventeen

TRAGEDY

Aristotle defined tragedy as a dramatization of a serious happening—not necessarily one ending with the death of the protagonist, and his definition remains among the best. But many plays have been written since Aristotle defined tragedy. When we think of Shakespeare's tragedies we cannot resist narrowing Aristotle's definition by adding something like "showing a struggle that rends the protagonist's whole being"; and when we think of the "problem plays" of the last hundred years—the serious treatments of such sociological problems as alcoholism and race prejudice—we cannot resist excluding some of them by adding to the definition something about the need for universal appeal. The question remains: Is there a single quality present in all works that we call tragedy and absent from works not called tragedy? If there is, no one has yet pointed it out to general satisfaction. But this failure does not mean that there is no such classification as tragedy. We sense that tragedies resemble each other as members of the same family resemble each other: two children have the mother's coloring and eyes, a third child has the mother's coloring but the father's eyes, a fourth child has the mother's eyes but the father's coloring.

The next few pages will examine three comments on tragedy, none of which is entirely acceptable, but each of which seems to have some degree of truth, and each of which can help us detect resemblances and differences among tragedies. The first comment is by Cyril Tourneur, a tragic dramatist of the early seventeenth century:

When the bad bleed, then is the tragedy good.

We think of Richard III ("that foul defacer of God's handiwork"), or even of Macbeth ("usurper," "butcher"). Macbeth, of course, is much more than a usurper and butcher, but it is undeniable that he is an offender against the moral order. Whatever the merits of

Tourneur's statement, however, if we think of Romeo and Juliet (to consider only one play), we realize its inadequacy. What Tourneur does is so stress the guilt of the protagonist that his suffering becomes mere retributive justice. But we cannot plausibly say, for example, that Romeo and Juliet deserved to die because they married without their parents' consent; it is much too simple to call them "bad." Romeo and Juliet are young, in love, nobler in spirit than their parents. Tourneur's view is probably derived ultimately from an influential passage in Aristotle's *Poetics* in which Aristotle speaks of **hamartia**, sometimes literally translated as "missing the target," sometimes as "vice" or "flaw" or "weakness," but perhaps best translated as "mistake." Aristotle seems to imply that the hero is undone because of some mistake he commits, but this mistake need not be the result of a moral fault; it may be simply a miscalculation—for example, failure to foresee the consequences of a deed. Brutus makes a strategic mistake when he lets Marc Antony speak at Caesar's funeral, but we can hardly call it a vice. Because Aristotle's *hamartia* includes mistakes of this sort, the common translation "**tragic flaw**" is erroneous. In many Greek tragedies the hero's *hamartia* is **hybris** (or **hubris**), usually translated as "overweening pride." The hero forgets that he is a fallible man, attributes to himself the power and wisdom of the gods, and is later humbled for his arrogance. On the other hand, a number of recent scholars have insisted that this self-assertiveness is not a vice but a virtue, not a weakness but a strength; if the hero is destroyed for his self-assertion, he is (they hold) nevertheless greater than the people around him, just as the man who tries to stem a lynch mob is greater than the mob although he too may be lynched for his virtue.

Next, here is a statement more or less the reverse of Tourneur's, by a Soviet critic, L. I. Timofeev:

> Tragedy in Soviet literature arouses a feeling of pride for the man who has accomplished a great deed for the people's happiness; it calls for continued struggle against the things which brought about the hero's death.

The distortions in Soviet criticism are often amusing: Hamlet is sometimes seen as an incipient Communist, undone by the decadent aristocracy; or Romeo and Juliet as young people of the future, undone by bourgeois parents. Recent Soviet drama so consistently shows the triumph of the worker that Western visitors to Russia have commented on the absence of contemporary tragic plays. Still, there is much in the idea that the tragic hero accomplishes "a great deed" and perhaps we do resent "the things which brought about the hero's death." The deceitfulness of Iago, the stubbornness of the Montagues and Capulets,

he fury of the mob which turns against Brutus, all of these would
em in some measure to call for our indignation. But do the plays
hat we call tragedies really make us want to struggle against things
n real life? After seeing *Othello*, do we go out of the theater hunting
or malicious deceivers?

The third comment is by Arthur Miller:

> If it is true to say that in essence the tragic hero is intent upon
> claiming his whole due as a personality, and if this struggle must
> be total and without reservation, then it automatically demon-
> strates the indestructible will of man to achieve his humanity.
> ... It is curious, although edifying, that the plays we revere,
> century after century, are the tragedies. In them, and in them
> alone, lies the belief—optimistic, if you will, in the perfectibility
> of man.

There is much in Mr. Miller's suggestions that the tragic hero makes
 large and total claim, and that the audience often senses triumph
ather than despair in tragedies. We often feel that we have witnessed
uman greatness, that the hero, despite profound suffering, has lived
ccording to his ideals. We may feel that we have achieved new insight
nto human greatness. But the perfectibility of man? Do we feel that
Macbeth or *Othello* have to do with human perfectibility? Don't these
lays suggest rather that man, whatever his nobility, has within him
he seeds of his own destruction? Without overstressing the guilt of
he protagonists, don't we feel that in part the plays dramatize the
mperfectibility of man? In much tragedy, after all, the destruction
omes from within, not from without:

> In tragic life, God wot,
> No villain need be! Passions spin the plot:
> We are betrayed by what is false within. (George Meredith)

Othello aims at justice when he kills Desdemona, but he performs an
ct of terrible injustice. What we are talking about is **tragic irony,**
he contrast between what is believed to be so and what is so, or
etween expectations and accomplishments.* Several examples from
Macbeth illustrate something of the range of tragic irony within a

Tragic irony is sometimes called **dramatic irony** or **Sophoclean irony**. The
rms are often applied to speeches or actions which the audience understands
 a sense fuller than or different from the sense in which the dramatic charters understand them. It is tragically ironic, for example, that the rope that
artley (in *Riders to the Sea*) uses as a bridle when he goes to sell the horses
 help support the family will presumably be used to lower his coffin. Sim-
arly, it is ironic that while Maurya is describing how Patch was carried in "in
he half of a red sail, and water dripping out of it," Bartley is being carried to
er door, "water dripping" from him, on a plank with "a bit of sail."

single play. In the first act, King Duncan bestows on Macbeth the title of Thane of Cawdor: by his kindness Duncan seals his own doom; Macbeth having achieved this rank will next want to achieve a higher one. Another example, from the third act: Macbeth, knowing that Banquo will soon be murdered, hypocritically urges Banquo to "fail not our feast." But Macbeth's hollow request is ironically fulfilled: the ghost of Banquo terrorizes Macbeth during the feast. The most pervasive irony of all, of course, is that Macbeth aims at happiness when he kills Duncan and takes the throne, but he wins only sorrow.

Aristotle's discussion of **peripeteia** (**reversal**) and **anagnorisis** (**recognition**) may be a way of getting at this sort of irony. He may simply have meant a reversal of fortune (*e.g.*, good luck ceases) and a recognition of who is who (*e.g.*, the pauper is really the prince), but more likely he meant profounder things. In *Macbeth* one can say that the reversal lies in the sorrow that Macbeth's increased power brings; the recognition comes when he realizes the consequences of his deeds:

> I have lived long enough: my way of life
> Is fall'n into the sere, the yellow leaf;
> And that which should accompany old age,
> As honor, love, obedience, troops of friends,
> I must not look to have; but, in their stead,
> Curses, not loud but deep, mouth-honor, breath
> Which the poor heart would fain deny, and dare not.

That a man's deeds often undo him, that a man aiming at his good can produce his ruin, was not, of course, a discovery of the tragic dramatists. The archetype is the story of Adam and Eve: these two aimed at becoming like God, and as a consequence they brought upon themselves corruption, death, the loss of their earthly paradise. The Bible is filled with stories of tragic irony. Here is a brief quotation from Ecclesiastes (10:8-9) that can stand as an epitome of these stories:

> He that diggeth a pit shall fall into it; and whoso breaketh an hedge, a serpent shall bite him.
> Whoso removeth stones shall be hurt therewith; and he that cleaveth wood shall be endangered thereby.

"He that cleaveth wood shall be endangered thereby." Activity involves danger. To be inactive is, often, to be ignoble, but to be active is necessarily to imperil oneself. Perhaps we can attempt a summary of tragic man: he acts, and he suffers, usually as a consequence of his action. It is not a question of his action's being particularly bad (Tourneur's view), or particularly good (Timofeev's view); the action is often both good and bad, a sign of man's courage and also of his arrogance, a sign of man's greatness and also of his limitations.

Finally, a brief consideration of the pleasure of tragedy: Why do we enjoy plays about suffering? Aristotle has some obscure comments on **catharsis** (**purgation**), which are often interpreted as saying that tragedy arouses in us both pity and fear and then purges us of these emotions. The idea, perhaps, is that just as we can harmlessly discharge our aggressive impulses by witnessing a prize fight or by shouting at an umpire, so we can harmlessly discharge our impulses to pity and to fear by witnessing the dramatization of a man's destruction. The theater in this view is an outlet for emotions that elsewhere would be harmful. But, it must be repeated, Aristotle's comments on catharsis are obscure; perhaps, too, they are wrong. Most later theories on the pleasure of tragedy are footnotes to Aristotle's words on catharsis. Some say that our pleasure is sadistic (we enjoy the sight of suffering); some, that our pleasure is masochistic (we enjoy lacerating ourselves); some, that it lies in sympathy (we enjoy extending pity and benevolence to the wretched); some, that it lies in self-congratulation (we are reminded, when we see suffering, of our own good fortune); some, that we take pleasure in tragedy because the tragic hero acts out our secret desires, and we rejoice in his aggression, expiating our guilt in his suffering. And so on. But this is all rather uncertain psychology, and it mostly neglects the distinction between real suffering and dramatized suffering. In the latter, surely, part of the pleasure is in the contemplation of an esthetic object, an object that is unified and complete. The chaos of real life seems, for a few moments in drama, to be ordered: the protagonist's action, his subsequent suffering, and the total cosmos seem somehow related. Tragedy has no use for the passerby who is killed by a falling brick. The events (the man's walk, the brick's fall) have no meaningful relation. But suppose a man chooses to climb a mountain, and in making the ascent sets in motion an avalanche that destroys him. Here we find (however slight the illustration) something closer to tragedy. We do not say that men should avoid mountains, or that mountain-climbers deserve to die by avalanches. But we feel that the event is unified, as the accidental conjunction of brick and passer-by is not. Tragedy, thus, presents some sort of ordered action; tragic drama itself is orderly. As we see or read it we feel it cannot be otherwise; word begets word, deed begets deed, and every moment is exquisitely appropriate. Whatever the relevance of sadism, masochism, sympathy, and the rest, the pleasure of tragedy surely comes in part from the artistic shaping of the material.

A NOTE ON GREEK TRAGEDY. Little or nothing is known for certain of the origin of Greek tragedy. The most common hypothesis holds that it developed from improvised speeches during choral dances honoring Dionysus, a Greek nature god associated with spring, fertility, and wine. Thespis (who perhaps never existed) is said to have introduced an actor into these choral performances in the sixth century B.C. Aeschylus (525-456 B.C.), Greece's first great writer of tragedies, added the second actor, and Sophocles (496-406 B.C.) added the third actor and fixed the size of the chorus at fifteen. (Because the chorus leader often functioned as an additional actor, and because the actors sometimes doubled in their parts, a Greek tragedy could have more characters than might at first be thought.)

All of the extant great Greek tragedy is of the fifth century B.C. It was performed at religious festivals in the winter and early spring, in large outdoor amphitheaters built on hillsides. Some of these theaters were enormous; the one at Epidaurus held about fifteen thousand people. The audience sat in tiers, looking down on the **orchestra** (a dancing place), the acting area behind it, and the **skene** (the scene-building) yet farther back. The scene-building served as dressing-room, background (suggesting a palace or temple), and place for occasional entrances and exits. Furthermore, this building helped to provide good acoustics, for speech travels well if there is a solid barrier behind the speaker and a hard, smooth surface in front of him, and if the audience sits in tiers. The wall of the scene-building provided the barrier; the orchestra provided the surface in front of the actors; and the seats on the hillside fulfilled the third demand. Moreover, the acoustics were somewhat improved by slightly elevating the actors above the orchestra, but it is not known exactly when this platform was first constructed in front of the scene-building.

A tragedy commonly begins with a **prologos** (prologue), during which the exposition is given; next comes the **parodos**, the chorus' ode of entrance, sung while the chorus marches into the theater, down the side aisles and onto the orchestra. The **epeisodion** (episode) is the ensuing scene; it is followed by a **stasimon** (choral song, ode). Usually there are four or five **epeisodia**, alternating with **stasima**. Each of these choral odes has a **strophe** (lines presumably sung while the chorus dances in one direction) and an **antistrophe** (lines presumably sung while the chorus retraces its steps). Sometimes a third part, an **epode**, concludes an ode. (In addition to odes that are *stasima*, there can be odes within episodes; the fourth episode of *Antigone* contains an ode complete with *epode*.) After the last part of the last ode comes the **exodos**, the epilogue or final scene.

The actors (all male) wore masks, and seem to have chanted much of the play. Perhaps the total result of combining speech with music and dancing was a sort of music-drama roughly akin to opera with some spoken dialogue, such as Mozart's *Magic Flute*.

SOPHOCLES (496?-406 B.C.)

Antigone

An English Version by Dudley Fitts and Robert Fitzgerald

RSONS REPRESENTED

Antigonê
Ismenê
Eurydicê
Creon
Haimon
Teiresias
A Sentry
A Messenger
Chorus

ENE. *Before the Palace of Creon, King of Thebes. A central double door, and two lateral doors. A platform extends the length of the façade, and from this platform three steps lead down into the "orchestra," or chorus-ground.*

ME. *Dawn of the day after the repulse of the Argive army from the assault on Thebes.*

PROLOGUE

[*Antigonê and Ismenê enter from the central door of the Palace.*]

itigonê. Ismenê, dear sister,
   You would think that we had already suffered enough
   For the curse on Oedipus:[1]
   I cannot imagine any grief
   That you and I have not gone through. And now—   5
   Have they told you of the new decree of our King Creon?
nenê. I have heard nothing: I know
   That two sisters lost two brothers, a double death
   In a single hour; and I know that the Argive army
   Fled in the night; but beyond this, nothing.   10

Dedipus, once King of Thebes, was the father of Antigonê and Ismenê, and
   their brothers Polyneicês and Eteoclês. Oedipus unwittingly killed his
ther, Laios, and married his own mother, Iocastê. When he learned what he
d done, he blinded himself and left Thebes. Eteoclês and Polyneicês
arrelled, Polyneicês was driven out but returned to assault Thebes. In the
ttle each brother killed the other; Creon became king and ordered that
ilyneicês be left to rot unburied on the battlefield as a traitor. [Editors' note]

Antigonê. I thought so. And that is why I wanted you
  To come out here with me. There is something we must do.
Ismenê. Why do you speak so strangely?
Antigonê. Listen, Ismenê:
  Creon buried our brother Eteoclês   15
  With military honors, gave him a soldier's funeral,
  And it was right that he should; but Polyneicês,
  Who fought as bravely and died as miserably,—
  They say that Creon has sworn
  No one shall bury him, no one mourn for him,   20
  But his body must lie in the fields, a sweet treasure
  For carrion birds to find as they search for food.
  That is what they say, and our good Creon is coming here
  To announce it publicly; and the penalty—
  Stoning to death in the public square!
                                              There it is,   25
  And now you can prove what you are:
  A true sister, or a traitor to your family.
Ismenê. Antigonê, you are mad! What could I possibly do?
Antigonê. You must decide whether you will help me or not.
Ismenê. I do not understand you. Help you in what?   30
Antigonê. Ismenê, I am going to bury him. Will you come?
Ismenê. Bury him! You have just said the new law forbids it.
Antigonê. He is my brother. And he is your brother, too.
Ismenê. But think of the danger! Think what Creon will do!
Antigonê. Creon is not strong enough to stand in my way.   35
Ismenê. Ah sister!
  Oedipus died, everyone hating him
  For what his own search brought to light, his eyes
  Ripped out by his own hand; and Iocastê died,
  His mother and wife at once: she twisted the cords   40
  That strangled her life; and our two brothers died,
  Each killed by the other's sword. And we are left:
  But oh, Antigonê,
  Think how much more terrible than these
  Our own death would be if we should go against Creon   45
  And do what he has forbidden! We are only women,
  We cannot fight with men, Antigonê!
  The law is strong, we must give in to the law
  In this thing, and in worse. I beg the Dead
  To forgive me, but I am helpless: I must yield   50
  To those in authority. And I think it is dangerous business
  To be always meddling.
Antigonê.   If that is what you think,
  I should not want you, even if you asked to come.
  You have made your choice, you can be what you want to be.
  But I will bury him; and if I must die,   55

I say that this crime is holy: I shall lie down
With him in death, and I shall be as dear
To him as he to me.
                    It is the dead,
Not the living, who make the longest demands:
We die for ever . . .
                    You may do as you like,   60
Since apparently the laws of the gods mean nothing to you.

Ismenê. They mean a great deal to me; but I have no strength
    To break laws that were made for the public good.

Antigonê. That must be your excuse, I suppose. But as for me,
    I will bury the brother I love.

Ismenê.   Antigonê,   65
    I am so afraid for you!

Antigonê.   You need not be:
    You have yourself to consider, after all.

Ismenê. But no one must hear of this, you must tell no one!
    I will keep it a secret, I promise!

Antigonê.   Oh tell it! Tell everyone!
    Think how they'll hate you when it all comes out   70
    If they learn that you knew about it all the time!

Ismenê. So fiery! You should be cold with fear.

Antigonê. Perhaps. But I am doing only what I must.

Ismenê. But can you do it? I say that you cannot.

Antigonê. Very well: when my strength gives out, I shall do no more. 75

Ismenê. Impossible things should not be tried at all.

Antigonê. Go away, Ismenê:
    I shall be hating you soon, and the dead will too,
    For your words are hateful. Leave me my foolish plan:
    I am not afraid of the danger; if it means death,   80
    It will not be the worst of deaths—death without honor.

Ismenê. Go then, if you feel that you must.
    You are unwise,
    But a loyal friend indeed to those who love you.

[*Exit into the Palace. Antigonê goes off, L. Enter the Chorus.*]

PÁRODOS

Chorus. Now the long blade of the sun, lying   [*Strophe 1*]   85
    Level east to west, touches with glory
    Thebes of the Seven Gates. Open, unlidded
    Eye of golden day! O marching light
    Across the eddy and rush of Dircê's stream,[2]
    Striking the white shields of the enemy   90
    Thrown headlong backward from the blaze of morning!

2 Dircê: a stream west of Thebes. [Editors' note]

Choragos.[3] Polyneicês their commander
    Roused them with windy phrases,
    He the wild eagle screaming
    Insults above our land,   95
    His wings their shields of snow,
    His crest their marshalled helms.

Chorus. Against our seven gates in a yawning ring   [*Antistrophe 1*]
    The famished spears came onward in the night;
    But before his jaws were sated with our blood,   100
    Or pinefire took the garland of our towers,
    He was thrown back; and as he turned, great Thebes—
    No tender victim for his noisy power—
    Rose like a dragon behind him, shouting war.
Choragos. For God hates utterly   105
    The bray of bragging tongues;
    And when he beheld their smiling,
    Their swagger of golden helms,
    The frown of his thunder blasted
    Their first man from our walls.   110

Chorus. We heard his shout of triumph high in the air   [*Strophe 2*]
    Turn to a scream; far out in a flaming arc
    He fell with his windy torch, and the earth struck him.
    And others storming in fury no less than his
    Found shock of death in the dusty joy of battle.   115
Choragos. Seven captains at seven gates
    Yielded their clanging arms to the god
    That bends the battle-line and breaks it
    These two only, brothers in blood,
    Face to face in matchless rage,   120
    Mirroring each the other's death,
    Clashed in long combat.

Chorus. But now in the beautiful morning of victory   [*Antistrophe 2*]
    Let Thebes of the many chariots sing for joy!
    With hearts for dancing we'll take leave of war: 125
    Our temples shall be sweet with hymns of praise,
    And the long night shall echo with our chorus.

SCENE I

Choragos. But now at last our new King is coming:
    Creon of Thebes, Menoikeus' son.

[3] Leader of the Chorus. [Editors' note]

In this auspicious dawn of his reign   130
What are the new complexities
That shifting Fate has woven for him?
What is his counsel? Why has he summoned
The old men to hear him?

[*Enter Creon from the Palace, C. He addresses the Chorus from
the top step.*]

Creon. Gentlemen: I have the honor to inform you that our Ship   135
of State, which recent storms have threatened to destroy,
has come safely to harbor at last, guided by the merciful
wisdom of Heaven. I have summoned you here this morning because I know that I can depend upon you: your
devotion to King Laïos was absolute; you never hesitated   140
in your duty to our late ruler Oedipus; and when Oedipus
died, your loyalty was transferred to his children. Unfortunately, as you know, his two sons, the princes Eteoclês and
Polyneicês, have killed each other in battle; and I, as the
next in blood, have succeeded to the full power of the   145
throne.

I am aware, of course, that no Ruler can expect complete loyalty from his subjects until he has been tested in
office. Nevertheless, I say to you at the very outset that I
have nothing but contempt for the kind of Governor who is   150
afraid, for whatever reason, to follow the course that he
knows is best for the State; and as for the man who sets
private friendship above the public welfare,—I have no use
for him, either. I call God to witness that if I saw my
country headed for ruin, I should not be afraid to speak   155
out plainly; and I need hardly remind you that I would
never have any dealings with an enemy of the people. No
one values friendship more highly than I; but we must remember that friends made at the risk of wrecking our Ship
are not real friends at all.   160

These are my principles, at any rate, and that is why I
have made the following decision concerning the sons of
Oedipus: Eteoclês, who died as a man should die, fighting
for his country, is to be buried with full military honors,
with all the ceremony that is usual when the greatest heroes 165
die; but his brother Polyneicês, who broke his exile to come
back with fire and sword against his native city and the
shrines of his fathers' gods, whose one idea was to spill the
blood of his blood and sell his own people into slavery—
Polyneicês, I say, is to have no burial: no man is to touch   170
him or say the least prayer for him; he shall lie on the plain,
unburied; and the birds and the scavenging dogs can do with
him whatever they like.

This is my command, and you can see the wisdom behind
it. As long as I am King, no traitor is going to be honored   175
with the loyal man. But whoever shows by word and deed
that he is on the side of the State,—he shall have my respect
while he is living and my reverence when he is dead.

Choragos. If that is your will, Creon son of Menoikeus,
You have the right to enforce it: we are yours.   180

Creon. That is my will. Take care that you do your part.

Choragos. We are old men: let the younger ones carry it out.

Creon. I do not mean that: the sentries have been appointed.

Choragos. Then what is it that you would have us do?

Creon. You will give no support to whoever breaks this law.   185

Choragos. Only a crazy man is in love with death!

Creon. And death it is; yet money talks, and the wisest
Have sometimes been known to count a few coins too many.

[Enter Sentry from L.]

Sentry. I'll not say that I'm out of breath from running, King, because every time I stopped to think about what I have to tell   190
you, I felt like going back. And all the time a voice kept
saying, "You fool, don't you know you're walking straight
into trouble?"; and then another voice: "Yes, but if you let
somebody else get the news to Creon first, it will be even
worse than that for you!" But good sense won out, at least   195
I hope it was good sense, and here I am with a story that
makes no sense at all; but I'll tell it anyhow, because, as they
say, what's going to happen's going to happen, and—

Creon. Come to the point. What have you to say?

Sentry. I did not do it. I did not see who did it. You must not   200
punish me for what someone else has done.

Creon. A comprehensive defense! More effective, perhaps,
If I knew its purpose. Come: what is it?

Sentry. A dreadful thing . . . I don't know how to put it—

Creon. Out with it!

Sentry.   Well, then;
The dead man—

            Polyneicês—

[Pause. The Sentry is overcome, fumbles for words. Creon
waits impassively.]

                    out there—

                        someone,—   205

New dust on the slimy flesh!

[Pause. No sign from Creon.]

Someone has given it burial that way, and
Gone . . .

[*Long pause. Creon finally speaks with deadly control.*]

eon. And the man who dared do this?

ntry. I swear I   210
Do not know! You must believe me!
                  Listen:
The ground was dry, not a sign of digging, no,
Not a wheeltrack in the dust, no trace of anyone.
It was when they relieved us this morning: and one of them,
The corporal, pointed to it.
                  There it was,   215
The strangest—
        Look:
The body, just mounded over with light dust: you see?
Not buried really, but as if they'd covered it
Just enough for the ghost's peace. And no sign
Of dogs or any wild animal that had been there.   220

And then what a scene there was! Every man of us
Accusing the other: we all proved the other man did it,
We all had proof that we could not have done it.
We were ready to take hot iron in our hands,
Walk through fire, swear by all the gods,
It was not I!   225
I do not know who it was, but it was not I!

[*Creon's rage has been mounting steadily, but the Sentry is too intent upon his story to notice it.*]

And then, when this came to nothing, someone said
A thing that silenced us and made us stare
Down at the ground: you had to be told the news,
And one of us had to do it! We threw the dice,   230
And the bad luck fell to me. So here I am,
No happier to be here than you are to have me:
Nobody likes the man who brings bad news.

horagos. I have been wondering, King: can it be that the gods
have done this?   235

reon. Stop!   [*Furiously.*]
Must you doddering wrecks
Go out of your heads entirely? "The gods!"
Intolerable!
The gods favor this corpse? Why? How had he served them?   240
Tried to loot their temples, burn their images,
Yes, and the whole State, and its laws with it!
Is it your senile opinion that the gods love to honor bad
men?
A pious thought!—
           No, from the very beginning

There have been those who have whispered together,   245
Stiff-necked anarchists, putting their heads together,
Scheming against me in alleys. These are the men,
And they have bribed my own guard to do this thing.
Money!   [*Sententiously.*]
There's nothing in the world so demoralizing as money.   250
Down go your cities,
Homes gone, men gone, honest hearts corrupted,
Crookedness of all kinds, and all for money!

                                        [*To Sentry.*]
                        But you—!
I swear by God and by the throne of God,
The man who has done this thing shall pay for it!   255
Find that man, bring him here to me, or your death
Will be the least of your problems: I'll string you up
Alive, and there will be certain ways to make you
Discover your employer before you die;
And the process may teach you a lesson you seem to have
          missed: 260
The dearest profit is sometimes all too dear:
That depends on the source. Do you understand me?
A fortune won is often misfortune.
Sentry. King, may I speak?
Creon.   Your very voice distresses me.
Sentry. Are you sure that it is my voice, and not your conscience? 265
Creon. By God, he wants to analyze me now!
Sentry. It is not what I say, but what has been done, that hurts you.
Creon. You talk too much.
Sentry.   Maybe; but I've done nothing.
Creon. Sold your soul for some silver: that's all you've done.
Sentry. How dreadful it is when the right judge judges wrong!   270
Creon. Your figures of speech
          May entertain you now; but unless you bring me the man,
          You will get little profit from them in the end.
                              [*Exit Creon into the Palace.*]
Sentry. "Bring me the man"—!
          I'd like nothing better than bringing him the man!   275
          But bring him or not, you have seen the last of me here.
          At any rate, I am safe!   [*Exit Sentry.*]

ODE I

Chorus. Numberless are the world's wonders, but none   [*Strophe 1*]
          More wonderful than man; the stormgray sea
          Yields to his prows, the huge crests bear him high;   280

Earth, holy and inexhaustible, is graven
With shining furrows where his plows have gone
Year after year, the timeless labor of stallions.

The lightboned birds and beasts that cling   [*Antistrophe 1*]
    to cover,
The lithe fish lighting their reaches of dim water,   285
All are taken, tamed in the net of his mind;
The lion on the hill, the wild horse windy-maned,
Resign to him; and his blunt yoke has broken
The sultry shoulders of the mountain bull.

Words also, and thought as rapid as air,   [*Strophe 2*]   290
He fashions to his good use; statecraft is his,
And his the skill that deflects the arrows of snow,
The spears of winter rain: from every wind
He has made himself secure—from all but one:
In the late wind of death he cannot stand.

O clear intelligence, force beyond all measure! [*Antistrophe 2*]   295
O fate of man, working both good and evil!
When the laws are kept, how proudly his city stands!
When the laws are broken, what of his city then?
Never may the anárchic man find rest at my hearth,
Never be it said that my thoughts are his thoughts.   300

SCENE II

[*Re-enter Sentry leading Antigonê.*]

Choragos. What does this mean? Surely this captive woman
    Is the Princess, Antigonê. Why should she be taken?
Sentry. Here is the one who did it! We caught her
    In the very act of burying him.—Where is Creon?
Choragos. Just coming from the house.

                                        [*Enter Creon, C.*]
Creon.   What has happened?   305
    Why have you come back so soon?
Sentry.   O King,   [*Expansively.*]
    A man should never be too sure of anything:
    I would have sworn
    That you'd not see me here again: your anger
    Frightened me so, and the things you threatened me with;   310
    But how could I tell then
    That I'd be able to solve the case so soon?

No dice-throwing this time: I was only too glad to come!

Here is this woman. She is the guilty one:
We found her trying to bury him.   315
Take her, then; question her; judge her as you will.
I am through with the whole thing now, and glád óf it.
Creon. But this is Antigonê! Why have you brought her here?
Sentry. She was burying him, I tell you!

                                                    [*Severely.*]
Creon.   Is this the truth?
Sentry. I saw her with my own eyes. Can I say more?   320
Creon. The details: come, tell me quickly!
Sentry.   It was like this:
After those terrible threats of yours, King,
We went back and brushed the dust away from the body.
The flesh was soft by now, and stinking,   325
So we sat on a hill to windward and kept guard.
No napping this time! We kept each other awake.
But nothing happened until the white round sun
Whirled in the center of the round sky over us:
Then, suddenly,
A storm of dust roared up from the earth, and the sky   330
Went out, the plain vanished with all its trees
In the stinging dark. We closed our eyes and endured it.
The whirlwind lasted a long time, but it passed;
And then we looked, and there was Antigonê!
I have seen   335
A mother bird come back to a stripped nest, heard
Her crying bitterly a broken note or two
For the young ones stolen. Just so, when this girl
Found the bare corpse, and all her love's work wasted,
She wept, and cried on heaven to damn the hands   340
That had done this thing.
                            And then she brought more dust
And sprinkled wine three times for her brother's ghost.

We ran and took her at once. She was not afraid,
Not even when we charged her with what she had done.
She denied nothing.
                            And this was a comfort to me,   345
And some uneasiness: for it is a good thing
To escape from death, but it is no great pleasure
To bring death to a friend.
                            Yet I always say
There is nothing so comfortable as your own safe skin!
Creon. And you, Antigonê,   [*Slowly, dangerously.*] 350
You with your head hanging,—do you confess this thing?

Antigonê. I do. I deny nothing.

[*To Sentry:*]

Creon.   You may go.

[*Exit Sentry. To Antigonê:*]

Tell me, tell me briefly:
Had you heard my proclamation touching this matter?

Antigonê. It was public. Could I help hearing it?   355

Creon. And yet you dared defy the law.

Antigonê.   I dared.
It was not God's proclamation. That final Justice
That rules the world below makes no such laws.

Your edict, King, was strong,
But all your strength is weakness itself against   360
The immortal unrecorded laws of God.
They are not merely now: they were, and shall be,
Operative for ever, beyond man utterly.

I knew I must die, even without your decree:
I am only mortal. And if I must die   365
Now, before it is my time to die,
Surely this is no hardship: can anyone
Living, as I live, with evil all about me,
Think Death less than a friend? This death of mine
Is of no importance; but if I had left my brother   370
Lying in death unburied, I should have suffered.
Now I do not.
                    You smile at me. Ah Creon,
Think me a fool, if you like; but it may well be
That a fool convicts me of folly.

Choragos. Like father, like daughter: both headstrong, deaf to   375
            reason!
She has never learned to yield.

Creon.   She has much to learn.
The inflexible heart breaks first, the toughest iron
Cracks first, and the wildest horses bend their necks
At the pull of the smallest curb.
                              Pride? In a slave?
This girl is guilty of a double insolence,   380
Breaking the given laws and boasting of it.
Who is the man here,
She or I, if this crime goes unpunished?
Sister's child, or more than sister's child,
Or closer yet in blood—she and her sister   385
Win bitter death for this!

[*To servants:*]

                    Go, some of you,

Arrest Ismenê. I accuse her equally.
Bring her: you will find her sniffling in the house there.

Her mind's a traitor: crimes kept in the dark
Cry for light, and the guardian brain shudders;   390
But how much worse than this
Is brazen boasting of barefaced anarchy!
Antigonê. Creon, what more do you want than my death?
Creon.   Nothing.
That gives me everything.
Antigonê.   Then I beg you: kill me.
This talking is a great weariness: your words   395
Are distasteful to me, and I am sure that mine
Seem so to you. And yet they should not seem so:
I should have praise and honor for what I have done.
All these men here would praise me
Were their lips not frozen shut with fear of you.   400
                                          [*Bitterly.*]
Ah the good fortune of kings,
Licensed to say and do whatever they please!
Creon. You are alone here in that opinion.
Antigonê. No, they are with me. But they keep their tongues in leash.
Creon. Maybe. But you are guilty, and they are not.   405
Antigonê. There is no guilt in reverence for the dead.
Creon. But Eteoclês—was he not your brother too?
Antigonê. My brother too.
Creon.   And you insult his memory?
Antigonê. The dead man would not say that I insult it.   [*Softly.*]
Creon. He would: for you honor a traitor as much as him.   410
Antigonê. His own brother, traitor or not, and equal in blood.
Creon. He made war on his country. Eteoclês defended it.
Antigonê. Nevertheless, there are honors due all the dead.
Creon. But not the same for the wicked as for the just.
Antigonê. Ah Creon, Creon,   415
Which of us can say what the gods hold wicked?
Creon. An enemy is an enemy, even dead.
Antigonê. It is my nature to join in love, not hate.
Creon. Go join them, then; if you must   [*Finally losing patience.*]
         have your love,
Find it in hell!   420
Choragos. But see, Ismenê comes:
                              [*Enter Ismenê, guarded.*]
Those tears are sisterly, the cloud
That shadows her eyes rains down gentle sorrow.
Creon. You too, Ismenê,
Snake in my ordered house, sucking my blood   425

Stealthily—and all the time I never knew
That these two sisters were aiming at my throne!
Ismenê,
Do you confess your share in this crime, or deny it?
Answer me.
Ismenê. Yes, if she will let me say so. I am guilty.   430
Antigonê. No, Ismenê. You have no right to say so.   [*Coldly.*]
You would not help me, and I will not have you help me.
Ismenê. But now I know what you meant; and I am here
To join you, to take my share of punishment.
Antigonê. The dead man and the gods who rule the dead   435
Know whose act this was. Words are not friends.
Ismenê. Do you refuse me, Antigonê? I want to die with you:
I too have a duty that I must discharge to the dead.
Antigonê. You shall not lessen my death by sharing it.
Ismenê. What do I care for life when you are dead?   440
Antigonê. Ask Creon. You're always hanging on his opinions.
Ismenê. You are laughing at me. Why, Antigonê?
Antigonê. It's a joyless laughter, Ismenê.
Ismenê.   But can I do nothing?
Antigonê. Yes. Save yourself. I shall not envy you.
There are those who will praise you; I shall have honor, too.   445
Ismenê. But we are equally guilty!
Antigonê.   No more, Ismenê.
You are alive, but I belong to Death.
Creon. Gentlemen, I beg you to observe these   [*To the Chorus:*]
girls:
One has just now lost her mind; the other,
It seems, has never had a mind at all.   450
Ismenê. Grief teaches the steadiest minds to waver, King.
Creon. Yours certainly did, when you assumed guilt with the guilty!
Ismenê. But how could I go on living without her?
Creon.   You are.
She is already dead.
Ismenê.   But your own son's bride!
Creon. There are places enough for him to push his plow.   455
I want no wicked women for my sons!
Ismenê. O dearest Haimon, how your father wrongs you!
Creon. I've had enough of your childish talk of marriage!
Choragos. Do you really intend to steal this girl from your son?
Creon. No; Death will do that for me.
Choragos.   Then she must die?   460
Creon. You dazzle me.   [*Ironically.*]
—But enough of this talk!

[*To Guards:*]
You, there, take them away and guard them well:

For they are but women, and even brave men run
When they see Death coming.

[*Exeunt Ismenê, Antigonê, and Guards.*]

ODE II

Chorus. Fortunate is the man who has never tasted   [*Strophe 1*]   465
      God's vengeance!
Where once the anger of heaven has struck, that house is
      shaken
For ever: damnation rises behind each child
Like a wave cresting out of the black northeast,
When the long darkness under sea roars up
And bursts drumming death upon the windwhipped sand.   470

I have seen this gathering sorrow from time   [*Antistrophe 1*]
      long past
Loom upon Oedipus' children: generation from generation
Takes the compulsive rage of the enemy god.
So lately this last flower of Oedipus' line
Drank the sunlight! but now a passionate word   475
And a handful of dust have closed up all its beauty.

    What mortal arrogance   [*Strophe 2*]
    Transcends the wrath of Zeus?
Sleep cannot lull him, nor the effortless long months
Of the timeless gods: but he is young for ever,   480
And his house is the shining day of high Olympos.
      All that is and shall be,
      And all the past, is his.
No pride on earth is free of the curse of heaven.

The straying dreams of men   [*Antistrophe 2*]   485
    May bring them ghosts of joy:
But as they drowse, the waking embers burn them;
Or they walk with fíxed éyes, as blind men walk.
But the ancient wisdom speaks for our own time:
    Fate works most for woe   490
    With Folly's fairest show.
Man's little pleasure is the spring of sorrow.

SCENE III

Choragos. But here is Haimon, King, the last of all your sons.
    Is it grief for Antigonê that brings him here,
    And bitterness at being robbed of his bride?   495
                               [*Enter Haimon.*]
Creon. We shall soon see, and no need of diviners.
                               —Son,
    You have heard my final judgment on that girl:
    Have you come here hating me, or have you come
    With deference and with love, whatever I do?
Haimon. I am your son, father. You are my guide.   500
    You make things clear for me, and I obey you.
    No marriage means more to me than your continuing
        wisdom.
Creon. Good. That is the way to behave: subordinate
    Everything else, my son, to your father's will.
    This is what a man prays for, that he may get   505
    Sons attentive and dutiful in his house,
    Each one hating his father's enemies,
    Honoring his father's friends. But if his sons
    Fail him, if they turn out unprofitably,
    What has he fathered but trouble for himself   510
    And amusement for the malicious?
                         So you are right
    Not to lose your head over this woman.
    Your pleasure with her would soon grow cold, Haimon,
    And then you'd have a hellcat in bed and elsewhere.
    Let her find her husband in Hell!   515
    Of all the people in this city, only she
    Has had contempt for my law and broken it.

    Do you want me to show myself weak before the people?
    Or to break my sworn word? No, and I will not.
    The woman dies.   520
    I suppose she'll plead "family ties." Well, let her.
    If I permit my own family to rebel,
    How shall I earn the world's obedience?
    Show me the man who keeps his house in hand,
    He's fit for public authority.
                     I'll have no dealings   525
    With law-breakers, critics of the government:
    Whoever is chosen to govern should be obeyed—
    Must be obeyed, in all things, great and small,
    Just and unjust! O Haimon,
    The man who knows how to obey, and that man only,   530
    Knows how to give commands when the time comes.

You can depend on him, no matter how fast
The spears come: he's a good soldier, he'll stick it out.

Anarchy, anarchy! Show me a greater evil!
This is why cities tumble and the great houses rain down,   535
This is what scatters armies!

No, no: good lives are made so by discipline.
We keep the laws then, and the lawmakers,
And no woman shall seduce us. If we must lose,
Let's lose to a man, at least! Is a woman stronger than we?   540
Choragos. Unless time has rusted my wits,
What you say, King, is said with point and dignity.
Haimon. Father: [*Boyishly earnest.*]
Reason is God's crowning gift to man, and you are right
To warn me against losing mine. I cannot say—
I hope that I shall never want to say!—that you   545
Have reasoned badly. Yet there are other men
Who can reason, too; and their opinions might be helpful.
You are not in a position to know everything
That people say or do, or what they feel:
Your temper terrifies them—everyone   550
Will tell you only what you like to hear.
But I, at any rate, can listen; and I have heard them
Muttering and whispering in the dark about this girl.
They say no woman has ever, so unreasonably,
Died so shameful a death for a generous act: 555
"She covered her brother's body. Is this indecent?
She kept him from dogs and vultures. Is this a crime?
Death?—She should have all the honor that we can
     give her!"

This is the way they talk out there in the city.

You must believe me: 560
Nothing is closer to me than your happiness.
What could be closer? Must not any son
Value his father's fortune as his father does his?
I beg you, do not be unchangeable:
Do not believe that you alone can be right.   565
The man who thinks that,
The man who maintains that only he has the power
To reason correctly, the gift to speak, the soul—
A man like that, when you know him, turns out empty.

It is not reason never to yield to reason!   570

In flood time you can see how some trees bend,

502 SOPHOCLES

And because they bend, even their twigs are safe,
While stubborn trees are torn up, roots and all.
And the same thing happens in sailing:
Make your sheet fast, never slacken,—and over you go,   575
Head over heels and under: and there's your voyage.
Forget you are angry! Let yourself be moved!
I know I am young; but please let me say this:
The ideal condition
Would be, I admit, that men should be right by instinct;   580
But since we are all too likely to go astray,
The reasonable thing is to learn from those who can teach.

horagos. You will do well to listen to him, King,
If what he says is sensible. And you, Haimon,
Must listen to your father.—Both speak well.   585

reon. You consider it right for a man of my years and experience
To go to school to a boy?

aimon.   It is not right
If I am wrong. But if I am young, and right,
What does my age matter?

reon. You think it right to stand up for an anarchist?   590

[aimon. Not at all. I pay no respect to criminals.

reon. Then she is not a criminal?

[aimon. The City would deny it, to a man.

reon. And the City proposes to teach me how to rule?

[aimon. Ah. Who is it that's talking like a boy now?   595

reon. My voice is the one voice giving orders in this City!

[aimon. It is no City if it takes orders from one voice.

reon. The State is the King!

[aimon.   Yes, if the State is a desert.

[*Pause.*]

reon. This boy, it seems, has sold out to a woman.

[aimon. If you are a woman: my concern is only for you.   600

reon. So? Your "concern"! In a public brawl with your father!

[aimon. How about you, in a public brawl with justice?

reon. With justice, when all that I do is within my rights?

[aimon. You have no right to trample on God's right.

reon. Fool, adolescent fool! Taken   [*Completely out of control.*] 605
In by a woman!

[aimon. You'll never see me taken in by anything vile.

reon. Every word you say is for her!

[aimon.   And for you.   [*Quietly, darkly.*]
And for me. And for the gods under the earth.

reon. You'll never marry her while she lives.

Haimon. Then she must die.—But her death will cause another.   610

reon. Another?
Have you lost your senses? It this an open threat?

Haimon. There is no threat in speaking to emptiness.

Creon. I swear you'll regret this superior tone of yours!
    You are the empty one!
Haimon.   If you were not my father,   615
    I'd say you were perverse.
Creon. You girlstruck fool, don't play at words with me!
Haimon. I am sorry. You prefer silence.
Creon.   Now, by God—!
    I swear, by all the gods in heaven above us,
    You'll watch it, I swear you shall!

                        [*To the Servants:*]
                    Bring her out!   620
    Bring the woman out! Let her die before his eyes!
    Here, this instant, with her bridegroom beside her!
Haimon. Not here, no; she will not die here, King.
    And you will never see my face again.
    Go on raving as long as you've a friend to endure you.   625
                        [*Exit Haimon.*]
Choragos. Gone, gone.
    Creon, a young man in a rage is dangerous!
Creon. Let him do, or dream to do, more than a man can.
    He shall not save these girls from death.
Choragos.   These girls?
    You have sentenced them both?
Creon.   No, you are right.   630
    I will not kill the one whose hands are clean.
Choragos. But Antigonê?
Creon.   I will carry her far away   [*Somberly.*]
    Out there in the wilderness, and lock her
    Living in a vault of stone. She shall have food,
    As the custom is, to absolve the State of her death.   635
    And there let her pray to the gods of hell:
    They are her only gods:
    Perhaps they will show her an escape from death,
    Or she may learn,
               though late,
    That piety shown the dead is pity in vain.   640
                        [*Exit Creon.*]

ODE III

Chorus. Love, unconquerable   [*Strophe*]
    Waster of rich men, keeper
    Of warm lights and all-night vigil
    In the soft face of a girl:
    Sea-wanderer, forest-visitor!
    Even the pure Immortals cannot escape you,   645
    And mortal man, in his one day's dusk,
    Trembles before your glory.

Surely you swerve upon ruin   [Antistrophe]
    The just man's consenting heart,   650
    As here you have made bright anger
    Strike between father and son—
    And none has conquered but Love!
    A girl's glánce wórking the will of heaven:
    Pleasure to her alone who mocks us,   655
    Merciless Aphroditê.[4]

SCENE IV

Choragos. But I can no longer   [As Antigonê enters guarded.]
        stand in awe of this,
    Nor, seeing what I see, keep back my tears.
    Here is Antigonê, passing to that chamber
    Where all find sleep at last.   660

Antigonê. Look upon me, friends, and pity me   [Strophe 1]
    Turning back at the night's edge to say
    Good-by to the sun that shines for me no longer;
    Now sleepy Death
    Summons me down to Acheron,[5] that cold shore: 665
    There is no bridesong there, nor any music.
Chorus. Yet not unpraised, not without a kind of honor,
    You walk at last into the underworld;
    Untouched by sickness, broken by no sword.
    What woman has ever found your way to death?   670

Antigonê. How often I have heard the story of   [Antistrophe 1]
        Niobê,[6]
    Tantalos' wretched daughter, how the stone
    Clung fast about her, ivy-close: and they say
    The rain falls endlessly
    And sifting soft snow; her tears are never done.   675
    I feel the loneliness of her death in mine.
Chorus. But she was born of heaven, and you
    Are woman, woman-born. If her death is yours,
    A mortal woman's, is this not for you
    Glory in our world and in the world beyond?   680

---

[4] Goddess of Love. [Editors' note]
[5] A river of the underworld, which was ruled by Hades. [Editors' note]
[6] Niobê boasted of her numerous children, provoking Leto, the mother of
Apollo, to destroy them. Niobê wept profusely, and finally was turned into a
stone on Mount Sipylus, whose streams are her tears. [Editors' note]

Antigonê. You laugh at me. Ah, friends, friends,   [*Strophe* 2]
        Can you not wait until I am dead? O Thebes,
        O men many-charioted, in love with Fortune,
        Dear springs of Dircê, sacred Theban grove,
        Be witnesses for me, denied all pity,   685
        Unjustly judged! and think a word of love
        For her whose path turns
        Under dark earth, where there are no more tears.
Chorus. You have passed beyond human daring and come at last
        Into a place of stone where Justice sits.   690
        I cannot tell
        What shape of your father's guilt appears in this.

Antigonê. You have touched it at last: that bridal bed   [*Antistrophe* 2]
        Unspeakable, horror of son and mother mingling:
        Their crime, infection of all our family!   695
        O Oedipus, father and brother!
        Your marriage strikes from the grave to murder mine.
        I have been a stranger here in my own land:
        All my life
        The blasphemy of my birth has followed me.   700
Chorus. Reverence is a virtue, but strength
        Lives in established law: that must prevail.
        You have made your choice,
        Your death is the doing of your conscious hand.

Antigonê. Then let me go, since all your words are bitter, [*Epode*]   705
        And the very light of the sun is cold to me.
        Lead me to my vigil, where I must have
        Neither love nor lamentation; no song, but silence.
                                    [*Creon interrupts impatiently.*]
Creon. If dirges and planned lamentations could put off death,
        Men would be singing for ever.

                                    [*To the Servants:*]
                        Take her, go!   710
        You know your orders: take her to the vault
        And leave her alone there. And if she lives or dies,
        That's her affair, not ours: our hands are clean.

Antigonê. O tomb, vaulted bride-bed in eternal rock,
        Soon I shall be with my own again   715
        Where Persephonê [7] welcomes the thin ghosts underground:
        And I shall see my father again, and you, mother,
        And dearest Polyneicês—
                                    dearest indeed

[7] Queen of the underworld. [Editors' note]

To me, since it was my hand
That washed him clean and poured the ritual wine: 720
And my reward is death before my time!

And yet, as men's hearts know, I have done no wrong,
I have not sinned before God. Or if I have,
I shall know the truth in death. But if the guilt
Lies upon Creon who judged me, then, I pray,   725
May his punishment equal my own.
horagos.   O passionate heart,
  Unyielding, tormented still by the same winds!
reon. Her guards shall have good cause to regret their delaying.
ntigonê. Ah! That voice is like the voice of death!
reon. I can give you no reason to think you are mistaken.   730
ntigonê. Thebes, and you my fathers' gods,
  And rulers of Thebes, you see me now, the last
  Unhappy daughter of a line of kings,
  Your kings, led away to death. You will remember
  What things I suffer, and at what men's hands,   735
  Because I would not transgress the laws of heaven.
                         [*To the Guards, simply:*]
Come: let us wait no longer.
                         [*Exit Antigonê, L., guarded.*]

ODE IV

Chorus. All Danaê's beauty was locked away   [*Strophe 1*]
  In a brazen cell where the sunlight could not come:
  A small room, still as any grave, enclosed her.   740
  Yet she was a princess too,
  And Zeus in a rain of gold poured love upon her.
  O child, child,
  No power in wealth or war
  Or tough sea-blackened ships   745
  Can prevail against untiring Destiny!

And Dryas' son [8] also, that furious king,   [*Antistrophe 1*]
  Bore the god's prisoning anger for his pride:
  Sealed up by Dionysos in deaf stone,
  His madness died among echoes.   750
  So at the last he learned what dreadful power
  His tongue had mocked:
  For he had profaned the revels,

[8] Dryas' son: Lycurgus, King of Thrace. [Editors' note]

And fired the wrath of the nine
Implacable Sisters [9] that love the sound of the flute. 755

And old men tell a half-remembered tale   [*Strophe 2*]
Of horror where a dark ledge splits the sea
And a double surf beats on the gráy shóres:
How a king's new woman,[10] sick
With hatred for the queen he had imprisoned,   760
Ripped out his two sons' eyes with her bloody hands
While grinning Arês[11] watched the shuttle plunge
Four times: four blind wounds crying for revenge,

Crying, tears and blood mingled.—Piteously born,   [*Antistrophe 2*]
Those sons whose mother was of heavenly birth!   765
Her father was the god of the North Wind
And she was cradled by gales,
She raced with young colts on the glittering hills
And walked untrammeled in the open light:
But in her marriage deathless Fate found means   770
To build a tomb like yours for all her joy.

SCENE V

[*Enter blind Teiresias, led by a boy. The opening speeches of
Teiresias should be in singsong contrast to the realistic lines
of Creon.*]

Teiresias. This is the way the blind man comes, Princes, Princes,
    Lock-step, two heads lit by the eyes of one.
Creon. What new thing have you to tell us, old Teiresias?
Teiresias. I have much to tell you: listen to the prophet, Creon.   775
Creon. I am not aware that I have ever failed to listen.
Teiresias. Then you have done wisely, King, and ruled well.
Creon. I admit my debt to you. But what have you to say?
Teiresias. This, Creon: you stand once more on the edge of fate.
Creon. What do you mean? Your words are a kind of dread.   780
Teiresias. Listen, Creon:
    I was sitting in my chair of augury, at the place

[9] The Muses. [Editors' note]
[10] Eidothea, second wife of King Phineus, blinded her stepsons. (Their
mother, Cleopatra, had been imprisoned in a cave.) Phineus was the son of
a king, and Cleopatra, his first wife, was the daughter of Boreas, the North
Wind; but this illustrious ancestry could not protect his sons from violence
and darkness. [Editors' note]
[11] God of war. [Editors' note]

Where the birds gather about me. They were all a-chatter,
As is their habit, when suddenly I heard
A strange note in their jangling, a scream, a   785
Whirring fury; I knew that they were fighting,
Tearing each other, dying
In a whirlwind of wings clashing. And I was afraid.
I began the rites of burnt-offering at the altar,
But Hephaistos [12] failed me: instead of bright flame,   790
There was only the sputtering slime of the fat thigh-flesh
Melting: the entrails dissolved in gray smoke,
The bare bone burst from the welter. And no blaze!

This was a sign from heaven. My boy described it,
Seeing for me as I see for others.   795

I tell you, Creon, you yourself have brought
This new calamity upon us. Our hearths and altars
Are stained with the corruption of dogs and carrion birds
That glut themselves on the corpse of Oedipus' son.
The gods are deaf when we pray to them, their fire   800
Recoils from our offering, their birds of omen
Have no cry of comfort, for they are gorged
With the thick blood of the dead.
                      O my son,
These are no trifles! Think: all men make mistakes,
But a good man yields when he knows his course is wrong,   805
And repairs the evil. The only crime is pride.

Give in to the dead man, then: do not fight with a corpse—
What glory is it to kill a man who is dead?
Think, I beg you:
It is for your own good that I speak as I do.   810
You should be able to yield for your own good.

Creon. It seems that prophets have made me their especial province.
All my life long
I have been a kind of butt for the dull arrows
Of doddering fortune-tellers!
                No, Teiresias: 815
If your birds—if the great eagles of God himself
Should carry him stinking bit by bit to heaven,
I would not yield. I am not afraid of pollution:
No man can defile the gods.
             Do what you will,
Go into business, make money, speculate   820
In India gold or that synthetic gold from Sardis,
Get rich otherwise than by my consent to bury him.

---

[12] God of fire. [Editors' note]

Teiresias, it is a sorry thing when a wise man
Sells his wisdom, lets out his words for hire!
Teiresias. Ah Creon! Is there no man left in the world— 825
Creon. To do what?—Come, let's have the aphorism!
Teiresias. No man who knows that wisdom outweighs any wealth?
Creon. As surely as bribes are baser than any baseness.
Teiresias. You are sick, Creon! You are deathly sick!
Creon. As you say: it is not my place to challenge a prophet. 830
Teiresias. Yet you have said my prophecy is for sale.
Creon. The generation of prophets has always loved gold.
Teiresias. The generation of kings has always loved brass.
Creon. You forget yourself! You are speaking to your King.
Teiresias. I know it. You are a king because of me. 835
Creon. You have a certain skill; but you have sold out.
Teiresias. King, you will drive me to words that—
Creon.   Say them, say them!
Only remember: I will not pay you for them.
Teiresias. No, you will find them too costly.
Creon.   No doubt. Speak:
Whatever you say, you will not change my will. 840
Teiresias. Then take this, and take it to heart!
The time is not far off when you shall pay back
Corpse for corpse, flesh of your own flesh.
You have thrust the child of this world into living night,
You have kept from the gods below the child that is theirs: 845
The one in a grave before her death, the other,
Dead, denied the grave. This is your crime:
And the Furies and the dark gods of Hell
Are swift with terrible punishment for you.

Do you want to buy me now, Creon?

                                    Not many days, 850
And your house will be full of men and women weeping,
And curses will be hurled at you from far
Cities grieving for sons unburied, left to rot
Before the walls of Thebes.

These are my arrows, Creon: they are all for you. 855

                                    [*To Boy:*]

But come, child: lead me home.
Let him waste his fine anger upon younger men.
Maybe he will learn at last
To control a wiser tongue in a better head.

                                    [*Exit Teiresias.*]

Choragos. The old man has gone, King, but his words 860

510 SOPHOCLES

Remain to plague us. I am old, too,
But I cannot remember that he was ever false.
Creon. That is true. . . . It troubles me.
Oh it is hard to give in! but it is worse
To risk everything for stubborn pride.   865
Choragos. Creon: take my advice.
Creon.   What shall I do?
Choragos. Go quickly: free Antigonê from her vault
And build a tomb for the body of Polyneicês.
Creon. You would have me do this?
Choragos.   Creon, yes!
And it must be done at once: God moves   870
Swiftly to cancel the folly of stubborn men.
Creon. It is hard to deny the heart! But I
Will do it: I will not fight with destiny.
Choragos. You must go yourself, you cannot leave it to others.
Creon. I will go.
            —Bring axes, servants: 875
Come with me to the tomb. I buried her, I
Will set her free.
            Oh quickly!
My mind misgives—
The laws of the gods are mighty, and a man must
            serve them
To the last day of his life!   880

                    [*Exit Creon.*]

                    PÆAN [13]

Choragos. God of many names   [*Strophe 1*]
Chorus.   O Iacchos
                    son
        of Kadmeian Sémelê
                    O born of the Thunder!
        Guardian of the West
                    Regent
        of Eleusis' plain
                    O Prince of maenad Thebes
        and the Dragon Field by rippling Ismenos: [14]   885

[13] A hymn here dedicated to Iacchos (also called Dionysos). His father was
Zeus, his mother was Sémelê, daughter of Kadmos. Iacchos' worshippers were
the Maenads, whose cry was "*Evohé evohé.*" [Editors' note]
[14] A river east of Thebes. From a dragon's teeth (sown near the river) there
sprang men who became the ancestors of the Theban nobility. [Editors' note]

Choragos. God of many names   [Antistrophe 1]
Chorus.   the flame of torches
    flares on our hills
        the nymphs of Iacchos
  dance at the spring of Castalia: 15
  from the vine-close mountain
          come ah come in ivy:
  Evohé evohé! sings through the streets of Thebes   890

Choragos. God of many names   [Strophe 2]
Chorus.   Iacchos of Thebes
    heavenly Child
        of Sémelê bride of the Thunderer!
  The shadow of plague is upon us:
              come
  with clement feet
        oh come from Parnasos
  down the long slopes
        across the lamenting water   895

Choragos. Iô Fire! Chorister of the throbbing stars!   [Antistrophe 2]
  O purest among the voices of the night!
  Thou son of God, blaze for us!
Chorus. Come with choric rapture of circling Maenads
  Who cry Iô Iacche!   900
      God of many names!

EXODOS

[Enter Messenger, L.]

Messenger. Men of the line of Kadmos,[16] you who live
  Near Amphion's citadel:
           I cannot say
Of any condition of human life "This is fixed,
This is clearly good, or bad." Fate raises up,
And Fate casts down the happy and unhappy alike: 905
No man can foretell his Fate.
          Take the case of Creon:
Creon was happy once, as I count happiness:

15 A spring on Mount Parnasos. [Editors' note]
16 Kadmos, who sowed the dragon's teeth, was the founder of Thebes;
Amphion played so sweetly on his lyre that he charmed stones to form a wall
around Thebes. [Editors' note]

Victorious in battle, sole governor of the land,
Fortunate father of children nobly born.
And now it has all gone from him! Who can say   910
That a man is still alive when his life's joy fails?
He is a walking dead man. Grant him rich,
Let him live like a king in his great house:
If his pleasure is gone, I would not give
So much as the shadow of smoke for all he owns.   915

Choragos. Your words hint at sorrow: what is your news for us?
Messenger. They are dead. The living are guilty of their death.
Choragos. Who is guilty? Who is dead? Speak!
Messenger.   Haimon.
Haimon is dead; and the hand that killed him
Is his own hand.
Choragos.   His father's? or his own?   920
Messenger. His own, driven mad by the murder his father had done.
Choragos. Teiresias, Teiresias, how clearly you saw it all!
Messenger. This is my news: you must draw what conclusions you
     can from it.
Choragos. But look: Eurydicê, our Queen:
     Has she overheard us?   925

               [*Enter Eurydicê from the Palace, C.*]

Eurydicê. I have heard something, friends:
     As I was unlocking the gate of Pallas' [17] shrine,
     For I needed her help today, I heard a voice
     Telling of some new sorrow. And I fainted
     There at the temple with all my maidens about me.   930
     But speak again: whatever it is, I can bear it:
     Grief and I are no strangers.
Messenger.   Dearest Lady,
     I will tell you plainly all that I have seen.
     I shall not try to comfort you: what is the use,
     Since comfort could lie only in what is not true?   935
     The truth is always best.
                         I went with Creon
     To the outer plain where Polyneicês was lying,
     No friend to pity him, his body shredded by dogs.
     We made our prayers in that place to Hecatê
     And Pluto, [18] that they would be merciful. And we bathed   940
     The corpse with holy water, and we brought
     Fresh-broken branches to burn what was left of it,
     And upon the urn we heaped up a towering barrow
     Of the earth of his own land.

---

[17] Pallas Athene, goddess of wisdom. [Editors' note]
[18] Hecatê and Pluto (also known as Hades) were deities of the underworld.
[Editors' note]

When we were done, we ran
To the vault where Antigonê lay on her couch of stone.   945
One of the servants had gone ahead,
And while he was yet far off he heard a voice
Grieving within the chamber, and he came back
And told Creon. And as the King went closer,   950
The air was full of wailing, the words lost,
And he begged us to make all haste. "Am I a prophet?"
He said, weeping, "And must I walk this road,
The saddest of all that I have gone before?
My son's voice calls me on. Oh quickly, quickly!
Look through the crevice there, and tell me   955
If it is Haimon, or some deception of the gods!"

We obeyed; and in the cavern's farthest corner
We saw her lying:
She had made a noose of her fine linen veil
And hanged herself. Haimon lay beside her,   960
His arms about her waist, lamenting her,
His love lost under ground, crying out
That his father had stolen her away from him.

When Creon saw him the tears rushed to his eyes
And he called to him: "What have you done, child? Speak
      to me.   965
What are you thinking that makes your eyes so strange?
O my son, my son, I come to you on my knees!"
But Haimon spat in his face. He said not a word,
Staring—
            And suddenly drew his sword
And lunged. Creon shrank back, the blade missed; and
      the boy,   970
Desperate against himself, drove it half its length
Into his own side, and fell. And as he died
He gathered Antigonê close in his arms again,
Choking, his blood bright red on her white cheek.
And now he lies dead with the dead, and she is his   975
At last, his bride in the houses of the dead.
                    [*Exit Eurydicê into the Palace.*]
Choragos. She has left us without a word. What can this mean?
Messenger. It troubles me, too; yet she knows what is best,
      Her grief is too great for public lamentation,
      And doubtless she has gone to her chamber to weep   980
      For her dead son, leading her maidens in his dirge.
Choragos. It may be so: but I fear this deep silence.   [*Pause.*]
Messenger. I will see what she is doing. I will go in.
                    [*Exit Messenger into the Palace.*]

[Enter Creon with attendants,
bearing Haimon's body.]

Choragos. But here is the King himself: oh look at him,
Bearing his own damnation in his arms.   985
Creon. Nothing you say can touch me any more.
My own blind heart has brought me
From darkness to final darkness. Here you see
The father murdering, the murdered son—
And all my civic wisdom!   990

Haimon my son, so young, so young to die,
I was the fool, not you; and you died for me.
Choragos. That is the truth; but you were late in learning it.
Creon. This truth is hard to bear. Surely a god
Has crushed me beneath the hugest weight of heaven,   995
And driven me headlong a barbaric way
To trample out the thing I held most dear.

The pains that men will take to come to pain!
[Enter Messenger from the Palace.]
Messenger. The burden you carry in your hands is heavy,
But it is not all: you will find more in your house.   1000
Creon. What burden worse than this shall I find there?
Messenger. The Queen is dead.
Creon. O port of death, deaf world,
Is there no pity for me? And you, Angel of evil,
I was dead, and your words are death again.   1005
Is it true, boy? Can it be true?
Is my wife dead? Has death bred death?
Messenger. You can see for yourself.
[The doors are opened, and the body
of Eurydicê is disclosed within.]
Creon. Oh pity!
All true, all true, and more than I can bear!   1010
O my wife, my son!
Messenger. She stood before the altar, and her heart
Welcomed the knife her own hand guided,
And a great cry burst from her lips for Megareus [19] dead,
And for Haimon dead, her sons; and her last breath   1015
Was a curse for their father, the murderer of her sons.
And she fell, and the dark flowed in through her closing
eyes.
Creon. O God, I am sick with fear.
Are there no swords here? Has no one a blow for me?
Messenger. Her curse is upon you for the deaths of both.   1020

[19] Megareus, brother of Haimon, had died in the assault on Thebes. [Editors'
note]

Creon. It is right that it should be. I alone am guilty.
    I know it, and I say it. Lead me in,
    Quickly, friends.
    I have neither life nor substance. Lead me in.
Choragos. You are right, if there can be right in so much wrong.   1025
    The briefest way is best in a world of sorrow.
Creon. Let it come,
    Let death come quickly, and be kind to me.
    I would not ever see the sun again.
Choragos. All that will come when it will; but we, meanwhile,   1030
    Have much to do. Leave the future to itself.
Creon. All my heart was in that prayer!
Choragos. Then do not pray any more: the sky is deaf.
Creon. Lead me away. I have been rash and foolish.
    I have killed my son and my wife.   1035
    I look for comfort; my comfort lies here dead.
    Whatever my hands have touched has come to nothing.
    Fate has brought all my pride to a thought of dust.

[*As Creon is being led into the house, the Choragos advances and speaks directly to the audience.*]

Choragos. There is no happiness where there is no wisdom;
    No wisdom but in submission to the gods.   1040
    Big words are always punished,
    And proud men in old age learn to be wise.

QUESTONS: *Antigone*

1. Although Sophocles called his play *Antigonê*, many critics say that Creon is the real tragic hero, pointing out that Antigonê is absent from the last third of the play. Evaluate this view.

2. In some Greek tragedies, fate plays a great role in bringing about the downfall of the tragic hero. Though there are references to the curse on the House of Oedipus in *Antigonê*, do we feel that Antigonê goes to her death as a result of the workings of fate? Do we feel that fate is responsible for Creon's fall? Is the Messenger right (line 904) to introduce the notion of "fate"? Or are both Antigonê and Creon the creators of their own tragedy?

3. Are the words *hamartia* and *hybris* (page 482) relevant to Antigonê? To Creon? Be specific.

4. Antigonê and Haimon never appear together in a scene. Is this a weakness? How does Sophocles present their love for one another without submitting them to a passionate love scene? What, in fact, is gained by Haimon's presence in the play?

5. Why does Creon, contrary to the Chorus' advice (lines 867-868), bury the body of Polyneicês before he releases Antigonê? Does his action show a zeal for piety as short-sighted as his earlier zeal for law? Is his action plausible, in view of the facts that Teiresias has dwelt on the wrong done to Polyneicês, and that Antigonê has ritual food to sustain her? Or are we not to worry about Creon's motive?

6. Characterize the Chorus. Is its attitude toward Creon constant? Toward Antigonê? When the main character in a Greek tragedy is a heroine, the chorus is usually made up of women. What added impact is given in *Antigonê* by having old men form the Chorus?

7. A "foil" is a character who, by contrast, sets off or helps define another character. To what extent is Ismenê a foil to Antigonê? Is she entirely without courage? Explain.

8. What function does Eurydicê serve? How deeply do we feel about her fate? Explain.

9. No gods appear in the play; how is their presence communicated?

10. Some readers have been distressed by a passage, omitted from the present version, that follows line 721. It runs (in Paul Roche's translation) thus:

> No husband dead and gone,
> No children lisping "mother" ever could
> Have forced me to withstand the city to its face.
> On what principles do I assert so much?
> Just this:
> A husband dead, another can be found;
> A child, replaced; but once a brother's lost
> (Mother and father dead and buried too)
> No other brother can be born or grows again.
> That's my principle, which Creon stigmatized
> As criminal—my principle for honoring
> You my dearest brother.

Goethe, for example, says (*Conversations of Goethe with Eckermann*): "There is a passage in *Antigonê* which I always look upon as a blemish and I would give a great deal for an apt philologist to prove that it is interpolated and spurious. After the heroine has explained the noble motives for her action, and displayed the elevated purity of her soul, she at last, when she is led to death, brings forward a motive that is quite unworthy and almost borders upon the comic. . . . This passage, . . . in my opinion, when placed in the mouth of a heroine going to her death, disturbs the tragic tone and appears to me very far-fetched—to savor too much of dialectical calculation." On the other hand H. D. F. Kitto has justified the passage thus (*Form and Meaning in Drama*): "Antigonê is neither a philosopher nor a *dévote*, but a passionate impulsive girl, and we need not expect consistency from one such, when for doing what to her was her manifest duty she is about to be buried alive, without a gleam of understanding from anybody. She thought she was obeying a divine law—as of course she was; now the gods seem to have deserted her—as they have, for they do not work miracles. Therefore nothing is left to her but her deep instinct that she had to do it, and it is neither surprising nor undramatic that she should now find what reason she can for asserting that in this special case she had no choice." Evaluate these views.

Eighteen

COMEDY

Though etymology is not always helpful (after all, is it really illuminating to say that "tragedy" may come from a Greek word meaning "goat song"?), the etymology of "comedy" helps to reveal comedy's fundamental nature. **Comedy** (Greek: *komoidia*) is a revel-song; ancient Greek comedies are descended from fertility rituals, and they dramatize the joy of renewal, the joy of triumphing over obstacles, the joy of being (in a sense) reborn. The movement of tragedy, speaking roughly, is from prosperity to disaster; the movement of comedy is from some sort of minor disaster to prosperity.

To say, however, that comedy dramatizes the triumph over obstacles is to describe it as though it were melodrama, a play in which, after hair-breadth adventures, good prevails over evil, often in the form of the hero's unlikely last-minute rescue of the fair Belinda from the clutches of the villain. What distinguishes comedy from melodrama is the pervasive high spirits of comedy. The joyous ending in comedy— usually a marriage—is in the spirit of what has gone before; the entire play, and not only the end, is a celebration of fecundity.

The threats in the world of comedy are not taken very seriously; the parental tyranny that helps make *Romeo and Juliet* and *Antigone* tragedies is, in comedy, laughable throughout. Parents may fret, fume, and lock doors, but in doing so they make themselves ridiculous, for love will find a way. Villains may threaten, but the audience never takes the threats seriously.

In the first act of *As You Like It*, Rosalind, at the mercy of a cruel uncle who has driven her father from his own dukedom, says: "O, how full of briers is this working-day world." The immediate reply is, "They are but burrs, cousin, thrown upon thee in holiday foolery." And it is the spirit of holiday foolery that dominates the whole play and culminates in marriage, the symbol of life renewing itself. The banished duke lives zestfully in the green woods, plentifully supplied with meat and song; when Rosalind herself is banished to the woods, she disguises herself and has a good time teasing her lover. In the last act things work out—as from the start we knew they would. While *Antigone* concludes with Creon looking at the corpses of his wife, son, and intended daughter-in-law, *As You Like It* concludes with four marriages, the repentance of the wicked duke, and the return of the rightful duke to his dukedom.

These exiles, marriages, and renewals of society are most improbable, but they do not therefore weaken the comedy. The stuff of comedy is, in part, improbability. In *A Midsummer-Night's Dream* Puck speaks for the spectator when he says:

> And those things do best please me
> That befall preposterously.

In tragedy, probability is important; in comedy, the improbable is often desirable, for at least three reasons. First, comedy seeks to include as much as possible, to reveal the rich abundance of life. The four marriages (and the reunion of the duke with his people, and the union of the usurper with a better way of life) in *As You Like It* do not weaken the play but strengthen it; the motto of comedy (and the implication in the weddings with which it usually concludes) is the more the merrier. Second, the improbable is the surprising; surprise often evokes laughter, and laughter surely has a central place in comedy. Third, by getting his characters into improbable situations, the dramatist can show off the absurdity of their behavior—a point that needs amplification.

Comedy often shows the absurdity of man's ideals. The miser, the puritan, the health-faddist, and so on, are men of ideals, but their ideals are suffocating. The miser, for example, treats everything in terms of money; his ideal causes him to renounce much of the abundance and joy of life. He is in love, but is unwilling to support a wife; or he has a daughter, but is unwilling to marry her off because he will have to buy himself a dress suit. If a thief accosts him with "Your money or your life," he will prefer to give up his life—and that is what in fact he has been doing all the while. Now, by putting this miser in a series of improbable situations, the dramatist can continue to demonstrate entertainingly the miser's absurdity.*

The comic protagonist's tenacious hold on his ideals is not very

* A character who is dominated by a single trait—avarice, jealousy, timidity, etc.—is sometimes called a **humor character**. Medieval and Renaissance psychology held that a man's personality depended on the mixture of four liquids (humors): blood (Latin: *sanguis*), choler, phlegm, and bile. An overabundance of one fluid produced a dominant trait, and even today "sanguine," "choleric," "phlegmatic," and "bilious" describe personalities.

Not all comedy, of course, depends on humor characters placed in situations far from the tragic protagonist's desperate hold on his. In general, however, tragedy suggests the nobility of ideals; the tragic hero's ideals undo him, and they may be ideals about which we have serious reservations, but, still, we admire him for them and recognize them as part of his nobility. Romeo and Juliet will not put off their love for each other; Antigone will not yield to Creon, and Creon holds almost impossibly long to his stern position. But the comic protagonist who is always trying to keep his hands clean is funny; we laugh at his refusal to touch dirt with the rest of us, his refusal to enjoy the abundance life has to offer. The comic protagonist who is always talking about his beloved is funny; we laugh at his failure to see that the world is filled with girls more attractive than the one who obsesses him. In short, the ideals for which the tragic protagonist loses the world seem important to us; those for which the comic protagonist loses the world seem trivial compared with the rich variety that life has to offer. Put it this way: the ideals of the tragic figure gain, in large measure, our sympathy, but the ideals of the comic figure are presented in such a way that we laugh at their absurdity. The tragic figure makes a claim on our sympathy. The absurd comic figure continually sets up obstacles to our sympathetic interest; we feel detached from him, superior to him, and amused by him. Something along these lines is behind William Butler Yeats's insistence that character is always present in comedy but not in tragedy. Though Yeats is eccentric in his notion that individual character is obliterated in tragedy, he interestingly gets at one of the important elements in comedy:

> When the tragic reverie is at its height . . .[we do not say,] "How well that man is realized. I should know him were I to meet him in the street," for it is always ourselves that we see upon the [tragic] stage. . . . Tragedy must always be a drowning and breaking of the dikes that separate man from man, and . . . it is upon these dikes comedy keeps house.

One additional comparison between tragedy and comedy is in order. Although the happenings in tragedy seem inevitable, they seem also to have occurred partly because of the pressure of time. In the short time, things had to turn out this way, we feel; but if there had only been more time. . . . In *Romeo and Juliet*, Friar Laurence writes a letter to Romeo, explaining that Juliet will take a potion that will

---

that exhibit their absurdity. **High comedy** is largely verbal, depending on witty language; **farce**, at the other extreme, is dependent on inherently ludicrous situations, *e.g.*, a hobo is mistaken for a millionaire. **Comedy of situation**, then, may use humor characters, but it need not do so.

put her in a temporary, death-like trance, but the letter is delayed, Romeo mistakenly hears that Juliet is dead, and he kills himself. A few moments after his suicide Juliet revives. Had Friar Laurence's message arrived on schedule, or had Romeo not been so quick to commit suicide, no great harm would have been done. But throughout the play one feels oppressed by time. Romeo early anticipates an "untimely death"; when the lovers first swear their allegiance, Juliet fears that things are moving too quickly:

> Although I joy in thee,
> I have no joy of this contract tonight:
> It is too rash, too unadvised, too sudden;
> Too like the lightning, which doth cease to be
> Ere one can say it lightens.

In *Antigone*, after condemning his niece to death, Creon changes his mind, but before he releases her he performs the ritual of burying Polyneices. When he then turns to save Antigone, it is too late. A little more time and all might have been well, but as it is, there are three corpses at the end of the play, and Creon is left—now with years at his disposal—to lament his isolation. In comedy, however, there is usually a sense of leisure. Things are difficult now, but they will work themselves out. Sooner or later people will realize that the strange goings-on are due to the existence of identical twins. Sooner or later the stubborn parents will realize that they cannot further stand in the way of the young lovers, and all will be well. In the world of comedy, one is always safe in relying on time. Viola, in *Twelfth Night*, is an ingenious young lady, but even she cannot solve all the problems. She knows, however, that things have a way of working themselves out all right:

> O Time! thou must untangle this, not I;
> It is too hard a knot for me to untie!

Most important comic plays can roughly be sorted into one of three types, depending on who is the protagonist: satiric comedies, romantic comedies, rogue comedies. In **satiric comedy** (such as Molière's) attention is centered on a protagonist who interferes with the happy outcome. The jealous spouse, the demanding parent, the decrepit wooer, goes through his paces, revealing again and again his absurdity. The writer of this sort of comedy often justifies himself by claiming to reform society: misers and other antisocial members of the audience will see their image on the stage and reform themselves when they leave the theater. But it is hard to believe that this theory is rooted in fact. Jonathan Swift (as we mentioned earlier) was probably right when he said "Satire is a sort of glass wherein beholders do generally discover everybody's face but their own."

Near the conclusion of a satiric comedy, the obstructing characters are dismissed, often perfunctorily, when the lost letter turns up, and the happy but colorless young lovers—who have not much held our attention—are united. And so all-encompassing are the festivities at the end that even the obstructionists are invited to join in the wedding feast. (If they cannot be invited to join, they are kept off the stage, as is Shylock at the end of *The Merchant of Venice*.) The over-all movement, then, is from conflict to social harmony, joy, and abundance. Such an ending might be called romantic, but because the bulk of the play has been satiric, the term romantic comedy is reserved for another sort.

Where satiric comedy is critical, holding a mirror up to the real world so that it may reform itself closer to the ideal, **romantic comedy** presents the ideal world, a golden world, a world in which if there are any difficulties they are not briers but "burrs . . . thrown upon thee in holiday foolery." It is the world of most of Shakespeare's comedies, a world of Illyria, of the Forest of Arden, of Belmont. The protagonists are young lovers who dominate this world; the course of their love is not smooth, but the outcome is never in doubt and the course is the more fun for being a little bumpy. Portia teases Bassanio, Lysander and Demetrius sometimes pursue the wrong girls, but they are all pleasant people. Of course, there are villains and lions, but the villains are great bunglers, and the lions are rather like the lion that Snug impersonates in *A Midsummer-Night's Dream*.

Rogue comedy, or **picaresque comedy**, can be even more briefly treated because it is less common in English. Essentially, the protagonist in rogue comedy (such as Ben Jonson's *The Alchemist*) is the underdog who lives by outwitting his more prosperous but less astute neighbors. Probably much of its appeal is to the audience's lawless impulse: for a couple of hours the spectators can see fulfilled on the stage their impulse to win women, to tell off the boss, to outwit creditors. Like satiric comedy, rogue comedy often exhibits foolish types; like romantic comedy, its fanciful world—at least for an hour or two—affords a release from the real world.

George Bernard Shaw's *Major Barbara* is something of an unusual mixture of these types of comedy. Shaw (an ardent pamphleteer as well as a playwright) entertainingly deflates some of man's pretensions and offers what at least seems to be a reasonable view of poverty and munitions-making. Undershaft, though not a cadging rogue, is (despite his millions) something of the underdog found in most rogue comedy. And, finally, when Shaw insists that although human beings can try to inflate themselves with absurd patriotic and religious ideas, things will turn out all right because they are not really bad fellows after all, he is approaching the fantastic realm of romantic comedy.

GEORGE BERNARD SHAW (1856-1950)

Major Barbara

ACT I

It is after dinner in January 1906, in the library in Lady Britomart Undershaft's house in Wilton Crescent. A large and comfortable settee is in the middle of the room, upholstered in dark leather. A person sitting on it (it is vacant at present) would have, on his right, Lady Britomart's writing table, with the lady herself busy at it; a smaller writing table behind him on his left; the door behind him on Lady Britomart's side; and a window with a window seat directly on his left. Near the window is an armchair.

Lady Britomart is a woman of fifty or thereabouts, well dressed and yet careless of her dress, well bred and quite reckless of her breeding, well mannered and yet appallingly outspoken and indifferent to the opinion of her interlocutors, amiable and yet peremptory, arbitrary, and high-tempered to the last bearable degree, and withal a very typical managing matron of the upper class, treated as a naughty child until she grew into a scolding mother, and finally settling down with plenty of practical ability and worldly experience, limited in the oddest way with domestic and class limitations, conceiving the universe exactly as if it were a large house in Wilton Crescent, though handling her corner of it very effectively on that assumption, and being quite enlightened and liberal as to the books in the library, the pictures on the walls, the music in the portfolios, and the articles in the papers.

Her son, Stephen, comes in. He is a gravely correct young man under 25, taking himself very seriously, but still in some awe of his mother, from childish habit and bachelor shyness rather than from any weakness of character.

Stephen. Whats the matter?
Lady Britomart. Presently, Stephen.

> *Stephen submissively walks to the settee and sits down. He takes up a Liberal weekly called The Speaker.*

Lady Britomart. Dont begin to read, Stephen. I shall require all your attention.
Stephen. It was only while I was waiting—
Lady Britomart. Dont make excuses, Stephen. (*He puts down The*

Speaker.) Now! (*She finishes her writing; rises; and comes to the settee.*) I have not kept you waiting very long, I think.

Stephen. Not at all, mother.

Lady Britomart. Bring me my cushion. (*He takes the cushion from the chair at the desk and arranges it for her as she sits down on the settee.*) Sit down. (*He sits down and fingers his tie nervously.*) Dont fiddle with your tie, Stephen: there is nothing the matter with it.

Stephen. I beg your pardon. (*He fiddles with his watch chain instead.*)

Lady Britomart. Now are you attending to me, Stephen?

Stephen. Of course, mother.

Lady Britomart. No: it's not of course. I want something much more than your everyday matter-of-course attention. I am going to speak to you very seriously, Stephen. I wish you would let that chain alone.

Stephen (*hastily relinquishing the chain*). Have I done anything to annoy you, mother? If so, it was quite unintentional.

Lady Britomart (*astonished*). Nonsense! (*With some remorse.*) My poor boy, did you think I was angry with you?

Stephen. What is it, then, mother? You are making me very uneasy.

Lady Britomart (*squaring herself at him rather aggressively*). Stephen: may I ask how soon you intend to realize that you are a grown-up man, and that I am only a woman?

Stephen (*amazed*). Only a—

Lady Britomart. Dont repeat my words, please: it is a most aggravating habit. You must learn to face life seriously, Stephen. I really cannot bear the whole burden of our family affairs any longer. You must advise me: you must assume the responsibility.

Stephen. I!

Lady Britomart. Yes, you, of course. You were 24 last June. Youve been at Harrow and Cambridge. Youve been to India and Japan. You must know a lot of things, now; unless you have wasted your time most scandalously. Well, advise me.

Stephen (*much perplexed*). You know I have never interfered in the household—

Lady Britomart. No: I should think not. I dont want you to order the dinner.

Stephen. I mean in our family affairs.

Lady Britomart. Well, you must interfere now for they are getting quite beyond me.

Stephen (*troubled*). I have thought sometimes that perhaps I ought; but really, mother, I know so little about them; and what I do know is so painful! it is so impossible to mention some things to you—(*he stops, ashamed*).

Lady Britomart. I suppose you mean your father.

Stephen (*almost inaudibly*). Yes.

Lady Britomart. My dear: we cant go on all our lives not mentioning him. Of course you were quite right not to open the subject until I asked you to; but you are old enough now to be taken into my confidence, and to help me to deal with him about the girls.

Stephen. But the girls are all right. They are engaged.

Lady Britomart (*complacently*). Yes: I have made a very good match for Sarah. Charles Lomax will be a millionaire at 35. But that is ten years ahead; and in the meantime his trustees cannot under the terms of his father's will allow him more than £800 a year.

Stephen. But the will says also that if he increases his income by his own exertions, they may double the increase.

Lady Britomart. Charles Lomax's exertions are much more likely to decrease his income than to increase it. Sarah will have to find at least another £800 a year for the next ten years; and even then they will be as poor as church mice. And what about Barbara? I thought Barbara was going to make the most brilliant career of all of you. And what does she do? Joins the Salvation Army; discharges her maid; lives on a pound a week and walks in one evening with a professor of Greek whom she has picked up in the street, and who pretends to be a Salvationist, and actually plays the big drum for her in public because he has fallen head over ears in love with her.

Stephen. I was certainly rather taken aback when I heard they were engaged. Cusins is a very nice fellow, certainly: nobody would ever guess that he was born in Australia; but—

Lady Britomart. Oh, Adolphus Cusins will make a very good husband. After all, nobody can say a word against Greek: it stamps a man at once as an educated gentleman. And my family, thank Heaven, is not a pig-headed Tory one. We are Whigs, and believe in liberty. Let snobbish people say what they please: Barbara shall marry, not the man they like, but the man *I* like.

Stephen. Of course I was thinking only of his income. However, he is not likely to be extravagant.

Lady Britomart. Dont be too sure of that, Stephen. I know your quiet, simple, refined, poetic people like Adolphus: quite content with the best of everything! They cost more than your extravagant people, who are always as mean as they are second rate. No: Barbara will need at least £2000 a year. You see it means two additional households. Besides, my dear, you must marry soon. I dont approve of the present fashion of philandering bachelors and late marriages; and I am trying to arrange something for you.

Stephen. It's very good of you, mother but perhaps I had better arrange that for myself.

Lady Britomart. Nonsense! you are much too young to begin matchmaking: you would be taken in by some pretty little nobody. Of course I dont mean that you are not to be consulted: you know that as well as I do. (*Stephen closes his lips and is silent.*) Now dont sulk, Stephen.

Stephen. I am not sulking, mother. What has all this got to do
—with—with my father?

Lady Britomart. My dear Stephen: where is the money to come from?
It is easy enough for you and the other children to live on my
income as long as we are in the same house; but I cant keep four
families in four separate houses. You know how poor my father
is: he has barely seven thousand a year now; and really, if he
were not the Earl of Stevenage, he would have to give up society.
He can do nothing for us. He says, naturally enough, that it is
absurd that he should be asked to provide for the children of a
man who is rolling in money. You see, Stephen, your father must
be fabulously wealthy, because there is always a war going on
somewhere.

Stephen. You need not remind me of that, mother. I have hardly ever
opened a newspaper in my life without seeing our name in it. The
Undershaft torpedo! The Undershaft quick firers! The Undershaft ten inch! the Undershaft disappearing rampart gun! the
Undershaft submarine! and now the Undershaft aerial battleship!
At Harrow they called me the Woolwich Infant. At Cambridge it
was the same. A little brute at King's who was always trying to
get up revivals, spoilt my Bible—your first birthday present to
me—by writing under my name, 'Son and heir to Undershaft and
Lazarus. Death and Destruction Dealers: address Christendom
and Judea.' But that was not so bad as the way I was kowtowed
to everywhere because my father was making millions by selling
cannons.

Lady Britomart. It is not only the cannons, but the war loans that
Lazarus arranges under cover of giving credit for the cannons.
You know, Stephen, it's perfectly scandalous. Those two men,
Andrew Undershaft and Lazarus, positively have Europe under
their thumbs. That is why your father is able to behave as he does.
He is above the law. Do you think Bismarck or Gladstone or
Disraeli could have openly defied every social and moral obliga-
tion all their lives as your father has? They simply wouldnt have
dared. I asked Gladstone to take it up. I asked The Times to
take it up. I asked the Lord Chamberlain to take it up. But it
was just like asking them to declare war on the Sultan. They
wouldnt. They said they couldnt touch him. I believe they were
afraid.

Stephen. What could they do? He does not actually break the law.

Lady Britomart. Not break the law! He is always breaking the law.
He broke the law when he was born: his parents were not married.

Stephen. Mother! Is that true?

Lady Britomart. Of course it's true: that was why we separated.

Stephen. He married without letting you know that!

Lady Britomart (*rather taken aback by this inference*). Oh no. To do

Andrew justice, that was not the sort of thing he did. Besides, you know the Undershaft motto: Unashamed. Everybody knew.

Stephen. But you said that was why you separated.

Lady Britomart. Yes, because he was not content with being a foundling himself: he wanted to disinherit you for another foundling. That was what I couldnt stand.

Stephen (*ashamed*). Do you mean for—for—for—

Lady Britomart. Dont stammer, Stephen. Speak distinctly.

Stephen. But this is so frightful to me, mother. To have to speak to you about such things!

Lady Britomart. It's not pleasant for me, either, especially if you are still so childish that you must make it worse by a display of embarrassment. It is only in the middle classes, Stephen, that people get into a state of dumb helpless horror when they find that there are wicked people in the world. In our class, we have to decide what is to be done with wicked people; and nothing should disturb our self-possession. Now ask your question properly.

Stephen. Mother: have you no consideration for me? For Heaven's sake either treat me as a child, as you always do, and tell me nothing at all or tell me everything and let me take it as best I can.

Lady Britomart. Treat you as a child! What do you mean? It is most unkind and ungrateful of you to say such a thing. You know I have never treated any of you as children. I have always made you my companions and friends, and allowed you perfect freedom to do and say whatever you like, so long as you liked what I could approve of.

Stephen (*desperately*). I daresay we have been the very imperfect children of a very perfect mother; but I do beg you to let me alone for once, and tell me about this horrible business of my father wanting to set me aside for another son.

Lady Britomart (*amazed*). Another son! I never said anything of the kind. I never dreamt of such a thing. This is what comes of interrupting me.

Stephen. But you said—

Lady Britomart (*cutting him short*). Now be a good boy, Stephen, and listen to me patiently. The Undershafts are descended from a foundling in the parish of St Andrew Undershaft in the city. That was long ago, in the reign of James the First. Well, this foundling was adopted by an armorer and gun-maker. In the course of time the foundling succeeded to the business; and from some notion of gratitude, or some vow or something, he adopted another foundling, and left the business to him. And that foundling did the same. Ever since that, the cannon business has always been left to an adopted foundling named Andrew Undershaft.

Stephen. But did they never marry? Were there no legitimate sons?

Lady Britomart. Oh yes: they married just as your father did; and they were rich enough to buy land for their own children and leave them well provided for. But they always adopted and trained some foundling to succeed them in the business; and of course they always quarrelled with their wives furiously over it. Your father was adopted in that way and he pretends to consider himself bound to keep up the tradition and adopt somebody to leave the business to. Of course I was not going to stand that. There may have been some reason for it when the Undershafts could only marry women in their own class, whose sons were not fit to govern great estates. But there could be no excuse for passing over my son.

Stephen (dubiously). I am afraid I should make a poor hand of managing a cannon foundry.

Lady Britomart. Nonsense! you could easily get a manager and pay him a salary.

Stephen. My father evidently had no great opinion of my capacity.

Lady Britomart. Stuff, child! you were only a baby: it had nothing to do with your capacity. Andrew did it on principle, just as he did every perverse and wicked thing on principle. When my father remonstrated, Andrew actually told him to his face that history tells us of only two successful institutions: one the Undershaft firm, and the other the Roman Empire under the Antonines. That was because the Antonine emperors all adopted their successors. Such rubbish! The Stevenages are as good as the Antonines, I hope: and you are a Stevenage. But that was Andrew all over. There you have the man! Always clever and unanswerable when he was defending nonsense and wickedness: always awkward and sullen when he had to behave sensibly and decently!

Stephen. Then it was on my account that your home life was broken up, mother. I am sorry.

Lady Britomart. Well, dear, there were other differences. I really cannot bear an immoral man. I am not a Pharisee, I hope; and I should not have minded his merely doing wrong things: we are none of us perfect. But your father didnt exactly do wrong things: he said them and thought them: that was what was so dreadful. He really had a sort of religion of wrongness. Just as one doesnt mind men practising immorality so long as they own that they are in the wrong by preaching morality; so I couldnt forgive Andrew for preaching immorality while he practised morality. You would all have grown up without principles, without any knowledge of right and wrong, if he had been in the house. You know, my dear, your father was a very attractive man in some ways. Children did not dislike him; and he took advantage of it to put the wickedest ideas into their heads, and make them quite unmanageable. I did not dislike him myself: very far from it; but nothing can bridge over moral disagreement.

Major Barbara 529

Stephen. All this simply bewilders me, mother. People may differ about matters of opinion, or even about religion; but how can they differ about right and wrong? Right is right; and wrong is wrong; and if a man cannot distinguish them properly, he is either a fool or a rascal: thats all.

Lady Britomart (*touched*). Thats my own boy (*she pats his cheek*)! Your father never could answer that: he used to laugh and get out of it under cover of some affectionate nonsense. And now that you understand the situation, what do you advise me to do?

Stephen. Well, what can you do?

Lady Britomart. I must get the money somehow.

Stephen. We cannot take money from him. I had rather go and live in some cheap place like Bedford Square or even Hampstead than take a farthing of his money.

Lady Britomart. But after all, Stephen, our present income comes from Andrew.

Stephen (*shocked*). I never knew that.

Lady Britomart. Well, you surely didnt suppose your grandfather had anything to give me. The Stevenages could not do everything for you. We gave you social position. Andrew had to contribute something. He had a very good bargain, I think.

Stephen (*bitterly*). We are utterly dependent on him and his cannons, then?

Lady Britomart. Certainly not: the money is settled. But he provided it. So you see it is not a question of taking money from him or not: it is simply a question of how much. I dont want any more for myself.

Stephen. Nor do I.

Lady Britomart. But Sarah does; and Barbara does. That is, Charles Lomax and Adolphus Cusins will cost them more. So I must put my pride in my pocket and ask for it, I suppose. That is your advice, Stephen, is it not?

Stephen. No.

Lady Britomart (*sharply*). Stephen!

Stephen. Of course if you are determined—

Lady Britomart. I am not determined: I ask your advice; and I am waiting for it. I will not have all the responsibility thrown on my shoulders.

Stephen (*obstinately*). I would die sooner than ask him for another penny.

Lady Britomart (*resignedly*). You mean that *I* must ask him. Very well, Stephen: it shall be as you wish. You will be glad to know that your grandfather concurs. But he thinks I ought to ask Andrew to come here and see the girls. After all, he must have some natural affection for them.

Stephen. Ask him here!!!

Lady Britomart. Do not repeat my words, Stephen. Where else can I ask him?

Stephen. I never expected you to ask him at all.

Lady Britomart. Now dont tease, Stephen. Come! you see that it is necessary that he should pay us a visit, dont you?

Stephen (*reluctantly*). I suppose so, if the girls cannot do without his money.

Lady Britomart. Thank you, Stephen: I knew you would give me the right advice when it was properly explained to you. I have asked your father to come this evening. (*Stephen bounds from his seat.*) Dont jump, Stephen: it fidgets me.

Stephen (*in utter consternation*). Do you mean to say that my father is coming here tonight—that he may be here at any moment?

Lady Britomart (*looking at her watch*). I said nine. (*He gasps. She rises.*) Ring the bell, please. (*Stephen goes to the smaller writing table; presses a button on it; and sits at it with his elbows on the table and his head in his hands, outwitted and overwhelmed.*) It is ten minutes to nine yet; and I have to prepare the girls. I asked Charles Lomax and Adolphus to dinner on purpose that they might be here. Andrew had better see them in case he should cherish any delusion as to their being capable of supporting their wives. (*The butler enters: Lady Britomart goes behind the settee to speak to him.*) Morrison: go up to the drawing room and tell everybody to come down here at once. (*Morrison withdraws. Lady Britomart turns to Stephen.*) Now remember, Stephen: I shall need all your countenance and authority. (*He rises and tries to recover some vestige of these attributes.*) Give me a chair, dear. (*He pushes a chair forward from the wall to where she stands, near the smaller writing table. She sits down; and he goes to the armchair, into which he throws himself.*) I dont know how Barbara will take it. Ever since they made her a major in the Salvation Army she has developed a propensity to have her own way and order people about which quite cows me sometimes. It's not lady-like: I'm sure I dont know where she picked it up. Anyhow, Barbara shant bully me but still it's just as well that your father should be here before she has time to refuse to meet him or make a fuss. Dont look nervous, Stephen: it will only encourage Barbara to make difficulties. *I* am nervous enough, goodness knows; but I don't shew it.

Sarah and Barbara come in with their respective young men, Charles Lomax and Adolphus Cusins. Sarah is slender, bored, and mundane. Barbara is robuster, jollier, much more energetic. Sarah is fashionably dressed: Barbara is in Salvation Army uniform. Lomax, a young man about town, is like many other young men about town. He is afflicted with a frivolous sense of humor which plunges him at the most inopportune moments into paroxysms of imperfectly suppressed laughter. Cusins is a spectacled student, slight, thin haired, and sweet voiced, with a more complex form of Lomax's complaint. His sense of humor is intellectual and subtle, and is complicated by an appalling temper. The lifelong struggle of a benevolent temperament and a high conscience against impulses of inhuman ridicule and fierce impatience has set up a chronic strain which has visibly wrecked his constitution. He is a most implacable, determined, tenacious, intolerant person who by mere force of character presents himself as—and indeed actually is—considerate, gentle, explanatory, even mild and apologetic, capable possibly of murder, but not of cruelty or coarseness. By the operation of some instinct which is not merciful enough to blind him with the illusions of love, he is obstinately bent on marrying Barbara. Lomax likes Sarah and thinks it will be rather a lark to marry her. Consequently he has not attempted to resist Lady Britomart's arrangements to that end.

All four look as if they had been having a good deal of fun in the drawing room. The girls enter first, leaving the swains outside. Sarah comes to the settee. Barbara comes in after her and stops at the door.

Barbara. Are Cholly and Dolly to come in?

Lady Britomart (forcibly). Barbara: I will not have Charles called Cholly: the vulgarity of it positively makes me ill.

Barbara. It's all right, mother: Cholly is quite correct nowadays. Are they to come in?

Lady Britomart. Yes, if they will behave themselves.

Barbara (through the door). Come in, Dolly; and behave yourself.

Barbara comes to her mother's writing table. Cusins enters smiling, and wanders towards Lady Britomart.

Sarah (calling). Come in, Cholly. (*Lomax enters, controlling his features very imperfectly, and places himself vaguely between Sarah and Barbara.*)

Lady Britomart (peremptorily). Sit down, all of you. (*They sit. Cusins crosses to the window and seats himself there. Lomax takes a chair. Barbara sits at the writing table and Sarah on the settee.*) I dont in the least know what you are laughing at, Adolphus. I am surprised at you, though I expected nothing better from Charles Lomax.

Cusins (in a remarkably gentle voice). Barbara has been trying to teach me the West Ham Salvation March.

Lady Britomart. I see nothing to laugh at in that; nor should you if you are really converted.

Cusins (sweetly). You were not present. It was really funny, I believe.

Lomax. Ripping.

Lady Britomart. Be quiet, Charles. Now listen to me, children. Your father is coming here this evening.

> *General stupefaction. Lomax, Sarah, and Barbara rise: Sarah scared, and Barbara amused and expectant.*

Lomax (remonstrating). Oh I say!

Lady Britomart. You are not called on to say anything, Charles.

Sarah. Are you serious, mother?

Lady Britomart. Of course I am serious. It is on your account, Sarah, and also on Charles's. (*Silence, Sarah sits, with a shrug. Charles looks painfully unworthy.*) I hope you are not going to object, Barbara.

Barbara. I! why should I? My father has a soul to be saved like everybody else. He's quite welcome as far as I am concerned. (*She sits on the table, and softly whistles 'Onward, Christian Soldiers'.*)

Lomax (still remonstrant). But really, dont you know! Oh I say!

Lady Britomart (frigidly). What do you wish to convey, Charles?

Lomax. Well, you must admit that this is a bit thick.

Lady Britomart (turning with ominous suavity to Cusins). Adolphus: you are a professor of Greek. Can you translate Charles Lomax's remarks into reputable English for us?

Cusins (cautiously). If I may say so, Lady Brit, I think Charles has rather happily expressed what we all feel. Homer, speaking of Autolycus, uses the same phrase. πυκινον δόμον ελθειν means a bit thick.

Lomax (handsomely). Not that I mind, you know, if Sarah dont. (*He sits.*)

Lady Britomart (crushingly). Thank you. Have I your permission, Adolphus, to invite my own husband to my own house?

Cusins (gallantly). You have my unhesitating support in everything you do.

Lady Britomart. Tush! Sarah: have you nothing to say?

Sarah. Do you mean that he is coming regularly to live here?

Lady Britomart. Certainly not. The spare room is ready for him if he likes to stay for a day or two and see a little more of you; but there are limits.

Sarah. Well, he cant eat us, I suppose. *I* dont mind.

Lomax (chuckling). I wonder how the old man will take it.

Lady Britomart. Much as the old woman will, no doubt, Charles.

Lomax (abashed). I didnt mean—at least—

Lady Britomart. You didnt think, Charles. You never do; and the result is, you never mean anything. And now please attend to me, children. Your father will be quite a stranger to us.

Lomax. I suppose he hasnt seen Sarah since she was a little kid.

Lady Britomart. Not since she was a little kid, Charles, as you express it with that elegance of diction and refinement of thought that

Major Barbara 533

seem never to desert you. Accordingly—er—(*impatiently*). Now
I have forgotten what I was going to say. That comes of your
provoking me to be sarcastic, Charles. Adolphus: will you kindly
tell me where I was.

Cusins (*sweetly*). You were saying that as Mr Undershaft has not
seen his children since they were babies, he will form his opinion
of the way you have brought them up from their behavior tonight,
and that therefore you wish us all to be particularly careful to
conduct ourselves well, especially Charles.

Lady Britomart (*with emphatic approval*). Precisely.

Lomax. Look here, Dolly: Lady Brit didnt say that.

Lady Britomart (*vehemently*). I did, Charles. Adolphus's recollection
is perfectly correct. It is most important that you should be good;
and I do beg you for once not to pair off into opposite corners
and giggle and whisper while I am speaking to your father.

Barbara. All right, mother. We'll do you credit. (*She comes off the
table, and sits in her chair with ladylike elegance.*)

Lady Britomart. Remember, Charles, that Sarah will want to feel
proud of you instead of ashamed of you.

Lomax. Oh I say! theres nothing to be exactly proud of, dont you
know.

Lady Britomart. Well, try and look as if there was.

*Morrison, pale and dismayed, breaks into the room in uncon-
cealed disorder.*

Morrison. Might I speak a word to you, my lady?

Lady Britomart. Nonsense! Shew him up.

Morrison. Yes, my lady. (*He goes.*)

Lomax. Does Morrison know who it is?

Lady Britomart. Of course. Morrison has always been with us.

Lomax. It must be a regular corker for him, dont you know.

Lady Britomart. Is this a moment to get on my nerves, Charles, with
your outrageous expressions?

Lomax. But this is something out of the ordinary, really—

Morrison (*at the door*). The—er—Mr Undershaft. (*He retreats in
confusion.*)

*Andrew Undershaft comes in. All rise. Lady Britomart meets him
in the middle of the room behind the settee.*

    *Andrew is, on the surface, a stoutish, easygoing elderly man,
with kindly patient manners, and an engaging simplicity of character. But he has a watchful, deliberate, waiting, listening face,
and formidable reserves of power, both bodily and mental, in his
capacious chest and long head. His gentleness is partly that of a
strong man who has learnt by experience that his natural grip*

hurts ordinary people unless he handles them very carefully, and partly the mellowness of age and success. He is also a little shy in his present very delicate situation.

Lady Britomart. Good evening, Andrew.

Undershaft. How d'ye do, my dear.

Lady Britomart. You look a good deal older.

Undershaft (apologetically). I am somewhat older. (*Taking her hand with a touch of courtship.*) Time has stood still with you.

Lady Britomart (throwing away his hand). Rubbish! This is your family.

Undershaft (surprised). Is it so large? I am sorry to say my memory is failing very badly in some things. (*He offers his hand with paternal kindness to Lomax.*)

Lomax (jerkily shaking his hand). Ahdedoo.

Undershaft. I can see you are my eldest. I am very glad to meet you again, my boy.

Lomax (remonstrating). No, but look here dont you know—(*Overcome.*) Oh I say!

Lady Britomart (recovering from momentary speechlessness). Andrew: do you mean to say that you dont remember how many children you have?

Undershaft. Well, I am afraid I—. They have grown so much—er. Am I making any ridiculous mistake? I may as well confess: I recollect only one son. But so many things have happened since, of course—er—

Lady Britomart (decisively). Andrew: you are talking nonsense. Of course you have only one son.

Undershaft. Perhaps you will be good enough to introduce me, my dear.

Lady Britomart. That is Charles Lomax, who is engaged to Sarah.

Undershaft. My dear sir, I beg your pardon.

Lomax. Notatall. Delighted, I assure you.

Lady Britomart. This is Stephen.

Undershaft (bowing). Happy to make your acquaintance, Mr Stephen. Then (*going to Cusins*) you must be my son. (*Taking Cusin's hands in his.*) How are you, my young friend? (*To Lady Britomart.*) He is very like you, my love.

Cusins. You flatter me, Mr Undershaft. My name is Cusins: engaged to Barbara. (*Very explicitly.*) That is Major Barbara Undershaft, of the Salvation Army. This is Sarah, your second daughter. This is Stephen Undershaft, your son.

Undershaft. My dear Stephen, I beg your pardon.

Stephen. Not at all.

Undershaft. Mr Cusins: I am much indebted to you for explaining so precisely. (*Turning to Sarah.*) Barbara, my dear—

Major Barbara 535

Sarah (prompting him). Sarah.

Undershaft. Sarah, of course. (*They shake hands. He goes over to Barbara.*) Barbara—I am right this time, I hope?

Barbara. Quite right. (*They shake hands.*)

Lady Britomart (resuming command). Sit down, all of you. Sit down, Andrew. (*She comes forward and sits on the settee. Cusins also brings his chair forward on her left. Barbara and Stephen resume their seats. Lomax gives his chair to Sarah and goes for another.*)

Undershaft. Thank you, my love.

Lomax (conversationally, as he brings a chair forward between the writing table and the settee, and offers it to Undershaft). Takes you some time to find out exactly where you are, dont it?

Undershaft (accepting the chair, but remaining standing). That is not what embarrasses me, Mr Lomax. My difficulty is that if I play the part of a father, I shall produce the effect of an intrusive stranger; and if I play the part of a discreet stranger, I may appear a callous father.

Lady Britomart. There is no need for you to play any part at all, Andrew. You had much better be sincere and natural.

Undershaft (submissively). Yes, my dear: I daresay that will be best. (*He sits down comfortably.*) Well, here I am. Now what can I do for you all?

Lady Britomart. You need not do anything, Andrew. You are one of the family. You can sit with us and enjoy yourself.

A painfully conscious pause. Barbara makes a face at Lomax, whose too long suppressed mirth immediately explodes in agonized neighings.

Lady Britomart (outraged). Charles Lomax: if you can behave yourself, behave yourself. If not, leave the room.

Lomax. I'm awfully sorry, Lady Brit; but really you know, upon my soul! (*He sits on the settee between Lady Britomart and Undershaft, quite overcome.*)

Barbara. Why dont you laugh if you want to, Cholly? It's good for your inside.

Lady Britomart. Barbara: you have had the education of a lady. Please let your father see that; and dont talk like a street girl.

Undershaft. Never mind me, my dear. As you know, I am not a gentleman; and I was never educated.

Lomax (encouragingly). Nobody'd know it, I assure you. You look all right, you know.

Cusins. Let me advise you to study Greek, Mr Undershaft. Greek scholars are privileged men. Few of them know Greek; and none of them know anything else; but their position is unchallengeable. Other languages are the qualifications of waiters and commercial travellers: Greek is to a man of position what the hallmark is to silver.

Barbara. Dolly: dont be insincere. Cholly: fetch your concertina and play something for us.

Lomax (jumps up eagerly, but checks himself to remark doubtfully to Undershaft). Perhaps that sort of thing isnt in your line, eh?

Undershaft. I am particularly fond of music.

Lomax (delighted). Are you? Then I'll get it. (*He goes upstairs for the instrument.*)

Undershaft. Do you play, Barbara?

Barbara. Only the tambourine. But Cholly's teaching me the concertina.

Undershaft. Is Cholly also a member of the Salvation Army?

Barbara. No: he says it's bad form to be a dissenter. But I dont despair of Cholly. I made him come yesterday to a meeting at the dock gates, and take the collection in his hat.

Undershaft (looks whimsically at his wife)!!

Lady Britomart. It is not my doing, Andrew. Barbara is old enough to take her own way. She has no father to advise her.

Barbara. Oh yes she has. There are no orphans in the Salvation Army.

Undershaft. Your father there has a great many children and plenty of experience, eh?

Barbara (looking at him with quick interest and nodding). Just so. How did you come to understand that? (*Lomax is heard at the door trying the concertina.*)

Lady Britomart. Come in, Charles. Play us something at once.

Lomax. Righto! (*He sits down in his former place, and preludes.*)

Undershaft. One moment, Mr Lomax. I am rather interested in the Salvation Army. Its motto might be my own: Blood and Fire.

Lomax (shocked). But not your sort of blood and fire, you know.

Undershaft. My sort of blood cleanses: my sort of fire purifies.

Barbara. So do ours. Come down tomorrow to my shelter—the West Ham shelter—and see what we're doing. We're going to march to a great meeting in the Assembly Hall at Mile End. Come and see the shelter and then march with us: it will do you a lot of good. Can you play anything?

Undershaft. In my youth I earned pennies, and even shillings occasionally, in the streets and in public house parlors by my natural talent for stepdancing. Later on, I became a member of the Undershaft orchestral society, and performed passably on the tenor trombone.

Lomax (scandalized—putting down the concertina). Oh I say!

Barbara. Many a sinner has played himself into heaven on the trombone, thanks to the Army.

Lomax (to Barbara, still rather shocked). Yes, but what about the cannon business, dont you know? (*To Undershaft.*) Getting into heaven is not exactly in your line, is it?

Lady Britomart. Charles!!!

Lomax. Well; but it stands to reason, dont it? The cannon business may be necessary and all that: we cant get on without cannons; but it isnt right, you know. On the other hand, there may be a certain amount of tosh about the Salvation Army—I belong to the Established Church myself—but still you cant deny that it's religion; and you cant go against religion, can you? At least unless youre downright immoral, dont you know.

Undershaft. You hardly appreciate my position, Mr Lomax—

Lomax (hastily). I'm not saying anything against you personally—

Undershaft. Quite so, quite so. But consider for a moment. Here I am, a profiteer in mutilation and murder. I find myself in a specially amiable humor just now because, this morning, down at the foundry, we blew twenty-seven dummy soldiers into fragments with a gun which formerly destroyed only thirteen.

Lomax (leniently). Well, the more destructive war becomes, the sooner it will be abolished, eh?

Undershaft. Not at all. The more destructive war becomes the more fascinating we find it. No, Mr Lomax: I am obliged to you for making the usual excuse for my trade; but I am not ashamed of it. I am not one of those men who keep their morals and their business in watertight compartments. All the spare money my trade rivals spend on hospitals, cathedrals, and other receptacles for conscience money, I devote to experiments and researches in improved methods of destroying life and property. I have always done so; and I always shall. Therefore your Christmas card moralities of peace on earth and goodwill among men are of no use to me. Your Christianity, which enjoins you to resist not evil, and to turn the other cheek, would make me a bankrupt. My morality—my religion—must have a place for cannons and torpedoes in it.

Stephen (coldly—almost sullenly). You speak as if there were half a dozen moralities and religions to choose from, instead of one true morality and one true religion.

Undershaft. For me there is only one true morality; but it might not fit you, as you do not manufacture aerial battleships. There is only one true morality for every man; but every man has not the same true morality.

Lomax (overtaxed). Would you mind saying that again? I didnt quite follow it.

Cusins. It's quite simple. As Euripides says, one man's meat is another man's poison morally as well as physically.

Undershaft. Precisely.

Lomax. Oh, that! Yes, yes, yes. True. True.

Stephen. In other words, some men are honest and some are scoundrels.

Barbara. Bosh! There are no scoundrels.

Undershaft. Indeed? Are there any good men?

Barbara. No. Not one. There are neither good men nor scoundrels: there are just children of one Father; and the sooner they stop calling one another names the better. You neednt talk to me: I know them. Ive had scores of them through my hands: scoundrels, criminals, infidels, philanthropists, missionaries, county councillors, all sorts. Theyre all just the same sort of sinner; and theres the same salvation ready for them all.

Undershaft. May I ask have you ever saved a maker of cannons?

Barbara. No. Will you let me try?

Undershaft. Well, I will make a bargain with you. If I go to see you tomorrow in your Salvation Shelter, will you come the day after to see me in my cannon works?

Barbara. Take care. It may end in your giving up the cannons for the sake of the Salvation Army.

Undershaft. Are you sure it will not end in your giving up the Salvation Army for the sake of the cannons?

Barbara. I will take my chance of that.

Undershaft. And I will take my chance of the other. (*They shake hands on it.*) Where is your shelter?

Barbara. In West Ham. At the sign of the cross. Ask anybody in Canning Town. Where are your works?

Undershaft. In Perivale St Andrews. At the sign of the sword. Ask anybody in Europe.

Lomax. Hadnt I better play something?

Barbara. Yes. Give us Onward, Christian Soldiers.

Lomax. Well, thats rather a strong order to begin with, dont you know. Suppose I sing Thourt passing hence, my brother. It's much the same tune.

Barbara. It's too melancholy. You get saved, Cholly; and youll pass hence, my brother, without making such a fuss about it.

Lady Britomart. Really, Barbara, you go on as if religion were a pleasant subject. Do have some sense of propriety.

Undershaft. I do not find it an unpleasant subject, my dear. It is the only one that capable people really care for.

Lady Britomart (*looking at her watch*). Well, if you are determined to have it, I insist on having it in a proper and respectable way. Charles: ring for prayers.

General amazement. Stephen rises in dismay.

Lomax (*rising*). Oh I say!

Undershaft (*rising*). I am afraid I must be going.

Lady Britomart. You cannot go now, Andrew: it would be most improper. Sit down. What will the servants think?

Undershaft. My dear: I have conscientious scruples. May I suggest a compromise? If Barbara will conduct a little service in the drawing room, with Mr Lomax as organist, I will attend it willingly. I will even take part, if a trombone can be procured.

Lady Britomart. Dont mock, Andrew.

Undershaft (*shocked—to Barbara*). You dont think I am mocking, my love, I hope.

Barbara. No, of course not; and it wouldnt matter if you were: half the Army came to their first meeting for a lark. (*Rising.*) Come along. (*She throws her arm round her father and sweeps him out, calling to the others from the threshold.*) Come, Dolly. Come, Cholly.

Lady Britomart. I will not be disobeyed by everybody. Adolphus: sit down. (*He does not.*) Charles: you may go. You are not fit for prayers: you cannot keep your countenance.

Lomax. Oh I say! (*He goes out.*)

Lady Britomart (*continuing*). But you, Adolphus, can behave yourself if you choose to. I insist on your staying.

Cusins. My dear Lady Brit: there are things in the family prayer book that I couldnt bear to hear you say.

Lady Britomart. What things, pray?

Cusins. Well, you would have to say before all the servants that we have done things we ought not to have done, and left undone things we ought to have done, and that there is no health in us. I cannot bear to hear you doing yourself such an injustice, and Barbara such an injustice. As for myself, I flatly deny it: I have done my best. I shouldnt dare to marry Barbara—I couldnt look you in the face—if it were true. So I must go to the drawing room.

Lady Britomart (*offended*). Well, go. (*He starts for the door.*) And remember this, Adolphus (*he turns to listen*): I have a very strong suspicion that you went to the Salvation Army to worship Barbara and nothing else. And I quite appreciate the very clever way in which you systematically humbug me. I have found you out. Take care Barbara doesnt. Thats all.

Cusins (*with ruffled sweetness*). Dont tell on me. (*He steals out.*)

Lady Britomart. Sarah: if you want to go, go. Anything's better than to sit there as if you wished you were a thousand miles away.

Sarah (*languidly*). Very well, mamma. (*She goes.*)

Lady Britomart, with a sudden flounce, gives way to a little gust of tears.

Stephen (*going to her*). Mother: whats the matter?

Lady Britomart (*swishing away her tears with her handkerchief*). Nothing. Foolishness. You can go with him, too, if you like, and leave me with the servants.

Stephen. Oh, you mustnt think that, mother. I—I dont like him.

Lady Britomart. The others do. That is the injustice of a woman's lot. A woman has to bring up her children; and that means to restrain them, to deny them things they want, to set them tasks, to punish them when they do wrong, to do all the unpleasant things. And then the father, who has nothing to do but pet them and spoil them, comes in when all her work is done and steals their affection from her.

Stephen. He has not stolen our affection from you. It is only curiosity.

Lady Britomart (*violently*). I wont be consoled, Stephen. There is nothing the matter with me. (*She rises and goes towards the door.*)

Stephen. Where are you going, mother?

Lady Britomart. To the drawing room, of course. (*She goes out. Onward, Christian Soldiers, on the concertina, with tambourine accompaniment, is heard when the door opens.*) Are you coming, Stephen?

Stephen. No. Certainly not. (*She goes. He sits down on the settee, with compressed lips and an expression of strong dislike.*)

ACT II

The yard of the West Ham shelter of the Salvation Army is a cold place on a January morning. The building itself, an old warehouse, is newly whitewashed. Its gabled end projects into the yard in the middle, with a door on the ground floor, and another in the loft above it without any balcony or ladder, but with a pulley rigged over it for hoisting sacks. Those who come from this central gable end into the yard have the gateway leading to the street on their left, with a stone horse-trough just beyond it, and, on the right, a penthouse shielding a table from the weather. There are forms at the table; and on them are seated a man and a woman, both much down on their luck, finishing a meal of bread (one thick slice each, with margarine and golden syrup) and diluted milk.

The man, a workman out of employment, is young, agile, a talker, a poser, sharp enough to be capable of anything in reason except honesty or altruistic considerations of any kind. The woman is a commonplace old bundle of poverty and hard-worn humanity. She looks sixty and probably is forty-five. If they were rich people, gloved and muffed and well wrapped up in furs and overcoats, they would be numbed and miserable; for it is a grindingly cold raw January day; and a glance at the background of grimy warehouses and leaden sky visible over the whitewashed walls of the yard would drive any idle rich person straight to the Mediterranean. But these two, being no more troubled with visions of the Mediterranean than of the moon, and being compelled to keep more of their clothes in the pawnshop, and less on their persons, in winter than in summer, are not depressed by the cold: rather are they stung into vivacity, to which their meal has just now given an almost jolly turn. The man takes a pull at his mug, and then gets up and moves about the yard with his hands deep in his pockets, occasionally breaking into a stepdance.

The Woman. Feel better arter your meal, sir?

The Man. No. Call that a meal! Good enough for you, praps; but wot is it to me, an intelligent workin man.

The Woman. Workin man! Wot are you?

The Man. Painter.

The Woman (*sceptically*). Yus, I dessay.

The Man. Yus, you dessay! I know. Every loafer that cant do nothink calls isself a painter. Well, I'm a real painter: grainer, finisher, thirty-eight bob a week when I can get it.

The Woman. Then why dont you go and get it?

The Man. I'll tell you why. Fust: I'm intelligent—fffff! it's rotten cold here (*he dances a step or two*)—yes: intelligent beyond the station o life into which it has pleased the capitalists to call me and they dont like a man that sees through em. Second, an intelligent bein needs a doo share of appiness; so I drink somethink cruel when I get the chawnce. Third, I stand by my class and do as little as I can so's to leave arf the job for me fellow workers. Fourth, I'm fly enough to know wots inside the law and wots outside it; and inside it I do as the capitalists do: pinch wot I can lay me ands on. In a proper state of society I am sober, industrious and honest: in Rome, so to speak, I do as the Romans do. Wots the consequence? When trade is bad—and it's rotten bad just now—and the employers az to sack arf their men, they generally start on me.

The Woman. Whats your name?

The Man. Price. Bronterre O'Brien Price. Usually called Snobby Price, for short.

The Woman. Snobby's a carpenter, aint it? You said you was a painter.

Price. Not that kind of snob, but the genteel sort. I'm too uppish, owing to my intelligence, and my father being a Chartist and a reading, thinking man: a stationer, too. I'm none of your common hewers of wood and drawers of water and dont you forget it. (*He returns to his seat at the table, and takes up his mug.*) Wots your name?

The Woman. Rummy Mitchens, sir.

Price (*quaffing the remains of his milk to her*). Your elth, Miss Mitchens.

Rummy (*correcting him*). Missis Mitchens.

Price. Wot! Oh Rummy, Rummy! Respectable married woman, Rummy, gittin rescued by the Salvation Army by pretendin to be a bad un. Same old game!

Rummy. What am I to do? I can't starve. Them Salvation lasses is dear good girls; but the better you are, the worse they likes to think you were before they rescued you. Why shouldnt they av a bit o credit, poor loves? theyre worn to rags by their work. And where would they get the money to rescue us if we was to let on we're no worse than other people? You know what ladies and gentlemen are.

Price. Thievin swine! Wish I ad their job, Rummy, all the same. Wot does Rummy stand for? Pet name praps?

Rummy. Short for Romola.

Price. For wot!?

Rummy. Romola. It was out of a new book. Somebody me mother wanted me to grow up like.

Price. We're companions in misfortune, Rummy. Both on us got names that nobody cawnt pronounce. Consequently I'm Snobby and youre Rummy because Bill and Sally wasnt good enough for our parents. Such is life!

Rummy. Who saved you, Mr Price? Was it Major Barbara?

Price. No: I come here on my own. I'm going to be Bronterre O'Brien Price, the converted painter. I know wot they like. I'll tell em how I blasphemed and gambled and wopped my poor old mother—

Rummy (shocked). Used you to beat your mother?

Price. Not likely. She used to beat me. No matter: you come and listen to the converted painter, and youll hear how she was a pious woman that taught me me prayers at er knee, an how I used to come home drunk and drag her out o bed be er snow white airs, an lam into er with the poker.

Rummy. Thats whats so unfair to us women. Your confessions is just as big lies as ours: you dont tell what you really done no more than us; but you men can tell your lies right out at the meetins and be made much of for it, while the sort o confessions we az to make az to be whispered to one lady at a time. It aint right, spite of all their piety.

Price. Right! Do you spose the Army'd be allowed if it went and did right? Not much. It combs our air and makes us good little blokes to be robbed and put upon. But I'll play the game as good as any of em. I'll see somebody struck by lightnin, or hear a voice sayin 'Snobby Price: where will you spend eternity?' I'll av a time of it, I tell you.

Rummy. You wont be let drink, though.

Price. I'll take it out in gorspellin, then. I dont want to drink if I can get fun enough any other way.

Jenny Hill, a pale, overwrought, pretty Salvation lass of 18, comes in through the yard gate, leading Peter Shirley, a half hardened, half worn-out elderly man, weak with hunger.

Jenny (supporting him). Come! pluck up. I'll get you something to eat. Youll be all right then.

Price (rising and hurrying officiously to take the old man off Jenny's hands). Poor old man! Cheer up, brother: youll find rest and peace and appiness ere. Hurry up with the food, miss: e's fair done. (*Jenny hurries into the shelter.*) Ere, buck up, daddy! she's fetchin y'a thick slice of breadn treacle, an a mug o skyblue. (*He seats him at the corner of the table.*)

Rummy (*gaily*). Keep up your old art! Never say die!

Shirley. I'm not an old man. I'm only 46. I'm as good as ever I was. The grey patch come in my hair before I was thirty. All it wants is three pennorth o hair dye: am I to be turned on the streets to starve for it? Holy God! Ive worked ten to twelve hours a day since I was thirteen, and paid my way all through; and now am I to be thrown into the gutter and my job given to a young man that can do it no better than me because Ive black hair that goes white at the first change?

Price (*cheerfully*). No good jawrin about it. Youre ony a jumped-up, jerked-off orspittle-turned-out incurable of an ole workin man: who cares about you? Eh? Make the thievin swine give you a meal: theyve stole many a one from you. Get a bit o your own back. (*Jenny returns with the usual meal.*) There you are, brother. Awsk a blessin an tuck that into you.

Shirley (*looking at it ravenously but not touching it, and crying like a child*). I never took anything before.

Jenny (*petting him*). Come, come! the Lord sends it to you: he wasnt above taking bread from his friends; and why should you be? Besides, when we find you a job you can pay us for it if you like.

Shirley (*eagerly*). Yes, yes: thats true. I can pay you back: it's only a loan. (*Shivering.*) Oh Lord! oh Lord! (*He turns to the table and attacks the meal ravenously.*)

Jenny. Well, Rummy, are you more comfortable now?

Rummy. God bless you, lovey! youve fed my body and saved my soul, havent you? (*Jenny, touched, kisses her.*) Sit down and rest a bit: you must be ready to drop.

Jenny. Ive been going hard since morning. But theres more work than we can do. I mustnt stop.

Rummy. Try a prayer for just two minutes. Youll work all the better after.

Jenny (*her eyes lighting up*). Oh isnt it wonderful how a few minutes prayer revives you! I was quite lightheaded at twelve o'clock, I was so tired; but Major Barbara just sent me to pray for five minutes; and I was able to go on as if I had only just begun. (*To Price.*) Did you have a piece of bread?

Price (*with unction*). Yes, miss; but Ive got the piece that I value more; and thats the peace that passeth hall hanner-stennin.

Rummy (*fervently*). Glory Hallelujah!

Bill Walker, a rough customer of about 25, appears at the yard gate and looks malevolently at Jenny.

Jenny. That makes me so happy. When you say that, I feel wicked for loitering here. I must get to work again.

She is hurrying to the shelter, when the new-comer moves quickly up to the door and intercepts her. His manner is so threatening that she retreats as he comes at her truculently, driving her down the yard.

Bill. Aw knaow you. Youre the one that took awy maw girl. Youre the one that set er agen me. Well, I'm gowin to ev er aht. Not that Aw care a carse for er or you: see? Bat Aw'll let er knaow; and Aw'll let you knaow. Aw'm gowing to give her a doin thatll teach er to cat awy from me. Nah in wiv you and tell er to cam aht afore Aw cam in and kick er aht. Tell er Bill Walker wants er. She'll knaow wot thet means; and if she keeps me witin itll be worse. You stop to jawr beck at me; and Aw'll stawt on you: d'ye eah? Theres your wy. In you gow. (*He takes her by the arm and slings her towards the door of the shelter. She falls on her hand and knee. Rummy helps her up again.*)

Price (rising, and venturing irresolutely towards Bill). Easy there, mate. She aint doin you no arm.

Bill. Oo are you callin mite? (*Standing over him threateningly*). Youre gowin to stend ap for er, aw yer? Put ap your ends.

Rummy (running indignantly to him to scold him). Oh, you great brute—(*He instantly swings his left hand back against her face. She screams and reels back to the trough, where she sits down, covering her bruised face with her hands and rocking herself and moaning with pain.*)

Jenny (going to her). Oh, God forgive you! How could you strike an old woman like that?

Bill (seizing her by the hair so violently that she also screams, and tearing her away from the old woman). You Gawd forgimme again an Aw'll Gawd forgive you one on the jawr thetll stop you pryin for a week. (*Holding her and turning fiercely on Price.*) Ev you ennything to sy agen it?

Price (intimidated). No, matey: she aint anything to do with me.

Bill. Good job for you! Aw'd pat two meals into you and fawt you with one finger arter, you stawved cur. (*To Jenny.*) Nah are you gowin to fetch aht Mog Ebbijem; or em Aw to knock your fice off you and fetch her meself?

Jenny (writhing in his grasp). Oh please someone go in and tell Major Barbara—(*she screams again as he wrenches her head down; and Price and Rummy flee into the shelter*).

Bill. You want to gow in and tell your Mijor of me, do you?

Jenny. Oh please dont drag my hair. Let me go.

Bill. Do you or downt you? (*She stifles a scream.*) Yus or nao?

Jenny God give me strength—

Bill (striking her with his fist in the face). Gow an shaow her thet, and tell her if she wants one lawk it to cam and interfere with me. (*Jenny, crying with pain, goes into the shed. He goes to the form and addresses the old man.*) Eah: finish your mess; an git aht o mah wy.

Shirley (springing up and facing him fiercely, with the mug in his hand). You take a liberty with me, and I'll smash you over the face with the mug and cut your eye out. Aint you satisfied—young whelps like you—with takin the bread out o the mouths of your elders that have brought you up and slaved for you, but you must come shovin and cheekin and bullyin in here, where the bread o charity is sickenin in our stummicks?

Bill (contemptuously, but backing a little). Wot good are you, you aold palsy mag? Wot good are you?

Shirley. As good as you and better. I'll do a day's work agen you or any fat young soaker of your age. Go and take my job at Horrockses, where I worked for ten year. They want young men there: they cant afford to keep men over forty-five. Theyre very sorry—give you a character and happy to help you to get anything suited to your years—sure a steady man wont be long out of a job. Well, let em try you. Theyll find the differ. What do you know? Not as much as how to beeyave yourself—layin your dirty fist across the mouth of a respectable woman!

Bill. Downt provowk me to ly it acrost yours: d'ye eah?

Shirley (with blighting contempt). Yes: you like an old man to hit, dont you, when youve finished with the women. I ain't seen you hit a young one yet.

Bill (stung). You loy, you aold soupkitchener, you. There was a yang menn eah. Did Aw offer to itt him or did Aw not?

Shirley. Was he starvin or was he not? Was he a man or only a cross-eyed thief an a loafer? Would you hit my son-in-law's brother?

Bill. Oo's ee?

Shirley. Todger Fairmile o Balls Pond. Him that won £20 off the Japanese wrastler at the music hall by standin out 17 minutes 4 seconds agen him.

Bill (sullenly). Aw'm nao music awl wrastler. Ken he box?

Shirley. Yes: an you cant.

Bill. Wot! Aw cawnt, cawnt Aw? Wots thet you sy (*threatening him*)?

Shirley (not budging an inch). Will you box Todger Fairmile if I put him on to you? Say the word.

Bill (subsiding with a slouch). Aw'll stend ap to enny menn alawy, if he was ten Todger Fairmawls. But Aw dont set ap to be a perfeshnal.

Shirley (looking down on him with unfathomable disdain). You box! Slap an old woman with the back o your hand! You hadnt even the sense to hit her where the magistrate couldnt see the mark of it, you silly young lump of conceit and ignorance. Hit a girl in the jaw and ony make her cry! If Todger Fairmile'd done it, she wouldnt a got up inside o ten minutes, no more than you would if he got on to you. Yah! I'd set about you myself if I had a week's feedin in me instead o two months' starvation. (*He turns his back on him and sits down moodily at the table.*)

Bill (*following him and stooping over him to drive the taunt in*). You loy! youve the bread and treacle in you that you cam eah to beg.

Shirley (*bursting into tears*). Oh God! it's true: I'm only an old pauper on the scrap heap. (*Furiously.*) But you'll come to it yourself; and then youll know. Youll come to it sooner than a teetotaller like me, fillin yourself with gin at this hour o the mornin!

Bill. Aw'm nao gin drinker, you oald lawr; but wen Aw want to give my girl a bloomin good awdin Aw lawk to ev a bit o devil in me: see? An eah Aw emm, talkin to a rotten aold blawter like you sted o givin her wot for. (*Working himself into a rage.*) Aw'm gowin in there to fetch her aht. (*He makes vengefully for the shelter door.*)

Shirley. Youre going to the station on a stretcher, more likely; and theyll take the gin and the devil out of you there when they get you inside. You mind what youre about: the major here is the Earl o Stevenage's granddaughter.

Bill (*checked*). Garn!

Shirley. Youll see.

Bill (*his resolution oozing*). Well, Aw aint dan nathin to er.

Shirley. Spose she said you did! who'd believe you?

Bill (*very uneasy, skulking back to the corner of the penthouse*). Gawd! theres no jastice in this cantry. To think wot them people can do! Aw'm as good as er.

Shirley. Tell her so. It's just what a fool like you would do.

Barbara, brisk and businesslike, comes from the shelter with a note book, and addresses herself to Shirley. Bill, cowed, sits down in the corner on a form, and turns his back on them.

Barbara. Good morning.

Shirley (*standing up and taking off his hat*). Good morning, miss.

Barbara. Sit down: make yourself at home. (*He hesitates; but she puts a friendly hand on his shoulder and makes him obey.*) Now then! since youve made friends with us, we want to know all about you. Names and addresses and trades.

Shirley. Peter Shirley. Fitter. Chucked out two months ago because I was too old.

Barbara (*not at all surprised*). Youd pass still. Why didnt you dye your hair?

Shirley. I did. Me age come out at a coroner's inquest on me daughter.

Barbara. Steady?

Shirley. Teetotaller. Never out of a job before. Good worker. And sent to the knackers like an old horse!

Barbara. No matter: if you did your part God will do his.

Shirley (suddenly stubborn). My religion's no concern of anybody but myself.

Barbara (guessing). I know. Secularist?

Shirley (hotly). Did I offer to deny it?

Barbara. Why should you? My own father's a Secularist, I think. Our Father—yours and mine—fulfils himself in many ways; and I daresay he knew what he was about when he made a Secularist of you. So buck up, Peter! we can always find a job for a steady man like you. (*Shirley, disarmed and a little bewildered, touches his hat. She turns from him to Bill.*) Whats your name?

Bill (insolently). Wots thet to you?

Barbara (calmly making a note). Afraid to give his name. Any trade?

Bill. Oo's afride to give is nime? (*Doggedly, with a sense of heroically defying the House of Lords in the person of Lord Stevenage.*) If you want to bring a chawge agen me, bring it. (*She waits, unruffled.*) Moy nime's Bill Walker.

Barbara (as if the name were familiar: trying to remember how). Bill Walker? (*Recollecting.*) Oh, I know: youre the man that Jenny Hill was praying for inside just now. (*She enters his name in her note book.*)

Bill. Oo's Jenny Ill? And wot call as she to pry for me?

Barbara. I dont know. Perhaps it was you that cut her lip.

Bill (defiantly). Yus, it was me that cat her lip. Aw aint afride o you.

Barbara. How could you be, since youre not afraid of God? Youre a brave man, Mr Walker. It takes some pluck to do our work here; but none of us dare lift our hand against a girl like that, for fear of her father in heaven.

Bill (sullenly). I want nan o your kentin jawr. I spowse you think Aw cam eah to beg from you, like this demmiged lot eah. Not me. Aw downt want your bread and scripe and ketlep. Aw dont believe in your Gawd, no more than you do yourself.

Barbara (sunnily apologetic and ladylike, as on a new footing with him). Oh, I beg your pardon for putting your name down, Mr Walker. I didnt understand. I'll strike it out.

Bill (taking this as a slight, and deeply wounded by it). Eah! you let maw nime alown. Aint it good enaff to be in your book?

Barbara (considering). Well, you see, theres no use putting down your name unless I can do something for you, is there? Whats your trade?

Bill (still smarting). Thets nao concern o yours.

Barbara. Just so. (*Very businesslike.*) I'll put you down as (*writing*) the man who—struck—poor little Jenny Hill—in the mouth.

Bill (rising threateningly). See eah. Awve ed enaff o this.

Barbara (quite sunny and fearless). What did you come to us for?

Bill. Aw cam for maw gel, see? Aw cam to tike her aht o this and to brike er jawr for er.

Barbara (complacently). You see I was right about your trade. (*Bill, on the point of retorting furiously, finds himself, to his great shame and terror, in danger of crying instead. He sits down again suddenly.*) Whats her name?

Bill (*dogged*). Er nime's Mog Ebbijem: thets wot her nime is.

Barbara. Mog Habbijam! Oh, she's gone to Canning Town, to our barracks there.

Bill (*fortified by his resentment of Mog's perfidy*). Is she? (*Vindictively*). Then Aw'm gowin to Kennintahn arter her. (*He crosses to the gate; hesitates; finally comes back at Barbara.*) Are you loyin to me to git shat o me?

Barbara. I dont want to get shut of you. I want to keep you here and save your soul. Youd better stay: youre going to have a bad time today, Bill.

Bill. Oo's gowin to give it to me? You, preps?

Barbara. Someone you dont believe in. But youll be glad afterwards.

Bill (*slinking off*). Aw'll gow to Kennintahn to be aht o reach o your tangue. (*Suddenly turning on her with intense malice.*) And if Aw downt fawnd Mog there, Aw'll cam beck and do two years for you, selp me Gawd if Aw downt!

Barbara (*a shade kindlier, if possible*). It's no use, Bill. She's got another bloke.

Bill. Wot!

Barbara. One of her own converts. He fell in love with her when he saw her with her soul saved, and her face clean, and her hair washed.

Bill (*surprised*). Wottud she wash it for, the carroty slat? It's red.

Barbara. It's quite lovely now, because she wears a new look in her eyes with it. It's a pity youre too late. The new bloke has put your nose out of joint, Bill.

Bill. Aw'll put his nowse aht o joint for him. Not that Aw care a carse for er, mawnd thet. But Aw'll teach her to drop me as if Aw was dirt. And Aw'll teach him to meddle with maw judy. Wots iz bleedin nime?

Barbara. Sergeant Todger Fairmile.

Shirley (*rising with grim joy*). I'll go with him, miss. I want to see them two meet. I'll take him to the infirmary when it's over.

Bill (*to Shirley, with undissembled misgiving*). Is thet im you was speakin on?

Shirley. Thats him.

Bill. Im that wrastled in the music awl?

Shirley. The competitions at the National Sportin Club was worth nigh a hundred a year to him. He's gev em up now for religion; so he's a bit fresh for want of the exercise he was accustomed to. He'll be glad to see you. Come along.

Bill. Wots is wight?

Shirley. Thirteen four. (*Bill's last hope expires.*)

Barbara. Go and talk to him, Bill. He'll convert you.

Shirley. He'll convert your head into a mashed potato.

Bill (sullenly). Aw aint afride of im. Aw aint afride of ennybody. But e can lick me. She's dan me. (*He sits down moodily on the edge of the horse trough.*)

Shirley. You aint going. I thought not. (*He resumes his seat.*)

Barbara (calling). Jenny!

Jenny (appearing at the shelter door with a plaster on the corner of her mouth). Yes, Major.

Barbara. Send Rummy Mitchens out to clear away here.

Jenny. I think she's afraid.

Barbara (her resemblance to her mother flashing out for a moment). Nonsense! she must do as she's told.

Jenny (calling into the shelter). Rummy: the Major says you must come.

Jenny comes to Barbara, purposely keeping on the side next Bill, lest he should suppose that she shrank from him or bore malice.

Barbara. Poor little Jenny! Are you tired? (*Looking at the wounded cheek.*) Does it hurt?

Jenny. No: it's all right now. It was nothing.

Barbara (critically). It was as hard as he could hit, I expect. Poor Bill! You dont feel angry with him, do you?

Jenny. Oh no, no, no: indeed I dont, Major, bless his poor heart! (*Barbara kisses her; and she runs away merrily into the shelter. Bill writhes with an agonizing return of his new and alarming symptoms, but says nothing. Rummy Mitchens comes from the shelter.*)

Barbara (going to meet Rummy). Now Rummy, bustle. Take in those mugs and plates to be washed; and throw the crumbs about for the birds.

Rummy takes the three plates and mugs; but Shirley takes back his mug from her, as there is still some milk left in it.

Rummy. There aint any crumbs. This aint a time to waste good bread on birds.

Price (appearing at the shelter door). Gentleman come to see the shelter, Major. Says he's your father.

Barbara. All right. Coming. (*Snobby goes back into the shelter, followed by Barbara.*)

Rummy (stealing across to Bill and addressing him in a subdued voice, but with intense conviction). I'd av the lor of you, you flat eared pignosed potwalloper, if she'd let me. Youre no gentleman, to hit a lady in the face. (*Bill, with greater things moving in him, takes no notice.*)

Shirley (following her). Here! in with you and dont get yourself into more trouble by talking.

Rummy (*with hauteur*). I aint ad the pleasure o being hintroduced to you, as I can remember. (*She goes into the shelter with the plates.*)

Shirley. Thats the—

Bill (*savagely*). Downt you talk to me, d'ye eah? You lea me alown, or Aw'll do you a mischief. Aw'm not dirt under your feet, ennywy.

Shirley (*calmly*). Dont you be afeerd. You aint such prime company that you need expect to be sought after. (*He is about to go into the shelter when Barbara comes out, with Undershaft on her right.*)

Barbara. Oh, there you are, Mr Shirley! (*Between them.*) This is my father: I told you he was a Secularist, didnt I? Perhaps youll be able to comfort one another.

Undershaft (*startled*). A Secularist! Not the least in the world: on the contrary, a confirmed mystic.

Barbara. Sorry, I'm sure. By the way, papa, what is your religion? in case I have to introduce you again.

Undershaft. My religion? Well, my dear, I am a Millionaire. That is my religion.

Barbara. Then I'm afraid you and Mr Shirley wont be able to comfort one another after all. Youre not a Millionaire, are you, Peter?

Shirley. No; and proud of it.

Undershaft (*gravely*). Poverty, my friend, is not a thing to be proud of.

Shirley (*angrily*). Who made your millions for you? Me and my like. Whats kep us poor? Keepin you rich. I wouldnt have your conscience, not for all your income.

Undershaft. I wouldnt have your income, not for all your conscience, Mr Shirley. (*He goes to the penthouse and sits down on a form.*)

Barbara (*stopping Shirley adroitly as he is about to retort*). You wouldnt think he was my father, would you, Peter? Will you go into the shelter and lend the lasses a hand for a while: we're worked off our feet.

Shirley (*bitterly*). Yes: I'm in their debt for a meal, aint I?

Barbara. Oh, not because youre in their debt, but for love of them, Peter, for love of them. (*He cannot understand, and is rather scandalized.*) There! dont stare at me. In with you; and give that conscience of yours a holiday (*bustling him into the shelter*).

Shirley (*as he goes in*). Ah! it's a pity you never was trained to use your reason, miss. Youd have been a very taking lecturer on Secularism.

Undershaft. Never mind me, my dear. Go about your work; and let me watch it for a while.

Barbara. All right.

Undershaft. For instance, whats the matter with that outpatient over there?

Barbara (*looking at Bill, whose attitude has never changed, and whose expression of brooding wrath has deepened*). Oh, we shall cure him in no time. Just watch. (*She goes over to Bill and waits. He glances up at her and casts his eyes down again, uneasy, but grimmer than ever.*) It would be nice to just stamp on Mog Habbijam's face, wouldnt it, Bill?

Bill (*starting up from the trough in consternation*). It's a loy: Aw never said so. (*She shakes her head.*) Oo taold you wot was in moy mawnd?

Barbara. Only your new friend.

Bill. Wot new friend?

Barbara. The devil, Bill. When he gets round people they get miserable, just like you.

Bill (*with a heartbreaking attempt at devil-may-care cheerfulness*). Aw aint miserable. (*He sits down again, and stretches his legs in an attempt to seem indifferent.*)

Barbara. Well, if youre happy, why dont you look happy, as we do?

Bill (*his legs curling back in spite of him*). Aw'm eppy enaff, Aw tell you. Woy cawnt you lea me alown? Wot ev I dan to you? Aw aint smashed your fice, ev Aw?

Barbara (*softly: wooing his soul*). It's not me thats getting at you, Bill.

Bill. Oo else is it?

Barbara. Somebody that doesnt intend you to smash women's faces, I suppose. Somebody or something that wants to make a man of you.

Bill (*blustering*). Mike a menn o me! Aint Aw a menn? eh? Oo sez Aw'm not a menn?

Barbara. Theres a man in you somewhere, I suppose. But why did he let you hit poor little Jenny Hill? That wasnt very manly of him, was it?

Bill (*tormented*). Ev dan wiv it, Aw tell you. Chack it. Aw'm sick o your Jenny Ill and er silly little fice.

Barbara. Then why do you keep thinking about it? Why does it keep coming up against you in your mind? Youre not getting converted, are you?

Bill (*with conviction*). Not ME. Not lawkly.

Barbara. Thats right, Bill. Hold out against it. Put out your strength. Dont lets get you cheap. Todger Fairmile said he wrestled for three nights against his salvation harder than he ever wrestled with the Jap at the music hall. He gave in to the Jap when his arm was going to break. But he didnt give in to his salvation until his heart was going to break. Perhaps youll escape that. You havnt any heart, have you?

Bill. Wot d'ye mean? Woy aint Aw got a awt the sime as ennybody else?

Barbara. A man with a heart wouldnt have bashed poor little Jenny's face, would he?

Bill (*almost crying*). Ow, will you lea me alown? Ev Aw ever offered to meddle with you, that you cam neggin and provowkin me lawk this? (*He writhes convulsively from his eyes to his toes.*)

Barbara (*with a steady soothing hand on his arm and a gentle voice that never lets him go*). It's your soul thats hurting you, Bill, and not me. Weve been through it all ourselves. Come with us, Bill. (*He looks wildly round.*) To brave manhood on earth and eternal glory in heaven. (*He is on the point of breaking down.*) Come. (*A drum is heard in the shelter; and Bill, with a gasp, escapes from the spell as Barbara turns quickly. Adolphus enters from the shelter with a big drum.*) Oh! there you are, Dolly. Let me introduce a new friend of mine, Mr Bill Walker. This is my bloke, Bill: Mr Cusins. (*Cusins salutes with his drumstick.*)

Bill. Gowin to merry im?

Barbara. Yes.

Bill (*fervently*). Gawd elp im! Gaw-aw-aw-awd elp im!

Barbara. Why? Do you think he wont be happy with me?

Bill. Awve aony ed to stend it for a mawnin: e'll ev to stend it for a lawftawm.

Cusins. That is a frightful reflection, Mr Walker. But I cant tear myself away from her.

Bill. Well, Aw ken. (*To Barbara.*) Eah do you knaow where Aw'm gowin to, and wot Aw'm gowin to do?

Barbara. Yes: youre going to heaven; and youre coming back here before the week's out to tell me so.

Bill. You loy. Aw'm gowin to Kennintahn, to spit in Todger Fairmawl's eye. Aw beshed Jenny Ill's fice; an nar Aw'll git me aown fice beshed and cam bec and shaow it to er. Ee'll itt me ardern Aw itt her. Thatll mike us square. (*To Adolphus.*) Is thet fair or is it not? Youre a genlmn: you oughter knaow.

Barbara. Two black eyes wont make one white one, Bill.

Bill. Aw didnt awst you. Cawnt you never keep your mahth shat? Oy awst the genlmn.

Cusins (*reflectively*). Yes: I think youre right, Mr Walker. Yes: I should do it. It's curious: it's exactly what an ancient Greek would have done.

Barbara. But what good will it do?

Cusins. Well, it will give Mr Fairmile some exercise; and it will satisfy Mr Walker's soul.

Bill. Rot! there aint nao sach a thing as a saoul. Ah kin you tell wevver Awve a saoul or not? You never seen it.

Barbara. Ive seen it hurting you when you went against it.

Bill (*with compressed aggravation*). If you was maw gel and took the word awt o me mahth lawk thet, Aw'd give you sathink youd feel urtin, Aw would. (*To Adolphus.*) You tike maw tip, mite. Stop er jawr or youll doy afoah your tawm (*With intense ex-*

pression.) Wore aht: thets wot youll be: wore aht. (*He goes away through the gate.*)

Cusins (*looking after him*). I wonder!

Barbara. Dolly! (*indignant, in her mother's manner*).

Cusins. Yes, my dear, it's very wearing to be in love with you. If it lasts, I quite think I shall die young.

Barbara. Should you mind?

Cusins. Not at all. (*He is suddenly softened, and kisses her over the drum, evidently not for the first time, as people cannot kiss over a big drum without practice. Undershaft coughs.*)

Barbara. It's all right, papa, weve not forgotten you. Dolly: explain the place to papa: I havnt time. (*She goes busily into the shelter.*)

Undershaft and Adolphus now have the yard to themselves. Undershaft, seated on a form, and still keenly attentive, looks hard at Adolphus. Adolphus looks hard at him.

Undershaft. I fancy you guess something of what is in my mind, Mr Cusins. (*Cusins flourishes his drumsticks as if in the act of beating a lively rataplan, but makes no sound.*) Exactly so. But suppose Barbara finds you out!

Cusins. You know, I do not admit that I am imposing on Barbara. I am quite genuinely interested in the views of the Salvation Army. The fact is, I am a sort of collector of religions; and the curious thing is that I find I can believe them all. By the way, have you any religion?

Undershaft. Yes.

Cusins. Anything out of the common?

Undershaft. Only that there are two things necessary to Salvation.

Cusins (*disappointed, but polite*). Ah, the Church Catechism. Charles Lomax also belongs to the Established Church.

Undershaft. The two things are—

Cusins. Baptism and—

Undershaft. No. Money and gunpowder.

Cusins (*surprised, but interested*). That is the general opinion of our governing classes. The novelty is in hearing any man confess it.

Undershaft. Just so.

Cusins. Excuse me: is there any place in your religion for honor, justice, truth, love, mercy and so forth?

Undershaft. Yes: they are the graces and luxuries of a rich, strong, and safe life.

Cusins. Suppose one is forced to choose between them and money or gunpowder?

Undershaft. Choose money and gunpowder; for without enough of both you cannot afford the others.

Cusins. That is your religion?

Undershaft. Yes.

The cadence of this reply makes a full close in the conversation, Cusins twists his face dubiously and contemplates Undershaft. Undershaft contemplates him.

Cusins. Barbara wont stand that. You will have to choose between your religion and Barbara.

Undershaft. So will you, my friend. She will find out that that drum of yours is hollow.

Cusins. Father Undershaft: you are mistaken: I am a sincere Salvationist. You do not understand the Salvation Army. It is the army of joy, of love, of courage: it has banished the fear and remorse and despair of the old hell-ridden evangelical sects: it marches to fight the devil with trumpet and drum, with music and dancing, with banner and palm, as becomes a sally from heaven by its happy garrison. It picks the waster out of the public house and makes a man of him: it finds a worm wriggling in a back kitchen, and lo! a woman! Men and women of rank too, sons and daughters of the Highest. It takes the poor professor of Greek, the most artificial and self-suppressed of human creatures, from his meal of roots, and lets loose the rhapsodist in him; reveals the true worship of Dionysos to him; sends him down the public street drumming dithyrambs (*he plays a thundering flourish on the drum*).

Undershaft. You will alarm the shelter.

Cusins. Oh, they are accustomed to these sudden ecstasies. However, if the drum worries you—(*he pockets the drumsticks; unhooks the drum and stands it on the ground opposite the gateway*).

Undershaft. Thank you.

Cusins. You remember what Euripides says about your money and gunpowder?

Undershaft. No.

Cusins (*declaiming*).

One and another
In money and guns may outpass his brother;
And men in their millions float and flow
And seethe with a million hopes as leaven;
And they win their will; or they miss their will;
And their hopes are dead or are pined for still;
But who'er can know
As the long days go
That to live is happy, has found his heaven.

My translation: what do you think of it?

Undershaft. I think, my friend, that if you wish to know, as the long days go, that to live is happy, you must first acquire money enough for a decent life, and power enough to be your own master.

Cusins. You are damnably discouraging. (*He resumes his declamation.*)
           Is it so hard a thing to see
           That the spirit of God—whate'er it be—
The law that abides and changes not, ages long,
The Eternal and Nature-born: these things be strong?
What else is Wisdom? What of Man's endeavor,
Or God's high grace so lovely and so great?
To stand from fear set free? to breathe and wait?
To hold a hand uplifted over Fate?
And shall not Barbara be loved for ever?

Undershaft. Euripides mentions Barbara, does he?

Cusins. It is a fair translation. The word means Loveliness.

Undershaft. May I ask—as Barbara's father—how much a year she is to be loved for ever on?

Cusins. As for Barbara's father, that is more your affair than mine. I can feed her by teaching Greek: that is about all.

Undershaft. Do you consider it a good match for her?

Cusins (*with polite obstinacy*). Mr Undershaft: I am in many ways a weak, timid, ineffectual person; and my health is far from satisfactory. But whenever I feel that I must have anything, I get it, sooner or later. I feel that way about Barbara. I dont like marriage: I feel intensely afraid of it; and I dont know what I shall do with Barbara or what she will do with me. But I feel that I and nobody else must marry her. Please regard that as settled.— Not that I wish to be arbitrary; but why should I waste your time in discussing what is inevitable?

Undershaft. You mean that you will stick at nothing: not even the conversion of the Salvation Army to the worship of Dionysos.

Cusins. The business of the Salvation Army is to save, not to wrangle about the name of the pathfinder. Dionysos or another: what does it matter?

Undershaft (*rising and approaching him*). Professor Cusins: you are a young man after my own heart.

Cusins. Mr Undershaft: you are, as far as I am able to gather, a most infernal old rascal; but you appeal very strongly to my sense of ironic humor.

Undershaft mutely offers his hand. They shake.

Undershaft (*suddenly concentrating himself*). And now to business.

Cusins. Pardon me. We are discussing religion. Why go back to such an uninteresting and unimportant subject as business?

Undershaft. Religion is our business at present, because it is through religion alone that we can win Barbara.

Cusins. Have you, too, fallen in love with Barbara?

Undershaft. Yes, with a father's love.

Cusins. A father's love for a grown-up daughter is the most dangerous of all infatuations. I apologize for mentioning my own pale, coy, mistrustful fancy in the same breath with it.

Undershaft. Keep to the point. We have to win her; and we are neither of us Methodists.

Cusins. That doesnt matter. The power Barbara wields here—the power that wields Barbara herself—is not Calvinism, not Presbyterianism, not Methodism—

Undershaft. Not Greek Paganism either, eh?

Cusins. I admit that. Barbara is quite original in her religion.

Undershaft (*triumphantly*). Aha! Barbara Undershaft would be. Her inspiration comes from within herself.

Cusins. How do you suppose it got there?

Undershaft (*in towering excitement*). It is the Undershaft inheritance. I shall hand on my torch to my daughter. She shall make my converts and preach my gospel—

Cusins. What! Money and gunpowder!

Undershaft. Yes, money and gunpowder. Freedom and power. Command of life and command of death.

Cusins (*urbanely: trying to bring him down to earth*). This is extremely interesting, Mr Undershaft. Of course you know that you are mad.

Undershaft (*with redoubled force*). And you?

Cusins. Oh, mad as a hatter. You are welcome to my secret since I have discovered yours. But I am astonished. Can a madman make cannons?

Undershaft. Would anyone else than a madman make them? And now (*with surging energy*) question for question. Can a sane man translate Euripides?

Cusins. No.

Undershaft (*seizing him by the shoulder*). Can a sane woman make a man of a waster or a woman of a worm?

Cusins (*reeling before the storm*). Father Colossus—Mammoth Millionaire—

Undershaft (*pressing him*). Are there two mad people or three in this Salvation shelter today?

Cusins. You mean Barbara is as mad as we are?

Undershaft (*pushing him lightly off and resuming his equanimity suddenly and completely*). Pooh, Professor! let us call things by their proper names. I am a millionaire; you are a poet: Barbara is a savior of souls. What have we three to do with the common mob of slaves and idolators? (*He sits down again with a shrug of contempt for the mob.*)

Cusins. Take care! Barbara is in love with the common people. So am I. Have you never felt the romance of that love?

Undershaft (*cold and sardonic*). Have you ever been in love with Poverty, like St Francis? Have you ever been in love with

Dirt, like St Simeon! Have you ever been in love with disease and suffering, like our nurses and philanthropists? Such passions are not virtues, but the most unnatural of all the vices. This love of the common people may please an earl's granddaughter and a university professor; but I have been a common man and a poor man; and it has no romance for me. Leave it to the poor to pretend that poverty is a blessing: leave it to the coward to make a religion of his cowardice by preaching humility: we know better than that. We three must stand together above the common people: how else can we help their children to climb up beside us? Barbara must belong to us, not to the Salvation Army.

Cusins. Well, I can only say that if you think you will get her away from the Salvation Army by talking to her as you have been talking to me, you dont know Barbara.

Undershaft. My friend: I never ask for what I can buy.

Cusins (*in a white fury*). Do I understand you to imply that you can buy Barbara?

Undershaft. No; but I can buy the Salvation Army.

Cusins. Quite impossible.

Undershaft. You shall see. All religious organizations exist by selling themselves to the rich.

Cusins. Not the Army. That is the Church of the poor.

Undershaft. All the more reason for buying it.

Cusins. I dont think you quite know what the Army does for the poor.

Undershaft. Oh yes I do. It draws their teeth: that is enough for me as a man of business.

Cusins. Nonsense! It makes them sober—

Undershaft. I prefer sober workmen. The profits are larger.

Cusins—honest—

Undershaft. Honest workmen are the most economical.

Cusins—attached to their homes—

Undershaft. So much the better: they will put up with anything sooner than change their shop.

Cusins—happy—

Undershaft. An invaluable safeguard against revolution.

Cusins—unselfish—

Undershaft. Indifferent to their own interests, which suits me exactly.

Cusins—with their thoughts on heavenly things—

Undershaft (*rising*). And not on Trade Unionism nor Socialism. Excellent.

Cusins (*revolted*). You really are an infernal old rascal.

Undershaft (*indicating Peter Shirley, who has just come from the shelter and strolled dejectedly down the yard between them*). And this is an honest man!

Shirley. Yes; and what av I got by it? (*he passes on bitterly and sits on the form, in the corner of the penthouse*).

Snobby Price, beaming sanctimoniously, and Jenny Hill, with a
tambourine full of coppers, come from the shelter and go to the
drum, on which Jenny begins to count the money.

Undershaft (*replying to Shirley*). Oh, your employers must have got
a good deal by it from first to last. (*He sits on the table, with*
one foot on the side form, Cusins, overwhelmed, sits down on
the same form nearer the shelter. Barbara comes from the shelter
to the middle of the yard. She is excited and a little overwrought.)

Barbara. Weve just had a splendid experience meeting at the other
gate in Cripps's lane. Ive hardly ever seen them so much moved
as they were by your confession, Mr Price.

Price. I could almost be glad of my past wickedness if I could believe
that it would elp to keep hathers stright.

Barbara. So it will, Snobby. How much, Jenny?

Jenny. Four and tenpence, Major.

Barbara. Oh Snobby, if you had given your poor mother just one
more kick, we should have got the whole five shillings!

Price. If she heard you say that, miss, she'd be sorry I didnt. But
I'm glad. Oh what a joy it will be to her when she hears I'm
saved!

Undershaft. Shall I contribute the odd twopence, Barbara? The millionaire's mite, eh? (*He takes a couple of pennies from his pocket.*)

Barbara. How did you make that twopence?

Undershaft. As usual. By selling cannons, torpedoes, submarines, and
my new patent Grand Duke hand grenade.

Barbara. Put it back in your pocket. You cant buy your salvation here
for twopence: you must work it out.

Undershaft. Is twopence not enough? I can afford a little more, if
you press me.

Barbara. Two million millions would not be enough. There is bad
blood on your hands; and nothing but good blood can cleanse
them. Money is no use. Take it away. (*She turns to Cusins.*)
Dolly: you must write another letter for me to the papers. (*He*
makes a wry face.) Yes: I know you dont like it; but it must be
done. The starvation this winter is beating us: everybody is unemployed. The General says we must close this shelter if we cant
get more money. I force the collections at the meetings until I am
ashamed: dont I, Snobby?

Price. It's a fair treat to see you work it, miss. The way you got
them up from three-and-six to four-and-ten with that hymn, penny
by penny and verse by verse, was a caution. Not a Cheap Jack on
Mile End Waste could touch you at it.

Barbara. Yes; but I wish we could do without it. I am getting at last
to think more of the collection than of the people's souls. And
what are those hatfuls of pence and halfpence? We want thousands! tens of thousands! hundreds of thousands! I want to con-

vert people, not to be always begging for the Army in a way I'd die sooner than beg for myself.

Undershaft (*in profound irony*). Genuine unselfishness is capable of anything, my dear.

Barbara (*unsuspectingly, as she turns away to take the money from the drum and put it in a cash bag she carries*). Yes, isnt it? (*Undershaft looks sardonically at Cusins.*)

Cusins (*aside to Undershaft*). Mephistopheles! Machiavelli!

Barbara (*tears coming into her eyes as she ties the bag and pockets it*). How are we to feed them? I cant talk religion to a man with bodily hunger in his eyes. (*Almost breaking down.*) It's frightful.

Jenny (*running to her*). Major, dear—

Barbara (*rebounding*). No: dont comfort me. It will be all right. We shall get the money.

Undershaft. How?

Jenny. By praying for it, of course. Mrs Baines says she prayed for it last night; and she has never prayed for it in vain: never once. (*She goes to the gate and looks out into the street.*)

Barbara (*who has dried her eyes and regained her composure*). By the way, dad, Mrs Baines has come to march with us to our big meeting this afternoon and she is very anxious to meet you, for some reason or other. Perhaps she'll convert you.

Undershaft. I shall be delighted, my dear.

Jenny (*at the gate: excitedly*). Major! Major! heres that man back again.

Barbara. What man?

Jenny. The man that hit me. Oh, I hope he's coming back to join us.

Bill Walker, with frost on his jacket, comes through the gate, his hands deep in his pockets and his chin sunk between his shoulders, like a cleaned-out gambler. He halts between Barbara and the drum.

Barbara. Hullo, Bill! Back already!

Bill (*nagging at her*). Bin talkin ever sence, ev you?

Barbara. Pretty nearly. Well, has Todger paid you out for poor Jenny's jaw?

Bill. Nao e aint.

Barbara. I thought your jacket looked a bit snowy.

Bill. Sao it is snaowy. You want to knaow where the snaow cam from, downt you?

Barbara. Yes.

Bill. Well, it cam from orf the grahnd in Pawkinses Corner in Kennintahn. It got rabbed orf be maw shaoulders: see?

Barbara. Pity you didnt rub some off with your knees, Bill! That would have done you a lot of good.

Bill (*with sour mirthless humor*). Aw was sivin anather menn's knees at the tawm. E was kneelin on moy ed, e was.

Jenny. Who was kneeling on your head?

Bill. Todger was. E was pryin for me: pryin camfortable wiv me as a cawpet. Sow was Mog. Sao was the aol bloomin meeting. Mog she sez 'Ow Lawd brike is stabborn sperrit; bat downt urt is dear art.' Thet was wot she said. 'Downt urt is dear art'! An er blowk—thirteen stun four!—kneelin wiv all is wight on me. Fanny, aint it?

Jenny. Oh no. We're so sorry, Mr Walker.

Barbara (*enjoying it frankly*). Nonsense! of course it's funny. Served you right, Bill! You must have done something to him first.

Bill (*doggedly*). Aw did wot Aw said Aw'd do. Aw spit in is eye. E looks ap at the skoy and sez, 'Ow that Aw should be fahind worthy to be spit upon for the gospel's sike!' e sez; an Mog sez 'Glaory Allelloolier!'; and then e called me Braddher, an dahned me as if Aw was a kid and e was me mather worshin me a Setterda nawt. Aw ednt jast nao shaow wiv im at all. Arf the street pryed; an the tather arf larfed fit to split theirselves. (*To Barbara.*) There are you settisfawd nah?

Barbara (*her eyes dancing*). Wish I'd been there, Bill.

Bill. Yus: youd a got in a hextra bit o talk on me, wouldnt you?

Jenny. I'm so sorry, Mr Walker.

Bill (*fiercely*). Downt you gow being sorry for me: youve no call. Listen eah. Aw browk your jawr.

Jenny. No, it didnt hurt me: indeed it didnt, except for a moment. It was only that I was frightened.

Bill. Aw downt want to be forgive be you, or be ennybody. Wot Aw did Aw'll py for. Aw trawd to gat me aown jawr browk to settisfaw you—

Jenny (*distressed*). Oh no—

Bill (*impatiently*). Tell y' Aw did: cawnt you listen to wots being taold you? All Aw got be it was being mide a sawt of in the pablic street for me pines. Well, if Aw cawnt settisfaw you one wy, Aw ken another. Listen eah! Aw ed two quid sived agen the frost; an Awve a pahnd of it left. A mite o mawn last week ed words with the judy e's gowing to merry. E give er wot-for; an e's bin fawned fifteen bob. E ed a rawt to itt er cause they was gowin to be merrid; but Aw ednt nao rawt to itt you; sao put anather fawv bob on an call it a pahnd's worth. (*He produces a sovereign.*) Eahs the manney. Tike it; and lets ev no more o your forgivin an prying and your Mijor jawrin me. Let wot Aw dan be dan an pide for; and let there be a end of it.

Jenny. Oh, I couldn't take it, Mr Walker. But if you would give a shilling or two to poor Rummy Mitchens! you really did hurt her; and she's old.

Bill (*contemptuously*). Not lawkly. Aw'd give her anather as soon as look at er. Let her ev the lawr o me as she threatened! She aint forgiven me: not mach. Wot Aw dan to er is not on me mawnd —wot she (*indicating Barbara*) mawt call on me conscience—no more than stickin a pig. It's this Christian gime o yours that Aw wownt ev plyed agen me: this bloomin forgivin an neggin an jawrin that mikes a menn thet sore that iz lawf's a burdn to im. Aw wownt ev it, Aw tell you; sao tike your manney and stop thraowin your silly beshed fice hap agen me.

Jenny. Major: may I take a little of it for the Army?

Barbara. No: the Army is not to be bought. We want your soul, Bill; and we'll take nothing less.

Bill (*bitterly*). Aw knaow. Me an maw few shillins is not good enaff for you. Youre a earl's grendorter, you are. Nathink less than a andered pahnd for you.

Undershaft. Come, Barbara! you could do a great deal of good with a hundred pounds. If you will set this gentleman's mind at ease by taking his pound, I will give the other ninety-nine.

Bill, dazed by such opulence, instinctively touches his cap.

Barbara. Oh, youre too extravagant, papa. Bill offers twenty pieces of silver. All you need offer is the other ten. That will make the standard price to buy anybody who's for sale. I'm not; and the Army's not. (*To Bill.*) Youll never have another quiet moment, Bill, until you come round to us. You cant stand out against your salvation.

Bill (*sullenly*). Aw cawnt stend aht agen music awl wrastlers and awtful tangued women. Awve offered to py. Aw can do no more. Tike it or leave it. There it is. (*He throws the sovereign on the drum, and sits down on the horse-trough. The coin fascinates Snobby Price, who takes an early opportunity of dropping his cap on it.*)

Mrs Baines comes from the shelter. She is dressed as a Salvation Army Commissioner. She is an earnest looking woman of about 40, with a caressing, urgent voice, and an appealing manner.

Barbara. This is my father, Mrs Baines. (*Undershaft comes from the table, taking his hat off with marked civility.*) Try what you can do with him. He wont listen to me, because he remembers what a fool I was when I was a baby. (*She leaves them together and chats with Jenny.*)

Mrs Baines. Have you been shewn over the shelter, Mr Undershaft? You know the work we're doing, of course.

Undershaft (*very civilly*). The whole nation knows it, Mrs Baines.

Mrs Baines. No, sir: the whole nation does not know it, or we should not be crippled as we are for want of money to carry our work through the length and breadth of the land. Let me tell you that there would have been rioting this winter in London but for us.

Undershaft. You really think so?

Mrs Baines. I know it. I remember 1886, when you rich gentlemen hardened your hearts against the cry of the poor. They broke the windows of your clubs in Pall Mall.

Undershaft (gleaming with approval of their method). And the Mansion House Fund went up next day from thirty thousand pounds to seventy-nine thousand! I remember quite well.

Mrs Baines. Well, wont you help me to get at the people? They wont break windows then. Come here, Price. Let me shew you to this gentleman *(Price comes to be inspected).* Do you remember the window breaking?

Price. My ole father thought it was the revolution, maam.

Mrs Baines. Would you break windows now?

Price. Oh no, maam. The windows of eaven av bin opened to me. I know now that the rich man is a sinner like myself.

Rummy (appearing above at the loft door). Snobby Price!

Snobby. Wot is it?

Rummy. Your mother's askin for you at the other gate in Cripps's Lane. She's heard about your confession *(Price turns pale).*

Mrs Baines. Go, Mr Price; and pray with her.

Jenny. You can go through the shelter, Snobby.

Price (to Mrs Baines). I couldnt face her now, maam, with all the weight of my sins fresh on me. Tell her she'll find her son at ome, waitin for her in prayer. *(He skulks off through the gate, incidentally stealing the sovereign on his way out by picking up his cap from the drum.)*

Mrs Baines (with swimming eyes). You see how we take the anger and the bitterness against you out of their hearts, Mr Undershaft.

Undershaft. It is certainly most convenient and gratifying to all large employers of labor, Mrs Baines.

Mrs Baines. Barbara: Jenny: I have good news: most wonderful news. *(Jenny runs to her.)* My prayers have been answered. I told you they would, Jenny, didnt I?

Jenny. Yes, yes.

Barbara (moving nearer to the drum). Have we got money enough to keep the shelter open?

Mrs Baines. I hope we shall have enough to keep all the shelters open. Lord Saxmundham has promised us five thousand pounds—

Barbara. Hooray!

Jenny. Glory!

Mrs Baines. —if—

Barbara. 'If!' If what?

Mrs Baines. —if five other gentlemen will give a thousand each to make it up to ten thousand.

Barbara. Who is Lord Saxmundham? I never heard of him.

Undershaft (*who has pricked up his ears at the peer's name, and is now watching Barbara curiously*). A new creation, my dear. You have heard of Sir Horace Bodger?

Barbara. Bodger! Do you mean the distiller? Bodger's whisky!

Undershaft. That is the man. He is one of the greatest of our public benefactors. He restored the cathedral at Hakington. They made him a baronet for that. He gave half a million to the funds of his party: they made him a baron for that.

Shirley. What will they give him for the five thousand?

Undershaft. There is nothing left to give him. So the five thousand, I should think, is to save his soul.

Mrs Baines. Heaven grant it may! Oh Mr Undershaft, you have some very rich friends. Cant you help us towards the other five thousand? We are going to hold a great meeting this afternoon at the Assembly Hall in the Mile End Road. If I could only announce that one gentleman had come forward to support Lord Saxmundham, others would follow. Dont you know somebody? couldnt you? wouldnt you? (*her eyes fill with tears*) oh, think of those poor people, Mr Undershaft: think of how much it means to them, and how little to a great man like you.

Undershaft (*sardonically gallant*). Mrs Baines: you are irresistible. I cant disappoint you; and I cant deny myself the satisfaction of making Bodger pay up. You shall have your five thousand pounds.

Mrs Baines. Thank God!

Undershaft. You dont thank me?

Mrs Baines. Oh sir, dont try to be cynical: dont be ashamed of being a good man. The Lord will bless you abundantly; and our prayers will be like a strong fortification round you all the days of your life. (*With a touch of caution.*) You will let me have the cheque to shew at the meeting, wont you? Jenny: go in and fetch a pen and ink. (*Jenny runs to the shelter door.*)

Undershaft. Do not disturb Miss Hill: I have a fountain pen. (*Jenny halts. He sits at the table and writes the cheque. Cusins rises to make room for him. They all watch him silently.*)

Bill (*cynically, aside to Barbara, his voice and accent horribly debased*). Wot prawce selvytion nah?

Barbara. Stop. (*Undershaft stops writing: they all turn to her in surprise.*) Mrs Baines: are you really going to take this money?

Mrs Baines (*astonished*). Why not, dear?

Barbara. Why not! Do you know what my father is? Have you forgotten that Lord Saxmundham is Bodger the whisky man? Do you remember how we implored the County Council to stop him from writing Bodger's Whisky in letters of fire against the sky; so that the poor drink-ruined creatures on the Embankment could not wake up from their snatches of sleep without being reminded of their deadly thirst by that wicked sky sign? Do you know that the worst thing I have had to fight here is not the devil, but Bodger, Bodger, Bodger, with his whisky, his distilleries, and his tied houses? Are you going to make our shelter another tied house for him, and ask me to keep it?

Bill. Rotten dranken whisky it is too.

Mrs Baines. Dear Barbara: Lord Saxmundham has a soul to be saved like any of us. If heaven has found the way to make a good use of his money, are we to set ourselves up against the answer to our prayers?

Barbara. I know he has a soul to be saved. Let him come down here; and I'll do my best to help him to his salvation. But he wants to send his cheque down to buy us, and go on being as wicked as ever.

Undershaft (with a reasonableness which Cusins alone perceives to be ironical). My dear Barbara: alcohol is a very necessary article. It heals the sick—

Barbara. It does nothing of the sort.

Undershaft. Well, it assists the doctor: that is perhaps a less questionable way of putting it. It makes life bearable to millions of people who could not endure their existence if they were quite sober. It enables Parliament to do things at eleven at night that no sane person would do at eleven in the morning. Is it Bodger's fault that this inestimable gift is deplorably abused by less than one per cent of the poor? (*He turns again to the table; signs the cheque; and crosses it.*)

Mrs Baines. Barbara: will there be less drinking or more if all those poor souls we are saving come tomorrow and find the doors of our shelters shut in their faces? Lord Saxmundham gives us the money to stop drinking—to take his own business from him.

Cusins (impishly). Pure self-sacrifice on Bodger's part, clearly! Bless dear Bodger! (*Barbara almost breaks down as Adolphus, too, fails her.*)

Undershaft (tearing out the cheque and pocketing the book as he rises and goes past Cusins to Mrs Baines). I also, Mrs Baines, may claim a little disinterestedness. Think of my business! think of the widows and orphans! the men and lads torn to pieces with shrapnel and poisoned with lyddite! (*Mrs Baines shrinks; but he goes on remorselessly*) the oceans of blood, not one drop of which is shed in a really just cause! the ravaged crops! the peaceful peasants forced, women and men, to till their fields under the fire of opposing armies on pain of starvation! the bad blood of the fierce little cowards at home who egg on others to fight for the gratification of their national vanity! All this makes money for me: I am never richer, never busier than when the papers are full of it. Well, it is your work to preach peace on earth and good will to men. (*Mrs Baines's face lights up again.*) Every convert you make is a vote against war. (*Her lips move in prayer.*) Yet I give you this money to help you to hasten my own commercial ruin. (*He gives her the cheque.*)

Cusins (*mounting the form in an ecstasy of mischief*). The millennium will be inaugurated by the unselfishness of Undershaft and Bodger. Oh be joyful! (*He takes the drum-sticks from his pocket and flourishes them.*)

Mrs Baines (*taking the cheque*). The longer I live the more proof I see that there is an Infinite Goodness that turns everything to the work of salvation sooner or later. Who would have thought that any good could have come out of war and drink? And yet their profits are brought today to the feet of salvation to do its blessed work. (*She is affected to tears.*)

Jenny (*running to Mrs Baines and throwing her arms round her*). Oh dear! how blessed, how glorious it all is!

Cusins (*in a convulsion of irony*). Let us seize this unspeakable moment. Let us march to the great meeting at once. Excuse me just an instant. (*He rushes into the shelter. Jenny takes her tambourine from the drum head.*)

Mrs Baines. Mr Undershaft: have you ever seen a thousand people fall on their knees with one impulse and pray? Come with us to the meeting. Barbara shall tell them that the Army is saved, and saved through you.

Cusins (*returning impetuously from the shelter with a flag and a trombone, and coming between Mrs Baines and Undershaft*). You shall carry the flag down the first street, Mrs Baines (*he gives her the flag*). Mr Undershaft is a gifted trombonist: he shall intone an Olympian diapason to the West Ham Salvation March. (*Aside to Undershaft, as he forces the trombone on him.*) Blow, Machiavelli, blow.

Undershaft (*aside to him, as he takes the trombone*). The trumpet in Zion! (*Cusins rushes to the drum, which he takes up and puts on. Undershaft continues, aloud.*) I will do my best. I could vamp a bass if I knew the tune.

Cusins. It is a wedding chorus from one of Donizetti's operas; but we have converted it. We convert everything to good here, including Bodger. You remember the chorus. 'For thee immense rejoicing—immenso giubilo—immenso giubilo.' (*With drum obbligato.*) Rum tum ti tum tum, tum tum ti ta—

Barbara. Dolly: you are breaking my heart.

Cusins. What is a broken heart more or less here? Dionysos Undershaft has descended. I am possessed.

Mrs Baines. Come, Barbara: I must have my dear Major to carry the flag with me.

Jenny. Yes, yes, Major darling.

Cusins (*snatches the tambourine out of Jenny's hand and mutely offers it to Barbara*).

Barbara (*coming forward a little as she puts the offer behind her with a shudder, whilst Cusins recklessly tosses the tambourine back to Jenny and goes to the gate*). I cant come.

Jenny. Not come!

Mrs Baines (*with tears in her eyes*). Barbara: do you think I am wrong to take the money?

Barbara (*impulsively going to her and kissing her*). No, no: God help you, dear, you must: you are saving the Army. Go; and may you have a great meeting!

Jenny. But arnt you coming?

Barbara. No. (*She begins taking off the silver S brooch from her collar.*)

Mrs Baines. Barbara: what are you doing?

Jenny. Why are you taking your badge off? You cant be going to leave us, Major.

Barbara (*quietly*). Father: come here.

Undershaft (*coming to her*). My dear! (*Seeing that she is going to pin the badge on his collar, he retreats to the penthouse in some alarm.*)

Barbara (*following him*). Dont be frightened. (*She pins the badge on and steps back towards the table, shewing him to the others.*) There! It's not much for £5000, is it?

Mrs Baines. Barbara: if you wont come and pray with us, promise me you will pray for us.

Barbara. I cant pray now. Perhaps I shall never pray again.

Mrs Baines. Barbara!

Jenny. Major!

Barbara (*almost delirious*). I cant bear any more. Quick march!

Cusins (*calling to the procession in the street outside*). Off we go. Play up, there! Immenso giubilo. (*He gives the time with his drum; and the band strikes up the march, which rapidly becomes more distant as the procession moves briskly away.*)

Mrs Baines. I must go, dear. Youre overworked: you will be all right tomorrow. We'll never lose you. Now Jenny: step out with the old flag. Blood and Fire! (*She marches out through the gate with her flag.*)

Jenny. Glory Hallelujah! (*flourishing her tambourine and marching.*)

Undershaft (*to Cusins, as he marches out past him easing the slide of his trombone*). 'My ducats and my daughter'!

Cusins (*following him out*). Money and gunpowder!

Barbara. Drunkenness and Murder! My God: why hast thou forsaken me?

She sinks on the form with her face buried in her hands. The march passes away into silence. Bill Walker steals across to her.

Bill (*taunting*). Wot prawce selvytion nah?

Shirley. Dont you hit her when she's down.

Bill. She it me wen aw wiz dahn. Waw shouldnt Aw git a bit o me aown beck?

Barbara (*raising her head*). I didnt take your money, Bill. (*She crosses the yard to the gate and turns her back on the two men to hide her face from them.*)

Bill (*sneering after her*). Naow, it warnt enaff for you. (*Turning to the drum, he misses the money.*) Ellow! If you aint took it sammun else ez. Weres it gorn? Bly me if Jenny Ill didnt tike it arter all!

Rummy (*screaming at him from the loft*). You lie, you dirty blackguard! Snobby Price pinched it off the drum when he took up his cap. I was up here all the time an see im do it.

Bill. Wot! Stowl maw manney! Waw didnt you call thief on him, you silly aold macker you?

Rummy. To serve you aht for ittin me acrost the fice. It's cost y'pahnd, that az. (*Raising a pœan of squalid triumph.*) I done you. I'm even with you. Uve ad it aht o y—(*Bill snatches up Shirley's mug and hurls it at her. She slams the loft door and vanishes. The mug smashes against the door and falls in fragments.*)

Bill (*beginning to chuckle*). Tell us, aol menn, wot o'clock this mawnin was it wen im as they call Snobby Prawce was sived?

Barbara (*turning to him more composedly, and with unspoiled sweetness*). About half past twelve, Bill. And he pinched your pound at a quarter to two. I know. Well, you cant afford to lose it. I'll send it to you.

Bill (*his voice and accent suddenly improving*). Not if Aw wiz to stawve for it. Aw aint to be bought.

Shirley. Aint you? Youd sell yourself to the devil for a pint o beer; only there aint no devil to make the offer.

Bill (*unashamed*). Sao Aw would, mite, and often ev, cheerful. But she cawnt baw me. (*Approaching Barbara.*) You wanted maw soul, did you? Well, you aint got it.

Barbara. I nearly got it, Bill. But weve sold it back to you for ten thousand pounds.

Shirley. And dear at the money!

Barbara. No, Peter: it was worth more than money.

Bill (*salvationproof*). It's nao good: you cawnt get rahnd me nah. Aw downt blieve in it; and Awve seen today that Aw was rawt. (*Going.*) Sao long, aol soupkitchener! Ta, ta, Mijor Earl's Grendorter! (*Turning at the gate.*) Wot prawce selvytion nah? Snobby Prawce! Ha! ha!

Barbara (*offering her hand*). Goodbye, Bill.

Bill (*taken aback, half plucks his cap off; then shoves it on again defiantly*). Get aht. (*Barbara drops her hand, discouraged. He has a twinge of remorse.*) But thets aw rawt, you knaow. Nathink pasnl. Naow mellice. Sao long, Judy. (*He goes.*)

Barbara. No malice. So long, Bill.

Shirley (*shaking his head*). You make too much of him, miss, in your innocence.

Barbara (*going to him*). Peter: I'm like you now. Cleaned out, and lost my job.

Shirley. Youve youth an hope. Thats two better than me.

Barbara. I'll get you a job, Peter. Thats hope for you: the youth will have to be enough for me. (*She counts her money.*) I have just enough left for two teas at Lockharts, a Rowton doss for you, and my tram and bus home. (*He frowns and rises with offended pride. She takes his arm.*) Dont be proud, Peter: it's sharing between friends. And promise me youll talk to me and not let me cry. (*She draws him towards the gate.*)

Shirley. Well, I'm not accustomed to talk to the like of you—

Barbara (*urgently*). Yes, yes: you must talk to me. Tell me about Tom Paine's books and Bradlaugh's lectures. Come along.

Shirley. Ah, if you would only read Tom Paine in the proper spirit, miss! (*They go out through the gate together.*)

ACT III

Next day after lunch Lady Britomart is writing in the library in Wilton Crescent. Sarah is reading in the armchair near the window. Barbara, in ordinary fashionable dress, pale and brooding, is on the settee. Charles Lomax enters. He starts on seeing Barbara fashionably attired and in low spirits.

Lomax. Youve left off your uniform!

Barbara says nothing; but an expression of pain passes over her face.

Lady Britomart (*warning him in low tones to be careful*). Charles!

Lomax (*much concerned, coming behind the settee and bending sympathetically over Barbara*). I'm awfully sorry, Barbara. You know I helped you all I could with the concertina and so forth. (*Momentously.*) Still, I have never shut my eyes to the fact that there is a certain amount of tosh about the Salvation Army. Now the claims of the Church of England—

Lady Britomart. Thats enough, Charles. Speak of something suited to your mental capacity.

Lomax. But surely the Church of England is suited to all our capacities.

Barbara (*pressing his hand*). Thank you for your sympathy, Cholly. Now go and spoon with Sarah.

Lomax (*dragging a chair from the writing table and seating himself affectionately by Sarah's side*). How is my ownest today?

Sarah. I wish you wouldnt tell Cholly to do things, Barbara. He always comes straight and does them. Cholly: we're going to the works this afternoon.

Lomax. What works?

Sarah. The cannon works.

Lomax. What? your governor's shop!

Sarah. Yes.

Lomax. Oh I say!

> *Cusins enters in poor condition. He also starts visibly when he sees Barbara without her uniform.*

Barbara. I expected you this morning, Dolly. Didnt you guess that?

Cusins (*sitting down beside her*). I'm sorry. I have only just breakfasted.

Sarah. But weve just finished lunch.

Barbara. Have you had one of your bad nights?

Cusins. No: I had rather a good night: in fact, one of the most remarkable nights I have ever passed.

Barbara. The meeting?

Cusins. No: after the meeting.

Lady Britomart. You should have gone to bed after the meeting. What were you doing?

Cusins. Drinking.

Lady Britomart.	Adolphus!
Sarah.	Dolly!
Barbara.	Dolly!
Lomax.	Oh I say!

Lady Britomart. What were you drinking, may I ask?

Cusins. A most devilish kind of Spanish burgundy, warranted free from added alcohol: a Temperance burgundy in fact. Its richness in natural alcohol made any addition superfluous.

Barbara. Are you joking, Dolly?

Cusins (*patiently*). No. I have been making a night of it with the nominal head of this household: that is all.

Lady Britomart. Andrew made you drunk!

Cusins. No: he only provided the wine. I think it was Dionysos who made me drunk. (*To Barbara.*) I told you I was possessed.

Lady Britomart. Youre not sober yet. Go home to bed at once.

Cusins. I have never before ventured to reproach you, Lady Brit; but how could you marry the Prince of Darkness?

Lady Britomart. It was much more excusable to marry him than to get drunk with him. That is a new accomplishment of Andrew's, by the way. He usent to drink.

Cusins. He doesnt now. He only sat there and completed the wreck of my moral basis, the rout of my convictions, the purchase of my soul. He cares for you, Barbara. That is what makes him so dangerous to me.

Barbara. That has nothing to do with it, Dolly. There are larger loves and diviner dreams than the fireside ones. You know that, dont you?

Cusins. Yes: that is our understanding. I know it. I hold to it. Unless he can win me on that holier ground he may amuse me for a while; but he can get no deeper hold, strong as he is.

Barbara. Keep to that; and the end will be right. Now tell me what happened at the meeting?

Cusins. It was an amazing meeting. Mrs Baines almost died of emotion. Jenny Hill simply gibbered with hysteria. The Prince of Darkness played his trombone like a madman: its brazen roarings were like the laughter of the damned. 117 conversions took place then and there. They prayed with the most touching sincerity and gratitude for Bodger, and for the anonymous donor of the £5000. Your father would not let his name be given.

Lomax. That was rather fine of the old man, you know. Most chaps would have wanted the advertisement.

Cusins. He said all the charitable institutions would be down on him like kites on a battle-field if he gave his name.

Lady Britomart. Thats Andrew all over. He never does a proper thing without giving an improper reason for it.

Cusins. He convinced me that I have all my life been doing improper things for proper reasons.

Lady Britomart. Adolphus: now that Barbara has left the Salvation Army, you had better leave it too. I will not have you playing that drum in the streets.

Cusins. Your orders are already obeyed, Lady Brit.

Barbara. Dolly: were you ever really in earnest about it? Would you have joined if you had never seen me?

Cusins (*disingenuously*). Well—er—well, possibly, as a collector of religions—

Lomax (*cunningly*). Not as a drummer, though, you know. You are a very clearheaded brainy chap, Dolly; and it must have been apparent to you that there is a certain amount of tosh about—

Lady Britomart. Charles: if you must drivel, drivel like a grown-up man and not like a schoolboy.

Lomax (*out of countenance*). Well, drivel is drivel, dont you know, whatever a man's age.

Lady Britomart. In good society in England, Charles, men drivel at all ages by repeating silly formulas with an air of wisdom. Schoolboys make their own formulas out of slang, like you. When they reach your age, and get political private secretaryships and things of that sort, they drop slang and get their formulas out of the Spectator or The Times. You had better confine yourself to The Times. You will find that there is a certain amount of tosh about The Times; but at least its language is reputable.

Lomax (*overwhelmed*). You are so awfully strong-minded, Lady Brit—

Lady Britomart. Rubbish! (*Morrison comes in.*) What is it?

Morrison. If you please, my lady, Mr Undershaft has just drove up to the door.

Lady Britomart. Well, let him in. (*Morrison hesitates.*) Whats the matter with you?

Morrison. Shall I announce him, my lady; or is he at home here, so to speak, my lady?

Lady Britomart. Announce him.

Morrison. Thank you, my lady. You wont mind my asking, I hope. The occasion is in a manner of speaking new to me.

Lady Britomart. Quite right. Go and let him in.

Morrison. Thank you, my lady. (*He withdraws.*)

Lady Britomart. Children: go and get ready. (*Sarah and Barbara go upstairs for their out-of-door wraps.*) Charles: go and tell Stephen to come down here in five minutes: you will find him in the drawing room. (*Charles goes.*) Adolphus: tell them to send round the carriage in about fifteen minutes. (*Adolphus goes.*)

Morrison (*at the door*). Mr Undershaft.

Undershaft comes in. Morrison goes out.

Undershaft. Alone! How fortunate!

Lady Britomart (*rising*). Dont be sentimental, Andrew. Sit down. (*She sits on the settee: he sits beside her, on her left. She comes to the point before he has time to breathe.*) Sarah must have £800 a year until Charles Lomax comes into his property. Barbara will need more, and need it permanently, because Adolphus hasnt any property.

Undershaft (*resignedly*). Yes, my dear: I will see to it. Anything else? for yourself, for instance?

Lady Britomart. I want to talk to you about Stephen.

Undershaft (*rather wearily*). Dont, my dear. Stephen doesnt interest me.

Lady Britomart. He does interest me. He is our son.

Undershaft. Do you really think so? He has induced us to bring him into the world; but he chose his parents very incongruously, I think. I see nothing of myself in him, and less of you.

Lady Britomart. Andrew: Stephen is an excellent son, and a most steady, capable, highminded young man. You are simply trying to find an excuse for disinheriting him.

Undershaft. My dear Biddy: the Undershaft tradition disinherits him. It would be dishonest of me to leave the cannon foundry to my son.

Lady Britomart. It would be most unnatural and improper of you to leave it to anyone else, Andrew. Do you suppose this wicked and immoral tradition can be kept up for ever? Do you pretend that Stephen could not carry on the foundry just as well as all the other sons of the big business houses?

Undershaft. Yes: he could learn the office routine without understanding the business, like all the other sons and the firm would go by its own momentum until the real Undershaft—probably an Italian or a German—would invent a new method and cut him out.

Lady Britomart. There is nothing that any Italian or German could do that Stephen could not do. And Stephen at least has breeding.

Undershaft. The son of a foundling! Nonsense!

Lady Britomart. My son, Andrew! And even you may have good blood in your veins for all you know.

Undershaft. True. Probably I have. That is another argument in favour of a foundling.

Lady Britomart. Andrew: dont be aggravating. And dont be wicked. At present you are both.

Undershaft. This conversation is part of the Undershaft tradition, Biddy. Every Undershaft's wife has treated him to it ever since the house was founded. It is mere waste of breath. If the tradition be ever broken it will be for an abler man than Stephen.

Lady Britomart (pouting). Then go away.

Undershaft (deprecatory). Go away!

Lady Britomart. Yes: go away. If you will do nothing for Stephen, you are not wanted here. Go to your foundling, whoever he is; and look after him.

Undershaft. The fact is, Biddy—

Lady Britomart. Dont call me Biddy. I dont call you Andy.

Undershaft. I will not call my wife Britomart: it is not good sense. Seriously, my love, the Undershaft tradition has landed me in a difficulty. I am getting on in years; and my partner Lazarus has at last made a stand and insisted that the succession must be settled one way or the other; and of course he is quite right. You see, I havent found a fit successor yet.

Lady Britomart (obstinately). There is Stephen.

Undershaft. Thats just it: all the foundlings I can find are exactly like Stephen.

Lady Britomart. Andrew!!

Undershaft. I want a man with no relations and no schooling: that is, a man who would be out of the running altogether if he were not a strong man. And I cant find him. Every blessed foundling nowadays is snapped up in his infancy by Barnardo homes, or School Board officers, or Boards of Guardians; and if he shews the least ability he is fastened on by schoolmasters; trained to win scholarships like a racehorse; crammed with secondhand ideas; drilled and disciplined in docility and what they call good taste; and lamed for life so that he is fit for nothing but teaching. If you want to keep the foundry in the family, you had better find an eligible foundling and marry him to Barbara.

Lady Britomart. Ah! Barbara! Your Pet! You would sacrifice Stephen to Barbara.

Undershaft. Cheerfully. And you, my dear, would boil Barbara to make soup for Stephen.

Lady Britomart. Andrew: this is not a question of our likings and dislikings: it is a question of duty. It is your duty to make Stephen your successor.

Undershaft. Just as much as it is your duty to submit to your husband. Come, Biddy! these tricks of the governing class are of no use with me. I am one of the governing class myself; and it is waste of time giving tracts to a missionary. I have the power in this matter; and I am not to be hum-bugged into using it for your purposes.

Lady Britomart. Andrew: you can talk my head off; but you cant change wrong into right. And your tie is all on one side. Put it straight.

Undershaft (*disconcerted*). It wont stay unless it's pinned (*he fumbles at it with childish grimaces*)—

Stephen comes in.

Stephen (*at the door*). I beg your pardon (*about to retire*).

Lady Britomart. No: come in, Stephen. (*Stephen comes forward to his mother's writing table.*)

Undershaft (*not very cordially*). Good afternoon.

Stephen (*coldly*). Good afternoon.

Undershaft (*to Lady Britomart*). He knows all about the tradition, I suppose?

Lady Britomart. Yes. (*To Stephen.*) It is what I told you last night, Stephen.

Undershaft (*sulkily*). I understand you want to come into the cannon business.

Stephen. I go into trade! Certainly not.

Undershaft (*opening his eyes, greatly eased in mind and manner*). Oh! in that case—

Lady Britomart. Cannons are not trade, Stephen. They are enterprise.

Stephen. I have no intention of becoming a man of business in any sense. I have no capacity for business and no taste for it. I intend to devote myself to politics.

Undershaft (*rising*). My dear boy: this is an immense relief to me. And I trust it may prove an equally good thing for the country. I was afraid you would consider yourself disparaged and slighted. (*He moves towards Stephen as if to shake hands with him.*)

Lady Britomart (*rising and interposing*). Stephen: I cannot allow you to throw away an enormous property like this.

Stephen (*stiffly*). Mother: there must be an end of treating me as a child, if you please. (*Lady Britomart recoils, deeply wounded by his tone.*) Until last night I did not take your attitude seriously, because I did not think you meant it seriously. But I find now that you left me in the dark as to matters which you should have explained to me years ago. I am extremely hurt and offended. Any further discussion of my intentions had better take place with my father, as between one man and another.

Lady Britomart. Stephen! (*She sits down again, her eyes filling with tears.*)

Undershaft (*with grave compassion*). You see, my dear, it is only the big men who can be treated as children.

Stephen. I am sorry, mother, that you have forced me—

Undershaft (*stopping him*). Yes, yes, yes, yes: thats all right, Stephen. She wont interfere with you any more: your independence is achieved: you have won your latchkey. Dont rub it in; and above all, dont apologize. (*He resumes his seat.*) Now what about your future, as between one man and another—I beg your pardon, Biddy: as between two men and a woman.

Lady Britomart (*who has pulled herself together strongly*). I quite understand, Stephen. By all means go your own way if you feel strong enough. (*Stephen sits down magisterially in the chair at the writing table with an air of affirming his majority.*)

Undershaft. It is settled that you do not ask for the succession to the cannon business.

Stephen. I hope it is settled that I repudiate the cannon business.

Undershaft. Come, come! dont be so devilishly sulky: it's boyish. Freedom should be generous. Besides, I owe you a fair start in life in exchange for disinheriting you. You cant become prime minister all at once. Havnt you a turn for something? What about literature, art, and so forth?

Stephen. I have nothing of the artist about me, either in faculty or character, thank Heaven!

Undershaft. A philosopher, perhaps? Eh?

Stephen. I make no such ridiculous pretension.

Undershaft. Just so. Well, there is the army, the navy, the Church, the Bar. The Bar requires some ability. What about the Bar?

Stephen. I have not studied law. And I am afraid I have not the necessary push—I believe that is the name barristers give to their vulgarity—for success in pleading.

Undershaft. Rather a difficult case, Stephen. Hardly anything left but the stage, is there? (*Stephen makes an impatient movement.*) Well, come! is there anything you know or care for?

Stephen (*rising and looking at him steadily*). I know the difference between right and wrong.

Undershaft (*hugely tickled*). You dont say so! What! no capacity for business, no knowledge of law, no sympathy with art, no pretension to philosophy; only a simple knowledge of the secret that has puzzled all the philosophers, baffled all the lawyers, muddled all the men of business, and ruined most of the artists: the secret of right and wrong. Why, man, youre a genius, a master of masters, a god! At twentyfour, too!

Stephen (*keeping his temper with difficulty*). You are pleased to be facetious. I pretend to nothing more than any honorable English gentleman claims as his birthright (*he sits down angrily*).

Undershaft. Oh, thats everybody's birthright. Look at poor little Jenny Hill, the Salvation lassie! she would think you were laughing at her if you asked her to stand up in the street and teach grammar or geography or mathematics or even drawing room dancing; but it never occurs to her to doubt that she can teach morals and religion. You are all alike, you respectable people. You cant tell me the bursting strain of a ten-inch gun, which is a very simple matter; but you all think you can tell me the bursting strain of a man under temptation. You darent handle high explosives; but youre all ready to handle honesty and truth and justice and the whole duty of man, and kill one another at that game. What a country! What a world!

Lady Britomart (*uneasily*). What do you think he had better do, Andrew?

Undershaft. Oh, just what he wants to do. He knows nothing and he thinks he knows everything. That points clearly to a political career. Get him a private secretaryship to someone who can get him an Under Secretaryship; and then leave him alone. He will find his natural and proper place in the end on the Treasury Bench.

Stephen (*springing up again*). I am sorry, sir, that you force me to forget the respect due to you as my father. I am an Englishman, and I will not hear the Government of my country insulted. (*He thrusts his hands in his pockets, and walks angrily across to the window.*)

Undershaft (*with a touch of brutality*). The government of your country! I am the government of your country: I, and Lazarus. Do you suppose that you and half a dozen amateurs like you, sitting in a row in that foolish gabble shop, can govern Undershaft and Lazarus? No, my friend: you will do what pays us. You will make war when it suits us, and keep peace when it doesnt. You will find out that trade requires certain measures when we have decided on those measures. When I want anything to keep my dividends up, you will discover that my want is a national need. When other people want something to keep my dividends down, you will call out the police and military. And in return you shall have the support and applause of my newspapers, and the delight of imagining that you are a great statesman. Government of your country! Be off with you, my boy, and play with your caucuses and leading articles and historic parties and great leaders and burning questions and the rest of your toys. I am going back to my counting-house to pay the piper and call the tune.

Stephen (*actually smiling, and putting his hand on his father's shoulder with indulgent patronage*). Really, my dear father, it is impossible to be angry with you. You dont know how absurd all this sounds to me. You are very properly proud of having been industrious enough to make money; and it is greatly to your credit that you have made so much of it. But it has kept you in circles where you are valued for your money and deferred to for it, instead of in the doubtless very old-fashioned and behind-the-times public school and university where I formed my habits of mind. It is natural for you to think that money governs England; but you must allow me to think I know better.

Undershaft. And what does govern England, pray?

Stephen. Character, father, character.

Undershaft. Whose character? Yours or mine?

Stephen. Neither yours nor mine, father, but the best elements in the English national character.

Undershaft. Stephen: Ive found your profession for you. Youre a born journalist. I'll start you with a high-toned weekly review. There!

Before Stephen can reply Sarah, Barbara, Lomax, and Cusins come in ready for walking. Barbara crosses the room to the window and looks out. Cusins drifts amiably to the armchair. Lomax remains near the door, whilst Sarah comes to her mother.

Stephen goes to the smaller writing table and busies himself with his letters.

Sarah. Go and get ready, mamma: the carriage is waiting. (*Lady Britomart leaves the room.*)

Undershaft (*to Sarah*). Good day, my dear. Good afternoon, Mr Lomax.

Lomax (*vaguely*). Ahdedoo.

Undershaft (*to Cusins*). Quite well after last night, Euripides, eh?

Cusins. As well as can be expected.

Undershaft. Thats right. (*To Barbara.*) So you are coming to see my death and devastation factory, Barbara?

Barbara (*at the window*). You came yesterday to see my salvation factory. I promised you a return visit.

Lomax (*coming forward between Sarah and Undershaft*). Youll find it awfully interesting. Ive been through the Woolwich Arsenal and it gives you a ripping feeling of security, you know, to think of the lot of beggars we could kill if it came to fighting. (*To Undershaft, with sudden solemnity.*) Still, it must be rather an awful reflection for you, from the religious point of view as it were. Youre getting on, you know, and all that.

Sarah. You dont mind Cholly's imbecility, papa, do you?

Lomax (*much taken aback*). Oh I say!

Undershaft. Mr Lomax looks at the matter in a very proper spirit, my dear.

Lomax. Just so. Thats all I meant, I assure you.

Sarah. Are you coming, Stephen?

Stephen. Well, I am rather busy—er—(*Magnanimously.*) Oh well, yes: I'll come. That is, if there is room for me.

Undershaft. I can take two with me in a little motor I am experimenting with for field use. You wont mind its being rather unfashionable. It's not painted yet; but it's bullet proof.

Lomax (*appalled at the prospect of confronting Wilton Crescent in an unpainted motor*). Oh I say!

Sarah. The carriage for me, thank you. Barbara doesnt mind what she's seen in.

Lomax. I say, Dolly, old chap: do you really mind the car being a guy? Because of course if you do I'll go in it. Still—

Cusins. I prefer it.

Lomax. Thanks awfully, old man. Come, my ownest. (*He hurries out to secure his seat in the carriage. Sarah follows him.*)

Cusins (*moodily walking across to Lady Britomart's writing table*). Why are we two coming to this Works Department of Hell? that is what I ask myself.

Barbara. I have always thought of it as a sort of pit where lost creatures with blackened faces stirred up smoky fires and were driven and tormented by my father? Is it like that, dad?

Undershaft (*scandalized*). My dear! It is a spotlessly clean and beautiful hillside town.

Cusins. With a Methodist chapel? Oh do say theres a Methodist chapel.

Undershaft. There are two: a Primitive one and a sophisticated one. There is even an Ethical Society but it is not much patronized, as my men are all strongly religious. In the High Explosives Sheds they object to the presence of Agnostics as unsafe.

Cusins. And yet they dont object to you!

Barbara. Do they obey all your orders?

Undershaft. I never give them any orders. When I speak to one of them it is 'Well, Jones, is the baby doing well? and has Mrs Jones made a good recovery?' 'Nicely, thank you, sir.' And thats all.

Cusins. But Jones has to be kept in order. How do you maintain discipline among your men?

Undershaft. I dont. They do. You see, the one thing Jones wont stand is any rebellion from the man under him, or any assertion of social equality between the wife of the man with 4 shillings a week less than himself, and Mrs Jones! Of course they all rebel against me, theoretically. Practically, every man of them keeps the man just below him in his place. I never meddle with them. I never bully them. I dont even bully Lazarus. I say that certain things are to be done; but I dont order anybody to do them. I dont say, mind you, that there is no ordering about and snubbing and even bullying. The men snub the boys and order them about; the carmen snub the sweepers; the artisans snub the unskilled laborers; the foremen drive and bully both the laborers and artisans; the assistant engineers find fault with the foremen; the chief engineers drop on the assistants; the departmental managers worry the chiefs; and the clerks have tall hats and hymnbooks and keep up the social tone by refusing to associate on equal terms with anybody. The result is a colossal profit, which comes to me.

Cusins (*revolted*). You really are a—well, what I was saying yesterday.

Barbara. What was he saying yesterday?

Undershaft. Never mind, my dear. He thinks I have made you unhappy. Have I?

Barbara. Do you think I can be happy in this vulgar silly dress? I! who have worn the uniform. Do you understand what you have done to me? Yesterday I had a man's soul in my hand. I set him in the way of life with his face to salvation. But when we took your money he turned back to drunkenness and derision. (*With intense conviction.*) I will never forgive you that. If I had a child, and you destroyed its body with your explosives—if you murdered Dolly with your horrible guns—I could forgive you if my forgiveness would open the gates of heaven to you. But to take a human soul from me, and turn it into the soul of a wolf! that is worse than any murder.

Undershaft. Does my daughter despair so easily? Can you strike a man to the heart and leave no mark on him?

Barbara (*her face lighting up*). Oh, you are right: he can never be lost now: where was my faith?

Cusins. Oh, clever clever devil!

Barbara. You may be a devil; but God speaks through you sometimes. (*She takes her father's hands and kisses them.*) You have given me back my happiness: I feel it deep down now, though my spirit is troubled.

Undershaft. You have learnt something. That always feels at first as if you had lost something.

Barbara. Well, take me to the factory of death; and let me learn something more. There must be some truth or other behind all this frightful irony. Come, Dolly. (*She goes out.*)

Cusins. My guardian angel! (*To Undershaft.*) Avaunt! (*He follows Barbara.*)

Stephen (*quietly, at the writing table*). You must not mind Cusins, father. He is a very amiable good fellow; but he is a Greek scholar and naturally a little eccentric.

Undershaft. Ah, quite so, Thank you, Stephen. Thank you. (*He goes out.*)

Stephen smiles patronizingly; buttons his coat responsibly; and crosses the room to the door. Lady Britomart, dressed for out-of doors, opens it before he reaches it. She looks round for others looks at Stephen and turns to go without a word.

Stephen (*embarrassed*). Mother—

Lady Britomart. Dont be apologetic, Stephen. And dont forget tha you have outgrown your mother. (*She goes out.*)

Perivale St Andrews lies between two Middlesex hills, half climb ing the northern one. It is an almost smokeless town of white walls, roofs of narrow green slates or red tiles, tall trees, domes campaniles, and slender chimney shafts, beautifully situated and beautiful in itself. The best view of it is obtained from the cres of a slope about half a mile to the east, where the high explosive are dealt with. The foundry lies hidden in the depths between the tops of its chimneys sprouting like huge skittles into the middle distance. Across the crest runs an emplacement of con crete, with a firestep, and a parapet which suggests a fortification, because there is a huge cannon of the obsolete Woolwich Infant pattern peering across it at the town. The cannon is mounted on an experimental gun carriage: possibly the original model of the Undershaft disappearing rampart gun alluded to by Stephen The firestep, being a convenient place to sit, is furnished here and there with straw disc cushions; and at one place there is the additional luxury of a fur rug.

Barbara is standing on the firestep, looking over the parapet towards the town. On her right is the cannon; on her left the end of a shed raised on piles, with a ladder of three or four steps up to the door, which opens outwards and has a little wooden landing at the threshold, with a fire bucket in the corner of the landing. Several dummy soldiers more or less mutilated, with straw protruding from their gashes, have been shoved out of the way under the landing. A few others are nearly upright against the shed; and one has fallen forward and lies, like a grotesque corpse, on the emplacement. The parapet stops short of the shed, leaving a gap which is the beginning of the path down the hill through the foundry to the town. The rug is on the firestep near this gap. Down on the emplacement behind the cannon is a trolley carrying a huge conical bombshell with a red band painted on it. Further to the right is the door of an office, which, like the sheds, is of the lightest possible construction.

Cusins arrives by the path from the town.

Barbara. Well?

Cusins. Not a ray of hope. Everything perfect! wonderful! real! It only needs a cathedral to be a heavenly city instead of a hellish one.

Barbara. Have you found out whether they have done anything for old Peter Shirley?

Cusins. They have found him a job as gatekeeper and timekeeper. He's frightfully miserable. He calls the time-keeping brainwork, and says he isnt used to it; and his gate lodge is so splendid that he's ashamed to use the rooms, and skulks in the scullery.

Barbara. Poor Peter!

Stephen arrives from the town. He carries a fieldglass.

Stephen (enthusiastically). Have you two seen the place? Why did you leave us?

Cusins. I wanted to see everything I was not intended to see; and Barbara wanted to make the men talk.

Stephen. Have you found anything discreditable?

Cusins. No. They call him Dandy Andy and are proud of his being a cunning old rascal; but it's all horribly, frightfully, immorally, unanswerably perfect.

Sarah arrives.

Sarah. Heavens! what a place! (*She crosses to the trolley.*) Did you see the nursing home? (*She sits down on the shell.*)

Stephen. Did you see the libraries and schools?

Sarah. Did you see the ball room and the banqueting chamber in the Town Hall!?

Stephen. Have you gone into the insurance fund, the pension fund, the building society, the various applications of cooperation!?

Undershaft comes from the office, with a sheaf of telegrams in his hand.

Undershaft. Well, have you seen everything? I'm sorry I was called away. (*Indicating the telegrams.*) Good news from Manchuria.

Stephen. Another Japanese victory?

Undershaft. Oh, I dont know. Which side wins does not concern us here. No: the good news is that the aerial battleship is a tremendous success. At the first trial it has wiped out a fort with three hundred soldiers in it.

Cusins (from the platform). Dummy soldiers?

Undershaft (striding across to Stephen and kicking the prostrate dummy brutally out of his way). No: the real thing.

Cusins and Barbara exchange glances. Then Cusins sits on the step and buries his face in his hands. Barbara gravely lays her hand on his shoulder. He looks up at her in whimsical desperation.

Undershaft. Well, Stephen, what do you think of the place?

Stephen. Oh, magnificent. A perfect triumph of modern industry. Frankly, my dear father, I have been a fool: I had no idea of what it all meant: of the wonderful forethought, the power of organization, the administrative capacity, the financial genius, the colossal capital it represents. I have been repeating to myself as I came through your streets 'Peace hath her victories no less renowned than War.' I have only one misgiving about it all.

Undershaft. Out with it.

Stephen. Well, I cannot help thinking that all this provision for every want of your workmen may sap their independence and weaken their sense of responsibility. And greatly as we enjoyed our tea at that splendid restaurant—how they gave us all that luxury and cake and jam and cream for threepence I really cannot imagine!—still you must remember that restaurants break up home life. Look at the continent, for instance! Are you sure so much pampering is really good for the men's characters?

Undershaft. Well you see, my dear boy, when you are organizing civilization you have to make up your mind whether trouble and anxiety are good things or not. If you decide that they are, then, I take it, you simply dont organize civilization; and there you are with trouble and anxiety enough to make us all angels! But if you decide the other way, you may as well go through with it. However, Stephen, our characters are safe here. A sufficient dose of anxiety is always provided by the fact that we may be blown to smithereens at any moment.

Sarah. By the way, papa, where do you make the explosives?

Undershaft. In separate little sheds like that one. When one of them blows up, it costs very little; and only the people quite close to it are killed.

Stephen, who is quite close to it, looks at it rather scaredly, and moves away quickly to the cannon. At the same moment the door of the shed is thrown abruptly open; and a foreman in overalls and list slippers comes out on the little landing and holds the door for Lomax, who appears in the doorway.

Lomax (with studied coolness). My good fellow: you neednt get into a state of nerves. Nothing's going to happen to you; and I suppose it wouldnt be the end of the world if anything did. A little bit of British pluck is what you want, old chap. (*He descends and strolls across to Sarah.*)

Undershaft (to the foreman). Anything wrong, Bilton?

Bilton (with ironic calm). Gentleman walked into the high explosives shed and lit a cigaret, sir: thats all.

Undershaft. Ah, quite so. (*Going over to Lomax.*) Do you happen to remember what you did with the match?

Lomax. Oh come! I'm not a fool. I took jolly good care to blow it out before I chucked it away.

Bilton. The top of it was red hot inside, sir.

Lomax. Well, suppose it was! I didnt chuck it into any of your messes.

Undershaft. Think no more of it, Mr Lomax. By the way, would you mind lending me your matches.

Lomax (*offering his box*). Certainly.

Undershaft. Thanks. (*He pockets the matches.*)

Lomax (*lecturing to the company generally*). You know, these high explosives dont go off like gunpowder, except when theyre in a gun. When theyre spread loose, you can put a match to them without the least risk: they just burn quietly like a bit of paper. (*Warming to the scientific interest of the subject.*) Did you know that, Undershaft? Have you ever tried?

Undershaft. Not on a large scale, Mr Lomax. Bilton will give you a sample of gun cotton when you are leaving if you ask him. You can experiment with it at home. (*Bilton looks puzzled.*)

Sarah. Bilton will do nothing of the sort, papa. I suppose it's your business to blow up the Russians and Japs; but you might really stop short of blowing up poor Cholly. (*Bilton gives it up and retires into the shed.*)

Lomax. My ownest, there is no danger. (*He sits beside her on the shell.*)

Lady Britomart arrives from the town with a bouquet.

Lady Britomart (*impetuously*). Andrew: you shouldnt have let me see this place.

Undershaft. Why, my dear?

Lady Britomart. Never mind why: you shouldnt have: thats all. To think of all that (*indicating the town*) being yours! and that you have kept it to yourself all these years!

Undershaft. It does not belong to me. I belong to it. It is the Undershaft inheritance.

Lady Britomart. It is not. Your ridiculous cannons and that noisy banging foundry may be the Undershaft inheritance; but all that plate and linen, all that furniture and those houses and orchards and gardens belong to us. They belong to me: they are not a man's business. I wont give them up. You must be out of your senses to throw them all away; and if you persist in such folly, I will call in a doctor.

Undershaft (*stooping to smell the bouquet*). Where did you get the flowers, my dear?

Lady Britomart. Your men presented them to me in your William Morris Labor Church.

Cusins. Oh! It needed only that. A Labor Church! (*he mounts the firestep distractedly, and leans with his elbows on the parapet, turning his back to them.*)

Lady Britomart. Yes, with Morris's words in mosaic letters ten feet high round the dome. NO MAN IS GOOD ENOUGH TO BE ANOTHER MAN'S MASTER. The cynicism of it!

Undershaft. It shocked the men at first, I am afraid. But now they take no more notice of it than of the ten commandments in church.

Lady Britomart. Andrew: you are trying to put me off the subject of the inheritance by profane jokes. Well, you shant. I dont ask it any longer for Stephen: he has inherited far too much of your perversity to be fit for it. But Barbara has rights as well as Stephen. Why should not Adolphus succeed to the inheritance? I could manage the town for him and he can look after the cannons, if they are really necessary.

Undershaft. I should ask nothing better if Adolphus were a foundling. He is exactly the sort of new blood that is wanted in English business. But he's not a foundling; and theres an end of it. (*He makes for the office door.*)

Cusins (*turning to them*). Not quite. (*They all turn and stare at him.*) I think—Mind! I am not committing myself in any way as to my future course—but I think the foundling difficulty can be got over. (*He jumps down to the emplacement.*)

Undershaft (*coming back to him*). What do you mean?

Cusins. Well, I have something to say which is in the nature of a confession.

Sarah.

Lady Britomart.

Barbara.   }Confession!

Stephen.

Lomax. Oh I say! }

Cusins. Yes, a confession. Listen, all. Until I met Barbara I thought myself in the main an honorable, truthful man, because I wanted the approval of my conscience more than I wanted anything else. But the moment I saw Barbara, I wanted her far more than the approval of my conscience.

Lady Britomart. Adolphus!

Cusins. It is true. You accused me yourself, Lady Brit, of joining the Army to worship Barbara; and so I did. She bought my soul like a flower at a street corner; but she bought it for herself.

Undershaft. What! Not for Dionysos or another?

Cusins. Dionysos and all the others are in herself. I adored what was divine in her, and was therefore a true worshipper. But I was romantic about her too. I thought she was a woman of the people, and that a marriage with a professor of Greek would be far beyond the wildest social ambitions of her rank.

Lady Britomart. Adolphus!!

Lomax. Oh I say!!!

Cusins. When I learnt the horrible truth—

Lady Britomart. What do you mean by the horrible truth, pray?

Cusins. That she was enormously rich; that her grandfather was an earl; that her father was the Prince of Darkness—

Undershaft. Chut!

Cusins. —and that I was only an adventurer trying to catch a rich wife, then I stooped to deceive her about my birth.

Barbara (*rising*). Dolly!

Lady Britomart. Your birth! Now Adolphus, dont dare to make up a wicked story for the sake of these wretched cannons. Remember: I have seen photographs of your parents; and the Agent General for South Western Australia knows them personally and has assured me that they are most respectable married people.

Cusins. So they are in Australia; but here they are outcasts. Their marriage is legal in Australia, but not in England. My mother is my father's deceased wife's sister; and in this island I am consequently a foundling. (*Sensation.*)

Barbara. Silly! (*She climbs to the cannon, and leans, listening, in the angle it makes with the parapet.*)

Cusins. Is the subterfuge good enough, Machiavelli?

Undershaft (*thoughtfully*). Biddy: this may be a way out of the difficulty.

Lady Britomart. Stuff! A man cant make cannons any the better for being his own cousin instead of his proper self (*she sits down on the rug with a bounce that expresses her downright contempt for their casuistry*).

Undershaft (*to Cusins*). You are an educated man. That is against the tradition.

Cusins. Once in ten thousand times it happens that the schoolboy is a born master of what they try to teach him. Greek has not destroyed my mind: it has nourished it. Besides, I did not learn it at an English public school.

Undershaft. Hm! Well, I cannot afford to be too particular: you have cornered the foundling market. Let it pass. You are eligible, Euripides: you are eligible.

Barbara. Dolly: yesterday morning, when Stephen told us all about the tradition, you became very silent, and you have been strange and excited ever since. Were you thinking of your birth then?

Cusins. When the finger of Destiny suddenly points at a man in the middle of his breakfast, it makes him thoughtful.

Undershaft. Aha! You have had your eye on the business, my young friend, have you?

Cusins. Take care! There is an abyss of moral horror between me and your accursed aerial battleships.

Undershaft. Never mind the abyss for the present. Let us settle the practical details and leave your final decision open. You know that you will have to change your name. Do you object to that?

Cusins. Would any man named Adolphus—any man called Dolly!— object to be called something else?

Undershaft. Good. Now, as to money! I propose to treat you handsomely from the beginning. You shall start at a thousand a year.

Cusins (*with sudden heat, his spectacles twinkling with mischief*). A thousand! You dare offer a miserable thousand to the son-in-law of a millionaire! No, by Heavens, Machiavelli! you shall not cheat me. You cannot do without me; and I can do without you I must have two thousand five hundred a year for two years At the end of that time, if I am a failure, I go. But if I am a success, and stay on, you must give me the other five thousand

Undershaft. What other five thousand?

Cusins. To make the two years up to five thousand a year. The two thousand five hundred is only half pay in case I should turn out a failure. The third year I must have ten per cent on the profits.

Undershaft (*taken aback*). Ten per cent! Why, man, do you know what my profits are?

Cusins. Enormous, I hope: otherwise I shall require twenty-five per cent.

Undershaft. But, Mr Cusins, this is a serious matter of business. You are not bringing any capital into the concern.

Cusins. What! no capital! Is my mastery of Greek no capital? Is my access to the subtlest thought, the loftiest poetry yet attained by humanity, no capital? My character! my intellect! my life! my career! what Barbara calls my soul! are these no capital? Say another word; and I double my salary.

Undershaft. Be reasonable—

Cusins (*peremptorily*). Mr Undershaft: you have my terms. Take them or leave them.

Undershaft (*recovering himself*). Very well. I note your terms; and I offer you half.

Cusins (*disgusted*). Half!

Undershaft (*firmly*). Half.

Cusins. You call yourself a gentleman; and you offer me half!!

Undershaft. I do not call myself a gentleman but I offer you half.

Cusins. This to your future partner! your successor! your son-in-law!

Barbara. You are selling your own soul, Dolly, not mine. Leave me out of the bargain, please.

Undershaft. Come! I will go a step further for Barbara's sake. I will give you three fifths; but that is my last word.

Cusins. Done!

Lomax. Done in the eye! Why, *I* get only eight hundred, you know.

Cusins. By the way, Mac, I am a classical scholar, not an arithmetical one. Is three fifths more than half or less?

Undershaft. More, of course.

Cusins. I would have taken two hundred and fifty. How you can succeed in business when you are willing to pay all that money to a University don who is obviously not worth a junior clerk's wages!—well! What will Lazarus say?

Undershaft. Lazarus is a gentle romantic Jew who cares for nothing but string quartets and stalls at fashionable theatres. He will be blamed for your rapacity in money matters, poor fellow! as he has hitherto been blamed for mine. You are a shark of the first order, Euripides. So much the better for the firm!

Barbara. Is the bargain closed, Dolly? Does your soul belong to him now?

Cusins. No: the price is settled: that is all. The real tug of war is still to come. What about the moral question?

Lady Britomart. There is no moral question in the matter at all, Adolphus. You must simply sell cannons and weapons to people whose cause is right and just, and refuse them to foreigners and criminals.

Undershaft (*determinedly*). No: none of that. You must keep the true faith of an Armorer, or you dont come in here.

Cusins. What on earth is the true faith of an Armorer?

Undershaft. To give arms to all men who offer an honest price for them, without respect of persons or principles: to aristocrat and republican, to Nihilist and Tsar, to Capitalist and Socialist, to Protestant and Catholic, to burglar and policeman, to black man, white man and yellow man, to all sorts and conditions, all nationalities, all faiths, all follies, all causes and all crimes. The first Undershaft wrote up in his shop IF GOD GAVE THE HAND, LET NOT MAN WITHHOLD THE SWORD. The second wrote up ALL HAVE THE RIGHT TO FIGHT: NONE HAVE THE RIGHT TO JUDGE. The third wrote up TO MAN THE WEAPON: TO HEAVEN THE VICTORY. The fourth had no literary turn; so he did not write up anything; but he sold cannons to Napoleon under the nose of George the Third. The fifth wrote up PEACE SHALL NOT PREVAIL SAVE WITH A SWORD IN HER HAND. The sixth, my master, was the best of all. He wrote up NOTHING IS EVER DONE IN THIS WORLD UNTIL MEN ARE PRE-PARED TO KILL ONE ANOTHER IF IT IS NOT DONE. After that, there was nothing left for the seventh to say. So he wrote up, simply, UNASHAMED.

Cusins. My good Machiavelli. I shall certainly write something up on the wall; only, as I shall write it in Greek, you wont be able to read it. But as to your Armorer's faith, if I take my neck out of the noose of my own morality I am not going to put it into the noose of yours. I shall sell cannons to whom I please and refuse them to whom I please. So there!

Undershaft. From the moment when you become Andrew Undershaft, you will never do as you please again. Dont come here lusting for power, young man.

Cusins. If power were my aim I should not come here for it. You have no power.

Undershaft. None of my own, certainly.

Cusins. I have more power than you, more will. You do not drive this place: it drives you. And what drives the place?

Undershaft (*enigmatically*). A will of which I am a part.

Barbara (*startled*). Father! Do you know what you are saying; or are you laying a snare for my soul?

Cusins. Dont listen to his metaphysics, Barbara. The place is driven by the most rascally part of society, the money hunters, the pleasure hunters, the military promotion hunters; and he is their slave.

Undershaft. Not necessarily. Remember the Armorer's Faith. I will take an order from a good man as cheerfully as from a bad one. If you good people prefer preaching and shirking to buying my weapons and fighting the rascals, dont blame me. I can make cannons: I cannot make courage and conviction. Bah! you tire me, Euripides, with your morality mongering. Ask Barbara: she understands. (*He suddenly reaches up and takes Barbara's hands, looking powerfully into her eyes.*) Tell him, my love, what power really means.

Barbara (*hypnotized*). Before I joined the Salvation Army, I was in my own power and the consequence was that I never knew what to do with myself. When I joined it, I had not time enough for all the things I had to do.

Undershaft (*approvingly*). Just so. And why was that, do you suppose?

Barbara. Yesterday I should have said, because I was in the power of God. (*She resumes her self-possession, withdrawing her hands from his with a power equal to his own.*) But you came and shewed me that I was in the power of Bodger and Undershaft. Today I feel—oh! how can I put it into words? Sarah: do you remember the earthquake at Cannes, when we were little children? —how little the surprise of the first shock mattered compared to the dread and horror of waiting for the second? That is how I feel in this place today. I stood on the rock I thought eternal; and without a word of warning it reeled and crumbled under me. I was safe with an infinite wisdom watching me, an army marching to Salvation with me; and in a moment, at a stroke of your pen in a cheque book, I stood alone; and the heavens were empty. That was the first shock of the earthquake: I am waiting for the second.

Undershaft. Come, come, my daughter! dont make too much of your little tinpot tragedy. What do we do here when we spend years of work and thought and thousands of pounds of solid cash on a new gun or an aerial battleship that turns out just a hairsbreadth wrong after all? Scrap it. Scrap it without wasting another hour or another pound on it. Well, you have made for yourself something that you call a morality or a religion or what not. It doesnt fit the facts. Well, scrap it. Scrap it and get one that does fit. That is what is wrong with the world at present. It scraps its obsolete steam engines and dynamos; but it wont scrap its old prejudices and its old moralities and its old religions and its old political constitutions. Whats the result? In machinery it does very well; but in morals and religion and politics it is working at a loss that brings it nearer bankruptcy every year. Dont persist in that folly. If your old religion broke down yesterday, get a newer and a better one for tomorrow.

Barbara. Oh how gladly I would take a better one to my soul! But you offer me a worse one. (*Turning on him with sudden vehemence.*) Justify yourself: shew me some light through the darkness of this dreadful place, with its beautifully clean workshops, and respectable workmen, and model homes.

Undershaft. Cleanliness and respectability do not need justification, Barbara: they justify themselves. I see no darkness here, no dreadfulness. In your Salvation shelter I saw poverty, misery, cold and hunger. You gave them bread and treacle and dreams of heaven. I give from thirty shillings a week to twelve thousand a year. They find their own dreams but I look after the drainage.

Barbara. And their souls?

Undershaft. I save their souls just as I saved yours.

Barbara (revolted). You saved my soul! What do you mean?

Undershaft. I fed you and clothed you and housed you. I took care that you should have money enough to live handsomely—more than enough; so that you could be wasteful, careless, generous. That saved your soul from the seven deadly sins.

Barbara (bewildered). The seven deadly sins!

Undershaft. Yes, the deadly seven. (*Counting on his fingers.*) Food, clothing, firing, rent, taxes, respectability and children. Nothing can lift those seven millstones from Man's neck but money and the spirit cannot soar until the mill stones are lifted. I lifted them from your spirit. I enabled Barbara to become Major Barbara; and I saved her from the crime of poverty.

Cusins. Do you call poverty a crime?

Undershaft. The worst of crimes. All the other crimes are virtues beside it: all the other dishonors are chivalry itself by comparison. Poverty blights whole cities; spreads horrible pestilences; strikes dead the very souls of all who come within sight, sound, or smell of it. What you call crime is nothing: a murder here and a theft there, a blow now and a curse then: what do they matter? they are only the accidents and illnesses of life: there are not fifty genuine professional criminals in London. But there are millions of poor people, abject people, dirty people, ill fed, ill clothed people. They poison us morally and physically: they kill the happiness of society: they force us to do away with our own liberties and to organize unnatural cruelties for fear they should rise against us and drag us down into their abyss. Only fools fear crime: we all fear poverty. Pah! (*turning on Barbara*) you talk of your half-saved ruffian in West Ham: you accuse me of dragging his soul back to perdition. Well, bring him to me here; and I will drag his soul back again to salvation for you. Not by words and dreams; but by thirtyeight shillings a week, a sound house in a handsome street and a permanent job. In three weeks he will have a fancy waistcoat; in three months a tall hat and a chapel sitting; before the end of the year he will shake hands with a duchess at a Primrose League meeting, and join the Conservative Party.

Barbara. And will he be the better for that?

Undershaft. You know he will. Dont be a hypocrite, Barbara. He will be better fed, better housed, better clothed, better behaved; and his children will be pounds heavier and bigger. That will be better than an American cloth mattress in a shelter, chopping firewood, eating bread and treacle, and being forced to kneel down from time to time to thank heaven for it: knee drill, I think you call it. It is cheap work converting starving men with a Bible in one hand and a slice of bread in the other. I will undertake to convert West Ham to Mahometanism on the same terms. Try your hand on my men: their souls are hungry because their bodies are full.

Barbara. And leave the east end to starve?

Undershaft (*his energetic tone dropping into one of bitter and brooding remembrance*). I was an east ender. I moralized and starved until one day I swore that I would be a full-fed free man at all costs; that nothing should stop me except a bullet, neither reason nor morals nor the lives of other men. I said 'Thou shalt starve ere I starve'; and with that word I became free and great. I was a dangerous man until I had my will: now I am a useful, beneficent, kindly person. That is the history of most self-made millionaires, I fancy. When it is the history of every Englishman we shall have an England worth living in.

Lady Britomart. Stop making speeches, Andrew. This is not the place for them.

Undershaft (*punctured*). My dear: I have no other means of conveying my ideas.

Lady Britomart. Your ideas are nonsense. You got on because you were selfish and unscrupulous.

Undershaft. Not at all. I had the strongest scruples about poverty and starvation. Your moralists are quite unscrupulous about both: they make virtues of them. I had rather be a thief than a pauper. I had rather be a murderer than a slave. I dont want to be either; but if you force the alternative on me, then, by Heaven, I'll choose the braver and more moral one. I hate poverty and slavery worse than any other crimes whatsoever. And let me tell you this. Poverty and slavery have stood up for centuries to your sermons and leading articles: they will not stand up to my machine guns. Dont preach at them: dont reason with them. Kill them.

Barbara. Killing. Is that your remedy for everything?

Undershaft. It is the final test of conviction, the only lever strong enough to overturn a social system, the only way of saying Must. Let six hundred and seventy fools loose in the streets; and three policemen can scatter them. But huddle them together in a certain house in Westminster; and let them go through certain ceremonies and call themselves certain names until at last they get the courage to kill; and your six hundred and seventy fools become a government. Your pious mob fills up ballot papers and imagines it is governing its masters; but the ballot paper that really governs is the paper that has a bullet wrapped up in it.

Cusins. That is perhaps why like most intelligent people, I never vote.

Undershaft. Vote! Bah! When you vote, you only change the names of the cabinet. When you shoot, you pull down governments, inaugurate new epochs, abolish old orders and set up new. Is that historically true, Mr Learned Man, or is it not?

Cusins. It is historically true. I loathe having to admit it. I repudiate your sentiments. I abhor your nature. I defy you in every possible way. Still, it is true. But it ought not to be true.

Undershaft. Ought! ought! ought! ought! ought! Are you going to spend your life saying ought, like the rest of our moralists? Turn your oughts into shalls, man. Come and make explosives with me. Whatever can blow men up can blow society up. The history of the world is the history of those who had courage enough to embrace this truth. Have you the courage to embrace it, Barbara?

Lady Britomart. Barbara: I positively forbid you to listen to your father's abominable wickedness. And you, Adolphus, ought to know better than to go about saying that wrong things are true. What does it matter whether they are true if they are wrong?

Undershaft. What does it matter whether they are wrong if they are true?

Lady Britomart (*rising*). Children: come home instantly. Andrew: I am exceedingly sorry I allowed you to call on us. You are wickeder than ever. Come at once.

Barbara (*shaking her head*). It's no use running away from wicked people, mamma.

Lady Britomart. It is every use. It shews your disapprobation of them.

Barbara. It does not save them.

Lady Britomart. I can see that you are going to disobey me. Sarah: are you coming home or are you not?

Sarah. I daresay it's very wicked of papa to make cannons; but I dont think I shall cut him on that account.

Lomax (*pouring oil on the troubled waters*). The fact is, you know, there is a certain amount of tosh about this notion of wickedness. It doesn't work. You must look at facts. Not that I would say a word in favor of anything wrong; but then, you see, all sorts of chaps are always doing all sorts of things; and we have to fit them in somehow, dont you know. What I mean is that you cant go cutting everybody; and thats about what it comes to. (*Their rapt attention to his eloquence makes him nervous.*) Perhaps I dont make myself clear.

Lady Britomart. You are lucidity itself, Charles. Because Andrew is successful and has plenty of money to give to Sarah, you will flatter him and encourage him in his wickedness.

Lomax (*unruffled*). Well, where the carcase is, there will the eagles be gathered, dont you know. (*To Undershaft.*) Eh? What?

Undershaft. Precisely. By the way, may I call you Charles?

Lomax. Delighted. Cholly is the usual ticket.

Undershaft (*to Lady Britomart*). Biddy—

Lady Britomart (*violently*). Dont dare call me Biddy. Charles Lomax: you are a fool. Adolphus Cusins: you are a Jesuit. Stephen: you are a prig. Barbara: you are a lunatic. Andrew: you are a vulgar tradesman. Now you all know my opinion; and my conscience is clear, at all events (*she sits down with a vehemence that the rug fortunately softens*).

Undershaft. My dear: you are the incarnation of morality. (*She snorts.*) Your conscience is clear and your duty done when you have called everybody names. Come, Euripides! it is getting late; and we all want to go home. Make up your mind.

Cusins. Understand this, you old demon—

Lady Britomart. Adolphus!

Undershaft. Let him alone, Biddy. Proceed, Euripides.

Cusins. You have me in a horrible dilemma. I want Barbara.

Undershaft. Like all young men, you greatly exaggerate the difference between one young woman and another.

Barbara. Quite true, Dolly.

Cusins. I also want to avoid being a rascal.

Undershaft (*with biting contempt*). You lust for personal righteousness, for self-approval, for what you call a good conscience, for what Barbara calls salvation, for what I call patronizing people who are not so lucky as yourself.

Cusins. I do not: all the poet in me recoils from being a good man. But there are things in me that I must reckon with. Pity—

Undershaft. Pity! The scavenger of misery.

Cusins. Well, love.

Undershaft. I know. You love the needy and the outcast: you love the oppressed races, the negro, the Indian ryot, the underdog everywhere. Do you love the Japanese? Do you love the French? Do you love the English?

Cusins. No. Every true Englishman detests the English. We are the wickedest nation on earth; and our success is a moral horror.

Undershaft. That is what comes of your gospel of love, is it?

Cusins. May I not love even my father-in-law?

Undershaft. Who wants your love, man? By what right do you take the liberty of offering it to me? I will have your due heed and respect, or I will kill you. But your love! Damn your impertinence!

Cusins (*grinning*). I may not be able to control my affections, Mac.

Undershaft. You are fencing, Euripides. You are weakening: your grip is slipping. Come! try your last weapon. Pity and love have broken in your hand: forgiveness is still left.

Cusins. No: forgiveness is a beggar's refuge. I am with you there: we must pay our debts.

Undershaft. Well said. Come! you will suit me. Remember the words of Plato.

Cusins (*starting*). Plato! You dare quote Plato to me!

Undershaft. Plato says, my friend, that society cannot be saved until either the Professors of Greek take to making gunpowder, or else the makers of gunpowder become Professors of Greek.

Cusins. Oh, tempter, cunning tempter!

Undershaft. Come! choose, man, choose.

Cusins. But perhaps Barbara will not marry me if I make the wrong choice.

Barbara. Perhaps not.

Cusins (*desperately perplexed*). You hear!

Barbara. Father: do you love nobody?

Undershaft. I love my best friend.

Lady Britomart. And who is that, pray?

Undershaft. My bravest enemy. That is the man who keeps me up to the mark.

Cusins. You know, the creature is really a sort of poet in his way. Suppose he is a great man, after all!

Undershaft. Suppose you stop talking and make up your mind, my young friend.

Cusins. But you are driving me against my nature. I hate war.

Undershaft. Hatred is the coward's revenge for being intimidated. Dare you make war on war? Here are the means: my friend Mr Lomax is sitting on them.

Lomax (*springing up*). Oh I say! You dont mean that this thing is loaded, do you? My ownest: come off it.

Sarah (*sitting placidly on the shell*). If I am to be blown up, the more thoroughly it is done the better. Dont fuss, Cholly.

Lomax (*to Undershaft, strongly remonstrant*). Your own daughter, you know!

Undershaft. So I see. (*To Cusins.*) Well, my friend, may we expect you here at six tomorrow morning?

Cusins (*firmly*). Not on any account. I will see the whole establishment blown up with its own dynamite before I will get up at five. My hours are healthy, rational hours: eleven to five.

Undershaft. Come when you please: before a week you will come at six and stay until I turn you out for the sake of your health.

(*Calling.*) Bilton! (*He turns to Lady Britomart, who rises.*) **My** dear: let us leave these two young people to themselves for a moment. (*Bilton comes from the shed.*) I am going to take you through the gun cotton shed.

Bilton (*barring the way*). You cant take anything explosive in here, sir.

Lady Britomart. What do you mean? Are you alluding to me?

Bilton (*unmoved*). No, maam. Mr Undershaft has the other gentleman's matches in his pocket.

Lady Britomart (*abruptly*). Oh! I beg your pardon! (*She goes into the shed.*)

Undershaft. Quite right, Bilton, quite right: here you are. (*He gives Bilton the box of matches.*) Come, Stephen. Come, Charles. Bring Sarah. (*He passes into the shed.*)

Bilton opens the box and deliberately drops the matches into the fire-bucket.

Lomax. Oh! I say. (*Bilton stolidly hands him the empty box.*) Infernal nonsense! Pure scientific ignorance! (*He goes in.*)

Sarah. Am I all right, Bilton?

Bilton. Youll have to put on list slippers, miss: thats all. Weve got em inside. (*She goes in.*)

Stephen (*very seriously to Cusins*). Dolly, old fellow, think. Think before you decide. Do you feel that you are a sufficiently practical man? It is a huge undertaking, an enormous responsibility. All this mass of business will be Greek to you.

Cusins. Oh, I think it will be much less difficult than Greek.

Stephen. Well, I just want to say this before I leave you to yourselves. Dont let anything I have said about right and wrong prejudice you against this great chance in life. I have satisfied myself that the business is one of the highest character and a credit to our country. (*Emotionally.*) I am very proud of my father. I—(*Unable to proceed, he presses Cusins' hand and goes hastily into the shed, followed by Bilton.*)

Barbara and Cusins, left alone together, look at one another silently.

Cusins. Barbara: I am going to accept this offer.

Barbara. I thought you would.

Cusins. You understand, dont you, that I had to decide without consulting you. If I had thrown the burden of the choice on you, you would sooner or later have despised me for it.

Barbara. Yes: I did not want you to sell your soul for me any more than for this inheritance.

Cusins. It is not the sale of my soul that troubles me: I have sold it too often to care about that. I have sold it for a professorship. I have sold it for an income. I have sold it to escape being imprisoned for refusing to pay taxes for hangmen's ropes and unjust wars and things that I abhor. What is all human conduct but the daily and hourly sale of our souls for trifles? What I am now selling it for is neither money nor position nor comfort, but for reality and for power.

Barbara. You know that you will have no power, and that he has none.

Cusins. I know. It is not for myself alone. I want to make power for the world.

Barbara. I want to make power for the world too; but it must be spiritual power.

Cusins. I think all power is spiritual: these cannons will not go off by themselves. I have tried to make spiritual power by teaching Greek. But the world can never be really touched by a dead langauge and a dead civilization. The people must have power; and the people cannot have Greek. Now the power that is made here can be wielded by all men.

Barbara. Power to burn women's houses down and kill their sons and tear their husbands to pieces.

Cusins. You cannot have power for good without having power for evil too. Even mother's milk nourishes murderers as well as heroes. This power which only tears men's bodies to pieces has never been so horribly abused as the intellectual power, the imaginative power, the poetic, religious power that can enslave men's souls. As a teacher of Greek I gave the intellectual man weapons against the common man. I now want to give the common man weapons against the intellectual man. I love the common people. I want to arm them against the lawyers, the doctors, the priests, the literary men, the professors, the artists, and the politicians, who, once in authority, are more disastrous and tyrannical than all the fools, rascals, and impostors. I want a power simple enough for common men to use, yet strong enough to force the intellectual oligarchy to use its genius for the general good.

Barbara. Is there no higher power than that (pointing to the shell)?

Cusins. Yes; but that power can destroy the higher powers just as a tiger can destroy a man: therefore Man must master that power first. I admitted this when the Turks and Greeks were last at war. My best pupil went out to fight for Hellas. My parting gift to him was not a copy of Plato's Republic, but a revolver and a hundred Undershaft cartridges. The blood of every Turk he shot —if he shot any—is on my head as well as on Undershaft's. That act committed me to this place for ever. Your father's challenge has beaten me. Dare I make war on war? I must. I will. And now, is it all over between us?

Barbara (touched by his evident dread of her answer). Silly baby Dolly! How could it be!

Cusins (*overjoyed*). Then you—you—you—Oh for my drum! (*He flourishes imaginary drumsticks.*)

Barbara (*angered by his levity*). Take care, Dolly, take care. Oh, if only I could get away from you and from father and from it all! if I could have the wings of a dove and fly away to heaven!

Cusins. And leave me!

Barbara. Yes, you, and all the other naughty mischievous children of men. But I cant. I was happy in the Salvation Army for a moment. I escaped from the world into a paradise of enthusiasm and prayer and soul saving; but the moment our money ran short, it all came back to Bodger: it was he who saved our people: he, and the Prince of Darkness, my papa. Undershaft and Bodger: their hands stretch everywhere: when we feed a starving fellow creature, it is with their bread, because there is no other bread; when we tend the sick, it is in the hospitals they endow; if we turn from the churches they build, we must kneel on the stones of the streets they pave. As long as that lasts, there is no getting away from them. Turning our backs on Bodger and Undershaft is turning our backs on life.

Cusins. I thought you were determined to turn your back on the wicked side of life.

Barbara. There is no wicked side: life is all one. And I never wanted to shirk my share in whatever evil must be endured, whether it be sin or suffering. I wish I could cure you of middle-class ideas, Dolly.

Cusins (*gasping*). Middle cl—! A snub! A social snub to me from the daughter of a foundling!

Barbara. That is why I have no class, Dolly: I come straight out of the heart of the whole people. If I were middle-class I should turn my back on my father's business; and we should both live in an artistic drawing room, with you reading the reviews in one corner, and I in the other at the piano, playing Schumann: both very superior persons, and neither of us a bit of use. Sooner than that, I would sweep out the guncotton shed, or be one of Bodger's barmaids. Do you know what would have happened if you had refused papa's offer?

Cusins. I wonder!

Barbara. I should have given you up and married the man who accepted it. After all, my dear old mother has more sense than any of you. I felt like her when I saw this place—felt that I must have it—that never, never, never could I let it go; only she thought it was the houses and the kitchen ranges and the linen and china, when it was really all the human souls to be saved: not weak souls in starved bodies, sobbing with gratitude for a scrap of bread and treacle, but fullfed, quarrelsome, snobbish, uppish creatures, all standing on their little rights and dignities, and thinking that my father ought to be greatly obliged to them for making so much money for him—and so he ought. That is where salvation is really wanted. My father shall never throw it in my teeth again that my converts were bribed with bread. (*She is transfigured.*) I have got rid of the bribe of bread. I have got rid of the bribe of heaven. Let God's work be done for its own sake: the work he had to create us to do because it cannot be done except by living men and women. When I die, let him be in my debt, not I in his; and let me forgive him as becomes a woman of my rank.

Cusins. Then the way of life lies through the factory of death?

Barbara. Yes, through the raising of hell to heaven and of man to God, through the unveiling of an eternal light in the Valley of The Shadow. (*Seizing him with both hands.*) Oh, did you think my courage would never come back? did you believe that I was a deserter? that I, who have stood in the streets, and taken my people to my heart, and talked of the holiest and greatest things with them, could ever turn back and chatter foolishly to fashionable people about nothing in a drawing room? Never, never, never, never: Major Barbara will die with the colors. Oh! and I have my dear little Dolly boy still; and he has found me my place and my work. Glory Hallelujah! (*She kisses him.*)

Cusins. My dearest: consider my delicate health. I cannot stand as much happiness as you can.

Barbara. Yes: it is not easy work being in love with me, is it? But it's good for you. (*She runs to the shed, and calls, childlike.*) Mamma! Mamma! (*Bilton comes out of the shed, followed by Undershaft.*) I want Mamma.

Undershaft. She is taking off her list slippers, dear. (*He passes on to Cusins.*) Well? What does she say?

Cusins. She has gone right up into the skies.

Lady Britomart (*coming from the shed and stopping on the steps, obstructing Sarah, who follows with Lomax. Barbara clutches like a baby at her mother's skirt*). Barbara: when will you learn to be independent and to act and think for yourself? I know, as well as possible what that cry of 'Mamma, Mamma,' means. Always running to me!

Sarah (*touching Lady Britomart's ribs with her finger tips and imitating a bicycle horn*). Pip! pip!

Lady Britomart (*highly indignant*). How dare you say Pip! pip! to me, Sarah? You are both very naughty children. What do you want, Barbara?

Barbara. I want a house in the village to live in with Dolly. (*Dragging at the skirt.*) Come and tell me which one to take.

Undershaft (*to Cusins*). Six o'clock tomorrow morning, Euripides.

THE END

1. What is the basic comic situation in Lady Britomart's dialogue with Stephen at the beginning of the play? Do we laugh with her or at her, or both? Explain.

2. When Undershaft is confused about which persons are his children, do we laugh with him or at him, or both? Explain. What sort of man had we expected? What sort of man does he seem to be in this scene?

3. In a paragraph characterize Barbara on the basis of her lines in Act I.

4. The opening dialogue in Act II, between Snobby Price and Rummy Mitchens, suggests that those who seek help from the Salvation Army are hypocrites. How does Shaw make Rummy likeable, and how does he prevent us from seeing Jenny and Barbara as mere dupes?

5. Is it a defect that Stephen, who was prominent in Act I, plays only a small part in Act III? Should his rebellion against his mother, in a way foreshadowed in the first act, have been made more of? Or did Shaw rightly move to bigger game? Explain.

6. What arguments can be offered to support the view that Cusins, and not Barbara or Undershaft, is the central figure in the play? Do these arguments convince us that Cusins is as successfully created as Barbara and Undershaft, or do we find him less memorable?

7. Aristotle's terms *peripeteia* (reversal) and *anagnorisis* (recognition), are commonly used in discussions of tragedy (see p. 484), but they can also be useful in discussions of comedy. What reversals and recognitions occur in *Major Barbara*? When Bill Walker says, "Wot prawce selvytion nah?" is this recognition the point toward which the play has been moving? Has he a point? The whole point?

8. Shaw once said, "It is the business of a writer of comedy to wound the susceptibilities of his audience. The classic definition of his function is 'the chastening of morals by ridicule.' " Does *Major Barbara* wound susceptibilities? If so, to any purpose? Is the play a serious examination of capitalism, charity, and religion, or does the clowning (*e.g.*, Lady Britomart's "I know your quiet, simple, refined, poetic people like Adolphus: quite content with the best of everything") obliterate the ideological content? Explain. Consider Undershaft's speeches on power on p. 576 and p. 587. Are they contradictory? If so, do they indicate that Shaw is writing amusing speeches but is not seriously concerned with the development of an idea? Consider, too, Cusins' assertion (p. 595) that he wishes to help the common man by arming him against the lawyer, the doctor, the priest, the literary man, the professor, etc. How will the manufacture of weapons help the common man?

9. One of the chief theories of laughter is neatly stated in Thomas Hobbes's *Leviathan* (1651):

Sudden Glory, is the passion which maketh those *Grimaces* called Laughter; and is caused either by some sudden act of their own, that pleaseth them; or by the apprehension of some deformed thing in another, in comparison whereof they suddenly applaud themselves.

If *Major Barbara* evokes laughter, is the laughter of Hobbes's sort? Does Hobbes's theory cover any or all laughable occurrences?

Nineteen

TWO PLAYS FOR
FURTHER STUDY

Nothing has lessened the truth of the old saying that drama requires only four boards, two actors, and a passion. An acting area, impersonators, and an intense feeling are the basic components. But of course the four boards usually become a playhouse—maybe the vast Theater of Dionysus, maybe an abandoned coffeehouse; the two actors usually become a troupe; and the passion becomes speeches and gestures embodied in a plot. In a way, all drama is one, and in another way, every drama is unique—so unique that we might almost say there is no such thing as drama, only dramas. Certainly there is reason to get nervous about (for example) the idea of "tragedy," especially when one hears that a tragedy shows a noble hero who dies because of some flaw. The remarks on tragedy in Chapter 17 suggest that this is much too simple a view, and the reader or spectator will do well to forget such a formula if he wishes to enjoy plays. The plays produced in 2000 years of western civilization have extraordinary differences as well as extraordinary resemblances. *Othello* is mostly in verse and has an aristocratic hero and an exotic setting; *The Glass Menagerie* is in prose and has lower-middle-class characters and a tawdry urban setting. But in both plays we have images of life that somehow compel our attention and give us a sense of what it means to be a human being.

A NOTE ON THE ELIZABETHAN THEATER. Shakespeare's theater was wooden, round or polygonal (the Chorus in *Henry V* calls it a "wooden O"). About 800 spectators could stand in the yard in front of—and perhaps along the two sides of—the stage that jutted from the rear wall, and another fifteen hundred or so spectators could sit in the three roofed galleries that ringed the stage. That portion of the gal-

600

leries that was above the rear of the stage was sometimes used by actors; when Iago and Roderigo in the first scene of *Othello* rouse Brabantio, he appears "above," in his house, then disappears, and shortly enters the stage, which represents a street. Entry to the stage was normally gained by doors at the rear but some use was made of a curtained alcove—or perhaps a booth—between the doors, which allowed characters to be "discovered" (*i.e.*, revealed) as in the modern proscenium theater, which normally employs a curtain. A performance was probably uninterrupted by intermissions or by long pauses for the changing of scenery; a group of characters leaves the stage, another enters, and if the locale has changed, the new characters somehow tell us. (Modern editors customarily add indications of locales to help a reader, but it should be understood that the action of the Elizabethan stage was continuous.)

WILLIAM SHAKESPEARE (1564-1616)

The Tragedy of Othello

The Moor of Venice

THE NAMES OF THE ACTORS

Othello, the Moor
Brabantio, father to Desdemona
Cassio, an honorable lieutenant
Iago, a villain
Roderigo, a gulled gentleman
Duke of Venice
Senators
Montano, Governor of Cyprus
Gentlemen of Cyprus
Lodovico and Gratiano, two noble Venetians
Sailors
Clown
Desdemona, wife to Othello
Emilia, wife to Iago
Bianca, a courtesan
[*Messenger, Herald, Officers, Gentlemen,
    Musicians, Attendants*]
[SCENE. *Venice and Cyprus*]

Othello was first printed in 1621 in a small book of a kind called a quarto; it was printed again in 1623 in a large volume (a folio) containing 36 of

ACT I

Scene I. [*Venice. A street.*]

Enter Roderigo and Iago.

Roderigo. Tush! Never tell me? I take it much unkindly
    That thou, Iago, who hast had my purse
    As if the strings were thine, shouldst know of this.
Iago. 'Sblood,°¹ but you'll not hear me! If ever I did dream
    Of such a matter, abhor me.
Roderigo.   Thou told'st me   5
    Thou didst hold him in thy hate.
Iago.   Despise me
    If I do not. Three great ones of the city,
    In personal suit to make me his lieutenant,
    Off-capped° to him; and, by the faith of man,
    I know my price; I am worth no worse a place.   10
    But he, as loving his own pride and purposes,
    Evades them with a bombast circumstance,°
    Horribly stuffed with epithets of war;
    Nonsuits° my mediators. For, "Certes," says he,
    "I have already chose my officer." And what was he?   15
    Forsooth, a great arithmetician,°
    One Michael Cassio, a Florentine,
    (A fellow almost damned in a fair wife)°
    That never set a squadron in the field,
    Nor the division of a battle knows   20
    More than a spinster; unless the bookish theoric,
    Wherein the tonguèd° consuls can propose

Shakespeare's plays. There are numerous differences between the two texts of *Othello*, and scholars are divided about which text represents Shakespeare's final version of the play. The text we give is that prepared by Alvin Kernan for the Signet Shakespeare; it is based on the folio but it includes some readings from the quarto. Material added by the editor, such as indication of locale and some stage directions, is enclosed in square brackets, thus [ ].

¹ The degree sign (°) indicates a footnote, which is keyed to the text by the line number. Text references are printed in **boldface** type; the annotation follows in roman type. I.i.4 **'Sblood** by God's blood   9 **Off-capped** doffed their caps—as a mark of respect   12 **bombast circumstance** stuffed, roundabout speech   14 **Nonsuits** rejects   16 **arithmetician** theorist (rather than practical)   18 **A . . . wife** (a much-disputed passage, which is probably best taken as a general sneer at Cassio as a dandy and a ladies' man. But in the story from which Shakespeare took his plot the counterpart of Cassio is married, and it may be that at the beginning of the play Shakespeare had decided to keep him married but later changed his mind)   22 **tongued** eloquent

As masterly as he. Mere prattle without practice
Is all his soldiership. But he, sir, had th' election;
And I, of whom his eyes had seen the proof   25
At Rhodes, at Cyprus, and on other grounds
Christian and heathen, must be belee'd and calmed
By debitor and creditor. This counter-caster,°
He, in good time, must his lieutenant be,
And I—God bless the mark!—his Moorship's ancient.°   30
Roderigo. By heaven, I rather would have been his hangman.
Iago. Why, there's no remedy. 'Tis the curse of service:
Preferment goes by letter and affection,°
And not by old gradation,° where each second
Stood heir to th' first. Now, sir, be judge yourself,   35
Whether I in any just term am affined°
To love the Moor.
Roderigo.   I would not follow him then.
Iago. O, sir, content you.
I follow him to serve my turn upon him.
We cannot all be masters, nor all masters   40
Cannot be truly followed. You shall mark
Many a duteous and knee-crooking° knave
That, doting on his own obsequious bondage,
Wears out his time, much like his master's ass,
For naught but provender; and when he's old, cashiered.   45
Whip me such honest knaves! Others there are
Who, trimmed in forms and visages of duty,
Keep yet their hearts attending on themselves,
And, throwing but shows of service on their lords,
Do well thrive by them, and when they have lined their
      coats,   50
Do themselves homage. These fellows have some soul;
And such a one do I profess myself. For, sir,
It is as sure as you are Roderigo,
Were I the Moor, I would not be Iago.
In following him, I follow but myself.   55
Heaven is my judge, not I for love and duty,
But seeming so, for my peculiar° end;
For when my outward action doth demonstrate
The native° act and figure of my heart
In complement extern,° 'tis not long after   60

28 **counter-caster** i.e., a bookkeeper who *casts* (reckons up) figures on a *counter*
(abacus)   30 **ancient** standard-bearer; an under-officer   33 **letter and affection**
recommendations (from men of power) and personal preference   34 **old
gradation** seniority   36 **affined** bound   42 **knee-crooking** bowing   57 **peculiar** personal   59 **native** natural, innate   60 **complement extern** outward
appearance

But I will wear my heart upon my sleeve
For daws to peck at; I am not what I am.
Roderigo. What a full fortune does the thick-lips owe°
    If he can carry't thus!
Iago.   Call up her father,
    Rouse him. Make after him, poison his delight,   65
    Proclaim him in the streets, incense her kinsmen,
    And though he in a fertile climate dwell,
    Plague him with flies; though that his joy be joy,
    Yet throw such chances of vexation on't
    As it may lose some color.   70
Roderigo. Here is her father's house. I'll call aloud.
Iago. Do, with like timorous° accent and dire yell
    As when, by night and negligence, the fire
    Is spied in populous cities.
Roderigo. What, ho, Brabantio! Signior Brabantio, ho!   75
Iago. Awake! What, ho, Brabantio! Thieves! Thieves!
    Look to your house, your daughter, and your bags!
    Thieves! Thieves!

    Brabantio above° [*at a window*].

Brabantio. What is the reason of this terrible summons?
    What is the matter there?   80
Roderigo. Signior, is all your family within?
Iago. Are your doors locked?
Brabantio.   Why, wherefore ask you this?
Iago. Zounds, sir, y'are robbed. For shame. Put on your gown!
    Your heart is burst, you have lost half your soul.
    Even now, now, very now, an old black ram   85
    Is tupping your white ewe. Arise, arise!
    Awake the snorting citizens with the bell,
    Or else the devil will make a grandsire of you.
    Arise, I say!
Brabantio.   What, have you lost your wits?
Roderigo. Most reverend signior, do you know my voice?   90
Brabantio. Not I. What are you?
Roderigo. My name is Roderigo.
Brabantio.   The worser welcome!
    I have charged thee not to haunt about my doors.
    In honest plainness thou hast heard me say
    My daughter is not for thee; and now, in madness,   95
    Being full of supper and distemp'ring draughts,°

63 **owe** own   72 **timorous** frightening   78 s.d. **above** (i.e., on the small upper stage above and to the rear, of the main platform stage, which resembled the projecting upper story of an Elizabethan house)   96 **distemp'ring draughts** unsettling drinks

Upon malicious knavery dost thou come
To start° my quiet.
Roderigo. Sir, sir, sir——
Brabantio.   But thou must needs be sure
My spirits and my place° have in their power   100
To make this bitter to thee.
Roderigo.   Patience, good sir.
Brabantio. What tell'st thou me of robbing? This is Venice;
My house is not a grange.°
Roderigo.   Most grave Brabantio,
In simple and pure soul I come to you.
Iago. Zounds, sir, you are one of those that will not serve God if   105
the devil bid you. Because we come to do you service and
you think we are ruffians, you'll have your daughter covered
with a Barbary° horse, you'll have your nephews° neigh to you,
you'll have coursers for cousins,° and gennets for germans.°
Brabantio. What profane wretch art thou?   110
Iago. I am one, sir, that comes to tell you your daughter and the
Moor are making the beast with two backs.
Brabantio. Thou art a villain.
Iago.   You are—a senator.
Brabantio. This thou shalt answer. I know thee, Roderigo.
Roderigo. Sir, I will answer anything. But I beseech you,   115
If't be your pleasure and most wise consent,
As partly I find it is, that your fair daughter,
At this odd-even° and dull watch o' th' night,
Transported, with no worse nor better guard
But with a knave of common hire, a gondolier,   120
To the gross clasps of a lascivious Moor—
If this be known to you, and your allowance,
We then have done you bold and saucy wrongs;
But if you know not this, my manners tell me
We have your wrong rebuke. Do not believe   125
That from the sense of all civility°
I thus would play and trifle with your reverence.
Your daughter, if you have not given her leave,
I say again, hath made a gross revolt,
Tying her duty, beauty, wit, and fortunes   130
In an extravagant° and wheeling stranger
Of here and everywhere. Straight satisfy yourself.

98 **start** disrupt   100 **place** rank, i.e., of senator   103 **grange** isolated house
108 **Barbary** Arabian, i.e., Moorish   108 **nephews** i.e., grandsons   109 **cousins** relations   109 **gennets for germans** Spanish horses for blood relatives
118 **odd-even** between night and morning   126 **sense of all civility** feeling
of what is proper   131 **extravagant** vagrant, wandering (Othello is not
Venetian and thus may be considered a wandering soldier of fortune)

          If she be in her chamber, or your house,
          Let loose on me the justice of the state
          For thus deluding you.
Brabantio.   Strike on the tinder, ho!   135
          Give me a taper! Call up all my people!
          This accident° is not unlike my dream.
          Belief of it oppresses me already.
          Light, I say! Light!   *Exit [above].*
Iago.   Farewell, for I must leave you.
          It seems not meet, nor wholesome to my place,   140
          To be produced—as, if I stay, I shall—
          Against the Moor. For I do know the State,
          However this may gall him with some check,°
          Cannot with safety cast° him; for he's embarked
          With such loud reason to the Cyprus wars,   145
          Which even now stands in act,° that for their souls
          Another of his fathom° they have none
          To lead their business; in which regard,
          Though I do hate him as I do hell-pains,
          Yet, for necessity of present life,   150
          I must show out a flag and sign of love,
          Which is indeed but sign. That you shall surely find him,
          Lead to the Sagittary° the raisèd search;
          And there will I be with him. So farewell.   *Exit.*

     Enter Brabantio [in his nightgown], with Servants and torches.

Brabantio. It is too true an evil. Gone she is;   155
          And what's to come of my despisèd time
          Is naught but bitterness. Now, Roderigo,
          Where didst thou see her?—O unhappy girl!—
          With the Moor, say'st thou?—Who would be a father?—
          How didst thou know 'twas she?—O, she deceives me   160
          Past thought!—What said she to you? Get moe° tapers!
          Raise all my kindred!—Are they married, think you?
Roderigo. Truly I think they are.
Brabantio. O heaven! How got she out? O treason of the blood!
          Fathers, from hence trust not your daughters' minds   165
          By what you see them act.° Is there not charms
          By which the property° of youth and maidhood
          May be abused? Have you not read, Roderigo,
          Of some such thing?
Roderigo.   Yes, sir, I have indeed.
Brabantio. Call up my brother.—O, would you had had her!—   170

137 **accident** happening   143 **check** restraint   144 **cast** dismiss   146 **stands in act** takes place   147 **fathom** ability   153 **Sagittary** (probably the name of an inn)   161 **moe** more   166 **act** do   167 **property** true nature

Some one way, some another.—Do you know
Where we may apprehend her and the Moor?
Roderigo. I think I can discover him, if you please
To get good guard and go along with me.
Brabantio. Pray you lead on. At every house I'll call;   175
I may command at most.—Get weapons, ho!
And raise some special officers of might.—
On, good Roderigo; I will deserve your pains.°   *Exeunt.*

Scene II. [*A street.*]

Enter Othello, Iago, Attendants with torches.

Iago. Though in the trade of war I have slain men,
Yet do I hold it very stuff° o' th' conscience
To do no contrived murder. I lack iniquity
Sometime to do me service. Nine or ten times
I had thought t' have yerked° him here, under the ribs.   5
Othello. 'Tis better as it is.
Iago.   Nay, but he prated,
And spoke such scurvy and provoking terms
Against your honor, that with the little godliness I have
I did full hard forbear him. But I pray you, sir,
Are you fast married? Be assured of this,   10
That the magnifico° is much beloved,
And hath in his effect a voice potential
As double as the Duke's.° He will divorce you,
Or put upon you what restraint or grievance
The law, with all his might to enforce it on,   15
Will give him cable.°
Othello.   Let him do his spite.
My services which I have done the Signiory°
Shall out-tongue his complaints. 'Tis yet to know°—
Which when I know that boasting is an honor
I shall promulgate—I fetch my life and being   20
From men of royal siege;° and my demerits°
May speak unbonneted to as proud a fortune
As this that I have reached.° For know, Iago,
But that I love the gentle Desdemona,
I would not my unhousèd° free condition   25

178 **deserve your pains** be worthy of (and reward) your efforts   I.ii.2 **stuff**
essence   5 **yerked** stabbed   11 **magnifico** nobleman   12-13 **hath ... Duke's**
i.e., can be as effective as the Duke   16 **cable** range, scope   17 **Signiory** the
rulers of Venice   18 **yet to know** unknown as yet   21 **siege** rank   21 **demerits**
deserts   22-23 **May ... reached** i.e., are the equal of the family I have married into   25 **unhoused** unconfined

Put into circumscription and confine
For the seas' worth. But look, what lights come yond?

Enter Cassio, with [Officers and] torches.

Iago. Those are the raisèd father and his friends.
    You were best go in.
Othello.   Not I. I must be found.
    My parts, my title, and my perfect soul°   30
    Shall manifest me rightly. Is it they?
Iago. By Janus, I think no.
Othello. The servants of the Duke? And my lieutenant?
    The goodness of the night upon you, friends.
    What is the news?
Cassio.   The Duke does greet you, general;   35
    And he requires your haste-posthaste appearance
    Even on the instant.
Othello.   What is the matter, think you?
Cassio. Something from Cyprus, as I may divine.
    It is a business of some heat. The galleys
    Have sent a dozen sequent° messengers   40
    This very night at one another's heels,
    And many of the consuls, raised and met,
    Are at the Duke's already. You have been hotly called for.
    When, being not at your lodging to be found,
    The Senate hath sent about three several° quests   45
    To search you out.
Othello.   'Tis well I am found by you.
    I will but spend a word here in the house,
    And go with you.   [*Exit.*]
Cassio.   Ancient, what makes he here?
Iago. Faith, he tonight hath boarded a land carack.°
    If it prove lawful prize, he's made forever.   50
Cassio. I do not understand.
Iago.   He's married.
Cassio.   To who?

    [*Enter Othello.*]

Iago. Marry,° to—Come captain, will you go?
Othello.   Have with you.
Cassio. Here comes another troop to seek for you.

Enter Brabantio, Roderigo, with Officers and torches.

Iago. It is Brabantio. General, be advised.
    He comes to bad intent.

---

30 **perfect soul** clear, unflawed conscience   40 **sequent** successive   45 **several**
separate   49 **carack** treasure ship   52 **Marry** By Mary (an interjection)

Othello.   Holla! Stand there!   55
Roderigo. Signior, it is the Moor.
Brabantio.   Down with him, thief!
                      [*They draw swords.*]
Iago. You, Roderigo? Come, sir, I am for you.
Othello. Keep up your bright swords, for the dew will rust them.
    Good signior, you shall more command with years
    Than with your weapons.   60
Brabantio. O thou foul thief, where hast thou stowed my daughter?
    Damned as thou art, thou hast enchanted her!
    For I'll refer me to all things of sense,°
    If she in chains of magic were not bound,
    Whether a maid so tender, fair, and happy,   65
    So opposite to marriage that she shunned
    The wealthy, curlèd darlings of our nation,
    Would ever have, t'incur a general mock,°
    Run from her guardage to the sooty bosom
    Of such a thing as thou—to fear, not to delight.   70
    Judge me the world if 'tis not gross in sense°
    That thou has practiced° on her with foul charms,
    Abused her delicate youth with drugs or minerals
    That weaken motion.° I'll have't disputed on;
    'Tis probable, and palpable to thinking.   75
    I therefore apprehend and do attach° thee
    For an abuser of the world, a practicer
    Of arts inhibited and out of warrant.°
    Lay hold upon him. If he do resist,
    Subdue him at his peril.
Othello.   Hold your hands,   80
    Both you of my inclining and the rest.
    Were it my cue to fight, I should have known it
    Without a prompter. Whither will you that I go
    To answer this your charge?
Brabantio.   To prison, till fit time
    Of law and course of direct session   85
    Call thee to answer.
Othello.   What if I do obey?
    How may the Duke be therewith satisfied,
    Whose messengers are here about my side
    Upon some present° business of the state
    To bring me to him?
Officer.   'Tis true, most worthy signior.   90

---

63 **refer . . . sense** i.e., base (my argument) on all ordinary understanding of
nature   68 **general mock** public shame   71 **gross in sense** obvious   72 **prac-
ticed** used tricks   74 **motion** thought, i.e., reason   76 **attach** arrest   78 **in-
hibited . . . warrant** prohibited and illegal (black magic)   89 **present** immediate

The Duke's in council, and your noble self
I am sure is sent for.
Brabantio.   How? The Duke in council?
In this time of the night? Bring him away.
Mine's not an idle cause. The Duke himself,
Or any of my brothers° of the state,   95
Cannot but feel this wrong as 'twere their own;
For if such actions may have passage free,
Bondslaves and pagans shall our statesmen be.   *Exeunt.*

Scene III. [*A council chamber.*]

*Enter Duke, Senators, and Officers [set at a table, with lights and
Attendants].*

Duke. There's no composition° in this news
That gives them credit.°
First Senator.   Indeed, they are disproportioned.
My letters say a hundred and seven galleys.
Duke. And mine a hundred forty.
Second Senator.   And mine two hundred.
But though they jump° not on a just accompt°—   5
As in these cases where the aim° reports
'Tis oft with difference—yet do they all confirm
A Turkish fleet, and bearing up to Cyprus.
Duke. Nay, it is possible enough to judgment.°
I do not so secure me in the error,   10
But the main article I do approve
In fearful sense.°
Sailor (Within). What, ho! What, ho! What, ho!

Enter Sailor.

Officer. A messenger from the galleys.
Duke.   Now? What's the business?
Sailor. The Turkish preparation makes for Rhodes.
So was I bid report here to the State   15
By Signior Angelo.
Duke. How say you by this change?
First Senator.   This cannot be
By no assay of reason. 'Tis a pageant°

95 **brothers** i.e., the other senators   I.iii.1 **composition** agreement   2 **gives
them credit** makes them believable   5 **jump** agree   5 **just accompt** exact
counting   6 **aim** approximation   9 **to judgment** when carefully considered
10-12 **I do ... sense** i.e., just because the numbers disagree in the reports,
I do not doubt that the principal information (that the Turkish fleet is out)
is fearfully true   18 **pageant** show, pretense

To keep us in false gaze.° When we consider
Th' importancy of Cyprus to the Turk,   20
And let ourselves again but understand
That, as it more concerns the Turk than Rhodes,
So may he with more facile question° bear it,
For that it stands not in such warlike brace,°
But altogether lacks th' abilities   25
That Rhodes is dressed in. If we make thought of this,
We must not think the Turk is so unskillful
To leave that latest which concerns him first,
Neglecting an attempt of ease and gain
To wake and wage a danger profitless.   30
Duke. Nay, in all confidence he's not for Rhodes.
Officer. Here is more news.

    Enter a Messenger.

Messenger. The Ottomites, reverend and gracious,
    Steering with due course toward the isle of Rhodes,
    Have there injointed them with an after° fleet.   35
First Senator. Ay, so I thought. How many, as you guess?
Messenger. Of thirty sail; and now they do restem
    Their backward course, bearing with frank appearance
    Their purposes toward Cyprus. Signior Montano,
    Your trusty and most valiant servitor,   40
    With his free duty° recommends° you thus,
    And prays you to believe him.
Duke. 'Tis certain then for Cyprus.
    Marcus Luccicos, is not he in town?
First Senator. He's now in Florence.   45
Duke. Write from us to him; post-posthaste dispatch.
First Senator. Here comes Brabantio and the valiant Moor.

    Enter Brabantio, Othello, Cassio, Iago, Roderigo, and Officers.

Duke. Valiant Othello, we must straight° employ you
    Against the general° enemy Ottoman.
    [*To Brabantio*] I did not see you. Welcome, gentle signior.   50
    We lacked your counsel and your help tonight.
Brabantio. So I did yours. Good your grace, pardon me.
    Neither my place, nor aught I heard of business,
    Hath raised me from my bed; nor doth the general care
    Take hold on me; for my particular grief   55

19 **in false gaze** looking the wrong way   23 **facile question** easy struggle
24 **warlike brace** "military posture"   35 **after** following   41 **free duty** un-
limited respect   41 **recommends** informs   48 **straight** at once   49 **general**
universal

Is of so floodgate and o'erbearing nature
That it engluts and swallows other sorrows,
And it is still itself.
Duke. Why, what's the matter?
Brabantio. My daughter! O, my daughter!
Senators. Dead?
Brabantio. Ay, to me.
    She is abused, stol'n from me, and corrupted   60
    By spells and medicines bought of mountebanks;
    For nature so prepost'rously to err,
    Being not deficient, blind, or lame of sense,
    Sans° witchcraft could not.
Duke. Whoe'er he be that in this foul proceeding   65
    Hath thus beguiled your daughter of herself,
    And you of her, the bloody book of law
    You shall yourself read in the bitter letter
    After your own sense; yea, though our proper° son
    Stood in your action.°
Brabantio. Humbly I thank your Grace.   70
    Here is the man—this Moor, whom now, it seems,
    Your special mandate for the state affairs
    Hath hither brought.
All. We are very sorry for't.
Duke [*To Othello*]. What in your own part can you say to this?
Brabantio. Nothing, but this is so.   75
Othello. Most potent, grave, and reverend signiors,
    My very noble and approved° good masters,
    That I have ta'en away this old man's daughter,
    It is most true; true I have married her.
    The very head and front° of my offending   80
    Hath this extent, no more. Rude am I in my speech,
    And little blessed with the soft phrase of peace,
    For since these arms of mine had seven years' pith°
    Till now some nine moons wasted,° they have used
    Their dearest° action in the tented field;   85
    And little of this great world can I speak
    More than pertains to feats of broils and battle;
    And therefore little shall I grace my cause
    In speaking for myself. Yet, by your gracious patience,
    I will a round° unvarnished tale deliver   90
    Of my whole course of love—what drugs, what charms,
    What conjuration, and what mighty magic,

---

64 **Sans** without   69 **proper** own   70 **Stood in your action** were the accused in your suit   77 **approved** tested, proven by past performance   80 **head and front** extreme form (*front* = forehead)   83 **pith** strength   84 **wasted** past   85 **dearest** most important   90 **round** blunt

For such proceeding I am charged withal,
I won his daughter—
Brabantio.   A maiden never bold,
Of spirit so still and quiet that her motion   95
Blushed at herself;° and she, in spite of nature,
Of years, of country, credit, everything,
To fall in love with what she feared to look on!
It is a judgment maimed and most imperfect
That will confess perfection so could err   100
Against all rules of nature, and must be driven
To find out practices of cunning hell
Why this should be. I therefore vouch again
That with some mixtures pow'rful o'er the blood,
Or with some dram, conjured to this effect,   105
He wrought upon her.
Duke.   To vouch this is no proof,
Without more wider and more overt test
Than these thin habits° and poor likelihoods
Of modern° seeming do prefer against him.
First Senator. But, Othello, speak.   110
Did you by indirect and forcèd courses
Subdue and poison this young maid's affections?
Or came it by request, and such fair question°
As soul to soul affordeth?
Othello.   I do beseech you,
Send for the lady to the Sagittary   115
And let her speak of me before her father.
If you do find me foul in her report,
The trust, the office, I do hold of you
Not only take away, but let your sentence
Even fall upon my life.
Duke.   Fetch Desdemona hither.   120
Othello. Ancient, conduct them; you best know the place.
              [*Exit Iago, with two or three Attendants.*]
And till she come, as truly as to heaven
I do confess the vices of my blood,
So justly to your grave ears I'll present
How I did thrive in this fair lady's love,   125
And she in mine.
Duke.   Say it, Othello.
Othello. Her father loved me; oft invited me;
Still° questioned me the story of my life
From year to year, the battle, sieges, fortune
That I have passed.   130

95-96 **her motion/Blushed at herself** i.e., she was so modest that she blushed
at every thought (and movement)   108 **habits** clothing   109 **modern** trivial
113 **question** discussion   128 **Still** regularly

I ran it through, even from my boyish days
To th' very moment that he bade me tell it.
Wherein I spoke of most disastrous chances,
Of moving accidents by flood and field,
Of hairbreadth scapes i' th' imminent° deadly breach,   135
Of being taken by the insolent foe
And sold to slavery, of my redemption thence
And portance° in my travel's history,
Wherein of anters° vast and deserts idle,°
Rough quarries, rocks, and hills whose heads touch heaven,   140
It was my hint to speak. Such was my process.
And of the Cannibals that each other eat,
The Anthropophagi,° and men whose heads
Grew beneath their shoulders. These things to hear
Would Desdemona seriously incline;   145
But still the house affairs would draw her thence;
Which ever as she could with haste dispatch,
She'd come again, and with a greedy ear
Devour up my discourse. Which I observing,
Took once a pliant hour, and found good means   150
To draw from her a prayer of earnest heart
That I would all my pilgrimage dilate,°
Whereof by parcels she had something heard,
But not intentively.° I did consent,
And often did beguile her of her tears   155
When I did speak of some distressful stroke
That my youth suffered. My story being done,
She gave me for my pains a world of kisses.
She swore in faith 'twas strange, 'twas passing° strange;
'Twas pitiful, 'twas wondrous pitiful.   160
She wished she had not heard it; yet she wished
That heaven had made her such a man. She thanked me,
And bade me, if I had a friend that loved her,
I should but teach him how to tell my story,
And that would woo her. Upon this hint I spake.   165
She loved me for the dangers I had passed,
And I loved her that she did pity them.
This only is the witchcraft I have used.
Here comes the lady. Let her witness it.

Enter Desdemona, Iago, Attendants.

Duke. I think this tale would win my daughter too.   170
  Good Brabantio, take up this mangled matter at the best.°

135 **imminent** threatening   138 **portance** manner of acting   139 **anters** caves
139 **idle** empty, sterile   143 **Anthropophagi** man-eaters   152 **dilate** relate in
full   154 **intentively** at length and in sequence   159 **passing** surpassing
171 **Take . . . best** i.e., make the best of this disaster

Men do their broken weapons rather use
Than their bare hands.
Brabantio.   I pray you hear her speak.
If she confess that she was half the wooer,
Destruction on my head if my bad blame   175
Light on the man. Come hither, gentle mistress.
Do you perceive in all this noble company
Where most you owe obedience?
Desdemona.   My noble father,
I do perceive here a divided duty.
To you I am bound for life and education;   180
My life and education both do learn me
How to respect you. You are the lord of duty,
I am hitherto your daughter. But here's my husband,
And so much duty as my mother showed
To you, preferring you before her father,   185
So much I challenge° that I may profess
Due to the Moor my lord.
Brabantio.   God be with you. I have done.
Please it your Grace, on to the state affairs.
I had rather to adopt a child than get° it.
Come hither, Moor.   190
I here do give thee that with all my heart
Which, but thou hast already, with all my heart
I would keep from thee. For your sake,° jewel,
I am glad at soul I have no other child,
For thy escape would teach me tyranny,   195
To hang clogs on them. I have done, my lord.
Duke. Let me speak like yourself and lay a sentence°
Which, as a grise° or step, may help these lovers.
When remedies are past, the griefs are ended
By seeing the worst, which late on hopes depended.°   200
To mourn a mischief that is past and gone
Is the next° way to draw new mischief on.
What cannot be preserved when fortune takes,
Patience her injury a mock'ry makes.
The robbed that smiles, steals something from the thief;   205
He robs himself that spends a bootless° grief.
Brabantio. So let the Turk of Cyprus us beguile:
We lose it not so long as we can smile.
He bears the sentence well that nothing bears
But the free comfort which from thence he hears;   210
But he bears both the sentence and the sorrow

186 **challenge** claim as right   189 **get** beget   193 **For your sake** because of
you   197 **lay a sentence** provide a maxim   198 **grise** step   200 **late on
hopes depended** was supported by hope (of a better outcome) until lately
202 **next** closest, surest   206 **bootless** valueless

That to pay grief must of poor patience borrow.
These sentences, to sugar, or to gall,
Being strong on both sides, are equivocal.
But words are words. I never yet did hear   215
That the bruisèd heart was piercèd° through the ear.
I humbly beseech you, proceed to th' affairs of state.

Duke. The Turk with a most mighty preparation makes for Cyprus. Othello, the fortitude° of the place is best known to
you; and though we have there a substitute° of most allowed   220
sufficiency,° yet opinion, a more sovereign mistress of effects
throws a more safer voice on you.° You must therefore be
content to slubber° the gloss of your new fortunes with this
more stubborn and boisterous° expedition.

Othello. The tyrant Custom, most grave senators,   225
Hath made the flinty and steel couch of war
My thrice-driven° bed of down. I do agnize°
A natural and prompt alacrity
I find in hardness and do undertake
This present wars against the Ottomites.   230
Most humbly, therefore, bending to your state,
I crave fit disposition for my wife,
Due reference of place, and exhibition,°
With such accommodation and besort
As levels with° her breeding.

Duke.   Why, at her father's.   235
Brabantio. I will not have it so.
Othello.   Nor I.
Desdemona.   Nor would I there reside,
To put my father in impatient thoughts
By being in his eye. Most gracious Duke,
To my unfolding° lend your prosperous° ear,
And let me find a charter° in your voice,   240
T' assist my simpleness.
Duke.   What would you, Desdemona?
Desdemona. That I love the Moor to live with him,
My downright violence, and storm of fortunes,

216 **pierced** (some editors emend to *pieced*, i.e., "healed." But *pierced* makes
good sense: Brabantio is saying in effect that his heart cannot be further hurt
[pierced] by the indignity of the useless, conventional advice the Duke offers
him. *Pierced* can also mean, however, "lanced" in the medical sense, and
would then mean "treated")   219 **fortitude** fortification   220 **substitute**
viceroy   220-21 **most allowed sufficiency** generally acknowledged capability
221-22 **opinion . . . you** i.e., the general opinion, which finally controls affairs,
is that you would be the best man in this situation   223 **slubber** besmear
224 **stubborn and boisterous** rough and violent   227 **thrice-driven** i.e., softest
227 **agnize** know in myself   233 **exhibition** grant of funds   235 **levels with** is
suitable to   239 **unfolding** explanation   239 **prosperous** favoring   240 **charter** permission

May trumpet to the world. My heart's subdued
Even to the very quality of my lord.°   245
I saw Othello's visage in his mind,
And to his honors and his valiant parts
Did I my soul and fortunes consecrate.
So that, dear lords, if I be left behind,
A moth of peace, and he go to the war,   250
The rites° for why I love him are bereft me,
And I a heavy interim shall support
By his dear absence. Let me go with him.
Othello. Let her have your voice.°
    Vouch with me, heaven, I therefore beg it not   255
And to please the palate of my appetite,
Nor to comply with heat°—the young affects°
In me defunct—and proper satisfaction;°
But to be free and bounteous to her mind;
And heaven defend° your good souls that you think   260
I will your serious and great business scant
When she is with me. No, when light-winged toys
Of feathered Cupid seel° with wanton° dullness
My speculative and officed instrument,°
That my disports corrupt and taint my business,   265
Let housewives make a skillet of my helm,
And all indign° and base adversities
Make head° against my estimation!°—
Duke. Be it as you shall privately determine,
Either for her stay or going. Th' affair cries haste,   270
And speed must answer it.
First Senator.   You must away tonight.
Othello. With all my heart.
Duke. At nine i' th' morning here we'll meet again.
    Othello, leave some officer behind,
    And he shall our commission bring to you,   275
    And such things else of quality and respect
    As doth import you.
Othello.   So please your grace, my ancient;
    A man he is of honesty and trust.
    To his conveyance I assign my wife.

244-45 **My. . . lord** i.e., I have become one in nature and being with the man
I married (therefore, I too would go to the wars like a soldier) 251 **rites**
(may refer either to the marriage rites or to the rites, formalities, of war)
254 **voice** consent 257 **heat** lust 257 **affects** passions 258 **proper satisfaction** i.e., consummation of the marriage 260 **defend** forbid 263 **seel** sew up
263 **wanton** lascivious 264 **speculative . . . instrument** i.e., sight (and, by
extension, the mind) 267 **indign** unworthy 268 **Make head** form an army,
i.e., attack 268 **estimation** reputation

With what else needful your good grace shall think   280
        To be sent after me.
Duke.   Let it be so.
        Good night to every one. [*To Brabantio*] And, noble signior,
        If virtue no delighted° beauty lack,
        Your son-in-law is far more fair than black.
First Senator. Adieu, brave Moor. Use Desdemona well.   285
Brabantio. Look to her, Moor, if thou hast eyes to see:
        She has deceived her father, and may thee.
                        [*Exeunt Duke, Senators, Officers, & c.*]
Othello. My life upon her faith! Honest Iago,
        My Desdemona must I leave to thee.
        I prithee let thy wife attend on her,   290
        And bring them after in the best advantage.°
        Come, Desdemona. I have but an hour
        Of love, of worldly matter, and direction
        To spend with thee. We must obey the time.
                        Exit [Moor with Desdemona].
Roderigo. Iago?   295
Iago. What say'st thou, noble heart?
Roderigo. What will I do, think'st thou?
Iago. Why, go to bed and sleep.
Roderigo. I will incontinently° drown myself.
Iago. If thou dost, I shall never love thee after. Why, thou silly   300
        gentleman?
Roderigo. It is silliness to live when to live is torment; and then
        have we a prescription to die when death is our physician.
Iago. O villainous! I have looked upon the world for four times
        seven years, and since I could distinguish betwixt a benefit   305
        and an injury, I never found man that knew how to love him-
        self. Ere I would say I would drown myself for the love of a
        guinea hen, I would change my humanity with a baboon.
Roderigo. What should I do? I confess it is my shame to be so
        fond, but it is not in my virtue° to amend it.   310
Iago. Virtue? A fig? 'Tis in ourselves that we are thus, or thus.
        Our bodies are our gardens, to the which our wills are garden-
        ers; so that if we will plant nettles or sow lettuce, set hyssop
        and weed up thyme, supply it with one gender of herbs or
        distract° it with many—either to have it sterile with idleness   315
        or manured with industry—why, the power and corrigible°
        authority of this lies in our wills. If the balance of our lives
        had not one scale of reason to poise another of sensuality,
        the blood and baseness of our natures would conduct us to

---

283 **delighted** delightful   291 **advantage** opportunity   299 **incontinently** at
once   310 **virtue** strength (Roderigo is saying that his nature controls him)
315 **distract** vary   316 **corrigible** corrective

most prepost'rous conclusions.° But we have reason to cool ₃₂₀ our raging motions, our carnal sting or unbitted° lusts, whereof I take this that you call love to be a sect or scion.°

Roderigo. It cannot be.

Iago. It is merely a lust of the blood and a permission of the will. Come, be a man! Drown thyself? Drown cats and blind pup- ₃₂₅ pies! I have professed me thy friend, and I confess me knit to thy deserving with cables of perdurable toughness. I could never better stead° thee than now. Put money in thy purse. Follow thou the wars; defeat thy favor° with an usurped° beard. I say, put money in thy purse. It cannot be long that ₃₃₀ Desdemona should continue her love to the Moor. Put money in thy purse. Nor he his to her. It was a violent commencement in her and thou shalt see an answerable° sequestration—put but money in thy purse. These Moors are changeable in their wills—fill thy purse with money. The ₃₃₅ food that to him now is as luscious as locusts° shall be to him shortly as bitter as coloquintida.° She must change for youth; when she is sated with his body, she will find the errors of her choice. Therefore, put money in thy purse. If thou wilt needs damn thyself, do it a more delicate way than drowning. Make ₃₄₀ all the money thou canst. If sanctimony° and a frail vow betwixt an erring° barbarian and supersubtle Venetian be not too hard for my wits, and all the tribe of hell, thou shalt enjoy her. Therefore, make money. A pox of drowning thyself, it is clean out of the way. Seek thou rather to be hanged in ₃₄₅ compassing° thy joy than to be drowned and go without her.

Roderigo. Wilt thou be fast to my hopes, if I depend on the issue?

Iago. Thou art sure of me. Go, make money. I have told thee often, and I retell thee again and again, I hate the Moor. My cause is hearted;° thine hath no less reason. Let us be con- ₃₅₀ junctive° in our revenge against him. If thou canst cuckold him, thou dost thyself a pleasure, me a sport. There are many events in the womb of time, which will be delivered. Traverse, go, provide thy money! We will have more of this tomorrow. Adieu. ₃₅₅

Roderigo. Where shall we meet i' th' morning?

Iago. At my lodging.

Roderigo. I'll be with thee betimes.

Iago. Go to, farewell. Do you hear, Roderigo?

---

320 **conclusions** ends 321 **unbitted** i.e., uncontrolled 322 **sect or scion** offshoot 328 **stead** serve 329 **defeat thy favor** disguise your face 329 **usurped** assumed 333 **answerable** similar 336 **locusts** (a sweet fruit) 337 **coloquintida** a purgative derived from a bitter apple 341 **sanctimony** sacred bond (of marriage) 342 **erring** wandering 346 **compassing** encompassing, achieving 350 **hearted** deep-seated in the heart 350-51 **conjunctive** joined

Roderigo. I'll sell all my land.   *Exit.*   ₃₆₀
Iago. Thus do I ever make my fool my purse;
    For I mine own gained knowledge° should profane
    If I would time expend with such snipe
    But for my sport and profit. I hate the Moor,
    And it is thought abroad that 'twixt my sheets   ₃₆₅
    H'as done my office. I know not if't be true,
    But I, for mere suspicion in that kind,
    Will do, as if for surety.° He holds me well;
    The better shall my purpose work on him.
    Cassio's a proper° man. Let me see now: ₃₇₀
    To get his place, and to plume up my will°
    In double knavery. How? How? Let's see.
    After some time, to abuse Othello's ears
    That he is too familiar with his wife.
    He hath a person and a smooth dispose°   ₃₇₅
    To be suspected—framed° to make women false.
    The Moor is of a free and open nature
    That thinks men honest that but seem to be so;
    And will as tenderly be held by th' nose
    As asses are.   ₃₈₀
    I have't! It is engendered! Hell and night
    Must bring this monstrous birth to the world's light.

                                                       [Exit.]

ACT II

Scene I. [*Cyprus.*]

Enter Montano and two Gentlemen, [one above].°

Montano. What from the cape can you discern at sea?
First Gentleman. Nothing at all, it is a high-wrought flood.
    I cannot 'twixt the heaven and the main
    Descry a sail.
Montano. Methinks the wind hath spoke aloud at land;   ₅
    A fuller blast ne'er shook our battlements.
    If it hath ruffianed so upon the sea,

362 **gained knowledge** i.e., practical, worldly wisdom   368 **surety** certainty
370 **proper** handsome   371 **plume up my will** (many explanations have been
offered for this crucial line, which in Q1 reads "make up my will." The general
sense is something like "to make more proud and gratify my ego")
375 **dispose** manner   376 **framed** designed   II.i. s.d. (the Folio arrangement
of this scene requires that the First Gentleman stand above—on the upper stage
—and act as a lookout reporting sights which cannot be seen by Montano standing below on the main stage)

What ribs of oak, when mountains melt on them,
Can hold the mortise? What shall we hear of this?
Second Gentleman. A segregation° of the Turkish fleet.   10
For do but stand upon the foaming shore,
The chidden billow seems to pelt the clouds;
The wind-shaked surge, with high and monstrous main,°
Seems to cast water on the burning Bear
And quench the guards of th' ever-fixèd pole.°   15
I never did like molestation view
On the enchafèd flood.
Montano.   If that the Turkish fleet
Be not ensheltered and embayed, they are drowned;
It is impossible to bear it out.

Enter a [third] Gentleman.

Third Gentleman. News, lads! Our wars are done.   20
The desperate tempest hath so banged the Turks
That their designment halts. A noble ship of Venice
Hath seen a grievous wrack and sufferance°
On most part of their fleet.
Montano. How? Is this true?
Third Gentleman.   The ship is here put in,   25
A Veronesa; Michael Cassio,
Lieutenant to the warlike Moor Othello,
Is come on shore; the Moor himself at sea,
And is in full commission here for Cyprus.
Montano. I am glad on't. 'Tis a worthy governor.   30
Third Gentleman. But this same Cassio, though he speak of comfort
Touching the Turkish loss, yet he looks sadly
And prays the Moor be safe, for they were parted
With foul and violent tempest.
Montano.   Pray heavens he be;
For I have served him, and the man commands   35
Like a full soldier. Let's to the seaside, ho!
As well to see the vessel that's come in
As to throw out our eyes for brave Othello,
Even till we make the main and th' aerial blue
An indistinct regard.°
Third Gentleman.   Come, let's do so;   40
For every minute is expectancy
Of more arrivancie.°

---

10 **segregation** separation   13 **main** (both "ocean" and "strength")   14-15
Seems . . . pole (the constellation Ursa Minor contains two stars which are
the *guards*, or companions, of the *pole*, or North Star)   23 **sufferance** damage
39-40 **the main . . . regard** i.e., the sea and sky become indistinguishable
42 **arrivancie** arrivals

Enter Cassio.

Cassio. Thanks, you the valiant of the warlike isle,
  That so approve° the Moor. O, let the heavens
  Give him defense against the elements,   45
  For I have lost him on a dangerous sea.
Montano. Is he well shipped?
Cassio. His bark is stoutly timbered, and his pilot
  Of very expert and approved allowance;°
  Therefore my hopes, not surfeited to death,°   50
  Stand in bold cure.° (*Within*) A sail, a sail, a sail!
Cassio. What noise?
First Gentleman. The town is empty; on the brow o' th' sea
  Stand ranks of people, and they cry, "A sail!"
Cassio. My hopes do shape him for the governor.   55

                                                              [*A shot.*]

Second Gentleman. They do discharge their shot of courtesy:
  Our friends at least.
Cassio.   I pray you, sir, go forth
  And give us truth who 'tis that is arrived.
Second Gentleman. I shall.   *Exit.*
Montano. But, good lieutenant, is your general wived?   60
Cassio. Most fortunately. He hath achieved a maid
  That paragons° description and wild fame;°
  One that excels the quirks of blazoning pens,°
  And in th' essential vesture of creation°
  Does tire the ingener.°

Enter [Second] Gentleman.

                    How now? Who has put in?   65
Second Gentleman. 'Tis one Iago, ancient to the general.
Cassio. H'as had most favorable and happy speed:
  Tempests themselves, high seas, and howling winds,
  The guttered° rocks and congregated° sands,
  Traitors ensteeped° to enclog the guiltless keel,   70

---

44 **approve** ("honor" or, perhaps, "are as warlike and valiant as your governor")   49 **approved allowance** known and tested   50 **not surfeited to death** i.e., not so great as to be in danger   51 **Stand in bold cure** i.e., are likely to be restored   62 **paragons** exceeds   62 **wild fame** extravagant report   63 **quirks of blazoning pens** ingenuities of praising pens   64 **essential vesture of creation** i.e., essential human nature as given by the Creator   65 **tire the ingener** (a difficult line which probably means something like "outdo the human ability to imagine and picture")   69 **guttered** jagged   69 **congregated** gathered   70 **ensteeped** submerged

As having sense° of beauty, do omit
Their mortal° natures, letting go safely by
The divine Desdemona.
Montano.   What is she?
Cassio. She that I spake of, our great captain's captain,
    Left in the conduct of the bold Iago,   75
    Whose footing° here anticipates our thoughts
    A se'nnight's° speed. Great Jove, Othello guard,
    And swell his sail with thine own pow'rful breath,
    That he may bless this bay with his tall° ship.
    Make love's quick pants in Desdemona's arms,   80
    Give renewed fire to our extincted spirits.

    Enter Desdemona, Iago, Roderigo, and Emilia.

    O, behold! The riches of the ship is come on shore!
    You men of Cyprus, let her have your knees.   [*Kneeling.*]
    Hail to thee, lady! and the grace of heaven,
    Before, behind thee, and on every hand,   85
    Enwheel thee round.
Desdemona.   I thank you valiant Cassio.
    What tidings can you tell me of my lord?
Cassio. He is not yet arrived, nor know I aught
    But that he's well and will be shortly here.
Desdemona. O but I fear. How lost you company?   90
Cassio. The great contention of sea and skies
    Parted our fellowship. (*Within*) A sail, a sail!   [*A shot.*]
            But hark. A sail!
Second Gentleman. They give this greeting to the citadel;
    This likewise is a friend.
Cassio.   See for the news.   95
            [*Exit Gentleman*]
    Good ancient, you are welcome. [*To Emilia*] Welcome, mistress.
    Let it not gall your patience, good Iago,
    That I extend° my manners. 'Tis my breeding°
    That gives me this bold show of courtesy.   [*Kisses Emilia.*]
Iago. Sir, would she give you so much of her lips   100
    As of her tongue she oft bestows on me,
    You would have enough.
Desdemona.   Alas, she has no speech.
Iago. In faith, too much.
    I find it still when I have leave to sleep.°

---

71 **sense** awareness 72 **mortal** deadly 76 **footing** landing 77 **se'nnight's** week's 79 **tall** brave 98 **extend** stretch 98 **breeding** careful training in manners (Cassio is considerably more the polished gentleman than Iago, and aware of it) 104 **still . . . sleep** i.e., even when she allows me to sleep she continues to scold

Marry, before your ladyship,° I grant,   105
  She puts her tongue a little in her heart
  And chides with thinking.
Emilia.   You have little cause to say so.
Iago. Come on, come on! You are pictures° out of door,
  Bells in your parlors, wildcats in your kitchens,
  Saints in your injuries,° devils being offended,   110
  Players in your housewifery,° and housewives in your beds.
Desdemona. O, fie upon thee, slanderer!
Iago. Nay, it is true, or else I am a Turk:
  You rise to play, and go to bed to work.
Emilia. You shall not write my praise.
Iago.   No, let me not.   115
Desdemona. What wouldst write of me, if thou shouldst praise me?
Iago. O gentle lady, do not put me to't,
  For I am nothing if not critical.
Desdemona. Come on, assay. There's one gone to the harbor?
Iago. Ay, madam.
Desdemona [*Aside*]. I am not merry; but I do beguile   120
  The thing I am by seeming otherwise.—
  Come, how wouldst thou praise me?
Iago. I am about it; but indeed my invention
  Comes from my pate as birdlime° does from frieze°—
  It plucks out brains and all. But my Muse labors,   125
  And thus she is delivered:
  If she be fair° and wise: fairness and wit,
  The one's for use, the other useth it.
Desdemona. Well praised. How if she be black° and witty?
Iago. If she be black, and thereto have a wit,   130
  She'll find a white that shall her blackness fit.
Desdemona. Worse and worse!
Emilia. How if fair and foolish?
Iago. She never yet was foolish that was fair,
  For even her folly helped her to an heir.   135
Desdemona. These are old fond° paradoxes to make fools laugh
  i' th' alehouse. What miserable praise hast thou for her that's
  foul and foolish?
Iago. There's none so foul, and foolish thereunto,
  But does foul pranks which fair and wise ones do.   140
Desdemona. O heavy ignorance. Thou praisest the worst best.

105 **before your ladyship** in your presence   108 **pictures** models (of virtue)
110 **in your injuries** when you injure others   111 **housewifery** (this word can
mean "careful, economical household management," and Iago would then be
accusing women of only pretending to be good housekeepers, while in bed they
are either [1] economical of their favors, or more likely [2] serious and dedicated
workers)   124 **birdlime** a sticky substance put on branches to catch birds   124
frieze rough cloth   127 **fair** light-complexioned   129 **black** brunette   136
fond foolish

But what praise couldst thou bestow on a deserving woman indeed—one that in the authority of her merit did justly put on
the vouch of very malice itself?°

Iago. She that was ever fair, and never proud;   145
Had tongue at will, and yet was never loud;
Never lacked gold, and yet went never gay;
Fled from her wish, and yet said "Now I may";
She that being angered, her revenge being nigh,
Bade her wrong stay, and her displeasure fly;   150
She that in wisdom never was so frail
To change the cod's head for the salmon's tail;°
She that could think, and nev'r disclose her mind;
See suitors following, and not look behind:
She was a wight° (if such wights were)—   155

Desdemona. To do what?

Iago. To suckle fools and chronicle small beer.°

Desdemona. O most lame and impotent conclusion. Do not learn
of him, Emilia, though he be thy husband. How say you,
Cassio? Is he not a most profane and liberal° counselor?   160

Cassio. He speaks home,° madam. You may relish him more in°
the soldier than in the scholar. [*Takes Desdemona's hand.*]

Iago [*Aside*]. He takes her by the palm. Ay well said, whisper!
With as little a web as this will I ensnare as great a fly as
Cassio. Ay, smile upon her, do! I will gyve° thee in thine own   165
courtship.—You say true; 'tis so, indeed!—If such tricks as
these strip you out of your lieutenantry, it had been better
you had not kissed your three fingers so oft—which now again
you are most apt to play the sir° in. Very good! Well kissed!
An excellent curtsy!° 'Tis so, indeed. Yet again your fingers   170
to your lips? Would they were clyster pipes° for your sake!
[*Trumpets within.*] The Moor! I know his trumpet.°

Cassio. 'Tis truly so.

Desdemona. Let's meet him and receive him.

Cassio. Lo, where he comes.   175

    Enter Othello and Attendants.

Othello. O my fair warrior!

Desdemona.   My dear Othello.

Othello. It gives me wonder great as my content

143-44 **one . . . itself** i.e., a woman so honest and deserving that even malice
would be forced to approve of her   152 **To . . . tail** i.e., to exchange something
valuable for something useless   155 **wight** person   157 **chronicle small beer**
i.e., keep household accounts (the most trivial of occupations in Iago's opinion)
160 **liberal** licentious   161 **speaks home** thrusts deeply with his speech   161
relish him more in enjoy him more as   165 **gyve** bind   169 **the sir** the fashionable gentleman   170 **curtsy** courtesy, i.e., bow   171 **clyster pipes** enema
tubes   172 **his trumpet** (great men had their own distinctive calls)

To see you here before me. O my soul's joy!
If after every tempest come such calms,
May the winds blow till they have wakened death.　　　180
And let the laboring bark climb hills of seas
Olympus-high, and duck again as low
As hell's from heaven. If it were now to die,
'Twas now to be most happy; for I fear
My soul hath her content so absolute　　　　　　185
That not another comfort like to this
Succeeds in unknown fate.
Desdemona.　　　　　　　　The heavens forbid
But that our loves and comforts should increase
Even as our days do grow.
Othello.　　　　　　　　Amen to that, sweet powers!
I cannot speak enough of this content;　　　　　190
It stops me here [*touches his heart*]; it is too much of joy.
And this, and this, the greatest discords be　　　[*They kiss.*]
That e'er our hearts shall make!
Iago.　　　　　　　[*Aside*] O, you are well tuned now!
But I'll set down the pegs° that make this music,
As honest as I am.
Othello.　　　　　　　Come, let us to the castle.　　　195
News, friends! Our wars are done; the Turks are drowned.
How does my old acquaintance of this isle?
Honey, you shall be well desired in Cyprus;
I have found great love amongst them. O my sweet,
I prattle out of fashion, and I dote　　　　　　200
In mine own comforts. I prithee, good Iago,
Go to the bay and disembark my coffers.
Bring thou the master to the citadel;
He is a good one, and his worthiness
Does challenge° much respect. Come, Desdemona,　　205
Once more well met at Cyprus.

　　　Exit Othello and Desdemona [and all but Iago and Roderigo].

Iago [*To an Attendant*]. Do thou meet me presently at the harbor.
　　[*To Roderigo*] Come hither. If thou be'st valiant (as they
　　say base men being in love have then a nobility in their na-
　　tures more than is native to them), list me. The lieutenant　210
　　tonight watches on the court of guard.° First, I must tell
　　thee this: Desdemona is directly in love with him.
Roderigo. With him? Why, 'tis not possible.
Iago. Lay thy finger thus [*puts his finger to his lips*], and let thy
　　soul be instructed. Mark me with what violence she first　215
　　loved the Moor but for bragging and telling her fantastical

194 **set down the pegs** loosen the strings (to produce discord)　205 **challenge**
require, exact　211 **court of guard** guardhouse

lies. To love him still for prating? Let not thy discreet heart think it. Her eye must be fed. And what delight shall she have to look on the devil? When the blood is made dull with the act of sport, there should be a game° to inflame it and to give satiety a fresh appetite, loveliness in favor,° sympathy in years,° manners, and beauties; all which the Moor is defective in. Now for want of these required conveniences,° her delicate tenderness will find itself abused, begin to heave the gorge,° disrelish and abhor the Moor. Very nature will instruct her in it and compel her to some second choice. Now, sir, this granted—as it is a most pregnant° and unforced position—who stands so eminent in the degree of this fortune as Cassio does? A knave very voluble; no further conscionable° than in putting on the mere form of civil and humane° seeming for the better compass of his salt° and most hidden loose° affection. Why, none! Why, none! A slipper° and subtle knave, a finder of occasion, that has an eye can stamp and counterfeit advantages, though true advantage never present itself. A devilish knave. Besides, the knave is handsome, young, and hath all those requisites in him that folly and green minds look after. A pestilent complete knave, and the woman hath found him already.

Roderigo. I cannot believe that in her; she's full of most blessed condition.

Iago. Blessed fig's-end! The wine she drinks is made of grapes. If she had been blessed, she would never have loved the Moor. Blessed pudding! Didst thou not see her paddle with the palm of his hand? Didst not mark that?

Roderigo. Yes, that I did; but that was but courtesy.

Iago. Lechery, by this hand! [*Extends his index finger.*] An index° and obscure prologue to the history of lust and foul thoughts. They met so near with their lips that their breaths embraced together. Villainous thoughts, Roderigo. When these mutualities so marshal the way, hard at hand comes the master and main exercise, th' incorporate° conclusion: Pish! But, sir, be you ruled by me. I have brought you from Venice. Watch you tonight; for the command, I'll lay't upon you. Cassio knows you not. I'll not be far from you. Do you find some occasion to anger Cassio, either by speaking too loud, or tainting° his discipline, or from what other course you please which the time shall more favorably minister.

220
225
230
235
240
245
250
255

220 **game** sport (with the added sense of "gamey," "rank,")   221 **favor** countenance, appearance   221-22 **sympathy in years** sameness of age 223 **conveniences** advantages   224-25 **heave the gorge** vomit   227 **pregnant** likely   229 **no further conscionable** having no more conscience   230 **humane** polite   231 **salt** lecherous   232 **loose** immoral   232 **slipper** slippery   246 **index** pointer   251 **incorporate** carnal   256 **tainting** discrediting

Roderigo. Well.

Iago. Sir, he's rash and very sudden in choler,° and haply may
    strike at you. Provoke him that he may; for even out of that 260
    will I cause these of Cyprus to mutiny, whose qualification
    shall come into no true taste° again but by the displanting of
    Cassio. So shall you have a shorter journey to your desires by
    the means I shall then have to prefer them; and the impedi-
    ment most profitably removed without the which there were 265
    no expectation of our prosperity.

Roderigo. I will do this if you can bring it to my opportunity.

Iago. I warrant thee. Meet me by and by at the citadel. I must
    fetch his necessaries ashore. Farewell.

Roderigo. Adieu.   *Exit.* 270

Iago. That Cassio loves her, I do well believe 't;
    That she loves him, 'tis apt and of great credit.
    The Moor, howbeit that I endure him not,
    Is of a constant, loving, noble nature,
    And I dare think he'll prove to Desdemona 275
    A most dear° husband. Now I do love her too;
    Not out of absolute° lust, though peradventure°
    I stand accountant for as great a sin,
    But partly led to diet° my revenge,
    For that I do suspect the lusty Moor 280
    Hath leaped into my seat; the thought whereof
    Doth, like a poisonous mineral, gnaw my inwards;
    And nothing can or shall content my soul
    Till I am evened with him, wife for wife.
    Or failing so, yet that I put the Moor 285
    At least into a jealousy so strong
    That judgment cannot cure. Which thing to do,
    If this poor trash of Venice, whom I trace°
    For his quick hunting, stand the putting on,
    I'll have our Michael Cassio on the hip, 290
    Abuse him to the Moor in the right garb°
    (For I fear Cassio with my nightcap too),
    Make the Moor thank me, love me, and reward me
    For making him egregiously an ass
    And practicing upon° his peace and quiet, 295
    Even to madness. 'Tis here, but yet confused:
    Knavery's plain face is never seen till used.   *Exit.*

259 **choler** anger   261-62 **qualification . . . taste** i.e., appeasement will not be
brought about (wine was "qualified" by adding water)   276 **dear** expensive
277 **out of absolute** absolutely out of   277 **peradventure** perchance   279 **diet**
feed   288 **trace** (most editors emend to "trash," meaning to hang weights on
a dog to slow his hunting: but "trace" clearly means something like "put on
the trace" or "set on the track")   291 **right garb** i.e., "proper fashion"
295 **practicing upon** scheming to destroy

Scene II. [*A street.*]

Enter Othello's Herald, with a proclamation.

Herald. It is Othello's pleasure, our noble and valiant general, that
upon certain tidings now arrived importing the mere perdi-
tion° of the Turkish fleet, every man put himself into
triumph. Some to dance, some to make bonfires, each man to
what sport and revels his addition° leads him. For, besides   5
these beneficial news, it is the celebration of his nuptial. So
much was his pleasure should be proclaimed. All offices° are
open, and there is full liberty of feasting from this present
hour of five till the bell have told eleven. Bless the isle of
Cyprus and our noble general Othello!   *Exit.*   10

Scene III. [*The citadel of Cyprus.*]

Enter Othello, Desdemona, Cassio, and Attendants.

Othello. Good Michael, look you to the guard tonight.
   Let's teach ourselves that honorable stop,
   Not to outsport discretion.
Cassio. Iago hath discretion what to do;
   But notwithstanding, with my personal eye   5
   Will I look to't.
Othello.   Iago is most honest.
   Michael, good night. Tomorrow with your earliest
   Let me have speech with you. [*To Desdemona*] Come, my
      dear love,
   The purchase made, the fruits are to ensue,
   That profit's yet to come 'tween me and you.   10
   Good night.
         Exit [*Othello with Desdemona and Attendants*].

Enter Iago.

Cassio. Welcome, Iago. We must to the watch.
Iago. Not this hour, lieutenant; 'tis not yet ten o' th' clock. Our
   general cast° us thus early for the love of his Desdemona;
   who let us not therefore blame. He hath not yet made   15
   wanton the night with her, and she is sport for Jove.
Cassio. She's a most exquisite lady.
Iago. And, I'll warrant her, full of game.
Cassio. Indeed, she's a most fresh and delicate creature.

II.ii.2-3 **mere perdition** absolute destruction   5 **addition** rank   7 **offices**
kitchens and storerooms of food.   II.iii.14 **cast** dismissed

Iago. What an eye she has! Methinks it sounds a parley to 20
provocation.
Cassio. An inviting eye; and yet methinks right modest.
Iago. And when she speaks, is it not an alarum° to love?
Cassio. She is indeed perfection.
Iago. Well, happiness to their sheets! Come, lieutenant, I have a 25
stoup° of wine, and here without are a brace of Cyprus gal-
lants that would fain have a measure to the health of black
Othello.
Cassio. Not tonight, good Iago. I have very poor and unhappy
brains for drinking; I could well wish courtesy would invent 30
some other custom of entertainment.
Iago. O, they are our friends. But one cup! I'll drink for you.
Cassio. I have drunk but one tonight, and that was craftily
qualified° too; and behold what innovation it makes here.
I am unfortunate in the infirmity and dare not task my weak- 35
ness with any more.
Iago. What, man! 'Tis a night of revels, the gallants desire it.
Cassio. Where are they?
Iago. Here, at the door. I pray you call them in.
Cassio. I'll do't, but it dislikes me.   *Exit.* 40
Iago. If I can fasten but one cup upon him
With that which he hath drunk tonight already,
He'll be as full of quarrel and offense
As my young mistress' dog. Now, my sick fool Roderigo,
Whom love hath turned almost the wrong side out, 45
To Desdemona hath tonight caroused
Potations pottle-deep;° and he's to watch.
Three else° of Cyprus, noble swelling spirits,
That hold their honors in a wary distance,°
The very elements of this warlike isle, 50
Have I tonight flustered with flowing cups,
And they watch too. Now, 'mongst this flock of drunkards
Am I to put our Cassio in some action
That may offend the isle. But here they come.

Enter Cassio, Montano, and Gentlemen.

If consequence do but approve my dream, 55
My boat sails freely, both with wind and stream.
Cassio. 'Fore God, they have given me a rouse° already.
Montano. Good faith, a little one; not past a pint, as I am a
soldier.
Iago. Some wine, ho!

---

23 **alarum** the call to action, "general quarters"   26 **stoup** two-quart tankard
34 **qualified** diluted   47 **pottle-deep** to the bottom of the cup   48 **else** others
49 **hold . . . distance** are scrupulous in maintaining their honor   57 **rouse** drink

[*Sings*] And let me the canakin clink, clink;   60
    And let me the canakin clink.
        A soldier's a man;
        O man's life's but a span,
        Why then, let a soldier drink.   65
  Some wine, boys!

Cassio. 'Fore God, an excellent song!

Iago. I learned it in England, where indeed they are most potent
  in potting. Your Dane, your German, and your swag-bellied°
  Hollander—Drink, ho!—are nothing to your English.   70

Cassio. Is your Englishman so exquisite° in his drinking?

Iago. Why, he drinks you with facility your Dane dead drunk; he
  sweats not to overthrow your Almain; he gives your Hollander
  a vomit ere the next pottle can be filled.

Cassio. To the health of our general!   75

Montano. I am for it, lieutenant, and I'll do you justice.

Iago. O sweet England!
  [*Sings*] King Stephen was and a worthy peer;
        His breeches cost him but a crown;
        He held them sixpence all too dear,   80
        With that he called the tailor lown.°
        He was a wight of high renown,
        And thou art but of low degree:
        'Tis pride that pulls the country down;
        And take thine auld cloak about thee.   85
  Some wine, ho!

Cassio. 'Fore God, this is a more exquisite song than the other.

Iago. Will you hear't again?

Cassio. No, for I hold him to be unworthy of his place that does
  those things. Well, God's above all; and there be souls must   90
  be saved, and there be souls must not be saved.

Iago. It's true, good lieutenant.

Cassio. For mine own part—no offense to the general, nor any
  man of quality—I hope to be saved.

Iago. And so do I too, lieutenant.   95

Cassio. Ay, but, by your leave, not before me. The lieutenant is to
  be saved before the ancient. Let's have no more of this; let's
  to our affairs.—God forgive us our sins!—Gentlemen, let's
  look to our business. Do not think, gentlemen, I am drunk.
  This is my ancient; this is my right hand, and this is my left.   100
  I am not drunk now. I can stand well enough, and I speak
  well enough.

Gentlemen. Excellent well!

Cassio. Why, very well then. You must not think then that I am
  drunk.   *Exit.*   105

---

69 **swag-bellied** hanging   71 **exquisite** superb   81 **lown** lout

Montano. To th' platform, masters. Come, let's set the watch.
Iago. You see this fellow that is gone before.
  He's a soldier fit to stand by Caesar
  And give direction; and do but see his vice.
  'Tis to his virtue a just equinox,° 110
  The one as long as th' other. 'Tis pity of him.
  I fear the trust Othello puts him in,
  On some odd time of his infirmity,
  Will shake this island.
Montano.   But is he often thus?
Iago. 'Tis evermore his prologue to his sleep: 115
  He'll watch the horologe a double set°
  If drink rock not his cradle.
Montano.   It were well
  The general were put in mind of it.
  Perhaps he sees it not, or his good nature
  Prizes the virtue that appears in Cassio 120
  And looks not on his evils. Is not this true?

    Enter Roderigo.

Iago [*Aside*]. How now, Roderigo?
  I pray you after the lieutenant, go!   [*Exit Roderigo.*]
Montano. And 'tis great pity that the noble Moor
  Should hazard such a place as his own second 125
  With one of an ingraft° infirmity.
  It were an honest action to say so
  To the Moor.
Iago.   Not I, for this fair island!
  I do love Cassio well and would do much
  To cure him of this evil.   (Help! Help! *Within.*)
              But hark? What noise? 130

    Enter Cassio, pursuing Roderigo.

Cassio. Zounds, you rogue! You rascal!
Montano. What's the matter, lieutenant?
Cassio. A knave teach me my duty? I'll beat the knave into a
    twiggen° bottle.
Roderigo. Beat me? 135
Cassio. Dost thou prate, rogue?   [*Strikes him.*]
Montano. Nay, good lieutenant! I pray you, sir, hold your hand.
                            [*Stays him.*]
Cassio. Let me go, sir, or I'll knock you o'er the mazzard.°
Montano. Come, come, you're drunk!

---

110 **just equinox** exact balance (of dark and light) 116 **watch ... set** stay
awake twice around the clock 126 **ingraft** ingrained 134 **twiggen** wicker-
covered 138 **mazzard** head

Cassio. Drunk?   [*They fight.*] ¹⁴⁰
Iago [*Aside to Roderigo*]. Away, I say! Go out and cry a mutiny!
                                                  [*Exit Roderigo.*]

> Nay, good lieutenant. God's will, gentlemen!
> Help, ho! Lieutenant. Sir. Montano.
> Help, masters! Here's a goodly watch indeed!

                                                  [*A bell rung.*]

> Who's that which rings the bell? Diablo, ho!   ¹⁴⁵
> The town will rise. God's will, lieutenant,
> You'll be ashamed forever.

Enter Othello and Attendants.

Othello.   What is the matter here?
Montano. Zounds, I bleed still. I am hurt to the death.
> He dies.   [*He and Cassio fight again.*]
Othello. Hold for your lives!   ¹⁵⁰
Iago. Hold, ho! Lieutenant. Sir. Montano. Gentlemen!
> Have you forgot all place of sense and duty?
> Hold! The general speaks to you. Hold, for shame!
Othello. Why, how now, ho? From whence ariseth this?
> Are we turned Turks, and to ourselves do that   ¹⁵⁵
> Which heaven hath forbid the Ottomites?°
> For Christian shame put by this barbarous brawl!
> He that stirs next to carve for his own rage
> Holds his soul light;° he dies upon his motion.
> Silence that dreadful bell! It frights the isle   ¹⁶⁰
> From her propriety.° What is the matter, masters?
> Honest Iago, that looks dead with grieving,
> Speak. Who began this? On thy love, I charge thee.
Iago. I do not know. Friends all, but now, even now,
> In quarter° and in tears like bride and groom   ¹⁶⁵
> Devesting them for bed; and then, but now—
> As if some planet had unwitted men—
> Swords out, and tilting one at other's breasts
> In opposition bloody. I cannot speak
> Any beginning to this peevish odds,°   ¹⁷⁰
> And would in action glorious I had lost
> Those legs that brought me to a part of it!
Othello. How comes it, Michael, you are thus forgot?
Cassio. I pray you pardon me; I cannot speak.
Othello. Worthy Montano, you were wont to be civil;   ¹⁷⁵
> The gravity and stillness of your youth
> The world hath noted, and your name is great

---

156 **heaven . . . Ottomites** i.e., by sending the storm which dispersed the Turks
159 **Holds his soul light** values his soul lightly   161 **propriety** proper order
165 **In quarter** on duty   170 **odds** quarrel

In mouths of wisest censure.° What's the matter
That you unlace° your reputation thus
And spend your rich opinion° for the name   180
Of a night-brawler? Give me answer to it.

Montano. Worthy Othello, I am hurt to danger.
Your officer, Iago, can inform you,
While I spare speech, which something now offends° me,
Of all that I do know; nor know I aught   185
By me that's said or done amiss this night,
Unless self-charity be sometimes a vice,
And to defend ourselves it be a sin
When violence assails us.

Othello.   Now, by heaven,
My blood begins my safer guides to rule,   190
And passion, having my best judgment collied,°
Assays to lead the way. If I once stir
Or do but lift this arm, the best of you
Shall sink in my rebuke. Give me to know
How this foul rout began, who set it on;   195
And he that is approved in this offense,
Though he had twinned with me, both at a birth,
Shall lose me. What? In a town of war
Yet wild, the people's hearts brimful of fear,
To manage° private and domestic quarrel?   200
In night, and on the court and guard of safety?
'Tis monstrous. Iago, who began't?

Montano. If partially affined, or leagued in office,°
Thou dost deliver more or less than truth,
Thou art no soldier.

Iago.   Touch me not so near.   205
I had rather have this tongue cut from my mouth
Than it should do offense to Michael Cassio.
Yet I persuade myself to speak the truth
Shall nothing wrong him. This it is, general.
Montano and myself being in speech,   210
There comes a fellow crying out for help,
And Cassio following him with determined sword
To execute upon him. Sir, this gentleman
Steps in to Cassio and entreats his pause.
Myself the crying fellow did pursue,   215
Lest by his clamor—as it so fell out—
The town might fall in fright. He, swift of foot,

---

178 **censure** judgment   179 **unlace** undo (the term refers specifically to the
dressing of a wild boar killed in the hunt)   180 **opinion** reputation
184 **offends** harms, hurts   191 **collied** darkened   200 **manage** conduct
203 **If . . . office** if you are partial because you are related ("affined") or the
brother officer (of Cassio)

Outran my purpose; and I returned then rather
For that I heard the clink and fall of swords,
And Cassio high in oath; which till tonight   220
I ne'er might say before. When I came back—
For this was brief—I found them close together
At blow and thrust, even as again they were
When you yourself did part them.
More of this matter cannot I report;   225
But men are men; the best sometimes forget.
Though Cassio did some little wrong to him,
As men in rage strike those that wish them best,
Yet surely Cassio I believe received
From him that fled some strange indignity,   230
Which patience could not pass.°
Othello.   I know, Iago,
Thy honesty and love doth mince° this matter,
Making it light to Cassio. Cassio, I love thee;
But never more be officer of mine.

Enter Desdemona, attended.

Look if my gentle love be not raised up.   235
I'll make thee an example.
Desdemona.   What is the matter, dear.
Othello. All's well, sweeting; come away to bed.
    [*To Montano*] Sir, for your hurts, myself will be your
        surgeon.
    Lead him off.   [*Montano led off.*]
    Iago, look with care about the town   240
    And silence those whom this vile brawl distracted.
    Come, Desdemona: 'tis the soldiers' life
    To have their balmy slumbers waked with strife.
               Exit [with all but Iago and Cassio].
Iago. What, are you hurt, lieutenant?
Cassio. Ay, past all surgery.   245
Iago. Marry, God forbid!
Cassio. Reputation, reputation, reputation! O, I have lost my rep-
    utation! I have lost the immortal part of myself, and what
    remains is bestial. My reputation, Iago, my reputation.
Iago. As I am an honest man, I had thought you had received   250
    some bodily wound. There is more sense° in that than in
    reputation. Reputation is an idle and most false imposition,°
    oft got without merit and lost without deserving. You have
    lost no reputation at all unless you refute yourself such a
    loser. What, man, there are more ways to recover the general   255

---

231 **pass** allow to pass   232 **mince** cut up (i.e., tell only part of)   251 **sense**
physical feeling   252 **imposition** external thing

again. You are but now cast in his mood°—a punishment more in policy° than in malice—even so as one would beat his offenseless dog to affright an imperious lion. Sue to him again, and he's yours.

Cassio. I will rather sue to be despised than to deceive so good   260
a commander with so slight, so drunken, and so indiscreet an officer. Drunk! And speak parrot!° And squabble! Swagger! Swear! and discourse fustian° with one's own shadow! O thou invisible spirit of wine, if thou hast no name to be known by, let us call thee devil!   265

Iago. What was he that you followed with your sword? What has he done to you?

Cassio. I know not.

Iago. Is't possible?

Cassio. I remember a mass of things, but nothing distinctly: a   270
quarrel, but nothing wherefore. O God, that men should put an enemy in their mouths to steal away their brains! that we should with joy, pleasance, revel, and applause transform ourselves into beasts!

Iago. Why, but you are now well enough. How came you thus recovered?   275

Cassio. It hath pleased the devil drunkenness to give place to the devil wrath. One unperfectness shows me another, to make me frankly despise myself.

Iago. Come, you are too severe a moraler. As the time, the place,   280
and the condition of this country stands, I could heartily wish this had befall'n; but since it is as it is, mend it for your own good.

Cassio. I will ask him for my place again: he shall tell me I am a drunkard. Had I as many mouths as Hydra, such an answer   285
would stop them all. To be now a sensible man, by and by a fool, and presently a beast! O strange! Every inordinate cup is unblest, and the ingredient is a devil.

Iago. Come, come, good wine is a good familiar creature if it be well used. Exclaim no more against it. And, good lieutenant,   290
I think you think I love you.

Cassio. I have well approved it, sir. I drunk?

Iago. You or any man living may be drunk at a time, man. I tell you what you shall do. Our general's wife is now the general. I may say so in this respect for that he hath devoted and   295
given up himself to the contemplation, mark, and devotement of her parts° and graces. Confess yourself freely to her; importune her help to put you in your place again. She is of

256 **cast in his mood** dismissed because of his anger   257 **in policy** politically necessary   262 **speak parrot** gabble without sense   263 **discourse fustian** speak nonsense ("fustian" was a coarse cotton cloth used for stuffing)   296-97 **devotement of her parts** devotion to her qualities

so free, so kind, so apt, so blessed a disposition she holds it a
vice in her goodness not to do more than she is requested. 300
This broken joint between you and her husband entreat her
to splinter;° and my fortunes against any lay° worth naming,
this crack of your love shall grow stronger than it was before.
Cassio. You advise me well.
Iago. I protest, in the sincerity of love and honest kindness. 305
Cassio. I think it freely; and betimes in the morning I will be-
seech the virtuous Desdemona to undertake for me. I am
desperate of my fortunes if they check° me.
Iago. You are in the right. Good night, lieutenant; I must to the
watch. 310
Cassio. Good night, honest Iago. *Exit Cassio.*
Iago. And what's he then that says I play the villain,
  When this advice is free° I give, and honest,
  Probal to° thinking, and indeed the course
  To win the Moor again? For 'tis most easy 315
  Th' inclining° Desdemona to subdue
  In any honest suit; she's framed as fruitful°
  As the free elements.° And then for her
  To win the Moor—were't to renounce his baptism,
  All seals and symbols of redeemèd sin— 320
  His soul is so enfettered to her love
  That she may make, unmake, do what she list,
  Even as her appetite° shall play the god
  With his weak function.° How am I then a villain
  To counsel Cassio to this parallel course, 325
  Directly to his good? Divinity of hell!
  When devils will the blackest sins put on,°
  They do suggest at first with heavenly shows,°
  As I do now. For whiles this honest fool
  Plies Desdemona to repair his fortune, 330
  And she for him pleads strongly to the Moor,
  I'll pour this pestilence into his ear:
  That she repeals him° for her body's lust;
  And by how much she strives to do him good,
  She shall undo her credit with the Moor. 335
  So will I turn her virtue into pitch,
  And out of her own goodness make the net
  That shall enmesh them all. How now, Roderigo?

Enter Roderigo.

---

302 **splinter** splint   302 **lay** wager   308 **check** repulse   313 **free** generous
and open   314 **Probal to** provable by   316 **inclining** inclined (to be helpful)
317 **framed as fruitful** made as generous   318 **elements** i.e., basic nature
323 **appetite** liking   324 **function** thought   327 **put on** advance, further
328 **shows** appearances   333 **repeals him** asks for (Cassio's reinstatement)

Roderigo. I do not follow here in the chase, not like a hound that
    hunts, but one that fills up the cry.° My money is almost   340
    spent; I have been tonight exceedingly well cudgeled; and I
    think the issue will be, I shall have so much experience for
    my pains; and so, with no money at all, and a little more wit,
    return again to Venice.

Iago. How poor are they that have not patience!   345
    What wound did ever heal but by degrees?
    Thou know'st we work by wit, and not by witchcraft;
    And wit depends on dilatory time.
    Does't not go well? Cassio hath beaten thee,
    And thou by that small hurt hath cashiered Cassio.   350
    Though other things grow fair against the sun,
    Yet fruits that blossom first will first be ripe.
    Content thyself awhile. By the mass, 'tis morning!
    Pleasure and action make the hours seem short.
    Retire thee; go where thou art billeted.   355
    Away, I say! Thou shalt know more hereafter.
    Nay, get thee gone!   *Exit Roderigo.*
              Two things are to be done:
    My wife must move° for Cassio to her mistress;
    I'll set her on;
    Myself awhile° to draw the Moor apart   360
    And bring him jump° when he may Cassio find
    Soliciting his wife. Ay, that's the way!
    Dull not device by coldness and delay.   *Exit.*

ACT III

Scene I. [*A street.*]

Enter Cassio [*and*] *Musicians.*

Cassio. Masters, play here. I will content your pains.°
    Something that's brief; and bid "Good morrow, general."
                         [*They play.*]

    [*Enter Clown.*°]

Clown. Why, masters, have your instruments been in Naples°
    that they speak i' th' nose thus?

---

340 **fills up the cry** makes up one of the hunting pack, adding to the noise
but not actually tracking   358 **move** petition   360 **awhile** at the same time
361 **jump** at the precise moment and place   III.i.1 **content your pains**
reward your efforts   2 s.d. **Clown** fool   3 **Naples** this may refer either to the
Neapolitan nasal tone, or to syphilis—rife in Naples—which breaks down the
nose)

Musician. How, sir, how?   5
Clown. Are these, I pray you, wind instruments?
Musician. Ay, marry, are they, sir.
Clown. O, thereby hangs a tale.
Musician. Whereby hangs a tale, sir?
Clown. Marry, sir, by many a wind instrument that I know. But,   10
     masters, here's money for you; and the general so likes your
     music that he desires you, for love's sake, to make no more
     noise with it.
Musician. Well, sir, we will not.
Clown. If you have any music that may not be heard, to't again.   15
     But, as they say, to hear music the general does not greatly
     care.
Musician. We have none such, sir.
Clown. Then put up your pipes in your bag, for I'll away. Go,
     vanish into air, away!   *Exit Musicians.*   20
Cassio. Dost thou hear me, mine honest friend?
Clown. No. I hear not your honest friend. I hear you.
Cassio. Prithee keep up thy quillets.° There's a poor piece of gold
     for thee. If the gentlewoman that attends the general's wife
     be stirring, tell her there's one Cassio entreats her a little   25
     favor of speech. Wilt thou do this?
Clown. She is stirring, sir. If she will stir hither, I shall seem to
     notify unto her.°   *Exit Clown.*

     Enter Iago.

Cassio. In happy time, Iago.
Iago.   You have not been abed then?
Cassio. Why no, the day had broke before we parted.   30
     I have made bold, Iago, to send in to your wife;
     My suit to her is that she will to virtuous Desdemona
     Procure me some access.
Iago.   I'll send her to you presently,
     And I'll devise a mean to draw the Moor
     Out of the way, that your converse and business   35
     May be more free.
Cassio. I humbly thank you for't.   *Exit [Iago].*
                         I never knew
     A Florentine° more kind and honest.

     Enter Emilia.

Emilia. Good morrow, good lieutenant. I am sorry
     For your displeasure;° but all will sure be well.   40

---

23 **quillets** puns   27-28 **seem . . . her** (the Clown is mocking Cassio's overly
elegant manner of speaking)   38 **Florentine** i.e., Iago is as kind as if he
were from Cassio's home town, Florence   40 **displeasure** discomforting

The general and his wife are talking of it,
And she speaks for you stoutly. The Moor replies
That he you hurt is of great fame in Cyprus
And great affinity,° and that in wholesome wisdom
He might not but refuse you. But he protests he loves you,   45
And needs no other suitor but his likings
To bring you in again.
Cassio.   Yet I beseech you,
If you think fit, or that it may be done,
Give me advantage of some brief discourse
With Desdemona alone.
Emilia.   Pray you come in.   50
I will bestow you where you shall have time
To speak your bosom° freely.
Cassio.   I am much bound to you.

[*Exeunt.*]

Scene II. [*The citadel.*]

Enter Othello, Iago, and Gentlemen.

Othello. These letters give, Iago, to the pilot
And by him do my duties to the Senate.
That done, I will be walking on the works;
Repair° there to me.
Iago.   Well, my good lord, I'll do't.
Othello. This fortification, gentlemen, shall we see't?   5
Gentlemen. We'll wait upon your lordship.   *Exeunt.*

Scene III. [*The citadel.*]

Enter Desdemona, Cassio, and Emilia.

Desdemona. Be thou assured, good Cassio, I will do
All my abilities in thy behalf.
Emilia. Good madam, do. I warrant it grieves my husband
As if the cause were his.
Desdemona. O, that's an honest fellow. Do not doubt, Cassio,   5
But I will have my lord and you again
As friendly as you were.
Cassio.   Bounteous madam,
Whatever shall become of Michael Cassio,
He's never anything but your true servant.
Desdemona. I know't; I thank you. You do love my lord.   10

44 **affinity** family   52 **bosom** inmost thoughts   III.ii.4 **Repair** go

You have known him long, and be you well assured
He shall in strangeness stand no farther off
Than in a politic distance.°
Cassio.   Ay, but, lady,
That policy may either last so long,
Or feed upon such nice° and waterish diet,   15
Or breed itself so out of circumstances,°
That, I being absent, and my place supplied,°
My general will forget my love and service.
Desdemona. Do not doubt° that; before Emilia here
I give thee warrant of thy place. Assure thee,   20
If I do vow a friendship, I'll perform it
To the last article. My lord shall never rest;
I'll watch him tame° and talk him out of patience;
His bed shall seem a school, his board a shrift;°
I'll intermingle everything he does   25
With Cassio's suit. Therefore be merry, Cassio,
For thy solicitor shall rather die
Than give thy cause away.

        Enter Othello and Iago [at a distance].

Emilia. Madam, here comes my lord.
Cassio. Madam, I'll take my leave.   30
Desdemona. Why, stay, and hear me speak.
Cassio. Madam, not now. I am very ill at ease,
    Unfit for mine own purposes.
Desdemona. Well, do your discretion.   Exit Cassio.
Iago. Ha! I like not that.
Othello.   What dost thou say?   35
Iago. Nothing, my lord; or if—I know not what.
Othello. Was not that Cassio parted from my wife?
Iago. Cassio, my lord? No, sure, I cannot think it
    That he would steal away so guilty-like,
    Seeing your coming.
Othello.   I do believe 'twas he.   40
Desdemona [Coming to them]. How now, my lord?
    I have been talking with a suitor here,
    A man that languishes in your displeasure.
Othello. Who is't you mean?
Desdemona. Why, your lieutenant, Cassio. Good my lord,   45
    If I have any grace or power to move you,

III.iii.12-13 **He . . . distance** i.e., he shall act no more distant to you than is necessary for political reasons   15 **nice** trivial   16 **Or . . . circumstances** i.e., or grow so on the basis of accidental happenings and political needs   17 **supplied** filled   19 **doubt** imagine   23 **watch him tame** (animals were tamed by being kept awake)   24 **board a shrift** table (seem) a confessional

His present° reconciliation take.
For if he be not one that truly loves you,
That errs in ignorance, and not in cunning,
I have no judgment in an honest face.   50
I prithee call him back.

Othello.   Went he hence now?

Desdemona. I' sooth so humbled
That he hath left part of his grief with me
To suffer with him. Good love, call him back.

Othello. Not now, sweet Desdemon; some other time.   55

Desdemona. But shall't be shortly?

Othello.   The sooner, sweet, for you.

Desdemona. Shall't be tonight at supper?

Othello.   No, not tonight.

Desdemona. Tomorrow dinner then?

Othello.   I shall not dine at home;
I meet the captains at the citadel.

Desdemona. Why then, tomorrow night, on Tuesday morn,   60
On Tuesday noon, or night, on Wednesday morn.
I prithee name the time, but let it not
Exceed three days. In faith, he's penitent;
And yet his trespass, in our common reason
(Save that, they say, the wars must make example   65
Out of her best), is not almost a fault
T' incur a private check.° When shall he come?
Tell me, Othello. I wonder in my soul
What you would ask me that I should deny
Or stand so mamm'ring° on. What? Michael Cassio,   70
That came awooing with you, and so many a time,
When I have spoke of you dispraisingly,
Hath ta'en your part—to have so much to do
To bring him in? By'r Lady, I could do much—

Othello. Prithee no more. Let him come when he will!   75
I will deny thee nothing.

Desdemona.   Why, this is not a boon;
'Tis as I should entreat you wear your gloves,
Or feed on nourishing dishes, or keep you warm,
Or sue to you to do a peculiar profit°
To your own person. Nay, when I have a suit   80
Wherein I mean to touch your love indeed,
It shall be full of poise° and difficult weight,
And fearful to be granted.

Othello.   I will deny thee nothing!

---

47 **present** immediate   66-67 **is . . . check** is almost not serious enough for a
private rebuke (let alone a public disgrace)   70 **mamm'ring** hesitating   79
peculiar profit particularly personal good   82 **poise** weight

Whereon I do beseech thee grant me this,
To leave me but a little to myself.   85
Desdemona. Shall I deny you? No. Farewell, my lord.
Othello. Farewell, my Desdemona: I'll come to thee straight.°
Desdemona. Emilia, come. Be as your fancies teach you;
Whate'er you be, I am obedient.   *Exit [with Emilia].*
Othello. Excellent wretch! Perdition catch my soul   90
But I do love thee! And when I love thee not,
Chaos is come again.
Iago. My noble lord—
Othello.   What dost thou say, Iago?
Iago. Did Michael Cassio, when you wooed my lady,
Know of your love?   95
Othello. He did, from first to last. Why dost thou ask?
Iago. But for a satisfaction of my thought,
No further harm.
Othello.   Why of thy thought, Iago?
Iago. I did not think he had been acquainted with her.
Othello. O, yes, and went between us° very oft.   100
Iago. Indeed?
Othello. Indeed? Ay, indeed! Discern'st thou aught in that?
Is he not honest?
Iago.   Honest, my lord?
Othello.   Honest? Ay, honest.
Iago. My lord, for aught I know.
Othello. What dost thou think?
Iago.   Think, my lord?
Othello.   Think, my lord?   105
By heaven, thou echoest me,
As if there were some monster in thy thought
Too hideous to be shown. Thou dost mean something.
I heard thee say even now, thou lik'st not that,
When Cassio left my wife. What didst not like?   110
And when I told thee he was of my counsel°
Of my whole course of wooing, thou cried'st "Indeed?"
And didst contract and purse thy brow together,
As if thou then hadst shut up in thy brain
Some horrible conceit.° If thou dost love me,   115
Show me thy thought.
Iago. My lord, you know I love you.
Othello.   I think thou dost;
And, for I know thou'rt full of love and honesty
And weigh'st thy words before thou giv'st them breath,
Therefore these stops° of thine fright me the more;   ⌐120

---

87 **straight** at once   100 **between us** i.e., as messenger   111 **of my counsel** in
my confidence   115 **conceit** thought   120 **stops** interruptions

For such things in a false disloyal knave
Are tricks of custom;° but in a man that's just
They're close dilations,° working from the heart
That passion cannot rule.

Iago.   For Michael Cassio,
I dare be sworn, I think that he is honest.   125

Othello. I think so too.

Iago.   Men should be what they seem;
Or those that be not, would they might seem none!

Othello. Certain, men should be what they seem.

Iago. Why then, I think Cassio's an honest man.

Othello. Nay, yet there's more in this?   130
I prithee speak to me as to thy thinkings,
As thou dost ruminate, and give thy worst of thoughts
The worst of words.

Iago.   Good my lord, pardon me:
Though I am bound to every act of duty,
I am not bound to that all slaves are free to.   135
Utter my thoughts? Why, say they are vile and false,
As where's that palace whereinto foul things
Sometimes intrude not? Who has that breast so pure
But some uncleanly apprehensions
Keep leets and law days,° and in sessions sit   140
With meditations lawful?

Othello. Thou dost conspire against thy friend, Iago,
If thou but think'st him wronged, and mak'st his ear
A stranger to thy thoughts.

Iago.   I do beseech you—
Though I perchance am vicious in my guess   145
(As I confess it is my nature's plague
To spy into abuses, and of my jealousy
Shape faults that are not), that your wisdom
From one that so imperfectly conceits
Would take no notice, nor build yourself a trouble   150
Out of his scattering and unsure observance.
It were not for your quiet nor your good,
Nor for my manhood, honesty, and wisdom,
To let you know my thoughts.

Othello.   What dost thou mean?

Iago. Good name in man and woman, dear my lord,   155
Is the immediate jewel of their souls.
Who steals my purse steals trash; 'tis something, nothing;
'Twas mine, 'tis his, and has been slave to thousands;
But he that filches from me my good name

---

122 **of custom** customary   123 **close dilations** expressions of hidden thoughts
140 **leets and law days** meetings of local courts

Robs me of that which not enriches him   160
And makes me poor indeed.

Othello. By heaven, I'll know thy thoughts!

Iago. You cannot, if my heart were in your hand;
Nor shall not whilst 'tis in my custody.

Othello. Ha!

Iago.   O, beware, my lord, of jealousy!   165
It is the green-eyed monster, which doth mock
The meat it feeds on. That cuckold lives in bliss
Who, certain of his fate, loves not his wronger;
But O, what damnèd minutes tells° he o'er
Who dotes, yet doubts—suspects, yet fondly° loves!   170

Othello. O misery.

Iago. Poor and content is rich, and rich enough;
But riches fineless° is as poor as winter
To him that ever fears he shall be poor.
Good God the souls of all my tribe defend   175
From jealousy!

Othello.   Why? Why is this?
Think'st thou I'd make a life of jealousy,
To follow still° the changes of the moon
With fresh suspicions? No! To be once in doubt
Is to be resolved. Exchange me for a goat   180
When I shall turn the business of my soul
To such exsufflicate and blown° surmises,
Matching thy inference. 'Tis not to make me jealous
To say my wife is fair, feeds well, loves company,
Is free of speech, sings, plays, and dances;   185
Where virtue is, these are more virtuous.
Nor from mine own weak merits will I draw
The smallest fear or doubt of her revolt,
For she had eyes, and chose me. No, Iago;
I'll see before I doubt; when I doubt, prove;   190
And on the proof there is no more but this:
Away at once with love or jealousy!

Iago. I am glad of this; for now I shall have reason
To show the love and duty that I bear you
With franker spirit. Therefore, as I am bound,   195
Receive it from me. I speak not yet of proof.
Look to your wife; observe her well with Cassio;
Wear your eyes thus: not jealous nor secure.
I would not have your free and noble nature
Out of self-bounty° be abused. Look to't.   200

169 **tells** counts 170 **fondly** foolishly 173 **fineless** infinite 178 **To follow still** to change always (as the phases of the moon) 182 **exsufflicate and blown** inflated and flyblown 200 **self-bounty** innate kindness (which attributes his own motives to others)

I know our country disposition well:
In Venice they do let heaven see the pranks
They dare not show their husbands; their best conscience
Is not to leave't undone, but kept unknown.°

Othello. Dost thou say so?   205

Iago. She did deceive her father, marrying you;
And when she seemed to shake and fear your looks,
She loved them most.

Othello.   And so she did.

Iago.   Why, go to then!
She that so young could give out such a seeming
To seel° her father's eyes up close as oak°—   210
He thought 'twas witchcraft. But I am much to blame.
I humbly do beseech you of your pardon
For too much loving you.

Othello.   I am bound to thee forever.

Iago. I see this faith hath a little dashed your spirits.

Othello. Not a jot, not a jot.

Iago.   Trust me, I fear it has.   215
I hope you will consider what is spoke
Comes from my love. But I do see y' are moved.
I am to pray you not to strain° my speech
To grosser issues nor to larger reach°
Than to suspicion.   220

Othello. I will not.

Iago.   Should you do so, my lord,
My speech should fall into such vile success
Which my thoughts aimed not. Cassio's my worthy friend—
My lord, I see y' are moved.

Othello.   No, not much moved.
I do not think but Desdemona's honest.   225

Iago. Long live she so. And long live you to think so.

Othello. And yet, how nature erring from itself——

Iago. Ay there's the point, as (to be bold with you)
Not to affect many proposèd matches
Of her own clime, complexion, and degree,°   230
Whereto we see in all things nature tends°—
Foh! one may smell in such a will most rank,
Foul disproportions, thoughts unnatural.
But, pardon me, I do not in position°
Distinctly° speak of her; though I may fear   235

203-4 **their . . . unknown** i.e., their morality does not forbid adultery, but it
does forbid being found out   210 **seel** hoodwink   210 **oak** (a close-grained
wood)   218 **strain** enlarge the meaning of   219 **reach** meaning   230 **degree**
social station   231 **in . . . tends** i.e., all things in nature seek out their own kind
234 **position** general argument   235 **Distinctly** specifically

Her will, recoiling to her better judgment,
May fall to match° you with her country forms,°
And happily° repent.
Othello.   Farewell, farewell!
If more thou dost perceive, let me know more.
Set on thy wife to observe. Leave me, Iago.   240
Iago. My lord, I take my leave.   [*Going.*]
Othello. Why did I marry? This honest creature doubtless
Sees and knows more, much more, than he unfolds.
Iago [*Returns*]. My lord, I would I might entreat your honor
To scan this thing no further. Leave it to time.   245
Although 'tis fit that Cassio have his place,
For sure he fills it up with great ability,
Yet, if you please to hold him off awhile,
You shall by that perceive him and his means.
Note if your lady strain his entertainment°   250
With any strong or vehement importunity;
Much will be seen in that. In the meantime
Let me be thought too busy in my fears
(As worthy cause I have to fear I am)
And hold her free, I do beseech your honor.   255
Othello. Fear not my government.°
Iago.   I once more take my leave.
                                   Exit.

Othello. This fellow's of exceeding honesty,
And knows all qualities,° with a learnèd spirit
Of human dealings. If I do prove her haggard,°
Though that her jesses° were my dear heartstrings,   260
I'd whistle her off and let her down the wind°
To prey at fortune. Haply for° I am black
And have not those soft parts° of conversation
That chamberers° have, or for I am declined
Into the vale of years—yet that's not much—   265
She's gone. I am abused, and my relief
Must be to loathe her. O curse of marriage,
That we can call these delicate creatures ours,
And not their appetites! I had rather be a toad
And live upon the vapor of a dungeon   270

---

237 **fall to match** happen to compare   237 **country forms** i.e., the familiar appearance of her countrymen   238 **happily** by chance   250 **strain his entertainment** urge strongly that he be reinstated   256 **government** self-control   258 **qualities** natures, types of people   259 **haggard** a partly trained hawk which has gone wild again   260 **jesses** straps which held the hawk's legs to the trainer's wrist   261 **I'd . . . wind** I would release her (like an untamable hawk) and let her fly free   262 **Haply for** it may be because   263 **soft parts** gentle qualities and manners   264 **chamberers** courtiers—or perhaps, accomplished seducers

Than keep a corner in the thing I love
For others' uses. Yet 'tis the plague to great ones;
Prerogatived are they less than the base.
'Tis destiny unshunnable, like death.
Even then this forkèd° plague is fated to us   275
When we do quicken.° Look where she comes.

Enter Desdemona and Emilia.

If she be false, heaven mocked itself!
I'll not believe't.
Desdemona.   How now, my dear Othello?
  Your dinner, and the generous islanders
  By you invited, do attend° your presence.   280
Othello. I am to blame.
Desdemona.   Why do you speak so faintly?
  Are you not well?
Othello. I have a pain upon my forehead, here.°
Desdemona. Why that's with watching; 'twill away again,
  Let me but bind it hard, within this hour   285
  It will be well.
Othello.   Your napkin° is too little;
      [*He pushes the handkerchief away, and it falls.*]
  Let it° alone. Come, I'll go in with you.
Desdemona. I am very sorry that you are not well.
                                        Exit [*with Othello*].
Emilia. I am glad I have found this napkin;
  This was her first remembrance from the Moor.   290
  My wayward husband hath a hundred times
  Wooed me to steal it; but she so loves the token
  (For he conjured her she should ever keep it)
  That she reserves it evermore about her
  To kiss and talk to. I'll have the work ta'en out°   295
  And give't Iago. What he will do with it,
  Heaven knows, not I; I nothing° but to please his fantasy.°

Enter Iago.

Iago. How now? What do you here alone?
Emilia. Do not you chide; I have a thing for you.
Iago. You have a thing for me? It is a common thing——   300

---

275 **forked** horned (the sign of the cuckold was horns)   276 **do quicken** are
born   280 **attend** wait   283 **here** (he points to his imaginary horns)
286 **napkin** elaborately worked handkerchief   287 **it** (it makes a considerable
difference in the interpretation of later events whether this "it" refers to
Othello's forehead or to the handkerchief; nothing in the text makes the
reference clear)   295 **work ta'en out** needlework copied   297 **I nothing** I wish
nothing   297 **fantasy** fancy, whim

Emilia. Ha?
Iago. To have a foolish wife.
Emilia. O, is that all? What will you give me now
    For that same handkerchief?
Iago.   What handkerchief?
Emilia. What handkerchief!   305
    Why, that the Moor first gave to Desdemona,
    That which so often you did bid me steal.
Iago. Hast stol'n it from her?
Emilia. No, but she let it drop by negligence,
    And to th' advantage,° I, being here, took't up.   310
    Look, here 't is.
Iago.   A good wench. Give it me.
Emilia. What will you do with't, that you have been so earnest
    To have me filch it?
Iago.   Why, what is that to you?
                                        [*Takes it.*]
Emilia. If it be not for some purpose of import,°
    Give't me again. Poor lady, she'll run mad   315
    When she shall lack° it.
Iago.   Be not acknown on't.°
    I have use for it. Go, leave me.   *Exit Emilia.*
    I will in Cassio's lodging lose this napkin
    And let him find it. Trifles light as air
    Are to the jealous confirmations strong   320
    As proofs of Holy Writ. This may do something.
    The Moor already changes with my poison:
    Dangerous conceits are in their natures poisons,
    Which at the first are scarce found to distaste,°
    But, with a little,° act upon the blood,   325
    Burn like the mines of sulfur. I did say so.

    Enter Othello.

    Look where he comes! Not poppy nor mandragora,°
    Nor all the drowsy syrups of the world,
    Shall ever medicine thee to that sweet sleep
    Which thou owedst° yesterday.
Othello.   Ha! ha! False to me?   330
Iago. Why, how now, general? No more of that.
Othello. Avaunt! be gone! Thou hast set me on the rack.
    I swear 'tis better to be much abused
    Than but to know't a little.

---

310 **to th' advantage** being lucky   314 **import** importance   316 **lack** miss
316 **Be not acknown on't** forget you ever saw it   324 **are scarce found to distaste** scarcely can be tasted   325 **with a little** in a short time   327 **poppy nor
mandragora** (soporifics)   330 **owedst** possessed

Iago. How now, my lord?

Othello. What sense had I of her stol'n hours of lust? 335
    I saw't not, thought it not, it harmed not me;
    I slept the next night well, fed well, was free and merry;
    I found not Cassio's kisses on her lips.
    He that is robbed, not wanting° what is stol'n,
    Let him know't, and he's not robbed at all. 340

Iago. I am sorry to hear this.

Othello. I had been happy if the general camp,
    Pioners° and all, had tasted her sweet body,
    So I had nothing known. O now, forever
    Farewell the tranquil mind! Farewell content! 345
    Farewell the plumèd troops, and the big wars
    That make ambition virtue! O, farewell!
    Farewell the neighing steed and the shrill trump,
    The spirit-stirring drum, th' ear-piercing fife,
    The royal banner, and all quality, 350
    Pride, pomp, and circumstance° of glorious war!
    And O you mortal engines° whose rude throats
    Th' immortal Jove's dread clamors° counterfeit,
    Farewell! Othello's occupation's gone!

Iago. Is't possible, my lord? 355

Othello. Villain, be sure thou prove my love a whore!
    Be sure of it; give me the ocular proof;
    Or, by the worth of mine eternal soul,
    Thou hadst been better have been born a dog
    Than answer my waked wrath!

Iago. Is't come to this? 360

Othello. Make me to see't; or at the least so prove it
    That the probation° bear no hinge nor loop
    To hang a doubt on—or woe upon thy life!

Iago. My noble lord——

Othello. If thou dost slander her and torture me, 365
    Never pray more; abandon all remorse;
    On horror's head horrors accumulate;
    Do deeds to make heaven weep, all earth amazed;
    For nothing canst thou to damnation add
    Greater than that.

Iago. O grace! O heaven forgive me! 370
    Are you a man? Have you a soul or sense?
    God b' wi' you! Take mine office. O wretched fool,
    That lov'st to make thine honesty a vice!
    O monstrous world! Take note, take note, O world,

---

339 **wanting** missing   343 **Pioners** (the basest manual laborers in the army, who dug trenches and mines)   351 **circumstance** pageantry   352 **mortal engines** lethal weapons, i.e., cannon   353 **clamors** i.e., thunder   362 **probation** proof

To be direct and honest is not safe.   375
I thank you for this profit, and from hence
I'll love no friend, sith° love breeds such offense.
Othello. Nay, stay. Thou shouldst be honest.
Iago. I should be wise; for honesty's a fool
And loses that it works for.
Othello.   By the world,   380
I think my wife be honest, and think she is not;
I think that thou art just, and think thou are not.
I'll have some proof. My name, that was as fresh
As Dian's° visage, is now begrimed and black
As mine own face. If there be cords, or knives,   385
Poison, or fire, or suffocating streams,
I'll not endure it. Would I were satisfied!
Iago. I see you are eaten up with passion.
I do repent me that I put it to you.
You would be satisfied?
Othello.   Would? Nay, and I will.   390
Iago. And may; but how? How satisfied, my lord?
Would you, the supervisor,° grossly gape on?
Behold her topped?
Othello.   Death and damnation! O!
Iago. It were a tedious° difficulty, I think,
To bring them to that prospect.° Damn them then,   395
If ever mortal eyes do see them bolster°
More than their own! What then? How then?
What shall I say? Where's satisfaction?
It is impossible you should see this,
Were they as prime° as goats, as hot as monkeys,   400
As salt° as wolves in pride,° and fools as gross
As ignorance made drunk. But yet, I say,
If imputation and strong circumstances
Which lead directly to the door of truth
Will give you satisfaction, you might have't.   405
Othello. Give me a living reason she's disloyal.
Iago. I do not like the office.°
But sith I am entered in this cause so far,
Pricked° to't by foolish honesty and love,
I will go on. I lay with Cassio lately,   410
And being troubled with a raging tooth,
I could not sleep.
There are a kind of men so loose of soul
That in their sleeps will mutter their affairs.

377 **sith** since   384 **Dian's** Diana's (goddess of the moon and of chastity)
392 **supervisor** onlooker   394 **tedious** hard to arrange   395 **prospect** sight
(where they can be seen)   396 **bolster** go to bed   400-01 **prime, salt** lustful
401 **pride** heat   407 **office** duty   409 **Pricked** spurred

One of this kind is Cassio.   415
In sleep I heard him say, "Sweet Desdemona,
Let us be wary, let us hide our loves!"
And then, sir, would he gripe° and wring my hand,
Cry "O sweet creature!" Then kiss me hard,
As if he plucked up kisses by the roots   420
That grew upon my lips; laid his leg o'er my thigh,
And sigh, and kiss, and then cry, "Cursèd fate
That gave thee to the Moor!"
Othello. O monstrous! monstrous!
Iago.   Nay, this was but his dream.
Othello. But this denoted a foregone conclusion,°   425
   'Tis a shrewd doubt,° though it be but a dream.
Iago. And this may help to thicken other proofs
   That do demonstrate° thinly.
Othello.   I'll tear her all to pieces!
Iago. Nay, yet be wise. Yet we see nothing done;
   She may be honest yet. Tell me but this: 430
   Have you not sometimes seen a handkerchief
   Spotted with strawberries in your wife's hand?
Othello. I gave her such a one; 'twas my first gift.
Iago. I know not that; but such a handkerchief—
   I am sure it was your wife's—did I today   435
   See Cassio wipe his beard with.
Othello.   If it be that——
Iago. If it be that or any that was hers,
   It speaks against her with the other proofs.
Othello. O, that the slave had forty thousand lives!
   One is too poor, too weak for my revenge.   440
   Now do I see 'tis true. Look here, Iago:
   All my fond love thus do I blow to heaven.
   'Tis gone.
   Arise, black vengeance, from the hollow hell!
   Yield up, O love, thy crown and hearted° throne   445
   To tyrannous hate! Swell, bosom, with thy fraught,°
   For 'tis of aspics'° tongues.
Iago.   Yet be content.°
Othello. O, blood, blood, blood!
Iago. Patience, I say. Your mind may change.
Othello. Never, Iago. Like to the Pontic Sea.°   450
   Whose icy current and compulsive course

418 **gripe** seize   425 **foregone conclusion** consummated fact   426 **shrewd doubt** penetrating guess   428 **demonstrate** show, appear   445 **hearted** seated in the heart   446 **fraught** burden   447 **aspics'** asps'   447 **content** patient, quiet   450 **Pontic Sea** the Black Sea (famous for the strong and constant current with which it flows through the Bosporus into the Mediterranean, where the water level is lower)

Nev'r keeps retiring ebb, but keeps due on
To the Propontic and the Hellespont,
Even so my bloody thoughts, with violent pace,
Shall nev'r look back, nev'r ebb to humble love,   455
Till that a capable and wide° revenge
Swallow them up. [*He kneels.*] Now, by yond marble heaven,
In the due reverence of a sacred vow
I here engage my words.
Iago.   Do not rise yet.

                                             [*Iago kneels.*]
Witness, you ever-burning lights above,   460
You elements that clip° us round about,
Witness that here Iago doth give up
The execution° of his wit, hands, heart
To wronged Othello's service! Let him command,
And to obey shall be in me remorse,°   465
What bloody business ever.°   [*They rise.*]
Othello.   I greet thy love,
Not with vain thanks but with acceptance bounteous,°
And will upon the instant put thee to't.°
Within these three days let me hear thee say
That Cassio's not alive.   470
Iago. My friend is dead. 'Tis done at your request.
But let her live.
Othello.   Damn her, lewd minx! O, damn her! Damn her!
Come, go with me apart. I will withdraw
To furnish me with swift means of death
For the fair devil. Now art thou my lieutenant.   475
Iago. I am your own forever.   *Exeunt.*

Scene IV. [*A street.*]

Enter Desdemona, Emilia, and Clown.

Desdemona. Do you know, sirrah, where Lieutenant Cassio lies?°
Clown. I dare not say he lies anywhere.
Desdemona. Why, man?
Clown. He's a soldier, and for me to say a soldier lies, 'tis stabbing.
Desdemona. Go to. Where lodges he?   5
Clown. To tell you where he lodges is to tell where I lie.
Desdemona. Can anything be made of this?

---

456 **capable and wide** sufficient and far-reaching   461 **clip** enfold   463 **execution** workings, action   465 **remorse** pity   466 **ever** soever   467 **bounteous** absolute   468 **to't** i.e., to the work you have said you are prepared to do   III.iv.1 **lies** lodges

Clown. I know not where he lodges, and for me to devise a lodging, and say he lies here or he lies there, were to lie in mine
own throat.° 10
Desdemona. Can you enquire him out, and be edified° by report?
Clown. I will catechize the world for him; that is, make questions,
and by them answer.
Desdemona. Seek him, bid him come hither. Tell him I have
moved° my lord on his behalf and hope all will be well. 15
Clown. To do this is within the compass° of man's wit, and there-
fore I will attempt the doing it.   *Exit Clown.*
Desdemona. Where should° I lose the handkerchief, Emilia?
Emilia. I know not, madam.
Desdemona. Believe me, I had rather have lost my purse 20
Full of crusadoes.° And but my noble Moor
Is true of mind, and made of no such baseness
As jealous creatures are, it were enough
To put him to ill thinking.
Emilia.   Is he not jealous?
Desdemona. Who? He? I think the sun where he was born 25
Drew all such humors° from him.
Emilia.   Look where he comes.

    Enter Othello.

Desdemona. I will not leave him now till Cassio
Be called to him. How is't with you, my lord?
Othello. Well, my good lady. [*Aside*] O, hardness to dissemble!°—
How do you, Desdemona?
Desdemona.   Well, my good lord. 30
Othello. Give me your hand. This hand is moist,° my lady.
Desdemona. It hath felt no age nor known no sorrow.
Othello. This argues° fruitfulness and liberal° heart.
Hot, hot, and moist. This hand of yours requires
A sequester° from liberty; fasting and prayer; 35
Much castigation; exercise devout;
For here's a young and sweating devil here
That commonly rebels. 'Tis a good hand,
A frank one.

9-10 **lie in mine own throat** (to lie in the throat is to lie absolutely and completely) 11 **edified** enlightened (Desdemona mocks the Clown's overly
elaborate diction) 15 **moved** pleaded with 16 **compass** reach 18 **should**
might 21 **crusadoes** Portuguese gold coins 26 **humors** characteristics 29
hardness to dissemble (Othello may refer here either to the difficulty he
has in maintaining his appearance of composure, or to what he believes to be
Desdemona's hardened hypocrisy) 31 **moist** (a moist, hot hand was taken as
a sign of a lustful nature) 33 **argues** suggests 33 **liberal** free, open (but
also with a suggestion of "licentious"; from here on in this scene Othello's
words bear a double meaning, seeming to be normal but accusing Desdemona
of being unfaithful) 35 **sequester** separation

Desdemona.   You may, indeed, say so;
     For 'twas that hand that gave away my heart.   40
Othello. A liberal hand! The hearts of old gave hands,
     But our new heraldry° is hands, not hearts.
Desdemona. I have sent to bid Cassio come speak with you.
Othello. I have a salt and sorry rheum° offends me.
     Lend me thy handkerchief.
Desdemona.   Here, my lord.   45
Othello. That which I gave you.
Desdemona.   I have it not about me.
Othello. Not?
Desdemona. No, indeed, my lord.
Othello.   That's a fault.
     That handkerchief
     Did an Egyptian to my mother give.
     She was a charmer,° and could almost read   50
     The thoughts of people. She told her, while she kept it
     'Twould make her amiable° and subdue my father
     Entirely to her love; but if she lost it
     Or made a gift of it, my father's eye
     Should hold her loathèd, and his spirits should hunt   55
     After new fancies. She, dying, gave it me,
     And bid me, when my fate would have me wived,
     To give it her. I did so; and take heed on't;
     Make it a darling like your precious eye.
     To lose't or give't away were such perdition   60
     As nothing else could match.
Desdemona.   Is't possible?
Othello. 'Tis true. There's magic in the web° of it.
     A sibyl that had numbered in the world
     The sun to course two hundred compasses,
     In her prophetic fury° sewed the work;   65
     The worms were hallowed that did breed the silk,
     And it was dyed in mummy° which the skillful
     Conserved of maidens' hearts.
Desdemona.   Indeed? Is't true?
Othello. Most veritable. Therefore look to't well.
Desdemona. Then would to God that I had never seen't!   70
Othello. Ha! Wherefore?
Desdemona. Why do you speak so startingly and rash?
Othello. Is't lost? Is't gone? Speak, is it out o' th' way?
Desdemona. Heaven bless us!
Othello. Say you?   75

---

42 **heraldry** heraldic symbolism   44 **a salt and sorry rheum** a heavy, running
head cold   50 **charmer** magician   52 **amiable** desirable   62 **web** weaving
65 **prophetic fury** seized by the spirit and able to prophesy   67 **mummy** liquid
drained from embalmed bodies.

Desdemona. It is not lost. But what an if it were?
Othello. How?
Desdemona. I say it is not lost.
Othello. Fetch't, let me see't!
Desdemona. Why, so I can; but I will not now. 80
  This is a trick to put me from my suit:
  Pray you let Cassio be received again.
Othello. Fetch me the handkerchief! My mind misgives.
Desdemona. Come, come!
  You'll never meet a more sufficient° man—— 85
Othello. The handkerchief!
Desdemona.   A man that all his time
  Hath founded his good fortunes on your love,
  Shared dangers with you——
Othello. The handkerchief!
Desdemona. I'faith, you are to blame. 90
Othello. Away!   *Exit Othello.*
Emilia. Is not this man jealous?
Desdemona. I nev'r saw this before.
  Sure there's some wonder in this handkerchief;
  I am most unhappy in the loss of it. 95
Emilia. 'Tis not a year or two shows us a man.
  They are all but stomachs, and we all but food;
  They eat us hungerly, and when they are full,
  They belch us.

  Enter Iago and Cassio.

    Look you, Cassio and my husband.
Iago. There is no other way; 'tis she must do't. 100
  And lo the happiness! Go and importune her.
Desdemona. How now, good Cassio? What's the news with you?
Cassio. Madam, my former suit. I do beseech you
  That by your virtuous means I may again
  Exist, and be a member of his love 105
  Whom I with all the office° of my heart
  Entirely honor. I would not be delayed.
  If my offense be of such mortal kind
  That nor my service past, nor present sorrows,
  Nor purposed merit in futurity, 110
  Can ransom me into his love again,
  But to know so must be my benefit.°
  So shall I clothe me in a forced content,
  And shut myself up in some other course
  To fortune's alms.

85 **sufficient** complete, with all proper qualities 106 **office** duty 112 **benefit** good

Desdemona.　　　　　Alas, thrice-gentle Cassio, 　　　　　　115
　　My advocation° is not now in tune.
　　My lord is not my lord; nor should I know him
　　Were he in humor° as in humor altered.
　　So help me every spirit sanctified
　　As I have spoken for you all my best 　　　　　　　　　120
　　And stood within the blank° of his displeasure
　　For my free speech. You must awhile be patient.
　　What I can do I will; and more I will
　　Than for myself I dare. Let that suffice you.
Iago. Is my lord angry?
Emilia.　　　　　　He went hence but now, 　　　　　　125
　　And certainly in strange unquietness.
Iago. Can he be angry? I have seen the cannon
　　When it hath blown his ranks into the air
　　And, like the devil, from his very arm
　　Puffed his own brother. And is he angry? 　　　　　　130
　　Something of moment° then. I will go meet him.
　　There's matter in't indeed if he be angry.
Desdemona. I prithee do so. 　　　　　　　　*Exit [Iago].*
　　　　　　　　Something sure of state,°
　　Either from Venice or some unhatched practice°
　　Made demonstrable here in Cyprus to him, 　　　　　　135
　　Hath puddled° his clear spirit; and in such cases
　　Men's natures wrangle with inferior things,
　　Though great ones are their object. 'Tis even so.
　　For let our finger ache, and it endues°
　　Our other, healthful members even to a sense 　　　　　140
　　Of pain. Nay, we must think men are not gods,
　　Nor of them look for such observancy
　　As fits the bridal. Beshrew me much, Emilia,
　　I was, unhandsome warrior as I am,
　　Arraigning his unkindness with my soul; 　　　　　　145
　　But now I find I had suborned the witness,
　　And he's indicted falsely.
Emilia.　　　　　　Pray heaven it be
　　State matters, as you think, and no conception
　　Nor no jealous toy° concerning you.
Desdemona. Alas the day! I never gave him cause. 　　　　150
Emilia. But jealous souls will not be answered so;
　　They are not ever jealous for the cause,
　　But jealous for they're jealous. It is a monster
　　Begot upon itself, born on itself.

---

116 **advocation** advocacy　118 **favor** countenance　121 **blank** bull's-eye of a target　131 **moment** importance　133 **of state** state affairs　134 **unhatched practice** undisclosed plot　136 **puddled** muddied　139 **endues** leads　149 **toy** trifle

Desdemona. Heaven keep the monster from Othello's mind!   155
Emilia. Lady, amen.
Desdemona. I will go seek him. Cassio, walk here about.
    If I do find him fit,° I'll move your suit
    And seek to effect it to my uttermost.
Cassio. I humbly thank your ladyship.   160

                    Exit [Desdemona with Emilia].

    Enter Bianca.

Bianca. Save you, friend Cassio!
Cassio.   What make you from home?
    How is't with you, my most fair Bianca?
    I' faith, sweet love, I was coming to your house.
Bianca. And I was going to your lodging, Cassio.
    What, keep a week away? Seven days and nights?   165
    Eightscore eight hours? And lovers' absent hours
    More tedious than the dial eightscore times?
    O weary reck'ning.°
Cassio.   Pardon me, Bianca.
    I have this while with laden thoughts been pressed,
    But I shall in a more continuate° time   170
    Strike off this score° of absence. Sweet Bianca,
             [Gives her Desdemona's handkerchief.]
    Take me this work out.
Bianca.   O Cassio, whence came this?
    This is some token from a newer friend.
    To the felt absence now I feel a cause.
    Is't come to this? Well, well.
Cassio.   Go to, woman!   175
    Throw your vile guesses in the devil's teeth,
    From whence you have them. You are jealous now
    That this is from some mistress, some remembrance.
    No, by my faith, Bianca.
Bianca.   Why, whose is it?
Cassio. I know not neither; I found it in my chamber.   180
    I like the work well; ere it be demanded,°
    As like enough it will, I would have it copied.
    Take it and do't, and leave me for this time.
Bianca. Leave you? Wherefore?
Cassio. I do attend here on the general   185
    And think it no addition, nor my wish,
    To have him see me womaned.
Bianca.   Why, I pray you?

---

158 **fit** receptive   168 **reck'ning** addition   170 **continuate** uninterrupted   171
Strike off this score i.e., pay this bill (the *score* being the account of drinks kept
in a tavern)   181 **demanded** asked for (by the person who lost it)

Cassio. Not that I love you not.
Bianca.   But that you do not love me!
    I pray you bring° me on the way a little,
    And say if I shall see you soon at night.   190
Cassio. 'Tis but a little way that I can bring you,
    For I attend here; but I'll see you soon.
Bianca. 'Tis very good. I must be circumstanced.°

                         Exeunt omnes.

ACT IV

Scene I. [*A street.*]

    Enter Othello and Iago.

Iago. Will you think so?
Othello.   Think so, Iago?
Iago.   What,
    To kiss in private?
Othello.   An unauthorized° kiss?
Iago. Or to be naked with her friend in bed
    An hour or more, not meaning any harm?
Othello. Naked in bed, Iago, and not mean harm?   5
    It is hypocrisy against the devil.
    They that mean virtuously, and yet do so,
    The devil their virtue tempts, and they tempt heaven.
Iago. If they do nothing, 'tis a venial slip.
    But if I give my wife a handkerchief——   10
Othello. What then?
Iago. Why, then 'tis hers, my lord; and being hers,
    She may, I think, bestow't on any man.
Othello. She is protectress of her honor too.
    May she give that?   15
Iago. Her honor is an essence that's not seen;
    They have it very oft that have it not.
    But for the handkerchief——
Othello. By heaven, I would most gladly have forgot it!
    Thou said'st—O, it comes o'er my memory   20
    As doth the raven° o'er the infected house,
    Boding to all—he had my handkerchief.
Iago. Ay, what of that?
Othello.   That's not so good now.
Iago. What if I had said I had seen him do you wrong?

189 **bring** accompany   193 **circumstanced** accept things as they are IV.i.2
unauthorized illicit   21 **raven** (a harbinger of death)

Or heard him say—as knaves be such abroad°   25
Who having, by their own importunate suit,
Or voluntary dotage° of some mistress,
Convincèd or supplied° them, cannot choose
But they must blab——

Othello. Hath he said anything?

Iago. He hath, my lord; but be you well assured,   30
No more than he'll unswear.

Othello. What hath he said?

Iago. Why, that he did—I know not what he did.

Othello. What? what?

Iago. Lie——

Othello. With her?

Iago. With her, on her; what you will.   35

Othello. Lie with her? Lie on her?—We say lie on her when they
belie her.—Lie with her! Zounds, that's fulsome.°—Handkerchief—confessions—handkerchief!—To confess, and be
hanged for his labor—first to be hanged, and then to confess! I tremble at it. Nature would not invest herself in   40
such shadowing passion without some instruction.° It is
not words that shakes me thus.—Pish! Noses, ears, and lips?
Is't possible?—Confess?—Handkerchief?—O devil!

Falls in a trance.

Iago. Work on.
My med'cine works! Thus credulous fools are caught,   45
And many worthy and chaste dames even thus,
All guiltless, meet reproach.° What, ho! My lord!
My lord, I say! Othello!

Enter Cassio.

                   How now, Cassio?

Cassio. What's the matter?

Iago. My lord is fall'n into an epilepsy.   50
This is his second fit; he had one yesterday.

Cassio. Rub him about the temples.

Iago. The lethargy° must have his quiet course.
If not, he foams at mouth, and by and by
Breaks out to savage madness. Look, he stirs.   55
Do you withdraw yourself a little while.

---

25 **abroad** i.e., in the world   27 **voluntary dotage** weakness of the will   28 **Convinced or supplied** persuaded or gratified (the mistress)   37 **fulsome** foul, repulsive   40-41 **Nature . . . instruction** i.e., my mind would not become so darkened (with anger) unless there were something in this (accusation); (it should be remembered that Othello believes in the workings of magic and super-natural forces)   47 **reproach** shame   53 **lethargy** coma

He will recover straight. When he is gone,
I would on great occasion° speak with you.

[*Exit Cassio.*]

How is it, general? Have you not hurt your head?
Othello. Dost thou mock° me?
Iago.   I mock you not, by heaven.   60
Would you would bear your fortune like a man.
Othello. A hornèd man's a monster and a beast.
Iago. There's many a beast then in a populous city,
And many a civil° monster.
Othello. Did he confess it?
Iago.   Good, sir, be a man.   65
Think every bearded fellow that's but yoked
May draw° with you. There's millions now alive
That nightly lie in those unproper° beds
Which they dare swear peculiar.° Your case is better.
O, 'tis the spite of hell, the fiend's arch-mock,   70
To lip a wanton in a secure couch,
And to suppose her chaste. No, let me know;
And knowing what I am, I know what she shall be.
Othello. O, thou art wise! 'Tis certain.
Iago.   Stand you awhile apart;
Confine yourself but in a patient list.°   75
Whilst you were here, o'erwhelmèd with your grief—
A passion most unsuiting such a man—
Cassio came hither. I shifted him away°
And laid good 'scuses upon your ecstasy;°
Bade him anon return, and here speak with me;   80
The which he promised. Do but encave° yourself
And mark the fleers,° the gibes, and notable° scorns
That dwell in every region of his face.
For I will make him tell the tale anew:
Where, how, how oft, how long ago, and when   85
He hath, and is again to cope your wife.
I say, but mark his gesture. Marry patience,
Or I shall say you're all in all in spleen,°
And nothing of a man.
Othello.   Dost thou hear, Iago?
I will be found most cunning in my patience;   90
But—dost thou hear?—most bloody.

58 **great occasion** very important matter   60 **mock** (Othello takes Iago's comment as a reference to his horns—which it is)   64 **civil** city-dwelling   67 **draw** i.e., like the horned ox   68 **unproper** i.e., not exclusively the husband's   69 **peculiar** their own alone   75 **a patient list** the bounds of patience   78 **shifted him away** got rid of him by a stratagem   79 **ecstasy** trance (the literal meaning, "outside oneself," bears on the meaning of the change Othello is undergoing)   81 **encave** hide   82 **fleers** mocking looks or speeches   82 **notable** obvious   88 **spleen** passion, particularly anger

Iago.   That's not amiss;
     But yet keep time in all. Will you withdraw?

     [*Othello moves to one side, where his remarks are not audible
                                          to Cassio and Iago.*]

     Now will I question Cassio of Bianca,
     A huswife° that by selling her desires
     Buys herself bread and cloth. It is a creature   95
     That dotes on Cassio, as 'tis the strumpet's plague
     To beguile many and be beguiled by one.
     He, when he hears of her, cannot restrain
     From the excess of laughter. Here he comes.

     Enter Cassio.

     As he shall smile, Othello shall go mad;   100
     And his unbookish° jealousy must conster°
     Poor Cassio's smiles, gestures, and light behaviors
     Quite in the wrong. How do you, lieutenant?
Cassio. The worser that you give me the addition°
     Whose want even kills me.   105
Iago. Ply Desdemona well, and you are sure on't.
     Now, if this suit lay in Bianca's power,
     How quickly should you speed!
Cassio.   Alas, poor caitiff!°
Othello. Look how he laughs already!
Iago. I never knew woman love man so.   110
Cassio. Alas, poor rogue! I think, i' faith, she loves me.
Othello. Now he denies it faintly, and laughs it out.
Iago. Do you hear, Cassio?
Othello.   Now he importunes him
     To tell it o'er. Go to! Well said, well said!
Iago. She gives it out that you shall marry her.   115
     Do you intend it?
Cassio. Ha, ha, ha!
Othello. Do ye triumph, Roman? Do you triumph?
Cassio. I marry? What, a customer?° Prithee bear some charity to
     my wit; do not think it so unwholesome. Ha, ha, ha!   120
Othello. So, so, so, so. They laugh that win.
Iago. Why, the cry goes that you marry her.
Cassio. Prithee, say true.
Iago. I am a very villain else.
Othello. Have you scored° me? Well.   125

---

94 **huswife** housewife (but with the special meaning here of "prostitute")
101 **unbookish** ignorant   101 **conster** construe   104 **addition** title   108 **caitiff**
wretch   119 **customer** one who sells, a merchant (here, a prostitute)   125
scored marked, defaced

Cassio. This is the monkey's own giving out. She is persuaded I
  will marry her out of her own love and flattery, not out of my
  promise.
Othello. Iago beckons me; now he begins the story.
  [*Othello moves close enough to hear.*]
Cassio. She was here even now; she haunts me in every place. I   130
  was the other day talking on the sea bank with certain Vene-
  tians, and thither comes the bauble,° and falls me thus about
  my neck——
Othello. Crying "O dear Cassio!" as it were. His gesture imports it.
Cassio. So hangs, and lolls, and weeps upon me; so shakes and   135
  pulls me! Ha, ha, ha!
Othello. Now he tells how she plucked him to my chamber. O, I
  see that nose of yours, but not that dog I shall throw it to.
Cassio. Well, I must leave her company.
Iago. Before me!° Look where she comes.   140

  Enter Bianca.

Cassio. 'Tis such another fitchew!° Marry a perfumed one? What
  do you mean by this haunting of me?
Bianca. Let the devil and his dam haunt you! What did you mean
  by that same handkerchief you gave me even now? I was a
  fine fool to take it. I must take out the work? A likely piece of 145
  work that you should find it in your chamber and know not
  who left it there! This is some minx's token, and I must take
  out the work? There! [*She throws down the handkerchief.*]
  Give it your hobbyhorse.° Wheresoever you had it, I'll take
  out no work on't.   150
Cassio. How now, my sweet Bianca? How now? how now?
Othello. By heaven, that should be my handkerchief!
Bianca. If you'll come to supper tonight, you may; if you will not,
  come when you are next prepared for.°   *Exit.*
Iago. After her, after her!   155
Cassio. Faith, I must; she'll rail in the streets else.
Iago. Will you sup there?
Cassio. Yes, I intend so.
Iago. Well, I may chance to see you, for I would very fain speak
  with you.   160
Cassio. Prithee come. Will you?
Iago. Go to, say no more.   [*Exit Cassio.*]
Othello [*Comes forward*]. How shall I murder him, Iago?
Iago. Did you perceive how he laughed at his vice?
Othello. O Iago!   165

---

132 **bauble** plaything   140 **Before me!** (an exclamation of surprise)   141 **fitchew** polecat, i.e., strong-smelling creature   149 **hobbyhorse** prostitute   154
next prepared for next expected—i.e., never

Iago. And did you see the handkerchief?

Othello. Was that mine?

Iago. Yours, by his hand! And to see how he prizes the foolish woman your wife! She gave it him, and he hath giv'n it his whore. 170

Othello. I would have him nine years a-killing!—A fine woman, a fair woman, a sweet woman?

Iago. Nay, you must forget that.

Othello. Ay, let her rot, and perish, and be damned tonight; for she shall not live. No, my heart is turned to stone; I strike it, 175 and it hurts my hand. O, the world hath not a sweeter creature! She might lie by an emperor's side and command him tasks.

Iago. Nay, that's not your way.°

Othello. Hang her! I do but say what she is. So delicate with her 180 needle. An admirable musician. O, she will sing the savageness out of a bear! Of so high and plenteous wit and invention°——

Iago. She's the worse for all this.

Othello. O, a thousand, a thousand times. And then, of so gentle 185 a condition?°

Iago. Ay, too gentle.

Othello. Nay, that's certain. But yet the pity of it, Iago. O Iago, the pity of it, Iago.

Iago. If you are so fond over her iniquity, give her patent to offend; 190 for if it touch° not you, it comes near nobody.

Othello. I will chop her into messes!° Cuckold me!

Iago. O, 'tis foul in her.

Othello. With mine officer!

Iago. That's fouler. 195

Othello. Get me some poison, Iago, this night I'll not expostulate with her, lest her body and beauty unprovide my mind° again. This night, Iago!

Iago. Do it not with poison. Strangle her in her bed, even the bed she hath contaminated. 200

Othello. Good, good! The justice of it pleases. Very good!

Iago. And for Cassio, let me be his undertaker.° You shall hear more by midnight.

Othello. Excellent good!   [*A trumpet.*]
         What trumpet is that same?

Iago. I warrant something from Venice.

---

179 **way** proper course   182-3 **invention** imagination   185-6 **gentle a condition** (1) well born (2) of a gentle nature 191 **touch** affects   192 **messes** bits 197 **unprovide my mind** undo my resolution   202 **undertaker** (not "burier" but "one who undertakes to do something")

Enter Lodovico, Desdemona, and Attendants.

'Tis Lodovico.   205
This comes from the Duke. See, your wife's with him.
Lodovico. God save you, worthy general.
Othello.   With° all my heart, sir.
Lodovico. The Duke and the senators of Venice greet you.
                        [*Gives him a letter.*]
Othello. I kiss the instrument of their pleasures.
                    [*Opens the letter and reads.*]
Desdemona. And what's the news, good cousin Lodovico?   210
Iago. I am very glad to see you, signior.
    Welcome to Cyprus.
Lodovico. I thank you. How does Lieutenant Cassio?
Iago.   Lives, sir.
Desdemona. Cousin, there's fall'n between him and my lord
    An unkind° breach; but you shall make all well.   215
Othello. Are you sure of that?
Desdemona. My lord?
Othello [*Reads*]. "This fail you not to do, as you will——"
Lodovico. He did not call; he's busy in the paper.
    Is there division 'twixt my lord and Cassio?   220
Desdemona. A most unhappy one. I would do much
    T' atone° them, for the love I bear to Cassio.
Othello. Fire and brimstone!
Desdemona.   My lord?
Othello.   Are you wise?
Desdemona. What, is he angry?
Lodovico.   May be th' letter moved him;
    For, as I think, they do command him home,   225
    Deputing Cassio in his government.°
Desdemona. Trust me, I am glad on't.
Othello.   Indeed?
Desdemona.   My lord?
Othello. I am glad to see you mad.
Desdemona.   Why, sweet Othello——
Othello. Devil!   [*Strikes her.*]
Desdemona. I have not deserved this.   230
Lodovico. My lord, this would not be believed in Venice,
    Though I should swear I saw't. 'Tis very much.
    Make her amends; she weeps.
Othello.   O devil, devil!
    If that the earth could teem° with woman's tears,
    Each drop she falls° would prove a crocodile.°   235
    Out of my sight!

207 **With** i.e., I greet you with   215 **unkind** unnatural   222 **atone** reconcile
226 **government** office   234 **teem** conceive   235 **falls** drops   235 **crocodile**
(the crocodile was supposed to shed false tears to lure its victims)

Desdemona. I will not stay to offend you.   [*Going.*]
Lodovico. Truly, an obedient lady.
    I do beseech your lordship call her back.
Othello. Mistress!
Desdemona.   My lord?
Othello.   What would you with her, sir?
Lodovico. Who? I, my lord?   240
Othello. Ay! You did wish that I would make her turn.
    Sir, she can turn, and turn, and yet go on
    And turn again; and she can weep, sir, weep;
    And she's obedient; as you say, obedient.
    Concerning this, sir—O well-painted passion!   245
    I am commanded home.—Get you away;
    I'll send for you anon.—Sir, I obey the mandate
    And will return to Venice.—Hence, avaunt!
                        [*Exit Desdemona.*]
    Cassio shall have my place. And, sir, tonight
    I do entreat that we may sup together.
    You are welcome, sir, to Cyprus.—Goats and monkeys! *Exit.*
Lodovico. Is this the noble Moor whom our full Senate
    Call all in all sufficient? Is this the nature
    Whom passion could not shake? whose solid virtue
    The shot of accident nor dart of chance   255
    Could neither graze nor pierce?
Iago.   He is much changed.
Lodovico. Are his wits safe? Is he not light of brain?
Iago. He's that he is; I may not breathe my censure.
    What he might be (if, what he might, he is not)
    I would to heaven he were!
Lodovico.   What, strike his wife?   260
Iago. Faith, that was not so well; yet would I knew
    That stroke would prove the worst.
Lodovico.   Is it his use?°
    Or did the letters work upon his blood°
    And new-create his fault?
Iago.   Alas, alas!
    It is not honesty in me to speak   265
    What I have seen and known. You shall observe him,
    And his own courses° will denote him so
    That I may save my speech. Do but go after
    And mark how he continues.
Lodovico. I am sorry that I am deceived in him.   *Exeunt.* 270

262 **use** habit   263 **blood** passion   267 **courses** actions

Scene II. [*The citadel.*]

Enter Othello and Emilia.

Othello. You have seen nothing then?
Emilia. Nor ever heard, nor ever did suspect.
Othello. Yes, you have seen Cassio and she together.
Emilia. But then I saw no harm, and then I heard
    Each syllable that breath made up° between them.   5
Othello. What, did they never whisper?
Emilia.   Never, my lord.
Othello. Nor send you out o' th' way?
Emilia. Never.
Othello. To fetch her fan, her gloves, her mask, nor nothing?
Emilia. Never, my lord.   10
Othello. That's strange.
Emilia. I durst, my lord, to wager she is honest,
    Lay down my soul at stake.° If you think other,
    Remove your thought. It doth abuse your bosom.
    If any wretch have put this in your head,   15
    Let heaven requite it with the serpent's curse,°
    For if she be not honest,° chaste, and true,
    There's no man happy. The purest of their wives
    Is foul as slander.
Othello.   Bid her come hither, Go.   *Exit Emilia.*
    She says enough; yet she's a simple bawd°   20
    That cannot say as much. This is a subtle whore,
    A close lock and key of villainous secrets,
    And yet she'll kneel and pray; I have seen her do't.

Enter Desdemona and Emilia.

Desdemona. My lord, what is your will?
Othello.   Pray you, chuck, come hither.
Desdemona. What is your pleasure?
Othello.   Let me see your eyes.   25
    Look in my face.
Desdemona.   What horrible fancy's this?
Othello [*To Emilia*]. Some of your function,° mistress:
    Leave procreants alone and shut the door;
    Cough or cry if anybody come.
    Your mystery,° your mystery! Nay, dispatch!   30
                                        Exit Emilia.

IV.ii.5 **that breath made up** spoken   13 **at stake** as the wager   16 **serpent's curse** (God's curse on the serpent after the fall in Eden)   17 **honest** chaste   20 **bawd** procuress   27 **Some of your function** do your proper work (as the operator of a brothel)   30 **mystery** trade

Desdemona. Upon my knee, what doth your speech import?
    I understand a fury in your words.°
Othello. Why, what art thou?
Desdemona.   Your wife, my lord; your true
    And loyal wife.
Othello.   Come, swear it, damn thyself;
    Lest, being like one of heaven, the devils themselves   35
    Should fear to seize thee. Therefore be doubledamned:
    Swear thou art honest.
Desdemona.   Heaven doth truly know it.
Othello. Heaven truly knows that thou art false as hell.
Desdemona. To whom, my lord? With whom? How am I false?
Othello. Ah, Desdemon! Away! Away! Away!   40
Desdemona. Alas the heavy day! Why do you weep?
    Am I the motive° of these tears, my lord?
    If haply° you my father do suspect
    An instrument of this your calling back,
    Lay not your blame on me. If you have lost him,   45
    I have lost him too.
Othello.   Had it pleased heaven
    To try with affliction, had they rained
    All kinds of sores and shames on my bare head,
    Steeped° me in poverty to the very lips,
    Given to captivity me and my utmost hopes,   50
    I should have found in some place of my soul
    A drop of patience. But alas, to make me
    The fixèd figure for the time of scorn°
    To point his slow and moving finger at.
    Yet could I bear that too, well, very well.   55
    But there where I have garnered up my heart,
    Where either I must live or bear no life,
    The fountain from the which my current runs
    Or else dries up—to be discarded thence,
    Or keep it as a cistern for foul toads   60
    To knot and gender° in—turn thy complexion there,
    Patience, thou young and rose-lipped cherubin!
    I here look grim as hell!°
Desdemona. I hope my noble lord esteems me honest.
Othello. O, ay, as summer flies are in the shambles,°   65

---

32 **words** (Q1 adds to this line, "But not the words")   **42 motive** cause
43 **haply** by chance   49 **Steeped** submerged   53 **The . . . scorn** the very image of scorn in our time   61 **knot and gender** twist in bunches and procreate
61-63 **turn . . . hell** (the rough sense would seem to be, "even Patience would grow pale, turn complexion, at Desdemona's perfidy, but that Othello looks grimly on")   65 **shambles** abattoirs

That quicken even with blowing.° O thou weed,
Who art so lovely fair, and smell'st so sweet,
That the sense aches at thee, would thou hadst never been
    born!
Desdemona. Alas, what ignorant° sin have I committed?
Othello. Was this fair paper, this most goodly book,   70
Made to write "whore" upon? What committed?
Committed? O thou public commoner,°
I should make very forges of my cheeks
That would to cinders burn up modesty,
Did I but speak thy deeds. What committed?   75
Heaven stops the nose at it, and the moon winks;°
The bawdy wind that kisses all it meets
Is hushed within the hollow mine of earth
And will not hear 't. What committed?
Desdemona. By heaven, you do me wrong!   80
Othello. Are not you a strumpet?
Desdemona.   No, as I am a Christian!
If to preserve this vessel for my lord
From any other foul unlawful touch
Be not to be a strumpet, I am none.
Othello. What, not a whore?
Desdemona.   No, as I shall be saved!   85
Othello. Is't possible?
Desdemona. O, heaven forgive us!
Othello.   I cry you mercy° then.
I took you for that cunning whore of Venice
That married with Othello. [*Calling*] You, mistress,

    Enter Emilia.

That have the office opposite to Saint Peter   90
And keep the gate of hell! You, you, ay, you!
We have done our course; there's money for your pains.
          [*Throws her some coins.*]
I pray you turn the key and keep our counsel.
                    Exit.

Emilia. Alas, what does this gentleman conceive?
How do you, madam? How do you, my good lady?   95
Desdemona. Faith, half asleep.
Emilia. Good madam, what's the matter with my lord?
Desdemona. With who?
Emilia. Why, with my lord, madam.

---

66 **quicken even with blowing** become impregnated as soon as they lay their
eggs   69 **ignorant** unknowing   72 **commoner** prostitute   76 **winks** closes its
eyes (the moon was the symbol of chastity)   87 **cry you mercy** ask your
pardon

Desdemona. Who is thy lord?
Emilia. He that is yours, sweet lady.   ₁₀₀
Desdemona. I have none. Do not talk to me, Emilia.
    I cannot weep, nor answers have I none
    But what should go by water.° Prithee tonight
    Lay on my bed my wedding sheets, remember;
    And call thy husband hither.
Emilia. Here's a change indeed!   ₁₀₅

                                           Exit.

Desdemona. 'Tis meet I should be used so, very meet.
    How have I been behaved, that he might stick
    The small'st opinion on my least misuse?°

    Enter Iago and Emilia.

Iago. What is your pleasure, madam? How is't with you?
Desdemona. I cannot tell. Those that do teach young babes   ₁₁₀
    Do it with gentle means and easy tasks.
    He might have chid me so; for, in good faith,
    I am a child to chiding.
Iago. What is the matter, lady?
Emilia. Alas, Iago, my lord hath so bewhored her,
    Thrown such despite° and heavy terms upon her   ₁₁₅
    That true hearts cannot bear it.
Desdemona. Am I that name, Iago?
Iago. What name, fair lady?
Desdemona. Such as she said my lord did say I was.
Emilia. He called her a whore. A beggar in his drink
    Could not have laid such terms upon his callet.°   ₁₂₀
Iago. Why did he so?
Desdemona. I do not know; I am sure I am none such.
Iago. Do not weep, do not weep. Alas the day.
Emilia. Hath she forsook so many noble matches,
    Her father and her country, and her friends,   ₁₂₅
    To be called whore? Would it not make one weep?
Desdemona. It is my wretched fortune.
Iago. Beshrew° him for 't!
    How comes this trick upon him?
Desdemona. Nay, heaven doth know.
Emilia. I will be hanged if some eternal villain,
    Some busy and insinuating rogue,
    Some cogging,° cozening slave, to get some office,   ₁₃₀
    Have not devised this slander. I will be hanged else.

---

103 **water** tears   107–08 **stick . . . misuse** base any doubt on my smallest fault
115 **despite** abuse   120 **callet** slut   127 **Beshrew** curse   131 **cogging** cheating

Iago. Fie, there is no such man! It is impossible.
Desdemona. If any such there be, heaven pardon him.
Emilia. A halter pardon him! And hell gnaw his bones!   135
Why should he call her whore? Who keeps her company?
What place? What time? What form? What likelihood?
The Moor's abused by some most villainous knave,
Some base notorious knave, some scurvy fellow.
O heavens, that such companions° thou'dst unfold,°   140
And put in every honest hand a whip
To lash the rascals naked through the world
Even from the east to th' west!
Iago.   Speak within door.°
Emilia. O, fie upon them! Some such squire° he was
That turned your wit the seamy side without   145
And made you to suspect me with the Moor.
Iago. You are a fool. Go to.
Desdemona.   Alas, Iago,
What shall I do to win my lord again?
Good friend, go to him, for, by this light of heaven,
I know not how I lost him. Here I kneel: 150
If e'er my will did trespass 'gainst his love
Either in discourse of thought° or actual deed,
Or that mine eyes, mine ears, or any sense
Delighted them in any other form;
Or that I do not yet, and ever did,   155
And ever will (though he do shake me off
To beggarly divorcement) love him dearly,
Comfort forswear me. Unkindness may do much,
And his unkindness may defeat° my life,
But never taint my love. I cannot say "whore."   160
It does abhor me now I speak the word;
To do the act that might the addition earn
Not the world's mass of vanity could make me.
Iago. I pray you be content. 'Tis but his humor.°
The business of the state does him offense.   165
Desdemona. If 'twere no other.
Iago.   It is but so, I warrant.
                              [*Trumpets within.*]
Hark how these instruments summon to supper.
The messengers of Venice stay the meat.°
Go in, and weep not. All things shall be well.
                    [*Exeunt Desdemona and Emilia.*]

140 **companions** fellows, rogues   140 **unfold** disclose   143 **within door** more
quietly and moderately   144 **squire** (a term of contempt)   152 **discourse of
thought** thinking   159 **defeat** destroy   164 **humor** mood   168 **stay the meat**
await the meal

Enter Roderigo.

How now, Roderigo?   170
Roderigo. I do not find that thou deal'st justly with me.
Iago. What in the contrary?
Roderigo. Every day thou daff'st° me with some device,° Iago,
and rather, as it seems to me now, keep'st from me all con-
veniency° than suppliest me with the least advantage of   175
hope. I will indeed no longer endure it; nor am I yet persuaded to put up° in peace what already I have foolishly
suffered.
Iago. Will you hear me, Roderigo?
Roderigo. I have heard too much, and your words and perfor-   180
mances are no kin together.
Iago. You charge me most unjustly.
Roderigo. With naught but truth. I have wasted myself out of my
means. The jewels you have had from me to deliver Desdemona would half have corrupted a votarist.° You have told   185
me she hath received them, and returned me expectations
and comforts of sudden respect° and acquaintance; but I find
none.
Iago. Well, go to; very well.
Roderigo. Very well? Go to? I cannot go to, man; nor 'tis not very   190
well. Nay, I think it is scurvy, and begin to find myself
fopped° in it.
Iago. Very well.
Roderigo. I tell you 'tis not very well. I will make myself known
to Desdemona. If she will return me my jewels, I will give   195
over my suit and repent my unlawful solicitation. If not,
assure yourself I will seek satisfaction of you.
Iago. You have said now?
Roderigo. Ay, and said nothing but what I protest° intendment
of doing.   200
Iago. Why, now I see there's mettle° in thee, and even from this
instant do build on thee a better opinion than ever before.
Give me thy hand, Roderigo. Thou hast taken against me a
most just exception;° but yet I protest I have dealt most
directly° in thy affair.   205
Roderigo. It hath not appeared.
Iago. I grant indeed it hath not appeared, and your suspicion is
not without wit and judgment. But, Roderigo, if thou hast
that in thee indeed which I have greater reason to believe
now than ever—I mean purpose, courage, and valor—this   210

---

173 **daff'st** put off   173 **device** scheme   174-5 **conveniency** what is needful
177 **put up** accept   185 **votarist** nun   187 **sudden respect** immediate consideration   192 **fopped** duped   199 **protest** aver   201 **mettle** spirit   204 **exception** objection   205 **directly** straightforwardly

night show it. If thou the next night following enjoy not
Desdemona, take me from this world with treachery and
devise engines for° my life.
Roderigo. Well, what is it? Is it within reason and compass?°
Iago. Sir, there is especial commission come from Venice to   215
depute Cassio in Othello's place.
Roderigo. Is that true? Why, then Othello and Desdemona
return again to Venice.
Iago. O, no; he goes into Mauritania and taketh away with him
the fair Desdemona, unless his abode be lingered here by   220
some accident; wherein none can be so determinate° as the
removing of Cassio.
Roderigo. How do you mean, removing him?
Iago. Why, by making him uncapable of Othello's place—knocking out his brains.   225
Roderigo. And that you would have me to do?
Iago. Ay, if you dare do yourself a profit and a right. He sups
tonight with a harlotry,° and thither will I go to him. He
knows not yet of his honorable fortune. If you will watch his
going thence, which I will fashion to fall out° between   230
twelve and one, you may take him at your pleasure. I will
be near to second° your attempt, and he shall fall between
us. Come, stand not amazed at it, but go along with me.
I will show you such a necessity in his death that you shall
think yourself bound to put it on him. It is now high supper   235
time, and the night grows to waste. About it.
Roderigo. I will hear further reason for this.
Iago. And you shall be satisfied.   *Exeunt.*

Scene III. [*The citadel.*]

Enter Othello, Lodovico, Desdemona, Emilia, and Attendants.

Lodovico. I do beseech you, sir, trouble yourself no further.
Othello. O, pardon me; 'twill do me good to walk.
Lodovico. Madam, good night. I humbly thank your ladyship.
Desdemona. Your honor is most welcome.
Othello. Will you walk, sir? O, Desdemona.   5
Desdemona. My lord?
Othello. Get you to bed on th' instant; I will be returned forth-
with. Dismiss your attendant there. Look't be done.
Desdemona. I will, my lord.
              Exit [*Othello, with Lodovico and Attendants*].

213 **engines for** schemes against   214 **compass** possibility   221 **determinate**
effective   228 **harlotry** female   230 **fall out** occur   232 **second** support

Emilia. How goes it now? He looks gentler than he did.   10

Desdemona. He says he will return incontinent,°
    And hath commanded me to go to bed,
    And bade me to dismiss you.

Emilia.   Dismiss me?

Desdemona. It was his bidding; therefore, good Emilia,
    Give me my nightly wearing, and adieu.   15
    We must not now displease him.

Emilia. I would you had never seen him!

Desdemona. So would not I. My love doth so approve him
    That even his stubbornness, his checks,° his frowns—
    Prithee unpin me—have grace and favor.   20

Emilia. I have laid these sheets you bade me on the bed.

Desdemona. All's one.° Good Father, how foolish are our minds!
    If I do die before, prithee shroud me
    In one of these same sheets.

Emilia.   Come, come! You talk.

Desdemona. My mother had a maid called Barbary.   25
    She was in love; and he she loved proved mad
    And did forsake her. She had a song of "Willow";
    An old thing 'twas, but it expressed her fortune,
    And she died singing it. That song tonight
    Will not go from my mind; I have much to do   30
    But to go hang my head all at one side
    And sing it like poor Barbary. Prithee dispatch.

Emilia. Shall I go fetch your nightgown?

Desdemona. No, unpin me here.
    This Lodovico is a proper man.   35

Emilia. A very handsome man.

Desdemona. He speaks well.

Emilia. I know a lady in Venice would have walked barefoot to
    Palestine for a touch of his nether lip.

Desdemona [*Sings*].
            "The poor soul sat singing by a sycamore tree,   40
                Sing all a green willow;
            Her hand on her bosom, her head on her knee,
                Sing willow, willow, willow.
            The fresh streams ran by her and murmured her moans;
                Sing willow, willow, willow;   45
            Her salt tears fell from her, and soft'ned the stones—
                Sing willow, willow, willow—"
    Lay by these.   [*Gives Emilia her clothes.*]
            "Willow, Willow"——
    Prithee hie° thee; he'll come anon.°   50

IV.iii.11 **incontinent** at once   19 **checks** rebukes   22 **All's one** no matter
50 **hie** hurry   50 **anon** at once

            "Sing all a green willow must be my garland.
            Let nobody blame him; his scorn I approve"——
        Nay, that's not next. Hark! Who is't that knocks?
Emilia. It is the wind.
Desdemona [*Sings*].
            "I called my love false love; but what said he then?   55
                Sing willow, willow, willow:
            If I court moe° women, you'll couch with moe men."
        So, get thee gone; good night. Mine eyes do itch.
        Doth that bode weeping?
Emilia.   'Tis neither here nor there.
Desdemona. I have heard it said so. O, these men, these men.   60
        Dost thou in conscience think, tell me, Emilia,
        That there be women do abuse their husbands
        In such gross kind?
Emilia.   There be some such, no question.
Desdemona. Wouldst thou do such a deed for all the world?
Emilia. Why, would not you?
Desdemona.   No, by this heavenly light!   65
Emilia. Nor I neither by this heavenly light.
        I might do't as well i' th' dark.
Desdemona. Wouldst thou do such a deed for all the world?
Emilia. The world's a huge thing; it is a great price for a small
        vice.   70
Desdemona. In troth, I think thou wouldst not.
Emilia. In troth, I think I should; and undo't when I had done.
        Marry, I would not do such a thing for a joint-ring,° nor for
        measures of lawn,° nor for gowns, petticoats, nor caps, nor
        any petty exhibition,° but for all the whole world? Why,   75
        who would not make her husband a cuckold to make him a
        monarch? I should venture purgatory for't.
Desdemona. Beshrew me if I would do such a wrong for the whole
        world.
Emilia. Why, the wrong is but a wrong i' th' world; and having   80
        the world for your labor, 'tis a wrong in your own world,
        and you might quickly make it right.
Desdemona. I do not think there is any such woman.
Emilia. Yes, a dozen; and as many to th' vantage as would store°
        the world they played for.   85
        But I do think it is their husbands' faults
        If wives do fall. Say that they slack their duties
        And pour our treasures into foreign° laps;
        Or else break out in peevish jealousies,

---

57 **moe** more   73 **joint-ring** (a ring with two interlocking halves)   74 **lawn**
fine linen   75 **exhibition** payment   84 **to . . . store** in addition as would fill
88 **foreign** alien, i.e., other than the wife

Throwing restraint upon us; or say they strike us,   90
Or scant our former having in despite°—
Why, we have galls; and though we have some grace,
Yet we have some revenge. Let husbands know
Their wives have sense like them. They see, and smell,
And have their palates both for sweet and sour,   95
As husbands have. What is it that they do
When they change° us for others? Is it sport?
I think it is. And doth affection° breed it?
I think it doth. Is't frailty that thus errs?
It is so too. And have not we affections?   100
Desires for sport? and frailty? as men have?
Then let them use us well; else let them know,
The ills we do, their ills instruct us so.°
Desdemona. Good night, good night. Heaven me such uses° send,
Not to pick bad from bad, but by bad mend.   *Exeunt.*   105

ACT V

Scene I. [*A street.*]

Enter Iago and Roderigo.

Iago. Here, stand behind this bulk;° straight will he come.
Wear thy good rapier bare, and put it home.
Quick, quick! Fear nothing; I'll be at thy elbow.
It makes us, or it mars us, think on that,
And fix most firm thy resolution.   5
Roderigo. Be near at hand; I may miscarry in't.
Iago. Here, at thy hand. Be bold, and take thy stand.
                              [*Moves to one side.*]
Roderigo. I have no great devotion to the deed,
And yet he hath given me satisfying reasons.
'Tis but a man gone. Forth my sword! He dies!   10
Iago. I have rubbed this young quat° almost to the sense,°
And he grows angry. Now, whether he kill Cassio,
Or Cassio him, or each do kill the other,
Every way makes my gain. Live Roderigo,
He calls me to a restitution large   15
Of gold and jewels that I bobbed° from him
As gifts to Desdemona.

---

91 **scant . . . despite** reduce, in spite, our household allowance (?)   97 **change** exchange   98 **affection** strong feeling, desire   103 **instruct us so** teach us to do likewise   104 **uses** practices   V.i.1 **bulk** projecting stall of a shop   11 **quat** pimple   11 **to the sense** raw   16 **bobbed** swindled

It must not be. If Cassio do remain,
He hath a daily beauty in his life
That makes me ugly; and besides, the Moor   20
May unfold me to him; there stand I in much peril.
No, he must die. But so, I hear him coming.

Enter Cassio.

Roderigo. I know his gait. 'Tis he. Villain, thou diest!
                              [*Thrusts at Cassio.*]
Cassio. That thrust had been mine enemy indeed
    But that my coat° is better than thou know'st.   25
    I will make proof of thine.   [*Fights with Roderigo.*]
Roderigo.   O, I am slain!°
Cassio. I am maimed forever. Help, ho! Murder! Murder!

Enter Othello [to one side].

Othello. The voice of Cassio. Iago keeps his word.
Roderigo. O, villain that I am!
Othello.   It is even so.
Cassio. O help, ho! Light! A surgeon!   30
Othello. 'Tis he. O brave Iago, honest and just,
    That has such noble sense of thy friend's wrong!
    Thou teachest me. Minion,° your dear lies dead,
    And your unblest° fate hies.° Strumpet, I come.
    Forth of my heart those charms, thine eyes, are blotted. 35
    Thy bed, lust-stained, shall with lust's blood be spotted.
                              Exit Othello.

Enter Lodovico and Gratiano.

Cassio. What, ho? No watch? No passage?° Murder! Murder!
Gratiano. 'Tis some mischance. The voice is very direful.
Cassio. O, help!
Lodovico. Hark!   40
Roderigo. O wretched villain!
Lodovico. Two or three groan. 'Tis heavy night.
    These may be counterfeits. Let's think't unsafe
    To come into the cry without more help.
Roderigo. Nobody come? Then shall I bleed to death.   45

25 **coat** i.e., a mail shirt or bulletproof vest   26 **slain** (most editors add here a
stage direction which has Iago wounding Cassio in the leg from behind, but remaining unseen. However, nothing in the text requires this, and Cassio's wound
can be given him in the fight with Roderigo, for presumably when Cassio attacks Roderigo the latter would not simply accept the thrust but would parry.
Since Iago enters again at line 46, he must exit at some point after line 22)
33 **Minion** hussy, i.e., Desdemona   34 **unblest** unsanctified   34 **hies** approaches swiftly   37 **passage** passers-by

Lodovico. Hark!

    Enter Iago [with a light].

Gratiano. Here's one comes in his shirt, with light and weapons.
Iago. Who's there? Whose noise is this that cries on murder?
Lodovico. We do not know.
Iago.   Do not you hear a cry?
Cassio. Here, here! For heaven's sake, help me!
Iago.   What's the matter?   50
Gratiano. This is Othello's ancient, as I take it.
Lodovico. The same indeed, a very valiant fellow.
Iago. What are you here that cry so grievously?
Cassio. Iago? O, I am spoiled, undone by villains.
    Give me some help.   55
Iago. O me, lieutenant! What villains have done this?
Cassio. I think that one of them is hereabout
    And cannot make away.
Iago.   O treacherous villains!
    [*To Lodovico and Gratiano*] What are you there?
    Come in, and give some help.
Roderigo. O, help me there!   60
Cassio. That's one of them.
Iago.   O murd'rous slave! O villain!
                                     [*Stabs Roderigo.*]
Roderigo. O damned Iago! O inhuman dog!
Iago. Kill men i' th' dark?—Where be these bloody thieves?—
    How silent is this town!—Ho! Murder! Murder!—
    What may you be? Are you of good or evil?   65
Lodovico. As you shall prove us, praise us.
Iago. Signior Lodovico?
Lodovico. He, sir.
Iago. I cry you mercy. Here's Cassio hurt by villains.
Gratiano. Cassio?   70
Iago. How is't, brother?
Cassio. My leg is cut in two.
Iago.   Marry, heaven forbid!
    Light, gentlemen. I'll bind it with my shirt.

    Enter Bianca.

Bianca. What is the matter, ho? Who is't that cried?
Iago. Who is't that cried?   75
Bianca. O my dear Cassio! My sweet Cassio!
    O Cassio, Cassio, Cassio!
Iago. O notable strumpet!—Cassio, you may suspect
    Who they should be that have thus mangled you?
Cassio. No.   80
Gratiano. I am sorry to find you thus. I have been to seek you.

Iago. Lend me a garter. So. O for a chair
    To bear him easily hence.
Bianca. Alas, he faints! O Cassio, Cassio, Cassio!
Iago. Gentlemen all, I do suspect this trash   85
    To be a party in this injury.—
    Patience awhile, good Cassio.—Come, come.
    Lend me a light. Know we this face or no?
    Alas, my friend and my dear countryman
    Roderigo? No.—Yes, sure.—Yes, 'tis Roderigo!   90
Gratiano. What, of Venice?
Iago. Even he, sir. Did you know him?
Gratiano.   Know him? Ay.
Iago. Signior Gratiano? I cry your gentle pardon.
    These bloody accidents must excuse my manners
    That so neglected you.
Gratiano.   I am glad to see you.   95
Iago. How do you, Cassio?—O, a chair, a chair!
Gratiano. Roderigo?
Iago. He, he, 'tis he! [*A chair brought in.*] O, that's well said;°
    the chair.
    Some good man bear him carefully from hence.
    I'll fetch the general's surgeon. [*To Bianca*] For you,
    mistress,   100
    Save you your labor. [*To Cassio*] He that lies slain here,
    Cassio,
    Was my dear friend. What malice was between you?
Cassio. None in the world; nor do I know the man.
Iago. What, look you pale?—O, bear him out o' th' air.
                                      [*Cassio is carried off.*]
    Stay you, good gentlemen.—Look you pale, mistress?   105
    Do you perceive the gastness° of her eye?
    Nay, if you stare, we shall hear more anon.
    Behold her well; I pray you look upon her.
    Do you see, gentlemen? Nay, guiltiness will speak,
    Though tongues were out of use.°   110

    [*Enter Emilia.*]

Emilia. Alas, what is the matter? What is the matter, husband?
Iago. Cassio hath here been set on in the dark
    By Roderigo and fellows that are scaped.
    He's almost slain, and Roderigo quite dead.
Emilia. Alas, good gentleman! Alas good Cassio!   115
Iago. This is the fruits of whoring. Prithee, Emilia,
    Go know of Cassio where he supped tonight.
    [*To Bianca*] What, do you shake at that?

98 **well said** well done   106 **gastness** terror   110 **tongues were out of use**
men no longer spoke

Bianca. He supped at my house; but I therefore shake not.
Iago. O, did he so? I charge° you go with me.   120
Emilia. Oh fie upon thee, strumpet!
Bianca. I am no strumpet, but of life as honest
    As you that thus abuse me.
Emilia.   As I? Fie upon thee!
Iago. Kind gentlemen, let's go see poor Cassio dressed.°
    [*To Bianca*] Come, mistress, you must tell's another tale.   125
    Emilia, run you to the citadel
    And tell my lord and lady what hath happed.

                      [*Exit Emilia.*]
    Will you go on afore?   *Exeunt* [*all but Iago*].
            This is the night
    That either makes me or fordoes me quite.°   [*Exit.*]

Scene II. [*Desdemona's chamber.*]

Enter Othello [*with a light*]; *and Desdemona in her bed.*

Othello. It is the cause, it is the cause, my soul.
    Let me not name it to you, you chaste stars.
    It is the cause. Yet I'll not shed her blood,
    Nor scar that whiter skin of hers than snow
    And smooth as monumental alabaster.   5
    Yet she must die, else she'll betray more men.
    Put out the light, and then put out the light.
    If I quench thee, thou flaming minister,°
    I can again thy former light restore,
    Should I repent me; but once put out thy light,   10
    Thou cunning'st° pattern of excelling nature,
    I know not where is that Promethean heat°
    That can thy light relume.° When I have plucked the rose,
    I cannot give it vital° growth again;
    It needs must wither. I'll smell thee on the tree.   15
                  [*He kisses her.*]
    O balmy breath, that dost almost persuade
    Justice to break her sword. One more, one more!
    Be thus when thou art dead, and I will kill thee,
    And love thee after. One more, and that's the last!
    So sweet was ne'er so fatal. I must weep,   20

120 **charge** command   124 **dressed** bandaged   129 **fordoes me quite** completely ruins me   V.ii.8 **minister** worker, servant   11 **cunning'st** most intricate and skillfully wrought (by nature excelling itself)   12 **Promethean heat** divine fire (Prometheus is the Titan who stole fire from heaven and gave it to man)   13 **relume** relight   14 **vital** living

But they are cruel tears. This sorrow's heavenly;
It strikes where it doth love. She wakes.
Desdemona. Who's there? Othello?
Othello.   Ay, Desdemona.
Desdemona. Will you come to bed, my lord?
Othello. Have you prayed tonight, Desdemon?
Desdemona.   Ay, my lord. 25
Othello. If you bethink yourself of any crime
    Unreconciled as yet to heaven and grace,
    Solicit for it straight.
Desdemona. Alack, my lord, what may you mean by that?
Othello. Well, do it, and be brief; I will walk by.° 30
    I would not kill thy unprepared spirit.
    No, heavens forfend! I would not kill thy soul.
Desdemona. Talk you of killing?
Othello.   Ay, I do.
Desdemona.   Then heaven
    Have mercy on me!
Othello.   Amen, with all my heart.
Desdemona. If you say so, I hope you will not kill me. 35
Othello. Humh.
Desdemona. And yet I fear you; for you're fatal then
    When your eyes roll so. Why I should fear I know not,
    Since guiltiness I know not; but yet I feel I fear.
Othello. Think on thy sins.
Desdemona.   They are loves I bear to you. 40
Othello. Ay, and for that thou diest.
Desdemona. That death's unnatural that kills for loving.
    Alas, why gnaw you so your nether lip?
    Some bloody passion shakes your very frame.
    These are portents; but yet I hope, I hope, 45
    They do not point on me.
Othello.   Peace and be still.
Desdemona. I will so. What's the matter?
Othello. That handkerchief which I so loved and gave thee,
    Thou gav'st to Cassio.
Desdemona.   No, by my life and soul!
    Send for the man and ask him.
Othello.   Sweet soul, take heed, 50
    Take heed of perjury; thou art on thy deathbed.
Desdemona. Ay, but not yet to die.
Othello.   Presently.°
    Therefore confess thee freely of thy sin,
    For to deny each article° with oath

30 **by** nearby   52 **Presently** immediately   54 **article** item (of the charge of adultery. Othello makes heavy use of legal terms in this scene)

Cannot remove nor choke the strong conception 55
That I do groan withal. Thou art to die.
Desdemona. Then Lord have mercy on me.
Othello.   I say, amen.
Desdemona. And have you mercy too. I never did
    Offend you in my life; never loved Cassio
    But with such general warranty° of heaven 60
    As I might love. I never gave him token.
Othello. By heaven, I saw my handkerchief in's hand!
    O perjured woman! thou dost stone° my heart,
    And mak'st me call what I intend to do
    A murder, which I thought a sacrifice. 65
    I saw the handkerchief.
Desdemona.   He found it then.
    I never gave it him. Send for him hither.
    Let him confess a truth.
Othello.   He hath confessed.
Desdemona. What, my lord?
Othello. That he hath used thee.
Desdemona.   How? Unlawfully?
Othello   Ay. 70
Desdemona. He will not say so.
Othello.   No, his mouth is stopped.
    Honest Iago hath ta'en order for't.°
Desdemona. O, my fear interprets. What, is he dead?
Othello. Had all his hairs been lives, my great revenge
    Had stomach° for them all. 75
Desdemona. Alas, he is betrayed, and I undone!
Othello. Out, strumpet! Weep'st thou for him to my face?
Desdemona. O, banish me, my lord, but kill me not!
Othello. Down, strumpet!
Desdemona. Kill me tomorrow; let me live tonight! 80
Othello. Nay, if you strive——
Desdemona. But half an hour!
Othello.   Being done, there is no pause.
Desdemona. But while I say one prayer!
Othello.   It is too late.

Smothers her.

Emilia at the door.

Emilia [*Calls within*]. My lord, my lord! What, ho, my lord, my
    lord!
Othello. What noise is this? Not dead? Not yet quite dead? 85
    I that am cruel am yet merciful;

60 **warranty** allowance   63 **stone** turn to stone   72 **ta'en order for't** made
sure of it   75 **stomach** appetite

I would not have thee linger in thy pain.
So, so.
Emilia [*Within*]. What, ho! My lord, my lord!
Othello.   Who's there?
Emilia [*Within*]. O, good my lord, I would speak a word with you.
Othello. Yes, 'tis Emilia.—By and by.—She's dead.—   90
'Tis like she comes to speak of Cassio's death.
The noise was high.° Ha! No more moving?
Still as the grave.—Shall she come in? Were't good?—
I think she stirs again. No.— What's best to do?
If she come in, she'll sure speak to my wife.   95
My wife! My wife! What wife? I have no wife.
O, insupportable! O heavy hour!
Methinks it should be now a huge eclipse
Of sun and moon, and that th' affrighted globe
Should yawn° at alteration.
Emilia.   [*Within*] I do beseech you   100
That I may speak with you, O good my lord!
Othello. I had forgot thee. O, come in, Emilia.
Soft, by and by.—Let me the curtains draw.—
                    [*Draws the bed hangings and then opens the door.*]
Where art thou?

Enter Emilia.

                    What's the matter with thee now?
Emilia. O my good lord, yonder's foul murders done!   105
Othello. What? Now?
Emilia. But now, my lord.
Othello. It is the very error° of the moon.
She comes more nearer earth than she was wont
And makes men mad.   110
Emilia. Cassio, my lord, hath killed a young Venetian
Called Roderigo.
Othello.   Roderigo killed?
And Cassio killed?
Emilia.   No, Cassio is not killed.
Othello. Not Cassio killed? Then murder's out of tune,
And sweet revenge grows harsh.   115
Desdemona. O, falsely, falsely murdered!
Emilia.   O Lord! What cry is that?
Othello. That? What?

92 **high** loud (Q1 reads "here")   98–100 **Methinks . . . alteration** (the Elizabethans believed that great changes in human affairs were reflected by disorders
in nature)   100 **yawn** gape open (as in an earthquake)   108 **error** wandering
out of regular course (disorders in the heavens were believed by some to cause
disorders on earth, as well as vice versa)

Emilia. Out and alas! that was my lady's voice.
   Help! Help, ho! Help! O lady, speak again!
   Sweet Desdemona! O sweet mistress, speak!   120
Desdemona. A guiltless death I die.
Emilia. O, who hath done this deed?
Desdemona. Nobody—I myself. Farewell.
   Commend me to my kind lord. O, farewell!

                                          [*She dies.*]

Othello. Why, how should she be murd'red?
Emilia.   Alas, who knows?   125
Othello. You heard her say herself, it was not I.
Emilia. She said so. I must needs report the truth.
Othello. She's like a liar gone to burning hell!
   'Twas I that killed her.
Emilia.   O, the more angel she,
   And you the blacker devil!   130
Othello. She turned to folly, and she was a whore.
Emilia. Thou dost belie her, and thou art a devil.
Othello. She was false as water.
Emilia.   Thou art rash as fire to say
   That she was false. O, she was heavenly true!
Othello. Cassio did top her. Ask thy husband else.   135
   O, I were damned beneath all depth in hell
   But that I did proceed upon just grounds
   To this extremity. Thy husband knew it all.
Emilia. My husband?
Othello.   Thy husband.
Emilia.   That she was false to wedlock?
Othello. Ay, with Cassio. Had she been true,   140
   If heaven would make me such another world
   Of one entire and perfect chrysolite,°
   I'd not have sold her for it.
Emilia.   My husband?
Othello. Ay, 'twas he that told me on her first.
   An honest man he is, and hates the slime   145
   That sticks on filthy deeds.
Emilia.   My husband?
Othello. What needs this iterance? Woman, I say thy husband.
Emilia. O mistress, villainy hath made mocks with love!
   My husband say she was false?
Othello.   He, woman.
   I say, thy husband. Dost understand the word?   150
   My friend, thy husband; honest, honest Iago.
Emilia. If he say so, may his pernicious soul
   Rot half a grain a day! He lies to th' heart.
   She was too fond of her most filthy bargain.

142 **chrysolite** topaz

Othello. Hah? ¹⁵⁵

Emilia. Do thy worst.
  This deed of thine is no more worthy heaven
  Than thou wast worthy her.

Othello.   Peace, you were best.°

Emilia. Thou hast not half that pow'r to do me harm
  As I have to be hurt. O gull! O dolt! ¹⁶⁰
  As ignorant as dirt! Thou hast done a deed—
          [*Othello moves to draw his sword.*]
  I care not for thy sword; I'll make thee known,
  Though I lost twenty lives. Help! Help! Ho! Help!
  The Moor hath killed my mistress! Murder! murder!

Enter Montano, Gratiano, and Iago [and Others].

Montano. What is the matter? How now, general? ¹⁶⁵

Emilia. O, are you come, Iago? You have done well,
  That men must lay their murders on your neck.

Gratiano. What is the matter?

Emilia. Disprove this villain, if thou be'st a man.
  He says thou told'st him that his wife was false. ¹⁷⁰
  I know thou didst not; thou'rt not such a villain.
  Speak, for my heart is full.

Iago. I told him what I thought, and told no more
  Than what he found himself was apt and true.

Emilia. But did you ever tell him she was false? ¹⁷⁵

Iago. I did.

Emilia. You told a lie, an odious damnèd lie!
  Upon my soul, a lie! A wicked lie!
  She false with Cassio? Did you say with Cassio?

Iago. With Cassio, mistress. Go to, charm° your tongue. ¹⁸⁰

Emilia. I will not charm my tongue; I am bound to speak:
  My mistress here lies murdered in her bed.

All. O heavens forfend!

Emilia. And your reports have set the murder on.

Othello. Nay, stare not, masters. It is true indeed. ¹⁸⁵

Gratiano. 'Tis a strange truth.

Montano. O monstrous act!

Emilia.   Villainy, villainy, villainy!
  I think upon't—I think I smell't!—O villainy!
  I thought so then.—I'll kill myself for grief.—
  O villainy, villainy! ¹⁹⁰

Iago. What, are you mad? I charge you get you home.

Emilia. Good gentlemen, let me have leave to speak.
  'Tis proper I obey him, but not now.
  Perchance, Iago, I will ne'er go home.

158 **Peace, you were best** i.e., you had better be silent   180 **charm** control

Othello. O! O! O!   [*Falls on the bed.*]
Emilia.   Nay, lay thee down and roar,   195
    For thou hast killed the sweetest innocent
    That e'er did lift up eye.
Othello.   O, she was foul!   [*Rises.*]
    I scarce did know you, uncle. There lies your niece,
    Whose breath, indeed, these hands have newly stopped.
    I know this act shows horrible and grim.   200
Gratiano. Poor Desdemon! I am glad thy father's dead.
    Thy match was mortal to him, and pure grief
    Shore his old thread in twain. Did he live now,
    This sight would make him do a desperate turn;
    Yea, curse his better angel from his side,   205
    And fall to reprobation.°
Othello. 'Tis pitiful; but yet Iago knows
    That she with Cassio hath the act of shame
    A thousand times committed. Cassio confessed it;
    And she did gratify his amorous works   210
    With that recognizance and pledge of love,
    Which I first gave her. I saw it in his hand.
    It was a handkerchief, an antique token
    My father gave my mother.
Emilia. O God! O heavenly God!   215
Iago. Zounds, hold your peace!
Emilia.   'Twill out, 'twill out! I peace?
    No, I will speak as liberal as the north.°
    Let heaven and men and devils, let them all,
    All, all, cry shame against me, yet I'll speak.
Iago. Be wise, and get you home.
Emilia.   I will not.   220
                     [*Iago draws and threatens Emilia.*]
Gratiano. Fie! Your sword upon a woman?
Emilia. O thou dull Moor, that handkerchief thou speak'st of
    I found by fortune, and did give my husband;
    For often with a solemn earnestness—
    More than indeed belonged to such a trifle—   225
    He begged of me to steal't.
Iago.   Villainous whore!
Emilia. She give it Cassio? No, alas, I found it,
    And I did give't my husband.
Iago.   Filth, thou liest!
Emilia. By heaven, I do not, I do not, gentlemen.
    O murd'rous coxcomb! What should such a fool   230
    Do with so good a wife?

---

206 **reprobation** damnation   217 **liberal as the north** freely (and bitingly) as
the north wind blows

Othello.   Are there no stones° in heaven
        But what serves for the thunder? Precious villain!
              [*The Moor runs at Iago, but is disarmed by Montano.*
                          Iago kills his wife.]
Gratiano. The woman falls. Sure he hath killed his wife.
Emilia. Ay, ay. O, lay me by my mistress' side.

                                              [*Exit Iago.*]

Gratiano. He's gone, but his wife's killed.   235
Montano. 'Tis a notorious° villain. Take you this weapon,
        Which I have recovered from the Moor.
        Come, guard the door without. Let him not pass,
        But kill him rather. I'll after that same villain,
        For 'tis a damnèd slave.
                          Exit [*with all but Othello and Emilia*].
Othello.   I am not valiant neither;   240
        But every puny whipster° gets my sword.
        But why should honor outlive honesty?
        Let it go all.
Emilia.   What did thy song bode, lady?
        Hark, canst thou hear me? I will play the swan,
        And die in music. [*Sings*] "Willow, willow, willow."   245
        Moor, she was chaste. She loved thee, cruel Moor,
        So come my soul to bliss as I speak true.
        So speaking as I think, alas, I die.   [*She dies.*]
Othello. I have another weapon in this chamber;
        It was a sword of Spain, the ice-brook's temper.   250
        O, here it is.—Uncle, I must come forth.
Gratiano. [*Within*] If thou attempt it, it will cost thee dear.
        Thou hast no weapon, and perforce must suffer.
Othello. Look in upon me then and speak with me,
        Or, naked as I am, I will assault thee.   255

        [*Enter Gratiano.*]

Gratiano. What is the matter?
Othello.   Behold, I have a weapon;
        A better never did itself sustain
        Upon a soldier's thigh. I have seen the day
        That with this little arm and this good sword
        I have made my way through more impediments   260
        Than twenty times your stop. But O vain boast!
        Who can control his fate? 'Tis not so now.
        Be not afraid, though you do see me weaponed.
        Here is my journey's end, here is my butt,°
        And very seamark of my utmost sail.°   265

---

231 **stones** thunderbolts   236 **notorious** out-and-out   241 **puny whipster** small
top-whipping boy (?)   264 **butt** target, stopping place   265 **seamark of my
utmost sail** marker of my farthest journey

Do you go back dismayed? 'Tis a lost fear.
Man but a rush° against Othello's breast,
And he retires. Where should Othello go?
Now, how dost thou look now? O ill-starred wench!
Pale as thy smock! When we shall meet at compt,°   270
This look of thine will hurl my soul from heaven,
And fiends will snatch at it. Cold, cold, my girl?
Even like thy chastity.
O cursèd, cursèd slave! Whip me, ye devils,
From the possession of° this heavenly sight!   275
Blow me about in winds! roast me in sulfur!
Wash me in steep-down gulfs of liquid fire!
O Desdemon! Dead Desdemon; dead. O! O!

Enter Lodovico, Cassio, Montano, and Iago [as prisoner,]
with Officers.

Lodovico. Where is this rash and most unfortunate man?
Othello. That's he that was Othello? Here I am.   280
Lodovico. Where is that viper? Bring the villain forth.
Othello. I look down towards his feet°—but that's a fable.
    If that thou be'st a devil, I cannot kill thee.
                                        [*Wounds Iago.*]
Lodovico. Wrench his sword from him.

                                        [*Othello is disarmed.*]
Iago.   I bleed, sir, but not killed.
Othello. I am not sorry neither. I'd have thee live;   285
    For in my sense, 'tis happiness to die.
Lodovico. O thou Othello that was once so good,
    Fall'n in the practice° of a cursèd slave,
    What shall be said to thee?
Othello.   Why, anything:
    An honorable murderer, if you will;   290
    For naught I did in hate, but all in honor.
Lodovico. This wretch hath part confessed his villainy.
    Did you and he consent in Cassio's death?
Othello. Ay.
Cassio. Dear general, I never gave you cause.   295
Othello. I do believe it, and I ask your pardon.
    Will you, I pray, demand that demi-devil
    Why he hath thus ensnared my soul and body?
Iago. Demand me nothing. What you know, you know.
    From this time forth I never will speak word.   300

267 **Man but a rush** attack with only a reed   270 **compt** Judgment Day   275
the possession of being possessed by   282 **towards his feet** i.e., for his cloven
hoofs   288 **practice** plotting

Lodovico. What, not to pray?
Gratiano.   Torments will ope your lips.
Othello. Well, thou dost best.
Lodovico. Sir, you shall understand what hath befall'n,
　　Which, as I think, you know not. Here is a letter
　　Found in the pocket of the slain Roderigo;　　　　305
　　And here another. The one of them imports
　　The death of Cassio to be undertook
　　By Roderigo.
Othello. O villain!
Cassio.   Most heathenish and most gross!
Lodovico. Now here's another discontented paper　　　310
　　Found in his pocket too; and this, it seems,
　　Roderigo meant t' have sent this damnèd villain;
　　But that, belike, Iago in the interim
　　Came in and satisfied him.
Othello.   O thou pernicious caitiff!
　　How came you, Cassio, by that handkerchief　　　315
　　That was my wife's?
Cassio.   I found it in my chamber;
　　And he himself confessed it but even now
　　That there he dropped it for a special purpose
　　Which wrought to his desire.
Othello.   O fool! Fool! Fool!
Cassio. There is besides in Roderigo's letter,　　　320
　　How he upbraids Iago that he made him
　　Brave me upon the watch; whereon it came
　　That I was cast; and even but now he spake,
　　After long seeming dead—Iago hurt him,
　　Iago set him on.　　　　　　　　　　　　325
Lodovico. You must forsake this room and go with us.
　　Your power and your command is taken off,
　　And Cassio rules in Cyprus. For this slave,
　　If there be any cunning cruelty
　　That can torment him much and hold him long,　　330
　　It shall be his. You shall close prisoner rest
　　Till that the nature of your fault be known
　　To the Venetian state. Come, bring away.
Othello. Soft you, a word or two before you go.
　　I have done the state some service and they know't.　　335
　　No more of that. I pray you, in your letters,
　　When you shall these unlucky deeds relate,
　　Speak of me as I am. Nothing extenuate,
　　Nor set down aught in malice. Then must you speak
　　Of one that loved not wisely, but too well;　　　340
　　Of one not easily jealous, but, being wrought,
　　Perplexed in the extreme; of one whose hand,

Like the base Judean,° threw a pearl away
Richer than all his tribe; of one whose subdued eyes,
Albeit unusèd to the melting mood,   345
Drops tears as fast as the Arabian trees
Their med'cinable gum. Set you down this.
And say besides that in Aleppo once,
Where a malignant and a turbaned Turk
Beat a Venetian and transduced the state,   350
I took by th' throat the circumcisèd dog
And smote him—thus.   [He stabs himself.]
Lodovico. O bloody period!°
Gratiano.   All that is spoke is marred.
Othello. I kissed thee ere I killed thee. No way but this,
Killing myself, to die upon a kiss.   355
                         [He falls over Desdemona and dies.]
Cassio. This did I fear, but thought he had no weapon;
For he was great of heart.
Lodovico.   [To Iago] O Spartan dog,
More fell° than anguish, hunger, or the sea!
Look on the tragic loading of this bed.
This is thy work. The object poisons sight;   360
Let it be hid.   [Bed curtains drawn.]
            Gratiano, keep° the house,
And seize upon the fortunes of the Moor,
For they succeed on you. To you, lord governor,
Remains the censure of this hellish villain,
The time, the place, the torture. O, enforce it!   365
Myself will straight aboard, and to the state
This heavy act with heavy heart relate.   Exeunt.

FINIS

343 **Judean** (most editors use the Q1 reading, "Indian," here, but F is clear;
both readings point toward the infidel, the unbeliever   353 **period** end   358
fell cruel   361 **keep** remain in

QUESTIONS: *Othello*

Act I

1. Iago, contemptuous of dutiful servants, compares them in
I.i.44 to asses. What other animal images does he use in the first
scene? What does the use of such images tell us about Iago?

2. Is there any need to do more than knock loudly at Brabantio's
door? What does I.1.72-74 tell us about Iago?

3. In I.i.105ff., and in his next speech, Iago uses prose instead of blank verse. What effect is gained?

4. What is Iago trying to do to Othello in the first speech of I.ii? In I.ii.29 why does Iago urge Othello to "go in"? When Othello first speaks (I.ii.6) does he speak as we might have expected him to, given Iago's earlier comments about Othello? In Othello's second speech is there anything that resembles Iago's earlier description of him?

5. Is it incredible that a girl who has rejected "the wealthy, curlèd darlings" (I.ii.67) of Venice should choose a Moor?

6. Iago had said (I.i.12) that Othello uses "bombast circumstance." Is I.iii.127ff. an example? Why?

7. Brabantio in I.iii.207-216 speaks in couplets (pairs of rhyming lines), as the Duke has just done. What is the effect of the verse? Does it suggest grief? Mockery?

8. Is the love of Othello and Desdemona impetuous and irrational? What is its basis?

9. The last speech in I.iii. is in verse, though previous speeches are in prose. What is the effect of the change?

10. Is it a fault that Othello "thinks men honest that but seem to be so" (I.iii.378)?

Act II

1. In II.i.1-19, why does Shakespeare introduce a description of a storm? What symbolic overtones, if any, may it have?

2. What does Iago's description (II.i.145-157) of a good woman tell us about his attitude toward goodness?

3. In Iago's last speech in this act he gives several reasons why he hates Othello. List them, and add to the list any reasons he gave earlier. How convincing are they?

4. Again (II.i.271ff.) Shakespeare gives Iago verse, when alone, after prose dialogue. Why?

5. In II.iii.13-24, what sort of thing is Iago trying to get Cassio to say?

6. How does II.iii.189-202 prepare us for Othello's later tragic deed of killing Desdemona?

Act III

1. What is the point of the repetition (III.iii.97-129) of "thought," "think," "know," and "honest"?

2. Is it surprising that Othello speaks (III.iii.180) of a goat? In later scenes keep an eye out for his use of animal imagery.

3. Does one indeed smell "a will most rank" (III.iii.228-33) in Desdemona's choice? Or had her choice been based on other qualities?

4. Emilia gets possession of the handkerchief by accident (III.iii.286-90). Is it fair, then, to say that the tragic outcome is based on mere accident?

5. In III.iv.65-69 Othello is, of course, talking about a handkerchief, but he is also asking for the restoration of love. What words apply especially to love?

Act IV

1. In IV.i.36ff. Othello uses prose. What does this shift suggest about Othello's state of mind?

2. Othello says (IV.i.192) "I will chop her into messes! Cuckold me!" Do we feel that in this scene Othello's ferocity toward Desdemona is chiefly motivated by a sense of personal injury? What does Shakespeare do here to prevent us from merely loathing Othello?

3. What is Othello's emotional state in the first nineteen lines of IV.ii?

4. In IV.ii. Othello's baseness, very evident in the previous scene, continues here. But what lines in this scene tend to work against the view that he is merely base, and give him the stature of a tragic hero?

5. Why is it that Othello "looks gentler than he did" (IV.iii.10)?

6. What qualities in Desdemona's singing prevent us from regarding her as a merely pathetic figure here?

Act V

1. What do V.i.19-20 tell us about Iago? How much "daily beauty" have we seen in Cassio's life? Do we assume Iago judges him incorrectly?

2. What does V.ii.16-17 tell us about the spirit with which Othello is about to kill Desdemona? Is he acting from a sense of wounded pride?

3. In V.ii.123-24 Desdemona dies with a lie on her lips. Do we think the worse of her? Why?

4. Emilia calls Othello "gull," "dolt," "ignorant as dirt" (V.ii.160-61). Has she a point? Do these words prevent Othello from being a tragic hero?

5. T. S. Eliot, in "Shakespeare and the Stoicism of Seneca," *Selected Essays*, says of V.ii.334-52: "Othello . . . is *cheering himself up*. He is endeavoring to escape reality, he has ceased to think about

Desdemona, and is thinking about himself." Evaluate this view. To what does Othello in effect compare himself in the last line of this speech?

6. In Christian thought suicide is a sin. Do we judge it sinful here?

General Questions

1. W. H. Auden, in *The Dyer's Hand*, says that "in most tragedies the fall of the hero from glory to misery and death is the work, either of the gods, or of his own freely chosen acts, or, more commonly, a mixture of both. But the fall of Othello is the work of another human being; nothing he says or does originates with himself. In consequence we feel pity for him but no respect; our esthetic respect is reserved for Iago." Evaluate.

2. Harley Granville-Barker, in *Prefaces to Shakespeare*, says: "The mere sight of such beauty and nobility and happiness, all wickedly destroyed, must be a harrowing one. Yet the pity and terror of it come short of serving for the purgation of our souls, since Othello's own soul stays unpurged. . . . It is a tragedy without meaning, and that is the ultimate horror of it." Evaluate.

The Glass Menagerie

Nobody, not even the rain, has such small hands.

E. E. CUMMINGS

CHARACTERS

Amanda Wingfield, the mother
Laura Wingfield, her daughter
Tom Wingfield, her son
Jim O'Connor, the gentleman caller

SCENE. *An alley in St. Louis.*

PART I. *Preparation for a Gentleman Caller.*
PART II. *The Gentleman Calls.*

TIME. *Now and the Past.*

SCENE I

The Wingfield apartment is in the rear of the building, one of those vast hive-like conglomerations of cellular living-units that flower as warty growths in overcrowded urban centers of lower middle-class population and are symptomatic of the impulse of this largest and fundamentally enslaved section of American society to avoid fluidity and differentiation and to exist and function as one interfused mass of automatism.

The apartment faces an alley and is entered by a fire-escape, a structure whose name is a touch of accidental poetic truth, for all of these huge buildings are always burning with the slow and implacable fires of human desperation. The fire-escape is included in the set—that is, the landing of it and steps descending from it.

The scene is memory and is therefore nonrealistic. Memory takes a lot of poetic license. It omits some details; others are exaggerated, according to the emotional value of the articles it touches, for memory is seated predominantly in the heart. The interior is therefore rather dim and poetic.

At the rise of the curtain, the audience is faced with the dark, grim rear wall of the Wingfield tenement. This building, which runs parallel to the footlights, is flanked on both sides by dark, narrow alleys which run into murky canyons of tangled clothes-lines, garbage cans and the sinister latticework of neighboring fire-escapes. It is up and down these side alleys that exterior entrances and exits are made, during the play. At the end of Tom's opening commentary, the dark tenement wall slowly re-

veals (*by means of a transparency*) the interior of the ground floor Wingfield apartment.

Downstage is the living room, which also serves as a sleeping room for Laura, the sofa unfolding to make her bed. Upstage, center, and divided by a wide arch or second proscenium with transparent faded portieres (or second curtain), is the dining room. In an old-fashioned what-not in the living room are seen scores of transparent glass animals. A blown-up photograph of the father hangs on the wall of the living room, facing the audience, to the left of the archway. It is the face of a very handsome young man in a doughboy's First World War cap. He is gallantly smiling, ineluctably smiling, as if to say, "I will be smiling forever."

The audience hears and sees the opening scene in the dining room through both the transparent fourth wall of the building and the transparent gauze portieres of the dining-room arch. It is during this revealing scene that the fourth wall slowly ascends, out of sight. This transparent exterior wall is not brought down again until the very end of the play, during Tom's final speech.

The narrator is an undisguised convention of the play. He takes whatever license with dramatic convention as is convenient to his purposes.

Tom enters dressed as a merchant sailor from alley, stage left, and strolls across the front of the stage to the fire-escape. There he stops and lights a cigarette. He addresses the audience.

Tom. Yes, I have tricks in my pocket, I have things up my sleeve. But I am the opposite of a stage magician. He gives you illusion that has the appearance of truth. I give you truth in the pleasant disguise of illusion. To begin with, I turn back time. I reverse it to that quaint period, the thirties, when the huge middle class of America was matriculating in a school for the blind. Their eyes had failed them, or they had failed their eyes, and so they were having their fingers pressed forcibly down on the fiery Braille alphabet of a dissolving economy. In Spain there was revolution. Here there was only shouting and confusion. In Spain there was Guernica. Here there were disturbances of labor, sometimes pretty violent, in otherwise peaceful cities such as Chicago, Cleveland, Saint Louis. . . . This is the social background of the play.

(MUSIC.)

The play is memory. Being a memory play, it is dimly lighted, it is sentimental, it is not realistic. In memory everything seems to happen to music. That explains the fiddle in the wings. I am the narrator of the play, and also a character in it. The other characters are my mother, Amanda, my sister, Laura, and a gentleman caller who appears in the final scenes. He is the most realistic character in the play, being an emmissary from a world of reality that we were somehow set apart from. But since I have a poet's weakness for symbols, I am using this character also as a symbol; he is the long delayed but always expected something that we live for. There is a fifth character in the play who doesn't appear except in this larger-than-life photograph over the mantel. This is our father who left us a long time ago. He was a telephone man who fell in love with long distances; he gave up his job with the telephone company and skipped the light fantastic out of town . . . The last we heard of him was a picture post-card from Mazatlan, on the Pacific coast of Mexico, containing a message of two words—" Hello—Goodbye!" and an address. I think the rest of the play will explain itself. . . .

Amanda's voice becomes audible through the portieres.

(LEGEND ON SCREEN: "OÙ SONT LES NEIGES.")

He divides the portieres and enters the upstage area.

Amanda and Laura are seated at a drop-leaf table. Eating is indicated by gestures without food or utensils. Amanda faces the audience. Tom and Laura are seated in profile.

The interior has lit up softly and through the scrim we see Amanda and Laura seated at the table in the upstage area.

Amanda (*calling*). Tom?
Tom. Yes, Mother.
Amanda. We can't say grace until you come to the table!
Tom. Coming, Mother. (*He bows slightly and withdraws, reappearing a few moments later in his place at the table.*)
Amanda (*to her son*). Honey, don't *push* with your *fingers*. If you have to push with something, the thing to push with is a crust of bread. And chew—chew! Animals have sections in their stomachs which enable them to digest food without mastication, but human beings are supposed to chew their food before they swallow it down. Eat food leisurely, son, and really enjoy it. A well-cooked meal has lots of delicate flavors that have to be held in the mouth for appreciation. So chew your food and give your salivary glands a chance to function!

Tom deliberately lays his imaginary fork down and pushes his chair back from the table.

Tom. I haven't enjoyed one bite of this dinner because of your constant directions on how to eat it. It's you that makes me rush through meals with your hawk-like attention to every bite I take. Sickening—spoils my appetite—all this discussion of animals' secretion—salivary glands—mastication!

Amanda (*lightly*). Temperament like a Metropolitan star! (*He rises and crosses downstage.*) You're not excused from the table.

Tom. I'm getting a cigarette.

Amanda. You smoke too much.

Laura rises.

Laura. I'll bring in the blanc mange.

He remains standing with his cigarette by the portieres during the following.

Amanda (*rising*). No, sister, no, sister—you be the lady this time and I'll be the darky.

Laura. I'm already up.

Amanda. Resume your seat, little sister—I want you to stay fresh and pretty—for gentlemen callers!

Laura. I'm not expecting any gentlemen callers.

Amanda (*crossing out to kitchenette. Airily*). Sometimes they come when they are least expected! Why, I remember one Sunday afternoon in Blue Mountain—(*Enters kitchenette.*)

Tom. I know what's coming!

Laura. Yes. But let her tell it.

Tom. Again?

Laura. She loves to tell it.

Amanda returns with bowl of dessert.

Amanda. One Sunday afternoon in Blue Mountain—your mother received—*seventeen!*—gentlemen callers! Why, sometimes there weren't chairs enough to accommodate them all. We had to send the nigger over to bring in folding chairs from the parish house.

Tom (*remaining at portieres*). How did you entertain those gentlemen callers?

Amanda. I understood the art of conversation!

Tom. I bet you could talk.

Amanda. Girls in those days *knew* how to talk, I can tell you.

Tom. Yes?

(IMAGE: AMANDA AS A GIRL ON A PORCH GREETING CALLERS.)

Amanda. They knew how to entertain their gentlemen callers. It wasn't enough for a girl to be possessed of a pretty face and a graceful figure—although I wasn't slighted in either respect. She also needed to have a nimble wit and a tongue to meet all occasions.

Tom. What did you talk about?

Amanda. Things of importance going on in the world! Never anything coarse or common or vulgar. (*She addresses Tom as though he were seated in the vacant chair at the table though he remains by portieres. He plays this scene as though he held the book.*) My callers were gentlemen—all! Among my callers were some of the most prominent young planters of the Mississippi Delta—planters and sons of planters!

Tom motions for music and a spot of light on Amanda.

Her eyes lift, her face glows, her voice becomes rich and elegiac.

(SCREEN LEGEND: "OU SONT LES NEIGES.")

There was young Champ Laughlin who later became vice-president of the Delta Planters Bank. Hadley Stevenson who was drowned in Moon Lake and left his widow one hundred and fifty thousand in Government bonds. There were the Cutrere brothers, Wesley and Bates. Bates was one of my bright particular beaux! He got in a quarrel with that wild Wainright boy. They shot it out on the floor of Moon Lake Casino. Bates was shot through the stomach. Died in the ambulance on his way to Memphis. His widow was also well-provided for, came into eight or ten thousand acres, that's all. She married him on the rebound—never loved her—carried my picture on him the night he died! And there was that boy that every girl in the Delta had set her cap for! That beautiful, brilliant young Fitzhugh boy from Green County!

Tom. What did he leave his widow?

Amanda. He never married! Gracious, you talk as though all of my old admirers had turned up their toes to the daisies!

Tom. Isn't this the first you mentioned that still survives?

Amanda. That Fitzhugh boy went North and made a fortune—came to be known as the Wolf of Wall Street! He had the Midas touch, whatever he touched turned to gold! And I could have been Mrs. Duncan J. Fitzhugh, mind you! But—I picked your *father!*

Laura (rising). Mother, let me clear the table.

Amanda. No, dear, you go in front and study your typewriter chart. Or practice your shorthand a little. Stay fresh and pretty!—It's almost time for our gentlemen callers to start arriving. (*She flounces girlishly toward the kitchenette.*) How many do you suppose we're going to entertain this afternoon?

Tom throws down the paper and jumps up with a groan.

Laura (alone in the dining room). I don't believe we're going to receive any, Mother.

Amanda (reappearing, airily). What? No one—not one? You must be joking! (*Laura nervously echoes her laugh. She slips in a fugitive manner through the half-open portieres and draws them gently behind her. A shaft of very clear light is thrown on her face against the faded tapestry of the curtains.* MUSIC: "THE GLASS MENAGERIE" UNDER FAINTLY. *Lightly.*) Not one gentleman caller? It can't be true! There must be a flood, there must have been a tornado!

Laura. It isn't a flood, it's not a tornado, Mother. I'm just not popular like you were in Blue Mountain.... (*Tom utters another groan. Laura glances at him with a faint, apologetic smile. Her voice catching a little.*) Mother's afraid I'm going to be an old maid.

(THE SCENE DIMS OUT WITH "GLASS MENAGERIE" MUSIC.)

SCENE II

"Laura, Haven't You Ever Liked Some Boy?"

On the dark stage the screen is lighted with the image of blue roses.

Gradually Laura's figure becomes apparent and the screen goes out.

The music subsides.

Laura is seated in the delicate ivory chair at the small claw-foot table.

She wears a dress of soft violet material for a kimono—her hair tied back from her forehead with a ribbon.

She is washing and polishing her collection of glass.

Amanda appears on the fire-escape steps. At the sound of her ascent, Laura catches her breath, thrusts the bowl of ornaments away and seats herself stiffly before the diagram of the typewriter keyboard as though it held her spellbound. Something has happened to Amanda. It is written in her face as she climbs to the landing: a look that is grim and hopeless and a little absurd.

She has on one of those cheap or imitation velvety-looking cloth coats with imitation fur collar. Her hat is five or six years old, one of those dreadful cloche hats that were worn in the late twenties and she is clasping an enormous black patent-leather pocket-book with nickel clasp and initials. This is her full-dress outfit, the one she usually wears to the D.A.R.

Before entering she looks through the door.

She purses her lips, opens her eyes wide, rolls them upward and shakes her head.

Then she slowly lets herself in the door. Seeing her mother's expression Laura touches her lips with a nervous gesture.

Laura. Hello, Mother, I was—(*She makes a nervous gesture toward the chart on the wall. Amanda leans against the shut door and stares at Laura with a martyred look.*)

Amanda. Deception? Deception? (*She slowly removes her hat and gloves, continuing the swift suffering stare. She lets the hat and gloves fall on the floor—a bit of acting.*)

Laura (*shakily*). How was the D.A.R. meeting? (*Amanda slowly opens her purse and removes a dainty white handkerchief which she shakes out delicately and delicately touches to her lips and nostrils.*) Didn't you go to the D.A.R. meeting, Mother?

Amanda (*faintly, almost inaudibly*). —No.—No. (*Then more forcibly.*) I did not have the strength—to go to the D.A.R. In fact, I did not have the courage! I wanted to find a hole in the ground and hide myself in it forever! (*She crosses slowly to the wall and removes the diagram of the typewriter keyboard. She holds it in front of her for a second, staring at it sweetly and sorrowfully —then bites her lips and tears it in two pieces.*)

Laura (*faintly*). Why did you do that, Mother? (*Amanda repeats the same procedure with the chart of the Gregg Alphabet.*) Why are you—

Amanda. Why? Why? How old are you, Laura?

Laura. Mother, you know my age.

Amanda. I thought that you were an adult; it seems that I was mistaken. (*She crosses slowly to the sofa and sinks down and stares at Laura.*)

Laura. Please don't stare at me, Mother.

Amanda closes her eyes and lowers her head. Count ten.

Amanda. What are we going to do, what is going to become of us, what is the future?

Count ten.

Laura. Has something happened, Mother? (*Amanda draws a long breath and takes out the handkerchief again. Dabbing process.*) Mother, has—something happened?

Amanda. I'll be all right in a minute. I'm just bewildered—(*Count five.*)—by life. . . .

Laura. Mother, I wish that you would tell me what's happened.

Amanda. As you know, I was supposed to be inducted into my office at the D.A.R. this afternoon. (IMAGE: A SWARM OF TYPEWRITERS.) But I stopped off at Rubicam's Business College to speak to your teachers about your having a cold and ask them what progress they thought you were making down there.

Laura. Oh. . . .

Amanda. I went to the typing instructor and introduced myself as your mother. She didn't know who you were. Wingfield, she said. We don't have any such student enrolled at the school! I assured her she did, that you had been going to classes since early in January. "I wonder," she said, "if you could be talking about that terribly shy little girl who dropped out of school after only a few days' attendance?" "No," I said, "Laura, my daughter, has been going to school every day for the past six weeks!" "Excuse me," she said. She took the attendance book out and there was your name, unmistakably printed, and all the dates you were absent until they decided that you had dropped out of school. I still said, "No, there must have been some mistake! There must have been some mix-up in the records!" And she said, "No—I remember her perfectly now. Her hand shook so that she couldn't hit the right keys! The first time we gave a speed-test, she broke down completely—was sick at the stomach and almost had to be carried into the wash-room! After that morning she never showed up any more. We phoned the house but never got any answer—while I was working at Famous and Barr, I suppose, demonstrating those—Oh!" I felt so weak I could barely keep on my feet! I had to sit down while they got me a glass of water! Fifty dollars' tuition, all of our plans—my hopes and ambitions for you—just gone up the spout, just gone up the spout like that. (*Laura draws a long breath and gets awkwardly to her feet. She crosses to the victrola and winds it up.*) What are you doing?

Laura. Oh! (*She releases the handle and returns to her seat.*)

Amanda. Laura, where have you been going when you've gone out pretending that you were going to business college?

Laura. I've just been going out walking.

Amanda. That's not true.

Laura. It is. I just went walking.

Amanda. Walking? Walking? In winter? Deliberately courting pneumonia in that light coat? Where did you walk to, Laura?

Laura. All sorts of places—mostly in the park.

Amanda. Even after you'd started catching that cold?

Laura. It was the lesser of two evils, Mother. (IMAGE: WINTER SCENE IN PARK.) I couldn't go back up. I—threw up—on the floor!

Amanda. From half past seven till after five every day you mean to tell me you walked around in the park, because you wanted to make me think that you were still going to Rubicam's Business College?

Laura. It wasn't as bad as it sounds. I went inside places to get warmed up.

Amanda. Inside where?

Laura. I went in the art museum and the bird-houses at the Zoo. I visited the penguins every day! Sometimes I did without lunch and went to the movies. Lately I've been spending most of my afternoons in the Jewel-box, that big glass house where they raise the tropical flowers.

Amanda. You did all this to deceive me, just for the deception? (*Laura looks down.*) Why?

Laura. Mother, when you're disappointed, you get that awful suffering look on your face, like the picture of Jesus' mother in the museum!

Amanda. Hush!

The Glass Menagerie 701

Laura. I couldn't face it.

Pause. A whisper of strings.

(LEGEND: "THE CRUST OF HUMILITY.")

Amanda (*hopelessly fingering the huge pocketbook*). So what are we going to do the rest of our lives? Stay home and watch the parades go by? Amuse ourselves with the glass menagerie, darling? Eternally play those worn-out phonograph records your father left as a painful reminder of him? We won't have a business career—we've given that up because it gave us nervous indigestion! (*Laughs wearily.*) What is there left but dependency all our lives? I know so well what becomes of unmarried women who aren't prepared to occupy a position. I've seen such pitiful cases in the South—barely tolerated spinsters living upon the grudging patronage of sister's husband or brother's wife!—stuck away in some little mouse-trap of a room—encouraged by one in-law to visit another—little birdlike women without any nest— eating the crust of humility all their life! Is that the future that we've mapped out for ourselves? I swear it's the only alternative I can think of! It isn't a very pleasant alternative, is it? Of course —some girls *do* marry. (*Laura twists her hands nervously.*) Haven't you ever liked some boy?

Laura. Yes. I liked one once. (*Rises.*) I came across his picture a while ago.

Amanda (*with some interest*). He gave you his picture?

Laura. No, it's in the year-book.

Amanda (*disappointed*). Oh—a high-school boy.

(SCREEN IMAGE: JIM AS A HIGH-SCHOOL HERO BEARING A SILVER CUP.)

Laura. Yes. His name was Jim. (*Laura lifts the heavy annual from the claw-foot table.*) Here he is in *The Pirates of Penzance*.

Amanda (*absently*). The what?

Laura. The operetta the senior class put on. He had a wonderful voice and we sat across the aisle from each other Mondays, Wednesdays and Fridays in the Aud. Here he is with the silver cup for debating! See his grin?

Amanda (*absently*). He must have had a jolly disposition.

Laura. He used to call me—Blue Roses.

(IMAGE: BLUE ROSES.)

Amanda. Why did he call you such a name as that?

Laura. When I had that attack of pleurosis—he asked me what was the matter when I came back. I said pleurosis—he thought that I said Blue Roses! So that's what he always called me after that. Whenever he saw me, he'd holler, "Hello, Blue Roses!" I didn't care for the girl that he went out with. Emily Meisenbach. Emily was the best-dressed girl at Soldan. She never struck me, though, as being sincere . . . It says in the Personal Section—they're engaged. That's—six years ago! They must be married by now.

Amanda. Girls that aren't cut out for business careers usually wind up married to some nice man. (*Gets up with a spark of revival.*) Sister, that's what you'll do!

Laura utters a startled, doubtful laugh. She reaches quickly for a piece of glass.

Laura. But, Mother—
Amanda. Yes? (*Crossing to photograph.*)
Laura (*in a tone of frightened apology*). I'm—crippled!

(IMAGE: SCREEN.)

Amanda. Nonsense! Laura, I've told you never, never to use that word. Why, you're not crippled, you just have a little defect—hardly noticeable, even! When people have some slight disadvantage like that, they cultivate other things to make up for it—develop charm—and vivacity—and—*charm!* That's all you have to do! (*She turns again to the photograph.*) One thing your father had *plenty* of—was *charm!*

Tom motions to the fiddle in the wings.

(THE SCENE FADES OUT WITH MUSIC.)

SCENE III

(LEGEND ON SCREEN: "AFTER THE FIASCO—")

Tom speaks from the fire-escape landing.

Tom. After the fiasco at Rubicam's Business College, the idea of getting a gentleman caller for Laura began to play a more important part in Mother's calculations. It became an obsession. Like some archetype of the universal unconscious, the image of the gentleman caller haunted our small apartment. . . . (IMAGE: YOUNG MAN AT DOOR WITH FLOWERS.) An evening at home rarely passed without some allusion to this image, this spectre, this hope. . . . Even when he wasn't mentioned, his presence hung in Mother's preoccupied look and in my sister's frightened, apologetic manner—hung like a sentence passed upon the Wingfields! Mother was a woman of action as well as words. She began to take logical steps in the planned direction. Late that winter and in the early spring —realizing that extra money would be needed to properly feather the nest and plume the bird—she conducted a vigorous campaign on the telephone, roping in subscribers to one of those magazine for matrons called *The Home-maker's Companion*, the type o journal that features the serialized sublimations of ladies of letter who think in terms of delicate cup-like breasts, slim, tapering waists, rich, creamy thighs, eyes like wood-smoke in autumn, fin gers that soothe and caress like strains of music, bodies as power ful as Etruscan sculpture.

(SCREEN IMAGE: GLAMOR MAGAZINE COVER.)

Amanda enters with phone on long extension cord. She is spotted in the dim stage.

Amanda. Ida Scott? This is Amanda Wingfield! We *missed* you a the D.A.R. last Monday! I said to myself: She's probably suffer ing with that sinus condition! How is that sinus condition? Hor rors! Heaven have mercy!—You're a Christian martyr, yes, that's what you are, a Christian martyr! Well, I just now happened to notice that your subscription to the *Companion's* about to expire Yes, it expires with the next issue, honey!—just when that won derful new serial by Bessie Mae Hopper is getting off to such an exciting start. Oh, honey, it's something that you can't miss! You remember how *Gone With the Wind* took everybody by storm? You simply couldn't go out if you hadn't read it. All everybody *talked* was Scarlett O'Hara. Well, this is a book that critics al ready compare to *Gone With the Wind*. It's the *Gone With the Wind* of the post-World War generation!—What?—Burning?— Oh, honey, don't let them burn, go take a look in the oven and I'll hold the wire! Heavens—I think she's hung up!

(DIM OUT.)

(LEGEND ON SCREEN: "YOU THINK I'M IN LOVE WITH CONTINENTAL SHOEMAKERS?")

Before the stage is lighted, the violent voices of Tom and Amanda are heard.

They are quarreling behind the portieres. In front of them stands Laura with clenched hands and panicky expression.

A clear pool of light on her figure throughout this scene.

Tom. What in Christ's name am I—
Amanda (*shrilly*). Don't you use that—
Tom. Supposed to do!
Amanda. Expression! Not in my—
Tom. Ohhh!
Amanda. Presence! Have you gone out of your senses?
Tom. I have, that's true, *driven* out!

Amanda. What is the matter with you, you—big—big—IDIOT!

Tom. Look—I've got *no thing*, no single thing—

Amanda. Lower your voice!

Tom. In my life here that I can call my OWN! Everything is—

Amanda. Stop that shouting!

Tom. Yesterday you confiscated my books! You had the nerve to—

Amanda. I took that horrible novel back to the library—yes! That hideous book by that insane Mr. Lawrence. (*Tom laughs wildly.*) I cannot control the output of diseased minds or people who cater to them—(*Tom laughs still more wildly.*) BUT I WON'T ALLOW SUCH FILTH BROUGHT INTO MY HOUSE! No, no, no, no, no!

Tom. House, house! Who pays rent on it, who makes a slave of himself to—

Amanda (*fairly screeching*). Don't you DARE to—

Tom. No, no, I mustn't say things! *I've* got to just—

Amanda. Let me tell you—

Tom. I don't want to hear any more! (*He tears the portieres open. The upstage area is lit with a turgid smoky red glow.*)

Amanda's hair is in metal curlers and she wears a very old bathrobe, much too large for her slight figure, a relic of the faithless Mr. Wingfield.

An upright typewriter and a wild disarray of manuscripts is on the drop-leaf table. The quarrel was probably precipitated by Amanda's interruption of his creative labor. A chair lying overthrown on the floor.

Their gesticulating shadows are cast on the ceiling by the fiery glow.

Amanda. You *will* hear more, you—

Tom. No, I won't hear more, I'm going out!

Amanda. You come right back in—

Tom. Out, out out! Because I'm—

Amanda. Come back here, Tom Wingfield! I'm not through talking to you!

Tom. Oh, go—

Laura (*desperately*). —Tom!

Amanda. You're going to listen, and no more insolence from you! I'm at the end of my patience! (*He comes back toward her.*)

Tom. What do you think I'm at? Aren't I supposed to have any patience to reach the end of, Mother? I know, I know. It seems unimportant to you, what I'm *doing*—what I *want* to do—having a little *difference* between them! You don't think that—

Amanda. I think you've been doing things that you're ashamed of. That's why you act like this. I don't believe that you go every night to the movies. Nobody goes to the movies night after night.

Nobody in their right minds goes to the movies as often as you
pretend to. People don't go to the movies at nearly midnight
and movies don't let out at two A.M. Come in stumbling. Mutter
ing to yourself like a maniac! You get three hours sleep and then
go to work. Oh, I can picture the way you're doing down there
Moping, doping, because you're in no condition.

Tom (wildly). No, I'm in no condition!

Amanda. What right have you got to jeopardize your job? Jeopardize
the security of us all? How do you think we'd manage if you were—

Tom. Listen! You think I'm crazy *about* the *warehouse*? (*He bends
fiercely toward her slight figure.*) You think I'm in love with the
Continental Shoemakers? You think I want to spend fifty-five
years down there in that—*celotex interior!* with—*fluorescent—
tubes!* Look! I'd rather somebody picked up a crowbar and battered out my brains—than go back mornings! I *go!* Every time
you come in yelling that God damn *"Rise and Shine!" "Rise and
Shine!"* I say to myself "How *lucky dead* people are!" But I get
up. I *go!* For sixty-five dollars a month I give up all that I dream
of doing and being *ever!* And you say self—*self's* all I ever think
of. Why, listen, if self is what I thought of, Mother, I'd be where
he is—GONE! (*Pointing to father's picture.*) As far as the system
of transportation reaches! (*He starts past her. She grabs his arm.*)
Don't grab at me, Mother!

Amanda. Where are you going?

Tom. I'm going to the *movies!*

Amanda. I don't believe that lie!

*Tom (crouching toward her, overtowering her tiny figure. She backs
away, gasping).* I'm going to opium dens! Yes, opium dens, dens
of vice and criminals' hang-outs, Mother. I've joined the Hogan
gang, I'm a hired assassin, I carry a tommy-gun in a violin case! I
run a string of cat-houses in the Valley! They call me Killer, Killer
Wingfield, I'm leading a double-life, a simple, honest warehouse
worker by day, by night, a dynamic *czar* of the *underworld, Mother.*
I go to gambling casinos, I spin away fortunes on the roulette
table! I wear a patch over one eye and a false mustache, sometimes
I put on green whiskers. On those occasions they call me— *El
Diablo!* Oh, I could tell you things to make you sleepless! My
enemies plan to dynamite this place. They're going to blow us all
sky-high some night! I'll be glad, very happy, and so will you!
You'll go up, up on a broomstick, over Blue Mountain with
seventeen gentlemen callers! You ugly—babbling old—*witch.* . . .
(*He goes through a series of violent, clumsy movements, seizing
his overcoat, lunging to the door, pulling it fiercely open. The
women watch him, aghast. His arm catches in the sleeve of the
coat as he struggles to pull it on. For a moment he is pinioned
by the bulky garment. With an outraged groan he tears the coat
off again, splitting the shoulders of it, and hurls it across the*

room. *It strikes against the shelf of Laura's glass collection, there is a tinkle of shattering glass. Laura cries out as if wounded.*

(MUSIC LEGEND: "THE GLASS MENAGERIE.")

Laura (*shrilly*). *My glass!*—menagerie. . . . (*She covers her face and turns away.*)

But Amanda is still stunned and stupefied by the "ugly witch" so that she barely notices this occurrence. Now she recovers her speech.

Amanda (*in an awful voice*). I won't speak to you—until you apologize! (*She crosses through portieres and draws them together behind her. Tom is left with Laura. Laura clings weakly to the mantel with her face averted. Tom stares at her stupidly for a moment. Then he crosses to shelf. Drops awkwardly to his knees to collect the fallen glass, glancing at Laura as if he would speak but couldn't.*

"The Glass Menagerie" steals in as

(THE SCENE DIMS OUT.)

SCENE IV

The interior is dark. Faint light in the alley.

A deep-voiced bell in a church is tolling the hour of five as the scene commences.

Tom appears at the top of the alley. After each solemn boom of the bell in the tower, he shakes a little noise-maker or rattle as if to express the tiny spasm of man in contrast to the sustained power and dignity of the Almighty. This and the unsteadiness of his advance make it evident that he has been drinking.

As he climbs the few steps to the fire-escape landing light steals up inside. Laura appears in night-dress, observing Tom's empty bed in the front room.

Tom fishes in his pockets for the door-key, removing a motley assortment of articles in the search, including a perfect shower of movie-ticket stubs and an empty bottle. At last he finds the key, but just as he is about to insert it, it slips from his fingers. He strikes a match and crouches below the door.

Tom (*bitterly*). One crack—and it falls through!

Laura opens the door.

Laura. Tom! Tom, what are you doing?

Tom. Looking for a door-key.

Laura. Where have you been all this time?

Tom. I have been to the movies.

Laura. All this time at the movies?

Tom. There was a very long program. There was a Garbo picture and a Mickey Mouse and a travelogue and a newsreel and a preview of coming attractions. And there was an organ solo and a collection for the milk-fund—simultaneously—which ended up in a terrible fight between a fat lady and an usher!

Laura (innocently). Did you have to stay through everything?

Tom. Of course! And, oh, I forgot! There was a big stage show! The headliner on this stage show was Malvolio the Magician. He performed wonderful tricks, many of them, such as pouring water back and forth between pitchers. First it turned to wine and then it turned to beer and then it turned to whiskey. I know it was whiskey it finally turned into because he needed somebody to come up out of the audience to help him, and I came up—both shows! It was Kentucky Straight Bourbon. A very generous fellow, he gave souvenirs. (*He pulls from his back pocket a shimmering rainbow-colored scarf.*) He gave me this. This is his magic scarf. You can have it, Laura. You wave it over a canary cage and you get a bowl of gold-fish. You wave it over the gold-fish bowl and they fly away canaries. . . . But the wonderfullest trick of all was the coffin trick. We nailed him into a coffin and he got out of the coffin without removing one nail. (*He has come inside.*) There is a trick that would come in handy for me—get me out of this 2 by 4 situation! (*Flops onto bed and starts removing shoes.*)

Laura. Tom—Shhh!

Tom. What you shushing me for?

Laura. You'll wake up Mother.

Tom. Goody, goody! Pay 'er back for all those "Rise an' Shines." (*Lies down, groaning.*) You know it don't take much intelligence to get yourself into a nailed-up coffin, Laura. But who in hell ever got himself out of one without removing one nail?

As if in answer, the father's grinning photograph lights up.

(SCENE DIMS OUT.)

Immediately following: The church bell is heard striking six. At the sixth stroke the alarm clock goes off in Amanda's room, and after a few moments we hear her calling: "Rise and Shine! Rise and Shine! Laura, go tell your brother to rise and shine!"

Tom (Sitting up slowly). I'll rise—but I won't shine.

The light increases.

Amanda. Laura, tell your brother his coffee is ready.

Laura slips into front room.

Laura. Tom! it's nearly seven. Don't make Mother nervous. (*He stares at her stupidly. Beseechingly.*) Tom, speak to Mother this morning. Make up with her, apologize, speak to her!

Tom. She won't to me. It's her that started not speaking.

Laura. If you just say you're sorry she'll start speaking.

Tom. Her not speaking—is that such a tragedy?

Laura. Please—please!

Amanda (*calling from kitchenette*). Laura, are you going to do what I asked you to do, or do I have to get dressed and go out myself?

Laura. Going, going—soon as I get on my coat! (*She pulls on a shapeless felt hat with nervous, jerky movement, pleadingly glancing at Tom. Rushes awkwardly for coat. The coat is one of Amanda's, inaccurately made-over, the sleeves too short for Laura.*) Butter and what else?

Amanda (*entering upstage*). Just butter. Tell them to charge it.

Laura. Mother, they make such faces when I do that.

Amanda. Sticks and stones may break my bones, but the expression on Mr. Garfinkel's face won't harm us! Tell your brother his coffee is getting cold.

Laura (*at door*). Do what I asked you, will you, will you, Tom?

He looks sullenly away.

Amanda. Laura, go now or just don't go at all!

Laura (*rushing out*). Going—going! (*A second later she cries out. Tom springs up and crosses to the door. Amanda rushes anxiously in. Tom opens the door.*)

Tom. Laura?

Laura. I'm all right. I slipped, but I'm all right.

Amanda (*peering anxiously after her*). If anyone breaks a leg on those fire-escape steps, the landlord ought to be sued for every cent he possesses! (*She shuts door. Remembers she isn't speaking and returns to other room.*)

As Tom enters listlessly for his coffee, she turns her back to him and stands rigidly facing the window on the gloomy gray vault of the areaway. Its light on her face with its aged but childish features is cruelly sharp, satirical as a Daumier print.

(MUSIC UNDER: "AVE MARIA.")

Tom glances sheepishly but sullenly at her averted figure and slumps at the table. The coffee is scalding hot; he sips it and gasps and spits it back in the cup. At his gasp, Amanda catches her breath and half turns. Then catches herself and turns back to window.

Tom blows on his coffee, glancing sidewise at his mother. She clears her throat. Tom clears his. He starts to rise. Sinks back down again, scratches his head, clears his throat again. Amanda coughs. Tom raises his cup in both hands to blow on it, his eyes staring over the rim of it at his mother for several moments. Then he slowly sets the cup down and awkwardly and hesitantly rises from the chair.

Tom (*hoarsely*). Mother. I—I apologize. Mother. (*Amanda draws a quick, shuddering breath. Her face works grotesquely. She breaks into childlike tears.*) I'm sorry for what I said, for everything that I said, I didn't mean it.

Amanda (*sobbingly*). My devotion has made me a witch and so I make myself hateful to my children!

Tom. No, you *don't*.

Amanda. I worry so much, don't sleep, it makes me nervous!

Tom (*gently*). I understand that.

Amanda. I've had to put up a solitary battle all these years. But you're my right-hand bower! Don't fall down, don't fail!

Tom (*gently*). I try, Mother.

Amanda (*with great enthusiasm*). Try and you will SUCCEED! (*The notion makes her breathless.*) Why, you—you're just *full of* natural endowments! Both of my children—they're *unusual* children! Don't you think I know it? I'm so—*proud!* Happy and— feel I've—so much to be thankful for but—Promise me one thing, son!

Tom. What, Mother?

Amanda. Promise, son, you'll—never be a drunkard!

Tom (*turns to her grinning*). I will never be a drunkard, Mother.

Amanda. That's what frightened me so, that you'd be drinking! Eat a bowl of Purina!

Tom. Just coffee, Mother.

Amanda. Shredded wheat biscuit?

Tom. No. No, Mother, just coffee.

Amanda. You can't put in a day's work on an empty stomach. You've got ten minutes—don't gulp! Drinking too-hot liquids makes cancer of the stomach. . . . Put cream in.

Tom. No, thank you.

Amanda. To cool it.

Tom. No! No, thank you, I want it black.

Amanda. I know, but it's not good for you. We have to do all that we can to build ourselves up. In these trying times we live in, all that we have to cling to is—each other. . . . That's why it's so important to—Tom, I—I sent out your sister so I could discuss something with you. If you hadn't spoken I would have spoken to you. (*Sits down.*)

Tom (*gently*). What is it, Mother, that you want to discuss?

Amanda. Laura!

> *Tom puts his cup down slowly.*

> (LEGEND ON SCREEN: "LAURA.")

> (MUSIC: "THE GLASS MENAGERIE.")

Tom. —Oh.—Laura . . .

Amanda (touching his sleeve). You know how Laura is. So quiet but —still water runs deep! She notices things and I think she— broods about them. (*Tom looks up.*) A few days ago I came in and she was crying.

Tom. What about?

Amanda. You.

Tom. Me?

Amanda. She has an idea that you're not happy here.

Tom. What gave her that idea?

Amanda. What gives her any idea? However, you do act strangely. I—I'm not criticizing, understand *that!* I know your ambitions do not lie in the warehouse, that like everybody in the whole wide world—you've had to—make sacrifices, but—Tom—Tom—life's not easy, it calls for—Spartan endurance! There's so many things in my heart that I cannot describe to you! I've never told you but I—*loved* your father. . . .

Tom (gently). I know that, Mother.

Amanda. And you—when I see you taking after his ways! Staying out late—and—well, you *had* been drinking the night you were in that—terrifying condition! Laura says that you hate the apartment and that you go out nights to get away from it! Is that true, Tom?

Tom. No. You say there's so much in your heart that you can't describe to me. That's true of me, too. There's so much in my heart that I can't describe to *you!* So let's respect each other's—

Amanda. But, why—why, Tom—are you always so *restless?* Where do you go to, nights?

Tom. I—go to the movies.

Amanda. Why do you go to the movies so much, Tom?

Tom. I go to the movies because—I like adventure. Adventure is something I don't have much of at work, so I go to the movies.

Amanda. But, Tom, you go to the movies *entirely* too *much!*

Tom. I like a lot of adventure.

> *Amanda looks baffled, then hurt. As the familiar inquisition resumes he becomes hard and impatient again. Amanda slips back into her querulous attitude toward him.*

> (IMAGE ON SCREEN: SAILING VESSEL WITH JOLLY ROGER.)

Amanda. Most young men find adventure in their careers.

Tom. Then most young men are not employed in a warehouse.

Amanda. The world is full of young men employed in warehouses and offices and factories.

Tom. Do all of them find adventure in their careers?

Amanda. They do or they do without it! Not everybody has a craze for adventure.

Tom. Man is by instinct a lover, a hunter, a fighter, and none of those instincts are given much play at the warehouse!

Amanda. Man is by instinct! Don't quote instinct to me! Instinct is something that people have got away from! It belongs to animals! Christian adults don't want it!

Tom. What do Christian adults want, then, Mother?

Amanda. Superior things! Things of the mind and the spirit! Only animals have to satisfy instincts! Surely your aims are somewhat higher than theirs! Than monkeys—pigs—

Tom. I reckon they're not.

Amanda. You're joking. However, that isn't what I wanted to discuss.

Tom (*rising*). I haven't much time.

Amanda (*pushing his shoulders*). Sit down.

Tom. You want me to punch in red at the warehouse, Mother?

Amanda. You have five minutes. I want to talk about Laura.

(LEGEND: "PLANS AND PROVISIONS.")

Tom. All right! What about Laura?

Amanda. We have to be making plans and provisions for her. She's older than you, two years, and nothing has happened. She just drifts along doing nothing. It frightens me terribly how she just drifts along.

Tom. I guess she's the type that people call home girls.

Amanda. There's no such type, and if there is, it's a pity! That is unless the home is hers, with a husband!

Tom. What?

Amanda. Oh, I can see the handwriting on the wall as plain as I see the nose in front of my face! It's terrifying! More and more you remind me of your father! He was out all hours without explanation—Then *left! Good-bye!* And me with a bag to hold. I saw that letter you got from the Merchant Marine. I know what you're dreaming of. I'm not standing here blindfolded. Very well then. Then *do* it! But not till there's somebody to take your place.

Tom. What do you mean?

Amanda. I mean that as soon as Laura has got somebody to take care of her, married, a home of her own, independent—why, then you'll be free to go wherever you please, on land, on sea, whichever way the wind blows! But until that time you've got to look out for your sister. I don't say me because I'm old and don't matter! I say for your sister because she's young and dependent. I put her in business college—a dismal failure! Frightened her so it made her sick to her stomach. I took her over to the Young People's League at the church. Another fiasco. She spoke to nobody, nobody spoke to her. Now all she does is fool with those pieces of glass and play those worn-out records. What kind of a life is that for a girl to lead?

Tom. What can I do about it?

Amanda. Overcome selfishness! Self, self, self is all that you ever think of! (*Tom springs up and crosses to get his coat. It is ugly and bulky. He pulls on a cap with earmuffs.*) Where is your muffler? Put your wool muffler on! (*He snatches it angrily from the closet and tosses it around his neck and pulls both ends tight.*) Tom! I haven't said what I had in mind to ask you.

Tom. I'm too late to—

Amanda (*catching his arm—very importunately. Then shyly*). Down at the warehouse, aren't there some—nice young men?

Tom. No!

Amanda. There *must* be—*some* . . .

Tom. Mother—

Gesture.

Amanda. Find out one that's clean-living—doesn't drink and—ask him out for sister!

Tom. What?

Amanda. For *sister!* To *meet!* Get *acquainted!*

Tom (*stamping to door*). Oh, my *go-osh!*

Amanda. Will you? (*He opens door. Imploringly.*) Will you? (*He starts down.*) Will you? *Will* you, dear?

Tom (*calling back*). YES!

Amanda closes the door hesitantly and with a troubled but faintly hopeful expression.

(SCREEN IMAGE: GLAMOR MAGAZINE COVER.)

Spot Amanda at phone.

Amanda. Ella Cartwright? This is Amanda Wingfield! How are you, honey? How is that kidney condition? (*Count five.*) Horrors! (*Count five*). You're a Christian martyr, yes, honey, that's what you are, a Christian martyr! Well, I just happened to notice in my little red book that your subscription to the *Companion* has just run out! I knew that you wouldn't want to miss out on the wonderful serial starting in this new issue. It's by Bessie Mae Hopper, the first thing she's written since *Honeymoon for Three.* Wasn't that a strange and interesting story? Well, this one is even lovelier, I believe. It has a sophisticated society background. It's all about the horsey set on Long Island!

(FADE OUT.)

SCENE V

(LEGEND ON SCREEN: "ANNUNCIATION.") *Fade with music.*

It is early dusk of a spring evening. Supper has just been finished in the Wingfield apartment. Amanda and Laura in light colored dresses are removing dishes from the table, in the upstage area which is shadowy, their movements formalized almost as a dance or ritual, their moving forms as pale and silent as moths.

Tom, in white shirt and trousers, rises from the table and crosses toward the fire-escape.

Amanda (*as he passes her*). Son, will you do me a favor?

Tom. What?

Amanda. Comb your hair! You look so pretty when your hair is combed! (*Tom slouches on sofa with evening paper. Enormous caption "Franco Triumphs."*) There is only one respect in which I would like you to emulate your father.

Tom. What respect is that?

Amanda. The care he always took of his appearance. He never allowed himself to look untidy. (*He throws down the paper and crosses to fire-escape.*) Where are you going?

Tom. I'm going out to smoke.

Amanda. You smoke too much. A pack a day at fifteen cents a pack. How much would that amount to in a month? Thirty times fifteen is how much, Tom? Figure it out and you will be astounded at what you could save. Enough to give you a night-school course in accounting at Washington U! Just think what a wonderful thing that would be for you, son!

Tom is unmoved by the thought.

Tom. I'd rather smoke. (*He steps out on landing, letting the screen door slam.*)

Amanda (*sharply*). I know! That's the tragedy of it.... (*Alone, she turns to look at her husband's picture.*)

(DANCE MUSIC: "ALL THE WORLD IS WAITING FOR THE SUNRISE!")

Tom (*to the audience*). Across the alley from us was the Paradise Dance Hall. On evenings in spring the windows and doors were open and the music came outdoors. Sometimes the lights were turned out except for a large glass sphere that hung from the ceiling. It would turn slowly about and filter the dusk with delicate rainbow colors. Then the orchestra played a waltz or a tango, something that had a slow and sensuous rhythm. Couples would come outside, to the relative privacy of the alley. You could see them kissing behind ash-pits and telephone poles. This was the compensation for lives that passed like mine, without any change or adventure. Adventure and change were imminent in this year. They were waiting around the corner for all these kids. Suspended in the mist over Berchtesgaden, caught in the folds of Chamberlain's umbrella—In Spain there was Guernica! But here there was only hot swing music and liquor, dance halls, bars, and movies, and sex that hung in the gloom like a chandelier and flooded the world with brief, deceptive rainbows. . . . All the world was waiting for bombardments!

Amanda turns from the picture and comes outside.

Amanda (sighing). A fire-escape landing's a poor excuse for a porch. (*She spreads a newspaper on a step and sits down, gracefully and demurely as if she were settling into a swing on a Mississippi veranda.*) What are you looking at?

Tom. The moon.

Amanda. Is there a moon this evening?

Tom. It's rising over Garfinkel's Delicatessen.

Amanda. So it is! A little silver slipper of a moon. Have you made a wish on it yet?

Tom. Um-hum.

Amanda. What did you wish for?

Tom. That's a secret.

Amanda. A secret, huh? Well, I won't tell mine either. I will be just as mysterious as you.

Tom. I bet I can guess what yours is.

Amanda. Is my head so transparent?

Tom. You're not a sphinx.

Amanda. No, I don't have secrets. I'll tell you what I wished for on the moon. Success and happiness for my precious children! I wish for that whenever there's a moon, and when there isn't a moon, I wish for it, too.

Tom. I thought perhaps you wished for a gentleman caller.

Amanda. Why do you say that?

Tom. Don't you remember asking me to fetch one?

Amanda. I remember suggesting that it would be nice for your sister if you brought home some nice young man from the warehouse. I think I've made that suggestion more than once.

Tom. Yes, you have made it repeatedly.

Amanda. Well?

Tom. We are going to have one.

Amanda. *What?*

Tom. A gentleman caller!

(THE ANNUNCIATION IS CELEBRATED WITH MUSIC.)

Amanda rises.

(IMAGE ON SCREEN: CALLER WITH BOUQUET.)

Amanda. You mean you have asked some nice young man to come over?

Tom. Yep. I've asked him to dinner.

Amanda. You really did?

Tom. I did!

Amanda. You did, and did he—*accept?*

Tom. He did!

Amanda. Well, well—well, well! That's—lovely!

Tom. I thought that you would be pleased.

Amanda. It's definite, then?

Tom. Very definite.

Amanda. Soon?

Tom. Very soon.

Amanda. For heaven's sake, stop putting on and tell me some things will you?

Tom. What things do you want me to tell you?

Amanda. *Naturally* I would like to know when he's *coming!*

Tom. He's coming tomorrow.

Amanda. *Tomorrow?*

Tom. Yep. Tomorrow.

Amanda. But, Tom!

Tom. Yes, Mother?

Amanda. Tomorrow gives me no time!

Tom. Time for what?

Amanda. Preparations! Why didn't you phone me at once, as soon as you asked him, the minute that he accepted? Then, don't you see, I could have been getting ready!

Tom. You don't have to make any fuss.

Amanda. Oh, Tom, Tom, Tom, of course I have to make a fuss! I want things nice, not sloppy! Not thrown together. I'll certainly have to do some fast thinking, won't I?

Tom. I don't see why you have to think at all.

Amanda. You just don't know. We can't have a gentleman caller in a pig-sty! All my wedding silver has to be polished, the mono grammed table linen ought to be laundered! The windows have to be washed and fresh curtains put up. And how about clothes? We have to *wear* something, don't we?

Tom. Mother, this boy is no one to make a fuss over!

Amanda. Do you realize he's the first young man we've introduced to your sister? It's terrible, dreadful, disgraceful that poor little sister has never received a single gentleman caller! Tom, come inside! (*She opens the screen door.*)

Tom. What for?

Amanda. I want to ask you some things.

Tom. If you're going to make such a fuss, I'll call it off, I'll tell him not to come.

Amanda. You certainly won't do anything of the kind. Nothing offends people worse than broken engagements. It simply means I'll have to work like a Turk! We won't be brilliant, but we'll pass inspection. Come on inside. (*Tom follows, groaning.*) Sit down.

Tom. Any particular place you would like me to sit?

Amanda. Thank heavens I've got that new sofa! I'm also making payments on a floor lamp I'll have sent out! And put the chintz covers on, they'll brighten things up! Of course I'd hoped to have these walls re-papered. . . . What is the young man's name?

Tom. His name is O'Connor.

Amanda. That, of course, means fish—tomorrow is Friday! I'll have that salmon loaf—with Durkee's dressing! What does he do? He works at the warehouse?

Tom. Of course! How else would I—

Amanda. Tom, he—doesn't drink?

Tom. Why do you ask me that?

Amanda. Your father *did!*

Tom. Don't get started on that!

Amanda. He *does* drink, then?

Tom. Not that I know of!

Amanda. Make sure, be certain! The last thing I want for my daughter's a boy who drinks!

Tom. Aren't you being a little premature? Mr. O'Connor has not yet appeared on the scene!

Amanda. But will tomorrow. To meet your sister, and what do I know about his character? Nothing! Old maids are better off than wives of drunkards!

Tom. Oh, my God!

Amanda. Be still!

Tom (*leaning forward to whisper*). Lots of fellows meet girls whom they don't marry!

Amanda. Oh, talk sensibly, Tom—and don't be sarcastic! (*She has gotten a hairbrush.*)

Tom. What are you doing?

Amanda. I'm brushing that cow-lick down! What is this young man's position at the warehouse?

Tom (*submitting grimly to the brush and the interrogation*). This young man's position is that of a shipping clerk, Mother.

Amanda. Sounds to me like a fairly responsible job, the sort of a job *you* would be in if you just had more *get-up.* What is his salary? Have you got any idea?

Tom. I would judge it to be approximately eighty-five dollars a month.

Amanda. Well—not princely, but—

Tom. Twenty more than I make.

Amanda. Yes, how well I know! But for a family man, eighty-five dollars a month is not much more than you can just get by on. . . .

Tom. Yes, but Mr. O'Connor is not a family man.

Amanda. He might be, mightn't he? Some time in the future?

Tom. I see. Plans and provisions.

Amanda. You are the only young man that I know of who ignores the fact that the future becomes the present, the present the past, and the past turns into everlasting regret if you don't plan for it!

Tom. I will think that over and see what I can make of it.

Amanda. Don't be supercilious with your mother! Tell me some more about this—what do you call him?

Tom. James D. O'Connor. The D. is for Delaney.

Amanda. Irish on *both* sides! *Gracious!* And doesn't drink?

Tom. Shall I call him up and ask him right this minute?

Amanda. The only way to find out about those things is to make discreet inquiries at the proper moment. When I was a girl in Blue Mountain and it was suspected that a young man drank, the girl whose attentions he had been receiving, if any girl *was*, would sometimes speak to the minister of his church, or rather her father would if her father was living, and sort of feel him out on the young man's character. That is the way such things are discreetly handled to keep a young woman from making a tragic mistake!

Tom. Then how did you happen to make a tragic mistake?

Amanda. That innocent look of your father's had everyone fooled! He *smiled*—the world was *enchanted!* No girl can do worse than put herself at the mercy of a handsome appearance! I hope that Mr. O'Connor is not too good-looking.

Tom. No, he's not too good-looking. He's covered with freckles and hasn't too much of a nose.

Amanda. He's not right-down homely, though?

Tom. Not right-down homely. Just medium homely, I'd say.

Amanda. Character's what to look for in a man.

Tom. That's what I've always said, Mother.

Amanda. You've never said anything of the kind and I suspect you would never give it a thought.

Tom. Don't be suspicious of me.

Amanda. At least I hope he's the type that's up and coming.

Tom. I think he really goes in for self-improvement.

Amanda. What reason have you to think so?

Tom. He goes to night school.

Amanda (beaming). Splendid! What does he do, I mean study?

Tom. Radio engineering and public speaking!

Amanda. Then he has visions of being advanced in the world! Any young man who studies public speaking is aiming to have an executive job some day! And radio engineering? A thing for the future! Both of these facts are very illuminating. Those are the sort of things that a mother should know concerning any young man who comes to call on her daughter. Seriously or—not.

Tom. One little warning. He doesn't know about Laura. I didn't let on that we had dark ulterior motives. I just said, why don't you come have dinner with us? He said okay and that was the whole conversation.

Amanda. I bet it was! You're eloquent as an oyster. However, he'll know about Laura when he gets here. When he sees how lovely and sweet and pretty she is, he'll thank his lucky stars he was asked to dinner.

Tom. Mother, you mustn't expect too much of Laura.

Amanda. What do you mean?

Tom. Laura seems all those things to you and me because she's ours and we love her. We don't even notice she's crippled any more.

Amanda. Don't say crippled! You know that I never allow that word to be used!

Tom. But face facts, Mother. She is and—that's not all—

Amanda. What do you mean "not all"?

Tom. Laura is very different from other girls.

Amanda. I think the difference is all to her advantage.

Tom. Not quite all—in the eyes of others—strangers—she's terribly shy and lives in a world of her own and those things make her seem a little peculiar to people outside the house.

Amanda. Don't say peculiar.

Tom. Face the facts. She is.

(THE DANCE-HALL MUSIC CHANGES TO A TANGO THAT HAS A MINOR AND SOMEWHAT OMINOUS TONE.)

Amanda. In what way is she peculiar—may I ask?

Tom (*gently*). She lives in a world of her own—a world of—little glass ornaments, Mother. . . . (*Gets up. Amanda remains holding brush, looking at him, troubled.*) She plays old phonograph records and—that's about all—(*He glances at himself in the mirror and crosses to door.*)

Amanda (*sharply*). Where are you going?

Tom. I'm going to the movies. (*Out screen door.*)

Amanda. Not to the movies, every night to the movies! (*Follows quickly to screen door.*) I don't believe you always go to the movies! (*He is gone. Amanda looks worriedly after him for a moment. Then vitality and optimism return and she turns from the door. Crossing to portieres.*) Laura! Laura! (*Laura answers from kitchenette.*)

Laura. Yes, Mother.

Amanda. Let those dishes go and come in front! (*Laura appears with dish towel. Gaily.*) Laura, come here and make a wish on the moon!

Laura (*entering*). Moon—moon?

Amanda. A little silver slipper of a moon. Look over your left shoulder, Laura, and make a wish! (*Laura looks faintly puzzled as if called out of sleep. Amanda seizes her shoulders and turns her at an angle by the door.*) No! Now, darling, *wish!*

Laura. What shall I wish for, Mother?

Amanda (*her voice trembling and her eyes suddenly filling with tears*).
Happiness! Good Fortune!

The violin rises and the stage dims out.

SCENE VI

(IMAGE: HIGH SCHOOL HERO.)

Tom. And so the following evening I brought Jim home to dinner. I had known Jim slightly in high school. In high school Jim was a hero. He had tremendous Irish good nature and vitality with the scrubbed and polished look of white chinaware. He seemed to move in a continual spotlight. He was a star in basketball, captain of the debating club, president of the senior class and the glee club and he sang the male lead in the annual light operas. He was always running or bounding, never just walking. He seemed always at the point of defeating the law of gravity. He was shooting with such velocity through his adolescence that you would logically expect him to arrive at nothing short of the White House by the time he was thirty. But Jim apparently ran into more interference after his graduation from Soldan. His speed had definitely slowed. Six years after he left high school he was holding a job that wasn't much better than mine.

(IMAGE: CLERK.)

He was the only one at the warehouse with whom I was on friendly terms. I was valuable to him as someone who could remember his former glory, who had seen him win basketball games and the silver cup in debating. He knew my secret practice of retiring to a cabinet of the washroom to work on poems when business was slack in the warehouse. He called me Shakespeare. And while the other boys in the warehouse regarded me with suspicious hostility, Jim took a humorous attitude toward me. Gradually his attitude affected the others, their hostility wore off and they also began to smile at me as people smile at an oddly fashioned dog who trots across their path at some distance.

I knew that Jim and Laura had known each other at Soldan, and I had heard Laura speak admiringly of his voice. I didn't know if Jim remembered her or not. In high school Laura had been as unobtrusive as Jim had been astonishing. If he did remember Laura, it was not as my sister, for when I asked him to dinner, he grinned and said, "You know, Shakespeare, I never thought of you as having folks!"

He was about to discover that I did. . . .

(LIGHT UP STAGE.)

(LEGEND ON SCREEN: "THE ACCENT OF A COMING FOOT.")

Friday evening. It is about five o'clock of a late spring evening which comes "scattering poems in the sky."

A delicate lemony light is in the Wingfield apartment.

Amanda has worked like a Turk in preparation for the gentleman caller. The results are astonishing. The new floor lamp with its rose-silk shade is in place, a colored paper lantern conceals the broken light fixture in the ceiling, new billowing white curtains are at the windows, chintz covers are on chairs and sofa, a pair of new sofa pillows make their initial appearance.

Open boxes and tissue paper are scattered on the floor.

Laura stands in the middle with lifted arms while Amanda crouches before her, adjusting the hem of the new dress, devout and ritualistic. The dress is colored and designed by memory. The arrangement of Laura's hair is changed; it is softer and more becoming. A fragile, unearthly prettiness has come out in Laura: she is like a piece of translucent glass touched by light, given a momentary radiance, not actual, not lasting.

Amanda (*impatiently*). Why are you trembling?
Laura. Mother, you've made me so nervous!
Amanda. How have I made you nervous?
Laura. By all this fuss! You make it seem so important!
Amanda. I don't understand you, Laura. You couldn't be satisfied with just sitting home, and yet whenever I try to arrange something for you, you seem to resist it. (*She gets up.*) Now take a look at yourself. No, wait! Wait just a moment—I have an idea!
Laura. What is it now?

Amanda produces two powder puffs which she wraps in handkerchiefs and stuffs in Laura's bosom.

Laura. Mother, what are you doing?
Amanda. They call them "Gay Deceivers"!
Laura. I won't wear them!
Amanda. You will!
Laura. Why should I?
Amanda. Because, to be painfully honest, your chest is flat.
Laura. You make it seem like we were setting a trap.
Amanda. All pretty girls are a trap, a pretty trap, and men expect them to be. (LEGEND: "A PRETTY TRAP.") Now look at yourself, young lady. This is the prettiest you will ever be! I've got to fix myself now! You're going to be surprised by your mother's appearance! (*She crosses through portieres, humming gaily.*)

The Glass Menagerie 721

Laura moves slowly to the long mirror and stares solemnly at herself.

A wind blows the white curtains inward in a slow, graceful motion and with a faint, sorrowful sighing.

Amanda (*off stage*). It isn't dark enough yet. (*She turns slowly before the mirror with a troubled look.*)

(LEGEND ON SCREEN: "THIS IS MY SISTER: CELEBRATE HER WITH STRINGS!" MUSIC.)

Amanda (*laughing, off*). I'm going to show you something. I'm going to make a spectacular appearance!
Laura. What is it, mother?
Amanda. Possess your soul in patience—you will see! Something I've resurrected from that old trunk! Styles haven't changed so terribly much after all.... (*She parts the portieres.*) Now just look at your mother! (*She wears a girlish frock of yellowed voile with a blue silk sash. She carries a bunch of jonquils—the legend of her youth is nearly revived. Feverishly.*) This is the dress in which I led the cotillion. Won the cakewalk twice at Sunset Hill, wore one spring to the Governor's ball in Jackson! See how I sashayed around the ballroom, Laura? (*She raises her skirt and does a mincing step around the room.*) I wore it on Sundays for my gentlemen callers! I had it on the day I met your father—I had malaria fever all that spring. The change of climate from East Tennessee to the Delta—weakened resistance—I had a little temperature all the time—not enough to be serious—just enough to make me restless and giddy! Invitations poured in—parties all over the Delta!—"Stay in bed," said Mother, "you have fever!"—but I just wouldn't.—I took quinine but kept on going, going!—Evenings, dances!—Afternoons, long, long rides! Picnics—lovely! —So lovely, that country in May.—All lacy with dogwood, literally flooded with jonquils!—That was the spring I had the craze for jonquils. Jonquils became an absolute obsession. Mother said, "Honey, there's no more room for jonquils." And still I kept bringing in more jonquils. Whenever, wherever I saw them, I'd say, "Stop! Stop! I see jonquils!" I made the young men help me gather the jonquils! It was a joke, Amanda and her jonquils! Finally there were no more vases to hold them, every available space was filled with jonquils. No vases to hold them? All right, I'll hold them myself! And then I—(*She stops in front of the picture. MUSIC.*) met your father! Malaria fever and jonquils and then—this—boy.... (*She switches on the rose-colored lamp.*) I hope they get here before it starts to rain. (*She crosses upstage and places the jonquils in bowl on table.*) I gave your brother

a little extra change so he and Mr. O'Connor could take the service car home.

Laura (*with altered look*). What did you say his name was?

Amanda. O'Connor.

Laura. What is his first name?

Amanda. I don't remember. Oh, yes, I do. It was—Jim!

Laura sways slightly and catches hold of a chair.

(LEGEND ON SCREEN: "NOT JIM!")

Laura (*faintly*). Not—Jim!

Amanda. Yes, that was it, it was Jim! I've never known a Jim that wasn't nice!

(MUSIC: OMINOUS.)

Laura. Are you sure his name is Jim O'Connor?

Amanda. Yes. Why?

Laura. Is he the one that Tom used to know in high school?

Amanda. He didn't say so. I think he just got to know him at the warehouse.

Laura. There was a Jim O'Connor we both knew in high school— (*Then, with effort.*) If that is the one that Tom is bringing to dinner—you'll have to excuse me, I won't come to the table.

Amanda. What sort of nonsense is this?

Laura. You asked me once if I'd ever liked a boy. Don't you remember I showed you this boy's picture?

Amanda. You mean the boy you showed me in the year book?

Laura. Yes, that boy.

Amanda. Laura, Laura, were you in love with that boy?

Laura. I don't know, Mother. All I know is I couldn't sit at the table if it was him!

Amanda. It won't be him! It isn't the least bit likely. But whether it is or not, you will come to the table. You will not be excused.

Laura. I'll have to be, Mother.

Amanda. I don't intend to humor your silliness, Laura. I've had too much from you and your brother, both! So just sit down and compose yourself till they come. Tom has forgotten his key so you'll have to let them in, when they arrive.

Laura (*panicky*). Oh, Mother—*you* answer the door!

Amanda (*lightly*). I'll be in the kitchen—busy!

Laura. Oh, Mother, please answer the door, don't make me do it!

Amanda (*crossing into kitchenette*). I've got to fix the dressing for the salmon. Fuss, fuss—silliness!—over a gentleman caller!

Door swings shut. Laura is left alone.

(LEGEND: "TERROR!")

She utters a low moan and turns off the lamp—sits stiffly on the edge of the sofa, knotting her fingers together.

(LEGEND ON SCREEN: "THE OPENING OF A DOOR!")

Tom and Jim appear on the fire-escape steps and climb to landing. Hearing their approach, Laura rises with a panicky gesture. She retreats to the portieres.

The doorbell. Laura catches her breath and touches her throat. Low drums.

Amanda (*calling*). Laura, sweetheart! The door!

Laura stares at it without moving.

Jim. I think we just beat the rain.
Tom. Uh-huh. (*He rings again, nervously. Jim whistles and fishes for a cigarette.*)
Amanda. (*very, very gaily*). Laura, that is your brother and Mr. O'Connor! Will you let them in, darling?

Laura crosses toward kitchenette door.

Laura (*breathlessly*). Mother—you go to the door!

Amanda steps out of kitchenette and stares furiously at Laura. She points imperiously at the door.

Laura. Please, please!
Amanda (*in a fierce whisper*). What is the matter with you, you silly thing?
Laura (*desperately*). Please, you answer it, *please!*
Amanda. I told you I wasn't going to humor you, Laura. Why have you chosen this moment to lose your mind?
Laura. Please, please, please, you go!
Amanda. You'll have to go to the door because I can't!
Laura (*despairingly*). I can't either!
Amanda. Why?
Laura. I'm *sick!*
Amanda. I'm sick, too—of your nonsense! Why can't you and your brother be normal people? Fantastic whims and behavior! (*Tom gives a long ring.*) Preposterous goings on! Can you give me one reason—(*Calls out lyrically.*) COMING! JUST ONE SECOND!—why should you be afraid to open a door? Now you answer it, Laura!
Laura. Oh, oh, oh . . . (*She returns through the portieres. Darts to the victrola and winds it frantically and turns it on.*)
Amanda. Laura Wingfield, you march right to that door!
Laura. Yes—yes, Mother!

A faraway, scratchy rendition of "Dardanella" softens the air

*and gives her strength to move through it. She slips to the door
and draws it cautiously open.*

Tom enters with the caller, Jim O'Connor.

Tom. Laura, this is Jim. Jim, this is my sister, Laura.
Jim (*stepping inside*). I didn't know that Shakespeare had a sister!
Laura (*retreating stiff and trembling from the door*). How—how do
   you do?
Jim (*heartily extending his hand*). Okay!

Laura touches it hesitantly with hers.

Jim. Your hand's *cold*, Laura!
Laura. Yes, well—I've been playing the victrola. . . .
Jim. Must have been playing classical music on it! You ought to play
   a little hot swing music to warm you up!
Laura. Excuse me—I haven't finished playing the victrola. . . .

*She turns awkwardly and hurries into the front room. She pauses
a second by the victrola. Then catches her breath and darts
through the portieres like a frightened deer.*

Jim (*grinning*). What was the matter?
Tom. Oh—with Laura? Laura is—terribly shy.
Jim. Shy, huh? It's unusual to meet a shy girl nowadays. I don't be-
   lieve you ever mentioned you had a sister.
Tom. Well, now you know. I have one. Here is the *Post Dispatch*.
   You want a piece of it?
Jim. Uh-huh.
Tom. What piece? The comics?
Jim. Sports! (*Glances at it.*) Ole Dizzy Dean is on his bad behavior.
Tom (*disinterest*). Yeah? (*Lights cigarette and crosses back to fire-
   escape door.*)
Jim. Where are *you* going?
Tom. I'm going out on the terrace.
Jim (*goes after him*). You know, Shakespeare—I'm going to sell you
   a bill of goods!
Tom. What goods?
Jim. A course I'm taking.
Tom. Huh?
Jim. In public speaking! You and me, we're not the warehouse type.
Tom. Thanks—that's good news. But what has public speaking got
   to do with it?
Jim. It fits you for—executive positions!
Tom. Awww.
Jim. I tell you it's done a helluva lot for me.

(IMAGE: EXECUTIVE AT DESK.)

Tom. In what respect?

Jim. In every! Ask yourself what is the difference between you an' me and men in the office down front? Brains?—No!—Ability?—No! Then what? Just one little thing—

Tom. What is that one little thing?

Jim. Primarily it amounts to—social poise! Being able to square up to people and hold your own on any social level!

Amanda (off stage). Tom?

Tom. Yes, Mother?

Amanda. Is that you and Mr. O'Connor?

Tom. Yes, Mother.

Amanda. Well, you just make yourselves comfortable in there.

Tom. Yes, Mother.

Amanda. Ask Mr. O'Connor if he would like to wash his hands.

Jim. Aw—no—no—thank you—I took care of that at the warehouse. Tom—

Tom. Yes?

Jim. Mr. Mendoza was speaking to me about you.

Tom. Favorably?

Jim. What do you think?

Tom. Well—

Jim. You're going to be out of a job if you don't wake up.

Tom. I am waking up—

Jim. You show no signs.

Tom. The signs are interior.

(IMAGE ON SCREEN: THE SAILING VESSEL WITH JOLLY ROGER AGAIN.)

Tom. I'm planning to change. (*He leans over the rail speaking with quiet exhilaration. The incandescent marquees and signs of the first-run movie houses light his face from across the alley. He looks like a voyager.*) I'm right at the point of commiting myself to a future that doesn't include the warehouse and Mr. Mendoza or even a night-school course in public speaking.

Jim. What are you gassing about?

Tom. I'm tired of the movies.

Jim. Movies!

Tom. Yes, movies! Look at them—(*A wave toward the marvels of Grand Avenue.*) All of those glamorous people—having adventures—hogging it all, gobbling the whole thing up! You know what happens? People go to the *movies* instead of *moving*! Hollywood characters are supposed to have all the adventures for everybody in America, while everybody in America sits in a dark room and watches them have them! Yes, until there's a war. That's when adventure becomes available to the masses! *Everyone's* dish, not only Gable's! Then the people in the dark room come out of the dark room to have some adventures themselves—Goody, goody!—It's our turn now, to go to the South Sea Island—to make a safari—to be exotic, far-off!—But I'm not patient. I don't want to wait till then. I'm tired of the *movies* and I am *about* to *move*!

Jim (*incredulously*). Move?

Tom. Yes.

Jim. When?

Tom. Soon!

Jim. Where? Where?

(THEME THREE MUSIC SEEMS TO ANSWER THE QUESTION, WHILE TOM THINKS IT OVER. HE SEARCHES AMONG HIS POCKETS.)

Tom. I'm starting to boil inside. I know I seem dreamy, but inside— well, I'm boiling! Whenever I pick up a shoe, I shudder a little thinking how short life is and what I am doing!—Whatever that means. I know it doesn't mean shoes—except as something to wear on a traveler's feet! (*Finds paper.*) Look—

Jim. What?

Tom. I'm a member.

Jim (*reading*). The Union of Merchant Seamen.

Tom. I paid my dues this month, instead of the light bill.

Jim. You will regret it when they turn the lights off.

Tom. I won't be here.

Jim. How about your mother?

Tom. I'm like my father. The bastard son of a bastard! See how he grins? And he's been absent going on sixteen years!

Jim. You're just talking, you drip. How does your mother feel about it?

Tom. Shhh!—Here comes Mother! Mother is not acquainted with my plans!

Amanda (*enters portieres*). Where are you all?

Tom. On the terrace, Mother.

They start inside. She advances to them. Tom is distinctly shocked at her appearance. Even Jim blinks a little. He is making his first contact with girlish Southern vivacity and in spite of the night-school course in public speaking is somewhat thrown off the beam by the unexpected outlay of social charm.

Certain responses are attempted by Jim but are swept aside by Amanda's gay laughter and chatter. Tom is embarrassed but after the first shock Jim reacts very warmly. Grins and chuckles, is altogether won over.

(IMAGE: AMANDA AS A GIRL.)

Amanda (*coyly smiling, shaking her girlish ringlets*). Well, well, well, so this is Mr. O'Connor. Introductions entirely unnecessary. I've heard so much about you from my boy. I finally said to him, Tom —good gracious!—why don't you bring this paragon to supper? I'd like to meet this nice young man at the warehouse!—Instead of just hearing him sing your praises so much! I don't know why my son is so stand-offish—that's not Southern behavior! Let's sit down and—I think we could stand a little more air in here! Tom, leave the door open. I felt a nice fresh breeze a moment ago. Where has it gone? Mmm, so warm already! And not quite summer, even. We're going to burn up when summer really gets started. However, we're having—we're having a very light supper. I think light things are better fo' this time of year. The same as light clothes are. Light clothes an' light food are what warm weather calls fo'. You know our blood gets so thick during th' winter—it takes a while fo' us to *adjust* ou'selves!—when the season changes . . . It's come so quick this year. I wasn't prepared. All of a sudden—heavens! Already summer!—I ran to the trunk an' pulled out this light dress—Terribly old! Historical almost! But feels so good—so good an' co-ol, y'know. . . .

Tom. Mother—

Amanda. Yes, honey?

Tom. How about—supper?

Amanda. Honey, you go ask Sister if supper is ready! You know that Sister is in full charge of supper! Tell her you hungry boys are waiting for it. (*To Jim.*) Have you met Laura?

Jim. She—

Amanda. Let you in? Oh, good, you've met already! It's rare for a girl as sweet an' pretty as Laura to be domestic! But Laura is, thank heavens, not only pretty but also very domestic. I'm not at all. I never was a bit. I never could make a thing but angel-food cake. Well, in the South we had so many servants. Gone, gone, gone. All vestige of gracious living! Gone completely! I wasn't prepared for what the future brought me. All of my gentlemen callers were sons of planters and so of course I assumed that I would be married to one and raise my family on a large piece of land with plenty of servants. But man proposes—and woman accepts the proposal! —To vary that old, old saying a little bit—I married no planter! I married a man who worked for the telephone company!—That gallantly smiling gentleman over there! (*Points to the picture.*) A telephone man who—fell in love with long-distance!—Now he travels and I don't even know where!—But what am I going on for about my—tribulations? Tell me yours—I hope you don't have any! Tom?

Tom (*returning*). Yes, Mother?

Amanda. Is supper nearly ready?

Tom. It looks to me like supper is on the table.

Amanda. Let me look—(*She rises prettily and looks through portieres.*) Oh, lovely!—But where is Sister?

Tom. Laura is not feeling well and she says that she thinks she'd better not come to the table.

Amanda. What?—Nonsense!—Laura? Oh, Laura!

Laura (*Off stage, faintly*). Yes, Mother.

Amanda. You really must come to the table. We won't be seated until you come to the table! Come in, Mr. O'Connor. You sit over there and I'll—Laura? Laura Wingfield! You're keeping us waiting, honey! We can't say grace until you come to the table!

The back door is pushed weakly open and Laura comes in. She is obviously quite faint, her lips trembling, her eyes wide and staring. She moves unsteadily toward the table.

(LEGEND: "TERROR!")

Outside a summer storm is coming abruptly. The white curtains billow inward at the windows and there is a sorrowful murmur and deep blue dusk.

Laura suddenly stumbles—she catches at a chair with a faint moan.

Tom. Laura!

Amanda. Laura! (*There is a clap of thunder.*) (LEGEND: "AH!") (*Despairingly.*) Why, Laura, you *are* sick, darling! Tom, help your sister into the living room, dear! Sit in the living room, Laura—rest on the sofa. Well! (*To the gentleman caller.*) Standing over the hot stove made her ill!—I told her that it was just too warm this evening, but—(*Tom comes back in. Laura is on the sofa.*) Is Laura all right now?

Tom. Yes.

Amanda. What *is* that? Rain? A nice cool rain has come up! (*She gives the gentleman caller a frightened look.*) I think we may—have grace—now . . . (*Tom looks at her stupidly.*) Tom, honey—you say grace!

Tom. Oh . . . "For these and all thy mercies—" (*They bow their heads, Amanda stealing a nervous glance at Jim. In the living room Laura, stretched on the sofa, clenches her hand to her lips, to hold back a shuddering sob.*) God's Holy Name be praised—

(THE SCENE DIMS OUT.)

SCENE VII

(A Souvenir.)

Half an hour later. Dinner is just being finished in the upstage area which is concealed by the drawn portieres.

As the curtain rises Laura is still huddled upon the sofa, her feet drawn under her, her head resting on a pale blue pillow, her eyes wide and mysteriously watchful. The new floor lamp with its shade of rose-colored silk gives a soft, becoming light to her face bringing out the fragile, unearthly prettiness which usually escapes attention. There is a steady murmur of rain, but it is slackening and stops soon after the scene begins; the air outside becomes pale and luminous as the moon breaks out.

A moment after the curtain rises, the lights in both rooms flicker and go out.

Jim. Hey, there, Mr. Light Bulb!

Amanda laughs nervously.

(LEGEND: "SUSPENSION OF A PUBLIC SERVICE.")

Amanda. Where was Moses when the lights went out? Ha-ha. Do you know the answer to that one, Mr. O'Connor?
Jim. No, Ma'am, what's the answer?
Amanda. In the dark! (*Jim laughs appreciably.*) Everybody sit still. I'll light the candles. Isn't it lucky we have them on the table? Where's a match? Which of you gentlemen can provide a match?
Jim. Here.
Amanda. Thank you, sir.
Jim. Not at all, Ma'am!
Amanda. I guess the fuse has burnt out. Mr. O'Connor, can you tell a burnt-out fuse? I know I can't and Tom is a total loss when it comes to mechanics. (SOUND: GETTING UP: VOICES RECEDE A LITTLE TO KITCHENETTE.) Oh, be careful you don't bump into something. We don't want our gentleman caller to break his neck. Now wouldn't that be a fine howdy-do?
Jim. Ha-ha! Where is the fuse-box?
Amanda. Right here next to the stove. Can you see anything?
Jim. Just a minute.
Amanda. Isn't electricity a mysterious thing? Wasn't it Benjamin Franklin who tied a key to a kite? We live in such a mysterious universe, don't we? Some people say that science clears up all the mysteries for us. In my opinion it only creates more! Have you found it yet?
Jim. No, Ma'am. All these fuses look okay to me.
Amanda. Tom!
Tom. Yes, Mother?
Amanda. That light bill I gave you several days ago. The one I told you we got the notices about?
Tom. Oh.—Yeah.

(LEGEND: "HA!")

Amanda. You didn't neglect to pay it by any chance?

Tom. Why, I—

Amanda. Didn't! I might have known it!

Jim. Shakespeare probably wrote a poem on that light bill, Mrs. Wingfield.

Amanda. I might have known better than to trust him with it! There's such a high price for negligence in this world!

Jim. Maybe the poem will win a ten-dollar prize.

Amanda. We'll just have to spend the remainder of the evening in the nineteenth century, before Mr. Edison made the Mazda lamp!

Jim. Candlelight is my favorite kind of light.

Amanda. That shows you're romantic! But that's no excuse for Tom. Well, we got through dinner. Very considerate of them to let us get through dinner before they plunged us into everlasting darkness, wasn't it, Mr. O'Connor?

Jim. Ha-ha!

Amanda. Tom, as a penalty for your carelessness you can help me with the dishes.

Jim. Let me give you a hand.

Amanda. Indeed you will not!

Jim. I ought to be good for something.

Amanda. Good for something? (*Her tone is rhapsodic.*) You? Why, Mr. O'Connor, nobody, *nobody's* given me this much entertainment in years—as you have!

Jim. Aw, now, Mrs. Wingfield!

Amanda. I'm not exaggerating, not one bit! But sister is all by her lonesome. You go keep her company in the parlor! I'll give you this lovely old candelabrum that used to be on the altar at the church of the Heavenly Rest. It was melted a little out of shape when the church burnt down. Lightning struck it one spring. Gypsy Jones was holding a revival at the time and he intimated that the church was destroyed because the Episcopalians gave card parties.

Jim. Ha-ha.

Amanda. And how about coaxing Sister to drink a little wine? I think it would be good for her! Can you carry both at once?

Jim. Sure. I'm Superman!

Amanda. Now, Thomas, get into this apron!

The door of kitchenette swings closed on Amanda's gay laughter; the flickering light approaches the portieres.

Laura sits up nervously as he enters. Her speech at first is low and breathless from the almost intolerable strain of being alone with a stranger.

(THE LEGEND: "I DON'T SUPPOSE YOU REMEMBER ME AT ALL!")

In her first speeches in this scene, before Jim's warmth overcomes

The Glass Menagerie 731

her paralyzing shyness, Laura's voice is thin and breathless as though she has just run up a steep flight of stairs.

Jim's attitude is gently humorous. In playing this scene it should be stressed that while the incident is apparently unimportant, it is to Laura the climax of her secret life.

Jim. Hello, there, Laura.

Laura (faintly). Hello. (*She clears her throat.*)

Jim. How are you feeling now? Better?

Laura. Yes. Yes, thank you.

Jim. This is for you. A little dandelion wine. (*He extends it toward her with extravagant gallantry.*)

Laura. Thank you.

Jim. Drink it—but don't get drunk! (*He laughs heartily. Laura takes the glass uncertainly; laughs shyly.*) Where shall I set the candles?

Laura. Oh—oh, anywhere . . .

Jim. How about here on the floor? Any objections?

Laura. No.

Jim. I'll spread a newspaper under to catch the drippings. I like to sit on the floor. Mind if I do?

Laura. Oh, no.

Jim. Give me a pillow?

Laura. What?

Jim. A pillow!

Laura. Oh . . . (*Hands him one quickly.*)

Jim. How about you? Don't you like to sit on the floor?

Laura. Oh—yes.

Jim. Why don't you, then?

Laura. I—will.

Jim. Take a pillow! (*Laura does. Sits on the other side of the candelabrum. Jim crosses his legs and smiles engagingly at her.*) I can't hardly see you sitting way over there.

Laura. I can—see you.

Jim. I know, but that's not fair, I'm in the limelight. (*Laura moves her pillow closer.*) Good! Now I can see you! Comfortable?

Laura. Yes.

Jim. So am I. Comfortable as a cow. Will you have some gum?

Laura. No, thank you.

Jim. I think that I will indulge, with your permission. (*Musingly unwraps it and holds it up.*) Think of the fortune made by the guy that invented the first piece of chewing gum. Amazing, huh? The Wrigley Building is one of the sights of Chicago.—I saw it summer before last when I went up to the Century of Progress. Did you take in the Century of Progress?

Laura. No, I didn't.

Jim. Well, it was quite a wonderful exposition. What impressed me most was the Hall of Science. Gives you an idea of what the future will be in America, even more wonderful than the present time is! (*Pause. Smiling at her.*) Your brother tells me you're shy. Is that right, Laura?

Laura. I—don't know.

Jim. I judge you to be an old-fashioned type of girl. Well, I think that's a pretty good type to be. Hope you don't think I'm being too personal—do you?

Laura (*hastily, out of embarrassment*). I believe I *will* take a piece of gum, if you—don't mind. (*Clearing her throat.*) Mr. O'Connor, have you—kept up with your singing?

Jim. Singing? Me?

Laura. Yes. I remember what a beautiful voice you had.

Jim. When did you hear me sing?

(VOICE OFF STAGE IN THE PAUSE.)

Voice (*off stage*).
    O blow, ye winds, heigh-ho,
    A-roving I will go!
    I'm off to my love
    With a boxing glove—
    Ten thousand miles away!

Jim. You say you've heard me sing?

Laura. Oh, yes! Yes, very often . . . I—don't suppose you remember me—at all?

Jim (*smiling doubtfully*). You know I have an idea I've seen you before. I had that idea soon as you opened the door. It seemed almost like I was about to remember your name. But the name that I started to call you—wasn't a name! And so I stopped myself before I said it.

Laura. Wasn't it—Blue Roses?

Jim (*springs up, grinning*). Blue Roses! My gosh, yes—Blue Roses! That's what I had on my tongue when you opened the door! Isn't it funny what tricks your memory plays? I didn't connect you with the high school somehow or other. But that's where it was; it was high school. I didn't even know you were Shakespeare's sister! Gosh, I'm sorry.

Laura. I didn't expect you to. You—barely knew me!

Jim. But we did have a speaking acquaintance, huh?

Laura. Yes, we—spoke to each other.

Jim. When did you recognize me?

Laura. Oh, right away!

Jim. Soon as I came in the door?

Laura. When I heard your name I thought it was probably you. I knew that Tom used to know you a little in high school. So when you came in the door—Well, then I was—sure.

Jim. Why didn't you *say* something, then?

The Glass Menagerie 733

Laura (*breathlessly*). I didn't know what to say, I was—too surprised
Jim. For goodness' sakes! You know, this sure is funny!
Laura. Yes! Yes, isn't it, though . . .
Jim. Didn't we have a class in something together?
Laura. Yes, we did.
Jim. What class was that?
Laura. It was—singing—Chorus!
Jim. Aw!
Laura. I sat across the aisle from you in the Aud.
Jim. Aw.
Laura. Mondays, Wednesdays and Fridays.
Jim. Now I remember—you always came in late.
Laura. Yes, it was so hard for me, getting upstairs. I had that brace on
my leg—it clumped so loud!
Jim. I never heard any clumping.
Laura (*wincing at the recollection*). To me it sounded like—thunder!
Jim. Well, well, well. I never even noticed.
Laura. And everybody was seated before I came in. I had to walk in
front of all those people. My seat was in the back row. I had to go
clumping all the way up the aisle with everyone watching!
Jim. You shouldn't have been self-conscious.
Laura. I know, but I was. It was always such a relief when the singing
started.
Jim. Aw, yes, I've placed you now! I used to call you Blue Roses. How
was it that I got started calling you that?
Laura. I was out of school a little while with pleurosis. When I came
back you asked me what was the matter. I said I had pleurosis—
you thought I said Blue Roses. That's what you always called me
after that!
Jim. I hope you didn't mind.
Laura. Oh, no—I liked it. You see, I wasn't acquainted with many—
people. . . .
Jim. As I remember you sort of stuck by yourself.
Laura. I—I—never had much luck at—making friends.
Jim. I don't see why you wouldn't.
Laura. Well, I—started out badly.
Jim. You mean being—
Laura. Yes, it sort of—stood between me—
Jim. You shouldn't have let it!
Laura. I know, but it did, and—
Jim. You were shy with people!
Laura. I tried not to be but never could—
Jim. Overcome it?
Laura. No, I—I never could!
Jim. I guess being shy is something you have to work out of kind of
gradually.

Laura (*sorrowfully*). Yes—I guess it—

Jim. Takes time!

Laura. Yes—

Jim. People are not so dreadful when you know them. That's what you have to remember! And everybody has problems, not just you, but practically everybody has got some problems. You think of yourself as having the only problems, as being the only one who is disappointed. But just look around you and you will see lots of people as disappointed as you are. For instance, I hoped when I was going to high school that I would be further along at this time, six years later, than I am now—You remember that wonderful write-up I had in *The Torch*?

Laura. Yes! (*She rises and crosses to table.*)

Jim. It said I was bound to succeed in anything I went into! (*Laura returns with the annual.*) Holy Jeez! *The Torch*! (*He accepts it reverently. They smile across it with mutual wonder. Laura crouches beside him and they begin to turn through it. Laura's shyness is dissolving in his warmth.*)

Laura. Here you are in *Pirates of Penzance*!

Jim (*wistfully*). I sang the baritone lead in that operetta.

Laura (*rapidly*). So—beautifully!

Jim (*protesting*). Aw—

Laura. Yes, yes—beautifully—beautifully!

Jim. You heard me?

Laura. All three times!

Jim. No!

Laura. Yes!

Jim. All three performances?

Laura (*looking down*). Yes.

Jim. Why?

Laura. I—wanted to ask you to—autograph my program.

Jim. Why didn't you ask me to?

Laura. You were always surrounded by your own friends so much that I never had a chance to.

Jim. You should have just—

Laura. Well, I—thought you might think I was—

Jim. Thought I might think you was—what?

Laura. Oh—

Jim (*with reflective relish*). I was beleaguered by females in those days.

Laura. You were terribly popular!

Jim. Yeah—

Laura. You had such a—friendly way—

Jim. I was spoiled in high school.

Laura. Everybody—liked you!

Jim. Including you?

Laura. I—yes, I—I did, too—(*She gently closes the book in her lap.*)

The Glass Menagerie 735

Jim. Well, well, well!—Give me that program, Laura. (*She hands it to him. He signs it with a flourish.*) There you are—better late than never!

Laura. Oh, I—what a—surprise!

Jim. My signature isn't worth very much right now. But some day—maybe—it will increase in value! Being disappointed is one thing and being discouraged is something else. I am disappointed but I am not discouraged. I'm twenty-three years old. How old are you?

Laura. I'll be twenty-four in June.

Jim. That's not old age!

Laura. No, but—

Jim. You finished high school?

Laura (*with difficulty*). I didn't go back.

Jim. You mean you dropped out?

Laura. I made bad grades in my final examinations. (*She rises and replaces the book and the program. Her voice strained.*) How is—Emily Meisenbach getting along?

Jim. Oh, that kraut-head!

Laura. Why do you call her that?

Jim. That's what she was.

Laura. You're not still—going with her?

Jim. I never see her.

Laura. It said in the Personal Section that you were—engaged!

Jim. I know, but I wasn't impressed by that—propaganda!

Laura. It wasn't—the truth?

Jim. Only in Emily's optimistic opinion!

Laura. Oh—

(LEGEND: "WHAT HAVE YOU DONE SINCE HIGH SCHOOL?")

Jim lights a cigarette and leans indolently back on his elbows smiling at Laura with a warmth and charm which lights her inwardly with altar candles. She remains by the table and turns in her hands a piece of glass to cover her tumult.

Jim (*after several reflective puffs on a cigarette*). What have you done since high school? (*She seems not to hear him.*) Huh? (*Laura looks up.*) I said what have you done since high school, Laura?

Laura. Nothing much.

Jim. You must have been doing something these six long years.

Laura. Yes.

Jim. Well, then, such as what?

Laura. I took a business course at business college—

Jim. How did that work out?

Laura. Well, not very—well—I had to drop out, it gave me—indigestion—

Jim laughs gently.

Jim. What are you doing now?

Laura. I don't do anything—much. Oh, please don't think I sit around doing nothing! My glass collection takes up a good deal of my time. Glass is something you have to take good care of.

Jim. What did you say—about glass?

Laura. Collection I said—I have one—(*She clears her throat and turns away again, acutely shy.*)

Jim (*abruptly*). You know what I judge to be the trouble with you? Inferiority complex! Know what that is? That's what they call it when someone low-rates himself! I understand it because I had it, too. Although my case was not so aggravated as yours seems to be. I had it until I took up public speaking, developed my voice, and learned that I had an aptitude for science. Before that time I never thought of myself as being outstanding in any way whatsoever! Now I've never made a regular study of it, but I have a friend who says I can analyze people better than doctors that make a profession of it. I don't claim that to be necessarily true, but I can sure guess a person's psychology, Laura! (*Takes out his gum.*) Excuse me, Laura. I always take it out when the flavor is gone. I'll use this scrap of paper to wrap it in. I know how it is to get it stuck on a shoe. Yep—that's what I judge to be your principal trouble. A lack of confidence in yourself as a person. You don't have the proper amount of faith in yourself. I'm basing that fact on a number of your remarks and also on certain observations I've made. For instance that clumping you thought was so awful in high school. You say that you even dreaded to walk into class. You see what you did? You dropped out of school, you gave up an education because of a clump, which as far as I know was practically non-existent! A little physical defect is what you have. Hardly noticeable even! Magnified thousands of times by imagination! You know what my strong advice to you is? Think of yourself as *superior* in some way!

Laura. In what way would I think?

Jim. Why, man alive, Laura! Just look about you a little. What do you see? A world full of common people! All of 'em born and all of 'em going to die! Which of them has one-tenth of your good points! Or mine! Or anyone else's, as far as that goes—Gosh! Everybody excels in some one thing. Some in many! (*Unconsciously glances at himself in the mirror.*) All you've got to do is discover in *what*! Take me, for instance. (*He adjusts his tie at the mirror.*) My interest happens to lie in electro-dynamics. I'm taking a course in radio engineering at night school, Laura, on top of a fairly responsible job at the warehouse. I'm taking that course and studying public speaking.

Laura. Ohhhh.

Jim. Because I believe in the future of television! (*Turning back to her.*) I wish to be ready to go up right along with it. Therefore

I'm planning to get in on the ground floor. In fact, I've already made the right connections and all that remains is for the industry itself to get under way! Full steam—(*His eyes are starry.*) *Knowledge*—Zzzzzp! *Money*—Zzzzzzp!—*Power!* That's the cycle democracy is built on! (*His attitude is convincingly dynamic. Laura stares at him, even her shyness eclipsed in her absolute wonder. He suddenly grins.*) I guess you think I think a lot of myself!

Laura. No—o-o-o, I—

Jim. Now how about you? Isn't there something you take more interest in than anything else?

Laura. Well, I do—as I said—have my—glass collection—

A peal of girlish laughter from the kitchen.

Jim. I'm not right sure I know what you're talking about. What kind of glass is it?

Laura. Little articles of it, they're ornaments mostly! Most of them are little animals made out of glass, the tiniest little animals in the world. Mother calls them a glass menagerie! Here's an example of one, if you'd like to see it! This one is one of the oldest. It's nearly thirteen. (*He stretches out his hand.*) (MUSIC: "THE GLASS MENAGERIE.") Oh, be careful—if you breathe, it breaks!

Jim. I'd better not take it. I'm pretty clumsy with things.

Laura. Go on, I trust you with him! (*Places it in his palm.*) There now —you're holding him gently! Hold him over the light, he loves the light! You see how the light shines through him?

Jim. It sure does shine!

Laura. I shouldn't be partial, but he is my favorite one.

Jim. What kind of a thing is this one supposed to be?

Laura. Haven't you noticed the single horn on his forehead?

Jim. A unicorn, huh?

Laura. Mmm-hmmm!

Jim. Unicorns, aren't they extinct in the modern world?

Laura. I know!

Jim. Poor little fellow, he must feel sort of lonesome.

Laura (*smiling*). Well, if he does he doesn't complain about it. He stays on a shelf with some horses that don't have horns and all of them seem to get along nicely together.

Jim. How do you know?

Laura (*lightly*). I haven't heard any arguments among them!

Jim (*grinning*). No arguments, huh? Well, that's a pretty good sign! Where shall I set him?

Laura. Put him on the table. They all like a change of scenery once in a while!

Jim (*stretching*). Well, well, well, well—Look how big my shadow is when I stretch!

Laura. Oh, oh, yes—it stretches across the ceiling!

Jim (*crossing to door*). I think it's stopped raining. (*Opens fire-escape door.*) Where does the music come from?

Laura. From the Paradise Dance Hall across the alley.

Jim. How about cutting the rug a little, Miss Wingfield?

Laura. Oh, I—

Jim. Or is your program filled up? Let me have a look at it. (*Grasps imaginary card.*) Why, every dance is taken! I'll just have to scratch some out. (WALTZ MUSIC: "LA GOLONDRINA.") Ahhh, a waltz! (*He executes some sweeping turns by himself, then holds his arms toward Laura.*)

Laura (*breathlessly*). I—can't dance!

Jim. There you go, that inferiority stuff!

Laura. I've never danced in my life!

Jim. Come on, try!

Laura. Oh, but I'd step on you!

Jim. I'm not made out of glass.

Laura. How—how—how do we start?

Jim. Just leave it to me. You hold your arms out a little.

Laura. Like this?

Jim. A little bit higher. Right. Now don't tighten up, that's the main thing about it—relax.

Laura (*laughing breathlessly*). It's hard not to.

Jim. Okay.

Laura. I'm afraid you can't budge me.

Jim. What do you bet I can't? (*He swings her into motion.*)

Laura. Goodness, yes, you can!

Jim. Let yourself go, now, Laura, just let yourself go.

Laura. I'm—

Jim. Come on!

Laura. Trying!

Jim. Not so stiff—Easy does it!

Laura. I know but I'm—

Jim. Loosen th' backbone! There now, that's a lot better.

Laura. Am I?

Jim. Lots, lots better! (*He moves her about the room in a clumsy waltz.*)

Laura. Oh, my!

Jim. Ha-ha!

Laura. Goodness, yes you can!

Jim. Ha-ha-ha! (*They suddenly bump into the table. Jim stops.*) What did we hit on?

Laura. Table.

Jim. Did something fall off it? I think—

Laura. Yes.

Jim. I hope that it wasn't the little glass horse with the horn!

Laura. Yes.

Jim. Aw, aw, aw. Is it broken?

Laura. Now it is just like all the other horses.

Jim. It's lost its—

Laura. Horn! It doesn't matter. Maybe it's a blessing in disguise.

Jim. You'll never forgive me. I bet that that was your favorite piece of glass.

Laura. I don't have favorites much. It's no tragedy, Freckles. Glass breaks so easily. No matter how careful you are. The traffic jars the shelves and things fall off them.

Jim. Still I'm awfully sorry that I was the cause.

Laura (smiling). I'll just imagine he had an operation. The horn was removed to make him feel less—freakish! (*They both laugh.*) Now he will feel more at home with the other horses, the ones that don't have horns . . .

Jim. Ha-ha, that's very funny! (*Suddenly serious.*) I'm glad to see that you have a sense of humor. You know—you're—well—very different! Surprisingly different from anyone else I know! (*His voice becomes soft and hesitant with a genuine feeling.*) Do you mind me telling you that? (*Laura is abashed beyond speech.*) You make me feel sort of—I don't know how to put it! I'm usually pretty good at expressing things, but—This is something that I don't know how to say! (*Laura touches her throat and clears it— turns the broken unicorn in her hands.*) (*Even softer.*) Has anyone ever told you that you were pretty? (PAUSE: MUSIC.) (*Laura looks up slowly, with wonder, and shakes her head.*) Well, you are! In a very different way from anyone else. And all the nicer because of the difference, too. (*His voice becomes low and husky. Laura turns away, nearly faint with the novelty of her emotions.*) I wish that you were my sister. I'd teach you to have some confidence in yourself. The different people are not like other people, but being different is nothing to be ashamed of. Because other people are not such wonderful people. They're one hundred times one thousand. You're one times one! They walk all over the earth. You just stay here. They're common as—weeds, but—you—well, you're—*Blue Roses!*

(IMAGE ON SCREEN: BLUE ROSES.)

(MUSIC CHANGES.)

Laura. But blue is wrong for—roses . . .

Jim. It's right for you—You're—pretty!

Laura. In what respect am I pretty?

Jim. In all respects—believe me! Your eyes—your hair—are pretty! Your hands are pretty! (*He catches hold of her hand.*) You think I'm making this up because I'm invited to dinner and have to be nice. Oh, I could do that! I could put on an act for you, Laura, and say lots of things without being very sincere. But this time I am. I'm talking to you sincerely. I happened to notice you had this inferiority complex that keeps you from feeling comfortable with people. Somebody needs to build your confidence up and make you proud instead of shy and turning away and—blushing— Somebody ought to—Ought to—*kiss* you, Laura! (*His hand slips slowly up her arm to her shoulder.*) (MUSIC SWELLS TUMULTU-OUSLY.) (*He suddenly turns her about and kisses her on the lips. When he releases her Laura sinks on the sofa with a bright, dazed look. Jim backs away and fishes in his pocket for a cigarette.*) (LEGEND ON SCREEN: "SOUVENIR.") Stumble-john! (*He lights the cigarette, avoiding her look. There is a peal of girlish laughter from Amanda in the kitchen. Laura slowly raises and opens her hand. It still contains the little broken glass animal. She looks at it with a tender, bewildered expression.*) Stumble-john! I shouldn't have done that—That was way off the beam. You don't smoke, do you? (*She looks up, smiling, not hearing the question. He sits beside her a little gingerly. She looks at him speechlessly— waiting. He coughs decorously and moves a little farther aside as he considers the situation and senses her feelings, dimly, with perturbation. Gently.*) Would you—care for a—mint? (*She doesn't seem to hear him but her look grows brighter even.*) Pep-permint—Life Saver? My pocket's a regular drug store—wher-ever I go . . . (*He pops a mint in his mouth. Then gulps and decides to make a clean breast of it. He speaks slowly and gin-gerly.*) Laura, you know, if I had a sister like you, I'd do the same thing as Tom. I'd bring out fellows—introduce her to them. The right type of boys of a type to—appreciate her. Only—well— he made a mistake about me. Maybe I've got no call to be saying this. That may not have been the idea in having me over. But what if it was? There's nothing wrong about that. The only trouble is that in my case—I'm not in a situation to—do the right thing. I can't take down your number and say I'll phone. I can't call up next week and—ask for a date. I thought I had better explain the situation in case you misunderstood it and—hurt your feelings. . . . (*Pause. Slowly, very slowly, Laura's look changes, her eyes returning slowly from his to the ornament in her palm.*)

Amanda utters another gay laugh in the kitchen.

Laura (*faintly*). You—won't—call again?

Jim. No, Laura, I can't. (*He rises from the sofa.*) As I was just explain-ing, I've—got strings on me, Laura, I've—been going steady! I go out all the time with a girl named Betty. She's a home-girl like you, and Catholic, and Irish, and in a great many ways we—get along fine. I met her last summer on a moonlight boat trip up the river to Alton, on the *Majestic*. Well—right away from the start it was —love! (LEGEND: LOVE!) (*Laura sways slightly forward and grips the arm of the sofa. He fails to notice, now enrapt in his own comfortable being.*) Being in love has made a new man of me!

(*Leaning stiffly forward, clutching the arm of the sofa, Laura struggles visibly with her storm. But Jim is oblivious, she is a long way off.*) The power of love is really pretty tremendous! Love is something that—changes the whole world, Laura! (*The storm abates a little and Laura leans back. He notices her again.*) It happened that Betty's aunt took sick, she got a wire and had to go to Centralia. So Tom—when he asked me to dinner—I naturally just accepted the invitation, not knowing that you—that he—that I— (*He stops awkwardly.*) Huh—I'm a stumble-john! (*He flops back on the sofa. The holy candles in the altar of Laura's face have been snuffed out. There is a look of almost infinite desolation. Jim glances at her uneasily.*) I wish that you would—say something. (*She bites her lip which was trembling and then bravely smiles. She opens her hand again on the broken glass ornament. Then she gently takes his hand and raises it level with her own. She carefully places the unicorn in the palm of his hand, then pushes his fingers closed upon it.*) What are you—doing that for? You want me to have him?—Laura? (*She nods.*) What for?

Laura. A—souvenir . . .

She rises unsteadily and crouches beside the victrola to wind it up.

(LEGEND ON SCREEN: "THINGS HAVE A WAY OF TURNING OUT SO BADLY.")

(OR IMAGE: "GENTLEMAN CALLER WAVING GOODBYE!—GAILY.")

At this moment Amanda rushes brightly back in the front room. She bears a pitcher of fruit punch in an old-fashioned cut-glass pitcher and a plate of macaroons. The plate has a gold border and poppies painted on it.

Amanda. Well, well, well! Isn't the air delightful after the shower? I've made you children a little liquid refreshment. (*Turns gaily to the gentleman caller.*) Jim, do you know that song about lemonade?

"Lemonade, lemonade
     Made in the shade and stirred with a spade—
     Good enough for any old maid!"

Jim (*uneasily*). Ha-ha! No—I never heard it.
Amanda. Why, Laura! You look so serious!
Jim. We were having a serious conversation.
Amanda. Good! Now you're better acquainted!
Jim (*uncertainly*). Ha-ha! Yes.
Amanda. You modern young people are much more serious-minded than my generation. I was so gay as a girl!
Jim. You haven't changed, Mrs. Wingfield.
Amanda. Tonight I'm rejuvenated! The gaiety of the occasion, Mr.

O'Connor! (*She tosses her head with a peal of laughter. Spills lemonade.*) Oooo! I'm baptizing myself!

Jim. Here—let me—

Amanda (*setting the pitcher down*). There now. I discovered we had some maraschino cherries. I dumped them in, juice and all!

Jim. You shouldn't have gone to that trouble, Mrs. Wingfield.

Amanda. Trouble, trouble? Why it was loads of fun! Didn't you hear me cutting up in the kitchen? I bet your ears were burning! I told Tom how outdone with him I was for keeping you to himself so long a time! He should have brought you over much, much sooner! Well, now that you've found your way, I want you to be a very frequent caller! Not just occasional but all the time. Oh, we're going to have a lot of gay times together! I see them coming! Mmm, just breathe that air! So fresh, and the moon's so pretty! I'll skip back out—I know where my place is when young folks are having a—serious conversation!

Jim. Oh, don't go out, Mrs. Wingfield. The fact of the matter is I've got to be going.

Amanda. Going, now? You're joking! Why, it's only the shank of the evening, Mr. O'Connor!

Jim. Well, you know how it is.

Amanda. You mean you're a young workingman and have to keep workingmen's hours. We'll let you off early tonight. But only on the condition that next time you stay later. What's the best night for you? Isn't Saturday night the best night for you workingmen?

Jim. I have a couple of time-clocks to punch, Mrs. Wingfield. One at morning, another one at night!

Amanda. My, but you *are* ambitious! You work at night, too?

Jim. No, Ma'am, not work but—Betty! (*He crosses deliberately to pick up his hat. The band at the Paradise Dance Hall goes into a tender waltz.*)

Amanda. Betty? Betty? Who's—Betty! (*There is an ominous cracking sound in the sky.*)

Jim. Oh, just a girl. The girl I go steady with! (*He smiles charmingly. The sky falls.*)

(LEGEND: "THE SKY FALLS.")

Amanda (*a long-drawn exhalation*). Ohhhh . . . Is it a serious romance, Mr. O'Connor?

Jim. We're going to be married the second Sunday in June.

Amanda. Ohhhh—how nice! Tom didn't mention that you were engaged to be married.

Jim. The cat's not out of the bag at the warehouse yet. You know how they are. They call you Romeo and stuff like that. (*He stops at the oval mirror to put on his hat. He carefully shapes the brim and the crown to give a discreetly dashing effect.*) It's been a wonderful

evening, Mrs. Wingfield. I guess this is what they mean by Southern hospitality.

Amanda. It really wasn't anything at all.

Jim. I hope it don't seem like I'm rushing off. But I promised Betty I'd
pick her up at the Wabash depot, an' by the time I get my jalopy
down there her train'll be in. Some women are pretty upset if you
keep 'em waiting.

Amanda. Yes, I know—The tyranny of women! (*Extends her hand.*)
Good-bye, Mr. O'Connor. I wish you luck—and happiness—and
success! All three of them, and so does Laura!—Don't you Laura?

Laura. Yes!

Jim (*taking her hand*). Good-bye, Laura. I'm certainly going to treasure that souvenir. And don't you forget the good advice I gave
you. (*Raises his voice to a cheery shout.*) So long, Shakespeare!
Thanks again, ladies—Good night!

He grins and ducks jauntily out.

*Still bravely grimacing, Amanda closes the door on the gentleman
caller. Then she turns back to the room with a puzzled expression.
She and Laura don't dare to face each other. Laura crouches beside the victrola to wind it.*

Amanda (*faintly*). Things have a way of turning out so badly. I don't
believe that I would play the victrola. Well, well—well—Our
gentleman caller was engaged to be married! Tom!

Tom (*from back*). Yes, Mother?

Amanda. Come in here a minute. I want to tell you something awfully
funny.

Tom (*enters with macaroon and a glass of the lemonade*). Has the
gentleman caller gotten away already?

Amanda. The gentleman caller has made an early departure. What a
wonderful joke you played on us!

Tom. How do you mean?

Amanda. You didn't mention that he was engaged to be married.

Tom. Jim? Engaged?

Amanda. That's what he just informed us.

Tom. I'll be jiggered! I didn't know about that.

Amanda. That seems very peculiar.

Tom. What's peculiar about it?

Amanda. Didn't you call him your best friend down at the warehouse?

Tom. He is, but how did I know?

Amanda. It seems extremely peculiar that you wouldn't know your
best friend was going to be married!

Tom. The warehouse is where I work, not where I know things about
people!

Amanda. You don't know things anywhere! You live in a dream; you
manufacture illusions! (*He crosses to door.*) Where are you going?

744 TENNESSEE WILLIAMS

Tom. I'm going to the movies.

Amanda. That's right, now that you've had us make such fools of our-selves. The effort, the preparations, all the expense! The new floor lamp, the rug, the clothes for Laura! All for what? To entertain some other girl's fiancé! Go to the movies, go! Don't think about us, a mother deserted, an unmarried sister who's crippled and has no job! Don't let anything interfere with your selfish pleasure! Just go, go, go—to the movies!

Tom. All right, I will! The more you shout about my selfishness to me the quicker I'll go, and I won't go to the movies!

Amanda. Go, then! Then go to the moon—you selfish dreamer!

Tom smashes his glass on the floor. He plunges out on the fire-escape, slamming the door. Laura screams—cut by door.

Dance-hall music up. Tom goes to the rail and grips it desperately, lifting his face in the chill white moonlight penetrating the narrow abyss of the alley.

(LEGEND ON SCREEN: "AND SO GOOD-BYE . . .")

Tom's closing speech is timed with the interior pantomime. The interior scene is played as though viewed through soundproof glass. Amanda appears to be making a comforting speech to Laura who is huddled upon the sofa. Now that we cannot hear the mother's speech, her silliness is gone and she has dignity and tragic beauty. Laura's dark hair hides her face until at the end of the speech she lifts it to smile at her mother. Amanda's gestures are slow and graceful, almost dancelike, as she comforts the daugh-ter. At the end of her speech she glances a moment at the father's picture—then withdraws through the portieres. At close of Tom's speech, Laura blows out the candles, ending the play.

Tom. I didn't go to the moon, I went much further—for time is the longest distance between two places—Not long after that I was fired for writing a poem on the lid of a shoe-box. I left Saint Louis. I descended the steps of this fire-escape for a last time and followed, from then on, in my father's footsteps, attempting to find in motion what was lost in space—I traveled around a great deal. The cities swept about me like dead leaves, leaves that were brightly colored but torn away from the branches. I would have stopped, but I was pursued by something. It always came upon me unawares, taking me altogether by surprise. Perhaps it was a familiar bit of music. Perhaps it was only a piece of trans-parent glass—Perhaps I am walking along a street at night, in some strange city, before I have found companions. I pass the lighted window of a shop where perfume is sold. The window is filled with pieces of colored glass, tiny transparent bottles in delicate colors, like bits of a shattered rainbow. Then all at once my sister touches my shoulder. I turn around and look into her eyes . . . Oh, Laura, Laura, I tried to leave you behind me, but I am more faithful than I intended to be! I reach for a cigarette, I cross the street, I run into the movies or a bar, I buy a drink, I speak to the nearest stranger—anything that can blow your candles out! (*Laura bends over the candles.*)—for nowadays the world is lit by lightning! Blow out your candles, Laura—and so good-bye. . . .

She blows the candles out.

(THE SCENE DISSOLVES.)

PRODUCTION NOTES

Being a "memory play," *The Glass Menagerie* can be presented with unusual freedom of convention. Because of its considerably delicate or tenuous material, atmospheric touches and subtleties of direction play a particularly important part. Expressionism and all other unconventional techniques in drama have only one valid aim, and that is a closer approach to truth. When a play employs unconventional techniques, it is not, or certainly shouldn't be, trying to escape its responsibility of dealing with reality, or interpreting experience, but is actually or should be attempting to find a closer approach, a more penetrating and vivid expression of things as they are. The straight realistic play with its genuine frigidaire and authentic ice-cubes, its characters that speak exactly as its audience speaks, corresponds to the academic landscape and has the same virtue of a photographic likeness. Everyone should know nowadays the unimportance of the photographic in art: that truth, life, or reality is an organic thing which the poetic imagination can represent or suggest, in essence, only through transformation, through changing into other forms than those which were merely present in appearance.

These remarks are not meant as comments only on this particular play. They have to do with a conception of a new, plastic theater which must take the place of the exhausted theater of realistic conventions if the theater is to resume vitality as a part of our culture.

THE SCREEN DEVICE

There is *only one important difference between the original and acting version of the play* and that is the *omission* in the latter of the device which I tentatively included in my *original* script. This device was the use of a screen on which were projected magic-lantern slides bearing images or titles. I do not regret the omission of this device from the . . . Broadway production. The extraordinary power of Miss Taylor's performance made it suitable to have the utmost simplicity in the physical production. But I think it may be interesting to some readers to see how this device was conceived. So I am putting it into the published manuscript. These images and legends, projected from behind, were cast on a section of wall between the front-room and dining-room areas, which should be indistinguishable from the rest when not in use.

The purpose of this will probably be apparent. It is to give accent to certain values in each scene. Each scene contains a particular point (or several) which is structurally the most important. In an episodic play, such as this, the basic structure or narrative line may be obscured from the audience; the effect may seem fragmentary rather than architectural. This may not be the fault of the play so much as a lack of attention in the audience. The legend or image upon the screen will strengthen the effect of what is merely allusion in the writing and allow the primary point to be made more simply and lightly than if the entire responsibility were on the spoken lines. Aside from this structural value, I think the screen will have a definite emotional appeal, less definable but just as important. An imaginative producer or director may invent many other uses for this device than those indicated in the present script. In fact the possibilities of the device seem much larger to me than the instance of this play can possibly utilize.

THE MUSIC

Another extra-literary accent in this play is provided by the use of music. A single recurring tune, "The Glass Menagerie," is used to give emotional emphasis to suitable passages. This tune is like circus music, not when you are on the grounds or in the immediate vicinity of the parade, but when you are at some distance and very likely thinking of something else. It seems under those circumstances to continue almost interminably and it weaves in and out of your preoccupied consciousness; then it is the lightest, most delicate music in the world and perhaps the saddest. It expresses the surface vivacity of life with the underlying strain of immutable and inexpressible sorrow. When you look at a piece of delicately spun glass you think of two things: how beautiful it is and how easily it can be broken. Both of those ideas should be woven into the recurring tune, which dips in and out of the play as if it were carried on a wind that changes. It serves as a thread of connection and allusion between the narrator with his separate point in time and space and the subject of his story. Between each episode it returns as reference to the emotion, nostalgia, which is the first condition of the play. It is primarily Laura's music and therefore comes out most clearly when the play focuses upon her and the lovely fragility of glass which is her image.

THE LIGHTING

The lighting in the play is not realistic. In keeping with the atmosphere of memory, the stage is dim. Shafts of light are focused on selected areas or actors, sometimes in contradistinction to what is the apparent center. For instance, in the quarrel scene between Tom and Amanda, in which Laura has no active part, the clearest pool of light is on her figure. This is also true of the supper scene, when her silent figure on the sofa should remain the visual center. The light upon Laura should be distinct from the others, having a peculiar pristine clarity such as light used in early religious portraits of female saints or madonnas. A certain correspondence to light in religious paintings, such as El Greco's, where the figures are radiant in atmosphere that is relatively dusky, could be effectively used throughout the play. (It will also permit a more effective use of the screen.) A free, imaginative use of light can be of enormous value in giving a mobile, plastic quality to plays of a more or less static nature.

T. W.

QUESTIONS: *The Glass Menagerie*

1. When produced in New York, the magic-lantern slides were omitted. Is the device an extraneous gimmick? Might it even interfere with the play, by oversimplifying and thus in a way belittling the actions?

2. What does the victrola offer to Laura? Why is the typewriter a better symbol (for the purposes of the play) than, say, a piano? After all, Laura could have been taking piano lessons. Explain the symbolism of the unicorn, and the loss of its horn. What is Laura saying to Jim in the gesture of giving him the unicorn?

3. Laura escapes to her glass menagerie. To what do Amanda and Tom escape? How complete is Tom's escape at the end of the play?

4. Did Williams slip in having Amanda say Laura is "crippled" on p. 745?

5. There is an implication that had Jim not been going steady he might have rescued Laura, but Jim also seems to represent (for example in his lines about money and power) the corrupt outside world that no longer values humanity. Is this a slip on Williams' part, or is it an interesting complexity?

6. On p. 745 Williams says, in a stage direction, "Now that we cannot hear the mother's speech, her silliness is gone and she has dignity and tragic beauty." Is Williams simply dragging in the word

"tragic" because of its prestige, or is it legitimate? "Tragedy" is often distinguished from "pathos": in the tragic, the suffering is experienced by persons who act and are in some measure responsible for their suffering; in the pathetic, the suffering is experienced by the passive and the innocent. For example, in discussing Aeschylus' *The Suppliants*, H. D. F. Kitto says (*Greek Tragedy*): "The Suppliants are not only pathetic, as the victims of outrage, but also tragic, as the victims of their own misconceptions." Given this distinction, to what extent are Amanda and Laura tragic? Pathetic?

INDEX

Literary Terms

INDEX

Authors, Titles, First Lines of Poems

The number in *italic* type indicates the
page on which the selection appears.